LIVING WELL

Introductory Readings in Ethics

LIVING WELL

Introductory Readings in Ethics

Steven Luper

Trinity University

HARCOURT BRACE COLLEGE PUBLISHERS

Fort Worth   Philadelphia   San Diego   New York   Orlando   Austin   San Antonio
Toronto   Montreal   London   Sydney   Tokyo

Publisher	**Earl McPeek**
Executive Editor	**David Tatom**
Market Strategist	**Laura M. Brennan**
Developmental Editor	**Tracy Napper**
Project Editor	**Laura Miley**
Art Director	**Biatriz Chapa**
Production Manager	**Linda McMillan**

Cover Credit: Giraudon/Art Resource, NY. Auguste Renoir, *Le Moulin de la Galette*. Musée d'Orsay, Paris, France.

ISBN: 0-15-508459-3
Library of Congress Catalog Card Number: 98-88277

Address for Domestic Orders
Harcourt Brace College Publishers, 6277 Sea Harbor Drive, Orlando, FL 32887-6777
800-782-4479

Address for International Orders
International Customer Service
Harcourt Brace & Company, 6277 Sea Harbor Drive, Orlando, FL 32887-6777
407-345-3800
(fax) 407-345-4060
(e-mail) hbintl@harcourtbrace.com

Address for Editorial Correspondence
Harcourt Brace College Publishers, 301 Commerce Street, Suite 3700, Fort Worth, TX 76102

Web Site Address
http://www.hbcollege.com

Printed in the United States of America

9 0 1 2 3 4 5 6 7 8   016   9 8 7 6 5 4 3 2 1

Harcourt Brace College Publishers

DEDICATION

For Bonnie Polk, my Grandmother

PREFACE

More people than ever before are preoccupied with wealth, and no matter how wealthy people become, many yearn to gain still more wealth. This preoccupation suggests a belief by many that well-being comes with affluence. But psychologists deny that happiness is well-correlated with wealth.[1] Certainly people who live in absolute poverty face privations that reduce their happiness. It would be absurd to say that money is a completely unimportant consideration. But those who have enough money to meet basic needs find that extra wealth does little to raise their level of well-being. Apparently, it is a mistake to think that wealth itself will enable humans to live well. Indeed, money is a mere means to some needs for a person to flourish, and one would make a grave mistake by failing to look beyond the means and losing sight of the end.

But difficult analysis indeed is required to establish requirements for living life well. It is not a matter of being cheerful, although cheerfulness surely accompanies well-being. A successful career does not ensure it, although success can certainly enhance life. Nor is it a matter of living a morally exemplary life, although egregious immorality is such a substantial flaw as to preclude the possibility of living well. Presumably living well is not *any* one single thing. Instead, it consists in various things. This book is designed to help readers identify what they need to live life well. In this volume, a variety of materials address the perennial questions: Who am I, and who ought I be? What makes life worthwhile? What are my obligations? The book includes generous selections from both Eastern and Western philosophers such as Confucius, Laotzi, the Buddha, Aristotle, Kant, and John Stuart Mill, along with original introductory discussions by specialists who make these philosophers accessible to less familiar readers. Several fresh translations of important works have been provided: John Heil translated Book 1 of Aristotle's *Nicomachean Ethics;* P. J. Ivanhoe translated selections from the *Daodejing;* David Kalupahana translated various Buddhist scriptures; and Judith Norman translated Hegel's "Master and Slave." The final chapters include brief excerpts from Supreme Court cases to bring out how various important issues have been resolved in U.S. law.

At the broadest level, the essays in *Living Well* are organized under three headings: first, theory; second, the good (the nature of the worthwhile life); and third, the right (dealing with obligations). The essays in Part I present the world's most prominent theories concerning how best to live; these works, together with introductions that accompany them, provide readers with a theoretical orientation with which to confront discussions of more specific topics that follow in later parts of the book. In Part II, which deals with the good or worthwhile life, the chapters are organized around five categories under which the elements of a worthwhile life can be classified. Part II begins with discussions of the nature of the self, and then considers various good-making aspects of life: attributes such as pleasure, virtue (excellence), and life itself, and relationships such as those between friends, sex partners, lovers, spouses, and families. Part III considers right-making features of conduct or character. It surveys the central duties often attributed to people. The first set of essays in this third part of the book discuss aspects of the duty of fidelity: integrity, honesty, and loyalty. Then come essays that discuss nonmalevolence toward people and toward the rest of the world. Next are essays covering various forms of beneficence: humanitarianism, parentalism (or paternalism), and benevolent killing, as involved, for example, in euthanasia. Fairness is the last topic of Part III, and that chapter includes essays discussing equality, nondiscrimination, and punishment. The three essays discussing punishment—by Stephen Nathanson, Jeffrey Reiman, and Ernest van den Haag—were written especially for *Living Well.*

Except for Chapter 1, each chapter is preceded by a brief introduction that offers a succinct statement of the points raised in the selections and their relation to each other. Included as well are questions designed to provoke reflection about the readings, and a brief list of works that discuss the topics at hand in greater detail. An essay called "The Good, the Right, the Self" introduces the volume as a whole.

No doubt people who use this book will think of many ways in which it can be improved. I invite anyone who would like to offer constructive criticism to contact me at *sluper@trinity.edu* (or via regular mail). If I find an opportunity to implement changes, I will happily take into account any advice I receive.

The help of several people made the book possible. The staff at Harcourt Brace, particularly David Tatom, executive editor; Tracy Napper, senior developmental editor; Laura Miley, project editor; Linda McMillan, production manager, and Biatriz Chapa, art director, provided a great deal of patient assistance. I am especially grateful to all of the people who contributed to the volume: John Heil, P. J. Ivanhoe, David Kalupahana, Stephen Nathanson, Judith Norman, Jeffrey Reiman, Henry Rosemont, and Ernest van den Haag. Also, I thank the reviewers of the manuscript: William Davie, University of Oregon; Carlo Filice, SUNY Genesco; Craig Hanks, University of Arizona—Huntsville; Joan Whitman Hoff, Lock Haven University; and Hal Walberg, Mankato State University. And I owe special thanks to Karla Barnett, Margaret Carrasco, and the student workers in the Philosophy Department for their help in preparing the manuscript.

---

[1]See, for example, David Myers, *The Pursuit of Happiness* (New York: Avon Books, 1993), p. 32.

CONTENTS

THE GOOD, THE RIGHT, THE SELF

Boasts about the uniqueness of the human being have become less common since we have learned that we share about 99.5 percent of our evolutionary history with the chimpanzees. Whether or not we are unique in the world, human beings have remarkable features and abilities that we often overlook because they are so familiar to us. Perhaps the most remarkable thing we can do is also an entirely commonplace activity: We can take our lives into our own hands and shape them in light of our best visions or ideals. Out of the materials of our spirit, we can fashion ideals for ourselves and for the world around us, and we can strive to bring those visions into reality. As a reminder of just how profound this creative capacity is, consider one of the things it has recently enabled humans to do: We can reshape our bodies and the bodies of other animals using genetic engineering or recombinant DNA technology. In a few short years, we will gain the capacity for dramatic reshaping. Applying the creative capacity of the human being has led to this awesome power over the very structure of living things.

The exercise of our creative capacity has always stirred deep controversies. On the one hand, some philosophers such as the ancient Daoists, have been impressed with the natural world that has given human beings a home; these philosophers implore us to conform to the natural state, leaving things as they are. On the other hand, visionary philosophers, have inspired us to pursue new ideals and improve upon the status quo, forever changing the natural order. Taking charge of our genetic makeup to eliminate diseases and perhaps to improve upon the natural capacities of human beings is simply one of the latest projects of the visionary. Most people can appreciate *both* of these views, so they must navigate in the complicated, murky territory in between. They welcome departures from the natural order that will greatly increase human comfort, but they also know that many changes seemingly likely to improve our lives will make them worse in the end.

Of course, no one person is in a position to take charge of life itself and dictate answers to large-scale issues such as whether and how to change the order of life. However, each of us can contribute thoughtfully to debates over large-scale issues in the hope that others will do likewise. Moreover, each person can take charge of a small piece of the life on the planet: We can take our own lives into our hands and shape them as best we can. To make our lives as worthwhile as possible, we can ask key questions about life, such as: What is it to be a person? What sort of person should one be? How should we shape our lives so that they will be as worthwhile as possible? These

1

questions will lead inexorably to others, such as: What is the relationship between the identity of one individual and the identities of others? In order for an individual to flourish, how must that person's life involve friends, family members, fellow citizens, fellow human beings, and the nonhuman denizens of the world?

These questions are investigated by *ethics,* which is the study of the right and the good in relation to conduct and character. When you ask how you should shape your life, your question calls for an application of both the concept of the right and the concept of the good. Answering your question involves reaching conclusions about what the *good* or best life would be like, for you as well as for others, and it involves forming opinions concerning the *right* or obligatory ways of interacting with others. When you ask yourself what sort of life is most desirable, you probably think of such elements as fulfilling work, pleasurable activities, friendships, and loving personal relationships, among other things, and you are led to ask how these elements are related to each other. Here you are working out for yourself a conception of the good life, and with such a conception you can go a long way toward deciding how you should shape your life. But you will need to ask another sort of question before you can reach a defensible decision, for not everything you might choose to do in order to provide yourself with the best life is right or permissible for you to do. Money is a multipurpose means, since it enables you to do many desirable things, but killing people to take their money is morally wrong. You will need to ask what is right. You will need to know what you *must* and must *not* do, so that you can work out what you *may* do. Only when you have provided yourself with a conception of the right, as well as a conception of the good, will you be able to decide how you ought to shape your life.

But how might you decide what constitutes a good life, and how do you identify your obligations? Let us discuss the first of these questions now, leaving the matter of your duties for a bit later.

THE GOOD

To clarify the good, consider several notions that are extremely closely related to goodness.

1. A Tight Circle of Ideas

One example is the notion of happiness: Goodness and happiness are intimately connected. If you ask yourself what goodness consists in, you are likely to think of happiness. Nor is happiness the only notion that is closely related to the good. In fact, the italicized terms in each of the following claims can be quite satisfactorily inter-defined:

1. Such and such constitutes a *good* life for me.
2. Such and such is the sort of life that would make me *happy.*
3. It would be in my *interest* to live such and such a life.
4. Such and such is what it would be *important* to me to get out of life.
5. Such and such is what would make my life *worthwhile.*

The concepts of goodness, happiness, self-interest, and what is important or worthwhile are not identical, but they are all so closely related, each can be understood in terms of the others. For instance, what is good for me is also what is in my interest. This observation can support the effort to understand the good life, for the investigation can be expanded to include what we know about happiness, our interests, and so on.

However, there is a sharp limit to how much we can learn about one concept in this circle of ideas by explaining it in terms of the others. Explaining one in terms of the others is like clarifying one of the following terms using one of the others: *expensive, high-priced, dear,* and *costly.* To attach a label to the practice of defining one term using another that is not really any clearer, let us use the term *Quine-circularity,* in honor of the philosopher W. V. O. Quine, who described such a circle of terms in one of his essays.[1]

2. The Preference Account of the Good

To shed significant light on the nature of the good life, we will need to break out of this circle of ideas and explain the good in terms of something else. For example, we might consider the theory that the good is whatever you, the reader, want or desire. The concept of desire is sufficiently distant from the earlier list of notions—not too unlike them and not too like them—that it might actually teach us something about those notions.

To test the view that the good is whatever you want, begin by working out some of its consequences and ask whether these consequences are plausible upon reflection. If we can identify implausible consequences, we can attempt to alter the theory so as to improve it, or replace it entirely, and then begin the process of testing consequences all over again.

Is the good whatever you, the reader, want? Presumably not, since obviously this conception has implausible consequences. For example, everyone wants things that are not in their best interests. Satisfying your desire to tell a white lie to your friend might result in the loss of his or her trust. Satisfying your desire not to study might result in your failing a class. Satisfying your desire to inhale paint fumes (as some people like to do in order to get high) will severely damage your brain and might eventually kill you. In each case, you desire something that is not good. So the good is not simply what the reader desires.

One way to respond to this objection is to replace the theory under evaluation with one that defines the good directly in terms of self-interest: The good is what is in the reader's best interest. But that would be a retreat back into the circle of ideas we are trying to escape, for it would offer the third account of the good mentioned earlier. A different response (which will not lead back into the circle) would adjust the theory in light of the distinction between instrumental desires and noninstrumental desires. Your desire for X is *instrumental* when you are interested in X only because it helps you to satisfy some other desire. Your desire for aspirin, for example, is instrumental, since you want aspirin simply because it will satisfy your desire to be free from pain. By contrast, your desire to be free from pain is (perhaps) not an instrumental desire. When we desire something for its own sake, our desire is a *noninstrumental* desire. It is a desire for something we take to be *intrinsically* good, or good in itself. In this way an instrumental desire is less *basic* than a noninstrumental desire. Perhaps the good is the satisfaction of your noninstrumentalor, or basic, desires.

But the new theory has a problem, too. *You* might welcome the view that the good consists in satisfying *your* noninstrumental desires, but why should the rest of the world welcome that view? Why, for example, should *I* say that the good consists in satisfying *your* noninstrumental desires? Just how implausible your view will be depends in part on what your desires turn out to be: What if you are an unsavory character like Adolf Hitler, whose ambitions are fundamentally incompatible with those of others?

It might help to add an element of universality to the conception of the good under consideration. Why not say that the good *for you* is whatever satisfies *your* noninstrumental desires, but the good *for me* is whatever satisfies *my* noninstrumental desires, and so on? That is, the good for any given person P is whatever satisfies P's noninstrumental desires. This *preference* account of the good (as we might call it) avoids the implausible consequence that your interests define the good for everyone else. On the new approach, each person's basic desires define the good for that person, which is a result that everyone might accept.

The preference account of the good is extremely versatile; versions of it are sometimes defended in philosophical literature. It has features that are worrisome, as well, though, and we will want to examine some of these. However, before we raise concerns about the preference account, let us look at two other popular accounts of the good that are closely related to the preference account, in that they, too, understand the good largely in terms of human preferences.

3. Hedonism

Hedonism, or *ethical hedonism* as it is sometimes called, says that only one thing is *intrinsically* good for person P, that is, good in and of itself (as opposed to instrumentally good, or good as a means). The sole intrinsic good for P, according to hedonism, is P's pleasure (and the absence of P's pain). Ethical hedonism should be distinguished from a view call *psychological hedonism,* which states that as a matter of psychological fact, people always choose what they believe will give them pleasure or preclude their pain. This latter view is a *descriptive* theory: It purports to describe facts—in this case, facts about human motivation. By contrast, ethical hedonism is a *normative* view: It purports to say what is good or right.

In normal circumstances, people attain pleasure by satisfying desires, and they avoid pain by avoiding thwarted desires. In practical terms, hedonism and the preference account come to much the same thing. Nonetheless, the accounts are distinct from one another. The preference account is compatible with an assertion that various states of the world are (or would be) intrinsically good for a person, while hedonism says that only P's pleasure, which is a state of mind, is intrinsically good for P. On the preference account, I might regard the welfare of my children as intrinsically good, but the hedonist would say that their welfare can be good only instrumentally, as the means to my experiencing pleasure.

4. Self-Realization

Yet another account analyzes the good in terms of *self-realization,* and some of the possible versions of the self-realization account of the good are closely related to the preference account. All versions of the self-realization account analyze the good in terms of the self and identity, but one can understand the self in several ways, and some ways to understand the self do not rely on the notion of desire as heavily as other ways. Suppose that we understand the self in terms of the desires with which we *identify*. If we take this approach, we must clarify what it means to identify with a desire; perhaps we can understand the desires with which we identify as those that express what we *most* desire, or the projects to which we are most committed. Such desires, we might say, are essential to who we are and, hence, constitute our identity in part. Self-realization, in turn, we might understand as the satisfaction of the desires with which we identify. (As later discussion will show, one can understand self-realization in other ways, primarily because one can understand the difficult notion of "identifying" with desires in other ways.) Finally, we may be able to explain the good in terms of self-realization as we understand it: Our good is self-realization, which is the satisfaction of the desires to which we are most committed.

If interpreted in this way, the self-realization account is a version of the preference account of the good. For the desires with which we identify are likely to be basic desires. It is an important fact that the good, the satisfaction of basic desires, and at least one notion of the self are all closely related notions.

5. The Malleability of Desire

Hedonism, the self-realization account, and the preference account all suggest that people's basic desires largely determine what constitutes a good life. All of these accounts suggest that basic desires are the keys to understanding the good life. If we adopt any of these accounts of the good, then one of the first things we will want to know is how malleable our desires are, for changing them in some sense changes what is good for us.

We know that we can change some desires under certain circumstances; for example, we can often eliminate desires by changing beliefs, as when I cease to desire to eat the food in front of me upon discovering that it is poisoned. But can we alter our noninstrumental, basic desires, and if so how extensively can we change them? Unfortunately, the answer is unavailable; it will require extensive empirical investigation by researchers. However, while a few basic motivations are a part of normal human nature, such as the sex drive and hunger for food, what seems most impressive about people is the open-ended range of ways in which they can respond to drives such as these. Consider how amorphous the sex drive is, for example. What does someone desire as a result of possessing a sex drive? It is impossible to give a concrete answer. Finally, what people want as sexual beings depends on a host of facts about what they also want, value, and believe: Certain religious beliefs and associated desires might lead people to sublimate their sexual desires (although by no means will all religious perspectives have this result), while other beliefs and desires might lead people to favor very active sex lives.

To the extent that desires cannot be changed, the option of changing them does not present itself. Suppose, on the other hand, that our desires are thoroughly malleable. Then it seems sensible to ask what we *ought* to desire. Needless to say, it is no answer to say that we ought to desire things that are desirable. This answer involves

Quine-circularity. The concept of the desir*able,* of that which ought to be desired, is another concept to add to the five that are already in our expanding circle of ideas that are so alike that none shed much light on the others.

6. Evaluating Basic Desires

So how should we respond to the question: What ought we desire? The fact is that we can make only limited sense of this question if we accept the preference account, hedonism, or the self-realization account of the good, for all three suggest finally that the good is entirely or almost entirely a matter of what people *do* desire. Consider, for example, the preference account. (Recall that the preference account states that the good for person P is whatever satisfies P's noninstrumental desires.) If the preference account is correct, the fundamental point of view from which we assess or evaluate options is the satisfaction of our desires. We cannot assess our desires from any point of view that is *prior to and independent from* our desires. To defer to such a point of view is to reject the preference account and related accounts.

7. Optimizing, Adaptation, and the Manipulation of the Good

If desire is thoroughly malleable, options concerning the best way to live are greatly expanded, for then we can act to improve our lives using either of two very different strategies. Our usual strategy can be characterized as follows: We take our basic desires for granted and attempt to mold the world in ways that efficiently satisfy our desires. Call this strategy *optimizing.* But to the extent that desires are malleable, we could work the other way around: Take the basic features of the world for granted and mold our desires so that the world as it is satisfies them. Call this strategy *adapting desire.* Either strategy moves one closer to the good since either moves us closer to the situation in which the desires we have are satisfied. As the essays in this volume will show, the adaptation strategy for improving our lives has been favored more by Eastern philosophers than by Western philosophers, although it is also suggested by the hedonist philosopher Epicurus and the Stoic philosopher Epictetus. Optimizing, on the other hand, is the method most heavily emphasized in the West. Then again, one need not choose between the two; a mixture of the two is an option, as well.

Notice that adapting desires does not improve our lives as assessed from the standpoint of satisfying the desires we give up. Instead, we improve our lives by altering our desires so that we meet the goal of *having only desires that we satisfy.* Adaptation improves our lives, but only because we have altered in part our understanding of what it *takes* to have a good life.

Thus, the preference account turns out to have some surprising consequences. We can change the good by changing our desires. In theory, we may even manipulate what counts as good for *others* by manipulating *their* desires. That is, radically changing someone's desires would radically change what is good for them. Not everyone will welcome these consequences. If Mother Theresa were kidnapped and given the desire profile of Hitler, then the new, Nazi-style desires would define her good. Moreover, in view of the fact that her good has changed, it is not clear that she would benefit if someone reversed the process. (Of course, hedonism and the self-realization accounts will have the same surprising consequences. Consider hedonism: We attain pleasure and avoid pain almost entirely *by* satisfying our desires, so by changing what we desire, we change what gives us pleasure. Given the hedonist's equation of the good and the pleasant, changing what gives us pleasure changes what is needed to have a good life.)

That the good can be manipulated in this way will strike some people as an implausible idea. However, to avoid saying that the good can be manipulated, we will have to abandon the preference account and its kin. Instead of the preference account, we must look for an account that does not analyze the good in terms of desire or anything else under human control: If the good is not understood in terms of desire, then it will not change with changes in desires. For example, if the good is something "objective," such as God's will, then it cannot be manipulated by changing (human) desires. No doubt such reflections are partly responsible for some antipathy against "subjectivist" accounts of the good.

8. Subjectivity and Objectivity

The preference, hedonist, and self-realization accounts all suggest that judgments about the good are *subjective*. That is, whether something is good is settled by facts about people's points of view, such as the particulars concerning what they desire. Other accounts might portray judgments about the good as *objective*. On the objectivist view, we settle whether something is good or valuable by taking up an impersonal point of view, which is a standpoint that abstracts away from particular subjective views. What is valuable from that impersonal point of view settles what is good. For example, some objectivists suggest that goodness is determined by facts about the natural order, and some suggest that features of some sort of supernatural order determine goodness.

An objective account of the good might allow us to do something that is much more problematic on subjective accounts: assess basic desires. An objectivist account might also eliminate the possibility, discussed in the previous section, of changing the good by changing desires. Instead of understanding the good in terms of desire, like the subjectivists, objectivists work the other way around: They say that we should desire what is good, and they explain the nature of the good in terms of objective considerations.

Two especially influential objectivist accounts seek to define the good. The *theist* account identifies the good with God's will or with performing an assigned role in God's plan. Each creature's good consists in doing whatever God wants that creature to do. A second version of objectivism can be called *ethical functionalism*. Ethical functionalists assume that all creatures, including people, have certain structures or functional organizations which, given the creatures' contexts, allow them to flourish or live well. Functionalists also assume that a creature will flourish *only* when that creature acts in the ways it is designed to act. According to the functionalist, a creature's acting in accordance with its nature constitutes the good for that creature. For example, some people argue that human beings cannot live well if they isolate themselves from other people, for by nature we are social creatures. Many of the things human beings are designed to do can only be done in a social context.

An objection, which dates back at least to Plato, is often pressed against the theist's view that the good is whatever God wills. If we accept the theist's view, we must say that the good is arbitrary. Surely, the objection goes, God wills what God does because it is good, rather than the other way around: Surely things are not good just because God wills them. If things were good simply because God wills them, then murder, torture, and so on would have been good had God willed them. Moreover, God would have had no grounds for preferring love for others to hate for others; the choice would have been entirely an arbitrary gesture. Because this objection is powerful, theists often supplement their belief in the goodness of God with a separate account of the good. For example, people sometimes combine the theist and functionalist accounts. Some suggest that acting naturally, or in harmony with our nature, is all or part of what God, who is responsible for designing human nature, wants us to do. This position combines the theist and functionalist accounts. But one can also adopt one of these two accounts while rejecting the other. Someone who rejects theism could adopt a version of ethical functionalism and say that human beings have evolved characteristic features such as innate psychological drives that determine, at least in large part, what they must do to have good lives.

The functionalist account of the good can also be closely related to the preference and hedonist accounts of the good. One might argue that certain basic desires are, or ought to be, part of the innate motivation of all human beings, so that a good life is both a life in which they satisfy basic desires and one in which they act in natural ways. A good life is also a life of pleasure, since satisfying desires has a pleasant effect.

Although the point might be a bit less obvious, the functionalist account can also be related to the self-realization account. Earlier discussion cast self-realization as a subjective matter, but it could also work out along the lines suggested by the functionalist account, so that self-realization becomes an objective matter. To clarify the differences between these two views of self-realization, first we will need to distinguish between the sense in which the self is natural and the sense in which the self is subjective.

9. The Subjective Self and the Natural Self

In one sense, you are a temporally extended creature with certain (more or less malleable) drives who is capable of thought, memory, and decision making, as well as awareness of those thoughts and decisions. As such, you have a nature that is subject to empirical, scientific investigation. In another sense, you are whatever you define yourself to be, as when you establish part of your identity by deciding what to commit yourself to in life. In the extreme, you can even decide not to identify with the empirically discoverable part of your identity, which would then no longer be part of you. You can eliminate from your self-definition some (perhaps all) of the facts about the creature whose capacity for awareness and thought makes possible the project of self-definition. Disowning facts about the creature whose awareness makes self-definition possible will not alter those facts, but in theory it will mean that those facts are not part of the self as it defines itself. Call the *natural self* the self insofar as it has a given nature; the self insofar as it is its own creation is the *subjective self.* Thus, subjective selves are self-defining beings, creations of natural selves. You and I can understand *self* to mean either or both.

Now consider the point about self-realization mentioned in the previous section. Self-realization is a subjective matter when it is understood to result from satisfaction of the definitive desires of the subjective self. It is an objective matter when it results from satisfying the desires that are part of the constitutions of natural selves.

10. Goods

As we have seen, the question, How should you shape your life? can easily lead into new, fairly abstract questions about what makes something good. But however philosophers have answered these abstract questions, and whether or not those philosophers have defended objectivist or subjectivist accounts of the good, they have tended to agree about some good things. On virtually anyone's list of life's goods are these: activities such as contemplation and creative work; attributes such as pleasure, excellence, and (perhaps) life itself; and relationships such as those among friends, lovers, married people, families, and (perhaps) sex partners. The goodness of the self *per se* is considerably more controversial; the value of the self depends, in part, on how the self is defined, and is complicated by the fact that the self, self-realization, and the good are, as we have seen, closely related notions.

THE RIGHT

How shall we understand the concept of the right? Let us begin (as for the discussion of the good) with a look at a few closely related notions.

1. Quine-Circularity Again

Consider the following list of more or less equivalent claims:

1. Doing A is *obligatory.*
2. One *must* (one is *required* to) do A.
3. Doing A is one's *duty.*
4. Failing to do A is *impermissible.*
5. Failing to do A is not *right* (failing to do A is *wrong*).

Each of these claims involves notions that can be interdefined. But analyzing one in terms of the others would result in a Quine-circular account. A person who does not understand one will fail to understand the others. Such a person will be helped very little by a suggestion that each can be understood in terms of the others.

In order to avoid offering a Quine-circular account of the right, we might try to understand the right in terms of the good. Of course, this approach will stall without a clear account of the good on hand, and we have already examined some of the difficulties that accompany any attempt to clarify the good. But we certainly have not decided to give up the attempt to clarify the good; we need an account of the good in any case, and we might well then use it as the basis for an understanding of the right. Many philosophers have attempted to analyze the right in terms of a prior and independent notion of the good. Such theories—ones that account for the good independently from the right, and then account for the right in terms of the good—are called *teleological* theories.

2. Ethical Egoism

Offhand, saying that an action would be good certainly appears quite different from saying that it is an obligatory action. Consider your volunteering all of your resources and time (save what it takes just to sustain your life) to help unfortunate people. This surely would be an extremely *good* thing to do, but does the conclusion follow that you *must* (or are obligated to) do it? That judgment does not appear to follow, but perhaps the appearances mislead. Perhaps the right is much the same thing as the good.

Suppose we investigate the possibility that the right can be analyzed in terms of the good by trying to understand the right in terms of the accounts of the good discussed so far. For example, at one point we mentioned the view that person P's good is whatever is in P's best interest; now let us try out the analogous view that it is morally permissible for P to do A (or even, P must do A) when A is in P's best interest. This view is called *ethical egoism*. It should be distinguished from psychological egoism, which says that as a matter of psychological fact, each of us always attempts to do what is in our own best interest

How plausible is ethical egoism? Notice that as an egoist you may (or perhaps are morally required to) press your interests against those of others if and when a conflict between your interests and theirs occurs, and you have good reason to think that you can prevail. Suppose you can easily kill your neighbors, who are rich bankers, and obtain the money you need for your projects. You will not get caught, and you cannot easily get the money you need any other way. Arguably, it is in your interest to kill the bankers and take their money; if it serves your interest, then as an ethical egoist, you can morally proceed. Few people will find this result a plausible consequence.

3. (Re)shaping the Self

Rejecting egoism leaves several alternatives, one of which is to acknowledge the possibility of genuine conflicts of interest among people and insist that people restrain themselves when such conflicts occur. Nothing is wrong with the pursuit of individual interests, one might say, but it must be limited in reasonable ways. An account of moral obligation will tell us what constitutes reasonable restraints on the individual's pursuit of the good. This way of understanding the notion of moral obligation is common among Western philosophers today.

Eastern philosophers have tended to take a different approach. Instead of looking for a theory of moral obligation that will plausibly handle conflicts of interest among individuals, Eastern philosophers look to prevent conflicts of interest from arising in the first place. On their view, either (1) no genuine conflicts of interest ever exist, or (2) no genuine conflicts of interest ever *need* arise among people.

To bolster the suggestion that genuine conflicts never arise, it is possible to argue that communities do not consist of separate individuals. As for why, one might offer two very different reasons. First, people in communities might be *one:* They might share an identity. Second, people might not *be* at all! People might not have identities; there might be no such things as selves. For selves to have interests, they must exist, so if selves do not exist, there is no possibility that the interests of selves conflict. On the other hand, if people in some sense share an identity, this shared identity defines their genuine interests, so their interests are the same.

Suggestion (2) that implies conflicts of interest *need not* arise among people can be defended more easily than suggestion (1) that implies conflicts of interest never exist. To defend (2), we do not have to say that people lack an identity or that they share their identity, for we can rely on a less ambitions claim: Identity is *malleable,* so people are *capable* of being separate individuals with conflicting interests, but they are *also* capable of sharing an identity. Moreover, it is in their best interest to give their shared identity priority over their separate identities, perhaps eliminating the latter in the process. Why is it important to emphasize the shared identity? Because doing so is the only way to eliminate the tragedy of conflicting interests: Emphasizing the interests of our shared self prevents conflicts of interest (or rather the conflicts are resolved). If we do not, then conflicts cause disruptions among individual selves and between those individual selves and the shared self.

On either option—whether people cannot help but share an identity, or they just do share an identity—all would have the same interests, and interests either *could* not clash, or at least *would* not clash. Hence, we could do what is in our interest without creating the conflicts that make egoism objectionable. Indeed, there is a sense in which the collective self acts like an egoist when it pursues its own interests.

4. Who We Are

But who or what is this self whom we all might be? The Hindu literature offers the mysterious doctrine that each of us is a being who can be identified as follows: Think of the world itself, but while doing so do not employ any of the distinctions you normally use in order to distinguish the various components of the world. You now conceive your true self; all things form a unity. In some Daoist literature is the suggestion that each person can identify herself or himself as follows: Think of the world, but without employing any of the distinctions by which you normally distinguish yourself from the rest of the world. Now you are conceiving your true self; you are not separate from the actual world. The Buddhist literature suggests that selves do not exist at all. All three of these conceptions of the self are closely related in that they emphasize that no self remains apart from the rest of the world. Confucianism offers something like the suggestion that each of us is the community as a whole, existing as an individual only in the sense that each plays a separate role in the life of the community. Given this identity, true self-realization consists in doing an excellent job at playing one's role in the community.

The Confucian notions of the self and self-realization are closely related to views developed by Plato and Aristotle and by later Western philosophers such as Hegel and a group of recent theorists called *communitarians.* According to Plato and Aristotle, each person should identify with the community as a whole, even though each plays a separate role in the life of the community. Self-realization consists partly in excelling at the role played and partly in the unfolding life of the community as a whole. In *The Republic,* Plato advocates teaching the guardians of the state to feel for the community "the sort of concern that is felt for something so closely bound up with oneself that its interests and fortunes, for good or ill, are held to be identical with one's own." Later communitarian philosophers have argued in a similar vein, suggesting that people derive identities from the state, and its interests should take priority over those of individuals. Plato and Aristotle also develop the thesis of the ethical functionalist that each creature's good consists in acting in accordance with the creature's functional organization and context in the natural order. In early China, the functionalist thesis is split off from communitarianism: broadly speaking, Confucius pursues communitarianism and not functionalism, and Daoists pursue functionalism and not communitarianism.

5. The Natural Law View

After examining the varied views of the self, we might conclude that we cannot or ought not eliminate conflicts among people by (re)shaping the self and self-interest. If so, we will have to confront conflicts of interest among individuals anew. Unless we opt to embrace the egoist's suggestion that people may press their interests against each other regardless of the harm done, the next step would be to drop egoism in favor of some account of the right that limits people's pursuit of the good in reasonable ways. For example, we might replace egoism with a theistic account of the right. To say that we must do A, according to this version of theism, is to say that we have been commanded to do A by an agent who has authority over us, and the ultimate authority is God. This theist view is usually accompanied by the suggestion that the application of reason to evident facts about the natural world reveals many of God's commands or laws. For example, human beings have a certain structure, as suggested by Aristotle's functionalist account of the good, which tells us how God intends that we behave. Laws of God that become evident through reason and observation are called the *natural law* by theorists such as Cicero, Thomas Aquinas, and John Locke. The natural law could then serve as the framework for limiting the individual's tendency to press individual interests against those of others.

6. Doing without the Right

The natural law tradition helped shape the concept of right employed by most Western philosophers today. Contemporary theorists in the West tend to presuppose a background of conflicting interests among people, while rejecting the egoist's suggestion that people may press their interests against each other with impunity. The concept of the right is the concept of a form of obligation that *trumps* all considerations of self-interest. It sets *limits* on the pursuit of self-interest that reasonable people will acknowledge and willingly impose upon themselves (and to which *un*reasonable people are reasonably forced to conform). Due largely to the work of 17th-century figures such as John Locke, a pair of notions features prominently in this framework of obligation: duties and rights. The correlative notions of duties and rights limit the pursuit of self-interest through restrictions that reasonable people willingly impose upon themselves. While *duties* compel one to accommodate the interests of others, *rights* compel others to accommodate one's own interests, thus limiting the ways in which others may interfere with the pursuit of individual interests.

Conceived in these ways, the notion of *the* right and the notion of *rights* were not emphasized by Eastern or ancient Greek philosophers (with the possible exception of the Stoics). Ancient philosophers did not employ a framework that trumps all considerations of self-interest; instead, they relied on the idea that selves take a shape (perhaps through a process of accommodation) in which interests are harmonious across the community, and the self-realization of one does not interfere with the self-realization of another. Eliminating conflicts among people by (re)shaping the self, self-interest, and self-realization, as described by many Eastern and ancient Greek philosophers, would eliminate the need for the concept of the right as that concept is usually understood by contemporary Western philosophers.

Even if ethical approaches like Confucianism and Aristotelianism make no use of a framework that trumps all considerations of self-interest, these ancient approaches need not dispense with terms such as *obligation, duty, right,* and *wrong.* Confucians and Aristotelians might interpret these terms in light of their visions of self-realization, and say, roughly, that my doing A is *wrong* when, and in the sense that, A interferes with my self-realization, that is, when A interferes with the interests of the community that is my true self. These approaches focus on the characteristics of individuals that ideally suit them to take part in the community; such features are called *excellences* or *virtues.* We may evaluate specific conduct if we keep in mind the exemplary person, the person who embodies the virtues, for we should strive to act as the ideally good person would.

Of course, the world is very different than it was when Aristotle and Confucius lived. The unity of communities has broken down over time, and individuals have come to be seen (and to see themselves) as beings entitled to pursue interests they define for themselves. Consequently, the ancient emphasis on community can seem outdated, and the more modern conception of the right can seem indispensable. However, the failure of ancient figures to develop the modern conception of the right is not obviously an unqualified flaw. One of the great strengths of approaches such as Confucianism and Aristotelianism is their elimination or reduction in status of the question, Why be moral? Because these ancient philosophies aligned self-interest with the interest of the community, they would have said that to be moral is simply to do what is truly in one's own best interest. No one would ask, Why be moral? if that question amounted to, Why do what is in your best interest? This last question is very odd indeed, much like the question, Why do what you truly want to do?

Because they set morality in complete opposition to self-interest, many Western figures find that the question, Why be moral? is difficult to answer. One could say that in the final analysis, God himself makes it a good idea to obey the restrictions of morality by using the threat of punishment and the promise of rewards. On this self-interested explanation, one would obey the restrictions of morality only because a powerful agent provides incentives for doing so. This precarious reason disappears to the extent that faith in God is lost and to the extent that no secular authority provides the necessary incentives. In fact, the position gives no reason to act morally at all; one has a reason to obey the rules only when one cannot get away with breaking them. As we will see shortly, Immanuel Kant attempts to improve on the self-interested explanation of why we should be moral by suggesting that the reason to do our duty is that it *is* our duty. But some will say that this answer is simply an admission that no one give a reason to do our duty; we can explain the nature of duty to a skeptic, but if the skeptic understands duty and finds no compelling reason to do it, further discussion cannot resolve the matter.

7. Utilitarianism

The natural law tradition provides one way of understanding the impartial framework that might harmonize the competing interests of people. There are others, however. Another influential way to portray the impartial moral standpoint involves focussing on the good of the group. *Classical utilitarianism* claims that the right thing to do is whatever results in the most good for *everyone.*

Does utilitarianism, however, offer a way to eliminate conflicts among competing interests without making use of the ancient presupposition that everyone will identify with the group? On one reading, utilitarianism does make use of the ancient presupposition. The utilitarian says that we should act so as to maximize the good of all. Doesn't this view mean that we should identify with the community, that we should take the community to *be* us? Wouldn't this identification underlie any temptation to act in the collective interest, to maximize the good of all? Perhaps it would, but utilitarians traditionally do not attempt to persuade people that the community is their true self. In fact, the most influential utilitarian, J. S. Mill, was a staunch individualist, who thought that the utilitarian principle supplied the basis for limiting the individual's pursuit of self-interest as well as the basis for limiting the demands the community may make against individuals.

At least officially, then, contemporary utilitarians do not share the ancient assumption that individual identity is bound up with the identity of the group, so that everyone shares the interests of the group. Utilitarians address themselves to a world of mostly separate individuals who do not accept the total good as part of their best interest; they offer the principle of utility maximization as an impartial, hence reasonable, basis for establishing individual duties and rights. They suggest that each individual's interests or good should be important to me even though these interests are in no sense *mine.*

8. Kantianism

Different conceptions of the right may be classified in terms of the way they define the relationship between the right and the good. The most simple approach—that taken by egoism and classical utilitarianism—defines the right in terms of the good. Recall that theories which define the good independently of the right and then define the right in terms of the good are called *teleological* views. Theories that are not teleological are called *deontological* views. Deontological views either fail to define the good independently from the right or fail to define the right in terms of the good. Another way to contrast teleological views with deontological views is by noting their approaches to the consequences of people's choices. Teleologists tend to be *consequentialists,* that is, they define the right instrumentally as the option that promotes the good. Deonotologists tend to be *nonconsequentialists,* since they think the right option is not always the option that promotes the good.

Immanuel Kant maintained that we cannot fully specify the good without referring to a prior notion of the right. No matter how good something might seem to be, measured by pleasure or wealth or whatever, it is not good if it is obtained by morally wrong means. Pleasure obtained through rape and money obtained through theft are bad. So Kant is led to develop a deontological theory of the right.

This introduction earlier referred to a second deontological theory, theism, and the natural law tradition that branches from theism. According to theism, certain requirements trump considerations of self-interest through the binding force of God's commands. Like the theist, Kant also thought of duties as given by commands, although unlike the theist, Kant did not believe that the source of obligation is God's authority. The source or obligation is rationality itself, according to Kant, and one can identify one's duty by asking whether the intention behind an action is universalizable in a sense which Kant attempts to clarify. Roughly stated, Kant's suggestion is that we may not act in some way unless everyone could do so as well. Kant also attempted to supply an understanding of the right which did not invoke considerations of self-interest. On his view, a duty to do something trumps matters of self-interest; we must do our duty regardless of the consequences for our happiness or self-interest.

9. Duties

Justifying particular duties is, therefore, a somewhat vexatious issue, but all of the leading contemporary moral views take seriously the idea of obligation. Many duties have been suggested; among them are the following:

1. Be true to oneself and others.
2. Do not harm other people nor (perhaps) other living things.
3. Offer a reasonable amount of help to those in need.
4. Deal fairly with people. (Treat them as equals.)

Some philosophers would refine the formulations of these duties to ensure that they cannot conflict, for duties are binding, and people must be able to meet all duties. But other philosophers would suggest that duties may conflict; the claim that they are absolutely binding (and hence must always be obeyed) must be qualified. David Ross, for example, has suggested that duties are binding, other things being equal; they are *prima facie* duties. On this view, when one duty does not conflict with another, we must meet that duty, but when duties conflict, determining the final duty becomes a complicated matter of finessing competing obligations. Clear answers may be impossible to find.

It is instructive to see the project of clarifying duties by expressing them in the form of clear principles as an attempt to fill a gap in the more ancient virtue-based ethics. In his writings on government, Aristotle makes the point that the rule of law is superior to the rule of people, meaning that governments should express as explicit laws any requirements that they will enforce. Even if public officials are virtuous people, they should not coerce others in ways that are not provided for by law. Aristotle adds that the rule of law has shortcomings, creating a need for virtuous judges to handle situations that were unforeseen when laws were designed. But laws are indispensable requirements. A first step in the design of good laws would express moral virtues in the form of principles. These principles could then guide legislation. Consequently, even the virtue ethicist ought to acknowledge the importance of explicitly formulated moral principles, and others should acknowledge that these principles will likely have implausible implications in unforeseeable situations. Hence, principles cannot completely replace the judgement of morally sensible people. Still, people should strive to express the moral virtues in the form of moral principles, so that the requirements of morality can be made more explicit and clear, and more easily applicable to law. In fact, without too much strain, one might pair ancient virtues to modern moral duties:

VIRTUES	DUTIES
Integrity, honesty, loyalty	Be true.
Non-maleficence	Do not harm other people nor (perhaps) living things.
Benevolence	Offer reasonable help to those in need.
Justice	Deal fairly with people

---

[1]See his essay "Two Dogmas of Empiricism," in *From a Logical Point of View* (New York: Harper Torchbooks, 1953).

Theories of the Good and the Right

■━━━━■

INTRODUCTION

As this book's introduction noted, some moral traditions elevate their concept of the good into an entire moral conception, relying on the assumption that we can eliminate conflicts among people by shaping, or reshaping, the identity which binds individuals to the community and defines their interests. This emphasis on the importance of the good is characteristic of the ancient Greek moral tradition initiated by Aristotle and his teacher Plato (and by Plato's teacher Socrates). It is also characteristic of leading ancient moral traditions in the East, such as Buddhism, Daoism, and Confucianism.

Recall also that later moral traditions rely less heavily on the concept of the good. Some traditions suggest that a complete moral conception requires a second fundamental moral notion—the concept of the right. Beginning with the natural law tradition, whose roots extend to the ancient Stoics, some philosophers began to emphasize the importance of the individual's identity, to see individuals as equals, and to view the individual's interests as morally significant in their own right. The concept of right itself was thought to provide a framework of specific freedoms and obligations, or specific rights and duties, which limit the pursuit of self-interest and protect the pursuit of self-interest from interference by others: *Duties* compel us to accommodate the interests of others, while *rights* compel others to accommodate our interests. This framework was said to take absolute priority over all considerations of the interests of selves, whether individual or group selves. Many thinkers contributed to this quintessentially Western approach to morality, including Stoics such as Cicero, natural law theorists such as Aquinas, contractarians (in whose moral views the idea of a contract plays a central role) such as John Locke and Immanuel Kant, and utilitarians such as Jeremy Bentham and J. S. Mill.

This part of the book (limited to Chapter 1) will examine six of the most influential theories of morality, including three Western approaches and three Eastern approaches: the views of Aristotle, Mill, Kant, Confucius, Laotzi, and Gautama (the Buddha). For each of the six, the chapter provides an introductory essay and excerpts from central texts.

TRADITIONAL APPROACHES

ARISTOTELIANISM

J. F. HEIL

Aristotelianism

No other philosopher has exerted more influence, and in more areas, than Aristotle. He wrote in virtually every major field—logic and epistemology, psychology and literary theory, ethics and politics, biology and zoology, physics and cosmology, to name a few—and, in most cases, he was the first to *define* the field itself, to articulate its basic principles and methodology, and to distinguish it from other disciplines. The "departments" of study that we take for granted nowadays in colleges and universities owe their origin largely to Aristotle.

Aristotle (384–322 BCE) lived most of his adult life in a city that he was not a citizen of, the great cultural hub of the ancient world, Athens. Born in Stagira, in the kingdom of Macedonia, Aristotle grew up as the son of a physician to the royal court of Amyntas (whose son Philip, and grandson Alexander, were to make their own mark on the world in days to come). When he was seventeen, Aristotle went to Athens, where he spent 20 years (367–347) studying with Plato at the Academy. After Plato's death, he left Athens for 12 years, living in Assos and then in Mytilene, where he apparently devoted his time to research in zoology and marine biology. In 343, he accepted an appointment from Philip to serve as tutor to Alexander the Great. Soon after Philip's assassination in 336, when Alexander assumed the kingship, Aristotle returned to Athens and founded his own school at the Lyceum, a gymnasium on the opposite side of town from Plato's Academy. The school's outdoor walkway or *"peripatos,"* where Aristotle would frequently hold his classes, earned his followers the name "Peripatetics." When Alexander the Great died in 323, anti-Macedonian feeling surfaced and intensified in Athens. According to one account, Aristotle was charged with impiety and, "rather than let Athens sin twice against philosophy," went into voluntary exile. He died a year later in Chalcis.

TELEOLOGY AND THE HUMAN GOOD

The *Nicomachean Ethics* is Aristotle's principal work on *"ta ēthika,"* an expression he himself seems to have coined, meaning literally "matters pertaining to character." Indeed, portions of the *Ethics* read like a guidebook to virtues, vices and other character traits. As Aristotle tells us in his opening chapter, however, the larger field of study that *ta ēthika* falls under is the study of good—or, rather, as he is fond of emphasizing, the *human* good. This emphasis is a reaction to Plato, who famously posited a "Form of the Good," a highly abstract entity that could explain the goodness of *all* good things. Aristotle decisively rejects Plato's Form of the Good (in Bk. 1, Ch. 6, not included below) and for three basic reasons: (1) there simply is no such universal goodness common to all things we call good (what does good chocolate ice cream have in common with the good timing of a gymnast or a good spot for a picnic?); (2) even if there were a Form, it is clearly not the sort of thing we *pursue* in life (we pursue goods, not some abstract formula that may be truly predicated of them); and (3) the Form would not be anything specific enough even to help us *understand* what is better or worse to pursue. Aristotle's goal in the *Ethics*, then, is to redress these problems in the Platonic approach, and to articulate and defend a view of what the good is for human beings, i.e., what it is (a) that we actually pursue in life, (b) that would benefit us to understand, and (c) that, if obtained, would make our life good.

Aristotle's answer to this question of the human good is deceptively simple: our life is good if it achieves its *"telos"*—its aim or *end*. I say deceptively simple because Aristotle is actually packing two ideas into this single term. One is the notion of an aim or goal that we, as agents who choose our own actions, set before us "like archers who have a target" (Ch. 2). Our lives have a teleological structure in the sense that our choices and actions are purposive; they are carried out with certain ends in view. Many of our goals are pursued for some further reason: we might, for instance, pursue a certain sort of education for the sake of a particular career, and, in turn, pursue that particular career because it is most rewarding. At some point, however, we reach an end (e.g., accomplishing good work, enjoying ourselves, etc.) that we pursue for no further reason. If, says Aristotle, there is some *ultimate end* of all our choices, i.e., something we aim at by pursuing all our other ends, then this would be our good. Such an ultimate end need not be a single, monolithic goal; it may well be a package of several ends that we pursue for their own sake. The basic idea is that the good of our life as a whole lies in the achievement of the things we are ultimately aiming at in life.

In addition to this *agent* teleology, however, Aristotle is also assuming a *natural* teleology for us as human beings. This is the notion of achieving our end by developing and perfecting our distinctively human nature. On Aristotle's view, anything that has a nature—human beings, frogs, oak trees, etc.—also has an end, namely, the realization of its nature. Thus its good, we might say, lies in becoming what it is. The good of a frog or an oak tree, for instance, is achieved through its unimpeded development into a mature, fully functioning frog or oak tree. But, what does Aristotle think our distinctively human features are? One of them, no doubt, would be what we mentioned above: *agency*. We organize our lives teleologically by carrying out our choices and actions with certain ends in view. This distinguishes us from oak trees (although frogs, and especially more intelligent animals, might seem to exhibit a similar sort of agency). In addition to this, however, we also have *rationality*. We deliberate over our choices; we weigh ends and calculate goods; we discuss problems and solutions with each other. In short, we *think* about what we do in a way that distinguishes us from all other animals (but not, in Aristotle's view, from the gods). Thus the full development and exercise of rationality, he argues in Ch. 7, will be part of our good, since that is part of what it is to be human. One other aspect of our nature that Aristotle takes to be crucial is summed up in his famous slogan, "the human being is a *political animal*" (alluded to in Ch. 7). By "political" Aristotle means something broader than we do when we use that term. His claim is that we are by nature *social* creatures. Part of being human is living in a community with others, and thus sharing in a variety of relationships at a number of different levels, "parents and children and wife, and friends and fellow-citizens" (Ch. 7). This, he thinks, distinguishes us from the gods, who live a life of pure contemplation without need for interaction with others.

Our social nature has deep and immediate implications. If a good human life involves the complete development and exercise of our nature, and if it is our nature to live with others, then the human good will of necessity include living well with others. It cannot be obtained outside of society. According to Aristotle, anyone who is not part of society, "either because he is incapable of sharing in a community or because he is self-sufficient and in need of nothing, must be either a beast or a god" (*Politics* Bk. 1, Ch. 2). Our good is not detachable from the community because *we* are not detachable. This is why he says that the good "is the same for an individual and a state," and that politics—the art of fashioning and maintaining a good human society—is ultimately the field in charge of understanding and achieving the human good (Ch. 2).

Aristotle's natural teleology, then, leads him to take a communitarian approach to ethics. He does not, however, neglect the individual. Indeed, the *Ethics* is devoted entirely to questions concerning the good life for an individual human being, because only *after* examining this will we see what a good society should look like. That is why Aristotle ends the *Ethics* with the words, "Now, let us begin our discussion"—referring to what he considers part two of his study of the human good, the *Politics*. There he suggests that, although the individual must be understood as an organic part of society, the individual's good is not itself determined by the larger purposes of society. The purpose of society, he seems to say, *is* the good of its members: it "exists for the sake of living well" (*Politics* Bk. 1, Ch. 2). We are not like a hive of bees making honey. What we aim to produce in the community, rather, is the goodness of each of our lives, but we do so through such collective efforts as education, sound lawmaking, stable business and trade practices, nice recreation areas, festivals, and countless other social activities.

HAPPINESS AND THE HUMAN FUNCTION

But how does Aristotle's natural teleology fit with the earlier notion that our good is the ultimate end of our choices and actions? After all, different people aim at different things. Do they all equally well fulfill the basic requirements of our human nature? If so, then are there many different and incompatible human goods? These are the questions Aristotle addresses next, and he begins by noting that "nearly everyone agrees to the name" of our ultimate end, "since both the majority and the refined call it 'happiness' (*eudaimonia*) and suppose that living well and doing well are the same as being happy" (Ch. 4). Beyond this, however, there is substantial disagreement. Some pursue pleasure and amusement; others seek wealth; others set their sights on the honors of military or political life; others strive to become good people who do their jobs well; still others pursue a life of study and aim for knowledge above all. It seems that "living well and doing well" takes many forms.

Aristotle certainly thinks some of these lives are better than others—the life of mere enjoyment, for instance, is likened to that of "grazing animals," while the life of study is "god-like"—but rather than adjudicate between them on the basis of which one best expresses our human nature, he makes the striking claim that they are *all* wrong, and for a completely different reason. They are wrong, he argues, because none of them aims at a truly *ultimate* end. Though they are all aiming at good things, these goods fail to satisfy one or both of the two basic requirements something must meet in order to be an ultimate end: "completeness" and "self-sufficiency." Something is "complete," says Aristotle, if it is pursued for its own sake, and even "more complete" if it is also pursued for the sake of nothing further. Wealth, for instance, would be a textbook case of an incomplete end because, according to Aristotle, it is never pursued for its own sake. Though most of the other ends—e.g., pleasure, honor, virtue, knowledge— can be pursued for their own sake, Aristotle thinks that "we also choose them for the sake of happiness, supposing that we will be happy through them" (Ch. 7). The idea, then, seems to be that these goals do not provide the ultimate reason *why* the people who pursue them are pursuing them. By a "self-sufficient" good Aristotle means something that "by itself . . . makes life choiceworthy and lacking in nothing." (Ibid.) The idea here is that a truly ultimate end must be *all* that we want out of life. If we want more than pleasure (e.g., a few friends and something to do), then pleasure is not self-sufficient. If we want more than virtue (e.g., opportunities to exercise it), then virtue also fails to be self-sufficient. Happiness, by contrast, must be something that "the least little additional good" would not make any better.

Nonetheless, these other pursuits each have something to recommend, and Aristotle makes an effort to show that a proper conception of happiness will incorporate the values of pleasure, virtue, action, and thought. The famous "Function Argument" in Ch. 7 represents his attempt to go back to human nature and develop a broader conception of the good life that makes room for all of these other goods. We have already discussed what Aristotle takes our distinctively human features to be, but here he refines the question by asking whether there is any distinctive "function" or "work" (*ergon*) that we perform in virtue of our human features. His suggestion is that, if we consider a human life as a kind of occupation, on analogy with crafts such as flute-playing and shoemaking, then we might be able to spell out the human good in the same way that we do for crafts: doing the job well. But, is there anything that we could call the "job" of a human being? Yes, Aristotle argues, it is "some sort of *life of action* belonging to something that possesses *reason*" or "activity of the soul in accordance with, or not without, reason" (Ch. 7). As we found earlier, what Aristotle takes to be distinctive about us is that we think and deliberate about our actions, and carry them out within some sort of rationally ordered scheme (pursuing some ends for the sake of others, etc.). To do this *well*, however, requires that we possess certain abilities or "virtues" and, so, happiness can be characterized as rational activity "in accordance with virtue." The "virtue" Aristotle introduces here is intentionally left vague. It presumably includes all of the moral and prudential virtues that he will discuss later on. For Aristotle, a virtue is quite generally a capacity to do something well, and its particular field of operation (managing our personal affairs, helping others, etc.) will determine whether it aims at something right or merely at something beneficial to us.

With this broad characterization of happiness, Aristotle can unite the several goods proposed above: virtue, action, and thought. In Ch. 8, he will try to show how his conception of happiness achieves this synthesis, and how it accommodates pleasure as well: virtuous activity is intrinsically pleasant, he says. It might be thought that the conception of happiness Aristotle defends here is hopelessly vague and unhelpful. What it gains in theoretical strength by uniting a number of competing conceptions of the good life, it loses in practical strength by offering us no specific guidance on how to live. Aristotle, however, likes this result. He believes that the specific content of ethics depends on the concrete circumstances in which we live. Ethical theory, then, *should* be fuzzy and imprecise. It can address only what is true "for the most part" and "can indicate the truth roughly and in outline" (Ch. 3). We are ultimately responsible for filling in the details, and here again our social nature is crucial. Our knowledge of which virtues and values are most important comes not from abstract or theoretical reasoning, but from parents and friends and fellow-citizens.

LUCK AND THE FRAGILITY OF HAPPINESS

Aristotle's self-sufficiency requirement, combined with his drive to articulate a conception of happiness that incorporates the prevailing, common sense views about the basic goods in life, gets him into trouble. It is trouble that he welcomes, however, because it is trouble he thinks is inherent in a proper conception of happiness. Here's the problem. If happiness is to be truly self-sufficient, if it is to be *all* that we want out of life, then it must apply to the entire span of our lifetime. "One swallow does not make a spring" (Ch. 7). Life, however, is subject to changes in fortune: natural disasters, tragic losses of friends and family members, unexpected financial burdens, diseases and disabilities. It seems, then, that many components of our happiness are largely beyond our control, and their continued preservation is particularly vulnerable to the ravages of time and the fluctuations of circumstance. Aristotle refers to these as "external goods" (Ch. 8: freedom from disease and disability would belong to "goods of the body," but the fragility of health is surely no less than that of external goods). He is committed, however, to the view that happiness requires external goods, both because common sense tells us so and, more importantly, because his own view of happiness as good *activity* demands it: "It is impossible, or not easy, to perform fine actions without resources" (Ch. 8).

This might not create a problem, except that Aristotle thinks (and perhaps we agree) that happiness should be something that, with thought and effort, we can *earn*. It requires, above all else, rational activity "in accordance with virtue," and virtue is acquired by improving *ourselves* (our "souls," as Aristotle puts it), not our external prosperity. From this angle, then, it seems that happiness should be "something permanent and not at all changeable" (Ch. 10). People who are happy only if they win the lottery, we think, are not happy at all. Happiness is not the same as luck; it is a successful life that is earned by making a success of ourselves. How could changes in fortune ever affect this kind of achievement? The problem, then, is that Aristotle holds *both* that happiness requires external goods *and* that it should have the kind of permanence that external goods are incapable of living up to.

Many Greek philosophers, both before and after Aristotle, opted for permanence over prosperity. Socrates, for instance, had argued that *virtue* is sufficient (and, thus, external goods unnecessary) for happiness. Virtue is something that we acquire by our own efforts and that cannot be taken away from us. But, if happiness—the ultimate prize in life—is rightly held in even greater esteem than virtue, then how can we allow it to be something that lousy people might end up with more of than good people? Thus Socrates. Now, Aristotle does not allow that bad people can be happy, since for him virtuous activity is a necessary condition for happiness, but he is willing to say that two equally good people might not both end up happy. External goods, whose presence or absence is controlled as much by luck as by virtue, are also necessary for happiness. Aristotle is willing to bite the bullet and admit that our happiness may not be something that we fully earn, and that the highest value in human life may not be achieved even after we have devoted our entire lives to achieving it: "Clearly minor instances of good or bad fortune do not bear significantly on life, but large and numerous successes will make life happier, both because they themselves naturally add beauty to it and because the use of them is fine and outstanding. If things turn out the other way around, however, it can crush and maim our happiness. Great misfortune brings pain and impedes many activities." (Ch. 10).

VIRTUE

A virtue *(aretē)*, for all Greek philosophers, is most broadly understood to be an excellent quality of something that enables it to perform well. As Aristotle tells us, "it is the best disposition or state or ability of whatever has some use or function" (*Eudemian Ethics,* Bk. 2, Ch. 1). Hence, even inanimate objects can be said to have virtues: the virtue of a coat lies in its warm and well-sewn material; the virtue of a knife lies in its sharp and sure edge; and so forth. In the animate realm, the paradigm of a virtue, at least for philosophers in the Classical period, is the expertise of a craftsman. Aristotle thinks of a craft or *"technē"* not as a precise, axiomatic science, but as a special set of abilities, acquired by training and experience, that allow someone to create excellent products on a reliable basis.

Two important points to notice are (1) "virtue" is not a specifically *moral* term, though it does always refer to some praiseworthy excellence; and (2) particular virtues are always defined in reference to an existing practice or pursuit. We don't think up virtues and then go looking for uses for them. Rather, we have uses and then seek corresponding virtues. This second point, I think, explains why Aristotle chooses to discuss the particular virtues that he does: courage (for the fearful conditions of warfare), temperance (for the alluring pleasures of civilian life), justice (for our transactions and dealings with others), gentleness (for our response to the injustices of others), and so forth. For this reason, too, Aristotle should not be read as offering a complete or definitive catalog of human virtues. We should be aware that some of what he says about particular virtues, and the way he divides them up, will be influenced by ancient Greek practices and expectations.[1]

In the *Ethics,* Aristotle is concerned with the virtues that we need to live a good human life and, as I mentioned earlier, he doesn't show any interest in drawing a line between what we would call "moral" virtues (e.g., honesty or fairness, pertaining specifically to morally right action) and "prudential" virtues (e.g., intelligence or industry, pertaining to the efficient accomplishment of our ends). We shall have to ask in a moment how exactly Aristotle thinks the virtues are connected to the fairly restricted domain of *morally right* actions and, in general, what his account of right and wrong is. What we shall find, however, is that he never gives us anything that we could call a *theory* of right and wrong. To us modern readers, who have learned to equate ethics with the study of right and wrong, such an omission is baffling and absurd. If, however, we remember the larger scope of Aristotle's project—a study of human good and "matters pertaining to character"—it is not surprising to find that his account of right and wrong is only one among many of his concerns.

THE DIVIDED SOUL

Aristotle's concern, at this point, is to give an account of "human virtue" (Bk. 1, Ch. 13) and his aim is quite ambitious: to offer a single, unified theory of virtue that explains (1) the basic structure shared by all the virtues, (2) the kinds of modifications they involve in the person, and (3) how they can be acquired. He goes about this, first, by dividing the virtues into two kinds: "virtues of character" (e.g., courage and temperance) and "virtues of thought" (e.g., wisdom and intelligence). This distinction, he tells us, corresponds to a fundamental division in the human soul. Virtues of thought belong to the "rational part" of the soul, virtues of character to the "nonrational part" (Ch. 13). Why does Aristotle think that the soul has two parts?

There are times, he says, when people act against their own best judgment. They decide that it would be best to abstain from some pleasure, but then cave into their appetite. Anyone who has ever tried to go on a diet knows the experience. This simple and familiar phenomenon of incontinence, which the Greeks called *akrasia,* shows that there is "some other natural element in them besides reason, which is fighting and struggling against their reason." *(Ibid.)* Is Aristotle right? Not all philosophers have agreed that *akrasia* is even possible. Socrates famously denied that people ever act against their better judgment: caving into our desires is a matter of *changing our mind,* if only momentarily, about what is best. Aristotle, however, thinks that *akrasia* does happen and that it is best explained by the hypothesis that there are two, independent forces in us, each of which is capable by itself of moving us to action. Thus he develops a "bipartite" theory of the soul, strongly influenced by Plato's famous "tripartite" view in *The Republic.* Aristotle essentially collapses the two nonrational parts of Plato's soul (the "spirited" and "appetitive" parts) into one.

It is important to get this distinction between rational and nonrational right, but easy to get it wrong. Aristotle is not contrasting reason with instinct.[2] Instinct is something that we cannot change about ourselves, but the nonrational part of us is *malleable* and, indeed, if shaped properly, is the seat of the virtues of character. It can be shaped because it has "some sort of tendency to listen to reason, as though to a father" and, in this way, thinks Aristotle, it can "participate in reason." From this, we can also tell that he does not intend his distinction to be one between cognition and desire, between an information-processing unit and a power source. The nonrational part has a rich cognitive structure, given that it can be "persuaded by reason" and thus even come to "possess reason." What the nonrational part cannot do is engage in *reasoning*. It can possess reason only derivatively. Both parts also have their own drives. In "akratic" or incontinent people, reason struggles and "urges them towards what is best," while in "enkratic" or continent people (those who *win* their struggles with desire) reason successfully overpowers the nonrational part and gains control of their actions. So, what is the best way of describing the distinction Aristotle wants to draw? The crucial contrast, I suggest, is between two different ways in which we acquire the beliefs that inform our choices and actions: one by thinking and *figuring things out,* another by being trained or *conditioned in a certain way.* Aristotle thinks this difference is so fundamental that he proposes two parts of the soul to do the work

The rational and nonrational parts, of course, influence and interact with each other. After figuring something out, we acquire a tendency to continue believing it. When values are involved, once we reason that something is good, our desires tend to be shaped accordingly, though rarely with the same speed and surety as reason (and, in some cases, where strong competing desires already exist, not at all). That is why Aristotle thinks people who "are guided by reason in forming their desires" can benefit tremendously from the study of ethics (Bk. 1, Ch. 3). Conversely, any conditioned tendency we may have to desire certain things will influence what we take to be necessary or important to figure out. Someone who doesn't *care* about being good to his friend, for instance, won't worry about such things as whether or not he should lie to him about his bleak medical prognosis, what lying or telling the truth would entail in this situation, and so forth. Aristotle takes this point to be absolutely central to ethics. Indeed, he thinks that if we have not had a decent "upbringing," and thus if we do not share certain basic moral beliefs and desires, then there is no point in doing ethics (Bk. 1, Ch. 4). Why would anyone worry about virtue if she didn't want to do well?

HABITUATION AND THE "MEAN"

Now we are in position to run through Aristotle's theory of virtue. Virtues of character arise in the nonrational part, the part of us that is *conditioned* or, as Aristotle prefers to say, "habituated" (Bk. 2, Ch 1). This happens by coming to feel pleasure in relation to some things and pain in relation to others. The case of the parent who rewards and punishes the child is the most familiar example of habituation.[3] But this is not just a process of having our feelings molded in certain ways. Guided by these pleasures and pains, we acquire habits of doing certain things and avoiding others. By repeated exercise of good activities and good responses to various circumstances we acquire dispositions to act and respond well. After we develop our reason and are able to navigate the world, interpret situations, and make decisions on our own, then we refine our actions and responses, and thus make our dispositions more precise and accurate. For instance, we move from a vague disposition to be generous to a disposition, say, to be generous in cases where someone has suffered genuinely undeserved losses. When we have achieved the best possible degree of precision in the broad range of situations in life that call for action or response, then we have the virtues. In fact, at this point we achieve, simultaneously, the virtues of character and of thought.[4]

That's a very fast sketch, but the details can be found in the text. The net result is that, when we have virtue, we act and respond "at the right times, about the right objects, towards the right people, for the right reason, and in the right way" (Bk. 2, Ch. 6). The big question now is: how do we determine what "the right" is? Aristotle gives three answers to this questions, all of which seem closely connected with each other. His remarks do not address specifically *moral* right and wrong, but he clearly intends them to include that sphere of action, so this is where we will find his account of how the virtues are connected to what is morally right.

First, he tells us that good actions must "be performed in accordance with *correct reason*" (Bk. 2, Ch. 2). This states a general condition, but offers no specific guidance because, according to Aristotle, "these matters fall under no craft or set of precepts." Rather, "people themselves, the people engaged in action, always need to consider things in relation to the occasion, just as they do in medicine and navigation." There are, then, no universal or exceptionless laws (e.g., Kant's categorical imperative or Mill's greatest happiness principle) that we can apply to determine if an action is right or wrong. Second, however, there is a general feature that all right actions exhibit: they aim at and hit "the mean." Just as the right amount of food and drink is neither too much nor too little, so to "someone who flees from and fears everything, and endures nothing, becomes cowardly. But, someone who fears absolutely nothing, and faces everything, becomes rash." Only the brave person "aims at the intermediate." It is unclear (and much debated among scholars) why Aristotle thinks his notion of the mean is at all helpful in determining right action—especially since he describes the mean not as a quantifiable kind of *moderation* in our actions, but as the appropriate, i.e., *right* way of acting.

As if needing something to complete what is already a vicious circle, Aristotle mentions a third basis for determining right action. Consider his final definition of virtue at the end of Bk. 2, Ch. 6: "Virtue, then, is a state having to do with decision, lying in a mean relative to us and defined by reason, i.e., *in the way someone with practical wisdom would define it.*" Practical wisdom *(phronēsis)* is the capstone of virtue I alluded to above: its achievement involves the simultaneous achievement of the virtues of character. It seems, then, according to this definition of virtue, that both the mean and correct reason are determined by people who already have the virtues. Just as in the arts, it is the masters who set the standards, so too in the virtues. This suggestion seems to solve nothing, and perhaps even to compound Aristotle's problem. How do we know which people have virtue if we still need to know what the right actions are? Do we ultimately have to become virtuous in order to know how to be virtuous? That seems absurd.

One move that we might expect Aristotle to make here, given his teleology and his concept of happiness as the ultimate good, is to measure right and wrong in terms of what promotes or impedes happiness. Mill and other utilitarians recommend just such a teleological standard, but Aristotle would emphatically reject it. For him, happiness involves all that is good in life; it is the package of all the ends we pursue for their own sake, and among these are included right action. Happiness cannot serve as a moral standard, then, precisely because we need to know what is right and wrong before we can develop our conception of happiness. This does not mean that happiness is useless as a reference point for our decisions, but a big part of what makes it useful is that it includes our view of what is right, and the latter is obviously crucial to reflect on when making decisions.

What we seem to be left with, then, is the community. The social practices around us and, hence, the people who have mastered these practices, provide the standard for right and wrong action. If we want to know why our society engages in these practices and not others, then Aristotle will have a long story to tell and will refer us to the *Politics.* He will try to nail down as much as he can to human nature and, subsequently, to the institutions that naturally arise in any decently organized society, but he can't deduce a specific set of practices, much less a moral code, from this alone. There is room for a certain amount of variety and flexibility. Whether this is a good thing or not is up to us to decide.

WHY "VIRTUE ETHICS"?

Aristotle's ethics, with its emphasis on virtue and its broader range of concern for the good life rather than just the moral life, has experienced a strong and enthusiastic revival in the last few decades. Does he have something to offer that is missing in modern approaches to ethics, such as those of Kant and Mill? Does his view avoid certain problems that the others seem to be plagued by?

Some ethicists believe that Aristotle provides the best answer to skeptical worries about discovering any general and exceptionless moral laws. If we cannot discover any such laws, and yet we still think there is a difference between being good and bad—we see that there *are* good people and, moreover, that being good still *matters*—then, in our own effort to become good, we may have no other guide than the judgment and virtue of good people. I happen to believe that this was one of Aristotle's own motivations for putting such an emphasis on virtue. Socrates had sought necessary and sufficient *definitions* for things such as justice and courage and piety. Plato, however, in his dialogues, depicts the failure of Socrates to achieve such definitions, and begins to develop a view that makes virtue and character foundational. (In *The Republic,* he makes it clear that no one can grasp the Form of the Good until she achieves virtue.) In this regard, then, Aristotle seems to be following through on Plato's project.

Let me mention three other issues that some modern philosophers have raised. Bernard Williams argues that the standard moral theories of Kant and Mill presuppose a problematic view of human beings as moral agents. They imagine us as occupants of an inner citadel of freedom, in which we make our moral decisions and then issue them into the world. Aristotle, on the other hand, begins with the assumption that we are social creatures who grow up within a pre-existing framework of social practices and, thus, whose virtues are defined in large part by the community. This, thinks Williams, is a more plausible picture of who we are, and we would do well to recognize this in our ascriptions of moral worth and responsibility. Luck and circumstance, for instance, do play a role in the goodness of people, however much we may wish it to be otherwise.

Michael Stocker has made the accusation that modern ethical theory leads to a kind of "schizophrenia" in our moral decisions. On the one hand, it tells us that we ought to act on certain moral principles *impartially*, without favoritism or bias. On the other hand, we all know a good life involves the love and care for *particular* individuals, such as our friends and family members. Thus, in our effort to be "moral" we must ignore the other side of us that is making an effort to live a good life. How could this sort of clash and disharmony be a correct recipe for the good life? Aristotle, as we've seen, makes the good life foundational to ethics and, hence, is well positioned to fit the suitable contexts for impartiality into the larger framework of happiness, rather than the other way around.

Finally, it has become a common complaint nowadays that a theory like Kant's comes up short in its account of what a moral action amounts to. It would seem, for instance, that helping others out of a sense of moral duty (as Kant would have it) is *morally* inferior to helping them out of kindness and love. As we've seen, Aristotle's virtue ethics demands that good action flow from an engrained disposition to perform the action. To the extent, then, that you may think Kant is wrong to dismiss "inclination" as irrelevant to the moral worth of our actions, you may decide that a theory like Aristotle's should be given serious consideration.

---

[1]His discussion of the particular virtues is not included in this anthology, but for further reading see Book 2, Ch. 7, and Book 3, Ch. 6 through Book 6.

[2]Aristotle does think that *part* of our nonrational part is "vegetative" and is responsible for such things as nourishment, growth, and reproduction. This comes closest to being the source of what we might call "instincts," since it comes closest to being the kind of thing we attribute to our *bodily* nature. He is very careful, however, to distinguish this nonrational part of us from the part he thinks matters to virtue.

[3]Our upbringing is also the earliest—and, for that reason, Aristotle thinks, the most crucial—habituation we receive in life. Although institutions such as customs and laws serve this function throughout our adult lives, what happens in the first few years "makes a tremendous difference—indeed, all the difference" (Bk. 2, Ch 1).

[4]Aristotle discusses the unity of intellectual and character virtue in Bk. 6, not included in this anthology.

Further Reading

Aristotle's Ethics

Annas, J. 1993. *The Morality of Happiness.* Oxford. [This work covers broad trends in ancient Greek ethics, from Aristotle through the Hellenistic schools.]

Broadie, S. 1991. *Ethics with Aristotle.* New York / Oxford.

Cooper, J. 1975. *Reason and Human Good in Aristotle.* Cambridge, MA.

Irwin, T. 1985. "Permanent Happiness: Aristotle and Solon." *Oxford Studies in Ancient Philosophy* 3, 89-124.

Nussbaum, M. 1986. *The Fragility of Goodness: Luck and Ethics in Greek Tragedy and Philosophy.* Cambridge.

Rorty, A. (ed.). 1980. *Essays on Aristotle's Ethics.* Berkeley / Los Angeles.
Recent Developments in Virtue Ethics
Crisp, R. (ed.). 1996. *How Should One Live? Essays on the Virtues.* Oxford.
Foot, P. 1978. *Virtues and Vices.* Oxford.
French, P., Uehling, T., Jr., and Wettstein, H. (eds.). 1988. "Ethical Theory: Character and Virtue." *Midwest Studies in Philosophy* 13. Notre Dame.
Geach, P. 1977. *The Virtues.* Cambridge.
Kruschwitz, R., and Roberts, R. (eds.). 1987. *The Virtues: Contemporary Essays on Moral Character.* Belmont, CA.
MacIntyre, A. 1981. *After Virtue.* London.
McDowell, John. 1979. "Virtue and Reason." *The Monist* 62, 331–350.
Slote, M. 1995. *From Morality to Virtue.* Oxford.
Stocker, M. 1976. "The Schizophrenia of Modern Ethical Theories." *Journal of Philosophy* 73, 453–466.
Williams, B. 1985. *Ethics and the Limits of Philosophy.* London.

ARISTOTLE

translated by J. F. Heil

Selections from Book 1 of *Nicomachean Ethics*

CHAPTER 1

Every craft and every inquiry, like every action and decision, is thought to aim at some good. Hence, people have rightly declared the good to be "that at which everything aims." But, there is evidently some difference among the ends aimed at. Some are activities, while others are works beyond the activities themselves, and where there are ends beyond the actions, the works are by nature better than the activities. And, given that there are many actions and crafts and fields of expertise, there are also many ends. Health is the end of medicine, a boat of shipbuilding, victory of generalship, and wealth of household management. But, any craft of this sort that falls under a single ability—as, for instance, the making of bridles and other equipment for horses falls under horsemanship, and this, in turn, along with all military action, falls under generalship, and so on—in every such case, the ends of the master crafts are more choiceworthy than all of those that fall under them, since it is for their sake that those others are even pursued. Here it makes no difference whether the ends of the actions are the activities themselves or, as in the fields of expertise just mentioned something else beyond them.

CHAPTER 2

If, then, there is some end of the things we do, something that we wish for because of *itself,* while the others are things we wish for because of it, and if we do not choose everything because of something else—since, in that case, things will proceed *ad infinitum,* so that our desire will be empty and in vain—then it is clear that this end would be the good and the best thing. Indeed, wouldn't knowledge of it have tremendous importance for our lives and, like archers who have a target, wouldn't we tend more to hit the right mark? If so, then we should try, in outline at least, to grasp what it is and to which field of expertise or ability it belongs.

The good would seem to belong to the most authoritative field, the one that is, above all others, a master craft. Politics appears to be just such a craft, since it tells us which fields of expertise need to exist in the state, and who is to learn each one and up to what point. We also see that even the most highly esteemed abilities—e.g., generalship, household management, rhetoric—fall under it. And, since it makes use of the remaining fields of expertise pertaining to action, and further, since it legislates which actions we ought to perform and abstain from, its end would contain the ends of the others. Hence, its end would be the human good. For, even if it is the same for an individual and a state, the good of the state appears to be a greater and more complete thing to achieve and maintain. It is to be welcomed for a single individual, but it is finer and more divine for nations and states. Our inquiry, then, aims at these things, being a political inquiry of sorts.

CHAPTER 3

Our discussion, however, would be adequate if it could be given a clarity that corresponds to the subject matter. We should not, after all, seek the same precision in all discussions, any more than we do in the productions of artisans. What is fine and what is just, matters that politics investigates, exhibit so much difference and variation that they are thought to exist only by convention and not by nature. This sort of variation is exhibited by good things as well, because of the harms that befall many people as a result of them. After all, there have been people destroyed because of their wealth, and others because of their courage. It is to be welcomed, then, when discussions about, and based upon, such things, can indicate the truth roughly and in outline— that is, when discussions about, and based upon, things that hold only "for the most part" can also reach conclusions of that sort. Each of the claims under discussion also needs to be accepted in the same way. For, it is the mark of an educated person to seek as much precision in each kind of study as the nature of the thing permits. Accepting probable reasoning from a mathematician is apparently just as silly as demanding demonstrative proofs from an orator. . . .

CHAPTER 4

Let us take up our discussion again. Since all knowledge and every decision reaches out for some good, what is it that we say politics aims at? What is the highest of all the goods in the things we do? Now, nearly everyone agrees to the name, since both the majority and the refined call it "happiness" and suppose that living well and doing well are the same as being happy. But, they dispute over what happiness is, and the majority do not give the same account as the wise. The former consider it to be something plain and obvious—pleasure or wealth or honor—and something different for different people. Indeed, even the same person frequently considers it something different: when he is sick it is health, but when he is poor it is wealth. And, when people become conscious of their own ignorance, they are awestruck by those who speak of something grand and over their heads. Some, however, used to think that beyond these many good things is something different, good in itself, that is the cause of all these other things' being goods as well. . . .

CHAPTER 7

Let us return again to the good we are seeking and ask what it could be. It certainly appears to be different in different actions and crafts: in medicine it is one thing, in generalship something else, and so on. What, then, is the good in each case? Isn't it *that for the sake of which the rest of the things are done?* And in the case of medicine this is health, in generalship victory, in construction a house, etc., but in every action and decision it is *the end,* since everyone performs the rest of his actions for its sake. It follows that, if there is some end of all the things we do, this would be the good of what we do (and if there is more than one end, then these would be the good). Our discussion, then, has travelled around to the same point as before, but we should try to clarify this still further.

Since there appear to be many ends, but since we choose some of them—e.g., wealth, flutes, and instruments in general—because of something else, it is clear that not all ends are *complete.* But the best end appears to be something complete. So, if there is only one end that is complete, then this would be what we are seeking, while if there are more than one, then we seek the most complete among them. Now, we say that what is pursued in itself is more complete than what is pursued because of something else, and that what is never chosen because of another is more complete than things chosen both in themselves and because of it. What is *always chosen in itself and never because of anything else* is, therefore, complete without qualification.

Happiness, above all else, is thought to be such a thing, since we always choose it in itself and never because of something else. Honor, pleasure, thought, and all virtue, to be sure, we choose because of themselves (since we would choose each of them even if nothing further resulted), but we also choose them for the sake of happiness, supposing that we will be happy through them. No one, however, chooses happiness for the sake of these things, or because of anything else at all.

We appear to get the same result from a consideration of *self-sufficiency.* After all, the complete good is thought to be self-sufficient. By self-sufficient, however, we mean not what is sufficient for oneself alone, living a solitary life, but also for parents and children and wife, and friends and fellow-citizens in general, given that a human is by nature a political being. But some limit should be set for these: if we extend them to ancestors and descendants and friends' friends, then they will continue *ad infinitum. . . .* Let us set it down that something is self-sufficient if, *by itself, it makes life choiceworthy and lacking in nothing.* And we consider happiness to be just such a thing.

Furthermore, we consider happiness to be the *most choiceworthy* of all and not numbered among other goods. If it were numbered among others, then clearly it would become more choiceworthy with the least little additional good, since what is added becomes an extra amount of good, and the greater amount of good is always more choiceworthy.

Happiness, then, is evidently something complete and self-sufficient, being the end of the things we do.

To say that happiness is the best thing, however, might appear to be a platitude. What is badly needed is a clearer articulation of what the best good is. This might happen if we could grasp the *function* of a human being.[1] Just as for a flautist, a sculptor, or any craftsman—indeed, for anything at all that has a certain function and action— their good and their "doing well" is thought to lie in their function, so too, one should think, for a human being, if indeed there *is* a function here. Do a carpenter and shoemaker, then, have certain functions and actions, while a human being has none, but is by nature inactive?[2] Or shouldn't we suppose that, just as the eye, hand, foot, and quite generally each of the body parts appears to have a function, so too the human being has a function beyond all of these?

What, then, could this be? Just *to live* is apparently something shared even with plants, but we are seeking a unique characteristic. We should exclude, therefore, the life of nutrition and growth. Next would be some sort of life of perception, but this too appears to be shared with horses and oxen and all animals. There remains, then, some sort of *life of action* belonging to something that possesses *reason.* (Part of what possesses reason does so by being obedient to reason, another part by itself having reason and exercising thought.) And, since "life" is also spoken of in two ways, we should put "life as activity," since this is thought to be life in the stricter sense.[3]

Let us take the function of a human being to be *activity of the soul in accordance with, or not without, reason.* Now, we claim that the function of this or that thing is the same in kind as the function of an outstanding this or that. For instance, the function of a harpist is the same as that of an outstanding harpist, and this is certainly true without qualification in every case where the extra element of virtue is added to the function. The function of a harpist is to play the harp, and the function of an outstanding harpist is to play it well.

If so, and if we hold (a) that the function of a human being is a certain life, and (b) that this life is the soul's activity and actions accompanied by reason, and (c) that the function of an outstanding man is to do this well and in a fine manner, and (d) that each function is accomplished well when it is done in accordance with its own proper virtue—if all this is so, the human *good* turns out to be *the soul's activity in accordance with virtue.* And, if there are many virtues, then it will be in accordance with the best or most complete virtue. We should also add "in a complete life." One swallow does not make a spring, nor does one day. Likewise, one day or even a short span of time does not make someone blessed and happy. . . .

CHAPTER 8

We should examine this, however, not only on the basis of the premises and conclusion of our argument, but also on the basis of what is commonly said about it. With truth, all of reality sings in harmony—with falsehood, the truth is quick to clash.

Given that goods have been divided into three classes—some called external, and others of the soul and body—we say that goods of the soul are the chief and highest goods, and we put the soul's actions and activities in this class. So, our account is fine, at least according to this view, which is an old one and agreed upon by philosophers. It was also correct for us to say that certain actions and activities are the end, since in this way the end turns out to be among the goods of the soul and not among the external goods.

The view that the happy person lives well and does well also accords with our account, since we virtually identified happiness with a sort of living well and doing well. Indeed, it appears that all of the features sought for in happiness belong to what was given in our account. By some it is thought to be virtue, by others practical wisdom, by others a sort of theoretical wisdom, and by others all or one of these combined with pleasure, or not without pleasure. Others include external prosperity as well. Some of these are the majority and traditional views, while others are held by a few reputable men. It is reasonable to suppose, however, that neither of these groups is entirely mistaken, but rather that they've got at least one point right, or perhaps even most points.

Now, our account accords with those who say that happiness is virtue or some particular virtue. After all, activity in accordance with virtue belongs to virtue. Presumably, however, it makes no small difference whether we suppose that the best thing consists in possession or use, i.e., in a state or an activity. Though it is possible for a state to accomplish nothing good, e.g., when someone is sleeping or otherwise incapacitated, this isn't possible for an activity. An activity will necessarily *do* something, and a good activity will do it well. Just as in the Olympics it is not the finest or strongest who are crowned, but the competitors, since only among them will some achieve victory, so too in life the fine and good people who perform actions correctly are the ones who win the prize.

Their life is also pleasant in itself. After all, having pleasure is a condition of the soul, and what is pleasant to each person is related to whatever sort of thing he is said to be a lover of. A horse is pleasant to the horse-lover, a spectacle to the lover of sights, and in the same way just things are pleasant to the lover of justice and, in general, virtuous things to the lover of virtue. Now, the things that are pleasant to the majority of people conflict with one another because of the fact that they are not by nature pleasant. Those, however, that are pleasant to lovers of what is fine are by nature pleasant; and virtuous actions are this sort of thing and, hence, are pleasant both to them and in themselves. Their life, then, needs none of its pleasure added to it as an ornament, but has its pleasure within itself. Indeed, in addition to what we've already said, someone who does not enjoy fine actions is not a good person. No one would call a person just if he did not enjoy acting justly, or liberal if he did not enjoy liberal actions, and likewise with the rest of the virtues. And, if so, then virtuous actions would be pleasant in themselves. Of course, their actions are also good and fine—and they are that above all else—given that the outstanding person is right in his judgment about them, and that is his judgment.

Happiness, therefore, is best and finest and most pleasant, and these are not distinguished as they are in the inscription at Delos:

> What is most just is finest, to be healthy is best,
> but to get what we long for is naturally most pleasant.

All of these are present in the best activities, and we claim that happiness is these, or the best one of these, activities.

Nevertheless, happiness also evidently needs the addition of external goods, as we've said. It is impossible, or not easy, to perform fine actions without resources. After all, many actions are done through the use of friends and wealth and political power, as tools if you will. And the deprivation of some things—a good family, good children, beauty—spoils our happiness. Someone who is hideous in appearance or from a bad family or solitary or childless will not entirely have the character of happiness, and will presumably have it even less if his children and friends are thoroughly evil, or were good but have died. So, as we've said, happiness seems to need the addition of this sort of prosperity. Hence, some people classify good fortune as the same thing as happiness. Others, however, put virtue with happiness.

CHAPTER 9

This is also the source of the problem of whether happiness can be learned, either by acquiring habits or by another form of training, or whether it comes by some divine dispensation, or even by luck. Now, if the gods give any gift at all to human beings, it would be reasonable for happiness to be god-given as well, and more so than any other human thing, inasmuch as it is the best. This topic is presumably better suited to another investigation, but even if happiness is not heaven sent, and instead comes to us because of virtue and some sort of learning or training, it does appear to be one of the most divine things. After all, the prize of virtue, i.e., its end, appears to be the best thing, and something divine and blessed.

If our view is right, then happiness would be widely shared, since, with some learning and diligence, it can belong to anyone who is not crippled in his climb to virtue. And, if it is better to be happy in this way than by luck, then it is reasonable to suppose that this is the way things are—if in fact what accords with nature has attained its finest possible condition, and likewise too with what accords with craft and every cause and, above all, the best cause. To entrust the greatest and finest thing to luck would be deeply inappropriate.

The line we are pursuing is also put in plain view from our account of happiness. We said that it is a certain sort of activity of the soul in accordance with virtue. Of the remaining goods, some are necessary conditions for happiness, while others are natural helpers and instrumentally useful. This would also agree with our remarks at the beginning, where we set it down that the end of politics is best. Politics devotes most of its attention to producing people of a certain character, i.e., citizens who are good and able to perform fine actions.

We are probably right, then, in not calling an ox or a horse or any other animal happy, since none of them can share in this sort of activity. For this very reason, no child is happy either, since, because of his age, he is not yet able to perform such actions. When children are called happy, they are being congratulated because of the promise they hold. As we've said, happiness needs both complete virtue and a complete life. After all, there are many changes and fluctuating fortunes in life, and it is possible for someone who is utterly thriving to encounter tremendous disasters in old age, as we are told about Priam in the Trojan stories. But, when someone has been handed misfortunes of this sort and has met a miserable end, no one calls him happy.

CHAPTER 10

Should we, then, count no one happy while he is still living, but do as Solon says and wait to see the end? . . . We are unwilling to count living people happy because of changes in fortune, and because we suppose that happiness is something permanent and not at all changeable, whereas fortunes frequently cycle up and down for the same person. Indeed, it is clear that, if we were to follow his fortunes, we would frequently be calling the same person happy and then miserable again, representing the happy person as a kind of chameleon and insecurely based.

Surely, it is completely wrong to follow a person's fortunes, since his doing well or badly does not lie in these. These, as we said, are what a human life needs to have added to it. What is crucial for happiness, rather, are virtuous activities, and for its opposite, the opposite activities. Indeed, this problem we are sorting through now also confirms our account of happiness. After all, none of the works of humanity possess as much stability as virtuous activities. These are thought to be more permanent even than our fields of expertise, and the most honorable of them are the more permanent ones, because those who are happy spend their lives engaged in them most exclusively and more continually than anything else. Indeed, this is probably the cause of their not becoming shrouded from memory.

The stability we are seeking, then, will belong to the happy person, and he will remain such a person throughout his life. He will always and above all else think and do virtuous things. He will bear misfortunes in the finest way and altogether appropriately in every circumstance, since he is "truly good" and "foursquare beyond reproach." However, many things, both great and small, do happen by luck. Clearly minor instances of good or bad fortune do not bear significantly on life, but large and numerous successes will make life happier, both because they themselves naturally add beauty to it and because the use of them is fine and outstanding. If things turn out the other way around, however, it can crush and maim our happiness. Great misfortune brings pain and impedes many activities.

Nevertheless, even in these situations, what is fine shines through, whenever someone bears numerous and large misfortunes with good temper, not because of insensitivity to pain, but because he is noble and magnanimous. If, as we said, activities are what is crucial for life, then no happy person could become miserable, since he will never do things that are hateful or base. Indeed, we think that someone who is truly good and wise will bear all misfortunes with poise, and from his existing conditions will always perform the finest actions—just as a good general uses his present forces in the most effective military fashion, and a good shoemaker produces the finest shoe from the hides given to him, and so on with all other craftsmen. . . .

What prevents us, then, from saying that a happy person is one who functions in accordance with complete virtue and is adequately equipped with external goods, not for just any stretch of time, but for a complete life? . . .

---

[1] "Function" translates the Greek word *ergon* ("work," "job," "task"). Sometimes Aristotle finds it important to distinguish the *ergon* of something from its *energeia* or "activity." Recall, for instance, Ch. 1 above, where he is considering the *ergon* to be more specifically the distinct product or effect (e.g., a boat) aimed at by the activity (shipbuilding). Elsewhere, such as here, he employs the term more broadly to cover both the activity and, in cases where there is one, the resultant product.

[2] "Inactive" translates *argon*, the standard Greek word for "idle" or "lazy," but also a word that, in the context of Aristotle's argument, can mean quite literally "without a function" (formed, as it is, from the compound, *a - ergon*).

[3] As opposed to life in the sense of a mere capacity or state. See Ch. 8 above, where Aristotle puts this contrast in terms of the mere *possession* of something ("as a state") as opposed to the exercise or *use* of it ("as activity").

UTILITARIANISM

JUDITH NORMAN

Utilitarianism

Utilitarianism is one of the classic moral philosophies. It is a species of consequentialism, a type of ethical theory which judges action according to its consequences (or, perhaps, intended consequences). The specific consequences with which utilitarianism is traditionally concerned are the maximization of pleasure and the minimization of pain; these constitute the utility or disutility of the putative ethical action. Utilitarians generally equate pleasure with happiness and argue that this alone is good or desirable for its own sake; accordingly, action is judged to be morally praiseworthy only when it aims to maximize happiness. As John Stuart Mill writes: "The creed which accepts as the foundation of morals 'utility' or the 'greatest happiness principle' holds that actions are right in proportion as they tend to promote happiness; wrong as they tend to produce the reverse of happiness. By happiness is intended pleasure and the absence of pain; by unhappiness, pain and the privation of pleasure."

Given this general statement of the nature of utilitarianism, it is easy to locate ideas that anticipate utilitarianism throughout the history of philosophy. A variety of ancient moral theories held pleasure to be the goal of human action, although this was typically construed in an egoistic sense of personal pleasure or well-being. Aristotelian eudaimonism can also be considered a forerunner of sorts; the concept of happiness is central to Aristotle's ethics, and Aristotle theorizes it in a more or less consequentialist fashion. Happiness, according to Aristotle, is the only thing desirable for its own sake; as such, it is rightfully the goal of human endeavor. But although these beliefs bring Aristotle into proximity with utilitarianism, he carefully distinguished between happiness and pleasure in a way utilitarians generally do not. For Aristotle, happiness, in contrast to pleasure, is not a psychological state or feeling; rather, it involves thriving or prospering over the course of a lifetime. No single action can bring happiness and no single action can dispel it. Accordingly, Aristotle does not believe the proper object of moral concern to be the individual action; rather, he is concerned with human character, and character is morally good to the extent that it exhibits the virtues whose exercise is an integral part of the happiness of their possessor.

All this is quite foreign to utilitarianism, which traditionally focuses narrowly on particular actions as the chosen objects of moral praise or censure. These actions might reflect on the character of the agent, but this character does not itself directly come in for judgment. As a result, the utilitarian has a much more finely tuned set of moral distinctions that the Aristotelian, and a considerably more precise guide to ethical decision making. While the utilitarian can decide among actions with a quasi-mathematical precision, the Aristotelian must appeal to the rather aesthetic notions of virtue and character. As such, utilitarianism is a more characteristically modern theory, with its roots in scientific positivism and, more particularly, economic theory, where gains and losses can be closely monitored. Indeed, the Enlightenment economist and philosopher David Hume was the first to systematize certain utilitarian principles into an ethical theory.

Still, it was not until the 19th century that utilitarianism received its classic formulation in the works of the British moral philosophers Jeremy Bentham and James Mill, and, most famously, in *Utilitarianism* by John Stuart Mill. John Stuart Mill's connection to the utilitarianism movement was not contingent; he was carefully educated to serve as a leading exponent of Bentham's ideas by his father, James Mill. J. S. Mill's famously rigorous schooling in (amongst other things) classical letters, political economy, and British history had several effects on his development of the utilitarianism movement. For one thing, it gave him considerable faith in the ability of education to train the individual to find pleasure in higher pursuits and altruistic actions. Equally important, however, was Mill's adolescent reaction against his frankly tedious and analytic education. It was an age of literary Romanticism, and Mill found some satisfaction for his newly discovered emotional life in poetry. As a result, he was driven to reevaluate the rather dismissive role the earlier utilitarian theorists gave to such artistic pursuits. Against Bentham's strictly quantitative ranking of pleasures (and his claim that poetry was as good as "pushpin"), Mill came to believe that pleasures were qualitatively different. We must rank two pleasures by invoking the consensus of those who have experienced both as to their relative merits. Anyone acquainted with the advantages of culture "would rather be Socrates dissatisfied than a pig satisfied," as Mill famously claimed.

Much of the appeal of utilitarianism stems from its theoretical simplicity; all moral issues can be referred to a single decisive question: do they maximize utility? Moreover, utilitarians often claim that all ethical considerations ultimately boil down to this utility calculation—that most people naturally try to maximize utility. Although Bentham originally theorized that we are concerned exclusively with our own utility, Mill modified the theory to include the good of all; far from running counter to overall utility, Mill argues, our own pleasures are intimately linked to the pleasures of others. Once we realize this, he believes, we will wish to pursue strictly impersonal calculations of utility; our own interest and those of our loved ones will make no more moral demand on us than the interests of strangers. This principled lack of favoritism might seem harsh, but it certainly is an antidote to racism or other forms of personal chauvinism. Always optimistic about the power of a good education, Mill believes that proper training might be required to help us realize this natural harmony of interests, and various sanctions might be called upon to ensure that we find our greatest pleasure in actions which maximize overall utility. Principle among these sanctions are the fear of disapproval from others and the inner bite of conscience. Once instituted, Mill is convinced, these will make utilitarian principles second nature, to the extent that our nature doesn't initially conform with utilitarian doctrine.

Given such claims about human nature, utilitarianism is often seen to double as a descriptive, as well as a prescriptive moral theory; that is, it describes how we in fact (try to) behave, as well as determining principles to dictate how we ought to behave. Accordingly, Mill attempts to prove that happiness is the only thing people actually do desire. Other apparently desirable things, he argues, are ingredients of happiness. In other words, utilitarianism can acknowledge the intrinsic value people place on goods such as virtue; what utilitarianism denies is the distinction between such goods and happiness. To be virtuous is to possess a form of happiness. Utilitarianism, therefore, believes it can assimilate other conceptions of moral goods within its own theory, clarifying rather than denying apparently nonutilitarian moral intuitions.

Still, it is questionable whether utilitarianism draws any genuine advantage from its supposed affinity to popular wisdom or common sense. Even if we grant Mill the claim that happiness is the only thing people desire, this observation on human nature underdetermines the properly utilitarian imperative that we should maximize *universal* happiness, an imperative that separates utilitarianism as moral theory proper from a narrow statement of psychological egoism. But perhaps more problematically, Mill believes that by showing happiness to be the only thing people *do* desire, he has thereby established it to be the only thing *worthy* of desire, which is to say the only thing desir*able*. Against utilitarianism, we could claim that there are goods people *should* desire, but don't, goods such as order and discipline. Indeed, moral systems often consider happiness (particularly construed as pleasure) to be an inappropriate goal of human endeavor. The (German) philosopher Friedrich Nietzsche once remarked: "Man does not strive for pleasure; only the Englishman does."

Utilitarianism's exclusive concern with happiness gives it a very broad field of application in some ways, and a very narrow range of concern in other ways. It is broadly applicable in that it offers the resources to easily extend our notion of moral regard to nonsentient entities, so long as they experience pleasure and pain. For this reason, utilitarianism has been a popular approach to the issue of animal rights, where it encourages us to include the suffering of nonhuman animals in our ethical decisions. On the other hand, utilitarianism's exclusive focus on happiness results in a strikingly narrow notion of human nature as the receptacle of quantities of happiness and unhappiness, and a correlative disregard for other human features. For instance, the integrity or autonomy of a person is not a native feature of utilitarianism and does not function into its notion of the essential features of human nature. Of course, people might well experience a great deal of pleasure in having their integrity respected, and consequently a great deal of pain at being treated without respect. If so, utilitarianism will include these factors in calculating the utility of the people involved. Even so, utilitarianism will not be demonstrating any specific concern for integrity itself, but only for the pleasure or pain which integrity involves. In other words, utilitarianism will take integrity into moral consideration only to the extent that it stakes its claims in the currency of utility or disutility.

Perhaps the most controversial result of this narrow conception of human interest is the utilitarian attitude towards rights. Again, people's rights might well have a role to play in a calculation of utility, provided they involve pleasure and pain; the pleasure we experience in having our rights respected gives them some proportionate amount of moral consideration for a utilitarian. But rights-based considerations will be rejected as soon as other factors with greater utility enter the picture. For instance, if your pleasure in violating my rights exceeds the pain I will suffer in being so violated, then traditionally, a utilitarian will need to consider your action not only acceptable, but positively moral. As a result, it seems, it is morally praiseworthy to rape a sleeping or unconscious victim, provided the rapist receives positive pleasure in the act, and the victim remains ignorant.

Indeed, one of the greatest challenges to utilitarianism comes from Immanuel Kant's rights-based system of ethics. Kant rejects any consequentialist considerations in favor of a narrow consideration of rights and duties. For Kant, if a particular action has been proven to be a moral duty, then we are morally obliged to perform it, regardless of any consequences that might obtain. For instance, if moral reason tells us murder is wrong, then we may not ever commit murder, even if the murder would ultimately save a greater number of lives. For Mill, of course, the overall greater utility of saving several lives justifies the sacrifice of one. Mill explicitly addresses Kant's theory by claiming that the way in which Kant determines whether or not some duty is moral makes essential reference to consequences. Although Kant would deny that moral reason takes account of consequences, Mill believes Kant tacitly appeals to consequences nonetheless.

On Mill's reading then, Kant is applying consequentialist considerations to the choice of moral principles. Although this is a highly debatable reading of Kant, it brings him into proximity with certain contemporary versions of utilitarianism. For instance, "indirect" utilitarianism seeks to avoid the crude maxim that "the end (of greater utility) always justifies the means" from which classical utilitarianism seems unable to distance itself. Indirect forms include rule and disposition utilitarianism, both of which turn their attention from the utility of particular acts. Rule utilitarianism focuses on the relative utilities of general ethical principles rather than the utilities of specific acts themselves (although Mill did not formulate rule utilitarianism as such, he appeals to a rule-oriented approach to defend a utilitarian interest in rights). Disposition utilitarianism, on the other hand, aims to promote utility-maximizing personality traits, and thus focuses on character rather than action. The appeal of such indirect strategies is clear; not only do they avoid the specter of the constant, tedious felicific calculations to which classical utilitarianism is evidently committed, but they accord more readily with our specific intuitions about moral propriety. Rule utilitarianism, for instance, might compel us not to lie though the truth causes pain, since the overall policy of truthfulness promotes the greatest utility (perhaps in the form of greater universal trust), and the occasional lie would endanger this global utility, even though it might have beneficial immediate local consequences. The extent to which local utility might occasionally override global utility (for instance, if the local event remains private or unnoticed) is left for utilitarians to resolve, although it is not clear how such a resolution is to be effected.

Recent utilitarianism has increased the power of the theory by cashing out utility in terms of "preference satisfaction" rather than simply pleasure. Although our choices sometimes bring us pain, our utility consists in the very fact that we have satisfied our preferences. Yet any facile interpretation of utility in terms of preference satisfaction raises a number of significant problems. For one thing, it assumes that desirability of some consequence is directly proportionate to its utility, and this can be called into doubt. For instance, our happiness might be best secured by a state of affairs we don't yet know to want. More essentially, however, this interpretation of utility ignores the issue of inappropriate preferences; in other words, it is open to the objection that our preferences, if satisfied, might ultimately reduce our ability to thrive, in some sense. For instance, politically disempowered groups of people have often acceded to their own oppression. Historically discouraged from seeking an education, women have often internalized the prohibition and resisted attempts to broaden horizons left comfortably, but regrettably narrow. Although they are satisfying their preferences, we can ask a utilitarian whether these are genuinely the right preferences to have.

Contemporary "welfare" utilitarians try to answer these sorts of questions by enhancing the notion of utility to include counterfactual as well as actual preferences. So a utilitarian calculus should take into account not only the current desires of the parties involved, but their real interests, which is to say the preferences they *would* assert given all the relevant information and optimal rational faculties. Despite the initial attraction of such a reply, it risks imposing a normalizing or at least paternalizing conception of "true" interests on a recalcitrantly idiosyncratic individual, and thus act[ing] as a tool for enforcing social conformity. Still, this might be more a problem of properly implementing the program of welfare utilitarianism than a problem with the theory itself. If anything is clear from the past century of utilitarianism, it is that the theory has a remarkable resiliency, and ample resources to meet many of the critical challenges it faces.

Further Reading

Works by Mill

Mill, J. S. John M. Robson, ed., *The Collected Works of John Stuart Mill.* Toronto: University of Toronto Press, 1969.

Works on Mill

Berlin, Isaiah. *Four Essays on Liberty.* Oxford: Oxford University Press, 1969.

Lyons, David. *Rights, Welfare, and Mill's Moral Theory.* Oxford: Oxford University Press, 1994.

Okin, Susan Moller. *Women in Western Political Thought.* Princeton: Princeton University Press, 1979.

Ryan, Alan. *The Philosophy of John Stuart Mill.* London: Macmillan, 1970.

Works on Utilitarianism

Moore, G. E. *Principia Ethica.* Cambridge: Cambridge University Press, 1903.

Bentham, J. *An Introduction to the Principles of Morals and Legislation,* J. Burns and H. L. A. Hart, eds. London: Athlone Press, 1970.

Sidgwick, H. *The Methods of Ethics.* London: Macmillan, 1907.

Brandt, R. B. *A Theory of the Good and the Right.* Oxford: Clarendon Press, 1979.

Sen, A. and Williams, B., eds. *Utilitarianism and Beyond.* Cambridge: Cambridge University Press, 1982.

JOHN STUART MILL

Utilitarianism

CHAPTER II: WHAT UTILITARIANISM IS: ITS MEANING

. . . The creed which accepts as the foundation of morals, Utility, or the Greatest Happiness Principle, holds that actions are right in proportion as they tend to promote happiness, wrong as they tend to produce the reverse of happiness. By happiness is intended pleasure, and the absence of pain; by unhappiness, pain, and the privation of pleasure. To give a clear view of the moral standard set up by the theory, much more requires to be said; in particular, what things it includes in the ideas of pain and pleasure; and to what extent this is left an open question. But these supplementary explanations do not affect the theory of life on which this theory of morality is grounded—namely, that pleasure, and freedom from pain, are the only things desirable as ends; and that all desirable things (which are as numerous in the utilitarian as in any other scheme) are desirable either for the pleasure inherent in themselves, or as a means to the promotion of pleasure and the prevention of pain.

Now, such a theory of life excites in many minds, and among them in some of the most estimable in feeling and purpose, inveterate dislike. To suppose that life has (as they express it) no higher end than pleasure—no better and nobler object of desire and pursuit—they designate as utterly mean and groveling; as a doctrine worthy only of swine, to whom the followers of Epicurus were, at a very early period, contemptuously likened; and modern holders of the doctrine are occasionally made the subject of equally polite comparisons by its German, French, and English assailants.

When thus attacked, the Epicureans have always answered, that it is not they, but their accusers, who represent human nature in a degrading light; since the accusation supposes human beings to be capable of no pleasures except those of which swine are capable. If this supposition were true, the charge could not be gainsaid, but would then be no longer an imputation; for if the sources of pleasure were precisely the same to human beings and to swine, the rule of life which is good enough for the one would be good enough for the other. The comparison of the Epicurean life to that of beasts is felt as degrading, precisely because a beast's pleasures do not satisfy a human being's conceptions of happiness. Human beings have faculties more elevated than the animal appetites, and when once made conscious of them, do not regard anything as happiness which does not include their gratification. I do not, indeed, consider the Epicureans to have been by any means faultless in drawing out their scheme of consequences from the utilitarian principle. To do this in any sufficient manner, many Stoic, as well as Christian elements require to be included. But there is no known Epicurean theory of life which does not assign to the pleasures of the intellect, of the feelings and imagination, and of the moral sentiments, a much higher value as pleasures than to those of mere sensation. It must be admitted, however, that utilitarian writers in general have placed the superiority of mental over bodily pleasures chiefly in the greater permanency, safety, uncostliness, etc., of the former—that is, in their circumstantial advantages rather than in their intrinsic nature. And on all these points utilitarians have fully proved their case; but they might have taken the other, and, as it may be called, higher ground, with entire consistency. It is quite compatible with the principle of utility to recognise the fact, that some *kinds* of pleasure are more desirable and more valuable than others. It would be absurd that while, in estimating all other things, quality is considered as well as quantity, the estimation of pleasures should be supposed to depend on quantity alone.

If I am asked, what I mean by difference of quality in pleasures, or what makes one pleasure more valuable than another, merely as a pleasure, except its being greater in amount, there is but one possible answer. Of two pleasures, if there be one to which all or almost all who have experience of both give a decided preference, irrespective of any feeling of moral obligation to prefer it, that is the more desirable pleasure. If one of the two is, by those who are competently acquainted with both, placed so far above the other that they prefer it, even though knowing it to be attended with a greater amount of discontent, and would not resign it for any quantity of the other pleasure which their nature is capable of, we are justified in ascribing to the preferred enjoyment a superiority in quality, so far outweighing quantity as to render it, in comparison, of small account.

Now it is an unquestionable fact that those who are equally acquainted with, and equally capable of appreciating and enjoying, both, do give a most marked preference to the manner of existence which employs their higher faculties. Few human creatures would consent to be changed into any of the lower animals, for a promise of the fullest allowance of a beast's pleasures; no intelligent human being would consent to be a fool, no instructed person would be an ignoramus, no person of feeling and conscience would be selfish and base, even though they should be persuaded that the fool, the dunce, or the rascal is better satisfied with his lot than they are with theirs. They would not resign what they possess more than he, for the most complete satisfaction of all the desires which they have in common with him. If they ever fancy they would, it is only in cases of unhappiness so extreme, that to escape from it they would exchange their lot for almost any other, however undesirable in their own eyes. A being of higher faculties requires more to make him happy, is capable probably of more acute suffering, and is certainly accessible to it at more points, than one of an inferior type; but in spite of these liabilities, he can never really wish to sink into what he feels to be a lower grade of existence. We may give what explanation we please of this unwillingness; we may attribute it to pride, a name which is given indiscriminately to some of the most and to some of the least estimable feelings of which mankind are capable; we may refer it to the love of liberty and personal independence, an appeal to which was with the Stoics one of the most effective means for the inculcation of it; to the love of power, or to the love of excitement, both of which do really enter into and contribute to it: but its most appropriate appellation is a sense of dignity, which all human beings possess in one form or other, and in some, though by no means in exact, proportion to their higher faculties, and which is so essential a part of the happiness of those in whom it is strong, that nothing which conflicts with it could be, otherwise than momentarily, an object of desire to them. Whoever supposes that this preference takes place at a sacrifice of happiness—that the superior being, in anything like equal circumstances, is not happier than the inferior—confounds the two very different ideas, of happiness, and content. It is indisputable that the being whose capacities of enjoyment are low, has the greatest chance of having them fully satisfied; and a highly endowed being will always feel that any happiness which he can look for, as the world is constituted, is imperfect. But he can learn to bear its imperfections, if they are at all bearable; and they will not make him envy the being who is indeed unconscious of the imperfections, but only because he feels not at all the good which those imperfections qualify. It is better to be a human being dissatisfied than a pig satisfied; better to be Socrates dissatisfied than a fool satisfied. And if the fool, or the pig, is of a different opinion, it is because they only know their own side of the question. The other party to the comparison knows both sides. . . .

. . . On a question which is the best worth having of two pleasures, or which of two modes of existence is the most grateful to the feelings, apart from its moral attributes and from its consequences, the judgment of those who are qualified by knowledge of both, or, if they differ, that of the majority among them, must be admitted as final. And there needs be the less hesitation to accept this judgement respecting the quality of pleasures, since there is no other tribunal to be referred to even on the question of quantity. What means are there of determining which is the acutest of two pains, or the intensest of two pleasurable sensations, except the general suffrage of those who are familiar with both? Neither pains nor pleasures are homogeneous, and pain is always heterogeneous with pleasure. What is there to decide whether a particular pleasure is worth purchasing at the cost of a particular pain, except the feelings and judgment of the experienced? When, therefore, those feelings and judgment declare the pleasures derived from the higher faculties to be preferable *in kind,* apart from the question of intensity, to those of which the animal nature, disjoined from the higher faculties, is susceptible, they are entitled on this subject to the same regard.

I have dwelt on this point, as being a necessary part of a perfectly just conception of Utility or Happiness, considered as the directive rule of human conduct. But it is by no means an indispensable condition to the acceptance of the utilitarian standard; for that standard is not the agent's own greatest happiness, but the greatest amount of happiness altogether, and if it may possibly be doubted whether a noble character is always the happier for its nobleness, there can be no doubt that it makes other people happier, and that the world in general is immensely a gainer by it. Utilitarianism, therefore, could only attain its end by the general cultivation of nobleness of character, even if each individual were only benefited by the nobleness of others, and his own, so far as happiness is concerned, were a sheer deduction from the benefit. But the bare enunciation of such an absurdity as this last, renders refutation superfluous.

. . . The objectors to utilitarianism cannot always be charged with representing it in a discreditable light. On the contrary, those among them who entertain anything like a just idea of its disinterested character, sometimes find fault with its standard as being too high for humanity. They say it is exacting too much to require that people shall always act from the inducement of promoting the general interests of society. But this is to mistake the very meaning of a standard of morals, and to confound the rule of action with the motive of it. It is the business of ethics to tell us what are our duties, or by what test we may know them; but no system of ethics requires that the sole motive of all we do shall be a feeling of duty; on the contrary, ninety-nine hundredths of all our actions are done from other motives, and rightly so done, if the rule of duty does not condemn them. It is the more unjust to utilitarianism that this particular misapprehension should be made a ground of objection to it inasmuch as utilitarian moralists have gone beyond almost all others in affirming that the motive has nothing to do with the morality of the action, though much with the worth of the agent. He who saves a fellow creature from drowning does what is morally right, whether his motive be duty, or the hope of being paid for his trouble: he who betrays the friend that trusts him, is guilty of a crime, even if his object be to serve another friend to whom he is under greater obligations. But to speak only of actions done from the motive of duty, and in direct obedience to principle: it is a misapprehension of the utilitarian mode of thought, to conceive it as implying that people should fix their minds upon so wide a generality as the world, or society at large. The great majority of good actions are intended, not for the benefit of the world, but for that of individuals, of which the good of the world is made up; and the thoughts of the most virtuous man need not on these occasions travel beyond the particular persons concerned, except so far as is necessary to assure himself that in benefiting them he is not violating the rights—that is, the legitimate and authorized expectations—of any one else. The multiplication of happiness is, according to the utilitarian ethics, the object of virtue: the occasions on which any person (except one in a thousand) has it in his power to do this on an extended scale, in other words, to be a public benefactor, are but exceptional; and on these occasions alone is he called on to consider public utility; in every other case, private utility, the interest or happiness of some few persons, is all he has to attend to. . . .

The same considerations dispose of another reproach against the doctrine of utility, founded on a still grosser misconception of the purpose of a standard of morality, and of the very meaning of the words *right* and *wrong*. It is often affirmed that utilitarianism renders men cold and unsympathizing; that it chills their moral feelings towards individuals; that it makes them regard only the dry and hard consideration of the consequences of actions, not taking into their moral estimate the qualities from which those actions emanate. If the assertion means that they do not allow their judgment respecting the rightness or wrongness of an action to be influenced by their opinion of the qualities of the person who does it, this is a complaint not against utilitarianism, but against having any standard of morality at all; for certainly no known ethical standard decides an action to be good or bad because it is done by a good or a bad man, still less because done by an amiable, a brave, or a benevolent man, or the contrary. These considerations are relevant, not to the estimation of actions, but of persons; and there is nothing in the utilitarian theory inconsistent with the fact that there are other things which interest us in persons besides the rightness and wrongness of their actions. . . .

It may not be superfluous to notice a few more of the common misapprehensions of utilitarian ethics. . . .

We not uncommonly hear the doctrine of utility inveighed against as a *godless* doctrine. If it be necessary to say anything at all against so mere an assumption, we may say that the question depends upon what idea we have formed of the moral character of the Deity. If it be a true belief that God desires, above all things, the happiness of his creatures, and that this was his purpose in their creation, utility is not only not a godless doctrine, but more profoundly religious than any other. It if be meant that utilitarianism does not recognise the revealed will of God as the supreme law of morals, I answer, that an utilitarian who believes in the perfect goodness and wisdom of God, necessarily believes that whatever God has thought fit to reveal on the subject of morals, must fulfil the requirements of utility in a supreme degree. . . .

Again, Utility is often summarily stigmatized as an immoral doctrine by giving it the name of Expediency, and taking advantage of the popular use of that term to contrast it with Principle. But the Expedient, in the sense in which it is opposed to the Right, generally means that which is expedient for the particular interest of the agent himself; as when a minister sacrifices the interest of his country to keep himself in place. When it means anything better than this, it means that which is expedient for some immediate object, some temporary purpose, but which violates a rule whose observance is expedient in a much higher degree. The Expedient, in this sense, instead of being the same thing with the useful, is a branch of the hurtful. Thus, it would often be expedient, for the purpose of getting over some momentary embarrassment, or attaining some object immediately useful to ourselves or others, to tell a lie. But inasmuch as the cultivation in ourselves of a sensitive feeling on the subject of veracity, is one of the most useful, and the enfeeblement of that feeling one of the most hurtful, things to which our conduct can be instrumental; and inasmuch as any, even unintentional, deviation from truth, does that much towards weakening the trustworthiness of human assertion, which is not only the principal support of all present social well-being, but the insufficiency of which does more than any one thing that can be named to keep back civilization, virtue, everything on which human happiness on the largest scale depends; we feel that the violation, for a present advantage, of a rule of such transcendent expediency, is not expedient. . . .

Yet that even this rule, sacred as it is, admits of possible exceptions, is acknowledged by all moralists; the chief of which is when the withholding of some fact (as of information from a malefactor, or of bad news from a person dangerously ill) would preserve some one (especially a person other than oneself) from great and unmerited evil, and when the withholding can only be effected by denial. But in order that the exception may not extend itself beyond the need, and may have the least possible effect in weakening reliance on veracity, it ought to be recognized, and, if possible, its limits defined; and if the principle of utility is good for anything, it must be good for weighing these conflicting utilities against one another, and marking out the region within which one or the other preponderates. . . .

The remainder of the stock arguments against utilitarianism mostly consist in laying to its charge the common infirmities of human nature, and the general difficulties which embarrass conscientious persons in shaping their course through life. We are told that an utilitarian will be apt to make his own particular case an exception to moral rules, and, when under temptation, will see an utility in the breach of a rule, greater than he will see in its observance. But is utility the only creed which is able to furnish us with excuses for evil doing, and means of cheating our own conscience? They are afforded in abundance by all doctrines which recognize as a fact in morals the existence of conflicting considerations; which all doctrines do, that have been believed by sane persons. It is not the fault of any creed, but of the complicated nature of human affairs, that rules of conduct cannot be so framed as to require no exceptions, and that hardly any kind of action can safely be laid down as either always obligatory or always condemnable. . . .

There exists no moral system under which there do not arise unequivocal cases of conflicting obligation. . . .

They are overcome practically with greater or with less success according to the intellect and virtue of the individual; but it can hardly be pretended that any one will be the less qualified for dealing with them, from possessing an ultimate standard to which conflicting rights and duties can be referred. If utility is the ultimate source of moral obligations, utility may be invoked to decide between them when their demands are incompatible. . . .

CHAPTER III: OF THE ULTIMATE SANCTION OF THE PRINCIPLE OF UTILITY

The question is often asked, and properly so, in regard to any supposed moral standard—What is its sanction? what are the motives to obey it? or more specifically, what is the source of its obligation? whence does it derive its binding force? . . .

The principle of utility either has, or there is no reason why it might not have, all the sanctions which belong to any other system of morals. Those sanctions are either external or internal. Of the external sanctions it is not necessary to speak at any length. They are, the hope of favor and the fear of displeasure from our fellow creatures or from the Ruler of the Universe, along with whatever we may have of sympathy or affection for them, or of love and awe of Him, inclining us to do his will independently of selfish consequences. . . .

The internal sanction of duty, whatever our standard of duty may be, is one and the same—a feeling in our own mind; a pain, more or less intense, attendant on violation of duty, which in properly cultivated moral natures rises, in the more serious cases, into shrinking from it as an impossibility. This feeling, when disinterested, and connecting itself with the pure idea of duty, and not with some particular form of it, or with any of the merely accessory circumstances, is the essence of Conscience. . . .

The ultimate sanction, therefore, of all morality (external motives apart) being a subjective feeling in our own minds, I see nothing embarrassing to those whose standard is utility, in the question, what is the sanction of that particular standard? We may answer, the same as of all other moral standards—the conscientious feelings of mankind. Undoubtedly this sanction has no binding efficacy on those who do not possess the feelings it appeals to; but neither will these persons be more obedient to any other moral principle than to the utilitarian one. On them morality of any kind has no hold but through the external sanctions. . . .

There is, I am aware, a disposition to believe that a person who sees in moral obligation a transcendental fact, an objective reality belonging to the province of "Things in themselves," is likely to be more obedient to it than one who believes it to be entirely subjective, having its seat in human consciousness only. But whatever a person's opinion may be on this point of Ontology, the force he is really urged by is his own subjective feeling, and is exactly measured by its strength. . . .

It is not necessary, for the present purpose, to decide whether the feeling of duty is innate or implanted. Assuming it to be innate, it is an open question to what objects it naturally attaches itself; for the philosophic supporters of that theory are now agreed that the intuitive perception is of principles of morality, and not of the details. If there be anything innate in the matter, I see no reason why the feeling which is innate should not be that of regard to the pleasures and pains of others. . . .

If so, the intuitive ethics would coincide with the utilitarian, and there would be no further quarrel between them. . . .

On the other hand, if, as in my own belief, the moral feelings are not innate, but acquired, they are not for that reason the less natural. It is natural to man to speak, to reason, to build cities, to cultivate the ground, though these are acquired faculties. . . .

Like the other acquired capacities above referred to, the moral faculty, if not a part of our nature, is a natural outgrowth from it; capable, like them, in a certain small degree, of springing up spontaneously; and susceptible of being brought by cultivation to a high degree of development. Unhappily it is also susceptible, by a sufficient use of the external sanctions and of the force of early impressions, of being cultivated in almost any direction: so that there is hardly anything so absurd or so mischievous that it may not, by means of these influences, be made to act on the human mind with all the authority of conscience. To doubt that the same potency might be given by the same means to the principle of utility, even if it had no foundation in human nature, would be flying in the face of all experience.

But moral associations which are wholly of artificial creation, when intellectual culture goes on, yield by degrees to the dissolving force of analysis: and if the feeling of duty, when associated with utility, would appear equally arbitrary . . .

If there were not, in short, a natural basis of sentiment for utilitarian morality, it might well happen that this association also, even after it had been implanted by education, might be analyzed away.

But there *is* this basis of powerful natural sentiment; and this it is which, when once the general happiness is recognised as the ethical standard, will constitute the strength of the utilitarian morality. This firm foundation is that of the social feelings of mankind; the desire to be in unity with our fellow creatures, which is already a powerful principle in human nature, and happily one of those which tend to become stronger, even without express inculcation, from the influences of advancing civilization. The social state is at once so natural, so necessary, and so habitual to man, that, except in some unusual circumstances or by an effort of voluntary abstraction, he never conceives himself otherwise than as a member of a body; and this association is riveted more and more, as mankind are further removed from the state of savage independence. Any condition, therefore, which is essential to a state of society, becomes more and more an inseparable part of every person's conception of the state of things which he is born into, and which is the destiny of a human being. Now, society between human beings, except in the relation of master and slave, is manifestly impossible on any other footing than that the interests of all are to be consulted. Society between equals can only exist on the understanding that the interests of all are to be regarded equally. And since in all states of civilization, every person, except an absolute monarch, has equals, every one is obliged to live on these terms with somebody; and in every age some advance is made towards a state in which it will be impossible to live permanently on other terms with anybody. In this way people grow up unable to conceive as possible to them a state of total disregard of other people's interests. They are under a necessity of conceiving themselves as at least abstaining from all the grosser injuries, and (if only for their own protection) living in a state of constant protest against them. They are also familiar with the fact of co-operating with others, and proposing to themselves a collective, not an individual, interest, as the aim (at least for the time being) of their actions. So long as they are co-operating, their ends are identified with those of others; there is at least a temporary feeling that the interests of others are their own interests. Not only does all strengthening of social ties, and all healthy growth of society, give to each individual a stronger personal interest in practically consulting the welfare of others; it also leads him to identify his *feelings* more and more with their good, or at least with an ever greater degree of practical consideration for it. . . .

Neither is it necessary to the feeling which constitutes the binding force of the utilitarian morality on those who recognise it, to wait for those social influences which would make its obligation felt by mankind at large. In the comparatively early state of human advancement in which we now live, a person cannot indeed feel that entireness of sympathy with all others, which would make any real discordance in the general direction of their conduct in life impossible; but already a person in whom the social feeling is at all developed, cannot bring himself to think of the rest of his fellow creatures as struggling rivals with him for the means of happiness, whom he must desire to see defeated in their object in order that he may succeed in his. The deeply rooted conception which every individual even now has of himself as a social being, tends to make him feel it one of his natural wants that there should be harmony between his feelings and aims and those of his fellow creatures. If differences of opinion and of mental culture make it impossible for him to share many of their actual feelings—perhaps make him denounce and defy those feelings—he still needs to be conscious that his real aim and theirs do not conflict; that he is not opposing himself to what they really wish for, namely, their own good, but is, on the contrary, promoting it. This feeling in most individuals is much inferior in strength to their selfish feelings, and is often wanting altogether. But to those who have it, it possesses all the characters of a natural feeling. It does not present itself to their minds as a superstition of education, or a law despotically imposed by the power of society, but as an attribute which it would not be well for them to be without. This conviction is the ultimate sanction of the greatest-happiness morality. This it is which makes any mind, of well-developed feelings, work with, and not against, the outward motives to care for others, afforded by what I have called the external sanctions; and when those sanctions are wanting, or act in an opposite direction, constitutes in itself a powerful internal binding force, in proportion to the sensitiveness and thoughtfulness of the character; since few but those whose mind is a moral blank, could bear to lay out their course of life on the plan of paying no regard to others except so far as their own private interest compels.

CHAPTER IV: OF WHAT SORT OF PROOF THE PRINCIPLE OF UTILITY IS SUSCEPTIBLE

. . . The utilitarian doctrine is, that happiness is desirable, and the only thing desirable, as an end; all other things being only desirable as means to that end. What ought to be required of this doctrine—what conditions is it requisite that the doctrine should fulfil—to make good its claim to be believed?

The only proof capable of being given that an object is visible, is that people actually see it. The only proof that a sound is audible, is that people hear it: and so of the other sources of our experience. In like manner, I apprehend, the sole evidence it is possible to produce that anything is desirable, is that people do actually desire it. . . .

No reason can be given why the general happiness is desirable, except that each person, so far as he believes it to be attainable, desires his own happiness. This, however, being a fact, we have not only all the proof which the case admits of, but all which it is possible to require, that happiness is a good: that each person's happiness is a good to that person, and the general happiness, therefore, a good to the aggregate of all persons. Happiness has made out its title as *one* of the ends of conduct, and consequently one of the criteria of morality.

But it has not, by this alone, proved itself to be the sole criterion. To do that, it would seem, by the same rule, necessary to show, not only that people desire happiness, but that they never desire anything else. Now it is palpable that they do desire things which, in common language, are decidedly distinguished from happiness. They desire, for example, virtue, and the absence of vice, no less really than pleasure and the absence of pain. The desire of virtue is not as universal, but it is as authentic a fact, as the desire of happiness. And hence the opponents of the utilitarian standard deem that they have a right to infer that there are other ends of human action besides happiness, and that happiness is not the standard of approbation and disapprobation.

But does the utilitarian doctrine deny that people desire virtue, or maintain that virtue is not a thing to be desired? The very reverse. It maintains not only that virtue is to be desired, but that it is to be desired disinterestedly, for itself. Whatever may be the opinion of utilitarian moralists as to the original conditions by which virtue is made virtue; however they may believe (as they do) that actions and dispositions are only virtuous because they promote another end than virtue; yet this being granted, and it having been decided, from considerations of this description, what *is* virtuous, they not only place virtue at the very head of the things which are good as means to the ultimate end, but they also recognise as a psychological fact the possibility of its being, to the individual, a good in itself, without looking to any end beyond it; and hold, that the mind is not in a right state, not in a state conformable to Utility, not in the state most conducive to the general happiness, unless it does love virtue in this manner—as a thing desirable in itself, even although, in the individual instance, it should not produce those other desirable consequences which it tends to produce, and on account of which it is held to be virtue. This opinion is not, in the smallest degree, a departure from the Happiness principle. The ingredients of happiness are very various, and each of them is desirable in itself, and not merely when considered as swelling an aggregate. The principle of utility does not mean that any given pleasure, as music, for instance, or any given exemption from pain, as for example health, are to be looked upon as means to a collective something termed happiness, and to be desired on that account. They are desired and desirable in and for themselves; besides being means, they are a part of the end. Virtue, according to the utilitarian doctrine, is not naturally and originally part of the end, but it is capable of becoming so; and in those who love it disinterestedly it has become so, and is desired and cherished, not as a means to happiness, but as a part of their happiness. . . .

It results from the preceding considerations, that there is in reality nothing desired except happiness. Whatever is desired otherwise than as a means to some end beyond itself, and ultimately to happiness, is desired as itself a part of happiness, and is not desired for itself until it has become so. . . .

We have now, then, an answer to the question, of what sort of proof the principle of utility is susceptible. If the opinion which I have now stated is psychologically true—if human nature is so constituted as to desire nothing which is not either a part of happiness or a means of happiness, we can have no other proof, and we require no other, that these are the only things desirable. If so, happiness is the sole end of human action, and the promotion of it the test by which to judge of all human conduct; from whence it necessarily follows that it must be the criterion of morality, since a part is included in the whole. . . .

CHAPTER V: ON THE CONNEXION BETWEEN JUSTICE AND UTILITY

In all ages of speculation, one of the strongest obstacles to the reception of the doctrine that Utility or Happiness is the criterion of right and wrong, has been drawn from the idea of Justice. The powerful sentiment, and apparently clear perception, which that word recals with a rapidity and certainty resembling an instinct, have seemed to the majority of thinkers to point to an inherent quality in things; to show that the Just must have an existence in Nature as something absolute—generically distinct from every variety of the Expedient, and, in idea, opposed to it, though (as is commonly acknowledged) never, in the long run, disjoined from it in fact. . . .

To throw light upon this question, it is necessary to attempt to ascertain what is the distinguishing character of justice, or of injustice: what is the quality, or whether there is any quality, attributed in common to all modes of conduct designated as unjust (for justice, like many other moral attributes, is best defined by its opposite), and distinguishing them from such modes of conduct as are disapproved, but without having that particular epithet of disapprobation applied to them. If, in everything which men are accustomed to characterize as just or unjust, some one common attribute or collection of attributes is always present, we may judge whether this particular attribute or combination of attributes would be capable of gathering round it a sentiment of that peculiar character and intensity by virtue of the general laws of our emotional constitution, or whether the sentiment is inexplicable, and requires to be regarded as a special provision of Nature. If we find the former to be the case, we shall, in resolving this question, have resolved also the main problem: if the latter, we shall have to seek for some other mode of investigating it. . . .

. . . The idea of justice supposes two things; a rule of conduct, and a sentiment which sanctions the rule. The first must be supposed common to all mankind, and intended for their good. The other (the sentiment) is a desire that punishment may be suffered by those who infringe the rule. There is involved, in addition, the conception of some definite person who suffers by the infringement; whose rights (to use the expression appropriated to the case) are violated by it. And the sentiment of justice appears to me to be, the animal desire to repel or retaliate a hurt or damage to oneself, or to those with whom one sympathizes, widened so as to include all persons, by the human capacity of enlarged sympathy, and the human conception of intelligent self-interest. From the latter elements, the feeling derives its morality; from the former, its peculiar impressiveness, and energy of self-assertion.

. . . The idea of a *right* residing in the injured person, and violated by the injury, [is] not as a separate element in the composition of the idea and sentiment, but . . . one of the forms in which the other two elements clothe themselves. These elements are, a hurt to some assignable person or persons on the one hand, and a demand for punishment on the other. An examination of our own minds, I think, will show, that these two things include all that we mean when we speak of violation of a right. When we call anything a person's right, we mean that he has a valid claim on society to protect him in the possession of it, either by the force of law, or by that of education and opinion. . . .

To have a right, then, is, I conceive, to have something which society ought to defend me in the possession of. If the objector goes on to ask why it ought, I can give him no other reason that general utility. If that expression does not seem to convey a sufficient feeling of the strength of the obligation, nor to account for the peculiar energy of the feeling, it is because there goes to the composition of the sentiment, not a rational only but also an animal element, the thirst for retaliation; and this thirst derives its intensity, as well as its moral justification, from the extraordinarily important and impressive kind of utility which is concerned. The interest involved is that of security, to every one's feelings the most vital of all interests. . . .

The feelings concerned are so powerful, and we count so positively on finding a responsive feeling in others (all being alike interested), that *ought* and *should* grow into *must,* and recognised indispensability becomes a moral necessity, analogous to physical, and often not inferior to it in binding force. . . .

Is, then, the difference between the Just and the Expedient a merely imaginary distinction? . . . By no means. . . . Justice is a name for certain classes of moral rules, which concern the essentials of human well-being more nearly, and are therefore of more absolute obligation, than any other rules for the guidance of life; and the notion which we have found to be of the essence of the idea of justice, that of a right residing in an individual, implies and testifies to this more binding obligation.

The moral rules which forbid mankind to hurt one another (in which we must never forget to include wrongful interference with each other's freedom) are more vital to human well-being than any maxims, however important, which only point out the best mode of managing some department of human affairs. They have also the peculiarity, that they are the main element in determining the whole of the social feelings of mankind. It is their observance which alone preserves peace among human beings: if obedience to them were not the rule, and disobedience the exception, every one would see in every one else a probable enemy, against whom he must be perpetually guarding himself. What is hardly less important, these are the precepts which mankind have the strongest and most direct inducements for impressing upon one another. By merely giving to each other prudential instruction or exhortation, they may gain, or think they gain, nothing: in inculcating on each other the duty of positive beneficence they have an unmistakable interest, but far less in degree: a person may possibly not need the benefits of others; but he always needs that they should not do him hurt. Thus the moralities which protect every individual from being harmed by others, either directly or by being hindered in his freedom of pursuing his own good, are at once those which he himself has most at heart, and those which he has the strongest interest in publishing and enforcing by word and deed. . . .

Now it is these moralities primarily, which compose the obligations of justice. The most marked cases of injustice, and those which give the tone to the feeling of repugnance which characterizes the sentiment, are acts of wrongful aggression, or wrongful exercise of power over some one; the next are those which consist in wrongfully withholding from him something which is his due; in both cases, inflicting on him a positive hurt, either in the form of direct suffering, or of the privation of some good which he had reasonable ground, either of a physical or of a social kind, for counting upon.

The same powerful motives which command the observance of these primary moralities, enjoin the punishment of those who violate them; and as the impulses of self-defence, of defence of others, and of vengeance, are all called forth against such persons, retribution, or evil for evil, becomes closely connected with the sentiment of justice, and is universally included in the idea. Good for good is also one of the dictates of justice; and this, though its social utility is evident, and though it carries with it a natural human feeling, has not at first sight that obvious connexion with hurt or injury, which, existing in the most elementary cases of just and unjust, is the source of the characteristic intensity of the sentiment. But the connexion, though less obvious, is not less real. He who accepts benefits, and denies a return of them when needed, inflicts a real hurt, by disappointing one of the most natural and reasonable of expectations, and one which he must at least tacitly have encouraged, otherwise the benefits would seldom have been conferred. The important rank, among human evils and wrongs, of the disappointment of expectation, is shown in the fact that it constitutes the principal criminality of two such highly immoral acts as a breach of friendship and a breach of promise. . . .

. . . Justice is a name for certain moral requirements, which, regarded collectively, stand higher in the scale of social utility, and are therefore of more paramount obligation, than any others; though particular cases may occur in which some other social duty is so important, as to overrule any one of the general maxims of justice. Thus, to save a life, it may not only be allowable, but a duty, to steal, or take by force, the necessary food or medicine, or to kidnap, and compel to officiate, the only qualified medical practitioner. In such cases, as we do not call anything justice which in not a virtue, we usually say, not that justice must give way to some other moral principle, but that what is just in ordinary cases is, by reason of that other principle, not just in the particular case. By this useful accommodation of language, the character of indefeasibility attributed to justice is kept up, and we are saved from the necessity of maintaining that there can be laudable injustice.

The considerations which have now been adduced resolve, I conceive, the only real difficulty in the utilitarian theory of morals. It has always been evident that all cases of justice are also cases of expediency: the difference is in the peculiar sentiment which attaches to the former, as contradistinguished from the latter. If this characteristic sentiment has been sufficiently accounted for; if there is no necessity to assume for it any peculiarity of origin; if it is simply the natural feeling of resentment, moralized by being made coextensive with the demands of social good; and if this feeling not only does but ought to exist in all the classes of cases to which the idea of justice corresponds; that idea no longer presents itself as a stumbling-block to the utilitarian ethics. . . .

KANTIANISM

John Rawls

Themes in Kant's Moral Philosophy

I shall discuss several connected themes in Kant's moral philosophy. . . .

§I.   THE FOUR-STEP CI-PROCEDURE

1.   I begin with a highly schematic rendering of Kant's conception of the categorical imperative.[1] I assume that this imperative is applied to the normal conditions of human life by what I shall call the "categorical imperative procedure," or the "CI-procedure" for short. This procedure helps to determine the content of the moral law as it applies to us as reasonable and rational persons endowed with conscience and moral sensibility, and affected by, but not determined by, our natural desires and inclinations. These desires and inclinations reflect our needs as finite beings having a particular place in the order of nature.

Recall that the moral law, the categorical imperative, and the CI-procedure are three different things. The first is an idea of reason and specifies a principle that applies to all reasonable and rational beings whether or not they are like us finite beings with needs. The second is an imperative and as such it is directed only to those reasonable and rational beings who, because they are finite beings with needs, experience the moral law as a constraint. Since we are such beings, we experience the law in this way, and so the categorical imperative applies to us. The CI-procedure adapts the categorical imperative to our circumstances by taking into account the normal conditions of human life and our situation as finite beings with needs in the order of nature.

Keep in mind throughout that Kant is concerned solely with the reasoning of fully reasonable and rational and sincere agents. The CI-procedure is a schema to characterize the framework of deliberation that such agents use implicitly in their moral thought. He takes for granted that the application of this procedure presupposes a certain moral sensibility that is part of our common humanity.[2] It is a misconception to think of it either as an algorithm that yields more or less mechanically a correct judgment, or on the other hand, as a set of debating rules that will trap liars and cheats, cynics and other scoundrels, into exposing their hand.

2.   The CI-procedure has four steps as follows.[3] At the first step we have the agent's maxim, which is, by assumption, rational from the agent's point of view: that is, the maxim is rational given the agent's situation and the alternatives available together with the agent's desires, abilities, and beliefs (which are assumed to be rational in the circumstances). The maxim is also assumed to be sincere: that is, it reflects the agent's actual reasons (as the agent would truthfully describe them) for the intended action. Thus the CI-procedure applies to maxims that rational agents have arrived at in view of what they

regard as the relevant features of their circumstances. And, we should add, this procedure applies equally well to maxims that rational and sincere agents might arrive at given the normal circumstances of human life. To sum up: the agent's maxim at the first step is both rational and sincere. It is a particular hypothetical imperative (to be distinguished later from *the* hypothetical imperative) and it has the form:

1. I am to do X in circumstances C in order to bring about Y. (Here X is an action and Y a state of affairs.)

The second step generalizes the maxim at the first to get:

2. Everyone is to do X in circumstances C in order to bring about Y.

At the third step we are to transform the general precept at 2 into a law of nature to obtain:

3. Everyone always does X in circumstances C in order to bring about Y (as if by a law of nature).

The fourth step is the most complicated and raises questions that I cannot consider here. The idea is this:

4. We are to adjoin the law of nature at step 3 to the existing laws of nature (as these are understood by us) and then calculate as best we can what the order of nature would be once the effects of the newly adjoined law of nature have had a chance to work themselves out.

It is assumed that a new order of nature results from the addition of the law at step 3 to the other laws of nature, and that this new order of nature has a settled equilibrium state the relevant features of which we are able to figure out. Let us call this new order of nature a "perturbed social world," and let's think of this social world as associated with the maxim at step 1.

Kant's categorical imperative can now be stated as follows: We are permitted to act from our rational and sincere maxim at step 1 only if two conditions are satisfied: First, we must be able to intend, as a sincere reasonable and rational agent, to act from this maxim when we regard ourselves as a member of the perturbed social world associated with it (and thus as acting within that world and subject to its conditions); and second, we must be able to will this perturbed social world itself and affirm it should we belong to it.

Thus, if we cannot at the same time both will this perturbed social world and intend to act from this maxim as a member of it, we cannot now act from the maxim even though it is, by assumption, rational and sincere in our present circumstances. The principle represented by the CI-procedure applies to us no matter what the consequences may be for our rational interests as we now understand them. It is at this point that the force of the priority of pure practical reason over empirical practical reason comes into play. But let's leave this aside for the moment.

3. To illustrate the use of the four-step procedure, consider the fourth example in the *Grundlegung* (Gr 4:423). The maxim to be tested is one that expresses indifference to the well-being of others who need our help and assistance. We are to decide

whether we can will the perturbed social world associated with this maxim formulated as follows.

I am not to do anything to help others, or to support them in distress, unless at the time it is rational to do so, given my own interests.

The perturbed-social world associated with this maxim is a social world in which no one ever does anything to help others for the sake of their well-being. And this is true of everyone, past, present, and future. This is the relevant equilibrium state; and we are to imagine that this state obtains, like any other order of nature, in perpetuity, backwards and forwards in time. Kant takes for granted that everyone in the perturbed social world knows the laws of human conduct that arise from generalized maxims and that everyone is able to work out the relevant equilibrium state. Moreover, that everyone is able to do this is itself public knowledge. Thus, the operation at step 3 converts a general precept at step 2 into a publicly recognized law of (human) nature. That Kant takes these matters for granted is clearest from his second example, that of the deceitful promise.

Now Kant says that we cannot will the perturbed social world associated with the maxim of indifference because many situations may arise in the world in which we need the love and sympathy of others. In those situations, by a law originating from our own will, we would have robbed ourselves of what we require. It would be irrational for us to will a social world in which every one, as if by a law of nature, is deaf to appeals based on this need. Kant does not say much about how the idea of a rational will works in this example. In addition, the test as he applies it to the maxim of indifference is too strong: that is, the same test rejects those maxims that lead to any form of the precept (or duty) of mutual aid. The reason is this: any such precept enjoins us to help others when they are in need. But here also, in the perturbed social world associated with a precept to help others in need, situations may arise in which we very much want not to help them. The circumstances may be such that helping them seriously interferes with our plans. Thus, in these cases too, by a law originating from our own will, we would have prevented ourselves from achieving what we very much want. The difficulty is clear enough: in any perturbed social world all moral precepts will oppose our natural desires and settled intentions on at least some occasions. Hence the test of the CI-procedure, as Kant apparently understands it, is too strong: it appears to reject al maxims that lead to moral precepts (or duties).

4.   One way out, I think, but I don't say the only one, is to try to develop an appropriate conception of what we may call "true human needs," a phrase Kant uses several times in the *Metaphysics of Morals* (MM 6:393, 432; see also 452–58).[4] Once this is done, the contradiction in the will test as illustrated by the fourth example might be formulated as follows:

Can I will the perturbed social world associated with the precept of indifference rather than the perturbed social world associated with a precept of mutual aid, that is, a maxim enjoining me to help others in need? In answering this question I am to take account only of my true human needs (which by assumption, as part of the CI-procedure, I take myself to have and to be the same for everyone).

Thus, in applying the procedure as now revised we understand that any general precept will constrain our actions prompted by our desires and inclinations on some and perhaps many occasions. What we must do is to compare alternative social worlds and evaluate the overall consequences of willing one of these worlds rather than another. In order to do this, we are to take into account the balance of likely effects over time for our true human needs. Of course for this idea to work, we require an account of these needs. And here certain moral conceptions, rooted in our shared moral sensibility, may be involved.

I believe that Kant also assumes that the evaluation of perturbed social worlds at step 4 is subject to at least two limits on information. The first limit is that we are to ignore the more particular features of persons, including ourselves, as well as the specific content of their and our final ends and desires (Gr 4:433). The second limit is that when we ask ourselves whether we can will the perturbed social world associated with our maxim, we are to reason as if we do not know which place we may have in that world. . . . The CI-procedure is misapplied when we project into the perturbed social world either the specific content of our final ends, or the particular features of our present or likely future circumstances. We must reason at step 4 not only on the basis of true human needs but also from a suitably general point of view that satisfies these two limits on particular (as opposed to general) information. We must see ourselves as proposing the public moral law for an ongoing social world enduring over time.

5.   This brief schematic account of the CI-procedure is intended only to set the background for explaining the sequence of conceptions of the good in §2. . . . To serve this purpose, the procedure must meet two conditions: (1) it must not represent the requirements of the moral law as merely formal; otherwise, the moral law lacks sufficient content for a constructivist view; and (2) it must have features that enable us to see what Kant means when he says that the moral law discloses our freedom to us (considered in §5). . . .

It turns out that for the second condition to be met, the CI-procedure must display in how it works, on its face as it were, the way in which pure practical reason is prior to empirical practical reason. This enables us to understand the distinctive structure of Kant's moral conception and how it is possible for our freedom to be made manifest to us by the moral law.

What this priority means will become clearer as we proceed. For the present let's say that pure practical reason restricts empirical practical reason and subordinates it absolutely. This is an aspect of the unity of reason. The way in which pure practical reason restricts and subordinates empirical practical reason is expressed in imperative form by the CI-procedure: this procedure represents the requirements of pure practical reason in the manner appropriate for the conditions of human life. Empirical practical reason is the principle of rational deliberation that determines when particular hypothetical imperatives are rational. The CI-procedure restricts empirical practical reason by requiring the agent's rational and sincere deliberations to be conducted in accordance with the stipulations we have just surveyed. Unless a maxim passes the test of that procedure, acting from the maxim is forbidden. This outcome is final from the standpoint of practical reason as a whole, both pure and empirical. The survey of six conceptions of the good in Kant's doctrine is the next part (§ 3) will supplement these remarks about how the two forms of practical reason are combined in the unity of practical reason.

6.   Before turning to this survey, a few comments on the sketch of the CI-procedure. In characterizing human persons I have used the phrase "reasonable and rational." The intention here is to mark the fact that Kant's uses *vernünftig* to express a full-bodied conception that covers the terms "reasonable" and "rational" as we often use them. In English we know what is meant when someone says: "Their proposal is rational, given their circumstances, but it is unreasonable all the same." The meaning is roughly that the people referred to are pushing a hard and unfair bargain, which they know to be in their own interests but which they wouldn't expect us to accept unless they knew their position is strong. "Reasonable" can also mean "judicious," "ready to listen to reason," where this has the sense of being willing to listen to and consider the reasons offered by others. *Vernünftig* can have the same meanings in German: it can have the broad sense of "reasonable" as well as the narrower sense of "rational" to mean roughly furthering our interests in the most effective way. Kant's usage varies but when applied to persons it usually covers being both reasonable and rational. His use of "reason" often has the even fuller sense of the philosophical tradition. Think of what has *Vernunft* means in the title of *Critique of Pure Reason*! We are worlds away from "rational" in the narrow sense. It's a deep question (which I leave aside) whether Kant's conception of reason includes far more than reason.

It is useful, then, to use "reasonable" and "rational" as handy terms to mark the distinction that Kant makes between the two forms of practical reason, pure and empirical. The first is expressed as an imperative in *the* categorical imperative, the second in *the* hypothetical imperative. These forms of practical reason must also be distinguished from particular categorical and hypothetical imperatives (the particular maxims at step 1) that satisfy the corresponding requirements of practical reason in particular circumstances. The terms "reasonable" and "rational" remind us of the fullness of Kant's conception of practical reason and of the two forms of reason it comprehends.

7.   I conclude with some remarks about the relation between Kant's three different formulations of the categorical imperative. Some may think that to rely, as I shall, on the first formulation alone gives an incomplete idea of the content of the categorical imperative. It may be incomplete, but nevertheless I believe it is adequate for our purposes. Kant says (Gr 4:436-37) that the three formulations are "so many formulations of precisely the same law." He also says that there is a difference between the formulations, which is only subjectively rather than objectively practical. The purpose of having several formulations is to bring the idea of reason (the moral law) nearer to intuition in accordance with a certain analogy and so nearer to feeling. At the end of the passage (pars. 72-75 of ch. II), Kant says that if we wish to gain access (or entry) for the moral law[5] it is useful to bring one and the same action under all three formulations, and in this way, so far as we can, to bring "it [the action] nearer to intuition." We are also instructed that it is better when making a moral judgment to "proceed always in accordance with the strict method and take as our basis the universal formula of

the categorical imperative." This imperative we have interpreted in accordance with the law of nature formula (Gr 4:421). . . .

There are certain obscurities in Kant's view here. I shall not discuss them but simply state what I regard as his two main points. First, we are to use the four-step CI-procedure whenever we are testing whether our maxim is permitted by the categorical imperative. The other formulations cannot add to the content of the moral law as it applies to us. What is important here is that, however we interpret them, the second and third formulations must not yield any requirement that is not already accounted for by the CI-procedure. In particular, this holds for the second formulation concerning treating persons always as ends and never as means only (see Gr 4:429). With its use of the term "humanity" *(Menschheit),* this formulation seems strikingly different from the first and third. This appearance is misleading, since it is clear from the Introduction to the *Metaphysics of Morals* that "humanity" means the powers that characterize us as reasonable and rational beings who belong to the natural order. Our humanity is our pure practical reason together with our moral sensibility (our capacity for moral feeling). These two powers constitute moral personality, and include the power to set ends (MM 6:392); they make a good will and moral character possible. We have a duty to cultivate our natural capacities in order to make ourselves worthy of our humanity (MM 6:387). Thus, the duty to treat humanity, whether in our own person or in the person of others, always as an end, and never simply as a means, is the duty to respect the moral powers both in ourselves and in other persons, and to cultivate our natural capacities so that we can be worthy of those powers. Modulo shifts of points of view as described in the next paragraph, what particular duties are covered by this duty are ascertained by the first formulation of the categorical imperative. The first principle of the doctrine of virtue (MM 6:395) is a special case of this formulation. I think we cannot discern what Kant means by the second formulation apart from his account in the *Metaphysics of Morals.*

8. A second point about the relation of the three formulations: I believe that the purpose of the second and third formulations is to look at the application of the CI-procedure from two further points of view. The idea is this: each formulation looks at this procedure from a different point of view. In the first formulation, which is the strict method, we look at our maxim from our point of view. This is clear from how the procedure is described. We are to regard ourselves as subject to the moral law and we want to know what it requires of us. In the second formulation, however, we are to consider our maxim from the point of view of our humanity as the fundamental element in our person demanding our respect, or from the point of view of other persons who will be affected by our action. Humanity both in us and in other persons is regarded as *passive:* as that which will be affected by what we do. . . . But when this passive subject considers which laws can arise from its will, it must apply the CI-procedure. The point is simply that all persons affected must apply that procedure in the same way both to accept and to reject the same maxims. This ensures a universal agreement which prepares the way for the third formulation.

In this formulation we come back again to the agent's point of view, but this time we no longer regard ourselves as someone who is subject to the moral law but as someone who makes that law. The CI-procedure is seen as the procedure adherence to which with a full grasp of its meaning enables us to regard ourselves as legislators—as those who make universal public law for a possible moral community. This community Kant calls a realm of ends—a commonwealth and not a kingdom—the conception of which is also an idea of reason.

Finally, using all three formulations of the moral law is subjectively practical in two ways: first, having these formulations deepens our understanding of the moral law by showing how it regards actions from different points of view, and second, our deeper understanding of that law strengthens our desire to act from it. This is what Kant means, I think, by gaining entry or access for the moral law.[6]

§2.   THE SEQUENCE OF SIX CONCEPTIONS OF THE GOOD

1.   In order to understand Kant's constructivism and how he thinks that the moral law discloses our freedom to us, we need to look at the priority of pure practical reason over empirical practical reason, and to distinguish six conceptions of the good in Kant's doctrine. These conceptions are built up in a sequence one by one from the preceding ones. This sequence can be presented by referring to the four steps of the CI-procedure, since each conception can be connected with a particular step in this procedure. This provides a useful way of arranging these conceptions and clarifies the relations between them. It also enables us to explain what is meant by calling the realm of ends the necessary object of a will determined by the moral law, as well as what is meant by saying of this realm that it is an object given a priori to such a pure will (CP 5:4).

The first of the six conceptions of the good is given by unrestricted empirical practical reason. It is the conception of happiness as organized by the (as opposed to a particular) hypothetical imperative. This conception may be connected with step 1 of the CI-procedure, since the maxim at this step is assumed to be rational and sincere given that conception. Thus the maxim satisfies the principles of rational deliberation that characterize the hypothetical imperative, or what we may call "the rational." There are no restrictions on the information available to sincere and rational agents either in framing their conceptions of happiness or in forming their particular maxims: all the relevant particulars about their desires, abilities, and situation, as well as the available alternatives, are assumed to be known.

The second conception of the good is of the fulfillment of true human needs. I have suggested that at the fourth step of the CI-procedure we require some such idea. Otherwise the agent going through the procedure cannot compare the perturbed social worlds associated with different maxims. At first we might think this comparison can be made on the basis of the agent's conception of happiness. But even if the agent knows what this conception is, there is still a serious difficulty, since Kant supposes different agents to have different conceptions of their happiness. On his view, happiness is an ideal, not of reason but of the imagination, and so our conception of our happiness depends on the contingencies of our life, and on particular modes of thought and feeling we have developed as we come of age. Thus, if conceptions of happiness are used in judging social worlds at step 4, then whether a maxim passes the CI-procedure would depend on who applies it. This dependence would defeat Kant's view. For if our following the CI-procedure doesn't lead to approximate agreement when we apply it intelligently and conscientiously against the background of the same information, then that law lacks objective content. Here objective content means a content that is publicly recognized as correct, as based on sufficient reasons and as (roughly) the same for all reasonable and sincere human agents.

Observe that this second conception of the good based on true human needs is a special conception designed expressly to be used at step 4 of the CI-procedure. It is formulated to meet a need of reason: namely, that the moral law have sufficient objective content. Moreover, when this procedure is thought of as applied consistently by everyone over time in accordance with the requirement of complete determination (Gr 4:436), it specifies the content of a conception of right and justice that would be realized in a realm of ends. This conception, as opposed to the first, is restricted: that is, it is framed in view of the restrictions on information to which agents are subject at step 4.

The third conception of the good is the good as the fulfillment in everyday life of what Kant calls "permissible ends" (MM 6:388), that is, ends that respect the limits of the moral law. This means in practice that we are to revise, abandon, or repress desires and inclinations that prompt us to rational and sincere maxims at step 1 that are rejected by the CI-procedure. Here it is not a question of balancing the strength and importance to us of our natural desires against the strength and importance to us of the pure practical interest we take in acting from the moral law. Such balancing is excluded entirely. Rather, whenever our maxim is rejected, we must reconsider our intended course of action, for in this case the claim to satisfy the desires in question is rejected. At this point the contrast with utilitarianism is clear, since for Kant this third conception of the good presupposes the moral law and the principles of pure practical reason. Whereas utilitarianism starts with a conception of the good given prior to, and independent of, the right (the moral law), and it then works out from that independent conception its conceptions of the right and of moral worth, in that order. In Kant's view, however, unrestricted rationality, or the rational, is framed by, and subordinated absolutely to, a procedure that incorporates the constraints of the reasonable. It is by this procedure that admissible conceptions of the good and their permissible ends are specified.

2. The first of the three remaining conceptions of the good is the familiar conception of the good will. This is Kant's conception of moral worth: a completely good will is the supreme (although not the complete) good of persons and of their character as reasonable and rational beings. This good is constituted by a firm and settled highest-order desire that leads us to take an interest in acting from the moral law for its own sake, or, what comes in practice to the same thing, to further the realm of ends as the moral law requires. When we have a completely good will, this highest-order desire, however strongly it may be opposed by our natural desires and inclinations, is always strong enough by itself to insure that we act from (and not merely in accordance with) the moral law.

The next conception of the good is the good as the object of the moral law, which is, as indicated above, the realm of ends. This object is simply the social world that would come about (at least under reasonably favorable conditions) if everyone were to follow the totality of precepts that result from the correct application of the CI-procedure. Kant sometimes refers to the realm of ends as the necessary object of a will, which is determined by the moral law, or alternatively, as an object that is given a priori to a will determined by that law (CP 5:4). By this I think he means that the realm of ends is an object—a social world—the moral constitution and regulation of which is specified by the totality of precepts that meet the test of the CI-procedure (when these precepts are adjusted and coordinated by the requirement of complete determination). Put another way, the realm of ends is not a social world that can be described prior to and independent of the concepts and principles of practical reason and the procedure by which they are applied. That realm is not an already given describable object the nature of which determines the content of the moral law. This would be the case, for example, if this law were understood as stating what must be done in order to bring about a good society the nature and institutions of which are already specified apart from the moral law. That such a teleological conception is foreign to Kant's doctrine is plain from ch. II of the Analytic of the *Critique of Practical Reason*. The burden of that chapter is to explain what has been called Kant's "Copernican Revolution" in moral philosophy (CP 5:62–65).[7] Rather than starting from a conception of the good given independently of the right, we start from a conception of the right—of the moral law—given by pure (as opposed to empirical) practical reason. We then specify in the light of this conception what ends are permissible and what social arrangements are right and just. We might say: a moral conception is not to revolve around the good as an independent object, but around a conception of the right as constructed by our pure practical reason into which any permissible good must fit. . . .

Finally, there is Kant's conception of the complete good. This is the good that is attained when a realm of ends exists and each member of it not only has a completely good will but is also fully happy so far as the normal conditions of human life allow. Here, of course, happiness is specified by the satisfaction of ends that respect the requirements of the moral law, and so are permissible ends. Often Kant refers to this complete good as the highest good. This is his preferred term after the *Grundlegung,* especially when he is presenting his doctrine of reasonable faith in the second *Critique.* I shall use the secular term "realized realm of ends," and I assume that this complete good can be approximated to in the natural world, at least under reasonably favorable conditions. In this sense it is a natural good, one that can be approached (although never fully realized) within the order of nature.

Kant holds that in the complete good, the good will is the supreme good, that is, we must have a good will if the other goods we enjoy are to be truly good and our enjoyment of them fully appropriate. This applies in particular to the good of happiness, since he thinks that only our having a good will can make us worthy of happiness. Kant also believes that two goods so different in their nature, and in their foundations in our person, as a good will and happiness are incommensurable; and, therefore, that they can be combined into one unified and complete good only by the relation of the strict priority of one over the other.

3.   The preceding sketch of conceptions of the good in Kant's view indicates how they are built up, or constructed, in an ordered sequence one after the other, each conception (except the first) depending on the preceding ones. If we count the second (that of true human needs) as part of the CI-procedure itself, we can say that beginning with the third (that of permissible ends), these conceptions presuppose an independent conception of right (the reasonable). This conception of right is represented by the CI-procedure as the application of pure practical reason to the conditions of human life. Only the first conception of the good is entirely independent of the moral law, since it is the rational without restriction. Thus the sequence of conceptions beginning with the second exemplifies the priority of pure practical reason over empirical practical reason and displays the distinctive deontological and constructivist structure of Kant's view. We start with two forms of practical reason, the reasonable and the rational. The unity of practical reason is grounded in how the reasonable frames the rational and restricts it absolutely. Then we proceed step by step to generate different conceptions of the good and obtain at the last two steps the conceptions of the good will and of a complete good as a fully realized realm of ends. The contrast between the deontological and constructivist structure of Kant's doctrine and the linear structure of a teleological view starting from an independent conception of the good is so obvious as not to need comment. . . .

§5.   THE MORAL LAW AS A LAW OF FREEDOM

1.   The distinctive feature of Kant's view of freedom is the central place of the moral law as an idea of pure reason; and pure reason, both theoretical and practical, is free. For Kant there is no essential difference between the freedom of the will and freedom of thought. If our mathematical and theoretical reasoning is free, as shown in free judgments, then so is our pure practical reasoning as shown in free deliberative judgments. Here in both cases free judgments are to be distinguished from verbal utterances that simply give voice to, that are the (causal) upshot of, our psychological states and of our wants and attitudes. Judgments claim validity and truth, claims that can be supported by reasons. The freedom of pure reason includes the freedom of practical as well as of theoretical reason, since both are freedoms of one and the same reason (Gr 4:391; CP 5:91, 121). Kant's approach requires that the moral law exhibit features that disclose our freedom, and these features should be discernible in the CI-procedure, on its face, so to speak. The moral law serves as the *ratio cognoscendi* of freedom (CP 5:4n). Our task is simply to recall the features of this procedure (surveyed in §1) which Kant thinks enables us to recognize it as a law of freedom.[8]

Consider first the features through which the CI-procedure exhibits the moral law as unconditional. These are evident in the ways that the reasonable restricts the rational and subordinates it absolutely. The CI-procedure (the reasonable) restricts empirical practical reason (the rational) by requiring that unless the agent's rational and sincere maxim is accepted by the procedure, acting from that maxim is forbidden absolutely. This outcome is final from the standpoint of practical reason as a whole, both pure and empirical. Thus, the moral law, as represented by the CI-procedure, specifies a scope within which permissible ends must fall, as well as limits on the means that can be adopted in the pursuit of these ends. The scope and limits that result delineate the duties of justice. The moral law also imposes certain ends as ends that we have a duty to pursue and to give some weight to. These duties are duties of virtue. That the moral law as represented is unconditional simply means that the constraints of the CI-procedure are valid for all reasonable and rational persons, no matter what their natural desires and inclinations.

We might say: pure practical reason is a priori with respect to empirical practical reason. Here the term "a priori" applies, of course, to pure practical knowledge and not to the knowledge of objects given in experience. It expresses the fact that we know in advance, no matter what our natural desires may be, that the moral law imposes certain ends as well as restrictions on means, and that these requirements are always valid for us. This fits the traditional epistemological meaning of a priori once it is applied to practical knowledge, and it accords with Kant's definition of the priori at CP 5:12. Kant uses the unconditional and a priori aspects of the moral law to explain the sense in which our acting from that law shows our independence of nature and our freedom from determination by the desires and needs aroused in us by natural and psychological causes (so-called negative freedom).

2.   Next, let's ask how the CI-procedure exhibits the moral law as sufficient to itself to determine the will. Here we should be careful not to interpret this feature too strongly. I do not think Kant wants to say, and certainly he does not need to say, that the moral law determines all relevant aspects of what we are to do. Rather, the moral law specifies a scope *within* which permissible ends must fall, and also *limits* the means that may be used in their pursuit, and this goes part way to make the moral law sufficient of itself to determine the will. (Of course, particular desires determine which permissible ends it is rational for us to pursue, and they also determine, within the limits allowed, how it is rational for us to pursue them. This leeway I view as compatible with Kant's intentions.)

But beyond specifying a scope for permissible ends and limiting means in their pursuit, the moral law must further provide sufficient grounds to determine the will by identifying certain ends that are also duties and by requiring us to give at least some weight to those ends. Since the moral law determines both aspects of action, both ends and means, pure practical reason, through the moral law as an idea of reason, is *sufficient* to determine the will.[9] The point here is that for Kant action has an end; if the moral law failed to identify certain ends as also duties, it would not suffice to determine an essential feature of actions.

What is crucial for Kant's view is that the moral law must not be merely formal but have enough content to be, in a natural meaning of the word, sufficient of itself to determine ends: pure reason is not merely finding the most effective way to realize given ends but it criticizes and selects among proposed ends. Its doing this is what Kant has in mind when he says that the moral law specifies a positive concept of freedom. We are free not only in the sense that we are able to act independently of our natural desires and needs, but also free in the sense that we have a principle regulative of *both* ends and means from which to act, a principle of autonomy appropriate to us as reasonable and rational beings.

3.   So much for the way in which the CI-procedure exhibits the moral law as unconditional and sufficient of itself to determine the will. In addition to this procedure exhibiting how the moral law imposes ends that are also duties, it exhibits that law as doing reason's work in setting ends and in securing their ordered unity, so that it is not merely a principle of rationality. We can also see how the moral law constructs the realm of ends and thereby specifies the conception of its object. In short, the CI-procedure in its constructions models all the essential features of a principle doing the work of pure reason in the practical sphere.

This procedure also clarifies the more general aspects of pure practical reason to which Kant refers in a passage from the first *Critique.* Kant says:

> Reason does not . . . follow the order of things as they present themselves in appearance, but frames for itself with perfect spontaneity an order of its own according to ideas [of pure reason], to which it adapts the empirical conditions, and according to which it declares actions to be [practically] necessary (A548/B576).

We can grasp what Kant has in mind: namely, that pure practical reason constructs out of itself the conception of the realm of ends as an order of its own according to ideas of reason; and given the historical and material circumstances under which society exists, that conception guides us in fashioning institutions and practices in conformity with it.

The particular characteristics of a realm of ends are, then, to be adapted to empirical, that is, to historical and social conditions. What in particular is the content of citizens' permissible ends, and what specific institutions are best suited to establish a moral community regulated by the moral law, must wait upon circumstances. But what we do know in advance are certain general features of such a moral community: the nature of ends that are also duties, and the arrangement of these ends under the duty to cultivate our moral and natural perfection, and the duty to further the happiness (the permissible ends) of others. We also know that under favorable conditions, a realm of ends is some form of constitutional democracy. . . .

---

[1]Modulo a few minor variations, my account of the CI-procedure in §I follows closely that of Onora (Nell) O'Neill in her *Acting on Principle* (New York, 1975). See also Paul Dietrichson, "When is a Maxim Universalizable?" *Kant-Studien,* 56 (1964). I have followed Barbara Herman in supposing that when we apply the CI-procedure we are to assume that the agent's maxim is rational. See her "Morality as Rationality: A Study in Kant's Ethics," Ph.D. thesis, Harvard, 1976.

[2]On this presupposition, see the instructive discussion by Barbara Herman, "The Practice of Moral Judgment," *Journal of Philosophy,* 82 (1985).

[3]In describing these steps many refinements are glossed over. I am indebted to Reinhard Brandt for illuminating discussions on this score. But as I have said, the account need only be accurate enough to set the stage for the themes of moral constructivism and the authentication of the moral law, and the rest.

[4]In adopting this way out we are amending, or adding to, Kant's account. It is, I think, Kantian in spirit provided that, as I believe, it doesn't compromise the essential elements of his doctrine.

[5]The German is: "Will man aber dem sittlichen Gesetze zugleich Eingang verschaffen." Kant's meaning here is obscure; see below at last par. of §1.

[6]I am indebted to Michael Friedman for clarification on this point.

[7]John Silber, "The Copernican Revolution in Ethics: The Good Reexamined," *Kant-Studien,* 51 (1959).

[8]There are three ideas of freedom in Kant that need to be distinguished and related in an account of the practical point of view: those of acting under the idea of freedom, of practical freedom, and of transcendental freedom. Unhappily, I cannot consider them here.

[9]The third and strongest way in which the moral law might suffice to determine the will would seem to be this: we read Kant to say in the *Doctrine of Virtue* that the ends of all our actions must be ends that are also duties. The only leeway that now remains is in the weight we are allowed to give to these ends and in the choice of the most effective means to achieve them. The ordinary pleasures of life are permissible only insofar as they are required to preserve our self-respect and sense of well-being and good health, essential if we are conscientiously and intelligently to fulfill our duties. This is one interpretation of Kant's so-called rigorism, but I shall not pursue it here.

Further Reading

Kant's Ethics
Groundwork of the Metaphysics of Morals (1785). H. J. Paton, trans. London: Hutchinson, 1948.
Critique of Practical Reason (1788). L. W. Beck, trans. New York: Macmillan, Library of Liberal Arts, 1993.
The Metaphysics of Morals (1797). M. J. Gregor, trans. Cambridge: Cambridge University Press, 1991.

Work on Kant
Herman, Barbara. *The Practice of Moral Judgment.* Cambridge, MA: Harvard University Press, 1993.
Hill, T. E., Jr. *Dignity and Practical Reason in Kant's Moral Theory.* Ithaca, NY: Cornell University Press, 1992.
Korsgaard, Christina. *Creating the Kingdom of Ends.* Cambridge: Cambridge University Press, 1996.
O'Neill, O. *Constructions of Reason: Explorations of Kant's Practical Philosophy.* Cambridge: Cambridge University Press, 1989.

IMMANUEL KANT

Grounding for the Metaphysics of Morals

FIRST SECTION: TRANSITION FROM THE ORDINARY RATIONAL KNOWLEDGE OF MORALITY TO THE PHILOSOPHICAL

There is no possibility of thinking anything at all in the world, or even out of it, which can be regarded as good without qualification, except a *good will*. Intelligence, wit, judgment, and whatever talents of the mind one might want to name are doubtless in many respects good and desirable, as are such qualities of temperament as courage, resolution, perseverance. But they can also become extremely bad and harmful if the will, which is to make use of these gifts of nature and which in its special constitution is called character, is not good. . . .

The concept of a will estimable in itself and good without regard to any further end must now be developed. This concept already dwells in the natural sound understanding and needs not so much to be taught as merely to be elucidated. It always holds first place in estimating the total worth of our actions and constitutes the condition of all the rest. Therefore, we shall take up the concept of *duty,* which includes that of a good will, though with certain subjective restrictions and hindrances, which far from hiding a good will or rendering it unrecognizable, rather bring it out by contrast and make it shine forth more brightly. . . .

To be beneficent where one can is a duty; and besides this, there are many persons who are so sympathetically constituted that, without any further motive of vanity or self-interest, they find an inner pleasure in spreading joy around them and can rejoice in the satisfaction of others as their own work. But I maintain that in such a case an action of this kind, however dutiful and amiable it may be, has nevertheless no true moral worth. . . .

The second proposition is this: An action done from duty has its moral worth, not in the purpose that is to be attained by it, but in the maxim according to which the action is determined. The moral worth depends, therefore, not on the realization of the object of the action, but merely on the principle of volition according to which, without regard to any objects of the faculty of desire, the action has been done. . . .

The third proposition, which follows from the other two, can be expressed thus: Duty is the necessity of an action done out of respect for the law. I can indeed have an inclination for an object as the effect of my proposed action; but I can never have respect for such an object, just because it is merely an effect and is not an activity of the will. . . .

Thus the moral worth of an action does not lie in the effect expected from it nor in any principle of action that needs to borrow its motive from this expected effect. . . .

But what sort of law can that be the thought of which must determine the will without reference to any expected effect, so that the will can be called absolutely good without qualification? Since I have deprived the will of every impulse that might arise for it from obeying any particular law, there is nothing left to serve the will as principle except the universal conformity of its actions to law as such, i.e., I should never act except in such a way that I can also will that my maxim should become a universal law. Here mere conformity to law as such (without having as its basis any law determining particular actions) serves the will as principle and must so serve it if duty is not to be a vain delusion and a chimerical concept. The ordinary reason of mankind in its practical judgments agrees completely with this, and always has in view the aforementioned principle. . . .

SECOND SECTION: TRANSITION FROM POPULAR MORAL PHILOSOPHY TO A METAPHYSICS OF MORALS

. . . Now all imperatives command either hypothetically or categorically. The former represent the practical necessity of a possible action as a means for attaining something else that one wants (or may possibly want). The categorical imperative would be one which represented an action as objectively necessary in itself, without reference to another end. . . .

If I think of a hypothetical imperative in general, I do not know beforehand what it will contain until its condition is given. But if I think of a categorical imperative, I know immediately what it contains. For since, besides the law, the imperative contains only the necessity that the maxim should accord with this law, while the law contains no condition to restrict it, there remains nothing but the universality of a law as such with which the maxim of the action should conform. This conformity alone is properly what is represented as necessary by the imperative.

Hence there is only one categorical imperative and it is this: Act only according to that maxim whereby you can at the same time will that it should become a universal law.

Now if all imperatives of duty can be derived from this one imperative as their principle, then there can at least be shown what is understood by the concept of duty and what it means, even though there is left undecided whether what is called duty may not be an empty concept.

The universality of law according to which effects are produced constitutes what is properly called nature in the most general sense (as to form), i.e., the existence of things as far as determined by universal laws. Accordingly, the universal imperative of duty may be expressed thus: Act as if the maxim of your action were to become through your will a universal law of nature.

We shall now enumerate some duties, following the usual division of them into duties to ourselves and to others and into perfect and imperfect duties.

1. A man reduced to despair by a series of misfortunes feels sick of life but is still so far in possession of his reason that he can ask himself whether taking his own life would not be contrary to his duty to himself. Now he asks whether the maxim of his action could become a universal law of nature. But his maxim is this: from self-love I make as my principle to shorten my life when its continued duration threatens more evil than it promises satisfaction. There only remains the question as to whether this principle of self-love can become a universal law of nature. One sees at once a contradiction in a system of nature whose law would destroy life by means of the very same feeling that acts so as to stimulate the furtherance of life, and hence there could be no existence as a system of nature. Therefore, such a maxim cannot possibly hold as a universal law of nature and is, consequently, wholly opposed to the supreme principle of all duty.

2. Another man in need finds himself forced to borrow money. He knows well that he won't be able to repay it, but he sees also that he will not get any loan unless he firmly promises to repay it within a fixed time.

. . . The maxim of his action would then be expressed as follows: when I believe myself to be in need of money, I will borrow money and promise to pay it back, although I know that I can never do so.

. . . I then transform the requirement of self-love into a universal law and put the question thus: how would things stand if my maxim were to become a universal law? He then sees at once that such a maxim could never hold as a universal law of nature and be consistent with itself, but must necessarily be self-contradictory. For the universality of a law which says that anyone believing himself to be in difficulty could promise whatever he pleases with the intention of not keeping it would make promising itself and the end to be attained thereby quite impossible, inasmuch as no one would believe what was promised him but would merely laugh at all such utterances as being vain pretenses.

3. A third finds in himself a talent whose cultivation could make him a man useful in many respects. But he finds himself in comfortable circumstances and prefers to indulge in pleasure rather than to bother himself about broadening and improving his fortunate natural aptitudes. But he asks himself further whether his maxim of neglecting his natural gifts, besides agreeing of itself with his propensity to indulgence, might agree also with what is called duty. He then sees that a system of nature could indeed always subsist according to such a universal law, even though every man (like South Sea Islanders) should let his talents rust and resolve to devote his life entirely to idleness, indulgence, propagation, and, in a word, enjoyment. But he cannot possibly will that this should become a universal law of nature or be implanted in us as such a law by a natural instinct. For as a rational being he necessarily wills that all his faculties should be developed, inasmuch as they are given him for all sorts of possible purposes.

4. A fourth man finds things going well for himself but sees others (whom he could help) struggling with great hardships; and he thinks: what does it matter to me? Let everybody be as happy as Heaven wills or as he can make himself; I shall take nothing from him nor even envy him; but I have no desire to contribute anything to his well-being or to his assistance when in need. If such a way of thinking were to become a universal law of nature, the human race admittedly could very well subsist and doubtless could subsist even better than when everyone prates about sympathy and benevolence and even on occasion exerts himself to practice them but, on the other hand, also cheats when he can, betrays the rights of man, or otherwise violates them. But even though it is possible that a universal law of nature could subsist in accordance with that maxim, still it is impossible to will that such a principle should hold everywhere as a law of nature. For a will which resolved in this way would contradict itself, inasmuch as cases might often arise in which one would have need of the love and sympathy of others and in which he would deprive himself, by such a law of nature springing from his own will, of all hope of the aid he wants for himself.

These are some of the many actual duties, or at least what are taken to be such, whose derivation from the single principle cited above is clear. We must be able to will that a maxim of our action become a universal law; this is the canon for morally estimating any of our actions. Some actions are so constituted that their maxims cannot without contradiction even be thought as a universal law of nature, much less be willed as what should become one. In the case of others this internal impossibility is indeed not found, but there is still no possibility of willing that their maxim should be raised to the universality of a law of nature, because such a will would contradict itself. There is no difficulty in seeing that the former kind of action conflicts with strict or narrow [perfect] (irremissible) duty, while the second kind conflicts only with broad [imperfect] (meritorious) duty. By means of these examples there has thus been fully set forth how all duties depend as regards the kind of obligation (not the object of their action) upon the one principle.

If we now attend to ourselves in any transgression of a duty, we find that we actually do not will that our maxim should become a universal law—because this is impossible for us—but rather that the opposite of this maxim should remain a law universally. We only take the liberty of making an exception to the law for ourselves (or just for this one time) to the advantage of our inclination. . . .

. . . Let us suppose that there were something whose existence has in itself an absolute worth, something which as an end in itself could be a ground of determinate laws. In it, and in it alone, would there be the ground of a possible categorical imperative, i.e., of a practical law.

Now I say that man, and in general every rational being, exists as an end in himself and not merely as a means to be arbitrarily used by this or that will. He must in all his actions, whether directed to himself or to other rational beings, always be regarded at the same time as an end. All the objects of inclinations have only a conditioned value; for if there were not these inclinations and the needs founded on them, then their object would be without value. But the inclinations themselves, being sources of needs, are so far from having an absolute value such as to render them desirable for their own sake that the universal wish of every rational being must be, rather, to be wholly free from them. Accordingly, the value of any object obtainable by our action is always conditioned. Beings whose existence depends not on our will but on nature have, nevertheless, if they are not rational beings, only a relative value as means and are therefore called things. On the other hand, rational beings are called persons inasmuch as their nature already marks them out as ends in themselves, i.e., as something which is not to be used merely as means and hence there is imposed thereby a limit on all arbitrary use of such beings, which are thus objects of respect. . . .

This principle of humanity and of every rational nature generally as an end in itself is the supreme limiting condition of every man's freedom of action. This principle is not borrowed from experience, first, because of its universality, inasmuch as it applies to all rational beings generally, and no experience is capable of determining anything about them; and, secondly, because in experience (subjectively) humanity is not thought of as the end of men, i.e., as an object that we of ourselves actually make our end which as a law ought to constitute the supreme limiting condition of all subjective ends (whatever they may be); and hence this principle must arise from pure reason [and not from experience]. That is to say that the ground of all practical legislation lies objectively in the rule and in the form of universality, which (according to the first principle) makes the rule capable of being a law (say, for example, a law of nature). Subjectively, however, the ground of all practical legislation lies in the end; but (according to the second principle) the subject of all ends is every rational being as an end in himself. From this there now follows the third practical principle of the will as the supreme condition of the will's conformity with universal practical reason, viz., the idea of the will of every rational being as a will that legislates universal law.

According to this principle all maxims are rejected which are not consistent with the will's own legislation of universal law. The will is thus not merely subject to the law but is subject to the law in such a way that it must be regarded also as legislating for itself and only on this account as being subject to the law (of which it can regard itself as the author).

CONFUCIANISM

HENRY ROSEMONT, JR.

Confucius and the *Analects*

Confucius (551–479 BCE) may well be the most influential thinker in human history, if influence is determined by the sheer number of people who have lived their lives, and died, in accordance with that thinker's vision of how people ought to live, and die.

Long recognized and described as China's "First (or Premier) Teacher," his ideas have been the fertile soil in which the Chinese cultural tradition has been cultivated, although at the same time a number of the views and practices he championed were already evidenced in China centuries before his birth. Like many other epochal figures of the ancient world— Buddha, Socrates, Jesus—Confucius does not seem to have written anything that is clearly attributable to him; all that we know of his vision directly must be pieced together from the several accounts of his teachings, and his activities, found in the little work known as the *Analects.*

Beginning shortly after he died, a few of the disciples of Confucius began setting down what they remember the Master saying to them (very probably the present books 4-8). Some disciples of the disciples continued this process for the next 75 years or so, and an additional dozen little "books" were composed by we-know-not-whom during the following century, and it was to be still another century before a number of these little "books" were gathered together to make up the *Analects* as we have it today.

Thus it is not at all surprising that the text does not seem to form a coherent whole. Worse, if we take the writings of, say, Aristotle, or Spinoza, or Kant, as exemplary of philosophical texts, then the *Analects* does not seem to be properly philosophical, for it contains precious little metaphysics, puts forth no first principles, is not systematic, and the "sayings" which comprise it are not set down in a hypothetico-deductive mode of discourse.

On the other hand, if the New Testament—or the Hebrew scriptures, or the *Quran*—are taken as religious texts *par excellance,* then it would appear that the *Analects* isn't a religious text either, for it speaks not of God, nor of creation, salvation, or a transcendental realm of being; and no prophecies will be found in its pages.

However, if we are willing to construe philosophy and religion more broadly— i.e., as those domains that address the question "What kind of life should I live?"— then the *Analects* is both philosophical and religious, for it does indeed address this question; it does proffer models of what is right and what is good, models that are perhaps no less important and relevant today in the post-modern, post-industrial West than they were in pre-modern, pre-industrial China over two millennia ago. This is not at all to suggest that Confucius and his disciples were "just like us;" manifestly they were not. Hence, before coming to appreciate what they nevertheless may have to say to us today, we must first focus on how different they really were.

Given that Confucianism is generally known in the West as an ethical system, reading the *Analects* for the first time can be disappointing, for it does not seem to put forward any general ethical principles whatsoever. We are told specifically how to behave toward our parents here, and our children there; toward our friends here, strangers there; toward rulers and others of high station yet here again, and toward "mean" or "petty" people yet there again; but no guidelines are given (with one exception) of a universal sort to help us ascertain how to behave toward other human beings simply as human beings. There is a simple reason for this fact: Confucius presupposes a different view of what it is to be a human being than the view that is common in the West today.

Underlying virtually all contemporary Western moral, social, and political philosophy is the presupposition that human beings are, or should be seen as, rational, free, autonomous individuals. There is of course widespread disagreement among philosophers about how freedom and autonomy should be exercised, what it is most rational to do, and how individuals should relate to the state, and society; but they concur that we are, or should be seen as, essentially autonomous individuals, free and rational.

Given that there are no equivalent ancient Chinese terms for "freedom," "rational," "autonomy," or "individual," it should not be surprising that this view of human beings will not be found in the *Analects*. Nor are these close semantic cognates for "liberty," "objective," "subjective," "public," "private," "true," "dilemma," "choice," or even "ought" to be found in the text (even though some translators use these terms, misleadingly if unintentionally so). As a consequence, the *Analects* should not be read seeking answers to moral (social, political, spiritual) questions which vex us, for such "answers" would appear either wrong or hopelessly naive at best, or as unintelligible at worst. Rather should the text be approached asking "To what extent is the *Analects* suggesting we should be asking different moral (social, political, spiritual) questions?"

And to begin doing this we must first appreciate that for Confucius, we are fundamentally relational, not individual selves. The life of a hermit could not be a human life for him:

I cannot flock with the birds and beasts.
If I am not to a person in the midst of others,
what am I to be? (18:6)

In other words, Confucian selves are first and foremost sons and daughters; then siblings, friends, neighbors, students, teachers, lovers, spouses, and perhaps much else; but not autonomous individuals. In the contemporary West, these relationships are described in terms of roles, which we first consciously (i.e., rationally) choose, and thereafter "play;" just as actors and actresses play different roles on the theater stage, so do autonomous individuals play roles on the stage of life. These roles may be important for our lives, but are not of our essence.

Confucian selves, on the other hand, are the sum of the roles they *live*, not play, and when all the specific roles one lives have been specified, then that person has been fully accounted for as a unique person, with no remainder with which to construct a free, autonomous, individual self. Consider how Confucius would respond to the "identity crisis" so many undergraduate students undergo at some point during their college career. When Mary Smith asks "Who am I?" the Master will first respond straightforwardly "You are obviously the daughter of Mr. & Mrs. Smith, and the sister of Tom Smith; you are the friend of x, y, and z, the roommate of w, the student of professors a, b, c, and d," and so forth. To which Mary will undoubtedly reply "I don't mean *that*. I'm searching for the *real* me." To which Confucius could only respond sadly, shaking his head: "No wonder you call it a 'crisis,' for you have taken away everything that could possibly count as answers to your question."

This view of a fully relational rather than autonomous self has a number of immediate implications for moral philosophy. In Western thought the basis for moral analysis and evaluation is the *agent* and the *action*. "What did *you* do?" and "why did you do it?" are the central questions. But whereas the first question remains the same in a Confucian framework, the second becomes "with whom did you do it?" followed by a third, "When?" Put another way, Confucius focuses on interactions, not actions, and on specific, not general, interactors. Individual selves are agents who perform actions. Relational selves are always dynamically interacting in highly specific ways.

The roles we live are reciprocal (see *Analects* 4:15 and 15:2) and at the abstract level can be seen to hold between benefactors and beneficiaries. Thus we are, when young, beneficiaries of our parents, and when they age, become their benefactors; the converse holds with respect to our children. We are beneficiaries of our teachers, benefactors of our students, and are, at different times, benefactors and beneficiaries of and to our friends, spouses, neighbors, colleagues, lovers, and so on.

It is for these reasons that there can be no *general* answer to the question "What should I do?" except "Do what is *appropriate* (not "right") under the specific circumstances." Fairly careful readers of the *Analects* will note that Confucius sometimes gives a different answer to the same question asked by one of his disciples. But *very* careful readers of the text will also note that it is *different* disciples who ask the question, and the Master gives an answer appropriate for each questioner (see 11:21). To do this is neither dissembling, nor wrong. For example, your roommate asks you to read and comment on a paper she has just written for a course. You are not impressed with it. What do you say? Well, if your roommate is fairly intelligent, but having troubles at home right now, is experiencing her identity crisis, and is thinking of quitting school, your answer might run something like "There are problems with this paper, but you have a really good potential thesis here, and argument there, which you can develop along thus-and-such lines. And when you've done so, I'll be happy to read it again." But now suppose that your roommate is different. He has just received a few *A*s on exams he didn't really study for, and while he is basically a good person, is showing signs of arrogance and pomposity; in which case you might well be inclined to say "This paper is junk from start to finish. Why did you have me waste my time reading it?"

For a Confucian, these differing responses are not at all either inconsistent or hypocritical, but are both altogether appropriate responses with respect to the second Confucian moral question: "With whom did you do it?" The third question, "When?" is equally significant, because the benefactor–beneficiary relationships are not static. Having just failed an examination yourself, you schedule an appointment with your instructor to go over it, your basic question being "How can I improve next time?" But upon arriving at the appointed time, you find that your instructor—who does not drive—has just learned that his wife has had a heart attack, and been taken to the emergency room at the hospital. Not at all surprisingly, you do not ask your original question, but instead say "Please let me drive you to the hospital."

All of these little examples appear simple, everyday, common-sensical at best, perhaps even trivial when compared to these moral issues focused on in the West: abortion, euthanasia, draft resistance, suicide, and so forth. But as reading the *Analects* shows clearly, they are the basic "stuff" of our human interactions, and Confucius seems to be telling us that if we learn to get the little things right on a day-in and day-out basis, the "big" things will take care of themselves.

And we start out on the path of getting the little things right by focusing on our first, most important, and lifelong role: that of son or daughter. *Analects* 2:7 and 2:8 are key passages for understanding the vision of Confucius, for they deal with filial piety, one of the highest Confucian excellences, or virtues; unless we are first filial children, we cannot become good, for as the Master says "Proper behavior toward parents is the root of authoritative conduct" (1:2).

These passages are equally significant for appreciating Confucian morality more abstractly, because the Master clearly is telling us that we have obligations we have not freely chosen. We did not ask to come into this world, we did not choose to be offspring, but we nevertheless have manifold responsibilities toward our parents; we are responsible for their well-being even though we have not freely chosen to assume those responsibilities.

Another striking feature of these passages is that Confucius insists that we cannot merely rest content with seeing to the material needs of our parents: filial piety is "something much more than that" (2:8). We must not only meet our familial obligations, we must have the proper attitude toward them, we must *want* to meet our responsibilities; we must have feelings appropriate to the situation. This is why Confucius "could not bear to see the rituals of mourning conducted purely formally, without genuine grief" (3:26). This point is brought home forcefully when it is seen that our obligations to our parents do not cease when they die; we must continue to show respect for them, and honor their memory (1:11, 4:20). Only then will we know and show the extent of our true filiality (19:17).

By cultivating filial piety in our relational roles to our parents—as both beneficiaries and benefactors—we are on the way (better: the Confucian Way) to achieving *ren*, which is the highest excellence, or virtue, for Confucius. The term occurs over 100 times in the *Analects*, and is made up of two elemental graphs, which signify "person," and the numeral 2. Usually translated as "goodness," or "benevolence," it is perhaps best captured in English by "authoritativeness," which signifies both having to do with authoring, and authority. On the one hand, *ren* is easy (7:29), because we are human. On the other hand, it can be difficult to achieve in practice owing to our more basic—i.e., biological—desires (4:6). But once we set out on the path of *ren*, it is with us forever; as the Master informs us:

> Admirable people will not seek to live at the expense of their
> authoritativeness. They will even sacrifice their lives to preserve
> it. (15:8)

In order to achieve ren one must submit to li. This term has been variously translated as "rituals," "rites," "etiquette," "ceremony," "mores," "customs," "propriety," and "worship." When reading the Analects it is best to keep all of these meanings in mind whenever the term occurs. "Rituals" and "rites" are the two most common translations, and are acceptable so long as it is appreciated that the *li* are not only to be thought of in terms of a solemn high mass, wedding, bar mitzvah, or funeral; the *li* pertain equally to our manner of greeting, leave-taking, sharing food, and most other everyday interpersonal activities as well.

It is through rituals, custom, and tradition that one's roles are properly effected. There are customary rituals, large and small, by means of which we interact with our parents, grandparents, relatives, young children, neighbors, officials, friends. These rituals are different for the different people with whom we are relating, and they may differ across time as well (we wouldn't hug friends we saw every day, but probably would if we hadn't seen them for some time). It is through the rituals that we express our filial piety toward our parents, respect for elders, care and affection for the young, and love and friendship for lovers and friends. We cannot simply "go through the motions" of performing the rituals, for this would show both a lack of concern for the other(s), and a lack of sincerity as well. It is through rituals, properly performed, that our true attitudes and feelings shine forth, and we more nearly approach *ren.*

Consider meeting someone for the first time. Your right hand automatically is raised, as is theirs; then you clasp it. Your clasp can be such that your hand feels like a dead fish, or you can show off your strength by attempting to crack the other's knuckles, and in either case you can utter a flat "How do you do?" Or you can present a warm hand, squeezing only an appropriate amount; perhaps you will put your left hand over the handshake, after which you say "I'm very pleased to meet you," looking at the other directly. In short, it is not the case that when we've seen one introduction we've seen them all.

Rituals, and the proper performance thereof, have been largely neglected in developing theories of the right and the good in the Western philosophical tradition. Worse, the contemporary West is virtually anti-ritualistic. Rituals are seen as purely formal, empty, dead weights of the past, and detrimental to the full expression of individuality.

They are, however, absolutely central in Confucianism, and without an understanding of their potential for enriching human life, the *Analects* cannot come alive for the modern reader. We can only become fully human, for Confucius, by learning to restrain our impulses to accord with the prescriptions of rituals (6:25). Rituals are the templates within which we interact with our fellows: there are proper (customary) ways of being a father, a sister, a neighbor, a student, a teacher. These ways are constrained by rituals, but once mastered, are liberating, are the vehicle by means of which we express our uniqueness.

But unless we have guidelines (the rituals) our behaviors can only be random. (Listen to Beethoven's Fifth Symphony, first as conducted by Toscanini, then by Bernstein, then by Rostropovich; is it not easy to distinguish them despite the severe constraints imposed on them all by the score?) There are many ways to be a good parent, teacher, friend, etc.; if Confucian selves aren't autonomous, they are certainly not automatons either.

So, then, it is through ritual that we cultivate and enhance our authoritativeness, but this can only be done as we become full participants in the rituals, expressing our feelings thereby, and thereby in turn investing them—and consequently ourselves—with significance. If someone you know is getting married, the ritual tradition dictates the giving of a gift. But if you merely purchase the first thing you see—or worse, have someone else buy it for you—you may be "going through the ritual," but are not participating in it, and it will thus be largely devoid of meaning. You must, first, *want* to buy the betrothed a gift (evidenced even in the modern Western expression "It's the thought that counts"), but in order to be a full participant in the ritual, and express yourself relationally, you must devote the time and effort to secure a gift that is appropriate for that person. This is what Confucius is telling us when he says "Ritual, ritual! Is it no more than giving gifts of jade and silk?" (17:11)

It must also be noted that for Confucius, the significance of rituals is not confined to our interpersonal relations, rituals can also serve as the glue of a society. A people who accept and follow ritual prescriptions will not need much in the way of laws or punishments to achieve harmony (2:3), and no government that fails to submit to rituals will long endure (11:25); indeed, he even suggests that rituals can be sufficient for regulating a society (4:13). And true rulers, having a full measure of authoritativeness and submitting to ritual, will rule by personal example, not coercion; their formal duties are minimal (e.g., 2:1, 8:18, 15:4).

Excepting the sages and sage kings, Confucius gives his highest praise to the *jun zi,* usually rendered as "Gentleman," which can be highly misleading. The *jun zi* have traveled a goodly distance along the Confucian way, and live a goodly number of roles. Benefactors to many, they are still beneficiaries of others like themselves. While still capable of anger in the presence of wrongdoing, they are in their persons tranquil. They know many rituals (and much music) and perform all of their roles not only with skill, but with grace, dignity, and beauty, and they take delight in the performances. Still filial toward parents and elders, they now endeavor to take "All under heaven"—i.e., the world—as their province. Always proper in the conduct of their roles, that conduct is not forced, but rather effortless, spontaneous, creative.

Thus the best way to understand Confucius' concept of the *jun zi* is to render the term as "exemplary person." Having learned, submitted to, and mastered the rituals of the past, the *jun zi* re-authorizes them by making them his or her own, thus becoming their author, who can speak with authority in the present. The *jun zi* fully exemplify authoritativeness, and are content with it, no longer worrying about wealth, fame, or glory (4:5).

Against the background of the authoritative person as an ideal, we can appreciate that even though Confucianism is highly particularistic in defining our conduct in specific relational roles, it nevertheless bespeaks a universalistic vision. The one exception to the lack of general principles put forward in the *Analects* is the negative formulation of the Golden Rule: "Do not do unto others as you would not have them do unto you" (12:2 and 15:24). If our Golden Rule is universalistic, so is the Master's.

But more than that, it should be clear that Confucius had a strong sense of, empathy with, and concept of humanity writ large. All of the specific human relations of which we are a part, interacting with the dead as well as the living, will be mediated by the *li,* i.e., the rituals, customs, and traditions we come to share as our inextricably linked histories unfold, and by fulfilling the obligations defined by these relationships, we are, for Confucius, following the human way *(dao).*

It is a comprehensive way. By the manner in which we interact with others our lives will clearly have a moral dimension infusing *all,* not just some, of our conduct. By the ways in which this ethical interpersonal conduct is effected, with reciprocity, and governed by courtesy, respect, affection, custom, ritual, and tradition, our lives will also have an aesthetic dimension for ourselves and others. And by specifically meeting our defining traditional obligations to our parents, elders, and ancestors on the one hand, and to our contemporaries and descendants on the other, Confucius proffers an uncommon, but nevertheless spiritually authentic form of transcendence, a human capacity to go beyond the specific spatiotemporal circumstances in which we live, giving our personhood the sense of humanity shared in common and thereby a strong sense of continuity with what has gone before and what will come later. In the cosmic sense, Confucius never addresses the question of the meaning of life; he probably wouldn't even have understood it. But his vision of what it is to be a human being provided for everyone to find meaning *in* life, a not inconsiderable accomplishment. If we are social beings, and if this is the only life we have to live, then perhaps the *Analects* can have much to say today as we continue the philosophical and religious search for how we should live our lives.

A final note. For most of the past two millenia Chinese society has been seen largely as a Confucian society, and it was hierarchical, sexist, and homophobic. Further, Chinese history certainly had its share of authoritarian rulers, self-serving officials, exploitative parents, unfilial children, dull pedants, and more. But sympathizing with the Confucian vision no more requires justifying or apologizing for the sorrier dimensions of Chinese history than an appreciation of the moral and spiritual vision of Christianity requires justifying or apologizing for the Crusades, Inquisition, Thirty Years' War, and other sorry dimensions of Western history. The Confucian concepts of the right and the good were not realized in imperial China any more than Christian ideals have been realized in the imperial West.

Moreover, what are foundational for Confucianism are the concepts of family, and intergenerational relations. And of course the concept of the family can be kept without assigning women inferior status, and equally kept—along with intergenerational relations—by allowing for two or more adults of the same sex to nurture the young. Again, the family and intergenerationality are basic; the genders and sexual preferences of the relational selves are much less so. By thus modifying the traditions and accompanying rituals, we can re-authorize them for the present; the *jun zi* ideal need not be confined to the past. But the past must be brought to life for us before we can understand the present, and for this we need good teachers (2:11).

Confucius is such a teacher.

Further Reading

Translations

Ames, Roger T., & Henry Rosemont, Jr. *The Confucian Analects: A Philosophical Translation.* Ballantine Books, 1998.

Brooks, E. Bruce, & Taeko. *The Original Analects.* Columbia University Press, 1998.

Lau, D. C. *Confucius: The Analects.* Penguin, 1979.

Legge, James. *The Confucian Analects.* Various editions, 1893–1989.

Waley, Arthur. *The Analects of Confucius.* Modern Library, n.d.

Commentaries

Creel, H. G. *Confucius & the Chinese Way.* Harper & Bros., 1962.

Fingarette, Herbert. *Confucius—The Secular as Sacred.* Harper & Row, 1970.

Graham, Angus. *Disputers of the Tao.* Open Court, 1989.

Hall, David L., & Roger T. Ames. *Thinking through Confucius.* SUNY Press, 1987.

Hansen, Chad. *A Daoist Theory of Chinese Thought.* Oxford University Press, 1992.

Rosemont, Jr., Henry, *A Confucian Alternative.* University of Hawaii Press, 1999.

CONFUCIUS

translated by Roger T. Ames and Henry Rosemont, Jr.

Analects

1.2 Master You said: "It is a rare thing for someone who has a sense of filial and fraternal responsibility (*xiaod i*) to have a taste for defying authority. And it is unheard of for those who have no taste for defying authority to be keen on initiating rebellion. Exemplary persons (*junzi*) concentrate their efforts on the root, for the root having taken hold, the way (*dao*) will grow therefrom. As for filial and fraternal responsibility, it is, I suspect, the root of authoritative conduct (*ren*)."

1.12 Master You said: "Achieving harmony (*he*) is the most valuable function of observing ritual propriety (*li*). In the ways of the Former Kings, this achievement of harmony made them elegant, and was a guiding standard in all things large and small. But when things are not going well, to realize harmony just for its own sake without regulating the situation through observing ritual propriety will not work."

2.3 The Master said: "Lead the people with administrative injunctions (*zheng*) and keep them orderly with penal law (*xing*), and they will avoid punishments but will be without a sense of shame. Lead them with excellence (*de*) and keep them orderly through observing ritual propriety (*li*) and they will develop a sense of shame, and moreover, will order themselves."

2.5 Meng Yizi asked about filial conduct (*xiao*). The Master replied: "Do not act contrary." Fan Chi was driving the Master's chariot, and the Master informed him further: "Meng Yizi asked me about filial conduct, and I replied: 'Do not act contrary.'" Fan Chi asked, "What did you mean by that?" The Master replied: "While they are living, serve them according to the observances of ritual propriety (*li*); when they are dead, bury them and sacrifice to them according to the observances of ritual propriety."

2.6 Meng Wubo asked about filial conduct (*xiao*). The Master replied: "Give your mother and father nothing to worry about beyond your physical well-being."

2.7 Ziyou asked about filial conduct (*xiao*). The Master replied: "Those today who are filial are considered so because they are able to provide for their parents. But even dogs and horses are given that much care. If you do not respect your parents, what is the difference?"

4.18 The Master said, "In serving your father and mother, remonstrate with them gently. On seeing that they do not heed your suggestions, remain respectful and do not act contrary. Although concerned, voice no resentment."

4.20 The Master said, "A person who for three years refrains from reforming the ways (*dao*) of his late father can be called a filial son (*xiao*)."

6.30 Zigong said, "What about the person who is broadly generous with the people and is able to help the multitude—is this what we could call authoritative conduct (*ren*)?"

The Master replied, "Why stop at authoritative conduct? This is certainly a sage (*sheng*). Even a Yao or a Shun would find such a task daunting. Authoritative persons establish others in seeking to establish themselves and promote others in seeking to get there themselves. Correlating one's conduct with those near at hand can be said to be the method of becoming an authoritative person."

11.10 When Yan Hui died, the Master grieved for him with sheer abandon. His followers cautioned, "Sir, you grieve with such abandon." The Master replied, "I grieve with abandon? If I don't grieve with abandon for him, then for whom?"

11.12 Zilu asked how to serve the spirits and the gods. The Master replied, "Not yet being able to serve other people, how would you be able to serve the spirits?" Zilu said, "May I ask about death?" The Master replied, "Not yet understanding life, how could you understand death?"

12.1 Yan Hui inquired about authoritative conduct (*ren*). The Master replied, "Through self-discipline and observing ritual propriety (*li*) one becomes authoritative in one's conduct. If for the space of a day one were able to accomplish this, the whole empire would defer to this authoritative model. Becoming authoritative in one's conduct is self-originating—how could it originate with others?"

Yan Hui said, "Could I ask what becoming authoritative entails?" The Master replied, "Do not look at anything that violates the observance of ritual propriety; do not listen to anything that violates the observance of ritual propriety; do not speak about anything that violates the observance of ritual propriety; do not do anything that violates the observance of ritual propriety."

"Though I am not clever," said Yan Hui, "allow me to act on what you have said."

12.2 Zhonggong inquired about authoritative conduct (*ren*). The Master replied, "In your public life, behave as though you are receiving important visitors; employ the common people as though you are overseeing a great sacrifice. Do not impose upon others what you yourself do not want, and you will not incur personal or political ill will."

"Though I am not clever," said Zhonggong, "allow me to act on what you have said."

12.19 Ji Kangzi asked Confucius about governing effectively (*zhe*), saying, "What if I kill those who have abandoned the way (*dao*) to attract those who are on it?"

"If you govern effectively," Confucius replied, "what need is there for killing? If you want to be truly adept (*shar*), the people will also be adept. The excellence (*de*) of the exemplary person (*junzi*) is the wind, while that of the petty person is the grass. As the wind blows, the grass is sure to bend."

14.34 Someone asked, "What do you think about the saying: 'Repay ill will with beneficence (*de*)'?"

The Master replied, "Then how would one repay beneficence? Repay ill will by remaining true. Repay beneficence with gratitude (*de*)."

15.9 The Master said, "For the resolute scholar-apprentice (*shi*) and the authoritative person (*renren*), while they would not compromise their authoritative conduct to save their lives, they might well give up their lives in order to achieve it."

15.24 Zigong asked, "Is there one expression that can be acted upon until the end of one's days?"

The Master replied, "There is *shu*: do not impose on others what you yourself do not want."

17.21 Zaiwo inquired, "The three-year mourning period on the death of one's parents is already too long. If for three years exemplary persons (*junzi*) were to give up observing ritual propriety (*li*), the rites would certainly go to ruin. And if for three years they were to give up the performance of music (*yue*), music would certainly collapse. The old grain has been used up, the new crop is ready for harvest, and the different woods used ceremonially as drills for making fire have gone through their full cycle—surely a year is good enough."

The Master replied, "Would you then be comfortable eating fine rice and wearing colorful brocade?"

"I would indeed," responded Zaiwo.

"If you are comfortable, then do it," said the Master. "When exemplary persons (*junzi*) are in the mourning shed, it is because they can find no relish in fine-tasting food, no pleasure in the sound of music, and no comfort in their usual lodgings, that they do not abbreviate the mourning period to one year. Now if you are comfortable with these things, then by all means, enjoy them."

When Zaiwo had left, the Master remarked, "Zaiwo is really perverse (*bu ren*)! It is only after being tended by his parents for three years that an infant can finally leave their bosom. The ritual of a three-year mourning period for one's parents is practiced throughout the empire. Certainly Zaiwo received this three years of loving care from his parents!"

DAOISM

P. J. IVANHOE

Daoism

In this essay, "Daoism" is used to refer to the group of early Chinese thinkers who were among the first to use the term *dao* ("Way") in the grand sense of the underlying structure or pattern of the world. We will introduce some central aspects of Daoist philosophy by describing the basic ethical views found in the *Daodejing,* one of the earliest

Daoist classics. All references are to the chapter divisions in the standard version of the text.

Traditionally ascribed to the mythical *Laozi,* an older contemporary of Confucius, the *Daodejing* is a composite work consisting of short passages, from a variety of sources, over half of which are rhymed. These were collected together into a single volume of eighty-one chapters that were then divided into two books. Book I consists of chapters one through thirty-seven, the *dao* ("Way") half of the text; Book II consists of chapters thirty-eight through eighty-one, the *de* ("virtue") half. This division in no way reflects the contents of the chapters themselves, except that the first chapter begins with the word *dao* and the thirty-eighth chapter begins by describing the highest *de.* The text appears to have reached its present form sometime during the third century BC. Other versions of the text, similar in content and firmly dated to the middle of the second century BC, have been found in which the order of the books is reversed, giving us the *Dedaojing.*

Though is was probably cobbled together from different sources, the *Daodejing* may well have been assembled during a relatively short period of time and perhaps by a single editor. When it was put together, China was near the end of a prolonged era of fierce interstate rivalry known as the *Warring States* (403–221 BC). This period saw the first use of large armies of conscripted foot soldiers. Fortified cities along with their civilian populations and food supplies all became military targets. Whole cities were sometimes put to the sword even after having surrendered. The *Daodejing* can be understood at least in part as a reaction to this troubled age. In it we hear the lament of a time tired of war and chaos, one yearning for a bygone age of innocence, security, and peace.

Wars of expansion are fiercely denounced in the text. War is represented as an evil force, a spiritual miasma born of a ruler's insatiable desires for wealth and power (30, 31, 46). Government corruption is also condemned (53, 75). Both of these complaints rest on a common, deeper criticism of the unbounded greed and ambition of those in power. These ideas may well have motivated the view that excessive desire *per se* is bad and the related belief that our "real" or "natural" desires are actually quite modest and limited. These are some of the more important themes in the *Daodejing.* The idea that excess in any form is bad is poignantly captured in the image of the "tilting vessel" of Chapter 9. The text claims that it is unnatural to have excessive desires and having them will not only not lead to a satisfying life but paradoxically to destitution, want, alienation, and self-destruction. Therefore, the *Daodejing* counsels everyone, but especially those in power, to be frugal and modest (9, 46).

While excessive desires lead to profound misfortune, such calamity is not regarded as an inevitable feature of the human condition. People can pursue certain modest levels of satisfaction without incurring any bad consequences. But most are enticed to upset the natural balance, by pursuing excessive wealth, beauty, or power, values foisted upon them by social conditioning. These values blind us to our true and natural desires and lead to both physical and psychological distress (3, 12).

Pursuing what society recommends leads one to depart from one's authentic nature, to neglect one's "belly" in order to please one's "eyes." Socially sanctioned notions of beauty, music, good taste, and other sources of "satisfaction" are portrayed as corruptions of natural preferences. Society isolates and exaggerates certain goods and elevates these to preeminent positions of prestige. This disrupts the natural harmony and leads people to clash and contend with one another in a mad dash to secure these goods. The great *dao* of the Daoists eliminates the source of all such conflicts by embracing all things: the ugly as well as the beautiful, the high as well as the low, the humble as well as the eminent. This does not mean that for a given creature there are not better and worse ways of being or states of affairs. But the *Daodejing* insists that no creature can forsake its proper place and transgress its natural limits without upsetting the delicate balance of the Way. In the end, all such attempts prove self-defeating.

Daoists appeal to an earlier golden age in human history, before people made sharp distinctions among things. This was a time when values and qualities were not clearly distinguished, when things simply were as they were spontaneously. The next best state is when distinctions among things are made but neither side of the dichotomies that arise from such distinctions are held up as absolutely superior. The text makes a great deal of the notion that whenever one recognizes a given value or quality one brings into being the idea of that quality or value's opposite as well, e.g., a concept of beauty gives rise to a corresponding concept of ugliness, a notion of high brings with it a notion of low. The further claim is then made that whenever such paired concepts are sharply distinguished, there is a tendency to elevate and pursue one side while suppressing and rejecting the other. This in turn leads to an obsessive desire to possess what is favored and eliminate what is disliked. But because of the mutual dependence of such conceptual dichotomies, this is thought to be an impossible goal and such effort purportedly generates a contrary effect. We can imagine an example where the pursuit of some conception of the beautiful leads one to try to eradicate all that falls short of this ideal. In such a case, beauty itself not only gives rise to but in some sense becomes something ugly. This is why the state before such distinctions comes into being serves as the Daoist ideal. At the next stage, the best one can do is to recognize both poles of such pairs and seek a state of harmony and balance.

Many of Laozi's harshest criticisms are reserved for society's ethical values. These not only are regarded as deeply hypocritical but are blamed for supporting and lending credence to the entire misguided affair of contemporary society. All such "knowledge," so cherished by society, is actually a horrible and corrupting influence. The rituals of the Confucians, along with their notions of benevolence, rightness, and filial piety are all debased mutations of the Natural—gaudy substitutes for the real things.

Like almost all traditional Chinese thinkers, Daoists are ethical realists, though of an unusual sort. They believe that true and correct value judgments reflect objective features about the world. Though they insist that spoken *daos*—i.e., ways of life that can be described and codified—are incomplete and flawed, this does not entail the belief that there is no norm-providing *dao*. The text goes to considerable lengths describing how elusive and indistinct the true *dao* is. Among other things, it is ineffable, but again this does not mean either that it does not exist or that we cannot understand it.

The *Daodejing* can be read as describing a mystical ideal in the sense that those who realize the Way lose a strong sense of themselves and seem to some extent to merge in the *dao*'s underlying patterns and processes. In such a state, one does not conceive of oneself as apart from and independent of the rest of the world. While aware of herself and the things around her, such a person does not stand back to view and analyze the *dao* and does not act on pre-established or self-conscious policies or principles. Rather she is guided by pre-reflective intuitions and tendencies.

Chapter 38 describes the history of the decline of the Way from an earlier golden age to its present debased state. This decline is characterized by an increasingly rational picture of the world. I mean by rational, an explicit and consistent account of the world, the antithesis of the ideal described above. The *dao* declined as civilization arose. On the level of individuals, this means that as one becomes more self-conscious of one's actions, as one reflects upon the things one does and seeks to understand why one does them, one becomes increasingly alienated from one's own true nature and the world. More and more, one comes to see oneself as cut off from and independent of the greater patterns and processes of the *dao*. And through a course of increasingly complex and abstract intellectualization, one loses touch with one's most basic sensibilities and deepest promptings. Society represents this same phenomenon writ large.

Exactly why or how this process of alienation occurs in the first place is something the Daoists never adequately explain (and given their views perhaps they cannot). But the text insists on returning to an earlier natural state when the Way was fully realized in the world. There are repeated references to "untangling," "blunting," and "rounding off" the corners of our present life. We are to let our "wheels move one along old ruts." All of these references are recommending a way of life that purportedly once was and that can be again (4, 40, 52, 56).

Again like most classical East Asian thinkers, Daoists saw no essential conflict between an ethical "ought"—what is proper or fitting—and a certain sense of what naturally "is" the case. What "is"—what is considered as naturally so—provides the normative standard. But the natural state to which Daoists appeal is not the status quo but the *dao* which lies beneath successive layers of socialization. For those in the fallen state of society, the *dao* is not easy to discern or to follow. The challenge is to become aware of what we—in some deep sense—are and then work to live in light of this awareness.

The *dao* is the source, sustenance, and ideal state of all things in the world. It is "hidden" but not metaphysically transcendent. In the apt metaphor of the text, it is the "root" of all things. The *dao* is *ziran* ("so of itself," "spontaneous") and its unencumbered activity brings about various natural states of affairs through *wuwei* ("nonaction"). From the Daoist perspective, *ziran* is normative for states of affairs (i.e., *what* is appropriate); *wuwei* is normative for actions (i.e., *how* to act).

Human beings have a place in the *dao* but are not particularly exalted. They are simply things among things (a view well-represented by the marvelous landscape paintings inspired by Daoism). Because of their unbridled desires and their unique capacity to think, act intentionally, and alter their nature—thus acting contrary to *wuwei* and bringing about states that are not *ziran*—humans tend to forsake their proper place. They attempt to set themselves up over and in opposition to the natural state of affairs, i.e., the *dao*. Having abandoned the natural security and contentment of the *dao,* most are led to embark upon an ever-spiraling effort to find satisfaction in increasingly unnatural and perilous pursuits, e.g., prestige, wealth, power, and excessive sensual stimulation. This quest proves not only futile but harmful to those driven to pursue it. And because such activity disrupts the natural harmony of the *dao,* its injurious effects spill over to harm others as well. This has been the state of things ever since human beings first fell out of the agrarian utopia of the golden age. The purpose of, or perhaps the hoped-for natural effect of reading the *Daodejing* is to undo the consequences of such misguided human views and practices and "return" to the earlier ideal. The text is more a form of philosophical therapy than the presentation of a theory. We are to be challenged by its paradoxes and moved by its images and poetic cadence more than by any arguments it presents.

An appreciation of the historical context of the *Daodejing* can help us to understand its radical rejection of society and its call for a return to an earlier age of innocence, integrity, and peace. It is likely that the apparent profound disutility of innovation and achievement—culminating in massacre, famine, hypocrisy, cruelty, and terror—moved the author of the *Daodejing* to embrace the idea that the elimination of human "cleverness" and "scheming" would itself represent an improvement. Life in the much simpler, ideal Daoist world would not be perfect, human beings would still face hardships, and like the *dao* itself they must embrace the bad as well as the good. But one could believe that the natural difficulties and even the natural disasters they would have to face would be less severe and debilitating that the man-made catastrophes that were widespread at the time. One can imagine a similar frame of mind arising again in the aftermath of some future nuclear or biological holocaust or massive ecological disaster and one can see a similar widespread rejection of high culture, technology, and the intellect and a yearning for a more innocent and gentle time among North American youth in the 1960s.

In order to realize the kind of life the Daoist recommends, we must pare away our inherited notions of right and wrong and return to the pre-reflective simplicity of Nature (48). If people do this, society too will "return" to the earlier golden age of the *dao.* This ideal age is a primitive agrarian utopia, a low-tech, highly dispersed society of independent village communities in which people find and are satisfied with simple pleasures. A ruler who wishes to bring about this happy state of affairs must dedicate himself to *undoing* the things others have worked so hard to bring about and then insure that such pernicious ideas and practices never arise again. He must reduce the size and population of the state (80), work to empty the people's minds and fill their bellies, weaken their wills and strengthen their bones, and then keep them innocent from knowledge and free from desire (3). Here we see the implementation in state policy of the beliefs discussed earlier regarding what are the real or natural desires of human beings and what they need to live a contented life. The *Daodejing* assumes that what brings people the greatest overall satisfaction, what is in their true best interest, is to live an innocent agrarian life in which they are provided with basic necessities, kept ignorant of high culture and free from the physical and psychological suffering that is thought to follow inevitably when "desire raises its head."

Some Chinese commentators and modern interpreters have read the *Daodejing* in a more purposive or instrumental way, i.e., as a manual of various techniques that enable one to gain certain non-moral goods like long life, health, power, or control over others. These techniques are often thought to rely on indirection or the ability to turn an opponent's energy back upon him by employing the dynamic of "excess leading to its opposite" described above. For example, we are told that in order to weaken something, one must first strengthen it and that what is most submissive and weak can dominate the most forceful and strong (36, 43, 61). The text also argues that the most vulnerable creatures when properly understood are potentially the most vital, powerful, and secure (76).

Techniques for gaining certain non-moral advantages can be extracted from the *Daodejing* but when read in the context of the entire text, such purely instrumental readings appear less tenable. The *Daodejing* does claim that those who truly accord with the *dao* are protected from many common dangers and enjoy a range of enhanced abilities, benefits and advantages. But anyone who purposely attempts to "use" the dynamic of the *dao* to gain these or other limited, selfish goods—be they material or psychological—cannot possibly tap into its remarkable and mysterious power. Anyone who tries to pursue such aims would neither accord with the *dao* nor act with *de* "virtue." Hence they would utterly and completely fail to fulfull the message of the *dao* "Way" and *de* "virtue" *jing* "classic."

Those who attempt to make use of the *dao* cannot accord with it—and hence will be undone—because they operate on consciously held and pre-established policies or principles. They have to stand back from the great *dao* and regard other people and things as fundamentally unconnected with themselves, objects to be manipulated in their schemes. This violates the more mystical aspects of the text, discussed above, that describe the ideal of abandoning oneself to the pre-reflective promptings of the *dao,* a benign and bountiful power. The great *dao* produces things without seeking to possess them and accomplishes its task without claiming credit (2, 10, 34, 51). By following the *dao,* every thing will return to its root and proper destiny (16). Heaven will become clear, the earth tranquil, spiritual beings divine, the valley full, and all things will flourish and grow (32, 39).

Those who seek to manipulate the *dao* for their private advantage would also fail to generate and possess *de* "virtue" or "power," the personal charisma thought essential to the functioning of the entire Daoist project. The Daoist sage is submissive and yielding in the sense of being open, welcoming, and nurturing. Such excellences are often described in the text as distinctively female characteristics (10, 28). The sage is like a loving mother, who has unqualified and overflowing concern for all. Daoists believe that the cultivation of such dispositions not only enables one to discern and harmonize with the patterns and processes of the *dao,* it also—though unintentionally—generates *de. De* accrues to an individual who possesses natural calm, compassion, and confidence. It is a power thought capable of attracting, disarming, reassuring, and pacifying other people. *De* enables the sage to move others to abandon the insanity of normal society and return without coercion to the peace, contentment, and prosperity of the *dao. De* is even described as able to affect other creatures and inanimate objects in ways that facilitate the realization of the *dao.* Anyone who tried to remove the attributes or methods of a sage from this, their full context, and employ them to achieve more limited ends or personal gain would undermine the efficacy and *de* "power" of these teachings.

For those of us still stuck in the spiritually backward perspective of trying to "make sense" of the text, the *Daodejing* presents numerous paradoxes. One of its most pronounced and influential conundrums concerns its recommendation that we be "without desires." For those who still "have desires"—understood as meaning something like *excessive* desires—this teaching seems only to multiply their difficulties. For if they follow this advice, they then are *desiring* not to desire, simply adding fuel to their fire. There is an apparent paradox to advice that counsels us to *work* at being relaxed or try not to try. And those who are "without desires" are not much better off. For this teaching might well lead them to develop the prideful self-consciousness of their own goodness that elsewhere the text warns against.

However, if we understand this teaching in the greater context of the *Daodejing* the paradox dissolves. Instead of interpreting it as an imperative to act—which leads to the difficulties described above—we should understand this teaching in more psychological terms, as indicating where we should focus our attention. For if, as the text insists, we always have within us pre-reflective intuitions and tendencies that lead us to spontaneously grasp and accord with *dao,* then by becoming aware of these and by focusing on and following them, we will be led to lose interest in and abandon our excessive desires. And we will do so without developing the debilitating delusion that *we* are the source of these insights. We "do nothing yet nothing remains undone."

The paradoxical nature of the *Daodejing,* along with its poetic form, are themselves important parts of its message. The motivation for these stylistic attributes of the text is the belief that if we cannot reason our way out of certain problems we can at least hope that wrestling with such paradoxes will exhaust our rational nature and loosen its grip on us. In such moments, alternative sources of insight, the underlying rhythms of the *dao* within us, can slip free and yield understanding. But the *Daodejing* itself tends to resist any neat attempt at analyzing its message. It refuses to fall before human "cleverness" and is careful to deny even its own authority, insisting that, "One who speaks does not know; one who knows does not speak" (56).

In arguing that human beings by nature have few basic needs and a minimum set of desires, the *Daodejing* dramatically rejects what many have taken to be our most distinctive characteristics: our intellectual abilities, our creative capacities, and our strong sense of autonomy. It tells us that these in fact are the source of some of our worst troubles. It turns out that most of life's greatest difficulties are caused by our own propensity to make our lives more complicated than they need to be. Most of the wounds we suffer are self-inflicted and only by unlearning what we know and hold most dear can we heal ourselves. These are among the text's most dramatic claims. But the *Daodejing* also offers more modest and equally fascinating ideas concerning moral psychology and ethical justification. In regard to the former are its insights regarding how a strong sense of the moral worth of one's actions not only seems to diminish their value but may in fact have a corrosive effect on one's character. It seems a bit paradoxical, but many people believe that a morally excellent person cannot go around announcing just how good he is, and that if he entertains too strong a sense of his own moral superiority this will lower our opinion of him. One need not embrace the entire metaphysical picture or background beliefs of the *Daodejing* in order to understand and appreciate such ideas. They are perfectly comprehensive in terms of where the focus of one's motivation and attention lies. Another fascinating idea is the *Daodejing*'s distinctive conception of the cultivated person's *de* "virtue." The ability that certain ethically remarkable people have to attract others to them, to put them at ease and perhaps increase their level of self-awareness and sensitivity is again a phenomenon attested in our own age as well as in the ancient classic. And finally, in regard to ethical justification, a sense of having a place in the greater scheme of things, of finding a harmonious relationship not only between oneself and other human beings but with other creatures and things as well, might indeed be part of what defines a good life for creatures like us. If something like this view is not the case, then apart from appealing to problematic notions like the rights of other animals, plants and inanimate objects or the existence of non-natural or otherwise odd moral qualities, it is hard to find any plausible justification for environmental concern, above simple prudence. We may not be able to embrace a belief in the value of a harmonious relationship with Nature in the precise sense or with the apparent certainty of early Daoists but we might still confidently and with good reason cherish it as an important part of living well.

Further Reading

Translations and Studies of the *Daodejing*
Chan, Wing-tsit. *The Way of Lao Tzu (Tao te ching)*. Chicago: University of Chicago Press, 1963.
Hendricks, Robert G. *Lao-Tzu Te-Tao Ching*. New York: Ballantine, 1989.
Lau, D. C. *Tao Te Ching*. Baltimore: Penguin Books, 1963.
Waley, Arthur. *The Way and Its Power*. New York: Grove Press, 1963.
Kohn, Livia and Michael La Fargue, eds., *Lao-tzu and the Tao-te-ching*. Albany, NY: SUNY Press, 1998.
Csiskszentmihalyi, Mark, and Philip J. Ivanhoe, eds. *Essays on Religious and Philosophical Aspects of the Laozi*. Albany, NY: SUNY Press, 1998.
General Studies of Chinese Thought
Graham, Angus C. *Disputers of the Tao: Philosophical Argument in Ancient China*. La Salle, IL: Open Court Press, 1989.
Schwartz, Benjamin I. *The World of Thought in Ancient China*. Cambridge, MA: Belknap Press, 1985.

Laozi

Daodejing

CHAPTER 1

The way that can be spoken of
Is not the constant way:
The name that can be named
Is not the constant name.
The nameless was the beginning of heaven and earth;
The named was the mother of the myriad creatures . . .

CHAPTER 9

Rather than fill it to the brim by keeping it upright
Better to have stopped in time;
Hammer it to a point
And the sharpness cannot be preserved forever;
There may be gold and jade to fill a hall
But there is none who can keep them.
To be overbearing when one has wealth and position
Is to bring calamity upon oneself.
To retire when the task is accomplished
Is the way of heaven.

CHAPTER 12

The five colors blind the eyes;
The five notes deafen the ears;
The five tastes injure the palate;
Riding and hunting
Make one's mind go wild with excitement;
Goods hard to come by
Serve to hinder one's progress.
Hence the sage is
For the belly
Not for the eye . . .

CHAPTER 30

. . . Where troops have encamped
There will brambles grow;
In the wake of a mighty army
Bad harvests follow without fail . . .
A creature in its prime doing harm to the old
Is known as going against the way.
That which goes against the way will come to an early end.

CHAPTER 32

The way is forever nameless.
Though unhewn wood is insignificant,
No one in the world can claim to be its master.

Should lords and princes be able to hold fast to it,
The myriad creatures will submit of their own accord,
Heaven and earth will unite and sweet dew will fall,
And the people will be equitable, though no one so decrees . . .
The way is to the world as the River and Sea are to rivulets and streams.

CHAPTER 37

The way never acts yet nothing is left undone.
Should lords and princes be able to hold fast to it,
The myriad creatures will be transformed of their own accord.
After they are transformed, should desire raise its head,
I shall press it down with the weight of nameless unhewn wood.
Nameless unhewn wood is but freedom from desire.
And if I cease to desire and remain still,
The empire will be at peace of its own accord.

CHAPTER 38

Those of highest virtue do not keep to virtue and so they have it.
Those of lowest virtue never stray from virtue and so they lack it.
The former never act yet leave nothing undone.
The latter act but leave things undone.
Those of the highest benevolence act, but without ulterior motives.
Those who have mastered the rites act, but if others do not respond,
　　They roll up their sleeves and resort to force.
Hence when the way was lost there was virtue;
When virtue was lost there was benevolence;
When benevolence was lost there was rectitude;
When rectitude was lost there were the rites.
The rites are the wearing thin of loyalty and good faith
And the beginning of disorder . . .

CHAPTER 51

The way gives them life;
Virtue rears them;
Things give them shape;
Circumstances bring them to maturity.
Therefore the myriad creatures all revere the way and honor virtue.
Yet the way is revered and virtue honored not because this is decreed by any authority

But because it is natural for them to be treated so.
Thus the way gives them life and rears them;
Brings them up and nurses them;
Brings them to fruition and maturity;
Feeds and shelters them.
It gives them life yet claims no possession;
It benefits them yet exacts no gratitude;
It is the steward yet exercises no authority.
Such is called the mysterious virtue.

CHAPTER 53

. . . The court is resplendent,
Yet the fields are overgrown,
The granaries are empty;
Yet there are those dressed in finery,
With swords at their sides.
Filled with food and drink,
Possessing too much wealth.
This is known as taking the lead in robbery.
Far indeed is this from the way!

CHAPTER 80

Reduce the size and population of the state.
Ensure that even though the people have tools of war for a troop or a battalion they
    will not use them;
And also that they will be reluctant to move to distant places because they look on
    death as no light matter.
Even when they have ships and carts, they will have no use for them;
And even when they have armor and weapons, they will have no occasion to make a
    show of them.
Bring it about that the people will return to the use of the knotted rope,
Will find relish in their food
And beauty in their clothes,
Will be content in their abode
And happy in the way they live.
Though adjoining states are within sight of one another,
And the sound of dogs barking and cocks crowing in one state can be heard in
    another,
Yet the people of one state will grow old and die without having had any dealings
    with those of another.

BUDDHISM

DAVID J. KALUPAHANA

Buddhist Moral Philosophy

Almost every major philosopher of the world, with the rare exception of the Buddha and Confucius during ancient times and William James in the modern world, has claimed to discover what he called the truth or reality, formulated that discovery in his own way, and then presented a moral philosophy in relation to his view of reality. This procedure was followed by the traditional Indian philosophers who preceded the Buddha. In one of the earliest Upanisads, their aspirations are clearly expressed in three chanted statements that an officiating priest requests: "From the unreal lead me to the real; from darkness lead me to light; from death lead me to immortality."[1] The same tradition assumed that a permanent and eternal spiritual self called *atma* can be found in human beings, and recognized the social hierarchy that had evolved for centuries, consisting of priests, warriors, ordinary citizens, and servants, as the creation of an absolute ultimate reality called *brahma*. People who realize the union between these two realities were considered to achieve the highest possible freedom. The moral life is thus based on a rejection of the reality of the psychophysical personality, and on performing duties assigned to people as a result of their being placed in one of the four castes which is the work of *brahma*. Such duties had to be performed without an iota of self-interest, and with no concern whatsoever for consequences. Total self-sacrifice constituted the crown of the moral life. Deontological ethics of the most extreme form came to be justified.

The reclusive (*sramana*) tradition, failing to discover realities such as *atma* and *brahma,* gave naturalistic explanations of the world of experience, emphasizing the material and biological aspects. In formulating a moral philosophy on the basis of such truths, the reclusive tradition moved in two different directions. One group insisted that what is true or real in the world are the material and biological processes and that moral discourse is nothing more than foolish talk. However, unlike in the West, moral skepticism did not contribute to an extremely hedonistic way of life, for the proponents of such theories were recluses with large retinues who led austere lives. Their skepticism was a critical response to the absolutism of the Brahmanical moral philosophy. The second group followed what is generally known as the theory of the stages of life: studentship, household life, forest-dwelling, and renunciation. This theory can be considered the equivalent of utilitarianism in moral philosophy, and came to be developed into a sophisticated theory in Kautilya's *Arthasāstra*.

The common belief among the interpreters of Buddhism is that Siddhartha Gautama left his royal inheritance and the household life in order to discover the truth about the world including human life. According to his own account, he wanted to discover "what is good" and the "unsurpassable and noble path of peace."[2] This search was not abandoned at any point in his struggle. This is the reason why he left the two contemplatives, Ālāra Kālāma and Uddaka Rāmaputta, under whom he had initial training in the higher contemplations. The good and the peaceful that he was looking for would be relevant to a person while living in society, not while one is absorbed in higher contemplations which the two contemplatives were practicing.

The good and the peaceful he achieved were due to his realization of the *unfortunate consequences* of birth, decay, death, sorrow, and defilement.[3] With this realization he attained inner peace, generally referred to as freedom or nirvana, and this enabled him to adopt an attitude toward life that is opposed to the possessive individualism that is characteristic of utilitarianism, on the one hand, and absolute denial of self-interest, as in the deontological traditions, on the other. This is clearly expressed in his first discourse to the world entitled, "Spoken by the Tathagata"[4] and more popularly known as the "Discourse on the Rolling of the Wheel of Morals," wherein he says:

> Monks, these two extremes should not be cultivated by one who has gone forth. What two? Indulgence in the desire for pleasure of sense, which is low, vulgar, individualist, ignoble, and unfruitful, and indulgence in self-mortification, which is painful, ignoble, and unfruitful.
>
> Avoiding these two extremes the Tathagata has gained knowledge of that middle path which gives vision, which gives knowledge, leading to appeasement, higher knowledge, enlightenment, and freedom.
>
> And what, monks, is that middle path which gives vision . . . freedom?
>
> Verily, it is this noble eightfold path, to wit, right view, right conception, right speech, right profession, right living, right effort, right mindfulness, right concentration. This, monks, is that middle path which gives vision, which gives knowledge, leading to appeasement, higher knowledge, enlightenment, and freedom.

This eightfold path, while denying an ego and avoiding possessive individualism, recognizes human self-interest.[5] It involves his realization of no-self or no-substance. Two facts about his approach are especially significant. First, it is only after attaining freedom that he proceeded to formulate his conception of truth or reality. Secondly, his presentation of the four truths about the world was preceded by the above statement regarding the realization of the moral principle, even though that moral principle constituted the last of the four truths. What is important for our purpose is the manner in which he formulated this conception of truth or reality.

If the Buddha was concerned about the good and peaceful for human beings, his conception of truth had to take into consideration a variety of factors. *First,* it had to recognize the most important of all facts about the nature of life on earth under normal conditions, namely, the fact of suffering, the dissatisfactions or the evil consequences that follow whatever happiness and satisfaction one can experience in life. *Second,* his conception had to portray truth as public, not private; it had to portray truth as something anyone can experience and verify, and not something that is accessible only by a privileged few. Truth cannot be something that exists only in a totally different kind of world. It has to detectable in the world given to sense experience, not something that is available only to an exotic non-sensuous intuition or a purely rational faculty. *Third,* the Buddha's conception of truth had to account for change and continuity without positing the existence of anything that is permanent, for permanence is not part of human experience. In other words, his conception had to recognize impermanence as the natural condition of everything in the world of experience. *Fourth,* his conception of truth had to accommodate freedom without subjecting the human being to a supreme being or an incorruptible law, whether that law be physical (as in the case of the Indian materialists) or moral (as it was in the case of Brahmanical tradition). *Fifth,* in order for such freedom to exist, the conception of the world of experience itself had to be one of malleability, that is, one which accommodates such human freedom. *Sixth,* his explanation of the world had to provide a way to eliminate conflict and bring about goodness and peace. For he had renounced the household life in order to achieve goodness and peace for all, not just for himself. *Finally,* the Buddha had to avoid any form of conceptual absolutism, and he had to avoid suggesting that truth is ineffable. This was no easy task. However the Buddha was equal to it. Not only was he an enlightened and freed person, but before his attainment of enlightenment he had excellent training in the traditional Indian system of education including the science of linguistics.

After his enlightenment, the Buddha spent 1 week seated under the tree of enlightenment reflecting on how to formulate his conception of truth to satisfy the conditions listed above. This he achieved by coining several new terms that were not found in the Indian languages. The most important of these new terms were "dependent arising" and "conditionality." Of these he said:

> This occurred to me, monks: "This doctrine, comprehended by me, is deep, difficult to see, difficult to understand, peaceful, excellent, not subject to a priori reasoning, effective, and to be realized by the wise. These people are delighting in attachment, engrossed in attachment, nourished in attachment. By these people who are delighting in attachment, engrossed in attachment, and nourished by attachment, this standpoint, namely, conditionality, dependent arising, is perceived with difficulty. This standpoint too, namely, the appeasement of all dispositions, relinquishing of all bases (of becoming), spewing out of craving, dispassion, cessation, freedom, is perceived with difficulty."[6]

This passage refers to his understanding of the nature of the world as well as the freedom a human being can achieve in that context. The world of experience as well as human life are dependently arisen. Within that world of dependent arising, a human being can achieve happiness, not by trying to control the world, but by calming down one's dispositions, eliminating greed, hatred, and confusion. The world that is dependently arisen need not, therefore, cause suffering. It is unrestrained dispositions such as greed and hatred that render the world one of suffering. In presenting such an explanation the Buddha has formulated three truths about the world: suffering exists, suffering is caused by unrestrained dispositions, and suffering can be ended by restraining dispositions. By insisting that the cause of suffering is human greed or hatred the Buddha makes human beings responsible for whether or not the world suffers or is free of suffering.

One of the first requirements of a moral philosophy is the recognition that there is human suffering and that there is a way to end it. Neither pessimism nor optimism in their extreme forms will provide impetus to a moral life. The most satisfactory view needs to accommodate both the existence of suffering and the possibility that human beings can overcome suffering. Such an explanation is couched in one word, highlighted by James, namely, meliorism. For centuries, since the first formulation of the doctrine by the Buddha, the conception of suffering has been misunderstood and misinterpreted by classical Indian philosophers as well as by modern interpreters. This misunderstanding appeared as a result of two perspectives. The first is embodied in the statement: "Everything is suffering." This statement is absolutist in its implications and leads to a pessimistic view of life. The Buddha's own view was that "all dispositions are suffering." A disposition is formed as a result of people taking an interest in things. Taking an interest in things can grow into monstrous proportions in the form of greed, craving, and so on. However, the complete elimination of interest would prevent human beings from obtaining knowledge of the world for, as James explained, without choosing in terms of interest, sensory knowledge would not be possible.[7] Furthermore, the elimination of interest is tantamount to suicide. The second perspective is generated by the first. If everything in human life is suffering, then happiness and freedom from suffering has to be sought outside of human life. This combination of perspectives led to the belief that the happiness of enlightenment and freedom (which is the goal of the moral life) is a permanent and eternal state of existence that is in absolute opposition to the impermanent human life.

Another requirement of a moral philosophy is the recognition of a principle of causation, without which a good deed cannot be related to a good consequence and a bad deed to a bad consequence. In the Western philosophical arena, Aristotle's reluctance to recognize causal laws except in the sphere of physics made him abandon moral principles and remain satisfied with an enumeration of virtues. In order to prove the validity of causal laws, the Buddha formulated the principle of dependent arising. The principle of dependent arising is not mysterious. It is described as being deep and difficult to understand because of the attachments on the part of the human beings. At one point the Buddha says:

> Depending upon birth is decay and death, monks; whether there be the arising of a Tathagata or whether there be no arising of a Tathagata, this nature of things, this causal status, this causal orderliness, this conditionality *has remained*. The Tathagata comprehends it fully, understands it fully, and having comprehended it fully . . . , he declares it, teaches it, expresses it, sets it forth, clarifies it, analyses it, makes it plain, saying: "Behold!"[8]

This means that the mystery about the world of experience disappears as soon as one calms down one's dispositions. For this reason, the Buddha recommended restraining the sense of faculties, instead of rejecting sense experience as being unreliable. The restraint is placed not on the physical faculties themselves, but on the search one sets up *after* perceiving an object.

> Having seen a material object with the eye, one does not grasp on to the substance and qualities. (Repeated in regard to the other sense faculties, ear, nose, tongue, body and mind.)[9]

Needless to say, several centuries of philosophical endeavors in the modern world have been wasted on this problem of substance and qualities, and the realization of its meaninglessness came rather late in the 20th century.[10] The Buddha advised his disciple Bahiya:

> Bahiya, herein you must train yourself thus: "In the seen, there will be the *mere* seen; in the heard, there will be the *mere* heard; in the thought, there will be the *mere* thought; in the cognized, there will be the *mere* cognized."[11]

Is this enlightened perspective a mysterious one,[12] as is generally believed, or one in which the *assumed* mystery is avoided? The fact is that the Buddha's conception of truth does not require any special intuition that transcends sense experience or any rational faculty that operates without the aid of the sensory faculties.

The principle of dependent arising is said to be a middle standpoint between the theories of existence and non-existence,[13] between eternalism and annihilationism.[14] It clearly avoids the two popular human sentiments relating to the understanding of the world of experience. The first is the sentiment for parsimony, for simplicity that reduces the multiple world of experience into a rational whole, to an abstract law that explains everything. This sentiment has given rise to many conceptions. Conceptions such as God, soul, and matter, while serving various other functions, also served as simple categories intended to provide unity to our conception of the religious, the individual, and the external world. The Spinozas have been there in the East as well as in the West. In contrast, there is the human sentiment for making distinctions. This arises from an attitude that says: "Whatever is distinguishable is also separable." Humean proponents of this attitude have dominated modern philosophical thinking, especially as seemed substantiated by the ultimate reductionism of modern science with its discovery of atoms (whose ultimate constituents remain unclear). Dependent arising is placed between these two extremes, and if anything comes close to it in the modern world it is the radical empiricism of William James. In fact, the Buddha has the greatest of difficulties in explaining the principle of dependent arising because the very conception of time in the Indian context called for existential distinctions. The past is what has gone away. The future is what has not yet come. The present is what exists. Working within this conception of time, the Indian philosophers were compelled to accept either permanence or annihilation. On the one hand, if they were to connect the non-existent past and the future with the existing present, they had to assume an underlying substance. On the other hand, if they were to remain true to the real present, they had to accept distinctions or absence of connection. Such a conceptual dichotomy could be avoided only by redefining the experienced present which is not totally severed from the past, at least the immediate past. Hence the Buddha coining another term to express the present as "that which is arisen dependent upon." Relationships when placed in such a live context became real rather than the work of imagination.

This formulation of the principle of dependent arising is based upon the experience of what has transpired so far, as is expressed in the previous statement that this status *has remained*. This knowledge is then applied to explain future events and is called inductive knowledge.[15] This leaves the principle of dependent arising open-ended, and not as a theory that can be asserted with absolute dogmatism saying: "This alone is true; any other is falsehood," a claim that was often condemned by the Buddha.[16] This is the reason why the theory, as described in a previous quotation, is characterized as being "peaceful."

The principle of dependent arising, when applied in the explanation of the world of experience, allows room for flexibility within which a human being can act in order to achieve some measure of success and happiness. The same principle applied in the explanation of the human person leaves room for human freedom. That freedom is built into the stream of consciousness[17] or the stream of becoming[18] where a human being is compelled, by the very nature of cognition, to choose from a plurality of alternatives. Without such choosing cognition cannot function. Such choosing is done in terms of the person's interest. This interest is expressed in the discourses as dispositions. These dispositions, themselves dependently arisen, are the factors that determine the stream of consciousness and they provide an individuality to a person. As mentioned earlier, that interest can be carried to its extreme and it can turn out to be greed or craving producing what is generally referred to as possessive individualism. The Buddha's admonition is to appease the interests of dispositions, not to eliminate them altogether, as recommended in the deontological traditions, for that would be tantamount to suicide.

The appeasement of disposition is the highest moral ideal in early Buddhism, for it is another term for freedom.[19] At the same time it is also the foundation of the moral life in the social context. Those with appeased interests can function as a group of individuals, even though unrelated, but having mutual self-interests. Very often human beings are not related to one another except as members of one species. For there to be any moral sentiment, there needs to be at least *two loving persons.* It is this necessity that made the Buddha inculcate the idea that one should develop one's thoughts towards all living beings in the same way as a mother would protect her own bosom-born son as her own life.[20] Even if a person may not be directly related by way of a natural relationship as between a mother and a child, for the Buddha the broader principle of dependent arising, in fact, serves as the most natural of all relations. For example, members of a family are related to one another, first by love between the parents and then by blood; the family is then related to the neighborhood by way of dependence, for any family that attempts to cut itself off completely will be an outcast and cannot expect to receive any help when faced with a calamity. Neighborhoods are related as parts of a state. States are similarly dependent upon one another and thus constitute a country. Finally, we have what is called the republic of nations, that is, the United Nations. The moral sentiment that springs from two loving persons thus receives maximum extension because of the principle of dependence. This is the deeper meaning of the Buddha's statement: "Whosoever sees dependent arising, he sees the moral principle."[21]

The Buddha's determination that his theory of morals should never deteriorate into a dogmatic assertion as to what is right and wrong is well entrenched in his statement: "Monks, even the morally good things should be abandoned, let alone the morally bad things." He uses the example of the raft, which is used to cross the stream of suffering but which should not be carried on one's shoulders after achieving one's goal.[22] This is not a pragmatic ploy but a genuine attempt to avoid any form of dogmatism in morals and the resulting conflicts.

Along with the need and the ability to choose from among different alternatives, a human being also has the capacity to initiate action in regard to what it has chosen. While rejecting any absolute autonomy, as envisaged in the deontological traditions in the form of a metaphysical will, and condemning any school that denied the ability on the part of a human being to achieve anything, as was advocated by the materialistic and naturalistic schools in India as well as in the West, the Buddha's principle of dependent arising accommodated human dispositions as well as their capacity to affect the world of experience. In fact, the physical world of a monarch like Maha Sudassana that included the palaces, the pleasure groves, the ponds, etc. were referred to by the Buddha as nothing but dispositions,[23] all of them being dispositionally conditioned. This reminds us of Karl Popper's conception of the World III. In addition to the human dispositions, the Buddha recognized certain tendencies in the human being through which it is able to plan and initiate processes that may even go against the observed flow of events,[24] and the one who has achieved moral perfection is considered to be an embodiment of such behavior.

Finally, his interest in the good and the peaceful was clearly embodied in his understanding and use of language. Not only did he use certain linguistic forms that had gone out of use as a result of the essentialist enterprise that led to the development of the artificial language called Sanskrit, he also adopted an attitude toward language that would prevent conflict among speakers of different languages. First, in the process of trying to achieve clarity and precision in expressing absolute truths, the traditional grammarians had eliminated the use of the aorist and the imperfect verbs. Not recognizing the possibility of such clarity and precision, the Buddha reintroduced these verbs. Furthermore, his criticism of the metaphysical self of the Brahmanical thinkers led him to the profuse use of passive forms as well as past participles. The active voice of personal pronouns such as "I" or "mine," forms that could easily generate the belief in self, and therefore, egoism, were used very sparingly. Secondly, the Buddha was extremely concerned with the most significant as well as the most cumbersome issue relating to human conflict, namely, the means of communication or language. He recognized that the most important function of language is communication, the most sophisticated version of which makes the humans a unique species. The Buddha was reluctant to let this most valuable tool to be used for self-destruction, that is, to generate conflicts among the humans. He was a pragmatist who did not look for universal solutions. As such he was not proposing a universal language. Realizing that language of the community to which one is born is one's first and the foremost inheritance, and as such one is emotionally related to it, the Buddha condemned anyone who took a specific term occurring in a language and maintained: "This alone is true; any other is falsehood." He himself was familiar with many languages, which made it easy for him to communicate with people as he moved from one part of his vast country to another. Thus, he was able to cite seven dialectical variants for one object, namely, the "bowl." These are *pāti, patta, vittha, sarāva, dhāropa, poṇa,* and *pisila.* An essentialist is one who will have a specific term to refer to an object and will be ready to go on adding adjectives to qualify the term if the object happens to be slightly different from the one for which he utilized the original term. The Buddha's advice is that one should take into consideration the different uses of the object described even if it happened to be the same object. During his day a bowl was used to collect food, as an eating utensil, as a drinking bowl, and sometimes as a bucket when bathing in a river. It may even have different sizes and shapes. However, there is no ultimate meaning or signification of the term bowl. On the contrary, it does not mean that the term "bowl" does not express the reality of what is experienced as a bowl. The Buddha's advice to his disciples was "one should neither grasp on to a language nor overstretch it." The Buddha's use of the two terms "grasping" (*abhinivesa*) and "overstretching" (*atisāra*) is tinged with sarcasm. Being the linguist he was, he could not have been unaware that the term *atisāra* was the Indian medical term for "diarrhea," in which case *abhinivesa* (literally, excessive entering or entering and settling down) could mean "constipation." Therefore, these terms stand for "conceptual constipation" and "conceptual diarrhea," respectively, depicting the essentialist and transcendentalist perspectives. Essentialism and transcendentalism have caused enormous conflicts in the world. The Buddha recommended that one should recognize the use of the language in a particular country without grasping on to it, saying: "For this purpose, these venerable ones speak of it," that is, accept the pragmatic value of the language. Having explained which attitude toward language will lead to conflict and which will lead to non-conflict or peace, the Buddha proceeded to identify someone who is foremost in living this ideal life of non-conflict, namely, Subhuti.

The Buddha clearly recognized a gradual path to moral perfection.[25] It consists of three parts: (1) the basic virtues constitute the beginning, (2) the more advanced moral life is the eightfold path, and (3) the conclusion, which is enlightenment and freedom.[26] We may make the transition from the virtuous life to the moral life only after improving our understanding. A variety of virtues are enumerated in several lists, starting with the basic five precepts there are hundreds included in the longest list available in the "Discourse on Brahma's Net."[27] We present here a list of seven basic virtues.

1. Refraining from taking life, abandoning severe punishment and arms, being modest and loving, extending friendliness and compassion to all living beings.

2. Refraining from stealing, accepting what is given, hoping for the given, living with a self that has become pure.

3. Abandoning a lower life, leading a higher life, being remote and detached from vulgate sensuality.

4. Refraining from confusing speech; speaking the truth, being realistic, trustworthy, and non-conflicting with the world.

5. Refraining from malicious speech (that is, not creating dissension among the people); being one who unites those that are divided, promoting those that are united, delighting in harmony, delighted in harmony, enjoying harmony, and speaking harmonizing words.

6. Renouncing harsh speech; resorting to speech that is blameless, pleasing to the ear, lovable, appealing to the heart, urbane, attractive, and pleasing to the multitude.

7. Abandoning frivolous talk; speaking at the appropriate time, speaking what has come to be (that is, the truth), what contributed to welfare, to morality, to discipline; making statements that are referential, timely, with horizon, and fruitful.

In order to motivate and encourage the beginner, the cultivation or non-cultivation of virtues are presented in the context of rewards and punishments. The rewards are to be reaped in heavens (symbolizing extreme pleasures) and human life (with a mixture of happiness and suffering), these being good destinies, even though both of them are impermanent. The punishments are to be experienced by being born in the animal womb, in the sphere of the departed spirits, and in hell, these being full of suffering, yet impermanent. However, this life of virtues is clearly distinguished from the more advanced moral life consisting of the eightfold path, which, in fact, includes the virtues mentioned earlier, but which is practiced on the basis of an understanding of the four truths about the world mentioned earlier. Here there is no assumption that the consequence of a deed is a reward or a punishment, but rather a natural process of dependence.

Before presenting the more advanced moral life it may be appropriate to take a look at the Buddha's admonitions to a lay person who is expected to lead a virtuous life without having to renounce all the significant aspects of the economic and social life. In his discourse to Singala, the householder, the Buddha had the following to say:

> To one who moves accumulating wealth,
> as does the bee, wealth grows like an ant-hill.
> Having accumulated wealth in this manner,
> a satisfied householder in the family,
> should parcel his wealth into four parts.
> He indeed binds his friends.
> With one he should enjoy himself.
> With two, he should resort to work,
> the fourth should be put away
> so that it will be available in times of calamity.[28]

Contrary to the prevalent belief that the Buddha denounced every aspect of the life of the householder in favor of a life of complete renunciation, here we find the Buddha perceiving no wrong in the accumulation of wealth, so long as that wealth is righteously earned. In fact, those householders who have failed to do so are described by the Buddha as follows: "Without having lived the higher life, without having acquired wealth during their prime, (some) languish like decrepit cranes in a lake depleted of fish."[29] Householders, nay even monks and nuns, are not expected to abandon every bit of self-interest. Householders who are involved in such enterprises help to improve the quality of life in the community. Those who renounce the household life are not expected to be involved in such enterprises, because they have a greater contribution to make, namely, work for the moral welfare of the community. One who is involved in both is the monarch who is expected to promote the material as well as the moral welfare of the society.

According to the advice of Singala, one who accumulates wealth "binds friends," that is, brings them together. For the Buddha, "friendship" is not something restricted only for the acquaintances. Friendliness is to be extended to all living beings because all of us, as mentioned earlier, are dependently arisen. If such be the case, the calamities for which the fourth quarter of one's wealth is saved need not be solely for taking care of calamities that befall oneself. That would be utter selfishness. It should be spent on anyone who is in need, whether it is an acquaintance or a stranger. If the rich in the world can share one-fourth of their wealth with those who are in need, the world would be, to use the Buddha's terminology, "an appropriate environment for living."[30]

The eightfold path thus includes right view, rightness being determined by comprehensiveness. It calls for the understanding that human knowledge, whether it is derived from sensory experience, inference, or extraordinary forms such as retrocognition and clairvoyance, is limited. Right view is a middle standpoint between absolute certainty and absolute skepticism. The limitations of our knowledge compel us to keep our minds open about what truth or reality is and to be prepared to modify our views when they are no longer relevant in the light of new situations or discoveries.

Right conception is not one directed at realizing the truth or falsity of what the conceiving mind has discovered, but the moral value of the very conceptions. Thus wrong conceptions are those that are dominated by or lead to pleasures of sense, ill will, and injury, while right conceptions are those that contribute to thoughts of renunciation, good-will, and non-violence.

Immediately after right view and right conception is listed their expression, namely right speech. It may be noted that the last three items of the virtues mentioned earlier relate to right speech. Right speech, as highlighted in the discourse included in this selection, is one of the most important conditions for peace or non-conflict. Right profession and right livelihood are then specified, these being the summarization of the longest list of virtues referred to earlier.

With the Buddha's rejection of a mysterious agent or a metaphysical will behind human deeds, there was a need to account for the manner in which someone could initiate the practice of the moral life. As a result, right effort finds an important place in the eightfold path.

Right mindfulness is an extremely significant factor in the moral path. The Buddha's reluctance to recognize absolutely valid laws in any sphere of human experience and his emphasis on an open-ended universe as embodied in his principle of dependent arising, it was necessary for him to underscore the epistemological significance of vigilance or heedfulness. This is the function of mindfulness, which is sometimes referred to as the royal road to enlightenment and freedom.[31] Finally, right concentration, necessary for any fruitful activity, constitutes the eighth factor.

The ultimate states that one achieves as a result of cultivating the moral life are characterized as enlightenment and freedom. The former is defined as wisdom or the knowledge of what "has come to be" (note the use of the past participle). It has nothing to do with the knowledge of things "as they are" (which has essentialist implications). The latter is popularly known as nirvana, which is a negative term implying "absense of constraint." The major constraints eliminated as a result of following the moral path are greed, hatred, and confusion, which are the causes of much suffering in human life, individual or social. Sometimes nirvana is also described as the absence of craving for pleasures of sense, highlighted in the discourse presented here, as well as the absence of craving for becoming, that is, constantly setting up goals and striving to achieve them, and more significantly, the absence of craving for other-becoming, this latter implying the dissatisfaction with the impermanence associated with the present life and seeking for a permanent and eternal state of existence. This was immortality advocated by the pre-Buddhist Brahmanical tradition but for the Buddha immortality was no more than not being reborn. The more positive description of the state of freedom is that it is a state of happiness, stability, composure, and the ability to remain unmoved by gain or loss, good reputation or bad reputation, praise or blame, and happiness or suffering. In short to lead a life of peace and non-conflict is the theme of the two discourses included here and is also expressed in the Buddha's statement: "Monks, I do not conflict with the world, but the world conflicts with me."[32]

Given the preceding analysis, the best sample of a discourse that deals with the most salient features of the Buddha's moral reflections is the "Discourse on the Analysis of Non-conflict." It starts with the statement of the moral path, which was the topic of discussion in his very first discourse, and then proceeds to characterize the sort of happiness that people ought to pursue, carefully examining all the conditions that allow people to communicate well and to avoid conflict. Finally the discourse analyzes the attitude people should adopt with regard to language, the means of communication.

The next selection is a text from later Buddhism that has had tremendous influence on the continuity of the earlier tradition. This is the famous "Discourse on the Perfection of Wisdom, the Cutting with the Diamond" (*Vajracchedikā Prajñā-pāramitā Sūtra*). It was compiled at a time when substantialist and nominalist thinking emerged in the Buddhist tradition with the speculations of the Sarvastivadins and the Sautrantikas respectively. While the Sarvastivadins introduced the notion of substantial elements, the Sautrantika speculations led to the belief in a subtle personality, both of which were rejected by the Buddha because they were contrary to his discoveries in epistemology, ontology, and ethics. In order to reject these two traditions, the discourse applies a unique method of deconstructing conceptions with substantialist implications and then reconstructing them in order to underscore their pragmatic meaning. The Buddha's statement, referred to above, that theory should be used like a raft is quoted in this text. More significantly, the interlocutor in this discourse is Subhuti, the monk who is referred to in the earlier discourse as one who "dwells in peace." In fact, in the present discourse, Subhuti is made to reminisce this pronunciation of the Buddha, thereby revealing an extremely close relationship between the original discourse of the Buddha and what was compiled centuries later. Furthermore, this discourse greatly influenced the development of some of the later Buddhist traditions not only in India, but also in the Far East. There is no doubt that it was known to the Sixth Patriarch of Ch'an Buddhism, Hui-neng, whose *Platform Sutra* contains an analysis directed at deconstructing solidified concepts and rendering them flexible. The teachings and practices of the Lin-chi (Rinzai) school of Ch'an (Zen) Buddhism, one of the most popular traditions in East Asia, can be traced to the doctrines of early Buddhism through the "Discourse on the Perfection of Wisdom" under consideration.

[1]*Brhadaranyaka Upanisad* 1.3.28, in *The Principal Upanisads,* edited with Introduction, Text, Translation, and Notes by Sarvepalli Radhakrishnan (London: Allyn & Unwin, 1953, p. 162).

[2]*Majjhima-nikāya,* 1.163, 165–166.

[3]Ibid., 1.167.

[4]A technical term used to refer to someone who has attained enlightenment and freedom, literally meaning "thus gone one."

[5]For a more detailed analysis of the middle path, see my *Ethics in Early Buddhism* (Honolulu: University of Hawaii Press, 1995).

[6]*Majjhima-nikāya,* 1.167.

[7]*The Principles of Psychology* (Cambridge, Mass.: Harvard University Press, 1983), p. 220.

[8]*Samyutta-nikāya,* 2.25.

[9]*Digha-nikāya,* 1.70.

[10]See Hillary Putnam, *The Many Faces of Realism* (LaSalle, Ill.: Open Court, 1987), pp. 6–7.

[11]*Udana,* p. 8.

[12]It is more like the "mere post-scientific common sense" now being talked about, and which comes after several centuries of the scientific wild-goose chase for the real beyond what is available to the senses. See Putnam, p. 6.

[13]*Samyutta-nikāya,* 1.20.

[14]Ibid., 2.17.

[15]Ibid., 2.58.

[16]*Digha-nikāya,* 1.187, 199.

[17]Ibid., 3.105.

[18]*Samyutta-nikāya,* 1.15; 4.128.

[19]*Majjhima-nikāya,* 1.167; *Samyutta-nikāya,* 1.136.

[20]*Sutta-nipata,* 149.

[21]*Majjhima-nikāya,* 1.190–191.

[22]Ibid., 1.135.

[23]*Digha-nikāya,* 2.198.

[24]*Samyutta-nikāya,* 1.136; *Anguttara-nikāya,* 2.6.

[25]*Majjhima-nikāya,* 1.476; 3.1.

[26]*Digha-nikāya,* 2.155; *Majjhima-nikāya,* 3.8.

[27]*Digha-nikāya,* 1.4–12.

[28]Ibid., 3.188.

[29]*Dhammapada,* 155.

[30]*Sutta-nipata,* 260.

[31]Ibid., 2.290.

[32]*Samyutta-nikāya,* 3.138.

Further Reading

Radhakrishnan, Sarvepalli, ed. *The Principal Upanisads.* London: Allen & Unwin, 1953.

Griffiths, P. J. *On Being Buddha.* Albany, NY: State University of New York Press, 1994.

Kalupahana, David J. *Ethics in Early Buddhism.* Honolulu: University of Hawaii Press, 1995.

Kalupahana, D. J. *Buddhist Philosophy: A Historical Analysis.* Honolulu, HI: University of Hawaii Press, 1976.

Williams, P. *Mahayana Buddhism: The Doctrinal Foundations.* London: Routledge, 1989.

translated by David J. Kalupahana

The Discourse on Non-Conflict

(230) . . . Thus, has been heard by me. At one time the Fortunate One was staying near Sāvatthi in the Jeta Grove in Anāthapiṇḍika's monastery. While he was there the Fortunate One addressed the monks saying: "Monks." "Reverend Sir," these monks answered the Fortunate One in assent. The Fortunate One spoke thus: "I will teach you, monks, the analysis of non-conflict. Listen carefully to it, pay attention and I will speak." "Yes, reverend Sir," these monks answered the Fortunate One in assent.

The Fortunate One spoke thus: "You should not be involved in the happiness of the pleasures of sense which is low, vulgar, individualistic, ignoble, not conducive to welfare; you should not be involved in self-mortification which is painful, ignoble, and not conducive to welfare. Not approaching either of these two extremes, a middle way has been realized by the Tathāgata which is productive of vision, productive of knowledge and leads to appeasement, higher knowledge, enlightenment, and freedom. One should know approval and one should know disapproval, and having known approval, having known disapproval, one should indeed not approve and not disapprove—one should merely teach the moral principle itself. One should know how to judge happiness, and having known how to judge happiness, one should be intent on internal happiness. One should not utter secret speech. Face to face one should not say a vexatious thing. One should speak quite slowly, not hurriedly. One should not be committed to a language of a country, one should not transgress common parlance. This is the exposition of the analysis of non-conflict.

"When it is said, 'You should not be intent on the happiness of the pleasures of sense . . . and should not be intent on self-mortification . . . ,' in reference to what is it said?

"Whatever is the intent on delight on the part of one whose happiness is in association with the pleasures of sense and which is low, vulgar, individualistic, ignoble, not conducive to welfare, that is a phenomenon with suffering, trauma, distress, fever; that is a wrong way. Whatever is the non-intent on the delight on the part of one whose happiness is associated with the pleasures of sense (231) and which is low . . . , that phenomenon is without suffering, trauma, distress, and fever; it is the right way. Whatever is the intent on the practice of self-mortification which is painful . . . , that phenomenon is accompanied by suffering, trauma, distress, and fever; that is a wrong way. Whatever is the non-intent on the practice of self-mortification which is painful . . . , that phenomenon is not accompanied by suffering, trauma, distress, and fever; that is a right way.

"When it is said, 'You should not be intent on the happiness of the pleasures of sense . . . , and should not be intent on self-mortification . . . ,' it is said in reference to this.

"When it is said, 'Not approaching either of these extremes, there is a middle way realized by the Tathāgata which is productive of vision, productive of knowledge and which leads to appeasement, higher knowledge, enlightenment, and freedom,' in reference to what is it said?

"It is the noble eightfold path itself, that is to say: right view, right conception, right speech, right profession, right livelihood, right effort, right mindfulness, and right concentration. When it is said, 'Not approaching both of these extremes, there is a middle way . . . which leads to . . . freedom,' it is said in reference to this.

"When it is said, 'One should know approval and one should know disapproval, and having known approval, having known disapproval, one should neither approve nor disapprove—one should simply teach the moral principle itself,' in reference to what is it said?

"And what, monks, is approval and what is disapproval but not the teaching of the moral principle? One disapproves of some others here, saying: 'All those who are intent on the delights of those whose happiness is associated with the pleasures of sense which is low, vulgar, individualistic, ignoble, and not conducive to welfare, all of them are accompanied by suffering, trauma, distress, and fever; have set out on the wrong way.' One approves of some others here, saying: 'All those who are not intent on the delights of those whose happiness is associated with the pleasures of sense which is low, vulgar, individualistic, ignoble, and not conducive to welfare, all of them are without suffering, trauma, distress, and fever; are set out on the right way.' One disapproves of some others here, saying: 'All those who are intent on the practice of self-mortification which is painful, ignoble, and not conducive to welfare, (232) all of them are accompanied by suffering, trauma, distress, and fever; have set out on the wrong way.' One approves of some others here, saying: 'All those who are not intent on the practice of self-mortification which is painful, ignoble, and not conducive to welfare, all of them are without suffering, trauma, distress, and fever; have set out on the right way.' One disapproves of some others here, saying: 'All those whose fetter of becoming is not got rid of, all of them are accompanied by suffering, trauma, distress, and fever; have set out on the wrong way.' One approves of some others here, saying: 'All those whose fetter of becoming is got rid of, all of them are without suffering, trauma, distress, and fever; have set out on the right way.' This, monks, is what is approval and disapproval, but not the teaching of the moral principle itself.

"What, monks, is neither approval not disapproval, but the teaching of the moral principle itself? One does not say: 'All those who are intent on the delights of those whose happiness is associated with the pleasures of sense which is low, vulgar, individualistic, ignoble, and not conducive to welfare, all of them are accompanied by suffering, trauma, distress, and fever; have set out on the wrong way.' One teaches the moral principle itself, saying: 'It is the intentness that is a phenomenon accompanied by suffering, trauma, distress, and fever; is a wrong way.' One does not say: 'All those who are non-intent on the delights of those whose happiness is associated with the pleasures of sense which is low, vulgar, individualistic, ignoble, and not conducive to welfare, all of them are without suffering, trauma, distress, and fever; have set out on the right way.' One teaches the moral principle itself, saying: 'It is the non-intentness that is a phenomenon without suffering, trauma, distress, and fever; is the right way.' One does not say: 'All those who are intent on the practice of self-mortification which is painful, ignoble, and not conducive to welfare, all of them are accompanied by suffering, trauma, distress, and fever; have set out on the wrong way.' One teaches the moral principle itself, saying: 'It is the intentness that is a phenomenon accompanied by suffering, trauma, distress, and fever; is a wrong way.' One does not say: 'All those who are non-intent on the practice of self-mortification which is painful, ignoble, and not conducive to welfare, all of them are without suffering, trauma, distress, and fever; have set out on the right way.' One teaches the moral principle itself saying: 'It is the non-intentness that is a phenomenon without suffering, trauma, distress, and fever; is a right way.' One does not say: 'All those whose fetter of becoming is not got rid of, all of them are accompanied by suffering, trauma, distress, and fever; have set out on the wrong way.' (233) One teaches the moral principle itself saying: 'When the fetter of becoming is not gotten rid of, becoming is not gotten rid of.' One does not say: 'All those whose fetter of becoming is gotten rid of, all of them are without suffering, trauma, distress, and fever; is the right way.' One teaches the moral principle itself saying: 'When the fetter of becoming is gotten rid of, becoming is gotten rid of.' This, monks, is indeed not approval and not disapproval, but the teaching of the moral principle itself.

"When it is said, 'One should know approval and one should know disapproval, and having known approval, having known disapproval, one should indeed not approve and not disapprove—one should simply teach the moral principle itself,' it is said in reference to this.

"When it is said: 'One should know how to judge happiness, and having known how to judge happiness, one should be intent on internal happiness,' in reference to what is it said?

"These five, monks, are the sensual propensities. What five? Material form cognizable by the eye, agreeable, pleasant, appealing to the mind, enticing, leading on to the pleasures of sense, alluring; sounds cognizable by the ear . . . ; smells cognizable by the nose . . . ; tastes cognizable by the tongue . . . ; tangibles cognizable by the body, agreeable, pleasant, appealing to the mind, enticing, leading on to the pleasures of sense, alluring. These, monks, are the five sensual propensities. Whatever happiness and delight that arise depending upon these five sensual propensities, this is called happiness of sense-pleasures, a vile happiness, an individualistic happiness, an ignoble happiness. I say of this happiness that it is not to be pursued, cultivated, developed—it is to be feared. Herein, monks, a monk, aloof from the pleasures of sense, aloof from the bad tendencies, enters on and abides in the first contemplation, with reflection and investigation and with joy and happiness born of aloofness; through the appeasement of reflection and investigation, enters on and abides in the second contemplation which is subjectively tranquilizing one-pointedness of thought, without reflection and investigation and with joy and happiness born of concentration; through dispassion for joy, one remains considerate, mindful, and conscious and experiences happiness through the body, enters on and abides in the third contemplation which the noble ones characterize as the 'abiding in consideration, mindfulness, and happiness;' through the abandoning of happiness and suffering, and through the prior cessation of delight and dejection, one enters on and abides in the fourth contemplation which is not suffering and not happiness but which is purity of consideration and mindfulness. This is called the happiness of renunciation, happiness of aloofness, happiness of appeasement, and happiness of enlightenment. I say of this happiness that it is to be pursued, cultivated, and developed—it is not to be feared.

(234) "When it is said: 'One should know how to judge happiness, and having known how to judge happiness, one should be intent on internal happiness,' it is said in reference to this.

"When it is said: 'One should not utter secret speech. Face to face one should not say a vexatious thing,' in reference to what is it said?

"Therein, monks, whatever secret speech is known to be untrue, not factual, not conducive to welfare, one should not, if possible, utter that secret speech; whatever secret speech is known to be true, factual, and not conducive to welfare, one should train oneself not to speak it; whatever secret speech is known to be true, factual, and conducive to welfare, therein let one be the knower of time for the speaking of that secret speech. Therein, monks, whatever vexatious thing to be said face to face is untrue, not factual, and not conducive to welfare, that vexatious thing should not be said face to face; whatever vexatious thing to be said face to face is known to be true, factual, and not conducive to welfare, one should train oneself not to speak it; whatever vexatious thing to be said face to face is true, factual, and conducive to welfare, let one be the knower of time for the speaking of that vexatious thing face to face.

"When it is said: 'One should not utter secret speech. Face to face one should not say a vexatious thing,' it is said in reference to this.

"When it is said: 'One should speak very slowly, not hurriedly,' in reference to what is it said?

"Herein, monks, in the case of one who speaks hurriedly, the body tires, thought is disturbed, voice is destroyed, throat is affected, and the speech of one who is hurrying is unclear and incomprehensible. Herein, monks, in the case of one who speaks unhurriedly, the body does not tire, thought is not disturbed, voice is not destroyed, throat is not affected, and the speech of one who speaks unhurriedly is clear and comprehensible.

"When it is said: 'One should speak very slowly, and not hurriedly,' it is said in reference to this.

"When it is said: 'One should not commit oneself to the language of a country, one should not transgress common parlance,' in reference to what is it said?

"How, monks, is the commitment to the language of a country and the transgression of a common parlance? Herein, monks, that itself is recognized in certain countries (235) as *pāti*, as *patta*, as *vittha*, as *sarāva*, as *dhāropa*, as *poṇa*, as *pisila*.[1] Thus, as it is recognized in those countries, so does one obstinately clinging to it and adhering to it, speak of it: 'This alone is true, all else is falsehood.' Thus, monks, is the commitment to language of a country and the transgression of a common parlance. What, monks, is the non-commitment to the language of a country and the non-transgression of common parlance? Herein, monks, that itself is recognized in certain countries as *pāti*, as *patta*, as *vittha*, as *sarāva*, as *dhāropa*, as *poṇa*, as *pisila*. Just as it is recognized in those countries, so does one speak of it, without clinging: 'For this purpose these venerable ones speak of this.' Thus, monks, is the non-commitment to the language of a country and the non-transgression of common parlance.

"When it is said: 'One should not commit oneself to the language of a country and one should not transgress common parlance,' it is said in reference to this.

"Whatever is the intent on delight on the part of one whose happiness is in association with the pleasures of sense and which is low, vulgar, individualistic, ignoble, not conducive to welfare, that is a phenomenon accompanied by suffering, trauma, distress, and fever; it is a wrong way; therefore that is a phenomenon of **conflict.** Whatever is the non-intent on the delight on the part of one whose happiness is associated with the pleasures of sense and which is low . . . , that phenomenon is without suffering, trauma, distress, and fever; it is the right way; therefore that is a phenomenon of **non-conflict.** Whatever is the intent on the practice of self-mortification which is painful . . . , that phenomenon is accompanied by suffering, trauma, distress, and fever; that is a wrong way; therefore that is a phenomenon of **conflict.** Whatever is the non-intent on the practice of self-mortification which is painful . . . , that phenomenon is not accompanied by suffering, trauma, distress, and fever; that is a right way; **(236)** therefore it is a phenomenon of **non-conflict.** Therein, monks, whatever middle way that has been realized by the Tathāgata which is productive of vision, productive of knowledge, and leads to appeasement, higher knowledge, enlightenment, and freedom, that is without suffering, trauma, distress, and fever; is a right way; therefore it is a phenomenon of **non-conflict.** Therein, monks, whatever is the approval and non-approval but not the teaching of doctrine, that is a phenomenon with suffering, trauma, distress, and fever; is a wrong way; therefore it is a phenomenon of **conflict.** Therein, monks, whatever is neither approval nor disapproval but is the teaching of the doctrine, that is a phenomenon without suffering, trauma, distress, and fever; is a right way; therefore is a phenomenon of **non-conflict.** Therein, monks, whatever is this happiness of sense-pleasures, a vile happiness, a happiness of the individualistic, and ignoble happiness, that is a phenomenon with suffering, trauma, distress, and fever; is a wrong way; therefore is a phenomenon of **conflict.** Therein, monks, whatever is this happiness of renunciation, happiness of aloofness, happiness of appeasement, and happiness of enlightenment, that is a phenomenon without suffering, trauma, distress, and fever; is a right way; therefore is a phenomenon of **non-conflict.** Therein, monks, whatever secret speech is untrue, not factual, not conducive to welfare, that is a phenomenon with suffering, trauma, distress, and fever; therefore is a phenomenon of **conflict.** Therein, monks, whatever is secret speech which is true, factual, and not conducive to welfare, that too is a phenomenon with suffering, trauma, distress, and fever; is a wrong way; therefore is a phenomenon of **conflict.** Therein, monks, whatever is secret speech which is true, factual and conducive to welfare, that is a phenomenon without suffering, trauma, distress, and fever; is a right way; therefore is a phenomenon of **non-conflict.** Therein, monks, whatever vexatious speech uttered face to face is untrue, not factual, not conducive to welfare, that is a phenomenon with suffering, trauma, distress, and fever; is a wrong way; therefore is a phenomenon of **conflict.** Therein, monks, whatever vexatious speech uttered face-to-face **(237)** is untrue, not factual, not conducive to welfare, that is a phenomenon with suffering, trauma, distress, and fever; is a wrong way; therefore is a phenomenon of **conflict.** Therein, monks, whatever is vexatious speech uttered face-to-face which is true, factual, and conducive to welfare, that is a phenomenon without suffering, trauma, distress, and fever; is a right way; therefore is a phenomenon of **non-conflict.** Therein, monks, whatever is the speech of one who speaks hurriedly, that is a phenomenon with suffering, trauma, distress, and fever; is a wrong way, therefore is a phenomenon of **conflict.** Therein, monks, whatever is the speech of one who does not speak hurriedly, that is a phenomenon without suffering, trauma, distress, and fever; is a right way; therefore is a phenomenon of **non-conflict.** Therein, monks, whatever is the clinging to the dialect of a country and the transgression of common parlance, that is a phenomenon with suffering, trauma, distress, and fever; is a wrong way; therefore is a phenomenon of **conflict.** Therein, monks, whatever is the non-clinging to a dialect of a country and the non-transgression of common parlance, that is a phenomenon without suffering, trauma, distress, and fever; is a right way; therefore is a phenomenon of **non-conflict.**

"Therefore, monks, you should train yourselves thus: 'We will know a phenomenon of **conflict** and we will know a phenomenon of **non-conflict;** having known a phenomenon of **conflict** and having known a phenomenon of **non-conflict,** we will embark on a way of **non-conflict.** Monks, Subhūti, the son of family, is one who has embarked on a way of **non-conflict."**

The Fortunate One spoke thus. Delighted, these monks rejoiced in what the Fortunate One said.

---

[1]Dialectical variants for the word "bowl."

The Discourse on the Perfection of Wisdom, the Cutting with the Diamond[1]

[26] 1. Thus has been heard by me. At one time the Fortunate One was staying near Śrāvasti, in the Jeta's Grove at the monastery of Anāthapiṇḍada together with a large congregation of monks, with 1,250 monks and a large number of *bodhisattvas,*[2] the great beings . . .

2. Again at that time the venerable Subhūti had joined the assembly and was seated. Thereupon, the venerable Subhūti . . . said thus to the Fortunate One:

"Wondrous, O Fortunate One, exceedingly wondrous, O Well-gone One, is the manner in which the *bodhisattvas,* the great beings, have been favored by the Tathāgata, . . .

Sir, how should a son or a daughter of family, set out on the *bodhisattva* vehicle, take a stand, how should one conduct oneself, how should one take control of thought?" . . .

3. The Fortunate One said thus:

"Herein, Subhūti, one who has set out in the *bodhisattva* vehicle should produce a thought thus: 'As many beings as there are in the sphere of beings, comprehended by the concept of being, egg-born or womb-born or moisture-born or of spontaneous birth, with material form or without material form, with perception or without perception, not with perception and not without perception, as far as whatever is expressed when expressing the sphere of beings, all of them should, by me, made to be ultimately free in the sphere of freedom without residual objectivity. In this way, even after having freed innumerable beings, not any being has been freed.[3] What is the reason for this? If, Subhūti, for the *bodhisattva* there were to prevail any perception of a being, he should not be called a *bodhisattva.* What is the reason for this? Subhūti, that person should not be called a *bodhisattva,* in whom the perception of the self prevails, in whom the perception of being or the perception of soul or the perception of person prevails.

4. "Again, Subhūti, a gift should not be given by a *bodhisattva* who is committed to an object; a gift should not be given by one who is committed to anything; a gift should not be given by one who is committed to material form, to sound, to smell, to taste, to touch, and to concepts. Subhūti, a gift should be given by a *bodhisattva,* a great being, so that there will be no commitment to even a perception of object. What is the reason for this? Whosoever, Subhūti, gives a gift without being committed, it is not easy, Subhūti, to assess the measure of his heap of merit. What do you think, Subhūti, is it easy to measure the extent of the space in the eastern direction?"

Subhūti said, "No indeed, O Fortunate One." . . .

[30] The Fortunate One said: "Even so, Subhūti, a *bodhisattva* who gives a gift without commitment, it is not easy to assess the measure of his heap of merit. In the same way, Subhūti, should a gift be given by one who has embarked on the *bodhisattva* way so that there will be no commitment even to a perception of object.

5. "What do you think, Subhūti, should the Tathāgata be perceived through the possession of characteristics?"

Subhūti said: "No, indeed, O Fortunate One, the Tathāgata should not be perceived through the possession of characteristics. What is the reason for this? O Fortunate One, what has been declared by the Tathāgata, as possession of characteristics, that itself is a possession of non-characteristics."[4]

When this has been said, the Fortunate One said thus to the venerable Subhūti: "Subhūti, the extent to which there is possession of characteristics, to that extent there is confusion; the extent to which there is possession of non-characteristics, to that extent there is no confusion, and therefore the Tathāgata should be perceived through the characteristics of non-characteristics."

6. When this has been said, Subhūti said thus to the Fortunate One: "Will there be any beings in the future period, in the last time, in the last epoch, in the last 500 years during which time the destruction of the genuine doctrine takes place, who, when these and similar statements of the discourses are being preached, will produce a true perception?"

The Fortunate One said: "Subhūti, do not say thus. There will be beings in the future period, in the last time, in the last epoch, in the last 500 years during which time the destruction of the genuine doctrine takes place, who, when these and similar statements of the discourses are being preached, will produce a true perception. Furthermore in the future period, in the last time, in the last epoch, in the last 500 years during which time the destruction of the genuine doctrine takes place, [31] there will be *bodhisattvas,* the great beings, endowed with good qualities, possessed of virtues and wisdom who, when these and similar statements of the discourses are being preached, will produce a true perception. And again, Subhūti, these *bodhisattvas,* the great beings, are not those who have been associated with a single enlightened one and not those who have planted the roots of the good under a single enlightened one; instead they are those who have been associated with many hundreds and thousands of enlightened ones, and have planted the roots of the good under many hundreds and thousands of enlightened ones, such that when these and similar statements of the discourses are being preached, will obtain even a single serenity of thought. Subhūti, they have been known by the Tathāgata with the knowledge of enlightenment; they have been seen by the Tathāgata with the eye of enlightenment; they have been fully comprehended by the Tathāgata. And they all, Subhūti, will accumulate and obtain an immeasurable and incalculable heap of merit. What is the reason for this? For those *bodhisattvas,* the great beings, no perception of self prevails, no perception of being, no perception of soul, no perception of person prevails. For those *bodhisattvas,* the great beings, Subhūti, not even a perception of elements prevails, and similarly, no perception of non-elements. For them, Subhūti, no particular perception nor non-perception prevails. What is the reason for this? If, Subhūti, for those *bodhisattvas,* the great beings, a perception of elements were to prevail, that itself will be for them seizing of a self, will be a seizing of a being, a seizing of a soul, a seizing of a person. If a perception of non-elements were to prevail, that itself will be for them seizing of a self, will be a seizing of a being, a seizing of a soul, a seizing of a person. [32] What is the reason for this? Again by a *bodhisattva,* a great being, Subhūti, an element should not be seized upon, nor a non-element. Therefore, this word has been expressed by the Tathāgata: 'By those who know the doctrinal mode as being comparable to a raft an element has to be abandoned, not to speak of a non-element.'"[5]

7. Again the Fortunate One said thus to venerable Subhūti: "What do you think, Subhūti, is there some element that has been fully known by the Tathāgata as 'unsurpassed perfect enlightenment' or has some element been taught by the Tathāgata?'"

When this was said, venerable Subhūti said thus to the Fortunate One: "O Fortunate One, as I understand the meaning of what has been said by the Fortunate One, there is not some element that has been fully known by the Tathāgata as 'unsurpassed perfect enlightenment' and there is no element that has been taught by the Tathāgata. What is the reason for this? Whatever is that element fully known or taught by the Tathāgata, that should not be grasped, should not be spoken of excessively,[6] [33] it is not an element, not a non-element. What is the reason for this? The noble persons are those who have cultivated the dispositionally unconditioned."[7] . . .

9a. "What do you think, Subhūti? [34] Would it occur to one who has entered the stream:[8] 'The fruit of the stream-entrance has been attained by me'?"

Subhūti said: "It is not so, Fortunate One, it does not occur to one who has entered the stream: 'The fruit of stream entrance has been attained by me.' What is the reason for this? Fortunate One, he has not attained any element, hence called 'one who has entered the stream.' He is not one who has attained material form, one who has not attained sound, smell, taste, touch, and concepts. Therefore he is called 'one who has entered the stream.' Fortunate One, if it occurs to one who has entered the stream: 'stream entrance has been attained by me,' that itself will be for him the seizing of a self, the seizing of a being, the seizing of a soul, the seizing of a person."

9b. The Fortunate One said: "What do you think, Subhūti? Would it occur to the once-returner: 'The fruit of the once-returning has been attained by me'?"

Subhūti said: "It is not so Fortunate One, it does not occur to the once-returner: 'The fruit of the once-returning has been attained by me.' What is the reason for this? Fortunate One, he has not attained any element, hence called 'a once-returner.'"

9c. The Fortunate One said: "What do you think, Subhūti? Would it occur to the non-returner: 'The fruit of non-returning has been attained by me'?"

Subhūti said: "It is not so Fortunate One, it does not occur to the non-returner: 'The fruit of non-returning has been attained by me.' What is the reason for this? Fortunate One, he has not attained any element, hence called 'a non-returner.'"

9d. The Fortunate One said: "What do you think, Subhūti? Would it occur to the worthy one: 'Worthiness has been attained by me'?"

[35] Subhūti said: "It is not so Fortunate One, it does not occur to the worthy one: 'Worthiness has been attained by me.' What is the reason for this? Fortunate One, there is no element named 'worthy one,' hence called 'a worthy one.' Fortunate One, if it occurs to the worthy one: 'Worthiness has been attained by me,' that itself will be for him the seizing of a self, the seizing of a being, the seizing of a soul, the seizing of a person.

9e. "What is the reason for this? O Fortunate One, I have been designated as the chief among those who dwell in peace by the Tathāgata, the Worthy One, the Perfectly Enlightened One. Fortunate One, I am a worthy one, one who has abandoned lust. Fortunate One, if it were to occur to me: 'I am a worthy one, one who has abandoned lust.' Fortunate One, if it were to occur to me: 'Worthiness has been attained by me,' the Tathāgata would not declare of me: 'Subhūti, the son of family, who is the chief among those who dwell in peace, does not live anywhere.' Therefore, it is said: 'Dweller in peace, dweller in peace.'" . . .

12. "Subhūti, in whatever region of this earth, [someone], having taken at least a stanza of four lines from this doctrinal mode, were to teach and explain, that region of earth will have become a shrine for the world together with gods, humans and the non-godly; what could be said of those who would retain this doctrinal mode in its entirety, who will recite, study and explain it in full detail to others? They, Subhūti, will come to be associated the exceedingly wondrous. In that region of the earth, Subhūti, a Teacher dwells or any other intelligent teacher should be stationed."

13a. When this was said, venerable Subhūti said thus to the Fortunate One: "Fortunate One, what is the name of this doctrinal mode and how can I retain it?"

When this was said, the Fortunate One said thus to venerable Subhūti: "Perfection of wisdom, Subhūti, is the name of this doctrinal mode, retain it thus. What is the reason for this? Whatever is the perfection of wisdom [38] spoken of by the Tathāgata, that itself is spoken of by the Tathāgata as non-perfection of wisdom. Therefore it is said: 'Perfection of wisdom.'

13b. "What do you think, Subhūti? Is there some doctrine which has been spoken of by the Tathāgata?"

Subhūti said: "It is not so, Fortunate One. There is not some doctrine which has been spoken of by the Tathāgata."

13c. The Fortunate One said: "What do you think, Subhūti? Whatever be the dust of the earth in this three thousandfold major world system—would they be many?"

Subhūti said: "Many, Fortunate One, many, Well-gone One, would be the dust of the earth. What is the reason for this? Whatever, Fortunate One, be that dust of the earth spoken of by the Tathāgata, that, Fortunate One, has been spoken as non-dust by the Tathāgata. Therefore it is said: 'Dust of the earth.' Whatever be the world system spoken of by the Tathāgata, that has been spoken of as non-system by the Tathāgata. Therefore it is called: 'World system.' "

13d. The Fortunate One said: "What do you think, Subhūti? Should the Tathāgata, the Worthy One, the perfectly Enlightened One, be perceived through the thirty-two characteristics of a great person?"

Subhūti said: "The Tathāgata, the Worthy One, the perfectly Enlightened One, should not be perceived through the thirty-two characteristics of a great person. What is the reason for this? Whatever, Fortunate One, are the thirty-two characteristics of a great person spoken of by the Tathāgata, they have been spoken by the Tathāgata as non-characteristics. Therefore it is said: 'Thirty-two characteristics of a great person.' "

[39] 13e. The Fortunate One said: "Whosoever, Subhūti, a woman or a man were to abandon, day after day, personal being equal to the sands of the river Gaṅgā, and so abandoning, would abandon personal being equal to the sands of the river Gaṅgā for an aeon, and whosoever were to, having taken at least a stanza of four lines from this doctrinal mode, and would teach and explain in detail to others, and this latter, on the basis of that, accumulate a greater heap of merit, immeasurable and incalculable." . . .

[40] 14b. "It is not difficult for me, Fortunate One, that I should place confidence and be drawn to thus doctrinal mode when it is being spoken. Whosoever beings in the future period, in the last time, in the last epoch, in the last 500 years during which time the destruction of the genuine doctrine takes place, who will pick up, retain, recite, study, and explain to others in detail this doctrinal mode, they will come to be associated with the exceedingly wondrous.

14c. "Furthermore, Fortunate One, to them the no perception of a self will prevail, no perception of a being, no perception of a soul, no perception of a person will prevail; and again to them no particular perception, no non-perception will prevail." . . .

14d. When this had been said, the Fortunate One said thus to venerable Subhūti: "Yes it is, Subhūti, yes it is. Those beings come to be associated with the exceedingly wondrous, Subhūti, who, when this discourse is being spoken of, will not tremble, not be agitated, will not fall into agitation. What is the reason for this? This ultimate perfection, [41] Subhūti, has been spoken by the Tathāgata, for example, as non-perfection. Subhūti, whatever ultimate perfection the Tathāgata speaks of, that an unlimited number of enlightened ones, fortunate ones also speak of, therefore, it is called 'ultimate perfection.'

14e. "Furthermore, Subhūti, whatever is the Tathāgata's perfection of patience, that itself is non-perfection. What is the reason for this? Subhūti, when the king of Kāliṅga cut my large limbs, small limbs, and flesh, there was for me no perception of a self or perception of a being or perception of a soul or perception of a person, not even a particular perception or non-perception. What is the reason for this? If, Subhūti, at that time there was for me the perception of a self, at that time there will be for me the perception of malevolence as well. If there were to be for me the perception of a being, perception of a soul, perception of a person, at that time there will be for me the perception of malevolence as well. That is the reason for this? I know through higher knowledge, Subhūti, 500 births of the past time, when I was a sage, Advocate of Patience. Then too for me there was no perception of a self, there was no perception of a being, no perception of a soul, no perception of a person. Therefore, on such occasions, having abandoned all perceptions, a thought in regard to the unsurpassable perfect enlightenment should be developed by a *bodhisattva,* the great being. A thought established on material form should not be produced; a thought established on sound, smell, taste, touch, concept should not be produced; a thought established on an element should not be produced; a thought established on a nonelement should be produced; a thought established on any place [42] should not be produced. What is the reason for this? Whatever is established, that is non-established. For this reason itself, the Tathāgata says: 'A gift should be given by a *bodhisattva* who is non-established; a gift should be given not by one who is established on material form, sound, smell, taste, touch, concepts.

14f. "Furthermore, Subhūti, for the welfare of all beings, such a renunciation of gifts should be practiced by the *bodhisttattva.* What is the reason for this? Whatever, Subhūti, be such perception of a being, that itself is non-perception. Whosoever thus be all beings spoken of by the Tathāgata, they indeed are non-beings. What is the reason for this? Tathāgata, Subhūti, is a speaker of the become, a speaker of the truth, speaker of the objective, speaker of the invariable; the Tathāgata is not a speaker of the unnecessary.

14g. "Furthermore, Subhūti, whatever doctrine that is fully known, taught, and reflected upon by the Tathāgata, therein there is no truth, no confusion. Subhūti, just as one who has entered the darkness, will not see something, so should a *bodhisattva* who is committed to an object be seen, who renounces gifts while being committed to an object. Subhūti, just as a man with vision, when the night becomes light, when the sun has risen, will see various material forms, so should a *bodhisattva* who is committed to a non-object be seen, who renounces gifts while being committed to a non-object.

14h. "Furthermore, Subhūti, whosoever son or daughter of family [43] to pick up this doctrinal mode, retain, recite, study, and explain to others in detail, Subhūti, these have been known by the Tathāgata through the knowledge of the enlightened one; Subhūti, these have been seen by the Tathāgata through the vision of the enlightened one; they have been thoroughly understood by the Tathāgata. Subhūti, all of these beings accumulate and acquire an immeasurable and incalculable heap of merit.

15a. "Furthermore, Subhūti, a woman or a man, in the morning, were to abandon personal beings equal to the sands of the river Gaṅgā, and similarly during midday, abandon personal beings equal to the sands of the river Gaṅgā, and in the evening, abandon personal beings equal to the sands of the river Gaṅgā, and in this manner abandon personal beings for many hundreds of thousands of millions of aeons, and someone would, on hearing this doctrinal mode, would not reject it, and this one will, on the basis of that accumulate a greater heap of merit, immeasurable and incalculable. What could be said of one who, having recorded it, pick it up, recite, study, and explain in detail to others?

15b. "Furthermore, Subhūti, this doctrinal mode is unthinkable and incomparable. And this doctrinal mode has been spoken of by the Tathāgata for the welfare of those beings who have set out on the best vehicle, for the welfare of those beings who have set out on the superior vehicle, and whosoever were to pick up this doctrinal mode, retain, recite, study, and [44] explain it in detail to others, these have been known by the Tathāgata through the knowledge of the enlightened one; Subhūti, these have been seen by the Tathāgata through the vision of the enlightened one; they have been thoroughly understood by the Tathāgata. Subhūti, all these beings come to possess an immeasurable heap of merit; come to possess an unthinkable, incomparable, measureless, and limitless heap of merit. All of them, Subhūti, will retain an equal share of the enlightenment. What is the reason for this? It is not possible, Subhūti, for this doctrinal mode to be heard by those with low dispositions; it is not possible for this doctrinal mode to be heard by those who hold a view of self, not by those who hold a view of being, not by those who hold a view of soul, not by those who hold a view of person. It is not possible for this doctrinal mode to be heard or taken up or retained or recited or studied by the beings who have taken a vow of non-*bodhisattva*. This situation is not evident." . . .

17a. Then the venerable Subhūti said thus to the Fortunate One. "How should one who has set out on the *bodhisattva* vehicle take a stand, how should one conduct oneself, how should one take control of thought?"

[47] The Fortunate One said: "One who has set out on the *bodhisattva* vehicle should produce a thought thus: 'All beings should, by me, made to be ultimately free in the sphere of freedom without residual objectivity. Even after having ultimately freed the beings, no particular being is ultimately freed. What is the reason for this? If, Subhūti, for a *bodhisattva* the perception of a being prevails, he should not be called a *bodhisattva*. If the perception of a soul or the perception of a person were to prevail, he should not be called a *bodhisattva*. What is the reason for this? Subhūti, a particular thing named 'one who has set out on the *bodhisattva* vehicle' does not exist." . . .

17e. "Suppose, Subhūti, there were to be a man endowed with a body, a huge body."

The venerable Subhūti said: "Whosoever is spoken of by the Tathāgata as 'endowed with body, a huge body,' that has been spoken of by the Tathāgata as non-body. Therefore it is said: 'Endowed with body, a huge body.' "

17f. The Fortunate One said: "It is so, Subhūti, whosoever *bodhisattva* were to say: "I will make beings ultimately free," he should not be called a *bodhisattva*. What is the reason for this Subhūti? Is there any particular thing that is called *bodhisattva?*"

Subhūti said: "No, Fortunate One, there is no particular thing that is called *bodhisattva.*"

The Fortunate One said: " 'Beings, beings,' Subhūti, have been spoken of by the Tathāgata as non-beings. Therefore it is said: 'Beings.' Therefore, the Tathāgata says: 'All things are without self, without being, without soul, without person.' " . . .

21a. The Fortunate One said, "What do you think, Subhūti? Does it occur to the Tathāgata: 'The doctrine has been preached by me'?"

Subhūti said: "It is not so, Fortunate One, it does not occur to the Tathāgata: 'The doctrine has been preached by me.' "

The Fortunate One said: "Subhūti, whosoever were to say: 'The doctrine has been preached by the Tathāgata,' he would be speaking falsehood, and he would be misrepresenting me by seizing on what is non-existent. What is the reason for this? 'Preaching the doctrine, preaching the doctrine,' Subhūti, there is no particular doctrine which receives the appellation as preaching of the doctrine. . . .

22. What do you think, Subhūti? Is there a particular thing that has been fully known by the Tathāgata as supreme and perfect enlightenment?"

Subhūti said: "Fortunate One, there is no particular thing that has been fully known by the Tathāgata as supreme and perfect enlightenment."

The Fortunate One said: "It is so, Subhūti, it is so. Therein even a minute thing is not evident, is not obtained. Therefore it is called 'supreme and perfect enlightenment.'

23. "Moreover, Subhūti, the doctrine is equitable, therein there is nothing inequitable. Therefore it is called 'supreme and perfect enlightenment.' Equitable, supreme, perfect enlightenment, because of the absence of a self, absence of a being, absence of a soul, absense of a person, is experienced through all the good phenomena. What is the reason for this? 'Good phenomena, good phenomena,' Subhūti, these have been spoken of by the Tathāgata as non-phenomenon. Therefore it is said: 'good phenomena.' . . .

25. "What do you think, Subhūti? Does it occur to the Tathāgata thus: 'Beings have been caused to be released by me.' Again, Subhūti, it should not be seen thus. What is the reason for this? There is no particular being who has been caused to be released by the Tathāgata. If, Subhūti, there were to be a being who has been caused to be released by the Tathāgata, that itself will be a seizing of a self for the Tathāgata, will be a seizing of a being, seizing of a soul, seizing of a person. Seizing of a self, Subhūti, is spoken of by the Tathāgata as non-seizing. It has been grasped by the foolish individual persons. 'Foolish individual persons,' Subhūti, [56] have been spoken of by the Tathāgata as non-persons. Therefore it is said: 'foolish individual persons.' . . .

27. "What do you think, Subhūti, was the supreme and perfect enlightenment fully known by the Tathāgata through the possession of characteristics? Subhūti, it should not be seen by you thus. What is the reason for this? It does not happen, Subhūti, that the supreme and perfect enlightenment is fully known by the Tathāgata through the possession of characteristics. Moreover, Subhūti, one should not say thus to you: [58] 'The destruction and annihilation of a particular thing has been expressed by those who have set out on the *bodhisattva* vehicle.' "

28. "Again, Subhūti, it should not be seen by you thus. What is the reason for this? The destruction and annihilation of a particular thing has not been expressed by those who have set out on the *bodhisattva* vehicle. Furthermore, Subhūti, whosoever son or daughter of family, having filled the world systems equal to the grains of sand of the river Gangā, and offers as a gift to the Tathāgatas, the worthy ones, the perfectly enlightened ones, and whosoever *bodhisattva* were to generate tolerance in regard to the things that are without self and not of the nature of arising,[9] this person, on the basis of that, indeed will accumulate a greater heap of merit, immeasurable,

incalculable. Yet again, Subhūti, a heap of merit should not be accumulated by a *bod-hisattva,* a great being."

The venerable Subhūti, said: "Fortunate One, should not a heap of merit be accumulated by a *bodhisattva?*"

The Fortunate One said: "Should be accumulated, Subhūti, but not seized upon. [59] Therefore it is said: 'Should be accumulated.' "[10] . . .

30b. "Whatever has been spoken of by the Tathāgata as the three thousandfold great world system, that has been spoken of by the Tathāgata as a non-system. Therefore it is said 'the three thousandfold great world system.' What is the reason for this? If, Fortunate One, there were to be a world system, that itself will be a seizing on to an objective lump; whatever seizing of an objective lump has been spoken of by the Tathāgata, [60] that has been spoken of by the Tathāgata as non-seizing. Therefore it is said: 'seizing of an objective lump.' "

The Fortunate One said: "Subhūti, a seizing of an objective lump is a non-usage, and should not be over-spoken. It is no thing; it is no non-thing. It has been grasped by foolish individual persons."

31a. "What is the reason for this? Whosoever, Subhūti, says thus: 'View of self has been spoken of by the Tathāgata; view of being, view of soul, view of person has been spoken of by the Tathāgata, when saying thus, would he be speaking rightly?"

Subhūti said: "It is not so, Fortunate One, it is not so, Well-gone One, he would not be speaking rightly. What is the reason for this? Fortunate One, whatever is that view of self spoken of by the Tathāgata, that has been spoken by the Tathāgata as non-view. Therefore it is said: 'view of self.' "

The Fortunate One said: "Even so, Subhūti, by one who has set out on the *bod-hisattva* vehicle all phenomena should be known, should be seen, [61] should be re-solved. So should be known, should be seen, and should be resolved that one does not set up a perception of a phenomenon. What is the reason for this? 'Perception of a phenomenon, perception of a phenomenon,' Subhūti, that has been spoken of by the Tathāgata as non-perception. Therefore it is said: 'perception of a phenomenon.'

32a. "Furthermore, Subhūti, whosoever *bodhisattva,* a great being, having filled this world system with the seven gems, were to offer as gift to the Tathāgatas, the worthy ones, the perfectly enlightened ones, and whosoever son or daughter of family, having picked up at least a stanza of four lines from this 'perfection of wisdom' doctrinal mode, retain it, teach it, recite, study, and explain in detail to others, this person will, on the basis of that, accumulate a greater heap of merit, immeasurable and incalculable. How should one explain? So that one does not make known. Therefore it is said: 'should explain.' "

As stars, an eye-disease, a lamp,
An illusion, a dew drop, a bubble,
A dream, a lightening, a cloud,
So should be seen the dispositionally conditioned.

32b. The Fortunate One said thus. Delighted, the elder[11] Subhūti, those monks, nuns, male and female lay disciples, and those *bodhisattvas,* the world together with gods, humans, the non-godly, the *gandharvas*[12] rejoiced in what was spoken of by the Fortunate One.

---

[1]The Sanskrit text of this translation was edited by Edward Conze, Rome: Is. M. E. O, 1957.

[2]A term used to refer to one who has set out on a path to enlightenment, "a being intent on enlightenment."

[3]Conze refers to *A* 1.20 as a parallel passage but no such passage is found.

[4]We will continue to use the prefix non-, instead of no-, in order to emphasize the fact that what is involved here is an epistemological negation, rather than an ontological one. It would be comparable to the use of the terms non-theism and atheism.

[5]We assume that the terms *dharma* and *adharma* are not used in the sense in which the Buddha used them in "Discourse on the Simile of the Water-snake" (*Alazaddūpama-sutta, Majjhima-nikāya,* 1.135). In that context, the terms were used to refer to the good and the bad. The metaphysical reading of the term *dharma* as "element" came to be introduced by the Sarvāstivādins, and the present text is definitely a criticism of such a reading.

[6]The phrase, *anabhilāpya,* generally taken to mean "unspeakable," is better understood as implying excessive talk, for according to the Buddha "speaking overmuch" (*adhivutti*) is the reason for the 62 varieties of metaphysical views discussed by him in the "Discourse on Brahamā's Net" (*Brahmajāia-suttanta, D,* 1.13 ff.).

[7]The misinterpretation of the term *asaṁskṛta* (Pali, *asaṅkhata*) goes back to several decades, if not a century, of Buddhist studies in the modern world. As I have pointed out elsewhere that even a medieval interpreter of the word of the Buddha such as Buddhaghosa has interpreted the state of nirvana as one in which causation does not function (*hetuno abhāva. Visuddhimazza,* 509). It is such an understanding of nirvana that prompts Conze to translate the statement as "Because an Absolute exults the Holy Persons," (p. 70).

[8]First of the final four states attained by one who has entered the moral path. The other three are referred to below.

[9]This is a reference to the "element of freedom without a residual of objectivity" referred to earlier.

[10]These last two statements of the Buddha may generate a puzzle. First the Buddha is made to say that a heap of merit should not be accumulated. However a *bodhisattva,* if he were to perform his task, needs all the merit in the world. But the reason why the Buddha is saying that he should not try to accumulate is because he realizes that such accumulation can also lead to grasping. This is precisely the implication of his second statement.

[11]*Sthavira,* a strange title for someone who is supposed to be explaining the Mahāyāna, instead of Sthaviravāda.

[12]A term explained by some as "water-spirits" and by others as "musicians." In the early discourses, it is specifically used to refer to the surviving consciousness needed for the rebirth of a being.

PART II
What Is Good?

—————

INTRODUCTION

To clarify the nature of the good life, as noted in the opening introduction, it is useful to notice that the term *good,* as in

1. Such and such constitutes a *good* life for me,

is closely related to several other terms which appear in the following claims:

2. Such and such is the sort of life that would make me *happy.*
3. It would be in my best *interest* to live such and such a life.
4. Such and such is what it would be *important* to me to get out of life.
5. Such and such is what would make my life *worthwhile.*

Consequently, clarifying the nature of a good life simultaneously produces a better idea about happiness, about what is in my best interest, about what is important for me to get out of life, about what makes life worthwhile, and (due to the close relationship between interests and identities) about the self.

This part of the book focuses on the things that help make life go best—the good-making elements of life. Chapter 2 begins with an examination of the self whose life will improve. The readings consider the nature of the self and look at some of the normative implications of different views of the self. Chapter 3 considers some of the good-making attributes of people, such as pleasure, the moral virtues, and life itself. Finally, Chapter 4 discusses personal relationships, which, according to many people, are of central importance in a worthwhile life.

—————————

C H A P T E R   2

THE SELF

■ ══════ ■

INTRODUCTION

We have seen that the notions of our good, our interests, and our identity are tightly intertwined. In this chapter, which is the first of three that explore some of the things that make life worth living, we discuss the self whose life we seek to enhance. The readings in this chapter are grouped under three headings: the self as an individual, the self as a community, and selflessness. The first group of readings favors individualism in various senses of the term "individualism." The second group favors the idea that we should identify with the community. The third suggests that we are or ought to be selfless.

THE SELF AS INDIVIDUAL

Several positions concerning the self are considered by the first group of readings. Among these positions are the following: (1) By nature, each person just *is* an individual, separate from other individuals, and different to varying degrees. (2) It is *good* to be separate individuals who differ greatly. (3) Each individual must *decide* whether to prize individuality; it is up to each of us to decide whether we will try to differ greatly from others and whether it is good to stand out.

1.   WE ARE INDIVIDUALS: LOCKE AND SACKS ON IDENTITY AND MEMORY

This section begins with John Locke's views concerning personal identity. Locke (1632–1704) was a British philosopher whose book *Essay Concerning Human Understanding* (1689) is an influential defense of empiricism, the view that knowledge is derived from the senses. Locke's *Two Treatises of Government* (1690) is an influential contribution to the natural law tradition in political philosophy. Our selection, "Of Identity and Diversity," is from his *Essay*. In our selection Locke asks What is it to *be* a person? and What is it for a person to *remain in existence*?

The Person

Like his predecessor, the French philosopher René Descartes (1596–1650), Locke equated being a person with having consciousness. To be a person is to have reflective awareness, a kind of awareness that allows a person to "consider itself as itself, the same thinking thing, in different times and places" (Section 9).

Locke finds that he is unsure what things are capable of reflective awareness. The two main candidates are *spirits*, which are collections of immaterial constituents, and *human beings*, which are compositions of material substances that exhibit the functional organization typical of human bodies. Locke's contemporaries would probably have described a person as Descartes did: a conscious, indivisible (and hence indestructible) immaterial substance with private introspective access to itself. Locke's own view was heavily influenced by Descartes, but he finds himself unsure about the existence of, and nature of, particular spirits. Locke presses a skeptical point: For all we know, God might endow material things with the power of reflection. Nor can we rule out the possibility that spirits are composed of immaterial particles which are gradually replaced with new immaterial particles, in much the same way that the material particles out of which the body is composed are gradually replaced. So for all we know, people could be purely material things or changing immaterial things. In fact, if a parrot had the power of reflective awareness, it would be a person, too (although it would not be a human being). Locke's own best guess is that people are combinations of spirits and material bodies that are in "vital union" one with the other. Thus, limbs are as much a part of a person as are the constituents of the spirit; so long as each remains "vitally united" with the whole.

The Same Person

So far we have said that a person is anything capable of reflective awareness. But what is it for a person to remain in existence? In order to state Locke's answer to this question, it will be useful to introduce the notion of a temporal stage. Consider the *copy* of the book *Living Well* that you own. It is not the same thing as the book itself, which you do not own. Your copy has had a history before you came to read it today, and its history will continue after you put it down. It has been the same book copy, even though it certainly has undergone changes, some large and some small. Part of the ordinary notion of book copies assumes that they persist through time and survive many changes until finally they undergo such drastic changes that they cease to exist. A book copy cannot continue to exist once it is burned to ashes. It also could not continue to exist if, mysteriously, it were transformed into a duck. The book copy exists throughout its entire history, but we may also refer to arbitrarily selected *stages* of the book copy's history. These are its temporal stages, and a convenient description says that as a temporally extended thing, the book is the collection of its temporal stages.

Just as books have temporal stages (or book stages, for short), so people have temporal stages, for they, too, are temporally extended things. Now we may restate the question: What does it take for a later person stage to be part of the same continuing person as an earlier person stage?

Locke gives his answer in Section 9: Person Stage A is part of the same continuing person as later Stage B just in case B can remember being reflectively aware of an experience of which A was reflectively aware. This principle, Locke's criterion for personal identity, is called the *memory criterion*. He notes that the criterion for personal identity is quite different from the criterion of identity for human beings. According to Locke, a human being's identity reduces to that of the body, and the criterion for bodily identity is as follows: Body Stage A is part of the same continuing body as later body Stage B just in case B is spatio-temporally continuous with A, that is, an unbroken series of body stages link A and B, and the earlier stages are causally responsible for the existence of the later stages in the usual way.

By saying what it is for future stages to be part of the same continuing person as past stages, Locke's criterion also says how to tell someone apart from other people. Right now, I have introspective access to my own thoughts and memories, but not to yours; as new stages are added to my life, I will retain this access to many of my current thoughts and memories, but I will never have introspective access to yours. Thus, on Locke's view, one continues to be the same person only insofar as one can reach back into one's past through recollection, and intentions and plans are directly inherited by future stages since one can recall them. Because intentions and plans are inherited, we can plan our lives as integrated projects that we cause to unfold over time.

The essay "A Matter of Identity" by neurologist Oliver Sacks helps to bring out the plausibility of Locke's view that memory is critical to identity, but it can also reveal apparent paradox in Locke's view. Sacks writes about one of his patients, Mr. Thompson, whose capacity for short-term memory was destroyed by Korsakov's disease. Mr. Thompson is able to hold new experiences in mind only for moments before they are gone. Without the ability to add to his store of memories, he seems frozen in time, unable to extend his history; he seems unable to add new person stages to his *self*, and in that way he has ceased to be a continuing being. But if Mr. Thompson's history ends with his accident, then who is the confused man after the accident? In a powerful way, Sacks also brings out how Mr. Thompson's loss robs the man of his ability to feel, to connect with others, and to sense the importance of the events going on around him.

2. INDIVIDUALISM: NIETZSCHE

On Locke's view we are separate, continuing individuals. However, being an individual is not an accomplishment. Each person is separate from others because of the way he or she is built, and each continues to exist as a self so long as his or her faculties continue proper functioning. Essentially, then, Locke's "person" is the natural self discussed in the book's Introduction: The self is a temporally extended creature with the capacity for thought, memory, and decision making, as well as awareness of these thoughts and decisions. Personal identity is simply a factual matter, not something we decide for ourselves, and we will continue to exist, one and the same self, as long as our faculties continue proper functioning. Locke's view does not imply that an identity separate from others is a good thing—or a bad thing, for that matter. It is simply our situation.

Later philosophers called *existentialists* reject Locke's idea that an identity is simply something people find themselves with. According to them, there is a significant sense in which people construct their own identities. Two important existentialist philosophers are Friedrich Nietzsche and Jean-Paul Sartre.

Friedrich Nietzsche

Friedrich Nietzsche (1844–1900), a German philosopher, defended a highly individualistic and iconoclastic philosophy. He was deeply influenced by the German idealist philosopher Arthur Schopenhauer (1788–1860). In his earlier writings Nietzsche showed great respect for Schopenhauer, but his youthful enthusiasm soon dissipated, and he began to attack Schopenhauer's views, as well as the views of Eastern and Western philosophers who influenced Schopenhauer.

Nietzsche's initial enthusiasm for Schopenhauer was due to the latter's refreshing candor about the human condition. But Nietzsche deplored Schopenhauer's conclusion that life is not worth living, and he came to see Schopenhauer's pessimistic style of thinking in many of the religious and philosophical writings he encountered, especially Platonism, Buddhism, and Abrahamic religious thought, so he roundly criticized them, too. Nietzsche resolved to develop an approach that was simultaneously unflinchingly accurate and life-affirming. As he said in *Ecce Homo* (Chapter 3, Section 10), he took as his formula for greatness *amor fati*, love of fate: "that one wants nothing to be different, not forward, not backward, not in all eternity. Not merely bear what is necessary, still less conceal it. . . but love it."

Nietzsche devoted a great deal of effort to rooting out conceptions of the human situation that disparage life then exposing the despair that underlies them. Religious views, especially those of Christianity, were among his favorite targets. In Section 43 of *The Antichrist*, he suggested that when people glorify the afterlife, they reject and distrust their own lives:

> When one places life's center of gravity not in life but in the "beyond"—in nothingness—one deprives life of its center of gravity altogether. The great lie of personal immortality destroys all reason, everything natural in the instincts—whatever in the instincts is beneficent and life-promoting or guarantees a future now arouses mistrust. To live so, that there is no longer any *sense* in living, *that* now becomes the "sense" of life.

Nietzsche also consistently rejected the notion of the soul as well as the Cartesian view of the soul or self or subject as a free, conscious entity that is entirely separate from all of the things it is aware of (except itself), including the body. Nietzsche rejected Cartesian dualism, and thought of people as physical animals with built-in drives and desires. In large part, creating an identity is a matter of creating a unity out of these elements of the psyche, according to Nietzsche. We cannot be separated from our bodies and the motivations our bodies bring to us; and we must be conceived as parts of the physical world we inhabit, not as immaterial things occupying a nonphysical realm. Nietzsche is especially concerned to attack dualist accounts that align the good on one side of a divide and the bad on the other. Blurring such lines is one of his ways of elevating the status of aspects of life that are often condemned and lowering the status of aspects of life that are given inflated respect.

Nietzsche often focused on features of life generally ignored, deplored, or misunderstood by people who reject it. He attempted to portray those features in a positive light. A key element in his picture was his theory of motivation: the will to power. According to Nietzsche, everyone seeks power; the will to power is an inborn motivation. However, the concept of power is somewhat open-ended, and different people view it in different ways. Nonetheless, power is often a matter of relative standing. Each individual wants to rise to a position of superiority to others; each wants to excel, to be great—although the particular dimensions along which people wish to stand out vary from person to person. Some pursue rather esoteric and refined aspirations. Some, for example, want to be great novelists or composers—which requires that they outdo others in novel or music writing. The power involved in such refined aspirations was Nietzsche's chief focus. The aspirations of others, such as those of pugilists and warriors, may be more crude, but are manifestations of the will to power notwithstanding.

A great individual redeems life, in Nietzsche's view. To see why life is worth living, people must understand that the advent of the great individual is life's denouement and its significance. Moreover, the truly great are never content with accomplishment; once they reach great heights, they set out to overcome themselves and others all over again. Unfortunately, the powerless masses align themselves against the great and the values of the great. Out of envy for and revenge against the powerful, according to Nietzsche, the impotent tend to adopt a "slave morality" whereby they invert the value system of the powerful: *noble* or *superior* they redefine as *evil*, and *mediocre* or *helpful to the weak* they redefine as *good*.

3. INDIVIDUALISM: JEAN-PAUL SARTRE

In his essay "Existentialism and Humanism," as well as in his book *Being and Nothingness*, the French philosopher Jean-Paul Sartre (1905–1980) defends an influential form of existentialism. Whereas Nietzsche and Sartre both emphasize the importance of self-creation, they do not share the same view of the self, self-interest, and various other things. Sartre's own position concerning the capacity for self-creation is in some ways more radical than Nietzsche's, and in other ways less radical. Sartre defines existentialism as the doctrine that existence precedes essence, by which slogan he means to suggest views about the nature of the self, the motivation of the self, morality, and the human condition. The following paragraphs briefly examine each view.

God and the Human Condition

One thing Sartre meant to suggest in his slogan is the idea that we were not created to serve any purpose—a view he shared with Nietzsche. Sartre noted that tools such as scissors are created to serve some purpose. For tools, essence or definitive purpose precedes existence. Sartre also noted that many people believe that God created people to serve some sort of purpose; on the theistic functionalist account of the good, human essence or definitive purpose precedes human existence. But Sartre denied the existence of a creator. People were not created by God; instead, they simply find themselves in existence, with a need to give themselves a definitive purpose.

The Self

Like Descartes and Locke, Sartre thought that each person is a being (separate from all other beings) capable of thought, memory, decision making, and reflective awareness.

Sartre also said that consciousness is completely transparent to itself, so that if, upon checking, we do not find a particular desire or thought in our minds, then it is not there. This view, which Sartre took over from Descartes, is one that Nietzsche would have rejected. Following Schopenhauer, Nietzsche argued that people often live in the grip of beliefs and motivations of which they are unaware, and Nietzsche developed many of the conceptual tools later used by Sigmund Freud, such as the unconscious mind, sublimation, projection, and suppression. Sartre, by contrast, is deeply critical of the Freudian perspective on the unconscious.

However, unlike Descartes and Locke, Sartre emphasized the need for self-creation, but of course we do not make ourselves into the natural selves which we are; that is, we do not make ourselves into beings capable of consciousness and thought, for example. On Sartre's view, the self is a construction of consciousness. Through individual consciousness, each person is capable of establishing an identity, largely by choosing a life plan as well as the beliefs, values, and commitments on which that life plan is based. However, in constructing the self, one must accept that consciousness has a different kind of existence than does the body and the various objects of the world. Consciousness exists "for-itself," whereas each thing that we are conscious *of*—each of the objects of consciousness—exists "in-itself." They differ mainly because an in-itself is a part of the causal order, while a for-itself is free and self-determining. On Sartre's view, people are largely free to define themselves as they wish, so long as they view the self as continuous with consciousness, that is, so long as they acknowledge that the self is free and self-determining. That we are self-creating is one of the things Sartre means by "existence precedes essence."

The Self's Motivation

Sartre's slogan that existence precedes essence also suggests a third point: People sculpt subjective selves through completely free choices not causally determined by context or even by a pre-existing human nature. Here Sartre's position differs substantially from Nietzsche's, who thought that to develop identities, people must somehow come to terms with the raw materials of human nature, involving various sorts of motivations summed up in the phrase, "will to power." Sartre seems to have thought that people need not allow themselves to be influenced by in-built drives. Sartre even downplays the influence of emotions. He portrays the emotions behaviorally, claiming that individuals choose whether or not to display an emotion by choosing behavior. For example, one displays fear (or doesn't) when one chooses to run from danger (or not).

The Subjectivity of Value

A fourth point Sartre wishes to make through his slogan is the subjectivity of values. When we adopt the values and commitments that constitute the backbone of our selves, those values are inventions or choices, not discoveries. No objective values underlie the decisions through which we sculpt our selves. Prior to our choices, *nothing* determines that one way of life is better than another; instead, we *decide* what constitutes a worthwhile life.

Sartre's depiction of people as self-creating beings does not imply that separateness and difference from other people is a good thing; instead, it leaves the individual free to make this determination. In this way, Sartre's view diverges from Nietzsche's. However, Sartre suggests that we ought to be aware of the fact that separate individuals sculpt their selves by making radically free choices; to hide from individual responsibility for these choices by attempting to conceal responsibility from themselves would be "bad faith."

THE SELF AS COMMUNITY

A view that arises again and again in the history of ideas is the claim that individual identity is more or less identical to the identity of the community as a whole, and self-realization or the good is excelling in the role a person plays in the life of a community. A closely related view is the claim that we *derive* our identities from the community, and, as before, self-realization or the good is excelling at our roles in the community's life. As we have seen, Confucius defended the former position. The latter can be attributed to G. W. F. Hegel and his followers, such as the British idealist F. H. Bradley (1846–1924).

1.   WE ARE THE COMMUNITY: AMES ON CONFUCIANISM

Roger Ames, a sinologist at the University of Hawaii, attempts to correct a common misunderstanding of Confucianism that considers the relationship between the individual and the group as one of subordination: The individual is to subordinate personal interests to the interests of the group, requiring a selfless or self-abnegating attitude. As Ames points out, this characterization presupposes that individuals are selves with interests that clash with those of the group. However, this portrayal ignores the fact that selves are "irreducibly social" entities. The interests of people are not at odds with the interests of the group because people *are* the group. Hence, pursuing the group's interests is not selflessness or self-abnegation. As Ames points out, emphasizing the separate individual would be regarded as "retarded personal development" by the Confucian. The Confucian self, Ames says, is a "field of selves" or community in which human beings are brought together by participating in a unifying set of traditions or rituals. Central to those traditions is the patriarchal family, and the Confucian identifies with others largely by way of relating to them as an extended family.

2.   WE DERIVE OUR IDENTITY FROM THE COMMUNITY: HEGEL

According to the German idealist philosopher Georg Wilhelm Friedrich Hegel (1770–1831), when I identify myself, I set myself off from what I am not in a way I find plausible. However, Hegel adds, to believe in my identification of myself, I require the endorsement of other people: I require that members of my community identify me the way I propose to do. As a member of the community, I must give my endorsement to *them* if they are to identify themselves as *they* propose to do. Identity-giving is a reciprocal process. This *communal derivation* view of the self (as we might call it), which holds that success at taking on a particular identity requires others' endorsement of that self-identification, is related to Confucius' *communal identity* view, which holds that we just *are* the community. But the former view is certainly not encompassed by the latter: Even if one is in no sense a communal self, one might find it impossible to maintain an identity without the endorsement of others. Nonetheless, on both views, each person's identity is bound up with that of the community.

Hegel claims that a competitive process brings forth identities. No one wants to be the passive recipient of an identity assigned by others. Each wants to do the assigning, to be the subject determining identity, not an object or thing receiving it. Only then are we freely determining who we are. But to be subjects determining identity, we must master others, given that we require their endorsement of our self-identifications. So we struggle to be "masters" (existing in the mode of the "for-itself") who force others to take on our interpretations of ourselves and others, and they resist being "slaves" who are subjected to our interpretations (and who set aside their own "being-for-self").

SELFLESSNESS

Of the three groups of readings that discuss the self, the most puzzling will be the third and last group. These readings suggest that we are or ought to be selfless. More specifically, they examine the following related claims: (1) the self does not exist, or (2) it is best not to be a self.

1. THE SELF DOES NOT EXIST

Hume

In the appendix to his book *Treatise of Human Nature* (1739), the Scottish philosopher David Hume (1711–1776) raises doubts about the existence of the self. Hume begins by reminding the reader that as an empiricist, he thinks that we can sensibly use terms such as *self* only by association with ideas derived from "impressions" or sensory experiences. The term *self* has meaning only if one can perceive the self. Yet when we attempt to heed the experiencing and thinking self, we perceive only a collection of sensory experiences and thoughts that changes over time. We never perceive an entity or self that is distinct from these experiences; in particular, we never experience anything like a substance in which experiences inhere, nor anything else that brings together these experiences and not others (such as the experiences someone else is having). We seem to feel that our experiences are connected, for we feel a "determination of the thought to pass from one object to another." For example, when I think of the experience caused by a flame held against my skin, I feel determined to think of pain. However, we can perceive nothing that could explain this determination. But surely the self cannot be a mere collection of sensory experiences.

Hume challenges a notion that had seemed utterly straightforward to Descartes and Locke, and that was the cornerstone of their conception of the person: the agent who *has* the experiences—the thinker or reflective being to whom thoughts and reflections occur. Descartes and Locke thought that this agent could be directly inspected; indeed, they thought that every time we experience something, we simultaneously catch this agent in the act of experiencing.

Gautama

According to Gautama's doctrine of no-self, selves do not exist and human beings should not be understood as selves. What he has in mind seems to show close affinities to claims made by Locke and Hume. All three figures suggest that we have no good reason to believe that selves are immutable substances. Locke pointed out that bodies undergo gradual changes of materials, so that they are not immutable substances underlying our thoughts, and he suggested that we are unable to detect anything like a single immutable spiritual substance underlying our thoughts, either. Gautama's own doubts extend beyond selves. He questions the idea that animate or inanimate objects (such as chariots and bottles) can be thought of as substances in which properties inhere. Roughly speaking, Gautama meant to replace the ontology of substances and attributes with an ontology of events: the world consists of events occurring, rather than substances undergoing changes. In particular, a human being is a series of events occurring.

Parfit

Do Gautama's doubts about the ontology of substances and attributes show that there are no such things as selves? His doubts might well undermine some common ways of understanding selves, but the notion of the self probably can be rescued.

Derek Parfit, a contemporary British philosopher who teaches at Oxford University, takes an approach to the self that is somewhat in the spirit of Buddhism. According to Parfit, remaining the same person over time is not merely a matter of satisfying Locke's memory criterion, for retaining other psychological attributes is important to identity, as well. Remaining the same person involves retaining many sorts of psychological attributes. If this is what identify involves, then we can draw important conclusions about selves, and some of those conclusions challenge the ordinary notion of the self. Ordinarily, remaining the same person is an all or nothing matter: Either a future person stage is part of the same continuing person, or it is not. However, retaining psychological features is not an all or nothing matter. It is a matter of degree: Desires, intentions, and capacity to recall the past, etc., gradually change over time, so that the psychological profile of one person stage will probably resemble that of a later one less than will the profile of a intermediate stage. Since people retain psychological features to varying degrees, they stay the same people to varying degrees. Consequently, they ought to replace the ordinary all or nothing notion of the self with a new conception. It is useful to distinguish future selves from present selves when the psychological profile of future selves comes to differ substantially from that of present selves. Since distantly future selves may be quite unlike our present selves, it is entirely possible that my present self will resemble *your* present self, and other selves around me, about as much as it resembles my future self. Consequently, Parfit suggests, it can be a mistake to emphasize separateness from others. Moreover, if we stop taking the line between different persons seriously, we will have grounds for embracing utilitarianism. Among other things, utilitarians claim that one person's benefits can justify another person's burdens when the benefit is greater than the burden. Many of us are inclined to deny this claim, but we are also inclined to say that the benefits of my future self can justify the burdens of my present self, thus relying heavily on the significance of the boundaries between lives.

2.   IT IS BEST NOT TO BE A SELF

Gautama's no-self doctrine was not merely a denial of the existence of selves, as selves are ordinarily understood. Denying that point, as said earlier, leaves open the possibility of revising our notion of the selves we take ourselves to be. Gautama also suggests that once we adjust our concerns in life somewhat, we will have no good reason to find a defensible notion of the self. We will be better off selfless.

One important reason it is best to accept selflessness is doing so reduces the importance of remaining in existence, which in turn eliminates concern about mortality: If you do not value existing tomorrow, you will not care about the prospect of dying tonight. In fact, as Gautama adds, accepting selflessness precludes applying the concept of death to ourselves, for death applies only to things that exist over time and that at some point no longer continue.

To position ourselves so that we can accept the no-self doctrine, we must eliminate any commitments that might lead us to emphasize the importance of remaining in existence. We must drop desires that can be satisfied only if we remain in existence over an extended period of time, such as the desire to become a medical researcher or to raise a family. Without such desires, we will cease to care about the continued existence of the self, and as a consequence we will be incapable of selfishness. However, we will also lose the capacity to care about the well-being of others: If we took an interest in the welfare of others, we would have a powerful motivation to remain alive so that we could help them.

Questions for Reflection

1. Locke suggests that later selves deserve less blame for crimes committed by their earlier selves. Is he correct in this assertion?

2. Is Mr. Thompson (discussed by Oliver Sacks) a person? Does he have a continuing identity? What does the case of Mr. Thompson suggest about the relationship between being a person and having a continuing identity?

3. After condemning the "priestly caste" in Section 6 of his first essay in the *Genealogy*, Nietzsche adds that "it was on the soil of this *essentially dangerous* form of human existence, the priestly form, that man first became an *interesting animal*." Explain what Nietzsche means and evaluate his claim.

4. Nietzsche gives a new interpretation to loving one's enemies in Section 10, saying that the noble "desires his enemy for himself, as his mark of distinction." Explain what Nietzsche means, and evaluate his claim that he has described the only way possible to genuinely love one's enemies.

5. Explain and evaluate Nietzsche's remark in Section 13 that the vengeful "maintain no belief more ardently than the belief that the strong man is free to be weak and the bird of prey to be a lamb—for thus they gain the right to make the bird of prey accountable for being a bird of prey."

6. What does Sartre mean when he says that "what we choose is always the better; and nothing can be better for us unless it is better for all"? Is this claim consistent with Sartre's moral subjectivism?

7. Evaluate Sartre's claim that "everything is indeed permitted if God does not exist, and man is in consequence forlorn."

8. Explain and evaluate Hegel's remark (in Section 187) that "the relation of the two self-conscious individuals is such that they prove themselves and each other through a life-and-death struggle."

9. Is Hume correct when he says that "when I turn my reflection on myself, I never can perceive this self without some one or more perceptions; nor can I ever perceive anything but the perception"? Are you a self? How do you know? What do you mean by the term *self*?

10. Gautama expresses skepticism about the self. Clarify his skeptical view, and evaluate it.

11. Is Gautama correct in suggesting that we would be better off if we were not selves? Nietzsche seems to think that it is a good idea to create selves. Is his view more plausible than Gautama's? Why or why not?

12. Which view of identity is most plausible: the self as individual, the self as community, or the no-self view? Explain.

Suggested Readings

On Identity and Individualism

Dewey, John. "Nature, Mind and the Subject." In *Experience and Nature.* New York: Dover, 1958.
———. "Time and Individuality." In *On Experience, Nature and Freedom.* New York: Liberal Arts Press, 1960.

Parfit, Derek. *Reasons and Persons.* Oxford: Clarendon Press, 1984.

Perry, John, ed. *Personal Identity.* Berkeley: University of California Press, 1975.

Rorty, Amelie, ed. *The Identities of Persons.* Berkeley: University of California Press, 1976.

On Existentialism

Cooper, David. *Existentialism: A Reconstruction.* Oxford: Oxford University Press, 1990.

Howells, C., ed. *The Cambridge Companion to Sartre.* Cambridge: Cambridge University Press, 1992.

Warnock, Mary. *Existentialism.* Oxford: Oxford University Press, 1970.

On Hegel

MacIntyre, Alasdair, ed. *Hegel: A Collection of Critical Essays.* New York: Anchor Books, 1972.

Singer, Peter. *Hegel.* Oxford: Oxford University Press, 1983.

Solomon, Robert. *In the Spirit of Hegel.* New York: Oxford University Press, 1983.

INDIVIDUALISM AND THE SELF

JOHN LOCKE

Of Identity and Diversity

1. Another occasion the mind often takes of comparing, is the very being of things; when, considering anything as existing at any determined time and place, we compare it with itself existing at another time, and thereon form the ideas of identity and diversity. When we see anything to be in any place in any instant of time, we are sure (be it what it will) that it is that very thing, and not another, which at that same time exists in another place, how like and indistinguishable soever it may be in all other respects: and in this consists identity, when the ideas it is attributed to vary not at all from what they were that moment wherein we consider their former existence, and to which we compare the present. For we never finding, nor conceiving it possible, that two things of the same kind should exist in the same place at the same time, we rightly conclude, that, whatever exists anywhere at any time, excludes all of the same kind, and is there itself alone. When therefore we demand whether anything be the same or no, it refers always to something that existed such a time in such a place, which it was certain at that instant was the same with itself, and no other. From whence it follows, that one thing cannot have two beginnings of existence, nor two things one beginning; it being impossible for two things of the same kind to be or exist in the same instant, in the very same place, or one and the same thing in different places. That, therefore, that had one beginning, is the same thing; and that which had a different beginning in time and place from that, is not the same, but diverse. That which has made the difficulty about this relation has been the little care and attention used in having precise notions of the things to which it is attributed.

2. We have the ideas but of three sorts of substances: 1. God. 2. Finite intelligences. 3. Bodies. First, God is without beginning, eternal, unalterable, and everywhere; and therefore concerning his identity there can be no doubt. Secondly, Finite spirits having had each its determinate time and place of beginning to exist, the relation to that time and place will always determine to each of them its identity, as long as it exists. Thirdly, The same will hold of every particle of matter, to which no addition or subtraction of matter being made, it is the same. For, though these three sorts of substances, as we term them, do not exclude one another out of the same place, yet we cannot conceive but that they must necessarily each of them exclude any of the same kind out of the same place; or else the notions and names of identity and diversity would be in vain, and there could be no such distinctions of substances, or anything else one from another. . . .

3. From what has been said, it is easy to discover what is so much inquired after, the principium individuationis; and that, it is plain, is existence itself, which determines a being of any sort to a particular time and place, incommunicable to two beings of the same kind. This, though it seems easier to conceive in simple substances or modes, yet, when reflected on, is not more difficult in compound ones, if care be taken to what it is applied: v.g., let us suppose an atom, i.e., a continued body under one immutable superfices, existing in a determined time and place; it is evident, that, considered in any instant of its existence, it is in that instant the same with itself. For, being at that instant what it is, and nothing else, it is the same, and so must continue as long as its existence is continued; for so long it will be the same, and no other. In like manner, if two or more atoms be joined together into the same mass, every one of those atoms will be the same, by the foregoing rule: and whilst they exist united together, the mass, consisting of the same atoms, must be the same mass, or the same body, let the parts be ever so differently jumbled. But if one of these atoms be taken away, or one new one added, it is no longer the same mass or the same body. In the state of living creatures, their identity depends not on a mass of the same particles, but on something else. For in them the variation of great parcels of matter alters not the identity: an oak growing from a plant to a great tree, and then lopped, is still the same oak; and a colt grown up to a horse, sometimes fat, sometimes lean, is all the while the same horse: though, in both these cases, there may be a manifest change of the parts; so that truly they are not either of them the same masses of matter, though they be truly one of them the same oak, and the other the same horse. The reason whereof is, that, in these two cases, a mass of matter, and a living body, identity is not applied to the same thing.

4. We must therefore consider wherein an oak differs from a mass of matter, and that seems to me to be in this, that the one is only the cohesion of particles of matter any how united, the other such a disposition of them as constitutes the parts of an oak; and such an organization of those parts as is fit to receive and distribute nourishment, so as to continue and frame the wood, bark, and leaves, &c., of an oak, in which consists the vegetable life. That being then one plant which has such an organization of parts in one coherent body, partaking of one common life, it continues to be the same plant as long as it partakes of the same life, though that life be communicated to new particles of matter vitally united to the living plant, in a like continued organization conformable to that sort of plants. For this organization being at any one instant in any one collection of matter, is in that particular concrete distinguished from all other, and is that individual life, which existing constantly from that moment both forwards and backwards, in the same continuity of insensibly succeeding parts united to the living body of the plant, it has that identity which makes the same plant, and all the parts of it, parts of the same plant, during all the time that they exist united in that continued organization, which is fit to convey that common life to all the parts so united.

5. The case is not so much different in brutes, but that any one may hence see what makes an animal and continues it the same. Something we have like this in machines, and may serve to illustrate it. For example, what is a watch? It is plain it is nothing but a fit organization or construction of parts to a certain end, which, when a sufficient force is added to it, it is capable to attain. If we would suppose this machine one continued body, all whose organized parts were repaired, increased, or diminished by a constant addition or separation of insensible parts, with one common life, we should have something very much like the body of an animal; with this difference, that, in an animal the fitness of the organization, and the motion wherein life consists, begin together, the motion coming from within; but in machines, the force coming sensibly from without, is often away when the organ is in order, and well fitted to receive it.

6. This also shows wherein the identity of the same man consists; viz., in nothing but a participation of the same continued life, by constantly fleeting particles of matter, in succession vitally united to the same organized body. . . .

7. It is not therefore unity of substance that comprehends all sorts of identity, or will determine it in every case; but to conceive and judge of it aright, we must consider what idea the word it is applied to stands for: it being one thing to be the same substance, another the same man, and a third the same person, if person, man, and substance, are three names standing for three different ideas; for such as is the idea belonging to that name, such must be the identity; which, if it had been a little more carefully attended to, would possibly have prevented a great deal of that confusion which often occurs about this matter, with no small seeming difficulties, especially concerning personal identity, which therefore we shall in the next place a little consider.

8. An animal is a living organized body and consequently the same animal, as we have observed, is the same continued life communicated to different particles of matter, as they happen successively to be united to that organized living body. . . .

9. This being premised, to find wherein personal identity consists, we must consider what person stands for; which, I think, is a thinking intelligent being, that has reason and reflection, and can consider itself as itself, the same thinking thing, in different times and places; which it does only by that consciousness which is inseparable from thinking, and, as it seems to me, essential to it: it being impossible for any one to perceive without perceiving that he does perceive. When we see, hear, smell, taste, feel, meditate, or will anything, we know that we do so. Thus it is always as to our present sensations and perceptions: and by this every one is to himself that which he calls self; it not being considered, in this case, whether the same self be continued in the same or divers substances. For, since consciousness always accompanies thinking, and it is that which makes every one to be what he calls self, and thereby distinguishes himself from all other thinking things: in this alone consists personal identity, i.e., the sameness of a rational being; and as far as this consciousness can be extended backwards to any past action or thought, so far reaches the identity of that person; it is the same self now it was then; and it is by the same self with this present one that now reflects on it, that that action was done.

10. But it is further inquired, whether it be the same identical substance? This, few would think they had reason to doubt of, if these perceptions, with their consciousness, always remained present in the mind, whereby the same thinking thing would be always consciously present, and, as would be thought, evidently the same to itself. But that which seems to make the difficulty is this, that this consciousness being interrupted always by forgetfulness, there being no moment of our lives wherein we have the whole train of all our past actions before our eyes in one view, but even the best memories losing the sight of one part whilst they are viewing another; and we sometimes, and that the greatest part of our lives, not reflecting on our past selves, being intent on our present thoughts, and in sound sleep having no thoughts at all, or at least none with that consciousness which remarks our waking thoughts; I say, in all these cases, our consciousness being interrupted, and we losing the sight of our past selves, doubts are raised whether we are the same thinking thing, i.e., the same substance or no. Which, however reasonable or unreasonable, concerns not personal identity at all: the question being, what makes the same person, and not whether it be the same identical substance, which always thinks in the same person; which, in this case, matters not at all: different substances, by the same consciousness (where they do partake in it) being united into one person, as well as different bodies by the same life are united into one animal, whose identity is preserved in that change of substances by the unity of one continued life. For it being the same consciousness that makes a man be himself to himself, personal identity depends on that only, whether it be annexed solely to one individual substance, or can be continued in a succession of several substances. For as far as any intelligent being can repeat the idea of any past action with the same consciousness it had of it at first, and with the same consciousness it has of any present action; so far it is the same personal self. . . .

11. That this is so, we have some kind of evidence in our very bodies, all whose particles, whilst vitally united to this same thinking conscious self, so that we feel when they are touched and are affected by, and conscious of good or harm that happens to them, are a part of ourselves; i.e., of our thinking conscious self. Thus, the limbs of his body are to every one a part of himself; he sympathizes and is concerned for them. Cut off a hand, and thereby separate it from that consciousness he had of its heat, cold, and other affections, and it is then no longer a part of that which is himself, any more than the remotest part of matter. Thus, we see the substance whereof personal self consisted at one time may be varied at another, without the change of personal identity; there being no question about the same person, though the limbs which but now were a part of it, be cut off.

12. But the question is, "Whether, if the same substance, which thinks, be changed, it can be the same person; or, remaining the same, it can be different persons?"

And to this I answer: First, This can be no question at all to those who place thought in a purely material animal constitution, void of an immaterial substance. For, whether their supposition be true or no, it is plain they conceive personal identity preserved in something else than identity of substance; as animal identity is preserved in identity of life, and not of substance. And therefore those who place thinking in an immaterial substance only, before they can come to deal with these men, must show why personal identity cannot be preserved in the change of immaterial substances, or variety of particular immaterial substances, as well as animal identity is preserved in the change of material substances, or variety of particular bodies: unless they will say, it is one immaterial spirit that makes the same life in brutes, as it is one immaterial spirit that makes the same person in men; which the Cartesians at least will not admit, for fear of making brutes thinking things too.

13. But next, as to the first part of the question, "Whether, if the same thinking substance (supposing immaterial substances only to think) be changed, it can be the same person?" I answer, that cannot be resolved, but by those who know what kind of substances they are that do think, and whether the consciousness of past actions can be transferred from one thinking substance to another. I grant, were the same consciousness the same individual action, it could not: but it being a present representation of a past action, why it may not be possible that that may be represented to the mind to have been, which really never was, will remain to be shown. And therefore how far the consciousness of past actions is annexed to any individual agent, so that another cannot possibly have it, will be hard for us to determine, till we know what kind of action it is that cannot be done without a reflex act of perception accompanying it, and how performed by thinking substances, who cannot think without being conscious of it. But that which we call the same consciousness, not being the same individual act, why one intellectual substance may not have represented to it, as done by itself, what it never did, and was perhaps done by some other agent; why, I say, such a representation may not possibly be without reality of matter of fact, as well as several representations in dreams are, which yet whilst dreaming we take for true, will be difficult to conclude from the nature of things. And that it never is so, will by us, till we have clearer views of the nature of thinking substances, be best resolved into the goodness of God, who, as far as the happiness or misery of any of his sensible creatures is concerned in it, will not, by a fatal error of theirs, transfer from one to another that consciousness which draws reward or punishment with it. How far this may be an argument against those who would place thinking in a system of fleeting animal spirits, I leave to be considered. But yet, to return to the question before us, it must be allowed, that, if the same consciousness (which, as has been shown, is quite a different thing from the same numerical figure or motion in body) can be transferred from one thinking substance to another, it will be possible that two thinking substances may make but one person. For the same consciousness being preserved, whether in the same or different substances, the personal identity is preserved.

14. As to the second part of the question, "Whether the same immaterial substance remaining, there may be two distinct persons?" which question seems to me to be built on this, whether the same immaterial being, being conscious of the action of its past duration, may be wholly stripped of all the consciousness of its past existence, and lose it beyond the power of ever retrieving it again; and so as it were beginning a new account from a new period, have a consciousness that cannot reach beyond this new state. All those who hold pre-existence are evidently of this mind, since they allow the soul to have no remaining consciousness of what it did in that pre-existent state, either wholly separate from body, or informing any other body; and if they should not, it is plain experience would be against them. So that personal identity reaching no further than consciousness reaches, a pre-existent spirit not having continued so many ages in a state of silence, must needs make different persons. . . .

15. And thus may we be able, without any difficulty, to conceive the same person at the resurrection, though in a body not exactly in make or parts the same which he had here, the same consciousness going along with the soul that inhabits it. But yet the soul alone, in the change of bodies, would scarce to any one but to him that makes the soul the man, be enough to make the same man. For should the soul of a prince, carrying with it the consciousness of the prince's past life, enter and inform the body of a cobbler, as soon as deserted by his own soul, every one sees he would be the same person with the prince, accountable only for the prince's actions: but who would say it was the same man? The body too goes to the making the man. . . .

17. Self is that conscious thinking thing, whatever substance made up of, (whether spiritual or material, simple or compounded, it matters not,) which is sensible or conscious of pleasure and pain, capable of happiness or misery, and so is concerned for itself, as far as that consciousness extends. Thus every one finds, that, whilst comprehended under that consciousness, the little finger is as much a part of himself as what is most so. Upon separation of this little finger, should this consciousness go along with the little finger, and leave the rest of the body, it is evident the little finger would be the person, the same person, and self then would have nothing to do with the rest of the body. As in this case it is the consciousness that goes along with the substance, when one part is separate from another, which makes the same person, and constitutes this inseparable self; so it is in reference to substances remote in time. That with which the consciousness of this present thinking thing can join itself, makes the same person, and is one self with it, and with nothing else; and so attributes to itself, and owns all the actions of that thing as its own, as far as that consciousness reaches, and no further; as every one who reflects will perceive.

18. In this personal identity is founded all the right and justice of reward and punishment; happiness and misery being that for which every one is concerned for himself, and not mattering what becomes of any substance not joined to, or affected with that consciousness. For as it is evident in the instance I gave but now, if the consciousness went along with the little finger when it was cut off, that would be the same self which was concerned for the whole body yesterday, as making part of itself, whose actions then it cannot but admit as its own now. Though, if the same body should still live, and immediately from the separation of the little finger have its own peculiar consciousness, whereof the little finger knew nothing; it would not at all be concerned for it, as a part of itself, or could own any of its actions, or have any of them imputed to him. . . .

20. But yet possibly it will still be objected, suppose I wholly lose the memory of some parts of my life, beyond a possibility of retrieving them, so that perhaps I shall never be conscious of them again; yet am I not the same person that did those actions, had those thoughts that I once was conscious of, though I have now forgot them? To which I answer, that we must here take notice what the word I is applied to; which, in this case, is the man only. And the same man being presumed to be the same person, I is easily here supposed to stand also for the same person. But if it be possible for the same man to have distinct incommunicable consciousness at different times, it is past doubt the same man would at different times make different persons; which, we see, is the sense of mankind in the solemnest declaration of their opinions; human laws not punishing the mad man for the sober man's actions, nor the sober man for what the mad man did, thereby making them two persons: which is somewhat explained by our way of speaking in English, when we say such an one is not himself, or is beside himself; in which phrases it is insinuated, as if those who now, or at least first used them, thought that self was changed, the self-same person was no longer in that man. . . .

22. But is not a man drunk and sober the same person? why else is he punished for the fact he commits when drunk, though he be never afterwards conscious of it? Just as much the same person as a man that walks, and does other things in his sleep, is the same person, and is answerable for any mischief he shall do in it. Human laws punish both, with a justice suitable to their way of knowledge; because, in these cases, they cannot distinguish certainly what is real, what counterfeit: and so the ignorance in drunkenness or sleep is not admitted as a plea. For, though punishment be annexed to personality, and personality to consciousness, and the drunkard perhaps be not conscious of what he did, yet human judicatures justly punish him, because the fact is proved against him, but want of consciousness cannot be proved for him. . . .

OLIVER SACKS

A Matter of Identity

"What'll it be today?" he says, rubbing his hands. "Half a pound of Virginia, a nice piece of Nova?"

(Evidently he saw me as a customer—he would often pick up the phone on the ward, and say "Thompson's Delicatessen.")

"Oh Mr. Thompson!" I exclaim. "And who do you think I am?"

"Good heavens, the light's bad—I took you for a customer. As if it isn't my old friend Tom Pitkins . . . Me and Tom" (he whispers in an aside to the nurse) "was always going to the races together."

"Mr. Thompson, you are mistaken again."

"So I am," he rejoins, not put out for a moment. "Why would you be wearing a white coat if you were Tom? You're Hymie, the kosher butcher next door. No bloodstains on your coat though. Business bad today? You'll look like a slaughterhouse by the end of the week!"

Feeling a bit swept away myself in this whirlpool of identities, I finger the stethoscope dangling from my neck.

"A stethoscope!" he exploded. "And you pretending to be Hymie! You mechanics are all starting to fancy yourselves to be doctors, what with your white coats and stethoscopes—as if you need a stethoscope to listen to a car! So, you're my old friend Manners from the Mobil station up the block, come in to get your boloney-and-rye . . ."

William Thompson rubbed his hands again, in his salesman–grocer's gesture, and looked for the counter. Not finding it, he looked at me strangely again.

"Where am I?" he said, with a sudden scared look. "I thought I was in my shop, doctor. My mind must have wandered . . . You'll be wanting my shirt off, to sound me as usual?"

"No, not the usual. I'm *not* your usual doctor."

"Indeed you're not. I could see that straightaway! You're not my usual chest-thumping doctor. And, by God, you've a beard! You look like Sigmund Freud—have I gone bonkers, round the bend?"

"No, Mr. Thompson. Not round the bend. Just a little trouble with your memory—difficulties remembering and recognising people."

"My memory has been playing me some tricks," he admitted. "Sometimes I make mistakes—I take somebody for somebody else . . . What'll it be now—Nova or Virginia?"

So it would happen, with variations, every time—with improvisations, always prompt, often funny, sometimes brilliant, and ultimately tragic. Mr. Thompson would identify me—misidentify, pseudo-identify me—as a dozen different people in the course of 5 minutes. He would whirl, fluently, from one guess, one hypothesis, one belief, to the next, without any appearance of uncertainty at any point—he never knew who I was, or what and where *he* was, an ex-grocer, with severe Korsakov's, in a neurological institution.

He remembered nothing for more than a few seconds. He was continually disoriented. Abysses of amnesia continually opened beneath him, but he would bridge them, nimbly, by fluent confabulations and fictions of all kinds. For him they were not fictions, but how he suddenly saw, or interpreted, the world. Its radical flux and incoherence could not be tolerated, acknowledged, for an instant—there was, instead, this strange, delirious, quasi-coherence, as Mr. Thompson, with his ceaseless, unconscious, quick-fire inventions, continually improvised a world around him—an Arabian Nights world, a phantasmagoria, a dream, of ever-changing people, figures, situations—continual, kaleidoscopic mutations and transformations. For Mr. Thompson, however, it was not a tissue of ever-changing, evanescent fancies and illusion, but a wholly normal, stable, and factual world. So far as *he* was concerned, there was nothing the matter.

On one occasion, Mr. Thompson went for a trip, identifying himself at the front desk as the "Revd. William Thompson," ordering a taxi, and taking off for the day. The taxi-driver, whom we later spoke to, said he had never had so fascinating a passenger, for Mr. Thompson told him one story after another, amazing personal stories full of fantastic adventures. "He seemed to have been everywhere, done everything, met everyone. I could hardly believe so much was possible in a single life," he said. "It is not exactly a single life," we answered. "It is all very curious—a matter of identity."[1]

Jimmie G., another Korsakov's patient . . . had long since *cooled down* from his acute Korsakov's syndrome, and seemed to have settled into a state of permanent lostness (or, perhaps, a permanent now-seeming dream or reminiscence of the past). But Mr. Thompson, only just out of hospital—his Korsakov's had exploded just 3 weeks before, when he developed a high fever, raved, and ceased to recognise all his family—was still on the boil, was still in an almost frenzied confabulatory delirium (of the sort sometimes called "Korsakov's psychosis," though it is not really a psychosis at all), continually creating a world and self, to replace what was continually being forgotten and lost. Such a frenzy may call forth quite brilliant powers of invention and fancy—a veritable confabulatory genius—for such a patient *must literally make himself (and his world) up every moment*. We have, each of us, a life-story, an inner narrative—

whose continuity, whose sense, *is* our lives. It might be said that each of us constructs and lives, a "narrative," and that this narrative *is* us, our identities.

If we wish to know about a man, we ask "what is his story—his real, inmost story?"—for each of us *is* a biography, a story. Each of us *is* a singular narrative, which is constructed, continually, unconsciously, by, through, and in us—through our perceptions, our feelings, our thoughts, our actions; and, not least, our discourse, our spoken narrations. Biologically, physiologically, we are not so different from each other; historically, as narratives—we are each of us unique.

To be ourselves we must *have* ourselves—possess, if need be re-possess, our life-stories. We must "recollect" ourselves, recollect the inner drama, the narrative, of ourselves. A man *needs* such a narrative, a continuous inner narrative, to maintain his identity, his self.

This narrative need, perhaps, is the clue to Mr. Thompson's desperate tale-telling, his verbosity. Deprived of continuity, of a quiet, continuous, inner narrative, he is driven to a sort of narrational frenzy—hence his ceaseless tales, his confabulations, his mythomania. Unable to maintain a genuine narrative or continuity, unable to maintain a genuine inner world, he is driven to the proliferation of pseudo-narratives, in a pseudo-continuity, pseudo-worlds peopled by pseudo-people, phantoms.

What is it *like* for Mr. Thompson? Superficially, he comes over as an ebullient comic. People say, "He's a riot." And there *is* much that is farcical in such a situation, which might form the basis of a comic novel.[2] It *is* comic, but not just comic—it is terrible as well. For here is a man who, in some sense, is desperate, in a frenzy. The world keeps disappearing, losing meaning, vanishing—and he must seek meaning, *make* meaning, in a desperate way, continually inventing, throwing bridges of meaning over abysses of meaninglessness, the chaos that yawns continually beneath him.

But does Mr. Thompson himself know this, feel this? After finding him "a riot," "a laugh," "loads of fun," people are disquieted, even terrified, by something in him. "He never stops," they say. "He's like a man in a race, a man trying to catch something which always eludes him." And, indeed, he can never stop running, for the breach in memory, in existence, in meaning, is never healed, but has to be bridged, to be "patched," every second. And the bridges, the patches, for all their brilliance, fail to work—because they *are* confabulations, fictions, which cannot do service for reality, while also failing to correspond with reality. Does Mr. Thompson feel *this*? Or, again, what *is* his "feeling of reality"? Is he in a torment all the while—the torment of a man lost in unreality, struggling to rescue himself, but sinking himself, by ceaseless inventions, illusions, themselves quite unreal? It is certain that he is not at ease—there is a tense, taut look on his face all the while, as of a man under ceaseless inner pressure; and occasionally, not too often, or masked if present, a look of open, naked, pathetic bewilderment. What saves Mr. Thompson in a sense, and in another sense damns him, *is* the forced or defensive superficiality of his life: the way in which it is, in effect, reduced to a surface, brilliant, shimmering, iridescent, ever-changing, but for all that a surface, a mass of illusions, a delirium, without depth.

And with this, no feeling *that* he has lost feeling (for the feeling he has lost), no feeling *that* he has lost the depth, that unfathomable, mysterious, myriad-levelled depth which somehow defines identity or reality. This strikes everyone who has been in contact with him for any time—that under his fluency, even his frenzy, is a strange loss of feeling—that feeling, or judgment, which distinguishes between "real" and "unreal," "true" and "untrue" (one cannot speak of "lies" here, only of "non-truth"), important and trivial, relevant and irrelevant. What comes out, torrentially, in his ceaseless confabulation, has, finally, a peculiar quality of indifference . . . as if it didn't really matter what he said, or what anyone else did or said; as if nothing really mattered any more.

A striking example of this was presented one afternoon, when William Thompson, jabbering away, of all sorts of people who were improvised on the spot, said: "And there goes my younger brother, Bob, past the window," in the same, excited but even and indifferent tone, as the rest of his monologue. I was dumbfounded when, a minute later, a man peeked round the door, and said: "I'm Bob, I'm his younger brother—I think he saw me passing by the window." Nothing in William's tone or manner—nothing in his exuberant, but unvarying and indifferent, style of monologue—had prepared me for the possibility of . . . reality. William spoke of his brother, who *was* real, in precisely the same tone, or lack of tone, in which he spoke of the unreal—and now, suddenly, out of the phantoms, a real figure appeared! Further, he did not treat his younger brother as "real"—did not display any real emotion, was not in the least oriented or delivered from his delirium—but, on the contrary, instantly treated his brother *as* unreal, effacing him, losing him, in a further whirl of delirium—utterly different from the rare but profoundly moving times when Jimmie G. . . . met *his* brother, and while with him was unlost. This was intensely disconcerting to poor Bob—who said "I'm Bob, not Rob, not Dob," to no avail whatever. In the midst of confabulations—perhaps some strand of memory, of remembered kinship, or identity, was still holding (or came back for an instant)—William spoke of his *elder* brother, George, using his invariable present indicative tense.

"But George died 19 years ago!" said Bob, aghast.

"Aye, George is always the joker!" William quipped, apparently ignoring, or indifferent to, Bob's comment, and went on blathering of George in his excited, dead way, insensitive to truth, to reality, to propriety, to everything—insensitive too to the manifest distress of the living brother before him.

It was this which convinced me, above everything, that there was some ultimate and total loss of inner reality, of feeling and meaning, of soul, in William—and led me to ask the Sisters, as I had asked them of Jimmie G. "Do you think William *has* a soul? Or has he been pithed, scooped-out, de-souled, by disease?"

This time, however, they looked worried by my question, as if something of the sort were already in their minds: they could not say "Judge for yourself. See Willie in Chapel," because his wise-cracking, his confabulations continued even there. There is an utter pathos, a sad *sense* of lostness, with Jimmie G. which one does not feel, or feel directly, with the effervescent Mr. Thompson. Jimmie has *moods*, and a sort of brooding (or, at least, yearning) sadness, a depth, a soul, which does not seem to be present in Mr. Thompson. Doubtless, as the Sisters said, he had a soul, an immortal soul, in the theological sense; could be seen, and loved, as an individual by the Almighty; but, they agreed, something very disquieting had happened to him, to his spirit, his character, in the ordinary, human sense.

It is *because* Jimmie is "lost" that he *can* be redeemed or found, at least for a while, in the mode of a genuine emotional relation. Jimmie is in despair, a quiet despair (to use or adapt Kierkegaard's term), and therefore he has the possibility of salvation, of touching base, the ground of reality, the feeling and meaning he has lost, but still recognises, still yearns for . . .

But for William—with his brilliant, brassy surface, the unending joke which he substitutes for the world (which if it covers over a desperation, is a desperation he does not feel); for William with his manifest indifference to relation and reality caught in an unending verbosity, there may be nothing "redeeming" at all—his confabulations, his apparitions, his frantic search for meanings, being the ultimate barrier *to* any meaning.

Paradoxically, then, William's great gift—for confabulation—which has been called out to leap continually over the ever-opening abyss of amnesia—William's great gift is also his damnation. If only he could be *quiet*, one feels, for an instant; if only he could stop the ceaseless chatter and jabber; if only he could relinquish the deceiving surface of illusions—then (ah then!) reality might seep in; something genuine, something deep, something true, something felt, could enter his soul.

For it is not memory which is the final, "existential" casualty here (although his memory *is* wholly devastated); it is not memory only which has been so altered in him, but some ultimate capacity for feeling which is gone; and this is the sense in which he is "de-souled."

Luria speaks of such indifference as "equalisation"—and sometimes seems to see it as the ultimate pathology, the final destroyer of any world, any self. It exerted, I think, a horrified fascination on him, as well as constituting an ultimate therapeutic challenge. He was drawn back to this theme again and again—sometimes in relation to Korsakov's and memory, as in *The Neuropsychology of Memory*, more often in relation to frontal-lobe syndromes, especially in *Human Brain and Psychological Processes*, which contains several full-length case-histories of such patients, fully comparable in their terrible coherence and impact to "the man with a shattered world"—comparable, and, in a way, more terrible still, because they depict patients who do not realise that anything has befallen them, patients who have lost their own reality, without knowing it, patients who may not suffer, but be the most God-forsaken of all. Zazetsky (in *The Man with a Shattered World*) is constantly described as a *fighter*, always (even passionately) conscious of his state, and always fighting "with the tenacity of the damned" to recover the use of his damaged brain. But William (like Luria's frontal-lobe patients . . .) is so damned he does not know he is damned, for it is not just a faculty, or some faculties, which are damaged, but the very citadel, the self, the soul itself. William is "lost," in this sense, far more than Jimmie—for all his brio; one never feels, or rarely feels, that there is a *person* remaining, whereas in Jimmie there is plainly a real, moral being, even if disconnected most of the time. In Jimmie, at least, re-connection is *possible*—the therapeutic challenge can be summed up as "Only connect."

Our efforts to "re-connect" William all fail—even increase his confabulatory pressure. But when we abdicate our efforts, and let him be, he sometimes wanders out into the quiet and undemanding garden which surrounds the Home, and there, in its quietness, he recovers his own quiet. The presence of others, other people, excite and rattle him, force him into an endless, frenzied, social chatter, a veritable delirium of identity-making and -seeking; the presence of plants, a quiet garden, the non-human order, making no social or human demands upon him, allow this identity-delirium to relax, to subside; and by their quiet, non-human self-sufficiency and completeness allow him a rare quietness and self-sufficiency of his own, by offering (beneath, or beyond, all merely human identities and relations) a deep wordless communion with Nature itself, and with this the restored sense of being in the world, being real.

---

[1] A very similar story is related by Luria in *The Neuropsychology of Memory* (1976), in which the spell-bound cabdriver only realised that his exotic passenger was ill when he gave him, for a fare, a temperature chart he was holding. Only then did he realise that this Scheherazade, this spinner of 1001 tales, was one of "those strange patients" at the Neurological Institute.

[2] Indeed such a novel has been written. Shortly after "The Lost Mariner" was published, a young writer named David Gilman sent me the manuscript of his book *Croppy Boy*, the story of an amnesiac like Mr. Thompson, who enjoys the wild and unbridled license of creating identities, new selves, as he whims, and as he must—an astonishing imagination of an amnesiac genius, told with positively Joycean richness and gusto. I do not know whether it has been published; I am very sure it should be. I could not help wondering whether Mr. Gilman had actually met (and studied) a "Thompson"—as I have often wondered whether Borges'"Funes," so uncannily similar to Luria's Mnemonist, may have been based on a personal encounter with such a mnemonist.

FRIEDRICH NIETZSCHE

Untimely Meditations

Sometimes it is harder to accede to a thing than it is to see its truth; and that is how most people may feel when they reflect on the proposition: "Mankind must work continually at the production of individual great men—that and nothing else is its task." How much one would like to apply to society and its goals something that can be learned from observation of any species of the animal or plant world: that its only concern is the individual higher exemplar, the more uncommon, more powerful, more complex, more fruitful—how much one would like to do this if inculcated fancies as to the goal of society did not offer such tough resistance! We ought really to have no difficulty in seeing that, when a species has arrived at its limits and is about to go over into a higher species, the goal of its evolution lies, not in the mass of its exemplars and their wellbeing, let alone in those exemplars who happen to come last in point of time, but rather in those apparently scattered and chance existences which favourable conditions have here and there produced; and it ought to be just as easy to understand the demand that, because it can arrive at a conscious awareness of its goal, mankind ought to seek out and create the favourable conditions under which those great redemptive men can come into existence. But everything resists this conclusion: here the ultimate goal is seen to lie in the happiness of all or of the greatest number, there in the development of great communities; and though one may be ready to sacrifice one's life to a state, for instance, it is another matter if one is asked to sacrifice it on behalf of another individual. It seems to be an absurd demand that one man should exist for the sake of another man; "for the sake of all others, rather, or at least for as many as possible!" O worthy man! as though it were less absurd to let number decide when value and significance are at issue! For the question is this: how can your life, the individual life, receive the highest value, the deepest significance? How can it be least squandered? Certainly only by your living for the good of the rarest and most valuable exemplars, and not for the good of the majority, that is to say those who, taken individually, are the least-valuable exemplars. And the young person should be taught to regard himself as a failed work of nature but at the same time as a witness to the grandiose and marvellous intentions of this artist: nature has done badly, he should say to himself; but I will honour its great intentions by serving it so that one day it may do better.

By coming to this resolve he places himself within the circle of *culture*; for culture is the child of each individual's self-knowledge and dissatisfaction with himself. Anyone who believes in culture is thereby saying: "I see above me something higher and more human than I am; let everyone help me to attain it, as I will help everyone who knows and suffers as I do: so that at last the man may appear who feels himself perfect and boundless in knowledge and love, perception and power, and who in his completeness is at one with nature, the judge and evaluator of things." It is hard to create in anyone this condition of intrepid self-knowledge because it is impossible to teach love; for it is love alone that can bestow on the soul, not only a clear, discriminating and self-contemptuous view of itself, but also the desire to look beyond itself and to seek with all its might for a higher self as yet still concealed from it. Thus only he who has attached his heart to some great man is by that act *consecrated to culture*; the sign of that consecration is that one is ashamed of oneself without any accompanying feeling of distress, that one comes to hate one's own narrowness and shrivelled nature, that one has a feeling of sympathy for the genius who again and again drags himself up out of our dryness and apathy and the same feeling in anticipation for all those who are still struggling and evolving, with the profoundest conviction that almost everywhere we encounter nature pressing towards man and again and again failing to achieve him, yet everywhere succeeding in producing the most marvellous beginnings, individual traits and forms: so that the men we live among resemble a field over which is scattered the most precious fragments of sculpture where everything calls to us: come, assist, complete, bring together what belongs together, we have an immeasurable longing to become whole.

This sum of inner states is, I said, the first sign that one is consecrated to culture; now, however, I have to describe the *further* stage of this consecration, and I realize that here my task is more difficult. For now we have to make the transition from the inward event to an assessment of the outward event; the eye has to be directed outwards so as to rediscover in the great world of action that desire for culture it recognized in the experiences of the first stage just described; the individual has to employ his own wrestling and longing as the alphabet by means of which he can now read off the aspirations of mankind as a whole. But he may not halt even here; from this stage he has to climb up to a yet higher one; culture demands of him, not only inward experience, not only an assessment of the outward world that streams all around him, but finally and above all an act, that is to say a struggle on behalf of culture and hostility towards those influences, habits, laws, institutions in which he fails to recognize his goal: which is the production of genius.

Friedrich Nietzsche

On the Genealogy of Morals

FIRST ESSAY: "GOOD AND EVIL," "GOOD AND BAD"

4

The signpost to the *right* road was for me the question: what was the real etymological significance of the designations for "good" coined in the various languages? I found they all led back to the *same conceptual transformation*—that everywhere "noble," "aristocratic" in the social sense, is the basic concept from which "good" in the sense of "with aristocratic soul," "noble," "with a soul of a higher order," "with a privileged soul" necessarily developed: a development which always runs parallel with that other in which "common," "plebeian," "low" are finally transformed into the concept of "bad." . . .

5

With regard to *our* problem, which may on good grounds be called a *quiet* problem and one which fastidiously directs itself to few ears, it is of no small interest to ascertain that through those words and roots which designate "good" there frequently still shines the most important nuance by virtue of which the noble felt themselves to be men of a higher rank. Granted that, in the majority of cases, they designate themselves simply by their superiority in power (as "the powerful," "the masters," "the commanders") or by the most clearly visible signs of this superiority, for example, as "the rich," "the possessors" (this is the meaning of *arya*; and of corresponding words in Iranian and Slavic). But they also do it by a *typical character trait*: and this is the case that concerns us here. They call themselves, for instance, "the truthful"; this is so above all of the Greek nobility, whose mouthpiece is the Megarian poet Theognis.[1] The root of the word coined for this, *esthlos*,[2] signifies one who *is*, who possesses reality, who is actual, who is true; then, with a subjective turn, the true as the truthful: in this phase of conceptual transformation it becomes a slogan and catchword of the nobility and passes over entirely into the sense of "noble," as distinct from the *lying* common man, which is what Theognis takes him to be and how he describes him—until finally, after the decline of the nobility, the word is left to designate nobility of soul and becomes as it were ripe and sweet . . .

6

To this rule that a concept denoting political superiority always resolves itself into a concept denoting superiority of soul it is not necessarily an exception (although it provides occasions for exceptions) when the highest caste is at the same time the *priestly* caste and therefore emphasizes in its total description of itself a predicate that calls to mind its priestly function. It is then, for example, that "pure" and "impure" confront one another for the first time as designations of station; and here too there evolves a "good" and a "bad" in a sense no longer referring to station. One should be warned, moreover, against taking these concepts "pure" and "impure" too ponderously or broadly, not to say symbolically: all the concepts of ancient man were rather at first incredibly uncouth, coarse, external, narrow, straightforward, and altogether *unsymbolical* in meaning to a degree that we can scarcely conceive. The "pure one" is from the beginning merely a man who washes himself, who forbids himself certain foods that produce skin ailments, who does not sleep with the dirty women of the lower strata, who has an aversion to blood—no more, hardly more! On the other hand, to be sure, it is clear from the whole nature of an essentially priestly aristocracy why antithetical valuations could in precisely this instance soon become dangerously deepened, sharpened, and internalized; and indeed they finally tore chasms between man and man that a very Achilles of a free spirit would not venture to leap without a shudder. There is from the first something *unhealthy* in such priestly aristocracies and in the habits ruling in them which turn them away from action and alternate between brooding and emotional explosions, habits which seem to have as their almost invariable consequence that intestinal morbidity and neurasthenia which has afflicted priests at all times; but as to that which they themselvs devised as a remedy for this morbidity—must one not assert that it has ultimately proved itself a hundred times more dangerous in its effects than the sickness it was supposed to cure? Mankind itself is still ill with the effects of this priestly naïveté in medicine! Think, for example, of certain forms of diet (abstinence from meat), of fasting, of sexual continence, of flight "into the wilderness" (the Weir Mitchell isolation cure[3]—without, to be sure, the subsequent fattening and overfeeding which constitute the most effective remedy for the hysteria induced by the ascetic ideal): add to these the entire antisensualistic metaphysic of the priests that makes men indolent and overrefined, their autohypnosis in the manner of fakirs and Brahmins—Brahma used in the shape of a glass knob and a fixed idea—and finally the only-too-comprehensible satiety with all this, together with the radical cure for it, *nothingness* (or God—the desire for a *unio mystica* with God is the desire of the Buddhist for nothingness, Nirvana—and no more!). For with the priests *everything* becomes more dangerous, not only cures and remedies, but also arrogance, revenge, acuteness, profligacy, love, lust to rule, virtue, disease—but it is only fair to add that it was on the soil of this *essentially dangerous* form of human existence, the priestly form, that man first became *an interesting animal*, that only here did the human soul in a higher sense acquire *depth* and become *evil*—and these are the two basic respects in which man has hitherto been superior to other beasts!

7

One will have divined already how easily the priestly mode af valuation can branch off from the knightly-aristocratic and then develop into its opposite; this is particularly likely when the priestly caste and the warrior caste are in jealous opposition to one another and are unwilling to come to terms. The knightly-aristocratic value judgments presupposed a powerful physicality, a flourishing, abundant, even overflowing health, together with that which serves to preserve it: war, adventure, hunting, dancing, war games, and in general all that involves vigorous, free, joyful activity. The priestly-noble

mode of valuation presupposes, as we have seen, other things: it is disadvantageous
for it when it comes to war! As is well known, the priests are the *most evil enemies*—
but why? Because they are the most impotent. It is because of their impotence that in
them hatred grows to monstrous and uncanny proportions, to the most spiritual and
poisonous kind of hatred. The truly great haters in world history have always been
priests; likewise the most ingenious[4] haters: other kinds of spirit[5] hardly come into
consideration when compared with the spirit of priestly vengefulness. Human history
would be altogether too stupid a thing without the spirit that the impotent have introduced into it—let us take at once the most notable example. All that has been done
on earth against "the noble," "the powerful," "the masters," "the rulers," fades into nothing compared with what the *Jews* have done against them; the Jews, that priestly people, who in opposing their enemies and conquerors were ultimately satisfied with
nothing less than a radical revaluation of their enemies' values, that is to say, an act of
the *most spiritual revenge*. For this alone was appropriate to a priestly people, the
people embodying the most deeply repressed priestly vengefulness. It was the Jews
who, with awe-inspiring consistency, dared to invert the aristocratic value-equation
(good = noble = powerful = beautiful = happy = beloved of God) and to hang on to
this inversion with their teeth, the teeth of the most abysmal hatred (the hatred of impotence), saying "the wretched alone are the good; the poor, impotent, lowly alone
are the good; the suffering, deprived, sick, ugly alone are pious, alone are blessed by
God, blessedness is for them alone—and you, the powerful and noble, are on the contrary the evil, the cruel, the lustful, the insatiable, the godless to all eternity; and you
shall be in all eternity the unblessed, accursed, and damned!" . . . One knows *who* inherited this Jewish revaluation . . . In connection with the tremendous and immeasur-
ably fateful initiative provided by the Jews through this most fundamental of all
declarations of war, I recall the proposition I arrived at on a previous occasion (*Beyond Good and Evil*, section 195)—that with the Jews there begins *the slave revolt
in morality:* that revolt which has a history of 2,000 years behind it and which we no
longer see because it—has been victorious. . . .

10

The slave revolt in morality begins when *ressentiment* itself becomes creative and
gives birth to values: the *ressentiment* of natures that are denied the true reaction, that
of deeds, and compensate themselves with an imaginary revenge. While every noble
morality develops from a triumphant affirmation of itself, slave morality from the outset says No to what is "outside," what is "different," what is "not itself"; and *this* No is its
creative deed. This inversion of the value-positing eye—this *need* to direct one's view
outward instead of back to oneself—is of the essence of *ressentiment:* in order to
exist, slave morality always first needs a hostile external world; it needs, physiologically
speaking, external stimuli in order to act at all—its action is fundamentally reaction.

The reverse is the case with the noble mode of valuation: it acts and grows spontaneously, it seeks its opposite only so as to affirm itself more gratefully and
triumphantly—its negative concept "low," "common," "bad" is only a subsequently-
invented pale, contrasting image in relation to its positive basic concept—filled with

life and passion through and through—"we noble ones, we good, beautiful, happy ones!" When the noble mode of valuation blunders and sins against reality, it does so in respect to the sphere with which it is *not* sufficiently familiar, against a real knowledge of which it has indeed inflexibly guarded itself: in some circumstances it misunderstands the sphere it despises, that of the common man, of the lower orders; on the other hand, one should remember that, even supposing that the affect of contempt, of looking down from a superior height, *falsifies* the image of that which it despises, it will at any rate still be a much less serious falsification than that perpetrated on its opponent—*in effigie* of course—by the submerged hatred, the vengefulness of the impotent. There is indeed too much carelessness, too much taking lightly, too much looking away and impatience involved in contempt, even too much joyfulness, for it to be able to transform its object into a real caricature and monster.

One should not overlook the almost benevolent nuances that the Greek nobility, for example, bestows on all the words it employs to distinguish the lower orders from itself; how they are continuously mingled and sweetened with a kind of pity, consideration, and forbearance, so that finally almost all the words referring to the common man have remained as expressions signifying "unhappy," "pitiable" (compare *deilos*,[6] *deilaios*,[7] *poneros*,[8] *mochtheros*,[9] the last two of which properly designate the common man as work-slave and beast of burden)—and how on the other hand "bad," "low," "unhappy" have never ceased to sound to the Greek ear as one note with a tone-color in which "unhappy" preponderates: this as an inheritance from the ancient nobler aristocratic mode of evaluation, which does not belie itself even in its contempt (—philologists should recall the sense in which *oïzyros*,[10] *anolbos*,[11] *tlēmōn*,[12] *dystychein*,[13] *xymphora*,[14] are employed). The "well-born" *felt* themselves to be the "happy"; they did not have to establish their happiness artificially by examining their enemies, or to persuade themselves, *deceive* themselves, that they were happy (as all men of *ressentiment* are in the habit of doing); and they likewise knew, as rounded men replete with energy and therefore *necessarily* active, that happiness should not be sundered from action—being active was with them necessarily a part of happiness (whence *eu prattein*[15] takes its origin)—all very much the opposite of "happiness" at the level of the impotent, the oppressed, and those in whom poisonous and inimical feelings are festering, with whom it appears as essentially narcotic, drug, rest, peace, "sabbath," slackening of tension and relaxing of limbs, in short *passively*.

While the noble man lives in trust and openness with himself (*gennaios*[16] "of noble descent" underlines the nuance "upright" and probably also "naïve"), the man of *ressentiment* is neither upright nor naïve nor honest and straightforward with himself. His soul *squints*; his spirit loves hiding places, secret paths and back doors, everything covert entices him as *his* world, *his* security, *his* refreshment; he understands how to keep silent, how not to forget, how to wait, how to be provisionally self-deprecating and humble. A race of such men of *ressentiment* is bound to become eventually *cleverer* than any noble race; it will also honor cleverness to a far greater degree: namely, as a condition of existence of the first importance; while with noble men cleverness can easily acquire a subtle flavor of luxury and subtlety—for here it is far less essential than the perfect functioning of the regulating *unconscious* instincts or even than a certain imprudence, perhaps a bold recklessness whether in the face of danger or of the enemy, or that enthusiastic impulsiveness in anger, love, reverence, gratitude, and revenge by which noble souls have at all times recognized one another. *Ressentiment* itself, if it should appear in the noble man, consummates and exhausts itself in an immediate reaction, and therefore does not *poison*: on the other hand, it fails to appear at all on countless occasions on which it inevitably appears in the weak and impotent.

To be incapable of taking one's enemies, one's accidents, even one's misdeeds seriously for very long—that is the sign of strong, full natures in whom there is an excess of the power to form, to mold, to recuperate and to forget (a good example of this in modern times is Mirabeau,[17] who had no memory for insults and vile actions done him and was unable to forgive simply because he—forgot). Such a man shakes off with a *single* shrug many vermin that eat deep into others; here alone genuine "love of one's enemies" is possible—supposing it to be possible at all on earth. How much reverence has a noble man for his enemies!—and such reverence is a bridge to love.—For he desires his enemy for himself, as his mark of distinction; he can endure no other enemy than one in whom there is nothing to despise and *very much* to honor! In contrast to this, picture "the enemy" as the man of *ressentiment* conceives him—and here precisely is his deed, his creation: he has conceived "the evil enemy," "*the Evil One*," and this in fact is his basic concept, from which he then evolves, as an afterthought and pendant, a "good one"—himself!

11

This, then, is quite the contrary of what the noble man does, who conceives the basic concept "good" in advance and spontaneously out of himself and only then creates for himself an idea of "bad"! This "bad" of noble origin and that "evil" out of the cauldron of unsatisfied hatred—the former an after-production, a side issue, a contrasting shade, the latter on the contrary the original thing, the beginning, the distinctive *deed* in the conception of a slave morality—how different these words "bad" and "evil" are, although they are both apparently the opposite of the same concept "good." But it is *not* the same concept "good": one should ask rather precisely *who* is "evil" in the sense of the morality of *ressentiment*. The answer, in all strictness, is: *precisely* the "good man" of the other morality, precisely the noble, powerful man, the ruler, but dyed in another color, interpreted in another fashion, seen in another way by the venomous eye of *ressentiment*.

Here there is one thing we shall be the last to deny: he who knows these "good men" only as enemies knows only *evil enemies*, and the same men who are held so sternly in check *inter pares*[18] by custom, respect, usage, gratitude, and even more by mutual suspicion and jealousy, and who on the other hand in their relations with one another show themselves so resourceful in consideration, self-control, delicacy, loyalty, pride, and friendship—once they go outside, where the strange, the *stranger* is found, they are not much better than uncaged beasts of prey. There they savor a freedom from all social constraints, they compensate themselves in the wilderness for the tension engendered by protracted confinement and enclosure within the peace of society, they go *back* to the innocent conscience of the beast of prey, as triumphant monsters who perhaps emerge from a disgusting[19] procession of murder, arson, rape, and torture, exhilarated and undisturbed of soul, as if it were no more than a students' prank, convinced they have provided the poets with a lot more material for song and praise. One cannot fail to see at the bottom of all these noble races the beast of prey, the splendid *blond beast*[20] prowling about avidly in search of spoil and victory; this hidden core needs to erupt from time to time, the animal has to get out again and go back to the wilderness: the Roman, Arabian, Germanic, Japanese nobility, the Homeric heroes, the Scandanavian Vikings—they all shared this need. . . .

Supposing that what is at any rate believed to be the "truth" really is true, and the *meaning of all culture* is the reduction of the beast of prey "man" to a tame and civilized animal, a *domestic animal*, then one would undoubtedly have to regard all those instincts of reaction and *ressentiment* through whose aid the noble races and their ideals were finally confounded and overthrown as the actual *instruments of culture*; which is not to say that the *bearers* of these instincts themselves represent culture. Rather is the reverse not merely probable—no! today it is *palpable*! These bearers of the oppressive instincts that thirst for reprisal, the descendants of every kind of European and non-European slavery, and especially of the entire pre-Aryan populace— they represent the *regression* of mankind! These "instruments of culture" are a disgrace to man and rather an accusation and counterargument against "culture" in general! One may be quite justified in continuing to fear the blond beast at the core of all noble races and in being on one's guard against it: but who would not a hundred times sooner fear where one can also admire than *not* fear but be permanently condemned to the repellent sight of the ill-constituted, dwarfed, atrophied, and poisoned?[21] And is that not *our* fate? What today constitutes *our* antipathy to "man"?—for we *suffer* from man, beyond doubt.

Not fear; rather that we no longer have anything left to fear in man; that the maggot[22] "man" is swarming in the foreground; that the "tame man," the hopelessly mediocre and insipid[23] man, has already learned to feel himself as the goal and zenith, as the meaning of history, as "higher man"—that he has indeed a certain right to feel thus, insofar as he feels himself elevated above the surfeit of ill-constituted, sickly, weary, and exhausted people of which Europe is beginning to stink today, as something at least relatively well-constituted, at least still capable of living, at least affirming life.

12

At this point I cannot suppress a sigh and a last hope. What is it that I especially find utterly unendurable? That I cannot cope with, that makes me choke and faint? Bad air! Bad air! The approach of some ill-constituted thing; that I have to smell the entrails of some ill-constituted soul!

How much one is able to endure: distress, want, bad weather, sickness, toil, solitude. Fundamentaly one can cope with everything else, born as one is to a subterranean life of struggle; one emerges again and again into the light, one experiences again and again one's golden hour of victory—and then one stands forth as one was born, unbreakable, tensed, ready for new, even harder, remoter things, like a bow that distress only serves to draw tauter.

But grant me from time to time—if there are divine goddesses in the realm beyond good and evil—grant me the sight, but *one* glance of something perfect, wholly achieved, happy, mighty, triumphant, something still capable of arousing fear! Of a man who justifies *man*, of a complementary and redeeming lucky hit on the part of man for the sake of which one may still *believe in man*!

For this is how things are: the diminution and leveling of European man constitutes *our* greatest danger, for the sight of him makes us weary.—We can see nothing today that wants to grow greater, we suspect that things will continue to go down, down, to become thinner, more good-natured, more prudent, more comfortable, more mediocre, more indifferent, more Chinese, more Christian—there is no doubt that man is getting "better" all the time.

Here precisely is what has become a fatality for Europe—together with the fear of man we have also lost our love of him, our reverence for him, our hopes for him, even the will to him. The sight of man now makes us weary—what is nihilism today if it is not *that*?—We are weary *of man*.

13

But let us return: the problem of the *other* origin of the "good," of the good as conceived by the man of *ressentiment*, demands its solution.

That lambs dislike great birds of prey does not seem strange: only it gives no ground for reproaching these birds of prey for bearing off little lambs. And if the lambs say among themselves: "these birds of prey are evil; and whoever is least like a bird of prey, but rather its opposite, a lamb—would he not be good?" there is no reason to find fault with this institution of an ideal, except perhaps that the birds of prey might view it a little ironically and say: "*we* don't dislike them at all, these good little lambs; we even love them: nothing is more tasty than a tender lamb."

To demand of strength that it should *not* express itself as strength, that it should *not* be a desire to overcome, a desire to throw down, a desire to become master, a thirst for enemies and resistances and triumphs, is just as absurd as to demand of weakness that it should express itself as strength. A quantum of force is equivalent to a quantum of drive, will, effect—more, it is nothing other than precisely this very driving, willing, effecting, and only owing to the seduction of language (and of the fundamental errors of reason that are petrified in it) which conceives and misconceives all effects as conditioned by something that causes effects, by a "subject," can it appear otherwise. For just as the popular mind separates the lightning from its flash and takes the latter for an *action*, for the operation of a subject called lightning, so popular morality also seperates strength from expressions of strength, as if there were a neutral substratum behind the strong man, which was *free* to express the strength or not to do so. But there is no such substratum; there is no "being" behind doing, effecting, becoming; "the doer" is merely a fiction added to the deed—the deed is everything. The popular mind in fact doubles the deed; when it sees the lightning flash, it is the deed of a deed: it posits the same event first as cause and then a second time as its effect. Scientists do no better when they say "force moves," "force causes," and the like— all its coolness, its freedom from emotion notwithstanding, our entire science still lies under the misleading influence of language and has not disposed of that little changeling, the "subject" (the atom, for example, is such a changeling, as is the Kantian "thing-in-itself"); no wonder if the submerged, darkly glowering emotions of vengefulness and hatred exploit this belief for their own ends and in fact maintain no belief more ardently than the belief that *the strong man is free* to be weak and the bird of prey to be a lamb—for thus they gain the right to make the bird of prey *accountable* for being a bird of prey.

When the oppressed, downtrodden, outraged exhort one another with the vengeful cunning of impotence: "let us be different from the evil, namely good! And he is good who does not outrage, who harms nobody, who does not attack, who does not requite, who leaves revenge to God, who keeps himself hidden as we do, who avoids evil and desires little from life, like us, the patient, humble, and just"—this, listened to calmly and without previous bias, really amounts to no more than: "we weak ones are, after all, weak; it would be good if we did nothing *for which we are not strong enough*"; but this dry matter of fact, this prudence of the lowest order which even insects possess (posing as dead, when in great danger, so as not to do "too much"), has, thanks to the counterfeit and self-deception of impotence, clad itself in the ostentatious garb of the virtue of quiet, calm resignation, just as if the weakness of the weak—that is to say, their *essence*, their effects, their sole ineluctable, irremovable reality—were a voluntary achievement, willed, chosen, a *deed*, a *meritorious act*. This type of man *needs* to believe in a neutral independent "subject," prompted by an instinct for self-preservation and self-affirmation in which every lie is sanctified. The subject (or, to use a more popular expression, the *soul*) has perhaps been believed in hitherto more firmly than anything else on earth because it makes possible to the majority of mortals, the weak and oppressed of every kind, the sublime self-deception that interprets weakness as freedom, and their being thus-and-thus as a *merit*. . . .

16

Let us conclude. The two *opposing values* "good and bad," "good and evil" have been engaged in a fearful struggle on earth for thousands of years; and though the latter value has certainly been on top for a long time, there are still places where the struggle is as yet undecided. One might even say that it has risen ever higher and thus become more and more profound and spiritual: so that today there is perhaps no more decisive mark of a "*higher nature*," a more spiritual nature, than that of being divided in this sense and a genuine battleground of these opposed values. . . .

---

[1]Nietzsche's first publication, in 1867 when he was still a student at the University of Leipzig, was an article in a leading classical journal, *Rheinisches Museum*, on the history of the collection of the maxims of Theognis ("Zur Geschichte der Theognideischen Spruchsammlung"). Theognis of Megara lived in the 6th century B.C.

[2]Greek: good, brave . . .

[3]The cure developed by Dr. Silas Weir Mitchell (1829–1914, American) consisted primarily in isolation, confinement to bed, dieting, and massage.

[4]*Geistreich*.

[5]*Geist*.

[6]All of the footnoted words in this section are Greek. The first four mean *wretched*, but each has a separate note to suggest some of its other connotations. *Delios*: cowardly, worthless, vile.

[7]Paltry.

[8]Oppressed by toils, good for nothing, worthless, knavish, base, cowardly.

[9]Suffering hardship, knavish.

[10]Woeful, miserable, toilsome; wretch.

[11]Unblest, wretched, luckless, poor.

[12]Wretched, miserable.

[13]To be unlucky, unfortunate.

[14]Misfortune.

[15]To do well in the sense of faring well.

[16]High-born, noble, high-minded.

[17]Honoré Gabriel Riqueti, Comte de Mirabeau (1749–1791), was a celebrated French Revolutionary statesman and writer.

[18]Among equals.

[19]*Scheusslichen*.

[20]This is the first appearance in Nietzsche's writings of the notorious "blond beast." It is encountered twice more in the present section; a variant appears in Section 17 of the second essay; and then the *blond Bestie* appears once more in *Twilight*, "The 'Improvers' of Mankind," Section 2 (*Portable Nietzsche*, p. 502). That is all. For a detailed discussion of these passages see Kaufmann's *Nietzsche*, Chapter 7, section III: ". . . The 'blond beast' is not a racial concept and does not refer to the 'Nordic race' of which the Nazis later made so much. Nietzsche specifically refers to Arabs and Japanese . . .—and the 'blondness' presumably refers to the beast, the lion."

[21]If the present section is not clear enough to any reader, he might turn to *Zarathustra's* contrast of the *overman* and the *last man* (Prologue, sections 3–5) and, for good measure, read also the first chapter or two of Part One. Then he will surely see how Aldous Huxley's *Brave New World* and George Orwell's *1984*—but especially the former—are developments of Nietzsche's theme. Huxley, in his novel, uses Shakespeare as a foil; Nietzsche, in the passage above, Homer.

[22]*Gewürm* suggests wormlike animals; *wimmelt* can mean swarm or crawl but is particularly associated with maggots—in a cheese, for example.

[23]*Unerquicklich*.

JEAN-PAUL SARTRE

Existentialism and Humanism

There are two kinds of existentialists. There are, on the one hand, the Christians, amongst whom I shall name Jaspers and Gabriel Marcel, both professed Catholics; and on the other the existential atheists, amongst whom we must place Heidegger as well as the French existentialists and myself. What they have in common is simply the fact that they believe that *existence* comes before *essence*—or, if you will, that we must begin from the subjective. What exactly do we mean by that?

If one considers an article of manufacture—as, for example, a book or a paperknife—one sees that it has been made by an artisan who had a conception of it; and he has paid attention, equally, to the conception of a paper-knife and to the pre-existent technique of production which is a part of that conception and is, at bottom, a formula. Thus the paper-knife is at the same time an article producible in a certain manner and one which, on the other hand, serves a definite purpose, for one cannot suppose that a man would produce a paper-knife without knowing what it is for. Les us say, then, of the paper-knife that its essence—that is to say the sum of the formulae and the qualities which made its production and its definition possible—precedes its existence. The presence of such-and-such a paper-knife or book is thus determined before my eyes. Here, then, we are viewing the world from a technical standpoint, and we can say that production precedes existence.

When we think of God as the creator, we are thinking of him, most of the time, as a supernal artisan. Whatever doctrine we may be considering, whether it be a doctrine like that of Descartes, or of Leibnitz himself, we always imply that the will follows, more or less, from the understanding or at least accompanies it, so that when God creates he knows precisely what he is creating. Thus, the conception of man in the mind of God is comparable to that of the paper-knife in the mind of the artisan: God makes man according to a procedure and a conception, exactly as the artisan manufactures a paper-knife, following a definition and a formula. Thus each individual man is the realisation of a certain conception which dwells in the divine understanding. In the philosophic atheism of the 18th century, the notion of God is suppressed, but not, for all that, the idea that essence is prior to existence; something of that idea we still find everywhere, in Diderot, in Voltaire, and even in Kant. Man possesses a human nature; that "human nature," which is the conception of human being, is found in every man; which means that each man is a particular example of an universal conception, the conception of Man. In Kant, this universality goes so far that the wild man of the woods, man in the state of nature and the bourgeois are all contained in the same definition and have the same fundamental qualities. Here again, the essence of man precedes that historic existence which we confront in experience.

Atheistic existentialism, of which I am a representative, declares with greater consistency that if God does not exist there is at least one being whose existence comes before its essence, a being which exists before it can be defined by any conception of it. That being is man or, as Heidegger has it, the human reality. What do we mean by saying that existence precedes essence? We mean that man first of all exists, encounters himself, surges up in the world—and defines himself afterwards. If man as the existentialist sees him is not definable, it is because to begin with he is nothing. He will not be anything until later, and then he will be what he makes of himself. Thus, there is no human nature, because there is no God to have a conception of it. Man simply is. Not that he is simply what he conceives himself to be, but he is what he wills, and as he conceives himself after already existing—as he wills to be after that leap towards existence. Man is nothing else but that which he makes of himself. That is the first principle of existentialism. And this is what people call its "subjectivity," using the word as a reproach against us. But what do we mean to say by this, but that man is of a greater dignity than a stone or a table? For we mean to say that man primarily exists—that man is, before all else, something which propels itself towards a future and is aware that it is doing so. Man is, indeed, a project which possesses a subjective life, instead of being a kind of moss, or a fungus or a cauliflower. Before that projection of the self nothing exists; not even in the heaven of intelligence: man will only attain existence when he is what he purposes to be. Not, however, what he may wish to be. For what we usually understand by wishing or willing is a conscious decision taken—much more often than not—after we have made ourselves what we are. I may wish to join a party, to write a book or to marry—but in such a case what is usually called my will is probably a manifestation of a prior and more spontaneous decision. If, however, it is true that existence is prior to essence, man is responsible for what he is. Thus, the first effect of existentialism is that it puts every man in possession of himself as he is, and places the entire responsibility for his existence squarely upon his own shoulders. And, when we say that man is responsible for himself, we do not mean that he is responsible only for his own individuality, but that he is responsible for all men. The word "subjectivism" is to be understood in two senses, and our adversaries play upon only one of them. Subjectivism means, on the one hand, the freedom of the individual subject and, on the other, that man cannot pass beyond human subjectivity. It is the latter which is the deeper meaning of existentialism. When we say that man chooses himself, we *do* mean that every one of us must choose himself; but by that we *also* mean that in choosing for himself he chooses for all men. For in effect, of all the actions a man may take in order to create himself as he wills to be, there is not one which is not creative, at the same time, of an image of man such as he believes he ought to be. To choose between this or that is at the same time to affirm the value of that which is chosen; for we are unable ever to choose the worse. What we choose is always the better; and nothing can be better for us unless it is better for all. If, moreover, existence precedes essence and we will to exist at the same time as we fashion our image, that image is valid for all and for the entire epoch in which we find ourselves. Our responsibility is thus much greater than we had supposed, for it concerns mankind as a whole. If I am a worker, for instance, I may choose to join a Christian rather than a Communist trade union. And if, by the membership, I choose to signify that resignation is, after all, the attitude that best becomes a man, that man's kingdom is not upon this earth, I do not commit myself alone to that view. Resignation is my will for everyone, and my action is, in consequence, a commitment on behalf of all mankind. Or if, to take a more personal case, I decide to marry and to have children, even though this decision proceeds simply from my situation, from my passion or my desire, I am thereby committing not only myself, but humanity as a whole, to the practice of monogamy. I am thus responsible for myself and for all men, and I am creating a certain image of man as I would have him to be. In fashioning myself I fashion man.

This may enable us to understand what is meant by such terms—perhaps a little grandiloquent—as anguish, abandonment, and despair. As you will soon see, it is very simple. First, what do we mean by anguish? The existentialist frankly states that man is in anguish. His meaning is as follows—When a man commits himself to anything, fully realising that he is not only choosing what he will be, but is thereby at the same time a legislator deciding for the whole of mankind—in such a moment a man cannot escape from the sense of complete and profound responsibility. There are many, indeed, who show no such anxiety. But we affirm that they are merely disguising their anguish or are in flight from it. Certainly, many people think that in what they are doing they commit no one but themselves to anything: and if you ask them, "What would happen if everyone did so?" they shrug their shoulders and reply, "Everyone does not do so." But in truth, one ought always to ask oneself what would happen if everyone did as one is doing; nor can one escape from that disturbing thought except by a kind of self-deception. The man who lies in self-excuse, by saying "Everyone will not do it" must be ill at ease in his conscience, for the act of lying implies the universal value which it denies. . . .

And when we speak of "abandonment"—a favourite word of Heidegger—we only mean to say that God does not exist, and that it is necessary to draw the consequences of his absence right to the end. The existentialist is strongly opposed to a certain type of secular moralism which seeks to suppress God at the least possible expense. Towards 1880, when the French professors endeavoured to formulate a secular morality, they said something like this:—God is a useless and costly hypothesis, so we will do without it. However, if we are to have morality, a society, and a law-abiding world, it is essential that certain values should be taken seriously; they must have an *a priori* existence ascribed to them. It must be considered obligatory *a priori* to be honest, not to lie, not to beat one's wife, to bring up children, and so forth; so we are going to do a little work on this subject, which will enable us to show that these values exist all the same, inscribed in an intelligible heaven although, of course, there is no God. In other words—and this is, I believe, the purport of all that we in France call radicalism— nothing will be changed if God does not exist; we shall re-discover the same norms of honesty, progress, and humanity, and we shall have disposed of God as an out-of-date hypothesis which will die away quietly of itself. The existentialist, on the contrary, finds it extremely embarrassing that God does not exist, for there disappears with Him all possibility of finding values in an intelligible heaven. There can no longer be any good *a priori*, since there is no infinite and perfect consciousness to think it. It is nowhere written that "the good" exists, that one must be honest or must not lie, since we are now upon the plane where there are only men. Dostoievsky once wrote "If God did not exist, everything would be permitted"; and that, for existentialism, is the starting point. Everything is indeed permitted if God does not exist, and man is in consequence forlorn, for he cannot find anything to depend upon either within or outside himself. He discovers forthwith, that he is without excuse. For if indeed existence precedes essence, one will never be able to explain one's action by reference to a given and specific human nature; in other words, there is no determinism—man is free, man *is* freedom. Nor, on the other hand, if God does not exist, are we provided with any values or commands that could legitimise our behaviour. Thus we have neither behind us, nor before us in a luminous realm of values, any means of justification or excuse. We are left alone, without excuse. That is what I mean when I say that man is condemned to be free. Condemned, because he did not create himself, yet is nevertheless at liberty, and from the moment that he is thrown into this world he is responsible for everything he does. The existentialist does not believe in the power of passion. He will never regard a grand passion as a destructive torrent upon which a man is swept into certain actions as by fate, and which, therefore, is an excuse for them. He thinks that man is responsible for his passion. Neither will an existentialist think that a man can find help through some sign being vouchsafed upon earth for his orientation: for he thinks that the man himself interprets the sign as he chooses. He thinks that every man, without any support or help whatever, is condemned at every instant to invent man. . . .

COMMUNITY AND THE SELF

G. W. F. HEGEL

translated by Judith Norman

Master and Slave

Self-consciousness is, to begin with, simple being-for-self. It is equal to itself by virtue of excluding everything else. Its essence and its absolute object is the 'I'; and it is an *individual* in this immediacy (or being) of its being-for-self. Anything it considers as "other" is inessential, and characterized negatively. But the other is a self-consciousness too; an individual is confronting an individual. Confronting each other *immediately* in this manner, they are like ordinary objects to each other, independent forms [of consciousness] subsisting at the level of mere life—for the existing object has determined itself as life. They are consciousnesses immersed [in the immediacy of life], and have not completed for each other the movement of absolute abstraction in which immediate being is eradicated, and only the purely negative being of self-identical consciousness remains. They have not yet presented themselves to each other as pure *being-for-self*, that is, as *self-consciousness*. Each one is fully certain of itself, but not of the other, and therefore its own self-certainty has no truth yet; for such truth would only come if its own being-for-self presented itself as an independent object, or, in other words, if the object presented itself as pure self-certainty. But according to the concept of recognition, this is only possible if each is for the other as the other is for it; it is only possible when each one, in itself through its own action, and again through the action of the other, achieves this pure abstraction of being-for-self.

However, the presentation of itself as the pure abstraction of self-consciousness consists of showing itself as pure negation of its objective manner, or showing that it is not attached to any definite *existence*, certainly not to the general individuality of existence; [showing, in other words,] that it is not attached to life. This is a *two-fold* action: an action of the other, and an action through itself. Insofar as it is an action of the *other*, each one seeks the death of the other. But this involves the second type of action, *the action through itself* as well; for the first action entails the risking of one's own life. The relation of both self-consciousnesses thus dictates that they must *prove* themselves and each other through a struggle of life and death.—They must enter into this struggle, for they must raise the certainty of *being for themselves* to truth, both for the other as well as for themselves. Freedom is proven worthwhile only by risking one's life; such a risk also proves that the essence of self-consciousness is not [just] *being*, that it is not *immediate* as it appears to be, that it is not this submersion in the expanse of life; rather, it proves that it contains only vanishing moments, that it is simply pure *being-for-self*. The individual who has not wagered his life can indeed be recognized as a *person*, but he has not achieved the truth of this recognition by being recognized as an independent self-consciousness. Likewise, each must pursue the death of the other, just as each risks his own life; for he values the other no more than he values himself. His essence is presented to him as an other. It is outside of itself, and this exteriority must be overcome. The other is a consciousness entangled in a variety of ways and must regard its otherness as pure being-for-self or as absolute negation.

But this trial by death destroys the truth that was supposed to come from it, and in so doing it destroys the certainty of itself in general. For, just as life is the *natural* position of consciousness, independence without absolute negativity, likewise, death is the *natural* negation of consciousness, negation without independence, and consequently remains without the meaning required of recognition. Death has indeed shown with certainty that both risked their lives, disregarding both their own deaths as well as that of the other; but this has not been shown for those who survive the struggle. They overcome their consciousness to the extent that it has been placed in this alien element of natural existence; or, they overcome and are overcome as *extremes* that want to be for themselves. But the essential moment thereby disappears from the game, the moment of decomposition into extremes of opposing determinations; and the middle falls into a dead unity, which is decomposed in dead extremes that merely lie side by side without opposition; there is no interchange between them through consciousness. Instead, they are indifferent to each other like mere things, and leave each other alone. Their action is that of abstract negation; it is not a negation from consciousness that *overcomes* itself so that it *retains* and *preserves* the elements that are overcome, and thereby survives its own overcoming.

In this experience, self-consciousness learns that life is as essential to it as pure self-consciousness. The simple I is the absolute object in immediate self-consciousness; for us or in itself, however, this object is the absolute mediator, and has steadfast independence as an essential moment. The result of this first experience is the dissolution of that simple unity [of the simple I]; through [this dissolution,] a pure self-consciousness is posited, as well as a consciousness that is not purely for itself, but is rather for another; that is, as *existing* consciousness or consciousness in the shape proper to *things*. Both moments are essential; since they are at first unequal and opposed, and their reflection has not yet submitted to the unity, they are like two opposed forms of consciousness; the first is independent and its essence is being-for-self; the other is dependent, and its essence is life or existing for an other. The former is the *master*, the latter is the *slave*.

The master is the consciousness that is *for itself*, and no longer merely the concept of such a consciousness; rather, he is consciousness existing for itself and mediated by an *other* consciousness, one whose essence involves being synthesized with independent *being* or objects in general. The master is in a relation to both these moments: first, to the object, which he desires, and second, to the consciousness whose essence is bound up with objects. And to the extent that (a) as concept of self-consciousness he is an immediate relation of *being-for-itself*, but (b) henceforth concurrently as mediator, or as a being-for-self that is for itself only through an other, he is related (a) immediately to both, and (b) mediately to each through the other. The master is related *mediately* to the slave through the *independent object*, because the slave is held fast to such an object; it is the chain from which he could not break free in the struggle, thereby proving that he is dependent and has his independence in objects. But the master is the one with power over this being, since he proved in struggle that he can regard it as merely negative. By having power over this being which has power over the other [the slave], the outcome is that he subordinates the slave to himself. Likewise the master relates to the thing *mediately, through agency the slave*. The slave, as self-consciousness in general, relates to the thing negatively as well, and overcomes it; but from his perspective, the thing is also independent. For this reason, he cannot fully annihilate it through his negation. In other words, he only *labors* on it. For the master, on the other hand, the *immediate* relation *becomes* pure negation itself, or *enjoyment*, due to the mediating agency [of the slave]. He can achieve what desire failed to do—to have done with [the thing], and to satisfy himself by enjoying it. Desire could not achieve this, due to the thing's independence. But the master, with the slave interposed in between him and the thing, appropriates only the dependent aspect of the thing, and enjoys it fully; he leaves the independent side of the thing to the slave, who labors upon it.

In both of these moments, the master achieves recognition by way of an other consciousness, since this other posits itself as unessential in both moments: first, in laboring on the thing, and second, in its dependence upon a particular being. In neither of these moments can this other consciousness become master over this being and achieve absolute negation. A moment of recognition is thus at hand, because the other consciousness suppresses its being-for-self, and thereby does to itself what the first consciousness does to it. In the same way, the other moment is also at hand, in that the second consciousness' action [of self-suppression] is the first's own action; for what the slave does is actually the deed of the master. The master's essence is only being-for-self; he is the purely negative power and for him the thing is nothing; for this reason, he is the purely essential action in this relationship. The slave, on the other hand, is an impure, unessential action. But [this situation cannot be one of] genuine recognition, since it is missing the moment in which the master does to himself what he does to the slave, and the slave does to the master what [the slave] does to himself. Therefore, the result is a one-sided and unequal recognition.

In this [failed] recognition, the unessential consciousness is the object that constitutes the *truth* of the master's self-certainty. But it is clear that this object does not correspond to its concept; instead the object that the master has mastered is not an independent consciousness at all. The master is confronted with a dependent rather than an independent consciousness. Consequently, he is not certain of *being-for-self* as the truth; instead, his truth is in fact the unessential consciousness and its unessential action.

As a result, the *truth* of the independent consciousness is the *slavish consciousness*. To be sure, this slavish consciousness first appears *outside* itself and not as the truth of self-consciousness. But just as the master's experience has demonstrated that his essence is the reverse of what he would have it be, slavery also ultimately proves to be the opposite of what it is immediately; as a consciousness *that has been forced back* upon itself, it will return into itself and change into a truly independent self-consciousness.

We have seen only what slavery is in relation to mastery. But it is a self-consciousness [in its own right], and we must now observe what it is in and of itself. At first, the master is the essence for the slave; thus the consciousness *that exists independently and for itself* is the *truth* for [the slave], but nonetheless it is not apparent to the slave that this is its truth. The slave alone has the truth of pure negativity and of *being-for-self in fact in itself.* This is because the slave *experienced* this in its own self. [The slave's] consciousness was not afraid of this thing or that, at some time or another; instead, it feared for its entire being, because it has felt the fear of death, of the absolute master. It has been seized with terror, shaken to its very core; it has lost all its bearings. But this purely abstract moment where everything stable becomes fluid—this moment is the simple essence of self-consciousness, the absolute negativity, *the pure being-for-self,* that is consequently part of this consciousness [an diesem Bewusstsein]. This moment of pure being-for-self is *for* this consciousness as well, because this consciousness has this being-for-self as an *object* in the [form of the] master. Furthermore, it is not merely this abstract dissolution *in general*; it is actually achieved in servitude. Through his slavery he gets rid of all *particular* moments of his attachment to natural existence and labors his way through it.

But the feeling of absolute power, both in general and in the particulars of servitude, is only implicitly dissolution; and although fear of the lord is indeed the beginning of wisdom, consciousness is not aware [at first] that it is a *being-for-self.* But such awareness is gained through labor. In the moment that corresponds to desire in the master's consciousness, it seemed that the side of the unessential relation to the thing had indeed devolved upon the servile consciousness, since the thing retains its independence. Desire reserved for itself the [right to a] pure negation of the object, and consequently to an unadulterated feeling of self. But the satisfaction [gained by desire] is accordingly merely transient, for it is missing the *object-like* side, or *endurance.* Labor, to the contrary, is *repressed* desire, transience *delayed*, or a *formation.* The negative relation to the object becomes the *form* of the object, and becomes an [element of] *permanence*, because it is precisely to the laborer that the object has independence. This *negative medium* or the formative *action* is at the same time the *particularity* or the pure being-for-self of the consciousness, which now, in the labor outside of it, gains an element of permanence. The laboring consciousness can thereby perceive in independent being *its own self.*

But the formative activity does not only have the positive meaning that the servile consciousness, as pure *being-for-self*, gains an existence. In contrast to its first moment, it also has the negative meaning for fear. This is because, in producing the thing, his own negativity—his being-for-self—becomes an object for him only by canceling out the existing *form* confronting him. But this object-like *negative* is precisely the alien essence that he had feared. But now he destroys this alien negative, and posits *himself* as such in the element of permanence, and thereby becomes *for himself* something that *exists for himself.* In the master, the being-for-self is an "other" for the slave, or is only *for him*; in fear, the being-for-self is *in the slave himself.* In producing, the being-for-self becomes *his own* for him, and it occurs to consciousness that it is in and for itself. The form does not thereby become for him, since it is *externalized*, something other than himself; for precisely the form is his pure being-for-self, that becomes the truth for him. Through this rediscovery of himself by himself, the slave realizes that it is through his labor—where he seemed to have only an aliened existence—that his spirit is his own.

ROGER T. AMES

The Focus-Field Self in Classical Confucianism

Arthur Danto, a distinguished philosopher (and friend), in the context of discussing the difficulty in interpreting a philosophical text, remarks:

> one of my favorite passages in the *Analects* is where Confucius says that if he gives someone *three* corners who cannot find the *fourth* corner for himself, he cannot teach that person. (Emphasis mine)

Of course, the passage that Danto is referring to in fact reads:

> If I have shown someone *one* corner of a square and he is not able to infer from it the other *three*, I will not show him a second time. (Emphasis mine)

Apart from the rather obvious and amusing irony of getting the passage wrong when you are trying to tell people how to read a text, Danto is certainly understating the effort required to put the square together.

In this essay, I want to begin by looking critically at several interpretations of the Confucian conception of self, claiming that none of them is successful in giving Confucius his square. I then want to develop my own model of the Confucian self, and to argue that, in fact, what Confucius was really looking for was a circle, anyway.

THE HOLLOW MEN

In the early 19th century, Hegel, witnessing the European assault on a seemingly passive China, read the situation from a distance. I cite him at some length here because, although the tenor of his commentary might be blunt and offensive, in substance, it resonates rather closely with much of what is being said today. Describing the traditional Chinese conception of self, Hegel reports:

> moral distinctions and requirements are expressed as Laws, but so that the subjective will is governed by these Laws as by an external force. Nothing subjective in the shape of disposition, Conscience, formal Freedom, is recognized. Justice is administered only on the basis of external morality, and Government exists only as the prerogative of compulsion. . . . Morality is in the East likewise a subject of positive legislation, and although moral prescriptions (the *substance* of their Ethics) may be perfect, what should be internal subjective sentiment is made a matter of external arrangement. . . . While *we* obey, because what we are required to do is confirmed by an *internal* sanction, there the Law is regarded as inherently and absolutely valid without a sense of the want of this subjective confirmation.

Hegel's perception of the Chinese as animated by a top-down "totalitarianism" and hence as being shaped and justified entirely from without, is hardly obsolete. In fact, its most recent application is in the contemporary discussions on the Chinese response to human-rights talk.

Much if not most of the contemporary commentary available on Chinese attitudes toward human rights has interpreted the fundamental presupposition that the Chinese "self" is qualified by a kind of self-abnegation or "selflessness" in a manner that, in a more modern and subtle way, echoes the Hegelian "hollow men" characterization of the Chinese person cited above. Donald J. Munro, for example, argues that

> selflessness . . . is one of the oldest values in China, present in various forms in Taoism and Buddhism, but especially in Confucianism. The selfless person is always willing to subordinate his own interests, or that of some small group (like a village) to which he belongs, to the interest of a larger social group.

. . . Munro . . . and the legion of scholars who seem to share this interpretation are certainly right in assuming that the Chinese tradition has been largely persuaded by a Confucian-based relational—and hence social—definition of person, rather than by any notion of discrete individuality. And they are again unassailable in their assumption that this fact has profound implications for the way in which China has responded to any doctrine of human rights. But where we must take issue is with the assumption that, in the Chinese context, community interest and self-interest are mutually exclusive.

We can allow that there does not seem to be an adequate philosophical basis to justify self as a locus of interests independent of and prior to society. Under the sway of this relational understanding of human being, the mutuality and interdependence of personal, societal, and political realization in the classical Chinese model can and has been generally conceded. But it certainly does not follow that the consequence of this interdependence is selflessness. Under scrutiny, the consequence of attributing "selflessness" as an ideal to the Chinese tradition is to sneak in both the public/private and the individual/society distinctions by the back door. To be "selfless" in the sense presupposed by these commentators requires that an individual self first exist and then . . . that it be sacrificed for some higher public interest. And the suggestion that there are "higher interests" on the part of either person or society covertly establishes a boundary between them that justifies an adversarial relationship. The "selfless" interpretation of these commentators does not support the claim that "person" in the Chinese tradition is irreducibly social; ironically, it vitiates it.

These several commentators, in imposing a "selfless" ideal on the Chinese tradition, are appealing to a contest between state and individual—the struggle between advocates of group interests over the priority of individual interests—that has in large measure separated collectivist thinkers from the liberal democratic in the Western experience, but has perhaps only limited applicability to the Chinese model. While it is true that for the traditional Chinese model, self-realization does not require a high degree of individual autonomy, it does not follow that the alternative to autonomy is capitulation to the general will. Rather, Confucian "personalism," to use William Theodore de Bary's felicitous term, involves benefiting and being benefited by membership in a world of reciprocal loyalties and obligations that surround and stimulate a person and define a person's own worth.

This attribution of "selflessness" to the Chinese tradition, both ancient and modern, seems to arise out of an unfortunate equivocation between "selfish" and "selfless." To eschew selfish concerns does not necessarily lead to self-abnegation. The classical

Confucian position, as I understand it, contends that, because self-realization is fundamentally a social undertaking, "selfish" concerns are to be rejected as an impediment to one's own growth and self-realization.

In Chinese philosophy, a perennial issue that has spanned the centuries has been the likelihood of conflict between the pursuit of selfish advantage (*li*), and negotiation of that which is appropriate and meaningful to all concerned (*yi*), including oneself. Concern for selfish personal advantage is associated with retarded personal development (*hsiao-jen*) while the pursuit of what is broadly "appropriate"—including, of course, one's own interests—is the mainstay of the self-realized and exemplary person (*chün-tzu*).

It can be argued that "self" does necessarily entail a notion of individuality. But, exposed in the differences we have discovered between being "nonselfish" and being "selfless," there is an unnoticed conceptual equivocation on the term *individual* that plagues this whole discussion. "Individual" can mean either one of a *kind*, like one human being as a member of a class of human beings, or *one* of a kind, like Turner's unique *Seastorm*. That is, "individual" can refer to a single, separate and indivisible thing that, by virtue of some essential property or properties, qualifies as a member of a class. By virtue of its membership in a "kind," it is substitutable—"equal before the law," "entitled to equal opportunity," "a locus of unalienable rights," "one of God's children," and so on. It is this definition of individual that generates notions like autonomy, equality, liberty, freedom, and individuated will. By virtue of both its separability and its indivisibility, it relates to its world only extrinsically and hence, where animate, has dominion over its own interiority.

Individual can alternatively also mean uniqueness: the character of a single and unsubstitutable particular, such as a work of art, where it might be quantitatively comparable to other particulars but where it has literally nothing qualitatively in common with them. Under this definition of individual, equality can only mean parity—a comparable excellence.

In the model of the unique individual, determinacy, far from being individuation, lies in the achieved quality of a person's relationships. A person becomes "recognized," "distinguished," or "renowned" by virtue of one's relations and their quality. Much of the effort in coming to an understanding of the traditional Confucian conception of self has to do with clarifying this distinction and reinstating the unique individual in the Confucian picture. While the definition of self as "irreducibly social" certainly precludes autonomous individuality, it does not rule out the second, less familiar notion of unique individuality. . . .

SELF AS FOCUS AND FIELD IN A FOCUS-FIELD MODEL

As I have noted above, the Chinese assumption is that personal, societal, and political order are coterminous and mutually entailing. One method of outlining the focus-field model of self, then, is to follow Plato in using the analogy of political order to describe the articulation of the particular person.

The first volume of the *Cambridge History of China* describes the career of the Han empire from its emergence under Liu Pang to its gradual disintegration three and a half centuries later. In this volume, Yü Ying-shih uses the "five zones" (*wu-fu*) of submission as a device for describing the dynamics of the Han world order:

> According to this theory, China since the Hsia dynasty had been divided into five concentric and hierarchical zones or areas. The central zone (*tien-fu*) was the royal domain, under the direct rule of the king. The royal domain was immediately surrounded by the Chinese states established by the king, known collectively as the lords' zone (*hou-fu*). Beyond the *hou-fu* were Chinese states conquered by the reigning dynasty, which constituted the so-called pacified zone (*sui-fu* or *pin-fu*, guest zone). The last two zones were reserved for the barbarians. The Man and I barbarians lived outside the *sui-fu* or *pin-fu* in the controlled zone (*yao-fu*) which was so called because the Man and I were supposedly subject to Chinese control, albeit of a rather loose kind. Finally, beyond the controlled zone lay the Jung and Ti barbarians, who were basically their own master in the wild zone (*huang-fu*) where the sinocentric world order reached its natural end.

This hierarchical scheme also describes the descending degree of tribute—local products and services—provided to the court at the center. Although this five zone theory seems more complex, it is really a distinction that defines the relative focus of an "inner–outer (*nei-wai*)" circle:

> China was the inner region relative to the outer region of the barbarians, just as the royal domain was, relative to the outer lords' zone, an inner zone, and the controlled zone became the inner area relative to the wild zone on the periphery of Chinese civilization.

This solar system of a centripetal harmony with patterns of deference articulating a central focus seems pervasive in Chinese society. These concrete, functioning patterns of deference "contribute" in varying degrees and are constitutive of the authority at the center, shaping and bringing into focus the character of the social and political entity—its standards and values. This determinate, detailed, "center-seeking" focus fades off into an increasingly indeterminate and untextured field. The attraction of the center is such that, with varying degrees of success, it draws into its field and suspends the disparate and diverse centers that constitute its world. The dynamic tension that obtains among these various centers articulates and inscribes the Han character. Importantly, the quality of these suspended centers are constitutive of the harmony of the field.

This sense of order in which all of the diversity and difference characteristic of the multiple, competing centers of the Warring States period are lifted into the harmony of the Han dynasty translates readily into intellectual world. The intellectual geography of the Hundred Schools in the pre-Ch'in period gives way to a syncretic Confucianism-centered doctrine that absorbs into itself and to some degree conceals the richness of what were competing elements to articulate the philosophical character of the period. This shift is better expressed in the language of incorporation and accommodation than of suppression.

As the centripetal center weakens in the second century AD and as the political order gradually dissolves into a period of disunity, the disparate centers precipitate out of the harmony to reassert themselves, and what was their contribution to the now-weakened center becomes the energy of contest. What was a tightening spire in the early Han becomes a gyre, disgorging itself of its disassociated contents. In the same period, there is a resurgence and interplay of competing philosophical schools and religious movements that reflect a disintegration of the centrally driven intellectual harmony.

Reflection, I believe, would persuade us that this focus-field notion of order is precisely that captured in the fundamental Confucian concept of ritually ordered community, where ritual (*li*), defined at the center by the authority of the tradition, not only demands personalization and participation but, further, is always reflective of the quality of its participants. Similarly, the extent to which a "zone" is active or passive with respect to configuring order is a function of its own distinctive achievement and the quality of its contribution. In fact, in the language of this tradition, the meaning of ritually ordered community itself is made literal from the image of *she-hui*: "a deferential assembly gathering around the sacred pole erected in the center of the community." Nishijima Sadao tells us:

> Such community life, based on the hamlet, had its religious center in the altar (*she*) where the local deity was enshrined. In the same way there was an altar for the state community (*kuo-she*), and each county and district also had its own altar. The religious festivals which took place at the hamlet altar (*li-she*), at which meat was distributed to the participants, helped to strengthen the community spirit.

Above we have employed the Han court analogy as a means of articulating the Confucian self as a "field of selves," but then the court analogy is itself derived from the all-pervasive family model. The "family" as the Chinese model of order is a variation on this notion of a graduated, centripetal harmony. Ambrose King argues persuasively that in the Chinese world, all relationships are familial:

> Among the five cardinal relations, three belong to the kinship realm. The remaining two, though not family relationships, are conceived in terms of the family. The relationship between the ruler and the ruled is conceived of in terms of father (*chün-fu*) and son (*tzu-min*), and the relationship between friend and friend is stated in terms of elder brother (*wu-hsiung*) and younger brother (*wu-ti*).

The family as the "in-group," is determinate and focused at the center, but becomes increasingly vague as it stretches out both diachronically in the direction of one's lineage and synchronically as a society full of "uncles" and "aunties." It is articulated in terms of *lun*, a ritual "wheel" (*lun*) of social relations that "ripple out" (*lun*) in a field of discourse (*lun*) to define the person as a network of roles. King's critique on this model is insightful:

> What must be emphasized here is that while Confucian ethics teach how the individual should be related to other particular roles through the proper *lun*, the issue of how the individual should be related to the "group" is not closely examined. In other words, the individual's behavior is supposed to be *lun*-oriented; the *lun*-oriented role relations, however, are seen as personal, concrete, and particularistic in nature.

While King's insistence that the Confucian model of self is constructed in concrete, particular, and differentiated relationships between self and "other" is certainly on the mark, this allowedly parochial self is not entirely devoid of a sense of group. We must give King the observation that the concreteness and immediacy of one's own definition is, like graduated love, necessitated by the unwillingness in this tradition to disengage the theoretical from experience. A role is not something you "are" but something you "do." But King goes too far in suggesting that the self's sense of group is so vague as to preclude the possibility of a broader civil ethic. He states:

> It seems to me that Confucian social ethics has failed to provide a "viable linkage" between the individual and *ch'ün*; the nonfamilistic group. The root of the Confucian *Problematik* lies in the fact that the boundary between the self and the group has not been conceptually articulated.

King, in missing the link, echoes Bertrand Russell's reservations about the weight given to family relations in the Chinese world:

> Filial piety, and the strength of the family generally, are perhaps the weakest point in Confucian ethics, the only point where the system departs seriously from common sense. Family feeling has militated against public spirit, and the authority of the old has increased the tyranny of ancient customs. . . . In this respect, as in certain others, what is peculiar to China is the preservation of the old custom after a very high level of civilization had been attained.

The link that both King and Russell overlook here is that although the family, the society, the state, and even the tradition itself, as the extended "group" or "field," is indeed ambiguous *as a group or field*, the vagueness of the abstract nexus is focused and made immediate in the embodiment of the group or field by the particular father, the social exemplar, the ruler, and the historical model. The meaning of the group is made present in my father, my teacher, Mao Tse-tung, and Confucius. Each *lun* as the focus and articulation of a particular field of roles is holographic in that it construes its own field. Although the concreteness and immediacy of the centripetal center precludes any but the vaguest and indeterminate definitions of "Chineseness," this notion comes alive *to me* in the image of a Tseng Kuo-fan or a Yang Yu-wei. The totality is nothing more than the full range of particular foci, each focus defining itself and its own particular field.

A final foray. . . . We really must question the appropriateness of using "concept" language to discuss the Confucian self. Concept belongs to the one–many model, where "self" can be understood as having some univocal and hence formal definition— it reifies or entifies self as an ego or an ideal. Concept is dependent upon formal abstraction. Given the dependency of the Confucian model on the particular image, then, we might have to allow that the Confucian self is precisely that particular and detailed portrait of Confucius found in the middle books of the *Analects*, where each passage is a remembered detail contributed by one of the disciples who belonged to the conversation. And this portrait, as it attracts more disciples and plays a role in shaping unique self-images in the tradition, does the work of concept. . . .

SELFLESSNESS

---

translated by David Kalupahana

Characteristics of No-Self

[13] Thereupon the Fortunate One addressed the monks of the group of five:[1]

"Monks, material form is no-self; if this material form were to be self, then this material form will not lead to disease; it is also possible to obtain in regard to the material form: 'Let my material form be thus; let my material form not be thus.' Because, monks, material form is no-self; this material form leads to disease; it is also not possible to obtain in regard to the material form: 'Let my material form be thus; let my material form not be thus.' Monks, feeling is no-self; if this feeling were to be self, then this feeling will not lead to disease; it is also possible to obtain in regard to the feeling: 'Let my feeling be thus; let my feeling not be thus.' Because, monks, feeling is no-self; this feeling leads to disease; it is also not possible to obtain in regard to the feeling: 'Let my feeling be thus; let my feeling not be thus.' Monks, perception is no-self; if this perception were to be self, then this perception will not lead to disease; it is also possible to obtain in regard to the perception: 'Let my perception be thus; let my perception not be thus.' Because, monks, perception is no-self; this perception leads to disease; it is also not possible to obtain in regard to the perception: 'Let my perception be thus; let my perception not be thus.' Monks, dispositions are no-self; if these dispositions were to be self, then these dispositions will not lead to disease; it is also possible to obtain in regard to the dispositions: 'Let my dispositions be thus; let my dispositions not be thus.' Because, monks, dispositions are no-self; these dispositions lead to disease; it is also not possible to obtain in regard to the dispositions: 'Let my dispositions be thus; let my dispositions not be thus.' Monks, consciousness is no-self; if this consciousness were to be self, then this consciousness will not lead to disease; [14] it is also possible to obtain in regard to the consciousness: 'Let my consciousness be thus; let my consciousness not be thus.' Because, monks, consciousness is no-self; this consciousness leads to disease; it is also not possible to obtain in regard to the consciousness: 'Let my consciousness be thus; let my consciousness not be thus.'

"Monks, what do you think: Is material form permanent or impermanent?"

"Impermanent, Sir."

"Whatever is impermanent, is it suffering or happiness?"

"It is suffering."

"Whatever is impermanent, suffering, of the nature of transforming, is it proper to look upon it as: 'It is mine; he, I am; he is myself?'"

"It is not, Sir."

"Is feeling . . ."

"Is perception . . ."

"Are dispositions . . ."

"Is consciousness permanent or impermanent?"

"Impermanent, Sir."

"Whatever is impermanent, is it suffering or happiness?"

"It is suffering."

"Whatever is impermanent, suffering, of the nature of transforming, is it proper to look upon it as: 'It is mine; he, I am; he is myself?' "

"It is not, Sir."

"Therefore, monks, herein whatever material form, past, future, and present, internal or external, gross or subtle, low or lofty, whatever is far away or near, all material form: 'It is not mine; he, I am not; he is not my self.' Thus should it be seen, as it has come to be, through right wisdom."

"Whatever feeling . . ."

"Whatever perception . . ."

"Whatever dispositions . . ."

"Whatever consciousness, past future, present, . . . , whatever is far away or near, all consciousness: 'It is not mine; he, I am not; he is not my self.' Thus should it be seen, as it has come to be, through right wisdom."

"Perceiving thus, monks, a learned and noble disciple is disenchanted in regard to material form, is disenchanted in regard to feeling, is disenchanted in regard to perception, is disenchanted in regard to dispositions, is disenchanted in regard to consciousness. Being disenchanted, one becomes dispassionate, through dispassion, one is released. In one who is released, there is knowledge: 'Has been released.' One knows: 'Birth has been spewed out; done is what needs to be done; the superior life has been lived; there is no other this-ness.' "

The Fortunate One said thus. Delighted, the monks of the group of five rejoiced in what the Fortunate had said. When this explanation was being delivered, the thoughts of the monks of the group of five were released from influxes without grasping. At that time there were six worthy ones in the world.

---

[1]*pañcavaggiye bhikkhū.*

DAVID HUME

On the Self

. . . I had entertained some hopes, that however deficient our theory of the intellectual world might be, it would be free from those contradictions and absurdities which seem to attend every explication that human reason can give of the material world. But upon a more strict review of the section concerning *personal identity*, I find myself involved in such a labyrinth that, I must confess, I neither know how to correct my former opinions, nor how to render them consistent. If this be not a good *general* reason for scepticism, it is at least a sufficient one (if I were not already abundantly supplied) for me to entertain a diffidence and modesty in all my decisions. I shall propose the arguments on both sides, beginning with those that induced me to deny the strict and proper identity and simplicity of a self or thinking being.

When we talk of *self* or *subsistence,* we must have an idea annexed to these terms, otherwise they are altogether unintelligible. Every idea is derived from preceding impressions; and we have no impression of self or substance, as something simple and individual. We have, therefore, no idea of them in that sense.

Whatever is distinct is distinguishable, and whatever is distinguishable is separable by the thought or imagination. All perceptions are distinct. They are, therefore, distinguishable, and separable, and may be conceived as separately existent, and may exist separately, without any contradiction or absurdity.

When I view this table and that chimney, nothing is present to me but particular perceptions, which are of a like nature with all the other perceptions. This is the doctrine of philosophers. But this table, which is present to me, and that chimney, may, and do exist separately. This is the doctrine of the vulgar, and implies no contradiction. There is no contradiction, therefore, in extending the same doctrine to all the perceptions.

In general, the following reasoning seems satisfactory. All ideas are borrowed from preceding perceptions. Our ideas of objects, therefore, are derived from that source. Consequently no proposition can be intelligible or consistent with regard to objects, which is not so with regard to perceptions. But it is intelligible and consistent to say, that objects exist distinct and independent, without any common *simple* substance or subject of inhesion. This proposition, therefore, can never be absurd with regard to perceptions.

When I turn my reflection on *myself,* I never can perceive this *self* without some one or more perceptions; nor can I ever perceive anything but the preceptions. It is the composition of these, therefore, which forms the self.

We can conceive a thinking being to have either many or few perceptions. Suppose the mind to be reduced even below the life of an oyster. Suppose it to have only one perception, as of thirst or hunger. Consider it in that situation. Do you conceive anything but merely that perception? Have you any notion of *self* or *substance*? If not, the addition of other perceptions can never give you that notion.

The annihilation which some people suppose to follow upon death, and which entirely destroys this self, is nothing but an extinction of all particular perceptions; love and hatred, pain and pleasure, thought and sensation. These, therefore, must be the same with self, since the one cannot survive the other.

Is *self* the same as *substance*? If it be, how can that question have place, concerning the substance of self, under a change of substance? If they be distinct, what is the difference betwixt them? For my part, I have a notion of neither, when conceived distinct from particular perceptions.

Philosophers begin to be reconciled to the principle, *that we have no idea of external substance, distinct from the ideas of particular qualities.* This must pave the way for a like principle with regard to the mind, *that we have no notion of it, distinct from the particular perception.*

So far I seem to be attended with sufficient evidence. But having thus loosened all our particular perceptions, when I proceed to explain the principle of connection, which binds them together, and makes us attribute to them a real simplicity and identity, I am sensible that my account is very defective, and that nothing but the seeming evidence of the precedent reasonings could have induced me to receive it. If perceptions are distinct existences, they form a whole only by being connected together. But no connections among distinct existences are ever discoverable by human understanding. We only *feel* a connection or determination of the thought to pass from one object to another. It follows, therefore, that the thought alone feels personal identity, when reflecting on the train of past perceptions that compose a mind, the ideas of them are felt to be connected together, and naturally introduce each other. However extraordinary this conclusion may seem, it need not surprise us. Most philosophers seem inclined to think, that personal identity *arises* from consciousness, and consciousness is nothing but a reflected thought or perception. The present philosophy, therefore, has so far a promising aspect. But all my hopes vanish when I come to explain the principles that unite our successive perceptions in our thought or consciousness. I cannot discover any theory which gives me satisfaction on this head.

In short, there are two principles which I cannot render consistent, nor is it in my power to renounce either of them, viz. *that all our distinct perceptions are distinct existences*, and *that the mind never perceives any real connection among distinct existences*. Did our perceptions either inhere in something simple and individual, or did the mind perceive some real connection among them, there would be no difficulty in the case. For my part, I must plead the privilege of a sceptic, and confess that this difficulty is too hard for my understanding. I pretend not, however, to pronounce it absolutely insuperable. Others, perhaps, or myself, upon more mature reflections, may discover some hypothesis that will reconcile those contradictions. . . .

DEREK PARFIT

Later Selves and Moral Principles*

I shall first sketch different views about the nature of personal identity, then suggest that the views support different moral claims.

I

Most of us seem to have certain beliefs about our own identity. We seem for instance to believe that, whatever happens, any future person must be either us, or someone else.

These beliefs are like those that some of us have about a simpler fact. Most of us now think that to be a person, as opposed to a mere animal, is just to have certain more specific properties, such as rationality. These are matters of degree. So we might say that the fact of personhood is just the fact of having certain other properties, which are had to different degrees.

There is a different view. Some of us believe that personhood is a further, deep, fact, and cannot hold to different degrees.

This second view may be confused with some trivial claims. Personhood is, in a sense, a further fact. And there is a sense in which all persons are equally persons.

Let us first show how these claims may be trivial. We can use a different example. There is a sense in which all our relatives are equally our relatives. We can use the phrase "related to" so that what it means has no degrees; on this use, parents and remote cousins are as much relatives. It is obvious, though, that kinship has degrees. This is shown in the phrase "closely related to": remote cousins are, as relatives, less close. I shall summarize such remarks in the following way. On the above use, the fact of being someone's relative has in its *logic* no degrees. But in its *nature*—in what it involves—it does have degrees. So the fact's logic hides its nature. Hence the triviality of the claim that all our relatives are equally our relatives. (The last few sentences may be wrongly worded,[1] but I hope that the example suggests what I mean.)

To return to the claims about personhood. These were: that it is a further fact, and that all persons are equally persons. As claims about the fact's logic, these are trivial. Certain people think the claims profound. They believe them to be true of the fact's nature.

The difference here can be shown in many ways. Take the question, "When precisely does an embryo become a person?" If we merely make the claims about the fact's logic, we shall not believe that this question must have a precise answer. Certain people do believe this. They believe that an embryo must either be, or not be, a complete person. Their view goes beyond the "logical claims." It concerns the nature of personhood.

We can now return to the main argument. About the facts of both personhood and personal identity, there are two views. According to the first, these facts have a special nature. They are further facts, independent of certain more specific facts; and in every case they must either hold completely, or completely fail to hold. According to the second view, these facts are not of this nature. They consist in the holding of the more specific facts; and they are matters of degree.

Let us name such opposing views. I shall call the first kind "Simple" and the second "Complex."

Such views may affect our moral principles, in the following way. If we change from a Simple to a Complex View, we acquire two beliefs: we decide that a certain fact is in its nature less deep, and that it sometimes holds to reduced degrees. These beliefs may have two effects: the first belief may weaken certain principles, and the second give the principles a new scope.

Take the views about personhood. An ancient principle gives to the welfare of people absolute precedence over that of mere animals. If the difference between people and mere animals is in its nature less deep, this principle can be more plausibly denied. And if embryos are not people, and become them only by degrees, the principle forbidding murder can be more plausibly given less scope.

I have not defended these claims. They are meant to parallel what I shall defend in the case of the two views about personal identity.

II

We must first sketch these views. It will help to revive a comparison. What is involved in the survival of a nation are just certain continuities, such as those of a people and a political system. When there is a weakening of these continuities, as there was, say, in the Norman Conquest, it may be unclear whether a nation survives. But there is here no problem. And the reason is that the survival of a nation just involves these continuities. Once we know how the continuities were weakened, we need not ask, as a question about an independent fact, "Did a nation cease to exist?" There is nothing left to know.

We can add the following remarks. Though identity has no degrees, these continuities are matters of degree. So the identity of nations over time is only in its logic "all-or-nothing"; in its nature it has degrees.

The identity of people over time is, according to the "Complex View," comparable.[2] It consists in bodily and psychological continuity. These, too, are matters of degree. So we can add the comparable remark. The identity of people over time is only in its logic "all-or-nothing"; in its nature it has degrees.

How do the continuities of bodies and minds have degrees? We can first dismiss bodies, since they are morally trivial.[3] Let us next call "direct" the psychological relations which hold between: the memory of an experience and this experience, the intention to perform some later action and this action, and different expressions of some lasting character-trait. We can now name two general features of a person's life. One, "connectedness," is the holding, over time, of particular "direct" relations. The other, "continuity," is the holding of a chain of such relations. If, say, I cannot now remember some earlier day, there are no "connections of memory" between me now and myself on that day. But there may be "continuity of memory." This there is if, on every day between, I remembered the previous day.

Of these two general relations, I define "continuous with" so that, in its logic, it has no degrees. It is like "related to" in the use on which all our relatives are equally our relatives. But "connectedness" has degrees. Between different parts of a person's life, the connections of memory, character, and intention are—in strength and number—more or less. ("Connected to" is like "closely related to"; different relatives can be more or less close.)

We can now restate the Complex View. What is important in personal identity are the two relations we have just sketched. One of these, continuity, is in its logic all-or-nothing. But it just involves connectedness, which clearly has degrees. In its nature, therefore, continuity holds different degrees. So the fact of personal identity also, in its nature, has degrees.

To turn to the Simple View. Here the fact is believed to be, in its nature, all-or-nothing. This it can only be if it does not just consist in (bodily and) psychological continuity—if it is, in its nature, a further fact. To suggest why: These continuities hold, over time, to different degrees. This is true in actual cases, but is most clearly true in some imaginary cases. We can imagine cases where the continuities between each of us and a future person hold to every possible degree. Suppose we think, in imagining these cases, "Such a future person must be either, and quite simply, *me*, or *someone else*." (Suppose we think, "Whatever happens, any future experience must be either *wholly* mine, or *not* mine *at all*.") If the continuities can hold to every degree, but the fact of our identity must hold completely or not at all, then this fact cannot consist in these continuities. It must be a further, independent, fact.

It is worth repeating that the Simple View is about the nature of personal identity, not its logic. This is shown by the reactions most of us have to various so-called "problem cases." These reactions also show that even if, on the surface, we reject the Simple View, at a deeper level we assume it to be true.[4]

We can add this—rough—test of our assumptions. Nations are in many ways unlike people; for example, they are not organisms. But if we take the Complex View, we shall accept this particular comparison: the survival of a person, like that of a nation, is a matter of degree. If instead we reject this comparison, we take the Simple View.

One last preliminary. We can use "I," and the other pronouns, so that they cover only the part of our lives to which, when speaking, we have the strongest psychological connections. We assign the rest of our lives to what we call our "other selves." When, for instance, we have undergone any marked change in character, or conviction, or style of life, we might say, "It was not *I* who did that, but an earlier self."

Such talk can become natural. To quote three passages:

> Our dread of a future in which we must forego the sight of faces, the sound of voices, that we love, friends from whom we derive today our keenest joys, this dread, far from being dissipated, is intensified, if to the grief of such a privation we reflect that there will be added what seems to us now in anticipation an even more cruel grief: not to feel it as a grief at all—to remain indifferent: for if that should occur, our self would then have changed. It would be in a real sense the death of ourself, a death followed, it is true, by a resurrection, but in a different self, the life, the love of which are beyond the reach of those elements of the existing self that are doomed to die. . . .[5]

> It is not because other people are dead that our affection for them grows faint, it is because we ourself are dying. Albertine had no cause to rebuke her friend. The man who was usurping his name had merely inherited it. . . . My new self, while it grew up in the shadow of the old, had often heard the other speak of Albertine; through that other self . . . it thought that it knew her, it found her attractive . . . but this was merely an affection at second hand.[6]

> Nadya had written in her letter: "When you return. . . ." But that was the whole horror: that there would be no *return*. . . . A new, unfamiliar person would walk in bearing the name of her husband, and she would see that the man, her beloved, for whom she had shut herself up to wait for fourteen years, no longer existed. . . .[7]

Whether we are inclined to use such talk will depend upon our view about the nature of personal identity. If we take the Simple View, we shall not be so inclined, for we shall think it deeply true that all the parts of a person's life are as much parts of his life. If we take the Complex View, we shall be less impressed by this truth. It will seem like the truth that all the parts of a nation's history are as much parts of its history. Because this latter truth is superficial, we at times subdivide such a history into that of a series of successive nations, such as Anglo-Saxon, Medieval, or Post-Imperial England. The connections between these, though similar in kind, differ in degree. If we take the Complex View, we may also redescribe a person's life as the history of a series of successive selves. And the connections between these we shall also claim to be similar in kind, different in degree.

III

We can now turn to our question. Do the different views tend to support different moral claims?

I have space to consider only three subjects: desert, commitment, and distributive justice. And I am forced to oversimplify, and to distort. So it may help to start with some general remarks.

My suggestions are of this form: "The Complex View supports certain claims." By "supports" I mean both "makes more plausible" and "helps to explain." My suggestions thus mean: "If the true view is the Complex, not the Simple, View, certain claims are more plausible. We may therefore be, on the Complex View, more inclined to make these claims."

I shall be discussing two kinds of case: those in which the psychological connections are as strong as they ever are, and those in which they are markedly weak. I choose these kinds of case for the following reason. If we change from the Simple to the Complex View, we believe (I shall claim) that our identity is in its nature less deep, and that it sometimes holds to reduced degrees. The first of these beliefs covers every case, even those where there are the strongest connections. But the second of the two beliefs only covers cases where there are weak connections. So the two kinds of case provide separate testing-grounds for the two beliefs.

Let us start with the cases of weak connection. And our first principle can be that we deserve to be punished for certain crimes.

We can suppose that, between some convict now and himself when he committed some crime, there are only weak psychological connections. (This will usually be when conviction takes place after many years.) We can imply the weakness of these connections by calling the convict, not the criminal, but his later self.

Two grounds for detaining him would be unaffected. Whether a convict should be either reformed, or preventively detained, turns upon his present state, not his relation to the criminal. A third ground, deterrence, turns upon a different question. Do potential criminals care about their later selves? Do they care, for instance, if they do not expect to be caught for many years? If they do, then detaining their later selves could perhaps deter.

Would it be deserved? Locke thought that if we forget our crimes we deserve no punishment.[8] Geach considers this view "morally repugnant."[9] Mere loss of memory does seem to be insufficient. Changes of character would appear to be more relevant. The subject is, though, extremely difficult. Claims about desert can be plausibly supported with a great variety of arguments. According to some of these loss of memory would be important. And according to most the nature and cause of any change in character would need to be known.

I have no space to consider these details, but I shall make one suggestion. This appeals to the following assumption. When some morally important fact holds to a lesser degree, it can be more plausibly claimed to have less importance—even, in extreme cases, none.

I shall not here defend this assumption. I shall only say that most of us apply the assumption to many kinds of principle. Take, for example, the two principles that we have special duties to help our relatives, or friends. On the assumption, we might claim that we have less of a special duty to help our less close relatives, or friends, and, to those who are very distant, none at all.

My suggestion is this. If the assumption is acceptable, and the Complex View correct, it becomes more plausible to make the following claim: when the connections between convicts and their past criminal selves are less, they deserve less punishment; if they are very weak, they perhaps deserve none. This claim extends the idea of "diminished responsibility." It does not appeal to mental illness, but instead treats a later self like a sane accomplice. Just as a man's deserts correspond to the degree of his complicity with some criminal, so his deserts, now, for some past crime correspond to the degree of connectedness between himself now and himself when committing that crime.

If we add the further assumption that psychological connections are, in general, weaker over longer periods, the claim provides a ground for Statutes of Limitations. (They of course have other grounds.)

IV

We can next consider promises. There are here two identities involved. The first is that of the person who, once, made a promise. Let us suppose that between this person now and himself then there are only weak connections. Would this wipe away his commitment? Does a later self start with a clean slate?

On the assumption that I gave, the Complex View supports the answer, "yes." Certain people think that only short-term promises carry moral weight. This belief becomes more plausible on the Complex View.

The second relevant identity is that of the person who received the promise. There is here an asymmetry. The possible effect of the Complex View could be deliberately blocked. We could ask for promises of this form: "I shall help you, and all your later selves." If the promises that I *receive* take this form, they cannot be plausibly held to be later undermined by any change in *my* character, or by any other weakening, over the rest of *my* life, in connectedness.

The asymmetry is this: similar forms cannot so obviously stay binding on the *maker* of a promise. I might say, "I, and all my later selves, shall help you." But it is plausible to reply that I can only bind my present self. This is plausible because it is like the claim that I can only bind myself. No one, though, denies that I can promise you that I shall help someone else. So I can clearly promise you that I shall help your later selves.

Such a promise may indeed seem especially binding. Suppose that you change faster than I do. I may then regard myself as committed, not to you, but to your earlier self. I may therefore think that you cannot waive my commitment. (It would be like a commitment, to someone now dead, to help his children. We cannot be released from such commitments.)

Such a case would be rare. But an example may help the argument. Let us take a nineteenth-century Russian who, in several years, should inherit vast estates. Because he has socialist ideals, he intends, now, to give the land to the peasants. But he knows that in time his ideals may fade. To guard against this possibility, he does two things. He first signs a legal document, which will automatically give away the land, and which can only be revoked with his wife's consent. He then says to his wife, "If I ever change my mind, and ask you to revoke the document, promise me that you will not consent." He might add, "I regard my ideals as essential to me, If I lose these ideals, I want you to think that *I* cease to exist. I want you to regard your husband, then, not as me, the man who asks you for this promise, but only as his later self. Promise me that you would not do what he asks."

This plea seems understandable. And if his wife made this promise, and he later asked her to revoke the document, she might well regard herself as in no way released from her commitment. It might seem to her as if she has obligations to two different people. She might think that to do what her husband now asks would be to betray the young man whom she loved and married. And she might regard what her husband now says as unable to acquit her of disloyalty to this young man—of disloyalty to her husband's earlier self.

Such an example may seem not to require the distinction between successive selves. Suppose that I ask you to promise me never to give me cigarettes, even if I beg you for them. You might think that I cannot, in begging you, simply release you from this commitment. And to think this you need not deny that it is I to whom you are committed.

This seems correct. But the reason is that addiction clouds judgment. Similar examples might involve extreme stress or pain, or (as with Odysseus, tied to the mast) extraordinary temptation. When, though, nothing clouds a person's judgment, most of us believe that the person to whom we are committed can always release us. He can always, if in sound mind, waive our commitment. We believe this whatever the commitment may be. So (on this view) the content of a commitment cannot stop its being waived.

To return to the Russian couple. The man's ideals fade, and he asks his wife to revoke the document. Though she promised him to refuse, he declares that he now releases her from this commitment. We have sketched two ways in which she might think that she is not released. She might, first, take her husband's change of mind as proof that he cannot now make considered judgments. But we can suppose that she has no such thought. We can also suppose that she shares our view about commitment. If so, she will only believe that her husband is unable to release her if she thinks that it is, in some sense, not *he* to whom she is committed. We have sketched such a sense. She may regard the young man's loss of his ideals as involving his replacement by a later self.

The example is of a quite general possibility. We may regard some events within a person's life as, in certain ways, like birth or death. Not in all ways, for beyond these events the person has earlier or later selves. But it may be only one out of the series of selves which is the object of some of our emotions, and to which we apply some of our principles.

The young Russian socialist regards his ideals as essential to his present self. He asks his wife to promise to this present self not to act against these ideals. And, on this way of thinking, she can never be released from her commitment. For the self to whom she is committed would, in trying to release her, cease to exist.

The way of thinking may seem to be within our range of choice. We can indeed choose when to *speak* of a new self, just as we can choose when to speak of the end of Medieval England. But the way of speaking would express beliefs, And the wife in our example cannot choose her beliefs. That the young man whom she loved and married has, in a sense, ceased to exist, that her middle-aged and cynical husband is at most the later self of this young man—these claims may seem to her to express more of the truth than the simple claim, "but they are the same person." Just as we can give a more accurate description if we divide the history of Russia into that of the Empire and of the Soviet Union, so it may be more accurate to divide her husband's life into that of two successive selves.

V

I have suggested that the Complex View supports certain claims. It is worth repeating that these claims are at most more plausible on the Complex View (more, that is, than on the Simple View). They are not entailed by the Complex View.

We can sometimes show this in the following way. Some claims make sense when applied to successive generations. Such claims can obviously be applied to successive selves. For example, it perhaps makes sense to believe that we inherit the commitments of our parents. If so, we can obviously believe that commitments are inherited by later selves.

Other claims may be senseless when applied to generations. Perhaps we cannot intelligibly think that we deserve to be punished for all our parents' crimes. But even if this is so, it should still make sense to have the comparable thought about successive selves. No similarity in the form of two relations could force us to admit that they are morally equivalent, for we can always appeal to the difference in their content.

There are, then, no entailments. But there seldom are in moral reasoning. So the Complex View may still support certain claims. Most of us think that our children are neither bound by our commitments, nor responsible for all we do. If we take the Complex View, we may be more inclined to think the same about our later selves. And the correctness of the view might make such beliefs more defensible.

VI

What, next, of our present selves? What of the other kind of case, where there are the strongest psychological connections? Here it makes no difference to believe that our identity has, in its nature, degrees, for there is here the strongest degree. But in the change to the Complex View we acquire a second new belief. We decide that our identity is in its nature less deep, or involves less. This belief applies to every case, even those where there are the strongest connections.

It is worth suggesting why there must be this second difference between the two views. On the Complex View, our identity over time just involves bodily and psychological continuity. On the Simple View, it does not just involve these continuities; it is in its nature a further fact. If we stop believing that it is a further fact, then (by arithmetic) we believe that it involves less. There is still the bare possibility that we thought the further fact superficial.[10] But it seems to most of us peculiarly deep.[11] This is why, if we change to the Complex View, we believe that our identity is in its nature less deep.

Would this belief affect our principles? If it has effects, they would not be confined to the special cases where there are only weak psychological connections. They would hold in every case. The effects would not be that we give certain principles a different scope. They would be that we give the principles a different weight.

Such effects could be defended on the following assumption. When some morally important fact is seen to be less deep, it can be plausibly claimed to be less important. As the limiting case, it becomes more plausible to claim that it has no importance. (This assumption is a variant of the one I used earlier.) The implications are obvious. The principles of desert and commitment presuppose that personal identity is morally important. On the assumption I have just sketched, the Complex View supports the claim that it is—because less deep—less important. So it may tend to weaken these principles.

I shall not here discuss these possible effects. I shall only say that the principle of commitment seems to be the less threatened by this weakening effect. The reason may be that, unlike the principle of desert, it is a conventional or "artificial" principle. This may shield it from a change of view about the facts.

I shall now turn to my last subject, distributive justice. Here the consequences of a change to the Complex View seem harder to assess. The reason is this: in the case of the principles of desert and commitment, both the possible effects, the weakening and the change in scope, are in theory pro-utilitarian. (Since these principles compete with the principle of utility, it is obviously in theory pro-utilitarian if they are weakened.[12] And their new scope would be a reduced scope. This should also be pro-utilitarian.) Since both the possible effects would be in the same direction, we can make this general claim: if the change of view has effects upon these principles, these effects would be pro-utilitarian. In the case of distributive justice, things are different. Here, as I shall argue, the two possible effects seem to be in opposite directions. So there is a new question: which is the more plausible combined effect? My reply will again be: pro-utilitarian. Before defending this claim, I shall mention two related claims. These can be introduced in the following way.

Utilitarians reject distributive principles. They aim for the greatest net sum of benefits minus burdens, whatever its distribution. Let us say they "maximize."

There is, here, a well-known parallel. When we can affect only one person, we accept maximization. We do not believe that we ought to give a person fewer happy days so as to be more fair in the way we spread them out over the parts of his life. There are, of course, arguments for spreading out enjoyments. We remain fresh, and have more to look forward to. But these arguments do not count against maximization; they remind us how to achieve it.

When we can affect several people, utilitarians make similar claims. They admit new arguments for spreading out enjoyments, such as that which appeals to relative deprivation. But they treat equality as a mere means, not a separate aim.

Since their attitude to sets of lives is like ours to single lives, utilitarians disregard the boundaries between lives. We may ask, "Why?"

Here are three suggestions.–Their approach to morality leads them to overlook these boundaries.–They believe that the boundaries are unimportant, because they think that sets of lives are like single lives.–They take the Complex View.

The first suggestion has been made by Rawls. It can be summarized like this. Utilitarians tend to approach moral questions as if they were impartial observers. When they ask themselves, as observers, what is right, or what they prefer, they tend to *identify* with *all* the affected people. This leads them to ignore the fact that *different* people are affected, and so to reject the claims of justice.[13]

In the case of some utilitarians, Rawls's explanation seems sufficient. Let us call these the "identifying observers." But there are others who in contrast always seem *"detached* observers."These utilitarians do not seem to overlook the distinction between people. And, as Rawls remarks, there is no obvious reason why observers who remain *detached* cannot adopt the principles of justice. If we approach morality in a quite detached way—if we do not think of ourselves as potentially involved—we may, I think, be somewhat more inclined to reject these principles. But this particular approach to moral questions does not itself seem a sufficient explanation for utilitarian beliefs.

The Complex View may provide a different explanation. These two are quite compatible. Utilitarians may both approach morality as observers, and take the Complex View. (The explanations may indeed be mutually supporting.)

To turn to the remaining explanation. Utilitarians treat sets of lives in the way that we treat single lives. It has been suggested, not that they ignore the difference between people, but that they actually believe that a group of people is like a superperson. This suggestion is, in a sense, the reverse of mine. It imputes a different view about the facts. And it can seem the more plausible.

Let us start with an example. Suppose that we must choose whether to let some child undergo some hardship. If he does, this will either be for his own greater benefit in adult life, or for the similar benefit of someone else. Does it matter which?

Most of us would answer: "Yes. If it is for the child's own benefit, there can at least be no unfairness."We might draw the general conclusion that failure to relieve useful burdens is more likely to be justified if they are for a person's *own* good.

Utilitarians, confusingly, could accept this conclusion. They would explain it in a different way. They might, for instance, point out that such burdens are in general easier to bear.

To block this reply, we can suppose that the child in our example cannot be cheered up in this way. Let us next ignore other such arguments. This simplifies the disagreement. Utilitarians would say: "Whether it is right to let the child bear the burden only depends upon how great the benefit will be. It does not depend upon who benefits. It would make no moral difference if the benefit comes, not to the child himself, but to someone else." Non-utilitarians might reply: "On the contrary, if it comes to the child himself this helps to justify the burden. If it comes to someone else, that is unfair."

We can now ask: do the two views about the nature of personal identity tend to support different sides in this debate?

Part of the answer seems clear. Non-utilitarians think it a morally important fact that it be the child himself who, as an adult, benefits. This fact, if it seems more important on one of the views, ought to do so on the Simple View, for it is on this view that the identity between the child and the adult is in its nature deeper. On the Complex View, it is less deep, and holds, over adolescence, to reduced degrees. If we take the Complex View, we may compare the lack of connections between the child and his adult self to the lack of connections between different people. That it will be *he* who receives the benefit may thus seem less important. We might say, "It will not be *he*. It will only be his adult self."

The Simple View seems, then, to support the non-utilitarian reply. Does it follow that the Complex View tends to support utilitarian beliefs? Not directly. For we might say, "Just as it would be unfair if it is someone else who benefits, so if it won't be he, but only his adult self, that would also be unfair."

The point is a general one If we take the Complex View, we may regard the (rough) subdivisions within lives as, in certain ways, like the divisions between lives. We may therefore come to treat alike two kinds of distribution: within lives, and between lives. But there are two ways of treating these alike. We can apply distributive principles to both, or to neither.

Which of these might we do? I claim that we may abandon these principles. Someone might object: "If we do add, to the divisions between lives, subdivisions within lives, the effects could only be these. The principles that we now apply to the divisions we come to apply to the sub-divisions." (If, to use your own example, we believe that our sons do not inherit our commitments, we may come to think the same about our later selves.)

"The comparable effect would now be this. We demand fairness to later selves. We *extend* distributive principles. You instead claim that we may abandon these principles. Since this is *not* the comparable effect, your claim must be wrong."

The objection might be pressed. We might add: "If we did abandon these principles, we should be moving in reverse. We should not be treating parts of one life as we now treat different lives, but be treating different lives as we now treat one life. This, the reverse effect, could only come from the reverse comparison. Rather than thinking that a person's life is like the history of a nation, we must be thinking that a nation—or indeed any group—is like a person."

To review the arguments so far. Treating alike single people and groups may come from accepting some comparison between them. But there are two ways of treating them alike. We can demand fairness even within single lives, or reject this demand in the case of groups. And there are two ways of taking this comparison. We can accept the Complex View and compare a person's life to the history of a group, or accept the reverse view and compare groups to single people.

Of these four positions, I had matched the Complex View with the abandonment of fairness. The objection was that it seemed to be better matched with the demand for fairness even within lives. And the rejection of this demand, in the case of groups, seemed to require what I shall call "the Reverse View."

My reply will be this. Disregard for the principles of fairness could perhaps be supported by the Reverse View. But it does not have to be. And in seeing why we shall see how it may be supported by the Complex View.

Many thinkers have believed that a society, or nation, is like a person. This belief seems to weaken the demand for fairness. When we are thought to be mere parts of a social organism, it can seem to matter less how we are each treated.[14]

If the rejection of fairness has to be supported in this way, utilitarians can be justly ignored. This belief is at best superficially true when held about societies. And to support utilitarian views it would have to be held about the whole of mankind, where it is absurd.

Does the rejection of fairness need such support? Certain writers think that it does. Gauthier, for instance, suggests that to suppose that we should maximize for mankind "is to suppose that mankind is a super-person."[15] This suggestion seems to rest on the following argument. "We are free to maximize within one life only because it is *one* life. So we could only be free to maximize over different lives if they are like parts of a single life."

Given this argument, utilitarians would, I think, deny the premise. They would deny that it is the unity of a life which, within this life, justifies maximization. They can then think this justified over different lives without assuming mankind to be a super-person.

The connection with the Complex View is, I think, this. It is on this view, rather than the Simple View, that the premise is more plausibly denied. That is how the Complex View may support utilitarian beliefs.

To expand these remarks. There are two kinds of distribution: within lives, and between lives. And there are two ways of treating these alike. We can apply distributive principles to both, or to neither.

Utilitarians apply them to neither. I suggest that this may be (in part) because they take the Complex View. An incompatible suggestion is that they take the Reverse View.

My suggestion may seem clearly wrong if we overlook the following fact. There are two routes to the abandonment of distributive principles. We may give them no scope, or instead give them no weight.

Suppose we assume that the only route is the change in scope. Then it may indeed seem that utilitarians must either be assuming that any group of people is like a single person (Gauthier's suggestion), or at least be forgetting that it is not (Rawls's suggestion).

I shall sketch the other route. Utilitarians may not be denying that distributive principles have scope. They may be denying that they have weight. This, the second of the kinds of effect that I earlier distinguished, *may* be supported by the Complex View.

The situation, more precisely, may be this. If the Complex View supports a change in the scope of distributive principles, it perhaps supports giving them more scope. It perhaps supports their extension even within single lives. But the other possible effect, the weakening of these principles, may be the more strongly supported. That is how the net effect may be pro-utilitarian.

This suggestion differs from the other two in the following way. Rawls remarks that the utilitarian attitude seems to involve "conflating all persons into one."[16] This remark also covers Gauthier's suggestion. But the attitude may derive, not from the conflation of persons, but from their (partial) disintegration. It may rest upon the view that a person's life is less deeply integrated than we mostly think. Utilitarians may be treating benefits and burdens, not as if they all came within the same life, but as if it made no moral difference where they came. This belief may be supported by the view that the unity of each life, and hence the difference between lives, is in its nature less deep.

VIII

I shall next sketch a brief defence of this suggestion. And I shall start with a new distributive principle. Utilitarians believe that benefits and burdens can be freely weighed against each other, even if they come to different people. This is frequently denied.

We must first distinguish two kinds of weighing. The claim that a certain burden "factually outweighs" another is the claim that it is greater. The claim that it "morally outweighs" the other is the claim that we should relieve it even at the cost of failing to relieve the other. Similar remarks apply to the weighing of benefits against burdens, and against each other.

Certain people claim that burdens cannot even *factually* outweigh each other if they come to different people. (They claim that the sense of "greater than" can only be provided by a single person's preferences.) I am here concerned with a different claim. At its boldest this is that the burdens and benefits of different people cannot be *morally* weighed. I shall consider one part of this claim. This goes: "Someone's burden cannot be morally outweighed by mere benefits to someone else." I say "mere" benefits, because the claim is not intended to deny that it *can* be right to let a person bear a burden so as to benefit another. Such acts may, for instance, be required by justice. What the claim denies is that such acts can be justified solely upon utilitarian grounds. It denies that a person's burden can be morally outweighed by *mere* benefits to someone else.

This claim often takes qualified forms. It can be restricted to great burdens, or be made to require that the net benefit be proportionately great. I shall here discuss the simplest form, for my remarks could be adapted to the other forms. Rawls puts the claim as follows: "The reasoning which balances the gains and losses of different persons . . . is excluded." So I shall call this the "objection to balancing."

This objection rests in part on a different claim. This goes: "Someone's burden cannot be *compensated* by benefits to someone else." This second claim is, with qualifications, clearly true. We cannot say, "On the contrary, our burdens can be compensated by benefits to anyone else, even a total stranger."

Not only is this second claim clearly true; its denial is in no way supported by the Complex View. So if the change to this view has effects upon this claim, they would be these. We might, first, extend the claim even within single lives. We might say, in the example that I gave, "The child's burden cannot be compensated by benefits to his adult self." This claim would be like the claims that we are sometimes not responsible for, nor bound by, our earlier selves. It would apply to certain parts of one life what we now believe about different lives. It would therefore seem to be, as a change in scope, in the right direction.

We might, next, give the claim less weight. Our ground would be the one that I earlier gave. Compensation presupposes personal identity. On the Complex View, we may think that our identity is, because less deep, less morally important. We may therefore think that the fact of compensation is itself less morally important. Though it cannot be denied, the claim about compensation may thus be given less weight.

If we now return to the objection to balancing, things are different. The concept of "greater moral weight" does not presuppose personal identity. So this objection can be denied; and the Complex View seems to support this denial.

The denial might be put like this: "Our burdens cannot indeed be *compensated* by mere benefits to someone else. But they may be *morally outweighed* by such benefits. It may still be right to give the benefits rather than relieve the burdens. Burdens are morally outweighed by benefits if they are factually outweighed by these benefits. All that is needed is that the benefits be greater than the burdens. It is unimportant, in itself, to whom both come."

This is the utilitarian reply. I shall next suggest why the Complex View seems, more than the Simple View, to support this reply.

The objection to balancing rests in part on the claim about compensation. On the Complex View, this claim can more plausibly be thought less important. If we take this view, we may (we saw) think both that there is less scope for compensation and that it has less moral weight. If the possibilities of compensation are, in these two ways, less morally important, there would then be less support for the objection to balancing. It would be more plausible to make the utilitarian reply.

The point can be made in a different way. Even those who object to balancing think it justified to let us bear burdens for our own good. So their claim must be that a person's burden, while it can be morally outweighed by benefits to him, cannot ever be outweighed by mere benefits to others. This is held to be so even if the benefits are far greater than the burden. The claim thus gives to the boundaries between lives—or to the fact of non-identity—overwhelming significance. It allows within the same life what, for different lives, it totally forbids.

This claim seems to be more plausible on the Simple View. Since identity is, here, thought to involve more, non-identity could plausibly seem more important. On the Simple View, we are impressed by the truth that all of a person's life is as much his life. If we are impressed by this truth—by the unity of each life—the boundaries between lives will seem to be deeper. This supports the claim that, in the moral calculus, these boundaries cannot be crossed. On the Complex View, we are less impressed by this truth. We regard the unity of each life as in is nature less deep, and as a matter of degree. We may therefore think the boundaries between lives to be less like those between, say, the squares on a chess-board, and to be more like those between different countries. They may then seem less morally decisive.

IX

We can now turn to different principles, for example that of equal distribution. Most of us give such principles only *some* weight. We think, for instance, that unequal distribution can be justified if it brings an overall gain in social welfare. But we may insist that the gain be proportionately great.

We do not, in making such claims, forbid utilitarian policies. We allow that every gain in welfare has moral value. But we do restrain these policies. We insist that it also matters *who* gains. Certain distributions are, we claim, morally preferable. We thus claim that we ought to favour the worst off, and to incline towards equality.

Utilitarians would reply: "These claims are of course plausible. But the policies they recommend are the very policies which tend to increase total welfare. This coincidence suggests[17] that we ought to change our view about the status of these claims.

We should regard them, not as checks upon, but as guides to, utilitarian policy. We should indeed value equal distribution. But the value lies in its typical effects."

This reply might be developed in the following way. Most of us believe that a mere difference in *when* something happens, if it does not affect the nature of what happens, cannot be morally significant. Certain answers to the question "When?" are of course important. We cannot ignore the timing of events. And it is even plausible to claim that if, say, we are planning when to give or to receive benefits, we should aim for an equal distribution over time. But we aim for this only because of its effects. We do not believe that the equality of benefit at different times is, as such, morally important.

Utilitarians might say: "If it does not, as such, matter *when* something happens, why does it matter *to whom* it happens? Both of these are mere differences in position. What is important is the nature of what happens. When we choose between social policies, we need only be concerned with how *great* the benefits will be. *Where* they come, whether in space, or in time, or as between people, has in itself no importance."

Part of the disagreement is, then, this. Non-utilitarians take the question "Who?" to be quite unlike the question "When?" If they are asked for the simplest possible description of the morally relevant facts, they will sometimes give them in a form which is tenseless; but it will always be personal. They will say, "Someone gains, the same person loses, someone else gains. . . ." Utilitarians would instead say, "A gain, a loss, another gain. . . ."

There are many different arguments for and against these two positions. We are only asking: would a change to the Complex View tend to support either one?

It would seem so. On the Simple View, it is more plausible to insist upon the question "Who?" On the Complex View, it is more plausible to compare this to the question "When?", and to present the moral data in the second, or "impersonal," form.

It may help to return to our comparison. Most of us believe that the existence of a nation does not involve anything more than the existence of associated people. We do not deny the reality of nations. But we do deny that they are separately, or independently, real. They are entirely composed of associated people.

This belief seems to support certain moral claims. If there is nothing to a nation but its citizens, it is less plausible to regard the nation as itself a (primary) object of duties, or possessor of rights. It is more plausible to focus upon the citizens, and to regard them less as citizens, more as people. We may therefore, on this view, think a person's nationality less morally important.

On the Complex View, we hold similar beliefs. We regard the existence of a person as, in turn, involving nothing more than the occurrence of interrelated mental and physical events. We do not, of course, deny the reality of people (our own reality!). And we agree that we are not, strictly, series of events—that we are not thoughts, but thinkers, not actions, but agents. But we consider this a fact of grammar. And we do deny that we are not just conceptually distinct from our bodies, actions, and experiences, but also separately real. We deny that the identity of a person, of the so-called "subject" of mental and physical events, is a further, deep, fact, independent of the facts about the interrelations between these events.

This belief may support similar claims. We may, when thinking morally, focus less upon the person, the subject of experience, and instead focus more upon the experiences themselves. Just as we often ignore whether people come from the same or different nations, so we may more often ignore whether experiences come within the same or different lives.

Take, for example, the relief of suffering. Suppose that we can only help one of two people. We shall achieve more if we help the first; but it is the second who, in the past, suffered more.

Those who believe in fair shares may decide to help the second person. This will be less effective; so the amount of suffering in the two people's lives will, in sum, be greater; but the amounts in each life will be made more equal.

If we take the Complex View, we may reject this line of thought. We may decide to do the most we can to relieve suffering. To suggest why, we can vary the example. Suppose that we can only help one of two nations. Here again, the one that we can help most is the one whose history was, in earlier centuries, the more fortunate. Most of us would not believe that it could be right to allow mankind to suffer more, so that its suffering could be more equally divided between the histories of different nations.

On the Complex View, we compare the lives of people to the histories of nations. We may therefore think the same about them too. We may again decide to aim for the least possible suffering, whatever its distribution.

X

We can next explain what, earlier, may have seemed puzzling. Besides the Complex View, which compares people to nations, I mentioned a reverse view, which compares nations to people. How can these be different?

It will help to introduce two more terms. With respect to many types of thing, we may take one of two views. We may believe that the existence of this type of thing does not involve anything more than the existence of certain other (interrelated) things. Such a view can be called "atomistic." We may instead believe that the things in question have a quite separate existence, over and above that of these other things. Such a view can be called "holistic."

One example of an atomistic view is the one we mostly take about nations. Most of us do not (here and now) believe that there is more to nations than associated people. On the other hand, we mostly do seem to assume that there is more to us than a series of mental and physical events. We incline to what I call the Simple View. Most of us are therefore atomists about nations, holists about people.

It is the difference between these common views which explains the two comparisons. The claim that X is like Y typically assumes the common view of Y. We shall therefore say "People are like nations" if we are atomists about both. We shall instead say "Nations are like people" if we are holists about both. Either way, we assume one of the common views and deny the other.

We can end by considering a remark in Rawls. There is, he writes, "a curious anomaly":

It is customary to think of utilitarianism as individualistic, and certainly there are good reasons for this. The utilitarians . . . held that the good of society is constituted by the advantages enjoyed by individuals. Yet utilitarianism is not individualistic . . . in that . . . it applies to society the principle of choice for one man.

Our account suggests an explanation. Individualists claim that the welfare of society only consists in the welfare of its members, and that the members have rights to fair shares.

Suppose that we are holists about society. We believe that the existence of society transcends that of its members. This belief threatens the first of the individualist claims. It supports the view that the welfare of society also transcends that of its members. This in turn threatens the second claim, for in the pursuit of a transcendent social goal, fair shares may seem less important. Social holists may thus reject both of the individualist claims.

Utilitarians reject the second claim, but accept the first. This would indeed be anomalous if their attitude to these claims rested upon social holism. If this were their ground, we should expect them to reject *both* claims.

We have sketched a different ground. Rather than being holists about society, utilitarians may be atomists about people. This dissolves the anomaly. For they are also atomists about society, and this double atomism seems to support the two positions Rawls describes. If we are atomists about society, we can then more plausibly accept the first of the individualist claims, *viz.* that the welfare of society only consists in that of its members. If we are also atomists about people, we can then more plausibly reject the second claim, the demand for fair shares. We may tend to focus less upon the person, the subject of experience, and instead focus more upon the experiences themselves. We may then decide that it is only the nature of what happens which is morally important, not to whom it happens. We may thus decide that it is always right to increase benefits and reduce burdens, whatever their distribution.

"Utilitarianism," Rawls remarks, "does not take seriously the distinction between persons."[19] If "the separateness of persons . . . is *the* basic fact for morals,"[20] this is a grave charge. I have tried to show how one view about the nature of persons may provide *some* defence.

Notes

*I have been helped in writing this by T. Nagel; also by S. Blackburn, E. Borowitz, S. Clark, L. Francis, H. Frankfurt, J. Griffin, R. M. Hare, S. Lukes, J. Mackie, A. Orenstein, C. Peacocke, A. Rorty, A. Ryan, S. Shoemaker, D. Thomas, R. Walker, and others.

[1]Most of the end notes have been omitted—ed.

[2]Cf. Hume: "I cannot compare the soul more properly to anything than to a republic or commonwealth." (Hume, Book I, Part IV, Section 6, p. 261.)

[3]They cannot be so dismissed in a full account. The Complex View is not identical to Hume's view. It is even compatible with physicalism. See, for example, Quinton (1962), and Quinton (1972), pp. 88-102.

[4]That we are inclined to this view is shown in Williams. That the view is false I began to argue in Parfit (1971).

[5]Proust (1967), p. 349. (I have slightly altered the translation.)

[6]Proust (1949), p. 249.

[7]Solzhenitsyn, p. 232. (Curiously, Solzhenitsyn, like Keats (p. 322), seems to attach weight not just to psychological but to *cellular* change. Cf. Hume.)

[8]Locke, Book II, chapter XXVII, section 26. (Cf. also the "Defence of Mr. Locke's Opinion" in certain editions of Locke's *Works* (e.g. 11th edn, vol. 3).)

[9]Geach, p. 4.

[10]As, for example, Leibniz may have done. See the remark that Shoemaker quotes in Care, p. 127. Locke sometimes held a similar view. (I refer to his claim that "whether it be the same identical substance, which always thinks in the same person . . . matters not at all.")

[11]As Williams suggests. Cf. Bayle's reply to Leibniz quoted by Chisholm in Care, p. 139; and, for other statements, Geach, pp. 1-29, Penelhum, closing chapters (both implicit), Butler, pp. 385 ff., Reid, Essay III, chs 4 and 6, and Chisholm (more explicit).

[12]That it may in practice be anti-utilitarian is, for instance, emphasized in Sidgwick (1901), Book IV, ch. V. (In Sidgwick (1902), p. 114, he writes, "It may be—I think it is—true that Utilitarianism is only adapted for practical use by human beings at an advanced stage of intellectual development.")

[13]Rawls, p. 27, and pp. 183-9.

[14]Cf. the claim of Espinas, that society "is a living being like an individual" (Perry, p. 402). Good Hegelians do not argue in this way.

[15]Gauthier, p. 126.

[16]p. 27; cf. p. 191; cf. also Nagel, p. 134.

[17]See, for instance, Sidgwick (1901), p. 425 (or indeed pp. 199-457).

[18]Rawls, p. 29.

[19]Rawls, p. 27; cf. Nagel, p. 134.

[20]Findlay, p. 393; cf. p. 294.

Bibliography

Anschutz, R. P., *The Philosophy of J. S. Mill*, Oxford, Clarendon Press, 1953.

Butler, Joseph, "Of Personal Identity," appendix to *The Analogy of Natural Religion*, vol. 1, ed. W. E. Gladstone, Oxford, Frowde, 1897.

Care, N. and Grimm, R. H., *Perception and Personal Identity*, Cleveland, Press of Case-Western Reserve University, 1967.

Chisholm, R., "Problems of Identity," in *Identity and Individuation*, ed. M. K. Munitz, New York University Press, 1971.

Dummett, M., "The Reality of the Past," *Proceedings of the Aristotelian Society*, 69, 1968-9.

Findlay, J., *Values and Intentions*, London, Allen and Unwin, 1961.

Gauthier, D., *Practical Reasoning*, Oxford, Clarendon Press, 1963.

Geach, P. T., *God and the Soul*, London, Routledge & Kegan Paul, 1969.

Hare, R. M. (1963), *Freedom and Reason*, Oxford, Clarendon Press.

Hare, R. M. (1972), "Rules of War and Moral Reasoning," *Philosophy and Public Affairs*, Winter.

Hare, R. M. (1973), review of Rawls in *Philosophical Quarterly*.

Hart, H. L. A., *Punishment and Responsibility*, Oxford, Clarendon Press, 1968.

Hobhouse, L. T., *The Metaphysical Theory of the State*, London, Allen & Unwin, 1918.

Hume, David, "A Treatise of Human Nature," 1740.

Keats, John, *Letters*, ed. R. Gittings, London, Oxford University Press, 1970.

Kripke, S., "Naming and Necessity," in *Semantics of Natural Language*, eds. D. Davidson and G. Harman, Dordrecht, Reidel, 1972.

Lewis, C. I., *An Analysis of Knowledge and Valuation*, La Salle, Illinois, Open Court, 1962.

Locke, John, *Essay Concerning Human Understanding*, 1690.

Lukes, S., *Individualism*, Oxford, Blackwell, 1973.

Mackaye, J., *The Economy of Happiness*, Boston, Little, Brown, 1906.

Mill, J. S., *An Examination of Sir William Hamilton's Philosophy*, London, Longmans, 1872.

Nabokov, V., *Glory*, London, Weidenfeld & Nicolson, 1971.

Nagel, T., *The Possibility of Altruism*, Oxford, Clarendon Press, 1970.

Parfit, D. (1971), "Personal Identity," *Philosophical Review*, January.

Parfit, D. (1972), "On 'The Importance of Self-Identity'," *Journal of Philosophy*, 21 October.

Penelhum, T., *Survival and Disembodied Existence*, London, Routledge & Kegan Paul, 1970.

Perry, R., *General Theory of Value*, Cambridge, Mass., Harvard University Press, 1950.

Plamenatz, J., *Man and Society*, vol. 2, London, Longmans, 1963.

Proust, Marcel (1949), *The Sweet Cheat Gone*, trans. by C. K. Scott Moncrieff, London, Chatto & Windus.

Proust, Marcel (1967), *Within a Budding Grove*, vol. 1, trans. by C. K. Scott Moncrieff, London, Chatto & Windus.

Quinton, A. M. (1962), "The Soul," *Journal of Philosophy*, 59.

Quinton, A. M. (1972), *On the Nature of Things*, London, Routledge & Kegan Paul.

Rawls, J., *A Theory of Justice*, Cambridge, Mass., Harvard University Press, 1971.

Reid, Joseph, *Essays on the Intellectual Powers of Man*, Essay III., chs IV and VI.

Sidgwick, Henry (1901), *Methods of Ethics*, sixth edition, London, Macmillan.

Sidgwick, Henry (1902), *The Ethics of Green, Spencer, and Martineau*, London, Macmillan.

Solzhenitsyn, A., *The First Circle*, New York, Bantam Books, 1969.

Strawson, P. F., *Individuals*, London, Methuen, 1959.

Williams, B. A. O., "The Self and the Future," *Philosophical Review*, 1970.

CHAPTER 3

ATTRIBUTES

■════════■

INTRODUCTION

Part of what we mean when we say that our lives are good is that we enjoy certain favored attributes. We may say that these attributes are intrinsically good, or that they are essential to a good life. Among the attributes usually considered to be intrinsically good are pleasure and virtue or excellence. Some people would add life to this list. Others would say that life is not an intrinsically good attribute, but it is the most important instrumentally good attribute. Indeed, *long* life would be good, to the extreme of immortality. This chapter is devoted to readings that discuss the value of the attributes of pleasure, virtue, and life.

PLEASURE

Almost everyone will say that experiencing pleasure (and not pain) is *a* good thing. Other conditions being equal, people prefer to have fun, to enjoy themselves, to spend time pleasantly, and so on, even while taking on demanding tasks and challenges. Research even shows that good moods enhance health.[1] But is pleasure the *only* thing that matters? Is pleasure the only intrinsically good thing? The controversy between hedonists (who say that pleasure is the only good) and nonhedonists (who say that pleasure is not the only good) is difficult to resolve.

Consider an example to illustrate how the lines are drawn in this controversy: Suppose that you love Fred (who might be your father, brother, spouse, etc.), and you believe that Fred loves you. Although you do not know it, however, your enemies have told Fred elaborate lies about you. They have convinced him that you are a dreadful person who must be carefully tracked, and Fred has agreed to pretend to love you and to act as if nothing has changed. In fact, Fred now despises you, but suppose that for one reason or another you will never know. You will continue to believe that Fred loves you, and you will continue to enjoy all of your encounters with Fred. Let us add that you will not suffer any sort of pain due to the plot involving Fred. Does it *matter* to you that Fred's love is only feigned? Does this fact affect your happiness? Is it important to you?

According to the hedonist, the answer is clearly "no" since real love and the utterly convincing *appearance* of love are equally pleasant experiences. "What do I care?" the hedonist asks. "So long as I never find out and am never made to suffer, ersatz love is no worse than the real thing." The nonhedonist, however, recoils in horror, saying something like: "What is important to me, what gives me true happiness, is receiving *real* love. If I am the victim of the plot, I will not receive the love of someone I deeply care about. In fact, that person will hate and deceive me, which may be the worst disaster that could befall me, and I cannot do anything about it, since I don't even know what is happening to me!"

The hedonist is highly egocentric: Neither the love of others, nor their welfare, nor anything else other than personal pleasure is an intrinsically good thing. She cares about things only to the extent that they bring her pleasure, and since seeming to obtain those things brings as much pleasure as actually obtaining them, appearances are as good as the real thing. Getting at the truth, knowing what is really going on, is unimportant to such a person.

Moreover, their egocentrism can allow hedonists to be impervious to the outside world. As Epicurus brings out in his "Letter to Menoeceus," hedonists who are careful to limit what they care about can achieve a type of happiness that is nearly impervious to loss. Seen in this light, Epicurus's philosophy has much in common with Buddhism.

Unlike hedonists, nonhedonists may attribute intrinsic value to various states of affairs beyond their mental lives. For example, nonhedonists might consider someone's welfare and love to be intrinsically good, so they might worry about being deceived. Only if they are in touch with the truth will they have access to, and some control over, matters they consider important. Hedonism often strikes the nonhedonist as unworthy of human beings. Recall that in his book *Utilitarianism,* Mill struggled with precisely this worry about the life of pleasure. J. J. C. Smart, a contemporary philosopher at the Research School of Social Sciences, Australian National University, also suggests that hedonism is incompatible with human dignity, and the same suggestion is explored by Aldous Huxley (1894–1963) in his famous novel *Brave New World* (1932).

1. EPICURUS AND INVULNERABILITY

According to Epicurus (341–270 BCE), an ancient Greek philosopher, the main concern in life should be to minimize pain through a form of desire adaptation that involves eliminating all desires except those one must satisfy to avoid pain. For happiness or the good is *ataraxia* or tranquillity, that is, the absence of suffering; humans can achieve a nearly invulnerable state of tranquillity by properly adapting desires. On this view, something is good if it eliminates or prevents suffering, bad if it causes suffering, and a matter of indifference otherwise. The form of hedonism Epicurus advocates is negative in the sense that it portrays the best life as free of suffering rather than as filled with enjoyment and novel experiences (unlike the life of the modern "epicure").

Epicurean adaptation does not entail eliminating all desires. It would defeat the desired purpose to eliminate any desire to eat on occasion, for someone who lives without satisfying this desire will suffer from starvation. But one would do well to eliminate the desire for extremely rare and expensive fare, for suffering will result from having this desire and not satisfying it, but no suffering results from dropping it. One should also drop the desire to live, for not living would not cause suffering. Epicurus acknowledges no afterlife, so death is utter annihilation; unlike some of the events leading up to death, annihilation ends existence, so no self remains to suffer as a result of it.

Is Epicurean hedonism good advice? In its favor, it offers the prospect of reaching a state of happiness that is nearly invulnerable to circumstances. It would be wonderful to so situate ourselves that we could be virtually assured of everything we regard as important to us. But do we really want to prune back our desires as Epicurus advised? Suppose that you have children. You have good reason to believe that they will survive your death, and you are sure that your death will occur before next year. Can their welfare matter to you, as an Epicurean? In theory, you *could* take an indirect interest in how well they fare until next year, for their potential misfortune might cause you pain. But you must not care what happens to them after next year, for you know that nothing that happens to them then could possibly cause you to suffer. Is Epicurean invulnerability worth cultivating this sort of callousness?

2. J. J. C. SMART, ALDOUS HUXLEY, AND DIGNITY

Smart describes the "voluptuary of the future" as someone "with a number of electrodes protruding from his skull, one to give the physical pleasure of sex, one for that of eating, one for that of drinking, and so on." Using the technology of the future, Smart's voluptuary directly stimulates his pleasure centers. Soon, such an arrangement may become the most efficient way to give ourselves pleasure. If so, the hedonist seems committed to saying that the life of the electronic voluptuary is the best life for people. Yet many of us would reject this claim, just as we react with disdain to the future world portrayed in *Brave New World,* despite the satisfaction of those imagined future citizens. Pleasure is not the only good, we might say, and the electronic voluptuary is missing some other goods. Smart rejects the hedonist's claim for a somewhat different reason: A statement that someone who is enjoying a particular pursuit is happy involves expressing a favorable attitude to his enjoying that pursuit. Since some, like Mill, would not have a favorable attitude to the voluptuary's way of enjoying himself, one can refuse to pronounce him a happy person.

Would either reason phase the committed hedonist? Probably not. The hedonist is likely to say that both responses raise concerns which the voluptuary herself does not share: *We* might see goods other than pleasure, and *we* might disapprove of the voluptuary's form of enjoyment, but the voluptuary does not. Why should we question the happiness of people who have everything *they* think is important for life?

VIRTUE

Many philosophers have embraced some version of Aristotle's suggestion that virtue involves doing well what we are already inclined to do by nature, including fitting together with others into a community with which each individual identifies. In the West, the main exception is Kant, who thought that virtue is exercised in opposition to the inclinations of nature. As earlier readings have shown, Confucians portray human excellence as participation by individuals (who would otherwise be barbaric) in the community, with its civilizing rites and traditions. Daoists are suspicious of the influences of the community; they portray excellence as an expression of natural inclinations that is at once spontaneous and in harmony with the surrounding natural order.

1. ARISTOTLE

Broadly speaking, Aristotle thinks of the moral virtues as dispositions by which individuals choose to identify with, and act in the interest of, their community. In Book 2 of his *Nicomachean Ethics,* Aristotle describes the virtues in some detail, making these points:

1. People are neither virtuous nor bad by nature. Instead, they acquire virtues when, from youth onward, they habitually act as a virtuous person would; they acquire vices by habitually acting as a vicious person would.

2. Virtuous people (have been trained to) enjoy acting in virtuous ways.

3. Virtues in some sense involve a mean between excess and deficiency ("but viewed in its relation to what is best and right, it is the extreme of perfection"). Choosing under the influence of excess fear makes people cowards, and cowardice is a vice; choosing under the influence of insufficient fear makes people foolhardy, and foolhardiness is also a vice. Choosing under the influence of just the right amount of fear makes people brave, and bravery is a virtue. But the mean cannot be calculated, and the virtuous person is someone who is affected by fear, confidence, desire, anger, and pity "at the right times, and on the right occasions, and towards the right persons, and with the right object, and in the right fashion" (Chapter 6).

4. Some actions are by definition bad, and Aristotle's doctrine of the mean does not apply to them, for example, murder and envy.

Moral virtues (along with their corresponding vices) which Aristotle discusses in the *Ethics* include courage (cowardice, foolhardiness), temperance (self-indulgence, insensibility), liberality (prodigality, meanness), magnificence (vulgarity, niggardliness), pride (vanity, humility), moderate ambition, friendliness (obsequiousness, churlishness), truthfulness (boastfulness, false modesty), wittiness (buffoonery, boorishness), and justice.

2. THOMAS AQUINAS

In one of the following excerpts from Aquinas's (1225–1274) *Summa Theologica* (1265–1272), Aquinas suggests that God's law is in effect "imprinted" on people. He means that God has structured people with an inclination to act in accordance with reason, which in turn leads them to act in accordance with virtue. Aquinas explains that "this participation of the eternal law in the rational creature is called the natural law." The natural law is that part of God's law which we can work out for ourselves through correct application of reason; when we use reason to work out the prescriptions of the natural law, and conform to those prescriptions, we are acting in a virtuous way.

In a later section of the *Summa Theologica,* Aquinas discusses the cardinal virtues: prudence, temperance, fortitude, and justice. Unlike Aristotle, who thought that the behavior for which moral virtues are appropriate is beneath the gods, Aquinas attributes the cardinal virtues to God. Aquinas argues that human beings could become virtuous only if they could follow the example of a preexisting exemplar of virtue, and the first virtuous being was God. Aquinas goes on to endorse Aristotle's conception of human beings as social animals as well as his claim that the virtues are dispositions by which people act in the interest of the community. However, Aquinas clearly asserts that the virtues chiefly incline people toward God. For example, he says that "prudence, by contemplating the things of God, counts as nothing all things of the world, and directs all the thoughts of the soul to God alone."

3. ALASDAIR MacINTYRE

Alasdair MacIntyre, a contemporary philosopher who teaches at Notre Dame University, offers an analysis of virtue that is heavily influenced by Aristotle and Aquinas. Like other "communitarian" philosophers, discussed in Chapter 8, and like Hegel, MacIntyre rejects an individualist conception of the self according to which identity is a person's choice and entirely separable from social setting. Both *identity* and *moral virtue* can be understood only in the context of an on-going community pledged to certain traditions and practices that constitute an open-ended narrative that defines social roles. Cast into these roles, people are expected to continue the narrative as best they can, and their community provides them with virtues that help them to do so.

MacIntyre sets out his explanation of the concept of virtue in three stages:

1. He defines an "internal good" and a "practice." Consider the game of chess. Certain moves or strategies can be understood to count as good or excellent only as part of chess-playing; for example, moving a piece in a certain way might be a brilliant triumph if done by a master but simply an accident if done by a child who has not yet learned to play well. These *internal* goods can be contrasted with *external* goods, such as winning money. *Practices* are cooperative activities that allow participants to achieve internal goods. Virtues are qualities that help people achieve goods internal to practices.

2. He develops a concept of identity. MacIntyre tries to understand some societies in terms of narratives created by members over time. People find themselves immersed in this ongoing narrative and are expected to continue its development, but they are constrained by the narrative as it has already been created in the past. Only certain ways of continuing the narrative will cohere with the existing portion and ensure that the whole makes sense. MacIntyre suggests that people understand their identities as constituted by this narrative. In so doing, they find their identities tied up with the identities of others; we are parts of each others' stories and therefore accountable to each other. A quest for the good is a part of the unity of an individual life, and virtues "are to

be understood as those dispositions which will not only sustain practices and enable us to achieve the goods internal to practices, but which will also sustain us in the relevant kind of quest for the good."

3. He brings in tradition. MacIntyre suggests that the virtues, as described at the first and second stages, presuppose a larger context that creates the possibility of virtues. We derive our identities from membership in communities with histories we inherit and whose traditions we bear. "The individual's search for his or her good is . . . conducted within a context defined by those traditions of which the individual's life is a part."

4. MARY MIDGLEY

In her book *Wickedness,* British philosopher Mary Midgley, who teaches at the University of Newcastle-upon-Tyne, attempts to explain the nature of evil or viciousness. Like Hannah Arendt, who had discussed the character of the Nazi, Adolf Eichmann, in *Eichmann in Jerusalem,* Midgley suggests that evil should be thought of as a somewhat banal absence rather than a horrifying presence: "Evil is . . . the absence of good, and cannot be understood on its own." Evil is not a definite or positive tendency, unlike aggression (which Midgley defines as "a natural [and innate] tendency to attack others sometimes, which involves an emotional tendency sometimes to get angry with them"). Instead, evil occurs when natural (positive) motivations fail. Thus, Midgley defends two main theses: (a) People exhibit a human nature "with relatively specific capacities and incapacities, rather than total plasticity and indefiniteness"; most importantly, human beings act from natural motives (such as aggression, territoriality, possessiveness, competitiveness, dominance); (b) Evil is a certain kind of failing in this natural human motivation.

When things go well, we acknowledge all elements of our nature, including all of our motives, and develop an identity that harmonizes and gives an outlet to all aspects of our nature. Midgley says that evil results when we refuse to acknowledge some of our less glamorous motives and attempt to exclude them from our identities, whereupon we come to see those motives as alien forces which cause actions we cannot regard as *ours* and over which, therefore, *we* have no control. The life brought about by these rejected motives is the life led by a shadowy self that is not *us* and over which we have relinquished control. Sometimes we might even "project" the shadowy selves with their bad motives outside oneself, perhaps onto the bodies of people nearby, in a further effort to distance oneself from them.

5. IMMANUEL KANT

It is worth contrasting Kant's conception of virtue with those of the others. On Kant's view, as he says in "Duties of the Virtuous and the Vicious," part of his *Lectures on Ethics,* virtue is the perfect "ability and readiness to overcome our inclination to evil on moral principles." Vice, by contrast, is opposition to the moral law, as Kant says at one place, or "slavery to the power of inclination," as he says later. On Kant's view, we work out our moral duty without appealing to any prior conception of virtue, and then we attempt to take proper actions. However, Kant presupposes that natural inclinations urge us to take wrong actions. He also supposes that people cannot always resist these urges. They can only approximate a state of virtue. Thus, Kant rejects the Aristotelian (and Thomist) view that living well is basically a matter of doing well what we are already inclined to do. Kant says that only imperfect beings can display virtue, and "holy beings are not virtuous, for the reason that they have no evil inclinations to overcome."

(ETERNAL) LIFE

Let us say that we live as long as we survive with our identities intact. Thus, for example, if we continued to exist in an afterlife as the people we are now, we can say that we would be alive in the afterlife (as indeed the term *afterlife* suggests). Two questions arise. First, is life a good thing? Second, is dying a bad thing?

Almost everyone will say that life is good, although many will qualify their claim to acknowledge the possibility that circumstances might become so dire that they undermine the value of living. But is life an *intrinsic* good? If so, we would presumably want to live as long as possible, other things being equal—an important qualification. We probably can imagine circumstances in which we would rather not exist at all: We would not want to live in pain so severe that it blotted out the capacity to appreciate compensating goods and without any hope of relief. Few probably would want to live under those circumstances even if they thought that life was intrinsically good, for they would probably judge that the good of life would be overwhelmed by the bad circumstances in which it was lived. Only someone who thought that life was infinitely, or incomparably good would insist that no conceivable circumstances would justify forgoing life.

Even someone who says that life is merely instrumentally good may yet prefer to live as long as possible, other things being equal, believing that the goods that life makes possible are remarkable enough to enjoy them for the indefinite future. Under the right circumstances, we would be fortunate to live forever. Whether we really would be fortunate depends on the nature of the good things eternal life would allow. Whether it is *conceivable* that we could live forever depends on the nature of the self.

Assuming that life, or continuing existence, is a good thing, is dying, or ending existence, a bad one? Controversies have supplied a range of answers. Realize from the start, however, that many arguments for the claim that *dying* is not a bad thing are not arguments for the claim that *annihilation* is not a bad thing. If we ask whether utterly going out of existence would be a misfortune, many people will avoid the question, and instead insist that no one needs to worry, because we just *won't* go out of existence when we die. Epicurus did offer an answer to the question of whether being annihilated would be bad, saying it would be a matter of indifference. In response to Epicurus, however, someone might argue that so long as living on would be good, not living on—being annihilated—would be a misfortune. This position leaves one to come to terms with the evident fact that one's physical existence will end: Does this fact mean that we will completely cease to be?

As a rule, Westerners tend to individuate themselves more completely from other people and from the rest of the world than Easterners do. We tend not to extend our identities past our bodies. The realization that our bodies will be destroyed in time can then become quite worrisome, except insofar as we embrace the idea of an immaterial soul capable of surviving the demise of the body. If we tie our identities to our souls, emphasizing the importance of spiritual matters, the demise of the body will matter less. Easterners, by contrast, have tended not to sharply individuate themselves from others and from the world around them. They have tended to identify with the whole world or the whole community or not to identify with anything. On each of these approaches to identity, the demise of the body does not destroy a person, giving a degree of invulnerability even without positing souls.

1. PASCAL AND TOLSTOY

Pascal and Tolstoy accept the Christian view that eternal life is a great good, and that dying, in the sense of being utterly annihilated, would be a grave misfortune. They suggest that eternal life and the things it makes possible are unimaginably good; by contrast, the ordinary life that appears to be available to mortals is so worthless as not to be worth having. Hence, the thought that we are mortals who can expect to be annihilated should fill us with despair, and we should do everything in our power to secure immortality for ourselves. Both writers emphasize that the belief in immortality can only be a matter of faith, but faith allows happiness, and the alternative is utter despair.

Blaise Pascal (1623–1662), a French mathematician, began his *Pensées* in 1660, but he died before it was completed. The work was to be an intellectual defense of Christianity. Pascal pitied anyone who was not a Christian, and thus guaranteed immortality, but only idiots would not try very hard to discover whether or not they could achieve immortality, regardless of whether they ended up as Christians or not. Since, according to Pascal, we must "wager" one way or another on the question of the existence of a God who offers us immortality, we should bet on God's existence:

1. We have no information either way concerning God's existence, so the possibility that God does exist is as likely as the possibility that he does not, and vice versa.

2. We must wager: We must choose to believe (a) that God does exist or (b) that he does not. (Suspending judgment on the matter is tantamount to choosing to believe that God does not exist.)

3. Suppose that we choose to believe that God exists. Then if we are correct, we have gained much (infinite bliss forever) and sacrificed little (the effort of devoting our lives to God, becoming "faithful, honest, humble, grateful, generous, a sincere friend, truthful" and forgoing "glory and luxury"). If incorrect, we have gained nothing, but lost little (namely, devotion to a nonexistent god).

4. Suppose that we choose to believe that God does not exist (or to suspend judgment). If there is no god, we have sacrificed nothing but have gained little (namely freedom from devotion to a nonexistent god). But if God does exist, then though we have gained a little (freedom from devotion) we have lost much.

5. Since we stand to gain so much and to lose so little if we believe, and since we stand to lose so much and to gain so little if we do not believe, it is better to believe.

2. BUDDHISM

Gautama takes much the same attitude toward death as Epicurus: It is a matter of indifference. According to Gautama, it is a matter of indifference for two reasons: First, since we should not operate with a concept of a self by which we persist over time, the concept of death simply does not apply. One reason people yearn for immortality is because it prevents them from perishing. Gautama's doctrine of no-self is intended to give people this same benefit, for it emphasizes that the concept of death does not apply to them, so they cannot be said to perish. Second, wise people will have undertaken a form of desire adaptation, eliminating any desires or commitments that lead to thoughts of the importance of remaining in existence. Lack of ties to anything that life makes possible leaves no reason to be concerned about whether or not we live.

3. HERBERT FINGARETTE

In "Immortality, Selflessness," Chapter 3 of his book *Death,* contemporary philosopher Herbert Fingarette suggests that because the notion of the soul is incoherent, we ought not hope for eternal life through the survival of the soul. However, he brings out ways in which Eastern disregard for individuality can help people to face the prospect of annihilation. For "if one were truly selfless, what would be lost when death comes?—nothing."

---

[1]Shelly Taylor, *Positive Illusions: Creative Self-Deception and the Healthy Mind* (New York: Basic Books, 1989).

Questions for Reflection

1. Is pleasure the only thing that matters? If not, how are the other things that matter related to happiness?

2. Can something be bad or constitute a misfortune for you even if it never causes you to suffer? Would it be a misfortune for you to contract a disease that destroyed your mental abilities and reduced you to the state of a contented infant?

3. Why not give people drugs that make them enjoy menial tasks such as collecting garbage, as in *Brave New World?* Perhaps forcing people to take the mood-enhancing drugs would be wrong, but what about simply offering the drugs?

4. Assess the wager argument Pascal defends. Does it presuppose that the only relevant possibilities are Christianity and its denial? Should one consider other possibilities?

5. Does Pascal's argument presuppose *voluntary* belief? Is belief a voluntary act? (Can you will to believe anything you like? Could you, for example, believe that you are a duck's tongue?)

6. Plato and Aristotle suggest that the state should ensure that people are virtuous by overseeing their training from birth. Are they correct, or ought moral education be left to individual families? (Suppose that you are a parent and you disapprove of the moral training the state supports. Should you be allowed to insist on training your children yourself?)

7. Compare and contrast the understanding of virtue described by Aquinas, MacIntyre, and Kant. Which view is most plausible to you?

8. Given Midgley's negative characterization of vice, what is the best way to raise people so that they do not end up being "wicked"?

9. Are Pascal and Tolstoy correct in suggesting that a worthwhile life is impossible without immortality? Would 200 years allow one to live a worthwhile life? How about 2,000?

10. Evaluate the Daoist suggestion that dying is acceptable because it is a natural process. Can you think of natural misfortunes?

11. Critically evaluate Fingarette's suggestion that dying becomes more tolerable through Eastern philosophies that emphasize selflessness.

Suggested Readings

About Hedonism
Mitsis, P. *Epicurus' Ethical Theory.* Ithaca, N.Y.: Cornell University Press, 1988.
Annas, Julia. *The Morality of Happiness.* New York: Oxford University Press, 1993.
About Virtues
Kruschwitz, R., and R. Roberts, eds. *The Virtues: Contemporary Essays on Moral Character.* Belmont, Calif.: Wadsworth, 1987.
MacIntyre, Alasdair. *After Virtue.* South Bend, Ind.: University of Notre Dame Press, 1981.
Murdoch, Iris. *The Sovereignty of Good.* New York: Schocken Books, 1970.
About Death
Ferrater Mora, Jose. *Being and Death.* Berkeley: Berkeley University Press, 1965.
Fischer, John Martin. *The Metaphysics of Death.* Palo Alto, Calif.: Stanford University Press, 1993.

PLEASURE

EPICURUS

Letter to Menoeceus

Epicurus to Menoeceus, greeting.

Let no young man delay the study of philosophy, and let no old man become weary of it; for it is never too early nor too late to care for the well-being of the soul. The man who says that the season for this study has not yet come or is already past is like the man who says it is too early or too late for happiness. Therefore, both the young and the old should study philosophy, the former so that as he grows old he may still retain the happiness of youth in his pleasant memories of the past, the latter so that although he is old he may at the same time be young by virtue of his fearlessness of the future. We must therefore study the means of securing happiness, since if we have it we have everything, but if we lack it we do everything in order to gain it.

Practice and study without ceasing that which I was always teaching you, being assured that these are the first principles of the good life. After accepting god as the immortal and blessed being depicted by popular opinion, do not ascribe to him anything in addition that is alien to immortality or foreign to blessedness, but rather believe about him whatever can uphold his blessed immortality. The gods do indeed exist, for our perception of them is clear; but they are not such as the crowd imagines them to be, for most men do not retain the picture of the gods that they first receive. It is not the man who destroys the gods of popular belief who is impious, but he who describes the gods in the terms accepted by the many. For the opinions of the many about the gods are not perceptions but false suppositions. According to these popular suppositions, the gods send great evils to the wicked, great blessings [to the righteous], for they, being always well disposed to their own virtues, approve those who are like themselves, regarding as foreign all that is different.

Accustom yourself to the belief that death is of no concern to us, since all good and evil lie in sensation and sensation ends with death. Therefore the true belief that death is nothing to us makes a mortal life happy, not by adding to it an infinite time, but by taking away the desire for immortality. For there is no reason why the man who is thoroughly assured that there is nothing to fear in death should find anything to fear in life. So, too, he is foolish who says that he fears death, not because it will be painful when it comes, but because the anticipation of it is painful; for that which is no burden when it is present gives pain to no purpose when it is anticipated. Death, the most dreaded of evils, is therefore of no concern to us; for while we exist death is not present, and when death is present we no longer exist. It is therefore nothing either to the living or to the dead since it is not present to the living, and the dead no longer are.

But men in general sometimes flee death as the greatest of evils, sometimes [long for it] as a relief from [the evils] of life. [The wise man neither renounces life] nor fears its end; for living does not offend him, nor does he suppose that not to live is in any way evil. As he does not choose the food that is most in quantity but that which is most pleasant, so he does not seek the enjoyment of the longest life but of the happiest.

He who advises the young man to live well, the old man to die well, is foolish, not only because life is desirable, but also because the art of living well and the art of dying well are one. Yet much worse is he who says that it is well not to have been born, but once born, be swift to pass through Hades' gates. If a man says this and really believes it, why does he not depart from life? Certainly the means are at hand for doing so if this really be his firm conviction. If he says it in mockery, he is regarded as a fool among those who do not accept his teaching.

Remember that the future is neither ours nor wholly not ours, so that we may neither count on it as sure to come nor abandon hope of it as certain not to be.

You must consider that of the desires some are natural, some are vain, and of those that are natural, some are necessary, others only natural. Of the necessary desires, some are necessary for happiness, some for the ease of the body, some for life itself. The man who has a perfect knowledge of this will know how to make his every choice or rejection tend toward gaining health of body and peace [of mind], since this is the final end of the blessed life. For to gain this end, namely freedom from pain and fear, we do everything. When once this condition is reached, all the storm of the soul is stilled, since the creature need make no move in search of anything that is lacking, nor seek after anything else to make complete the welfare of the soul and the body. For we only feel the lack of pleasure when from its absence we suffer pain; [but when we do not suffer pain,] we no longer are in need of pleasure. For this reason we say that pleasure is the beginning and the end of the blessed life. We recognize pleasure as the first and natural good; starting from pleasure we accept or reject; and we return to this as we judge every good thing, trusting this feeling of pleasure as our guide.

For the very reason that pleasure is the chief and the natural good, we do not choose every pleasure, but there are times when we pass by pleasures if they are outweighed by the hardships that follow; and many pains we think better than pleasures when a greater pleasure will come to us once we have undergone the long-continued pains. Every pleasure is a good since it has a nature akin to ours; nevertheless, not every pleasure is to be chosen. Just so, every pain is an evil, yet not every pain is of a nature to be avoided on all occasions. By measuring and by looking at advantages and disadvantages, it is proper to decide all these things; for under certain circumstances we treat the good as evil, and again, the evil as good.

We regard self-sufficiency as a great good, not so that we may enjoy only a few things, but so that, if we do not have many, we may be satisfied with the few, being firmly persuaded that they take the greatest pleasure in luxury who regard it as least needed, and that everything that is natural is easily provided, while vain pleasures are hard to obtain. Indeed, simple sauces bring a pleasure equal to that of lavish banquets if once the pain due to need is removed; and bread and water give the greatest pleasure when one who is in need consumes them. To be accustomed to simple and plain living is conducive to health and makes a man ready for the necessary tasks of life. It also makes us more ready for the enjoyment of luxury if at intervals we chance to meet with it, and it renders us fearless against fortune.

When we say that pleasure is the end, we do not mean the pleasure of the profligate or that which depends on physical enjoyment—as some think who do not understand our teachings, disagree with them, or give them an evil interpretation—but by pleasure we mean the state wherein the body is free from pain and the mind from anxiety. Neither continual drinking and dancing, nor sexual love, nor the enjoyment of fish and whatever else the luxurious table offers brings about the pleasant life; rather, it is produced by the reason which is sober, which examines the motive for every choice and rejection, and which drives away all those opinions through which the greatest tumult lays hold of the mind.

Of all this the beginning and the chief good is prudence. For this reason prudence is more precious than philosophy itself. All the other virtues spring from it. It teaches that it is not possible to live pleasantly without at the same time living prudently, nobly, and justly, [nor to live prudently, nobly, and justly] without living pleasantly; for the virtues have grown up in close union with the pleasant life, and the pleasant life cannot be separated from the virtues.

Whom then do you believe to be superior to the prudent man: he who has reverent opinions about the gods, who is wholly without fear of death, who has discovered what is the highest good in life and understands that the highest point in what is good is easy to reach and hold and that the extreme of evil is limited either in time or in suffering and who laughs at that which some have set up as the ruler of all things, [Necessity? He thinks that the chief power of decision lies within us, although some things come about by necessity,] some by chance, and some by our own wills; for he sees that necessity is irresponsible and chance uncertain, but that our actions are subject to no power. It is for this reason that our actions merit praise or blame. It would be better to accept the myth about the gods than to be a slave to the determinism of the physicists; for the myth hints at a hope for grace through honors paid to the gods, but the necessity of determinism is inescapable. Since the prudent man does not, as do many, regard chance as a god (for the gods do nothing in disorderly fashion) or as an unstable cause [of all things], he believes that chance does [not] give man good and evil to make his life happy or miserable, but that it does provide opportunities for great good or evil. Finally, he thinks it is better to meet misfortune while acting with reason than to happen upon good fortune while acting senselessly; for it is better that what has been well-planned in our actions [should fail than that what has been ill-planned] should gain success by chance.

Meditate on these and like precepts, by day and by night, alone or with a like-minded friend. Then never, either awake or asleep, will you be dismayed; but you will live like a god among men; for life amid immortal blessings is in no way like the life of a mere mortal.

J. J. C. Smart

Hedonism

Let us consider Mill's contention that it is "better to be Socrates dissatisfied than a fool satisfied."[1] Mill holds that pleasure is not to be our sole criterion for evaluating consequences: the state of mind of Socrates might be less pleasurable than that of the fool, but, according to Mill, Socrates would be happier than the fool. . . .

A man who enjoys pushpin is likely eventually to become bored with it, whereas the man who enjoys poetry is likely to retain this interest throughout his life. Moreover the reading of poetry may develop imagination and sensitivity, and so as a result of his interest in poetry a man may be able to do more for the happiness of others than if he had played pushpin and let his brain deteriorate. In short, both for the man immediately concerned and for others, the pleasures of poetry are, to use Bentham's word, more *fecund* than those of pushpin.

Perhaps, then, our preference for poetry over pushpin is not one of intrinsic value, but is merely one of extrinsic value. Perhaps strictly in itself and at a particular moment, a contented sheep is as good as a contented philosopher. However it is hard to agree to this. If we did we should have to agree that the human population ought ideally to be reduced by contraceptive methods and the sheep population more than correspondingly increased. Perhaps just so many humans should be left as could keep innumerable millions of placid sheep in contented idleness and immunity from depredations by ferocious animals. Indeed if a contented idiot is as good as a contented philosopher, and if a contented sheep is as good as a contented idiot, then a contented fish is as good as a contented sheep, and a contented beetle is as good as a contented fish. Where shall we stop?

Maybe we have gone wrong in talking of pleasure as though it were no more than contentment. Contentment consists roughly in relative absence of unsatisfied desires; pleasure is perhaps something more positive and consists in a balance between absence of unsatisfied desires and presence of satisfied desires. We might put the difference in this way: pure unconsciousness would be a limiting case of contentment, but not of pleasure. A stone has no unsatisfied desires, but then it just has no desires. Nevertheless, this consideration will not resolve the disagreement between Bentham and Mill. No doubt a dog has as intense a desire to discover rats as the philosopher has to discover the mysteries of the universe. Mill would wish to say that the pleasures of the philosopher were more valuable intrinsically than those of the dog, however intense these last might be.

It appears, then, that many of us may well have a preference not only for enjoyment as such but for certain sorts of enjoyment. And this goes for many of the humane and beneficent readers whom I am addressing. I suspect that they too have an intrinsic preference for the more complex and intellectual pleasures. . . . Even the most avid television addict probably enjoys solving practical problems connected with his car, his furniture, or his garden. However unintellectual he might be, he would certainly resent the suggestion that he should, if it were possible, change places with a contented sheep, or even a lively and happy dog. Nevertheless, when all is said and done, we must not disguise the fact that disagreements in ultimate attitude are possible between those who like Mill have, and those who like Bentham have not, an intrinsic preference for the "higher" pleasures. However it is possible for two people to disagree about ultimate ends and yet agree in practice about what ought to be done. . . .

This [agreement in practice] need not always be so. Some years ago two psychologists, Olds and Milner, carried out some experiments with rats.[2] Through the skull of each rat they inserted an electrode. These electrodes penetrated to various regions of the brain. In the case of some of these regions the rat showed behaviour characteristics of pleasure when a current was passed from the electrode, in others they seemed to show pain, and in others the stimulus seemed neutral. That a stimulus was pleasure-giving was shown by the fact that the rat would learn to pass the current himself by pressing a lever. He would neglect food and make straight for this lever and start stimulating himself. In some cases he would sit there pressing the lever every few seconds for hours on end. This calls up a pleasant picture of the voluptuary of the future, a bald-headed man with a number of electrodes protruding from his skull, one to give the physical pleasure of sex, one for that of eating, one for that of drinking, and so on. Now is this the sort of life that all our ethical planning should culminate in? A few hours' work a week, automatic factories, comfort and security from disease, and hours spent at a switch, continually electrifying various regions of one's brain? Surely not. Men were made for higher things, one can't help wanting to say, even though one knows that men weren't made for anything, but are the product of evolution by natural selection.

It might be said that the objection to continual sensual stimulation of the above sort is that though it would be pleasant in itself it would be infecund of future pleasures. This is often so with the ordinary sensual pleasures. . . . Maybe if everyone became an electrode operator people would lose interest in everything else and the human race would die out.

Suppose, however, that the facts turned out otherwise: that a man could (and would) do his full share of work in the office or the factory and come back in the evening to a few hours contented electrode work, without bad aftereffects. This would be his greatest pleasure, and the pleasure would be so great intrinsically and so easily repeatable that its lack of fecundity would not matter. Indeed perhaps by this time human arts, such as medicine, engineering, agriculture and architecture will have been brought to a pitch of perfection sufficient to enable most of the human race to spend most of its time electrode operating, without compensating pains of starvation, disease and squalor. Would this be a satisfactory state of society? Would this be the millennium towards which we have been striving? Surely the pure hedonist would have to say that it was.

It is time, therefore, that we had another look at the concept of happiness. Should we say that the electrode operator was really happy? This is a difficult question to be clear about, because the concept of happiness is a tricky one. But whether we should call the electrode operator "happy" or not, there is no doubt (a) that he would be *contented* and (b) that he would be *enjoying himself.*

Perhaps a possible reluctance to call the electrode operator "happy" might come from the following circumstance. The electrode operator might be perfectly contented, might perfectly enjoy his electrode operating, and might not be willing to exchange his lot for any other. And we ourselves, perhaps, once we became electrode operators too, could become perfectly contented and satisfied. But nevertheless, as we are now, we just do not want to become electrode operators. We want other things, perhaps to write a book or get into a cricket team. If someone said "from tomorrow onwards you are going to be forced to be an electrode operator" we should not be pleased. Maybe from tomorrow onwards, once the electrode work had started, we should be perfectly contented, but we are not contented now at the prospect. We are not satisfied at being told that we would be in a certain state from tomorrow onwards, even though we may know that from tomorrow onwards we should be perfectly satisfied. . . .

This, I think, explains part of our hesitancy about whether to call the electrode operator "happy." The notion of happiness ties up with that of contentment: to be fairly happy at least involves being fairly contented, though it involves something more as well. Though we should be contented when we became electrode operators, we are not contented now with the prospect that we should become electrode operators. Similarly if Socrates had become a fool he might thereafter have been perfectly contented. Nevertheless if beforehand he had been told that he would in the future become a fool he would have been even more dissatisfied than in fact he was. This is part of the trouble about the dispute between Bentham and Mill. The case involves the possibility of (a) our being contented if we are in a certain state, and (b) our being contented at the prospect of being so contented. Normally situations in which we should be contented go along with our being contented at the prospect of our getting into such situations. In the case of the electrode operator and in that of Socrates and the fool we are pulled two ways at once.

Now to call a person "happy" is to say more than that he is contented for most of the time, or even that he frequently enjoys himself and is rarely discontented or in pain. It is, I think, in part to express a favourable attitude to the idea of such a form of contentment and enjoyment. That is, for *A* to call *B* "happy," *A* must be contented at the prospect of *B* being in his present state of mind and at the prospect of *A* himself, should the opportunity arise, enjoying that sort of state of mind. That is, "happy" is a word which is mainly descriptive (tied to the concepts of contentment and enjoyment) but which is also partly evaluative. It is because Mill approves of the "higher" pleasures, e.g. intellectual pleasures, so much more than he approves of the more simple and brutish pleasures, that, quite apart from consequences and side effects, he can pronounce the man who enjoys the pleasures of philosophical discourse as "more happy" than the man who gets enjoyment from pushpin or beer drinking.

The word "happy" is not wholly evaluative, for there would be something absurd, as opposed to merely unusual, in calling a man who was in pain, or who was not enjoying himself, or who hardly ever enjoyed himself, or who was in a more or less permanent state of intense dissatisfaction, a "happy" man. For a man to be happy he must, as a minimal condition, be fairly contented and moderately enjoying himself for much of the time. Once this minimal condition is satisfied we can go on to evaluate various types of contentment and enjoyment and to grade them in terms of happiness. Happiness is, of course, a long-term concept in a way that enjoyment is not. We can talk of a man enjoying himself at a quarter past two precisely, but hardly of a man being happy at a quarter past two precisely. Similarly we can talk of it raining at a quarter past two precisely, but hardly about it being a wet climate at a quarter past two precisely. But happiness involves enjoyment at various times, just as a wet climate involves rain at various times.

To be enjoying oneself, Ryle once suggested, is to be doing what you want to be doing and not to be wanting to do anything else,[3] or, more accurately, we might say that one enjoys oneself the more one wants to be doing what one is in fact doing and the less one wants to be doing anything else. A man will not enjoy a round of golf if (a) he does not particularly want to play golf, or (b) though he wants to play golf there is something else he wishes he were doing at the same time, such as buying the vegetables for his wife, filling in his income tax forms, or listening to a lecture on philosophy.

The hedonistic ideal would then appear to reduce to a state of affairs in which each person is enjoying himself. Since, as we noted, a dog may, as far as we can tell, enjoy chasing a rat as much as a philosopher or a mathematician may enjoy solving a problem, we must, if we adopt the purely hedonistic position, defend the higher pleasures on account of their fecundity. And that might not turn out to be a workable defence in a world made safe for electrode operators. . . .

So much for the issue between Bentham and Mill. What about that between Mill and Moore? Could a pleasurable state of mind have no intrinsic value at all, or perhaps even a *negative* intrinsic value?[4] Are there pleasurable states of mind towards which we have an unfavourable attitude, even though we disregard their consequences? In order to decide this question let us imagine a universe consisting of one sentient being only, who falsely believes that there are other sentient beings and that they are undergoing exquisite torment. So far from being distressed by the thought, he takes a great delight in these imagined sufferings. Is this better or worse than a universe containing no sentient being at all? Is it worse, again, than a universe containing only one sentient being with the same beliefs as before but who sorrows at the imagined tortures of his fellow creatures? I suggest, as against Moore, that the universe containing the deluded sadist is the preferable one. After all he is happy, and since there is no other sentient being, what harm can he do? Moore would nevertheless agree that the sadist was happy, and this shows how happiness, though partly an evaluative concept, is also partly not an evaluative concept.

It is difficult, I admit, not to feel an immediate repugnance at the thought of the deluded sadist. If throughout our childhood we have been given an electric shock whenever we had tasted cheese, then cheese would have become immediately distasteful to us. Our repugnance to the sadist arises, naturally enough, because in our universe sadists invariably do harm. If we lived in a universe in which by some extraordinary laws of psychology a sadist was always confounded by his own knavish tricks and invariably did a great deal of good, then we should feel better disposed towards the sadistic mentality. Even if we could de-condition ourselves from feeling an immediate repugnance to a sadist (as we could de-condition ourselves from a repugnance to cheese by going through a course in which the taste of cheese was invariably associated with a pleasurable stimulus) language might make it difficult for us to distinguish an extrinsic distaste for sadism, founded on our distaste for the consequences of sadism, from an immediate distaste for sadism as such. Normally when we call a thing "bad" we mean indifferently to express a dislike for it in itself or to express a dislike for what it leads to. When a state of mind is sometimes extrinsically good and sometimes extrinsically bad, we find it easy to distinguish between our intrinsic and extrinsic preferences for instances of it, but when a state of mind is always, or almost always, extrinsically bad, it is easy for us to confuse an extrinsic distaste for it with an intrinsic one. If we allow for this, it does not seem so absurd to hold that there are no pleasures which are intrinsically bad.

---

[1] *Utilitarianism*, p. 9. The problem of the unhappy sage and the happy fool is cleverly stated in Voltaire's "Histoire d'un bon Bramin," *Choix de Contes*, edited with an introduction and notes by F. C. Green (Cambridge University Press, London, 1951), pp. 245–7.

[2] James Olds and Peter Milner, "Positive reinforcement produced by electrical stimulation of the septal area and other regions of the rat brain," *Journal of Comparative and Physiological Psychology* 47 (1954): 419–27; James Olds, "A preliminary mapping of electrical reinforcing effect in the rat brain," *ibid.* 49 (1956): 281–5. I. J. Good has also used these results of Olds and Milner in order to discuss ethical hedonism. See his "A problem for the hedonist," in I. J. Good (ed.), *The Scientist Speculates* (Heinemann, London, 1962). Good takes the possibility of this sort of thing to provide a *reductio ad absurdum* of hedonism.

[3] Gilbert Ryle, *The Concept of Mind* (Hutchison, London, 1949), p. 108.

[4] Cf. G. E. Moore, *Principia Ethica*, pp. 209–10.

ALDOUS HUXLEY

Brave New World

. . . "But do you like being slaves?" the Savage was saying as they entered the Hospital. His face was flushed, his eyes bright with ardour and indignation. "Do you like being babies? Yes, babies. Mewling and puking," he added, exasperated by their bestial stupidity into throwing insults at those he had come to save. The insults bounced off their carapace of thick stupidity; they stared at him with a blank expression of dull and sullen resentment in their eyes. "Yes, puking!" he fairly shouted. Grief and remorse, compassion and duty—all were forgotten now and, as it were, absorbed into an intense overpowering hatred of these less than human monsters. "Don't you want to be free and men? Don't you even understand what manhood and freedom are?" Rage was making him fluent; the words came easily, in a rush. "Don't you?" he repeated, but got no answer to his question. "Very well then," he went on grimly. "I'll teach you; I'll *make* you be free whether you want to or not." And pushing open a window that looked on to the inner court of the Hospital, he began to throw the little pill-boxes of *soma* tablets in handfuls out into the area.

For a moment the khaki mob was silent, petrified, at the spectacle of this wanton sacrilege, with amazement and horror.

"He's mad," whispered Bernard, staring with wide open eyes. "They'll kill him. They'll . . ." A great shout suddenly went up from the mob; a wave of movement drove it menacingly towards the Savage. "Ford help him!" said Bernard, and averted his eyes.

"Ford helps those who help themselves." And with a laugh, actually a laugh of exultation, Helmholtz Watson pushed his way through the crowd.

"Free, free!" the Savage shouted, and with one hand continued to throw the *soma* into the area while, with the other, he punched the indistinguishable faces of his assailants. "Free!" And suddenly there was Helmholtz at his side—"Good old Helmholtz!"—also punching—"Men at last!"—and in the interval also throwing the poison out by handfuls through the open window. "Yes, men! men!" and there was no more poison left. He picked up the cash-box and showed them its black emptiness. "You're free!" . . .

The room into which the three were ushered was the Controller's study.

"His fordship will be down in a moment." The Gamma butler left them to themselves.

Helmholtz laughed aloud.

. . . "Cheer up, Bernard," he added, catching sight of his friend's green unhappy face. But Bernard would not be cheered. . . .

The Savage meanwhile wandered restlessly round the room, peering with a vague superficial inquisitiveness at the books in the shelves, at the soundtrack rolls and the reading machine bobbins in their numbered pigeon-holes. On the table under the window lay a massive volume bound in limp black leather-surrogate, and stamped with large golden T's. He picked it up and opened it. *My Life and Work*, by Our Ford. . . . Idly he turned the pages, . . . when the door opened, and the Resident World Controller for Western Europe walked briskly into the room.

Mustapha Mond shook hands with all three of them; but it was to the Savage that he addressed himself. "So you don't much like civilization, Mr. Savage," he said.

The Savage looked at him. He had been prepared to lie, to bluster, to remain sullenly unresponsive; but, reassured by the good-humoured intelligence of the Controller's face, he decided to tell the truth, straightforwardly. "No." He shook his head.

Bernard started and looked horrified. What would the Controller think? To be labelled as the friend of a man who said that he didn't like civilization—said it openly and, of all people, to the Controller—it was terrible. "But, John," he began. A look from Mustapha Mond reduced him to an abject silence.

"Of course," the Savage went on to admit, "there are some very nice things. All that music in the air, for instance . . ."

"Sometimes a thousand twangling instruments will hum about my ears and sometimes voices."

The Savage's face lit up with a sudden pleasure. "Have you read it too?" he asked. "I thought nobody knew about that book here, in England."

"Almost nobody. I'm one of the very few. It's prohibited, you see. But as I make the laws here, I can also break them. With impunity, Mr. Marx," he added, turning to Bernard. "Which I'm afraid you *can't* do."

Bernard sank into a yet more hopeless misery.

"But why is it prohibited?" asked the Savage. In the excitement of meeting a man who had read Shakespeare he had momentarily forgotten everything else.

The Controller shrugged his shoulders. "Because it's old; that's the chief reason. We haven't any use for old things here."

"Even when they're beautiful?"

"Particularly when they're beautiful. Beauty's attractive, and we don't want people to be attracted by old things. We want them to like the new ones."

"But the new ones are so stupid and horrible. Those plays, where there's nothing but helicopters flying about and you *feel* the people kissing." He made a grimace. "Goats and monkeys!" Only in Othello's words could he find an adequate vehicle for his contempt and hatred.

"Nice tame animals, anyhow," the Controller murmured parenthetically.

"Why don't you let them see *Othello* instead?"

"I've told you; it's old. Besides, they couldn't understand it." . . .

"Why not?" . . .

"Because our world is not the same as Othello's world. You can't make flivvers without steel—and you can't make tragedies without social instability. The world's stable now. People are happy; they get what they want, and they never want what they can't get. They're well off; they're safe; they're never ill; they're not afraid of death; they're blissfully ignorant of passion and old age; they're plagued with no mothers or fathers; they've got no wives, or children, or lovers to feel strongly about; they're so conditioned that they practically can't help behaving as they ought to behave. And if anything should go wrong, there's *soma*. Which you go and chuck out of the window in the name of liberty, Mr. Savage. *Liberty!*" He laughed. "Expecting Deltas to know what liberty is! And now expecting them to understand *Othello!* My good boy!" . . .

"I was wondering," said the Savage, ". . . Why don't you make everybody an Alpha Double Plus while you're about it?"

Mustapha Mond laughed. "Because we have no wish to have our throats cut," he answered. "We believe in happiness and stability. A society of Alphas couldn't fail to be unstable and miserable. Imagine a factory staffed by Alphas—that is to say by separate and unrelated individuals of good heredity and conditioned so as to be capable (within limits) of making a free choice and assuming responsibilities. Imagine it!" he repeated.

The Savage tried to imagine it, not very successfully.

"It's an absurdity. An Alpha-decanted, Alpha-conditioned man would go mad if he had to do Epsilon Semi-Moron work—go mad, or start smashing things up. Alphas can be completely socialized—but only on condition that you make them do Alpha work. Only an Epsilon can be expected to make Epsilon sacrifices, for the good reason that for him they aren't sacrifices; they're the line of least resistance. His conditioning has laid down rails along which he's got to run. He can't help himself; he's foredoomed. Even after decanting, he's still inside a bottle—an invisible bottle of infantile and embryonic fixations. Each one of us, of course," the Controller meditatively continued, "goes through life inside a bottle. But if we happen to be Alphas, our bottles are, relatively speaking, enormous. We should suffer acutely if we were confined in a narrower space. You cannot pour upper-caste champagne-surrogate into lower-caste bottles. It's obvious theoretically. But it has also been proved in actual practice. The result of the Cyprus experiment was convincing."

"What was that?" asked the Savage.

Mustapha Mond smiled. "Well, you can call it an experiment in rebottling if you like. It began in A.F. 473. The Controllers had the island of Cyprus cleared of all its existing inhabitants and re-colonized with a specially prepared batch of 22,000 Alphas. All agricultural and industrial equipment was handed over to them and they were left to manage their own affairs. The result exactly fulfilled all the theoretical predictions. . . . Within 6 years they were having a first-class civil war. When 19,000 out of the 22,000 had been killed, the survivors unanimously petitioned the World Controllers to resume the government of the island. Which they did. And that was the end of the only society of Alphas that the world has ever seen."

The Savage sighed, profoundly.

"The optimum population," said Mustapha Mond, "is modelled on the iceberg—eight-ninths below the water line, one-ninth above."

"And they're happy below the water line?"

"Happier than above it. Happier than your friend here, for example." He pointed.

"In spite of that awful work?"

"Awful? *They* don't find it so. On the contrary, they like it. It's light, it's childishly simple. No strain on the mind or the muscles. Seven and a half hours of mild, unexhausting labour, and then the *soma* ration and games and unrestricted copulation and the feelies. What more can they ask for? True," he added, "they might ask for shorter hours. And of course we could give them shorter hours. . . . The experiment was tried, more than a century and a half ago. The whole of Ireland was put on to the 4-hour day. What was the result? Unrest and a large increase in the consumption of *soma;* that was all. Those three and one-half hours of extra leisure were so far from being a source of happiness, that people felt constrained to take a holiday from them. The Inventions Office is stuffed with plans for labour-saving processes. Thousands of them."

Mustapha Mond made a lavish gesture. "And why don't we put them into execution? For the sake of the labourers; it would be sheer cruelty to afflict them with excessive leisure . . . Every discovery in pure science is potentially subversive; even science must sometimes be treated as a possible enemy. Yes, even science." . . .

"You've had no scientific training, so you can't judge. I was a pretty good physicist in my time. Too good—good enough to realize that all our science is just a cookery book, with an orthodox theory of cooking that nobody's allowed to question, and a list of recipes that mustn't be added to except by special permission from the head cook. I'm the head cook now. But I was an inquisitive young scullion once. I started doing a bit of cooking on my own. Unorthodox cooking, illicit cooking. A bit of real science, in fact." He was silent.

"What happened?" asked Helmholtz Watson.

The Controller sighed. "Very nearly what's going to happen to you young men. I was on the point of being sent to an island."

The words galvanized Bernard into a violent and unseemly activity. "Send *me* to an island?" He jumped up, ran across the room, and stood gesticulating in front of the Controller. "You can't send *me*. I haven't done anything. It was the others. I swear it was the others." . . . And in a paroxysm of abjection he threw himself on his knees before the Controller. Mustapha Mond tried to make him get up; but Bernard persisted in his grovelling; the stream of words poured out inexhaustibly. In the end the Controller had to ring for his fourth secretary.

"Bring three men," he ordered, "and take Mr. Marx into a bedroom. Give him a good *soma* vaporization and then put him to bed and leave him." . . .

"One would think he was going to have his throat cut," said the Controller, as the door closed. "Whereas, if he had the smallest sense, he'd understand that his punishment is really a reward. He's being sent to an island. That's to say, he's being sent to a place where he'll meet the most interesting set of men and women to be found anywhere in the world. All the people who, for one reason or another, have got too self-consciously individual to fit into community-life. All the people who aren't satisfied with orthodoxy, who've got independent ideas of their own. Every one, in a word, who's any one. I almost envy you, Mr. Watson." . . .

"But *you* didn't go to an island," said the Savage, breaking a long silence.

The Controller smiled. "That's how I paid. By choosing to serve happiness. Other people's—not mine. It's lucky," he added, after a pause, "that there are such a lot of islands in the world. I don't know what we should do without them. Put you all in the lethal chamber, I suppose. By the way, Mr. Watson, would you like a tropical climate? The Marquesas, for example; or Samoa? Or something rather more bracing?"

Helmholtz rose from his pneumatic chair. "I should like a thoroughly bad climate," he answered. "I believe one would write better if the climate were bad. If there were a lot of wind and storms, for example . . ."

The Controller nodded his approbation. "I like your spirit, Mr. Watson. I like it very much indeed. As much as I officially disapprove of it." He smiled. . . .

"Art, science—you seem to have paid a fairly high price for your happiness," said the Savage, when they were alone. "Anything else?"

"Well, religion, of course," replied the Controller. "There used to be something called God—before the Nine Years' War. But I was forgetting; you know all about God, I suppose."

"Well . . ." The Savage hesitated. He would have liked to say something about solitude, about night, about the mesa lying pale under the moon, about the precipice, the plunge into shadowy darkness, about death. He would have liked to speak; but there were no words. Not even in Shakespeare. . . .

"But God's the reason for everything noble and fine and heroic. If you had a God . . ."

"My dear young friend," said Mustapha Mond, "civilization has absolutely no need of nobility or heroism. These things are symptoms of political inefficiency. In a properly organized society like ours, nobody has any opportunities for being noble or heroic. Conditions have got to be thoroughly unstable before the occasion can arise. . . . And if ever, by some unlucky chance, anything unpleasant should somehow happen, why, there's always *soma* to give you a holiday from the facts. And there's always *soma* to calm your anger, to reconcile you to your enemies, to make you patient and long-suffering. In the past you could only accomplish these things by making a great effort and after years of hard moral training. Now, you swallow two or three half-gramme tablets, and there you are. Anybody can be virtuous now. You can carry at least half your morality about in a bottle. Christianity without tears—that's what *soma* is." . . .

"Exposing what is mortal and unsure to all that fortune, death and danger dare, even for an eggshell. Isn't there something in that?" he asked, looking up at Mustapha Mond. "Quite apart from God—though of course God would be a reason for it. Isn't there something in living dangerously?"

"There's a great deal in it," the Controller replied. "Men and women must have their adrenals stimulated from time to time."

"What?" questioned the Savage, uncomprehending.

"It's one of the conditions of perfect health. That's why we've made the V.P.S. treatments compulsory."

"V.P.S.?"

"Violent Passion Surrogate." Regularly once a month. We flood the whole system with adrenin. It's the complete physiological equivalent of fear and rage. All the tonic effects of murdering Desdemona and being murdered by Othello, without any of the inconveniences."

"But I like the inconveniences."

"We don't," said the Controller. "We prefer to do things comfortably."

"But I don't want comfort. I want God, I want poetry, I want real danger, I want freedom, I want goodness. I want sin."

"In fact," said Mustapha Mond, "you're claiming the right to be unhappy."

"All right then," said the Savage defiantly, "I'm claiming the right to be unhappy."

"Not to mention the right to grow old and ugly and impotent; the right to have syphilis and cancer; the right to have too little to eat; the right to be lousy; the right to live in constant apprehension of what may happen to-morrow; the right to catch typhoid; the right to be tortured by unspeakable pains of every kind."

There was a long silence.

"I claim them all," said the Savage at last.

Mustapha Mond shrugged his shoulders. "You're welcome," he said.

VIRTUE

ARISTOTLE

translated by J. F. Heil

Nicomachean Ethics,
Selections from Books 1 and 2

BOOK 1

CHAPTER 13

Since happiness is a certain activity of the soul in accordance with complete virtue, we should examine virtue. This might also be a way to get a better look at happiness. Indeed, the "true politician" is thought to devote more effort to virtue than anything else, since he wants to make the citizens good and obedient to the laws. . . .

It is clear that the virtue we should investigate is human virtue, since the good we started seeking was the human good, and the happiness, human happiness. By human virtue we mean that of the soul, not that of the body, and by happiness we mean activity of the soul. If this is the case, then it is clear that the politician needs to understand matters of the soul to some extent, just as someone who is going to heal the eyes needs to understand the body as a whole. All the more so for politics, inasmuch as it is better and more honorable than medicine. Even among physicians, however, the refined ones make knowledge of the body a large part of their business. The politician, then, should study the soul. . . .

Now, we have covered some points about the soul sufficiently even in our popular works, and we should make use of them here—for instance, that there is a part of it that is nonrational and another part that possesses reason. . . . It seems that one part of the nonrational part is shared even with plants, I mean that which is responsible for nourishment and growth. . . . However, we can dismiss this nutritive part, since it is not its nature to have any portion of human virtue.

There seems to be another nature in the soul that is nonrational and, yet, in a certain way participates in reason. After all, in both the continent and incontinent person, we praise their reason and that part of their soul that possesses reason, because it rightly urges them towards what is best. There is evidently some other natural element in them besides reason, which is fighting and struggling against their reason. It is just like the paralyzed limbs of a body: though we decide to move them to the right, they travel off in the opposite direction to the left. The same is true of the soul. After all, the impulses of incontinent people go in opposite directions. To be sure, in the case of bodies we *see* the part travelling off, while in the case of the soul we don't. Nonetheless, we should presumably hold that there is something besides reason in the soul, opposing and struggling against it. How it is a distinct thing does not matter here. What does matter, as we said, is that this part also appears to participate in reason. In the continent person, at any rate, it *obeys* reason. Presumably, in the temperate and brave person it is even more ready to listen, since it agrees with reason about everything.

It appears, then, that our nonrational part is twofold. The vegetative part has absolutely no share in reason, but the appetitive part, or quite generally the desiderative part, does participate in reason in a way, insofar as it listens to it and obeys it. Thus it possesses reason in the sense in which we say it is "rational" to listen to our father or friends, and not as we speak of mathematics as rational. That the nonrational part is persuaded in some way by reason is shown by the practice of admonishing, and every variety of reproach and exhortation. But, if we ought to say that this part too possesses reason, then "the part that possesses reason" will be twofold: one that has it in the strict sense within itself, and another that has it as some sort of tendency to listen to reason, as though to a father.

Virtue too is divided on the basis of this distinction. We call some of them virtues of thought and others virtues of character. Theoretical wisdom, comprehension, and practical wisdom are virtues of thought, while liberality and temperance are virtues of character. After all, when we are speaking of someone's character we don't say that he is wise or intelligent, but that he is gentle or temperate. However, we also praise the wise person on the basis of his state, and the states that are praiseworthy we call virtues.

BOOK 2

CHAPTER 1

Virtue, then, is twofold: virtue of thought and virtue of character. Virtue of thought has its birth and growth mostly from teaching, which is why it requires experience and time. Virtue of character (*ēthikē*), on the other hand, comes about from habit (*ethos*), hence it gets even its name from a slight variation on the word "habit."

From this it is also clear that none of the virtues of character arises in us by nature. Nothing that exists by nature is habituated into another condition. For instance, a stone, which by nature travels downward, could not be habituated to travel upwards, not even if you threw it up 10,000 times. Nor could fire be habituated to move downwards. Nor could anything else that is naturally in one condition be habituated into another condition.

The virtues, therefore, arise neither by nature nor contrary to nature, but rather by our being naturally constituted to acquire them, and by our bringing their development to completion through habit. A further argument is this: for anything that arises in us by nature, we first find ourselves with the capacity and then display the activity. This is particularly clear in the case of the senses. It isn't from frequent seeing or frequent hearing that we acquired these senses, but rather the reverse. We already had them when we began to use them; we didn't come to have them by using them. The virtues, however, we acquire only by exercising them first, as is true for the other crafts as well. Indeed, the things we must learn before doing we learn by doing. People become builders by building and harpists by playing the harp. So too, then, we become just by performing just actions, temperate by temperate ones and brave by brave ones.

This is corroborated by what goes on in states. The legislators make the citizens good by habituating them. This is the wish of every legislator, and those who fail to do it well miss their mark. Indeed, this is what distinguishes a good from a bad constitution.

Furthermore, the activities from which and through which every virtue is created are the very ones that can also destroy it. The same is true of a craft: from playing the harp, both good and bad harpists are created. Analogously with builders and all the rest: from building things well people will be good builders, from doing it badly they will be bad. If this were not the case, then there would have been no need for someone to *teach* the craft; everyone would simply have been born good or bad. This is also the case, then, for the virtues. By the actions we perform in our relationships with human beings, some of us become just, others unjust. By the actions we perform in fearful situations, and by our being habitually frightened or confident, some of us become brave, others cowardly. And likewise for actions involving our appetites and those involving our anger. Depending on how people react in those situations, some become temperate and gentle, others intemperate and harsh.

In short, our states of character are formed out of the activities that are like them. This is why we need to display activities of a certain kind, because our states follow along with the differences in these. It makes no small difference, then, whether we become habituated in this way or that way right from our youth. Rather, it makes a tremendous difference—indeed, all the difference.

CHAPTER 2

Now, our present study is not, as others are, for the sake of theoretical understanding. We are examining virtue not in order to know what virtue is, but in order to become good—otherwise it would have no benefit. We must, therefore, investigate the question of actions, namely, how they should be performed. These, as we've said, are crucial for the kinds of states of character that are formed.

That our actions should be performed in accordance with "correct reason" is a common view, and let it be assumed here. We will discuss later on what this correct reason is and how it is related to the other virtues.[1] Let it be agreed in advance, however, that, as a whole, our account of the actions that are to be done is bound to be stated in outline and not precisely. As we said at the beginning,[2] we should demand accounts that correspond to the subject matter, and in the realm of action, as well as with matters of benefit, nothing is fixed—anymore than in matters of health. And, when our general account is like this, then our account of the particulars has even less precision. *These matters fall under no craft or set of precepts.* People themselves, the people engaged in action, always need to consider things in relation to the occasion, just as they do in medicine and navigation. But, even though our present account is imprecise, we should try to offer some help.

Now, the first point we should consider is this: it is the nature of such things to be destroyed by deficiency and excess. We observe this—given that we need to use things that are evident as witnesses for the things that are not—in the case of strength and health. Both excessive and deficient exercising destroys strength. Likewise, drinking and eating too much or too little destroys health, while the proportionate amount produces, increases, and maintains it. Now, the same is true of temperance and courage and the other virtues. Someone who flees from and fears everything, and endures nothing, becomes cowardly. But, someone who fears absolutely nothing, and faces everything, becomes rash. Likewise, too, someone who enjoys every pleasure and abstains from none, becomes intemperate. But someone who, like those crude people, avoids all pleasure, becomes an insensitive sort. Temperance and courage, then, are destroyed by excess and deficiency, but are maintained by *the mean*.

But not only are their birth and growth produced from and caused by the same things as their destruction; their activities too will be displayed in the same things. This is certainly true of the other more evident cases. Strength, for instance, is produced as result of eating plenty of food and enduring plenty of labor, and the strong person is the one most able to *do* these very things. The same goes for the virtues. As a result of abstaining from pleasures we become temperate, and having become temperate we are most able to abstain from them. Likewise for courage: by being habituated to disdain and endure fearful things we become brave, and once we have become brave we will be most able to endure fearful things.

CHAPTER 3

The pleasure or pain that accompanies our actions should be considered a sign of our states of character. Someone who abstains from bodily pleasures and *enjoys* abstaining is temperate, while someone who finds it a burden is intemperate. Someone who endures fearful things and enjoys it, or at least is not pained by it, is brave, while someone who is pained by it is cowardly.

Indeed, virtue of character is concerned with pleasures and pains. It is because of pleasure that we do bad things and because of pain that we don't do fine things. This is why, as Plato says, we need to have been brought up in a certain way right from our youth, so as to take pleasure in and be pained by the things we should. This, indeed, is "Correct Education."

Furthermore, since the virtues are concerned with actions and affections, and since every affection and all action is accompanied by pleasure or pain, then, for this reason too, virtue is concerned with pleasures and pains. . . .

Let us set it down, therefore, that virtue is the sort of thing that is capable of doing what is best in regard to pleasures and pains, and that vice is the opposite. . . .

CHAPTER 5

Next, we should examine what virtue is. Since there are three things that occur in the soul—affections, capacities, and states—virtue would have to be one of these. By affections I mean appetite, anger, fear, confidence, envy, joy, love, hate, longing, jealousy, pity, and, in general, things accompanied by pleasure or pain. Capacities are those things on the basis of which we are said to be capable of these affections, e.g., capable of being angered or being pained or feeling pity. States are those things on the basis of which we are in a good or bad condition with respect to our affections. For instance, with respect to being angered, if we are affected too intensely or too weakly, then we are in a bad condition, but if in an intermediate way, then we are in a good condition. And likewise with respect to the other affections.

Now, neither the virtues nor the vices are affections. We do not call people outstanding or inferior on the basis of their affections, but we *do* call them this on the basis of their virtues or vices. Also, we are not praised or blamed on the basis of our affections. I mean no one is praised for being frightened or angry, nor is anyone blamed for just being angry, but for being angry in a certain way. But we are praised and blamed on the basis of our virtues and vices. Furthermore, we get angered and frightened without decision, but the virtues are decisions of a sort, or at least are not without decision. Finally, in reference to our affections we are said to be moved, whereas in reference to our virtues and vices we are said, not to be moved, but to be disposed in a certain way.

For the same reasons the virtues are not capacities either. We are not called good or bad simply by being capable of affections, nor are we praised or blamed for it. Furthermore, we have our capacities by nature, but we don't become good or bad by nature. We discussed that earlier, however.

So, if the virtues are neither affections nor capacities, it remains for them to be states. We have said, then, what virtue is in terms of its genus.

CHAPTER 6

We need to say not only that virtue is a state, but also what sort of state it is. We should say, then, that *every virtue perfects whatever it is a virtue of, and allows it to perform its function well.* For instance, the virtue of the eye makes both the eye and its function outstanding, since it is by the virtue of the eye that we see well. Similarly, the virtue of a horse makes a horse outstanding and good at running, carrying its rider, and standing steadfast against the enemy. If, therefore, this is true in every case, then the virtue of a human being, too, would be the state that makes a human being good and makes him perform his own function well.

We've already said how this will be true, but it will also be obvious by considering what the nature of virtue is. Now, with everything that is continuous and divisible it is possible to take more, less, or an equal amount—either with respect to the thing itself or relative to us. The equal amount is an intermediate between excess and deficiency. By an intermediate "of the thing itself" I mean what is equidistant from each of the extremes, which is one and the same for everyone. By "relative to us" I mean what neither exceeds nor falls short, and this is not one thing, nor is it the same for everyone. For example, if ten is a large amount and two is small, then the intermediate, taken with respect to the thing, is six, since it exceeds and is exceeded by an equal amount.[3] This is an intermediate with respect to numerical proportion, but this is not how we should take it relative to us. It isn't the case that, if ten pounds of food is too much to eat and two pounds too little, the trainer will prescribe six pounds. This might be too much for the one who is to take it, or too little. For Milo it is too little, but for the beginner in athletics it is too much, and likewise in the case of running and wrestling. In *this* sense, then, every expert in his field avoids excess and deficiency, and seeks and chooses the intermediate—not the intermediate of the thing, but relative to us.

This is how every field of expertise accomplishes its work well, namely, by looking to the intermediate and steering its works toward that. Hence, people tend to comment on good works that nothing could be added or subtracted, suggesting that excess and deficiency destroy the good, while the mean maintains it. Now, since we say that good craftsmen look to this when they work, and since virtue, like nature, is better and more precise than any craft, it follows that *virtue is something that aims at the intermediate.*

Here, however, I mean virtue of *character,* since this is the kind concerned with affections and actions, and in these there can be excess and deficiency and the intermediate. For instance, we can have fear, confidence, appetite, anger, pity, and, in general, pleasure and pain, both more and less, and in either way not well. But to have these at the right times, about the right objects, towards the right people, for the right reason, and in the right way—this is the intermediate and best condition, and this is the mark of virtue. Likewise, for our actions too, there can be excess and deficiency and an intermediate.

Again, virtue is concerned with affections and actions, in which excess goes wrong and deficiency is also blamed, while the intermediate is correct and is praised. But, both of these are features of virtue. Hence, virtue is a certain mean, since it is something that aims at the intermediate.

Furthermore, there are many ways we can go wrong. Indeed, the bad belongs to the unlimited (as the Pythagoreans used to imagine) and the good to the limited. There is only one way, however, to be correct. That is why it is easy to go wrong and hard to be correct, easy to miss the target and hard to hit it. For this reason too, then, excess and deficiency belong to vice, while the mean belongs to virtue. "For, we are good in a single way, but bad in all sorts."

Virtue, then, is a state having to do with decision, lying in a mean relative to us and defined by reason, i.e., in the way someone with practical wisdom would define it. . . .

Not every action and every affection admits of a mean, however. Indeed, some are given names that immediately imply badness, e.g., spite, shamelessness, envy, and, in the case of actions, adultery, theft, and murder. All of these are called such things because they themselves, and not their excesses and deficiencies, are bad. So, we can never be correct in them, but must always go wrong. We cannot do such things well or not well—by, say, committing adultery with the right woman, at the right time, and in the right way—but rather to do any of them under any condition is to do something wrong. To claim otherwise would be like claiming that there is a mean and an excess and a deficiency for actions such as doing injustice or being cowardly or acting intemperately. Indeed, if *that* were so, then there would be a mean of an excess or of a deficiency, and an excess of an excess, and a deficiency of a deficiency. But, just as there is no excess or deficiency of temperance or courage—because the intermediate is in a sense an extreme—so too there is no mean or excess or deficiency of these vicious actions; they are wrong however they are done. Indeed, generally speaking, there is no mean of an excess or of a deficiency, and no excess or deficiency of a mean.

---

[1]Aristotle returns to it in Book 6 (not included here), where he takes up the virtues of thought.

[2]See Book 1, Chapter 3 earlier in this anthology.

[3]That is, six exceeds the small amount by four, and is exceeded by the large amount by four.

THOMAS AQUINAS

On Virtue and Natural Law

SECOND ARTICLE

Law, being a rule and measure, can be in a person in two ways: in one way, as in him that rules and measures; in another way, as in that which is ruled and measured, since a thing is ruled and measured, in so far as it partakes of the rule or measure. Wherefore, since all things subject to Divine providence are ruled and measured by the eternal law . . . it is evident that all things partake somewhat of the eternal law, in so far as, namely, from its being imprinted on them, they derive their respective inclinations to their proper acts and ends. Now among all others, the rational creature is subject to Divine providence in the most excellent way, in so far as it partakes of a share of providence, by being provident both for itself and for others. Wherefore it has a share of the Eternal Reason, whereby it has a natural inclination to its proper act and end: and this participation of the eternal law in the rational creature is called the natural law. . . .

THIRD ARTICLE

We may speak of virtuous acts in two ways: first, under the aspect of virtuous; secondly, as such and such acts considered in their proper species. If then we speak of acts of virtue, considered as virtuous, thus all virtuous acts belong to the natural law. For it has been stated (A. 2) that to the natural law belongs everything to which a man is inclined according to his nature. Now each thing is inclined naturally to an operation that is suitable to it according to its form: thus fire is inclined to give heat. Wherefore, since the rational soul is the proper form of man, there is in every man a natural inclination to act according to reason: and this is to act according to virtue. Consequently, considered thus, all acts of virtue are prescribed by the natural law: since each one's reason naturally dictates to him to act virtuously. But if we speak of virtuous acts, considered in themselves, i.e., in their proper species, thus not all virtuous acts are prescribed by natural law: for many things are done virtuously, to which nature does not incline at first; but which, through the inquiry of reason, have been found by men to be conducive to well-living.

THOMAS AQUINAS

On the Cardinal Virtues

The soul needs to follow something in order to give birth to virtue: this something is God: if we follow Him we shall live aright. Consequently the exemplar of human virtue must needs pre-exist in God, just as in Him pre-exist the types of all things.

Accordingly virtue may be considered as existing originally in God, and thus we speak of *exemplar* virtues: so that in God the Divine Mind itself may be called prudence; while temperance is the turning of God's gaze on Himself, even as in us it is that which conforms the appetite to reason. God's fortitude is His unchangeableness; His justice is the observance of the Eternal Law in His works, as Plotinus states.

Again, since man by his nature is a social animal, these virtues, in so far as they are in him according to the condition of his nature, are called *social* virtues; since it is by reason of them that man behaves himself well in the conduct of human affairs. It is in this sense that we have been speaking of these virtues until now.

But since it behooves man to do his utmost to strive onward even to Divine things, as even the Philosopher declares in *Ethic.* x. 7, and as Scripture often admonishes us. . . . we must needs place some virtues between the social or human virtues, and the exemplar virtues which are Divine. Now these virtues differ by reason of a difference of movement and term: so that some are virtues of men who are on their way and tending towards the Divine similitude; and these are called *perfecting* virtues. Thus prudence, by contemplating the things of God, counts as nothing all things of the world, and directs all the thoughts of the soul to God alone;—temperance, so far as nature allows, neglects the needs of the body; fortitude prevents the soul from being afraid of neglecting the body and rising to heavenly things; and justice consists in the soul giving a wholehearted consent to follow the way thus proposed.—Besides these there are the virtues of those who have already attained to the Divine similitude: these are called the *perfect virtues.*—Thus prudence sees nought else but the things of God; temperance knows no earthly desires; fortitude has no knowledge of passion; and justice, by imitating the Divine Mind, is united thereto by an everlasting covenant. Such are the virtues attributed to the Blessed, or, in this life, to some who are at the summit of perfection.

ALASDAIR MACINTYRE

After Virtue

THE NATURE OF THE VIRTUES

. . . One of the features of the concept of a virtue . . . is that it always requires for its application the acceptance for some prior account of certain features of social and moral life in terms of which it has to be defined and explained. So in the Homeric account the concept of a virtue is secondary to that of *a social role,* in Aristotle's account it is secondary to that of *the good life for man* conceived as the *telos* of human action and in Franklin's much later account it is secondary to that of utility. What is it in the account which I am about to give which provides in a similar way the necessary background against which the concept of a virtue has to be made intelligible? It is in answering this question that the complex, historical, multi-layered character of the core concept of virtue becomes clear. For there are no less than three stages in the logical development of the concept which have to be identified in order, if the core conception of a virtue is to be understood, and each of these stages has its own conceptual background. The first stage requires a background account of what I shall call a practice, the second an account of what I have already characterized as the narrative order of a single human life and the third an account a good deal fuller than I have given up to now of what constitutes a moral tradition. Each later stage presupposes the earlier, but not *vice versa*. Each earlier stage is both modified by and reinterpreted in the light of, but also provides an essential constituent of each later stage. The progress in the development of the concept is closely related to, although it does not recapitulate in any straightforward way, the history of the tradition of which it forms the core.

In the Homeric account of the virtues—and in heroic societies more generally—the exercise of a virtue exhibits qualities which are required for sustaining a social role and for exhibiting excellence in some well-marked area of social practice: to excel is to excel at war or in the games, as Achilles does, in sustaining a household, as Penelope does, in giving counsel in the assembly, as Nestor does, in the telling of a tale, as Homer himself does. When Aristotle speaks of excellence in human activity, he sometimes though not always, refers to some well-defined type of human practice: flute-playing, or war, or geometry. I am going to suggest that this notion of a particular type of practice as providing the arena in which the virtues are exhibited and in terms of which they are to receive their primary, if incomplete, definition is crucial to the whole enterprise of identifying a core concept of the virtues. I hasten to add two *caveats* however.

The first is to point out that my argument will not in any way imply that virtues are *only* exercised in the course of what I am calling practices. The second is to warn that I shall be using the word "practice" in a specially defined way which does not completely agree with current ordinary usage, including my own previous use of that word. What am I going to mean by it?

By a "practice" I am going to mean any coherent and complex form of socially established cooperative human activity through which goods internal to that form of activity are realized in the course of trying to achieve those standards of excellence which are appropriate to, and partially definitive of, that form of activity, with the result that human powers to achieve excellence, and human conceptions of the ends and goods involved, are systematically extended. Tic-tac-toe is not an example of a practice in this sense, nor is throwing a football with skill; but the game of football is, and so is chess. Bricklaying is not a practice; architecture is. Planting turnips is not a practice; farming is. So are the enquiries of physics, chemistry and biology, and so is the work of the historian, and so are painting and music. In the ancient and medieval worlds the creation and sustaining of human communities—of households, cities, nations—is generally taken to be a practice in the sense in which I have defined it. Thus the range of practices is wide: arts, sciences, games, politics in the Aristotelian sense, the making and sustaining of family life, all fall under the concept. But the question of the precise range of practices is not at this stage of the first importance. Instead let me explain some of the key terms involved in my definition, beginning with the notion of goods internal to a practice.

Consider the example of a highly intelligent 7-year-old child whom I wish to teach to play chess, although the child has no particular desire to learn the game. The child does however have a very strong desire for candy and little chance of obtaining it. I therefore tell the child that if the child will play chess with me once a week I will give the child 50 cents worth of candy; moreover I tell the child that I will always play in such a way that it will be difficult, but not impossible, for the child to win and that, if the child wins, the child will receive an extra 50 cents worth of candy. Thus motivated the child plays and plays to win. Notice however that, so long as it is the candy alone which provides the child with a good reason for playing chess, the child has no reason not to cheat and every reason to cheat, provided he or she can do so successfully. But, so we may hope, there will come a time when the child will find in those goods specific to chess, in the achievement of a certain highly particular kind of analytical skill, strategic imagination, and competitive intensity, a new set of reasons, reasons now not just for winning on a particular occasion, but for trying to excel in whatever way the game of chess demands. Now if the child cheats, he or she will be defeating not me, but himself or herself.

There are thus two kinds of good possibly to be gained by playing chess. On the one hand there are those goods externally and contingently attached to chess-playing and to other practices by the accidents of social circumstance—in the case of the imaginary child candy, in the case of real adults such goods as prestige, status, and money. There are always alternative ways for achieving such goods, and their achievement is never to be had *only* by engaging in some particular kind of practice. On the other hand there are the goods internal to the practice of chess which cannot be had in any way but by playing chess or some other game of that specific kind. We call them internal for two reasons: first, as I have already suggested, because we can only specify them in terms of chess or some other game of that specific kind and by means of examples from such games (otherwise the meagerness of our vocabulary for speaking of such goods forces us into such devices as my own resort to writing of "a certain highly particular kind of"); and secondly because they can only be identified and recognized by the experience of participating in the practice in question. Those who lack the relevant experience are incompetent thereby as judges of internal goods. . . .

A practice involves standards of excellence and obedience to rules as well as the achievement of goods. To enter into a practice is to accept the authority of those standards and the inadequacy of my own performance as judged by them. It is to subject my own attitudes, choices, preferences, and tastes to the standards which currently and partially define the practice. Practices of course, as I have just noticed, have a history: games, sciences and arts all have histories. Thus the standards are not themselves immune from criticism, but nonetheless we cannot be initiated into a practice without accepting the authority of the best standards realized so far. If, on starting to listen to music, I do not accept my own incapacity to judge correctly, I will never learn to hear, let alone to appreciate, Bartok's last quartets. If, on starting to play baseball, I do not accept that others know better than I when to throw a fast ball and when not, I will never learn to appreciate good pitching let alone to pitch. In the realm of practices the authority of both goods and standards operates in such a way as to rule out all subjectivist and emotivist analyses of judgment. De gustibus *est* disputandum.

We are now in a position to notice an important difference between what I have called internal and what I have called external goods. It is characteristic of what I have called external goods that when achieved they are always some individual's property and possession. Moreover characteristically they are such that the more someone has of them, the less there is for other people. This is sometimes necessarily the case, as with power and fame, and sometimes the case by reason of contingent circumstance as with money. External goods are therefore characteristically objects of competition in which there must be losers as well as winners. Internal goods are indeed the outcome of competition to excel, but it is characteristic of them that their achievement is a good for the whole community who participate in the practice. So when Turner transformed the seascape in painting or W. G. Grace advanced the art of batting in cricket in a quite new way their achievement enriched the whole relevant community.

But what does all or any of this have to do with the concept of the virtues? It turns out that we are now in a position to formulate a first, even if partial and tentative definition of a virtue: *A virtue is an acquired human quality the possession and exercise of which tends to enable us to achieve those goods which are internal to practices and the lack of which effectively prevents us from achieving any such goods.* Later this definition will need amplification and amendment. But as a first approximation to an adequate definition it already illuminates the place of the virtues in human life. For it is not difficult to show for a whole range of key virtues that without them the goods internal to practices are barred to us, but not just barred to us generally, barred in a very particular way.

It belongs to the concept of a practice as I have outlined it—and as we are all familiar with it already in our actual lives, whether we are painters or physicists or quarterbacks or indeed just lovers of good painting or first-rate experiments or a well-thrown pass—that its goods can only be achieved by subordinating ourselves within the practice in our relationship to other practitioners. We have to learn to recognize what is due to whom; we have to be prepared to take whatever self-endangering risks are demanded along the way; and we have to listen carefully to what we are told about our own inadequacies and to reply with the same carefulness for the facts. In other words we have to accept as necessary components of any practice with internal goods and standards of excellence the virtues of justice, courage, and honesty. For not to accept these, to be willing to cheat as our imagined child was willing to cheat in his or her early days at chess, so far bars us from achieving the standards of excellence or the goods internal to the practice that it renders the practice pointless except as a device for achieving external goods.

We can put the same point in another way. Every practice requires a certain kind of relationship between those who participate in it. Now the virtues are those goods by reference to which, whether we like it or not, we define our relationships to those other people with whom we share the kind of purposes and standards which inform practices. Consider an example of how reference to the virtues has to be made in certain kinds of human relationship.

A, B, C, and D are friends in that sense of friendship which Aristotle takes to be primary: they share in the pursuit of certain goods. In my terms they share in a practice.

D dies in obscure circumstances, A discovers how D died and tells the truth about it to B while lying to C. C discovers the lie. What A cannot then intelligibly claim is that he stands in the same relationship of friendship to both B and C. By telling the truth to one and lying to the other he has partially defined a difference in the relationship. Of course it is open to A to explain this difference in a number of ways; perhaps he was trying to spare C pain or perhaps he is simply cheating C. But some difference in the relationship now exists as a result of the lie. For their allegiance to each other in the pursuit of common goods has been put in question.

Just as, so long as we share the standards and purposes characteristic of practices, we define our relationship to each other, whether we acknowledge it or not, by reference to standards of truthfulness and trust, so we define them too by reference to standards of justice and of courage. If A, a professor, gives B and C the grades that their papers deserve, but grades D because he is attracted by D's blue eyes or is repelled by D's dandruff, he has defined his relationship to D differently from his relationship to the other members of the class, whether he wishes it or not. Justice requires that we treat others in respect of merit or desert according to uniform and impersonal standards; to depart from the standards of justice in some particular instance defines our relationship with the relevant person as in some way special or distinctive.

The case with courage is a little different. We hold courage to be a virtue because the care and concern for individuals, communities and causes which is so crucial to so much in practices requires the existence of such a virtue. If someone says that he cares for some individual, community, or cause, but is unwilling to risk harm or danger on his, her, or its own behalf, he puts in question the genuineness of his care and concern. Courage, the capacity to risk harm or danger to oneself, has its role in human life because of this connection with care and concern. This is not to say that a man cannot genuinely care and also be a coward. It is in part to say that a man who genuinely cares and has not the capacity for risking harm or danger has to define himself, both to himself and to others, as a coward.

I take it then that from the standpoint of those types of relationship without which practices cannot be sustained truthfulness, justice, and courage—and perhaps some others—are genuine excellences, are virtues in the light of which we have to characterize ourselves and others, whatever our private moral standpoint or our society's particular code may be. . . .

The discussion so far I hope makes it clear that a practice, in the sense intended, is never just a set of technical skills, even when directed towards some unified purpose and even if the exercise of those skills can on occasion be valued or enjoyed for their own sake. What is distinctive in a practice is in part the way in which conceptions of the relevant goods and ends which the technical skills serve—and every practice does require the exercise of technical skills—are transformed and enriched by these extensions of human powers and by that regard for its own internal goods which are partially definitive of each particular practice or type of practice. Practices never have a goal or goals fixed for all time—painting has no such goal nor has physics—but the goals themselves are transmuted by the history of the activity. It therefore turns out not to be accidental that every practice has its own history and a history which is more and other than that of the improvement of the relevant technical skills. This historical dimension is crucial in relation to the virtues.

To enter into a practice is to enter into a relationship not only with its contemporary practitioners, but also with those who have preceded us in the practice, particularly those whose achievements extended the reach of the practice to its present point. It is thus the achievement, and *a fortiori* the authority, of a tradition which I then confront and from which I have to learn. And for this learning and the relationship to the past which it embodies the virtues of justice, courage, and truthfulness are prerequisite in precisely the same way and for precisely the same reasons as they are in sustaining present relationships within practices.

It is not only of course with sets of technical skills that practices ought to be contrasted. Practices must not be confused with institutions. Chess, physics, and medicine are practices; chess clubs, laboratories, universities, and hospitals are institutions. Institutions are characteristically and necessarily concerned with what I have called external goods. They are involved in acquiring money and other material goods; they are structured in terms of power and status, and they distribute money, power, and status as rewards. Nor could they do otherwise if they are to sustain not only themselves, but also the practices of which they are the bearers. For no practices can survive for any length of time unsustained by institutions. Indeed so intimate is the relationship of practices to institutions—and consequently of the goods external to the goods internal to the practices in question—that institutions and practices characteristically form a single causal order in which the ideals and the creativity of the practice are always vulnerable to the acquisitiveness of the institution, in which the cooperative care for common goods of the practice is always vulnerable to the competitiveness of the institution. In this context the essential function of the virtues is clear. Without them, without justice, courage, and truthfulness, practices could not resist the corrupting power of institutions.

Yet if institutions do have corrupting power, the making and sustaining of forms of human community—and therefore of institutions—itself has all the characteristics of a practice, and moreover of a practice which stands in a peculiarly close relationship to the exercise of the virtues in two important ways. The exercise of the virtues is itself apt to require a highly determinate attitude to social and political issues; and it is always within some particular community with its own specific institutional forms that we learn or fail to learn to exercise the virtues. There is of course a crucial difference between the way in which the relationship between moral character and political community is envisaged from the standpoint of liberal individualist modernity and the way in which that relationship was envisaged from the standpoint of the type of ancient and medieval tradition of the virtues which I have sketched. For liberal individualism a community is simply an arena in which individuals each pursue their own self-chosen conception of the good life, and political institutions exist to provide that degree of order which makes such self-determined activity possible. Government and law are, or ought to be, neutral between rival concepts as of the good life for man, and hence, although it is the task of government to promote law-abidingness, it is on the liberal view no part of the legitimate function of government to inculcate any one moral outlook.

By contrast, on the particular ancient and medieval view which I have sketched political community not only requires the exercise of the virtues for its own sustenance, but it is one of the tasks of parental authority to make children grow up so as to be virtuous adults. The classical statement of this analogy is by Socrates in the *Crito.* It does not of course follow from an acceptance of the Socratic view of political community and political authority that we ought to assign to the modern state the moral function which Socrates assigned to the city and its laws. Indeed the power of the liberal individualist standpoint partly derives from the evident fact that the modern state is indeed totally unfitted to act as moral educator of any community. But the history of how the modern state emerged is of course itself a moral history. If my account of the complex relationship of virtues to practices and to institutions is correct, it follows that we shall be unable to write a true history of practices and institutions unless that history is also one of the virtues and vices. For the ability of a practice to retain its integrity will depend on the way in which the virtues can be and are exercised in sustaining the institutional forms which are the social bearers of the practice. The integrity of a practice causally requires the exercise of the virtues by at least some of the individuals who embody it in their activities; and conversely the corruption of institutions is always in part at least an effect of the vices.

The virtues are of course themselves in turn fostered by certain types of social institution and endangered by others. Thomas Jefferson thought that only in a society of small farmers could the virtues flourish; and Adam Ferguson with a good deal more sophistication saw the institutions of modern commercial society as endangering at least some traditional virtues. It is Ferguson's type of sociology which is the empirical counterpart of the conceptual account of the virtues which I have given, a sociology which aspires to lay bare the empirical, causal connection between virtues, practices, and institutions. For this kind of conceptual account has strong empirical implications; it provides an explanatory scheme which can be tested in particular cases. Moreover my thesis has empirical content in another way; it does entail that without the virtues there could be a recognition only of what I have called external goods and not at all of internal goods in the context of practices. And in any society which recognized only external goods competitiveness would be the dominant and even exclusive feature. We have a brilliant portrait of such a society in Hobbes's account of the state of nature; and Professor Turnbull's report of the fate of the Ik suggests that social reality does in the most horrifying way confirm both my thesis and Hobbes's.

Virtues then stand in a different relationship to external and to internal goods. The possession of the virtues—and not only of their semblance and simulacra—is necessary to achieve the latter; yet the possession of the virtues may perfectly well hinder us in achieving external goods. I need to emphasize at this point that external goods genuinely are goods. Not only are they characteristic objects of human desire, whose allocation is what gives point to the virtues of justice and of generosity, but no one can despise them altogether without a certain hypocrisy. Yet notoriously the cultivation of truthfulness, justice, and courage will often, the world being what it contingently is, bar us from being rich or famous or powerful. Thus although we may hope that we can not only achieve the standards of excellence and the internal goods of certain practices by possessing the virtues *and* become rich, famous, and powerful, the virtues are always a potential stumbling block to this comfortable ambition. We should therefore expect that, if in a particular society the pursuit of external goods were to become dominant, the concept of the virtues might suffer first attrition and then perhaps something near total effacement, although simulacra might abound. . . .

I stressed earlier that any account of the virtues in terms of practices could only be a partial and first account. What is required to complement it? The most notable difference so far between my account and any account that could be called Aristotelian is that although I have in no way restricted the exercise of the virtues to the context of practices, it is in terms of practices that I have located their point and function. Whereas Aristotle locates that point and function in terms of the notion of a type of whole human life which can be called good. And it does seem that the question "What would a human being lack who lacked the virtues?" must be given a kind of answer which goes beyond anything which I have said so far. For such an individual would not merely fail *in a variety of particular ways* in respect of the kind of excellence which can be achieved through participation in practices and in respect of the kind of human relationship required to sustain such excellence. His own life *viewed as a whole* would perhaps be defective; it would not be the kind of life which someone would describe in trying to answer the question "What is the best kind of life for this kind of man or woman to live?" And that question cannot be answered without at least raising Aristotle's own question, "What is the good life for man?" Consider three ways in which human life informed only by the conception of the virtues sketched so far would be defective.

It would be pervaded, first of all, by *too many* conflicts and *too much* arbitrariness. I argued earlier that it is a merit of an account of the virtues in terms of a multiplicity of goods that it allows for the possibility of tragic conflict in a way in which Aristotle's does not. But it may also produce even in the life of someone who is virtuous and disciplined too many occasions when one allegiance points in one direction, another in another. The claims of one practice may be incompatible with another in such a way that one may find oneself oscillating in an arbitrary way, rather than making rational choices. So it seems to have been with T. E. Lawrence. Commitment to sustaining the kind of community in which the virtues can flourish may be incompatible with the devotion to a particular practice—of the arts, for example—requires. So there may be tensions between the claims of family life and those of the arts—the problem that Gauguin solved or failed to solve by fleeing to Polynesia, or between the claims of politics and those of the arts—the problem that Lenin solved or failed to solve by refusing to listen to Beethoven. . . .

Secondly without an overriding conception of the *telos* of a whole human life, conceived as a unity, our conception of certain individual virtues has to remain partial and incomplete. . . . Justice, on an Aristotelian view, is defined in terms of giving each person his or her due or desert. To deserve well is to have contributed in some substantial way to the achievement of those goods, the sharing of which and the common pursuit of which provide foundations for human community. But the goods internal to practices, including the goods internal to the practice of making and sustaining forms of community, need to be ordered and evaluated in some way if we are to assess relative desert. Thus any substantive application of an Aristotelian concept of justice requires an understanding of goods and of the good that goes beyond the multiplicity of goods which inform practices. . . .

I have suggested so far that unless there is a *telos* which transcends the limited goods of practices by constituting the good of a whole human life, the good of a human life conceived as a unity, it will *both* be the case that a certain subversive arbitrariness will invade the moral life *and* that we shall be unable to specify the context of certain virtues adequately. These two considerations are reinforced by a third: that there is at least one virtue recognized by the tradition which cannot be specified at all except with reference to the wholeness of a human life—the virtue of integrity or constancy. "Purity of heart," said Kierkegaard, "is to will one thing." This notion of singleness of purpose in a whole life can have no application unless that of a whole life does.

It is clear therefore that my preliminary account of the virtues in terms of practices captures much, but very far from all, of what the Aristotelian tradition taught about the virtues. It is also clear that to give an account that is at once more fully adequate to the tradition and rationally defensible, it is necessary to raise a question to which the Aristotelian tradition presupposed an answer, an answer so widely shared in the pre-modern world that it never had to be formulated explicitly in any detailed way. This question is: is it rationally justifiable to conceive of each human life as a unity, so that we may try to specify each such life as having its good and so that we may understand the virtues as having their function in enabling an individual to make of his or her life one kind of unity rather than another?

MARY MIDGLEY

Wickedness

CHAPTER 6: SELVES AND SHADOWS

1.   THE PROBLEM OF SELF-DECEPTION

. . . We try to avoid "owning" our bad motives, not just from vanity (though that is important) but because we feel that to own or acknowledge is to accept. We dread exposure to the hidden force whose power we sense. Our official idea of ourselves has no room for it. It therefore does not seem merely humiliating and depressing (as our known faults do), but alien, inhuman, and menacing to an indefinite degree. When this sense of menace gets severe, it is almost certain to get projected on to the outside world, supplying fuel for those irrational fears and hatreds which play so central a part in human destructiveness.

In what may be called contentedly wicked people—and in all of us so far as we are contentedly wicked—this process is far gone, and may involve no more conflict in the inner life than in the front shown to the world. It is the fact that no conflict is visible that makes this kind of case so opaque. But this need not force us either to assume a special alternative morality at work, or to give up the attempt at understanding altogether. Instead, we can approach this kind of case by way of the much less opaque ones where conflict is still visibly raging. Hard though this is, it seems necessary to attempt it since self-deception, in spite of its chronic obscurity, is a topic which we badly need to understand. Bishop Butler, at the end of his discussion of it, cries out suddenly:

> And, if people will be wicked, they had better of the two be so from the common vicious passions without such refinements, than from this deep and calm source of delusion, which undermines the whole principle of good, darkens that light, that *candle of the Lord within,* which is to direct our steps, and corrupts conscience, which is the guide of life.[1]

Does this mean that there are two quite separate alternatives, self-deception and vice? It seems not. Butler apparently takes "the common vicious passions" to be something conscious and acknowledged. But the more fully conscious they are, the nearer their owners come to what Aristotle called weakness, rather than vice.[2] They suffer spasms of (say) furious or covetous action alternating with fits of repentance. People who are weak in this sense are supposed still to keep so clear an intellectual grasp of the situation that they judge their own acts impartially, as they would other people's. This seems rather strange. The disadvantages of oscillating violently in this way are obvious, and in fact if we find people who seem to do it we tend to look for an explanation in some oscillation of their physical state. Without this extra factor, it is hard to see how the oscillator's clarity of vision can really be maintained. Some self-deception seems absolutely necessary, first so that he can have some kind of a story to tell himself during his vicious fits, but also, and more deeply, because the whole process of oscillation is going to need some justification of its own, and it will be uncommonly difficult to find an honest one. The question why one is behaving alternatively like two quite different people is one that cannot fail to arise. The answer "I just happen to be two people" has never been found to be very satisfactory. Butler's point, then, seems sound, but it is a matter of degree, not a complete dichotomy. The more chronic, continuous, and well-established is the self-deception, the deeper and more pernicious the vice. But some self-deception is probably needed if actions are to be called vicious at all.

2. INNER DIALOGUE AND DUALITY

I am suggesting that self-deception arises because we see motives which are in fact our own as alien to us and refuse to acknowledge them. This is not an isolated event, but is one possible outcome of a very common and pervasive inner dialogue, in which aspects of the personality appear to exchange views as if they were separate people. We are used to this interchange between alternating moods or viewpoints. (If we were not, we should probably find it much harder to disown some of them, because it would be harder to separate them from our official selves in the first place.) This inner dialogue is, I believe, the source of drama. Good plays and stories do not just show clashes between distinct individuals, externally related. They show ones which take place within us as well as outside. However black the villains, however strange the character-parts, we need to feel something within us respond to them. Drama helps inner conflict by crystallizing it. It can, of course, be used to help self-deception by externalizing villainy, but it can also help self-knowledge by showing up the participants clearly. Properly used, it always helps us to avoid that dangerous thing, an oversimple view of personal identity.

There is a great deal more to the problem of personal identity than meets the eye, or gets mentioned in current philosophical discussions. This connexion with inner conflict and the problem of evil, in particular, seems to have had very little academic attention of late. It is, however, very important, on account of the existence of shadows. In this century, academic philosophy, as much as psychology, has been reluctant to pay much attention to the shadow-side of human motivation. It has not occupied itself with the agonizing question "Can it really have been I who did that?" or with the genuine clash of reasons for answering yes or no to it. Nor has it dealt much with the still more startling division of the self into two or more embattled factions which marks the process of temptation. If we want to find a way into these problems, we had therefore better turn to those who have seriously and methodically considered them. Setting aside the religious traditions for a moment—because we are not sure how much of their conceptual equipment we shall want to accept—we are left, therefore, with works of imagination, and particularly of imaginative literature.

There is absolutely no shortage of shadows here. Resisting the urge to plunge in and round them all up, I shall deliberately start with a rather simple and schematic specimen, namely *The Strange Case of Dr. Jekyll and Mr. Hyde*. Critics have sometimes treated this story as a lightweight, but I think they are mistaken. Any crash course on evil must acknowledge a great debt to the Scots, and the debt to Stevenson here seems to be quite an important part of it. It is worth while, if one has not taken it very seriously, having another look.

What Stevenson brings out is the negativity of Hyde's character. Evil, in spite of its magnificent pretensions, turns out to be mostly a vacuum. That does not make it less frightening, but more so. Like darkness and cold, it destroys but it cannot replace. The thought is an old one, but we may have regarded it simply as a platitude. In the story, however, Hyde's first appearance shows it sharply:

> Street after street and all the folks asleep. . . . All at once I saw two figures; one a little man who was stumping along eastwards at a good walk, and the other a girl of maybe eight or ten who was running as hard as she was able down a cross street. Well sir, the two ran into one another naturally enough at the corner; and then came the horrible part of the thing; for the man trampled calmly over the child's body and left her screaming on the ground. It sounds nothing to hear, but it was hellish to see.[3]

What makes it so is not deliberate cruelty, but callousness—the total absence of a normal human response. David Hume (a Scot of a different kind) asked, "Would any man, who is walking along, tread as willingly on another's gouty toes, whom he has no quarrel with, as on the hard flint and pavement?"[4] Well, here is that man, and his total blindness to any feeling but his own is central to his character. As Jekyll puts it, when he is eventually driven to attempt a choice between his two lives:

> Hyde was indifferent to Jekyll, or but remembered him as the mountain bandit remembers the cavern is which he conceals himself from pursuit. Jekyll had more than a father's interest (because he shared Hyde's pleasures); Hyde had more than a son's indifference.[5]

This is why, although Hyde had

> a soul boiling with causeless hatreds, and a body that seemed not strong enough to contain the raging energies of life, [Jekyll] . . . thought of Hyde, for all his energy of life, as of something not only hellish but inorganic. This was the shocking thing; that the slime of the pit seemed to utter cries and voices; that what was dead and had no shape, should usurp the offices of life.[6]

This fearful limitation is, of course, the reason why he cannot choose to settle for Hyde, but must continue the doomed effort to be Jekyll. . . .

Of course Stevenson's story is somewhat crude and schematic. But by being so it gets past our defences and makes us pay some attention to its topic. Jekyll was partly right: we *are* each not only one but also many. Might not this fact deserve a little more philosophic attention? Some of us have to hold a meeting every time we want to do something only slightly difficult, in order to find the self who is capable of undertaking it. We often fail, and have to make do with an understudy who is plainly not up to the job. We spend a lot of time and ingenuity on developing ways of organizing the inner crowd, securing consent among it, and arranging for it to act as a whole. Literature shows that the condition is not rare. Others, of course, obviously do not feel like this at all, hear such descriptions with amazement, and are inclined to regard those who give them as dotty. There is not, however, the sort of difference between the conduct of those aware of constant internal debate and that of other people which would justify writing this awareness off as an aberration. When real difficulties arise, everybody becomes conscious of it, and has what is recognizably the same sort of trouble. There are then actually advantages in being used to it. Someone who has never felt gravely divided before is likely to be more bewildered than a habitual splitter. Most people, too, probably would recognize that serious troubles do give rise to such conflicts, that rather more of them go on than are sometimes noticed, and that, through the process of temptation, they do have an important bearing on wickedness. But just how does this connexion work? Can inner conflicts explain major crimes?

4.   THE POWER OF PROJECTION

The difficulty for thought here is this. We feel that motives ought to be adequate for the actions they produce. In the case of good actions they often are so; indeed, it is common to find that the people who did something good were trying to do much more than they achieved. The frustration of really good schemes by outside difficulties is a commonplace. But in the case of evil actions this is much less clear. When we look for someone who conceived them we often cannot find him at all; when we can, we often find a number of culprits with no clear connexion with each other, none of whom was apparently trying to do what actually resulted. In such cases, we are inclined to retire baffled, give up the search for causes rooted in human motivation, and fall back on other sorts of explanation, such as the economic. But this is clearly not very satisfactory, since the human conduct in question—for instance, that of launching the First World War, and of carrying it on in the way that was in fact followed—is not a rational response to the economic factors. Although a few people profited from it, the damage which it did was so enormous, and the chance for any individual of immunity from that damage so small, that Hobbesian calculators of en-lightened self-interest would not have been led to take such action. For instance, even the most selfish of politicians and generals did not want to lose their sons, nor to risk their careers in the chaos that follows defeat. The rational aims they were pur-suing could have been followed up by methods which did not involve these dangers. And anyway most of those involved were not simply and clear-headed selfish; they thought they were doing their duty. We have therefore to look for diffused human motives, not clearly recognized, which blind people to their own interests as well as to other people's, and incline them to see as their duty actions which, if they viewed them impartially, they would consider wrong.

What makes these motives hard to see is the very same fact which gives them their force—namely, their immense diffusion. The habitual, half-conscious, apparently mild hostility of one person towards another is as little noticed, consciously, as the air they breathe. It also resembles that air in being a vital factor in their lives, and in the fact that a slight shift in its quality can make enormous changes. Yet it differs from it in being something for which they are, at root, responsible. To take the crudest case at once, it is what makes war possible. And a very interesting and significant point about the way in which it does so is its versatility—the ease with which it can be shifted from one opponent to another. Orwell's caricature in *1984,* where a political speaker in the middle of a speech changes fulminations directed against one enemy into ones directed against another, in response to a slip handed up to him showing that the High Command has changed its policy, contains a truth with which history has made us fa-miliar, but whose oddness we need to notice. Alliances are changed far more easily than one might expect, and hostility is even more easily redirected. This is connected with another striking feature, the ease with which improbable charges are believed against anyone designated as an enemy, the invention of further charges when real data fail, and the general unreality with which enemy thought-processes are imagined. We need to notice again how contrary this habit of mind is to rational prudence. If one has enemies, it is surely of the first importance to discover their real intentions, to study them carefully, and assess realistically the dangers which they actually pose. No real enemy is unlimitedly hostile. All have particular aims, and between such aims compromise is nearly always possible. Certainly some enemies are more threatening, some conflicts of interest harder to reconcile than others. But this only makes it all the more important to discover realistically which sort one is facing at the moment.

When we consider people's frequent failure to do this, and the extraordinary flour-ishing of violent hostility where no real threat is posed at all, we are (as far as I can see) forced to look for an explanation within. People who seriously believe that they are being attacked when they are not, and who attribute hostile planning groundlessly to their supposed attackers, have to be projecting their own unrecognized bad mo-tives onto the world around them. For instance, the suspicion of witchcraft is a very common form for this projection, found in many cultures. The more convinced we are that witchcraft does not actually take place, the more necessary it surely is to account for this belief in terms of projection. In our own culture, the story of witch-hunting is a very remarkable one, since the early church actively discouraged it, and laid down rules which made the practice very difficult. In order to let loose the witch-hunting movement which was rife between the 15th and 17th centuries, it was necessary for those who saw witchcraft everywhere to break through established custom and reverse many ecclesiastical rulings. This and many similar cases show how shallow it would be to attribute these beliefs merely to chance tradition and primitive ignorance of causes. Other obvious cases are anti-semitism and persecution of religious minorities. When we turn to disputes between nations things are, of course, often more complicated, since real conflicts of interests, and real threats, may be involved as well as irrational hostility. But when we look at these apparently more solid causes, complications appear. How rational is resentment? When one country has previously attacked another—for instance in the case of France and Germany after the war of 1870—what follows? It is natural for the invaded party to fear that it will happen again, to want its provinces back, and in fact want revenge. But intense concentration of these aims is certainly not the best way to secure, in the end, harmonious relations with the neighbour. And those harmonious relations provide the only possible hope of arbitrating the conflict of interest effectively.

Even in the most reasonable kinds of dispute, uncontrolled, chronic hostility is a liability, not an asset, and this, again, gives us further grounds to suppose that it takes its rise in irrelevant, projected motives, not just in the specific, apparent causes of the outward dispute. Specific grievances wear out; the unchangingness of group hostilities marks them as fraudulent. They are not responses to real external dangers, but fantasies. We erect a glass at the border of our own group, and see our own anger reflected against the darkness behind it. Where we know a good deal about neighbouring groups, the darkness is not complete and the projection is imperfect. If we want to maintain it, we may then have to do quite a lot of arguing. But the more unfamiliar that group is, the deeper the darkness becomes. The illusion can then grow wholly convincing. This is the point at which even people who know perfectly well that the so-called *Protocols of the Elders of Zion* were deliberately forged by the Czarist police still find no difficulty in accepting them as evidence.[7] The dark vision is too vivid to be doubted; its force is its warrant. What we see out there is indeed real enough; it is our own viciousness, and it strikes us with quite appropriate terror. And by an unlucky chance, while it remains projected, there is no way to weaken or destroy it. Persecution and punishment of those to whom it is attributed do not soften it at all; indeed, to the persecutors' alarm, they often seem to intensify it. Hence the strange instability of persecution, the way in which suspicion seems to grow by being fed, and security never comes nearer.

5.   COMPLICITY BETWEEN LEADERS AND LED

This account of course raises many questions which we have still to deal with, notably about the origin of the projected feelings in the first place. But it has one great asset which, as it seems to me, makes some form of it a necessary move. This is that it resolves the difficulty about finding an adequate motive. The joint repressed aggression of a whole populace makes up a very powerful motive for communal crimes, such as pogroms, witch-hunts, or gratuitous wars. It is a cause suitable to such effects. By invoking it, we can avoid a very odd and unconvincing feature of those explanations

which ignore it, namely, that they divide populations sharply into a few guilty instiga-
tors and a majority of amazingly passive dupes or fools. Unless we think that a particular population is weak and foolish on all subjects, we must surely find it odd that they
become so as soon as some particular feared or persecuted group comes in question.
The picture of innocent passivity is not convincing because it is too selective. We
know very well that not every kind of political leader, and not every kind of cause,
finds this kind of uncritical passive obedience. And if the picture of the passive herd
is suspect, that of the wholly active, creative instigator, stamping his personality at
will upon this wax, is still more so. Mass leaders must use the causes they can find.
Konrad Heiden, in his life of Hitler, stresses the incoherence and vacillation of his
policies, the random, opportunistic way in which he picked up his ideas, largely according to their saleability:

> Rather than a means of directing the mass mind, propaganda is a technique for riding
> with the masses. It is not a machine to make wind, but a sail to catch the wind. . . .
> The more passionately Hitler harps on the value of personality, the more clearly he re-
> veals his nostalgia for something that is lacking. . . . Yes, he knows this mass world, he
> knows how to guide it by "compliance." . . . He did not have a plan and act accord-
> ingly; he acted, and out of his actions a plan arose.[8]

Influential psychopaths and related types, in fact, get their power not from originality,
but from a perception of just what unacknowledged motives lie waiting to be exploited, and just what aspects of the world currently provide a suitable patch of darkness on to which they can be projected. In order to catch the wind, they must (if
Heiden is right) be without any specific, positive motivation of their own which might
distract them from taking up and using skillfully whatever has most popular appeal at
the time. Many aspiring Caesars have come to grief here; they had too much individual character. They did not see the sharpness of the dilemma. To gain great popular
power, you must either be a genuinely creative genius, able to communicate new ideas
very widely, or you must manage to give a great multitude permission for things which
it already wants, but for which nobody else is currently prepared to give that permission. In order to find these things, and to handle skillfully the process of permitting
the unthinkable, absolute concentration on the main chance is required, and this
seems only possible to those without serious, positive aims of their own. There is
therefore a sense, and not a trivial one, in which such demagogues are themselves the
tools of their supporters. This becomes disturbingly plain in causes where they eventually lose their influence and are cast aside to end their days in obscurity, like Titus
Oates and Senator Joe McCarthy. It then becomes a mystery, even to many of those
who followed them, how they can ever have had such power. The only place where
solutions to this mystery can be sought for seems to be the unconscious motivation of
those who allowed themselves to be deceived. . . .

---

[1]Bishop Butler, *Fifteen Sermons,* Sermon X "Upon Self-Deceit," section 16.

[2]*Nicomachean Ethics* book VII, chapters 1–10.

[3]R. L. Stevenson, *The Strange Case of Dr. Jekyll and Mr. Hyde,* Chapter 1 (Nelson, London, 1956), p. 6.

[4]*Enquiry Concerning the Principles of Morals,* part ii, section V, 183.

[5]Stevenson, chapter 10, p. 86.

[6]Ibid., pp. 94–5, 96–7.

[7]For this extremely strange business, see Konrad Heiden, *Der Fuehrer: Hitler's Rise to Power* (trans. Ralph Mannheim, Gollancz, 1944), chapter 1.

[8]Ibid., p. 118.

(ETERNAL) LIFE

BLAISE PASCAL

Pensées

194

. . . The immortality of the soul is a matter which is of so great consequence to us, and which touches us so profoundly, that we must have lost all feeling to be indifferent as to knowing what it is. All our actions and thoughts must take such different courses, according as there are or are not eternal joys to hope for, that it is impossible to take one step with sense and judgment, unless we regulate our course by our view of this point which ought to be our ultimate end.

Thus our first interest and our first duty is to enlighten ourselves on this subject, whereon depends all our conduct. Therefore among those who do not believe, I make a vast difference between those who strive with all their power to inform themselves, and those who live without troubling or thinking about it.

I can have only compassion for those who sincerely bewail their doubt, who regard it as the greatest of misfortunes, and who, sparing no effort to escape it, make of this inquiry their principal and most serious occupations.

But as for those who pass their life without thinking of this ultimate end of life, and who, for this sole reason that they do not find within themselves the lights which convince them of it, neglect to seek them elsewhere, and to examine thoroughly whether this opinion is one of those which people receive with credulous simplicity, or one of those which, although obscure in themselves, have nevertheless a solid and immovable foundation, I look upon them in a manner quite different.

This carelessness in a matter which concerns themselves, their eternity, their all, moves me more to anger than pity; it astonishes and shocks me; it is to me monstrous. I do not say this out of the pious zeal of a spiritual devotion. I expect, on the contrary, that we ought to have this feeling from principles of human interest and self-love; for this we need only see what the least enlightened persons see.

We do not require great education of the mind to understand that there is no real and lasting satisfaction; that our pleasures are only vanity; that our evils are infinite; and, lastly, that death, which threatens us every moment, must infallibly place us within a few years under the dreadful necessity of being for ever either annihilated or unhappy.

There is nothing more real than this, nothing more terrible. Be we as heroic as we like, that is the end which awaits the noblest life in the world. Let us reflect on this, and then say whether it is not beyond doubt that there is no good in this life but in the hope of another; that we are happy only in proportion as we draw near it; and that, as there are no more woes for those who have complete assurance of eternity, so there is no more happiness for those who have no insight into it. . . .

If there is a God, He is infinitely incomprehensible, since, having neither parts nor limits, He has no affinity to us. We are then incapable of knowing either what He is or if He is. This being so, who will dare to undertake the decision of the question? Not we, who have no affinity to Him.

Who then will blame Christians for not being able to give a reason for their belief, since they profess a religion for which they cannot give a reason? They declare, in expounding it to the world, that it is a foolishness, *stultitiam;* and then you complain that they do not prove it! If they proved it, they would not keep their word; it is in lacking proofs, that they are not lacking in sense. "Yes, but although this excuses those who offer it as such, and takes away from them the blame of putting it forward without reason, it does not excuse those who receive it." Let us then examine this point, and say, "God is, or He is not." But to which side shall we incline? Reason can decide nothing here. There is an infinite chaos which separated us. A game is being played at the extremity of this infinite distance where heads or tails will turn up. What will you wager? According to reason, you can do neither one thing nor the other; according to reason, you can defend neither of the propositions.

Do not then reprove for error those who have made a choice; for you know nothing about it. "No, but I blame them for having made, not this choice, but a choice; for again both he who chooses heads and he who chooses tails are equally at fault, they are both in the wrong. The true course is not to wager at all."

Yes; but you must wager. It is not optional. You are embarked. Which will you choose then? Let us see. Since you must choose, let us see which interests you least. You have two things to lose, the true and the good; and two things at stake, your reason and your will, your knowledge and your happiness; and your nature has two things to shun, error and misery. Your reason is no more shocked in choosing one rather than the other, since you must of necessity choose. This is one point settled. But your happiness? Let us weigh the gain and the loss in wagering that God is. Let us estimate these two chances. If you gain, you gain all; if you lose, you lose nothing. Wager, then, without hesitation that He is.—"That is very fine. Yes, I must wager; but I may perhaps wager too much."—Let us see. Since there is an equal risk of gain and of loss, if you had only to gain two lives, instead of one, you might still wager. But if there were three lives to gain, you would have to play (since you are under the necessity of playing), and you would be imprudent, when you are forced to play, not to chance your life to gain three at a game where there is an equal risk of loss and gain. But there is an eternity of life and happiness. And this being so, if there were an infinity of chances, of which one only would be for you, you would still be right in wagering one to win two, and you would act stupidly, being obliged to play, by refusing to stake one life against three at a game in which out of an infinity of chances there is one for you, if there were an infinity of an infinitely happy life to gain. But there is here an infinity of an infinitely happy life to gain, a chance of gain against a finite number of chances of loss, and what you stake is finite. It is all divided; wherever the infinite is and there is not an infinity of chances of loss against that of gain, there is no time to hesitate, you must give all. And thus, when one is forced to play, he must renounce reason to preserve his life, rather than risk it for infinite gain, as likely to happen as the loss of nothingness.

For it is no use to say it is uncertain if we will gain, and it is certain that we risk, and that the infinite distance between the *certainty* of what is staked and the *uncertainty* of what will be gained, equals the finite good which is certainly staked against the uncertain infinite. It is not so, as every player stakes a certainty to gain an uncertainty, and yet he stakes a finite certainty to gain a finite uncertainty, without transgressing against reason. There is not an infinite distance between the certainty staked and the uncertainty of the gain; that is untrue. In truth, there is an infinity between the certainty of gain and the certainty of loss. But the uncertainty of the gain is proportioned to the certainty of the stake according to the proportion of the chances of gain and loss. Hence it comes that, if there are as many risks on one side as on the other, the course is to play even; and then the certainty of the stake is equal to the uncertainty of the gain, so far is it from fact that there is an infinite distance between them. And so our proposition is of infinite force, when there is the finite to stake in a game where there are equal risks of gain and of loss, and the infinite to gain. This is demonstrable; and if men are capable of any truths, this is one.

"I confess it, I admit it. But, still, is there no means of seeing the faces of the cards?"—Yes, Scripture and the rest, etc. "Yes, but I have my hands tied and my mouth closed; I am forced to wager, and am not free. I am not released, and am so made that I cannot believe. What, then, would you have me do?"

True. But at least learn your inability to believe, since reason brings you to this, and yet you cannot believe. Endeavour then to convince yourself, not by increase of proofs of God, but by the abatement of your passions. You would like to attain faith, and do not know the way; you would like to cure yourself of unbelief, and ask the remedy for it. Learn of those who have been bound like you, and who now stake all their possessions. These are people who know the way which you would follow, and who are cured of an ill of which you would be cured. Follow the way by which they began; by acting as if they believed, taking the holy water, having masses said, etc. Even this will naturally make you believe, and deaden your acuteness.—"But this is what I am afraid of."—And why? What have you to lose?

But to show you that this leads you there, it is this which will lessen the passions, which are your stumbling-blocks.

The end of this discourse.—Now, what harm will befall you in taking this side? You will be faithful, honest, humble, grateful, generous, a sincere friend, truthful. Certainly you will not have those poisonous pleasures, glory and luxury; but will you not have others? I will tell you that you will thereby gain in this life, and that, at each step you take on this road, you will see so great certainty of gain, so much nothingness in what you risk, that you will at last recognise that you have wagered for something certain and infinite, for which you have given nothing.

"Ah! This discourse transports me, charms me," etc.

If this discourse pleases you and seems impressive, know that it is made by a man who has knelt, both before and after it, in prayer to that Being, infinite and without parts, before whom he lays all he has, for you also to lay before Him all you have for your own good and for His glory, that so strength may be given to lowliness. . . .

LEO TOLSTOY

Confessions

Five years ago something very strange started happening to me. At first I began experiencing moments of bewilderment; my life would come to a standstill, as if I did not know how to live or what to do, and I felt lost and fell into despair. But they passed and I continued to live as before. Then these moments of bewilderment started to recur more frequently, always taking the same form. On these occasions, when life came to a standstill, the same questions always arose: "Why? What comes next? . . ."

All this was happening to me at a time when I was surrounded on all sides by what is considered complete happiness: I was not yet fifty, I had a kind, loving, and beloved wife, lovely children, and a large estate that was growing and expanding with no effort on my part. I was respected by relatives and friends far more than ever before. I was praised by strangers and could consider myself a celebrity without deceiving myself. Moreover I was not unhealthy in mind or body, but on the contrary enjoyed a strength of mind and body such as I had rarely witnessed in my contemporaries. Physically I could keep up with the peasants tilling the fields; mentally I could work for 8 or 10 hours at a stretch without suffering any ill effects from the effort. And in these circumstances I found myself at the point where I could no longer go on living and, since I feared death, I had to deceive myself in order to refrain from suicide.

I could not attribute any rational meaning to a single act, let alone to my whole life. I simply felt astonished that I had failed to realize this from the beginning. It had all been common knowledge for such a long time. Today or tomorrow sickness and death will come (and they had already arrived) to those dear to me, and to myself, and nothing will remain other than the stench and the worms. Sooner or later my deeds, whatever they may have been, will be forgotten and will no longer exist. What is all the fuss about then? How can a person carry on living and fail to perceive this? That is what is so astonishing! It is only possible to go on living while you are intoxicated with life; once sober it is impossible not to see that it is all a mere trick, and a stupid trick! That is exactly what it is: there is nothing either witty or amusing, it is only cruel and stupid.

There is an old Eastern fable about a traveller who is taken unawares on the steppes by a ferocious wild animal. In order to escape the beast the traveller hides in an empty well, but at the bottom of the well he sees a dragon with its jaws open, ready to devour him. The poor fellow does not dare to climb out because he is afraid of being eaten by the rapacious beast, neither does he dare drop to the bottom of the well for fear of being eaten by the dragon. So he seizes hold of a branch of a bush that is growing in the crevices of the well and clings on to it. His arms grow weak and he knows that he will soon have to resign himself to the death that awaits him on either side. Yet he still clings on, and while he is holding on to the branch he looks around and sees that two mice, one black and one white, are steadily working their way round the bush he is hanging from, gnawing away at it. Sooner or later they will eat through it and the branch will snap, and he will fall into the jaws of the dragon. The traveller sees this and knows that he will inevitably perish. But while he is still hanging there he sees some drops of honey on the leaves of the bush, stretches out his tongue and licks them. In the same way I am clinging to the tree of life, knowing full well that the dragon of death inevitably awaits me, ready to tear me to pieces, and I cannot understand how I have fallen into this torment. And I try licking the honey that once consoled me, but it no longer gives me pleasure.

In my search for answers to the question of life I felt just like a man who is lost in a wood.

I came to a clearing, climbed a tree, and saw clearly into the never-ending distance. But there was no house there, nor could there be. I walked into the thicket, into the gloom and saw the darkness, but there was no house there either.

In the same way I wandered in the forest of human knowledge, both amidst the bright rays of mathematical knowledge and experimental knowledge, where wide horizons were opened up to me, but in a direction where I could find no house, and amidst the darkness of speculative knowledge where I was immersed in ever deeper gloom the further I progressed. And I became quite convinced that there was not, and could not be, a way out.

When I inclined to the bright side of knowledge I realized that I was only avoiding facing the question. However bright and attractive those horizons spreading out before me were, and however tempting it was to immerse myself in the infinity of all this knowledge, I already knew that the clearer the knowledge was, the less I needed it, and the less it answered my question. "Well," I said to myself, "I know everything that science so urgently wants to know and along that path there is no answer to the question of the meaning of my life." In the speculative realm I knew that despite the fact, or rather precisely because of the fact, that the primary purpose of this knowledge is to answer my question, the answer given was none other than the one I had already given myself: what is the meaning of my life? It has none. Or: what will come of my life? Nothing. Or: why does everything there is exist, and why do I exist? Because it does.

When I put my questions to one branch of human knowledge I received a countless number of precise answers to things I had not asked: the chemical composition of the stars, the movement of the sun towards the constellation Hercules, the origin of the species and of man, the forms of infinitely tiny atoms, the fluctuations of infinitely small and imponderable particles of ether. But the only answer this branch of knowledge provided to my question concerning the meaning of life was this: you are that which you call your life; you are a temporary, incidental accumulation of particles. The mutual interaction and alteration of these particles produces in you something you refer to as your life. This accumulation can only survive for a limited length of time; when the interaction of these particles ceases, that which you call life will cease, bringing an end to all your questions. You are a randomly united lump of something. This lump decomposes and the fermentation is called your life. The lump will disintegrate and the fermentation will end, together with all your questions. This is the answer given by the exact side of knowledge, and if it adheres strictly to its principles, it cannot answer otherwise.

However, the truth is that this answer does not reply to the question. I need to know the meaning of my life, and the fact that it is a particle of infinity not only fails to give it any meaning, but eliminates any possible meaning.

The experimental side of knowledge vaguely compromises with the speculative side in saying that the meaning of life lies in development and in the encouragement of this development. But owing to the inaccuracies and obscurities these cannot be regarded as answers.

Whenever the other side of knowledge, the speculative realm, sticks firmly to its principles and gives direct answers to the question, it has always, throughout the ages, given the same answer: the universe is something infinite and incomprehensible. Man's life is an inscrutable part of this inscrutable "whole." . . .

Whether it was thanks to my somewhat strange and instinctive love of the true working people that I was forced to understand them and to realize that they are not as stupid as we thought; or whether it was thanks to the sincerity of my conviction that I knew of nothing better to do than hang myself, I sensed anyway that if I wanted to live and to understand the meaning of life I must not seek it among those who have lost it and wish to kill themselves, but among the millions of people living and dead who have created life, and who carry the weight of our lives together with their own. And I looked around at the enormous masses of simple, uneducated people without wealth, who have lived and who still live, and I saw something quite different. I saw that with a few exceptions all those millions do not fit into my divisions, and that I could not categorize them as people who did not understand the question because they themselves posed, and answered, the question with unusual clarity. Neither could I categorize them as epicureans, since their lives rest more on deprivation and suffering than on pleasure. I could still less regard them as living out their meaningless lives irrationally, since they could explain every act of their lives, including death. They considered suicide the greatest evil. It appeared that mankind as a whole had some kind of comprehension of the meaning of life that I did not acknowledge and derided. It followed that rational knowledge does not provide the meaning of life, but excludes it; while the meaning given to life by the millions of people, by humanity as a whole, is founded on some sort of knowledge that is despised and considered false. . . .

A contradiction arose from which there were only two ways out: either that which I called reasonable was not as reasonable as I thought, or that which I felt to be irrational was not as irrational as I thought. And I started to check the line of argument that stemmed from my rational knowledge.

As I checked this line of argument I found it to be entirely correct. The conclusion that life is nothing was inevitable, but I spotted a mistake. The mistake was that my thinking did not correspond to the question I had posed. The question was: why do I live? Or: is there anything that will remain and not be annihilated of my illusory and transitory life? Or: what meaning has my finite existence in an infinite universe? In order to answer this question I studied life.

Clearly the solution to all the possible questions of life could not satisfy me because my question, however simple it may seem at first, involves a demand for an explanation of the finite by means of the infinite and vice versa.

I had asked: what my life means beyond time, beyond space, beyond cause? And I was answered with the question: "What is the meaning of my life within time, space, and cause?" The result was that after long and laboured thought I could only answer: none.

In my deliberations I was continually drawing comparisons between the finite and the finite, and the infinite and the infinite, and I could not have done otherwise. Thus I reached the only conclusion I could reach: force is force, matter is matter, will is will, the infinite is the infinite, nothing is nothing; and I could go no further than that.

It was somewhat similar to what happens in mathematics when, trying to resolve an equation, we get an identity. The method of deduction is correct, but the only answer obtained is that a equals a, and x equals x, or o equals o. Precisely the same thing was happening with my reasoning concerning the meaning of life. The only answers the sciences give to this question are identities.

And really, strictly rational knowledge, such as that of Descartes, begins with complete doubt in everything and throws aside any knowledge founded on faith, reconstructing everything along laws of reason and experiment. And it can provide no answer other than the one I reached: an indefinite one. It was only at first that I thought knowledge had given an affirmative answer, Schopenhauer's answer that life has no meaning and is evil. But when I went into the matter I realized that this answer is not affirmative and that it was only my senses that had taken it to be so. Strictly expressed, as it is by the Brahmins, Solomon, and Schopenhauer, the answer is but a vague one, an identity: o equals o, life presented to me as nothing is nothing. Thus, philosophical knowledge denies nothing but simply replies that it cannot solve the question, and that as far as it is concerned any resolution remains indefinite.

Having understood this, I realized that it was impossible to search for an answer to my questions in rational knowledge; that the answer given by rational knowledge simply suggests that the answer can only be obtained by stating the question in another way, by introducing the question of the relation of the finite to the infinite. I realized that no matter how irrational and distorted the answers given by faith might be, they had the advantage of introducing to every answer a relationship between the finite and the infinite, without which there can be no solution. Whichever way I put the question: how am I to live? the answer is always: according to God's law. Or to the question: is there anything real that will come of my life? the answer is: eternal torment or eternal bliss. Or, to the question: what meaning is there that is not destroyed by death? the answer is: unity with the infinite, God, heaven.

Thus in addition to rational knowledge, which I had hitherto thought to be the only knowledge, I was inevitably led to acknowledge that there does exist another kind of knowledge—an irrational one—possessed by humanity as a whole: faith, which affords the possibility of living. Faith remained as irrational to me as before, but I could not fail to recognize that it alone provides mankind with the answers to the question of life, and consequently with the possibility of life.

Rational knowledge had led me to recognize that life is meaningless. My life came to a halt and I wanted to kill myself. As I looked around at people, at humanity as a whole, I saw that they lived and affirmed that they knew the meaning of life. I looked at myself. I had lived as long as I knew the meaning of life. For me, as for others, faith provided the meaning of life and the possibility of living.

Having looked around further at people in other countries and at my contemporaries and predecessors, I saw the same thing. Where there is life there is faith. Since the day of creation faith has made it possible for mankind to live, and the essential aspects of that faith are always and everywhere the same.

---

translated by David Kaḷupahana

Yamaka

(109) Thus have I heard: At one time venerable Sāriputta was staying near Sāvatthi in the Jeta Grove in Anāthapiṇḍika's monastery. Now at that time a pernicious entrenched view like this had arisen to the monk called Yamaka: "In so far as I understand the doctrine taught by the Fortunate One it is that a monk who has spewed influxes, at the break up of the body, will be annihilated, will be destroyed, and does not come to be after death." Many monks heard: "A pernicious entrenched view like this had arisen to the monk called Yamaka: 'In so far as I understand the doctrine taught by the Fortunate One it is that a monk who has spewed influxes, at the break up of the body, will be annihilated, will be destroyed, and does not come to be after death.'"

Then these monks approached the monk Yamaka; having approached, they exchanged greetings; having concluded the exchange of greetings of friendliness and courtesy, they sat on one side.

So seated these monks spoke thus to the monk Yamaka: "Is it true that a pernicious entrenched view like this has arisen to you, friend Yamaka: 'In so far as I understand (110) the doctrine taught by the Fortunate One, that a monk who has spewed influxes, at the break up of the body, will be annihilated, will be destroyed, and does not come to be after death'?"

"Even so do I, friends, understand the doctrine taught by the Fortunate One, that a monk who has spewed influxes, at the break up of the body, will be annihilated, will be destroyed, and does not come to be after death."

"Do not, friend Yamaka, speak thus, do not misrepresent the Fortunate One; misrepresentation of the Fortunate One is not good; the Fortunate One would not speak thus: 'A monk who has spewed influxes, at the break up of the body, will be annihilated, will be destroyed, and does not come to be after death.'"

Thus, the monk Yamaka, being spoken to by those monks, continued to express that pernicious entrenched view grasping on to it with great obstinacy [saying]: "In so far as I understand the doctrine taught by the Fortunate One, that a monk who has spewed influxes, at the break up of the body, will be annihilated, will be destroyed, and does not come to be after death."

Those monks could not free the monk Yamaka from that pernicious entrenched view. Then those monks approached venerable Sāriputta; having approached, said thus to venerable Sāriputta: "Venerable Sāriputta, such a pernicious entrenched view has arisen to the monk Yamaka: 'In so far as I understand the doctrine taught by the

Fortunate One, that a monk who has spewed influxes, at the break up of the body, will be annihilated, will be destroyed, and does not come to be after death.' It would be good! Let venerable Sāriputta approach the monk Yamaka through sympathy."

Venerable Sāriputta accepted (the request) with silence.

The venerable Sāriputta, in the evening, having arisen from seclusion, approached venerable Yamaka; having approached, exchanged greetings; having concluded the exchange of greetings of friendliness and courtesy, sat on one side.

Seated on one side, venerable Sāriputta said thus to venerable Yamaka: "Is it true that a pernicious entrenched view like this has arisen to you, friend Yamaka: 'In so far as I understand the doctrine taught by the Fortunate One, (111) that a monk who has spewed influxes, at the break up of the body, will be annihilated, will be destroyed, and does not come to be after death.'?"

"Even so do I, friends, understand the doctrine taught by the Fortunate One, that a monk who has spewed influxes, at the break up of the body, will be annihilated, will be destroyed, and does not come to be after death."

"What do you think, friend Yamaka, is material form permanent or impermanent?"

"Impermanent, friend."

"What do you think, friend Yamaka, is feeling . . . perception . . . (are) dispositions . . . consciousness permanent or impermanent?"

"Impermanent, friend."

"Therefore, monks, herein whatever material form, past, future, and present, internal or external, gross or subtle, low or lofty, whatever is far away or near, all material form: 'It is not mine; he, I am not; he is not my self.' Thus should it be seen, as it has come to be, through right wisdom.

"Whatever feeling . . . .

"Whatever perception . . . .

"Whatever dispositions . . . .

"Whatever consciousness, past, future, present, . . . , whatever is far away or near, all consciousness: 'It is not mine; he, I am not; he is not my self.' Thus should it be seen, as it has come to be, through right wisdom.

"Perceiving thus, monks, a learned and noble disciple is disenchanted in regard to material form, is disenchanted in regard to feeling, is disenchanted in regard to perception, is disenchanted in regard to dispositions, is disenchanted in regard to consciousness. Being disenchanted, one becomes dispassionate, through dispassion, one is released. In one who is released, there is knowledge: 'Has been released.' One knows: 'Birth has been spewed out; done is what needs to be done; the superior life has been lived; there is no other this-ness.'

"What do you think, friend Yamaka, do you perceive: 'Tathāgata is material form'?"

"It is not so, friend."

"What do you think, friend Yamaka, do you perceive: 'Tathāgata is feeling . . . perception . . . dispositions . . . consciousness.'?"

"It is not so, friend."

"What do you think, friend Yamaka, do you perceive: 'Tathāgata is in material form'?"

"It is not so, friend."

"Do you perceive: 'Tathāgata is beside material form'?"

"It is not so, friend."

"What do you think, friend Yamaka, do you perceive: 'Tathāgata is in feeling . . . perception . . . dispositions . . . consciousness'?"

"It is not so, friend."

"Do you perceive: 'Tathāgata is beside feeling . . . perception . . . dispositions . . . consciousness'?"

"It is not so, friend."

"What do you think, friend Yamaka, do you perceive: 'On the basis of material form, feeling, perception, dispositions, and consciousness is a Tathāgata'?"

"It is not so, friend."

(112) "What do you think, friend Yamaka, do you perceive: 'This person of immaterial form, of non-feeling, of non-perception, of non-disposition, of non-consciousness is the Tathāgata'?"

"It is not so, friend."

"Therein, friend Yamaka, when a Tathāgata is not obtained by you in truth and reality in this very life, is your explanation appropriate: 'In so far as I understand the doctrine taught by the Fortunate One, that a monk who has spewed influxes, at the break up of the body, will be annihilated, will be destroyed, and does not come to be after death'?"

"Friend Sāriputta, that pernicious entrenched view was mine, the ignorant one in that past, and having listened to the teaching of the doctrine on the part of venerable Sāriputta, that pernicious entrenched view has been abandoned, the doctrine has been understood by me."

"Friend Yamaka, if you were to be questioned: 'Whosoever, friend Yamaka, is a monk, a worthy one, spewed out influxes, at the break of the body, after death, what will he become?' When questioned thus, friend Yamaka, how will you explain?"

"Friend, if I were to be questioned: 'Whosoever, friend Yamaka, is a monk, a worthy one, spewed out influxes, at the break of the body, after death, what will he become?' When questioned thus, friend, I will explain thus: 'Material form, friend, is impermanent; whatever is impermanent, that is suffering; whatever is suffering, that has ceased, has gone away. Feeling, . . . Perception . . . Dispositions . . . Consciousness is impermanent; whatever is impermanent, that is suffering; whatever is suffering, that has ceased, has gone away.' When questioned thus, friend, I will explain thus."

"Very good, friend Yamaka. In that case, friend Yamaka, I will present you with a simile for the sake of thoroughly knowing the meaning of it.

"Just as, friend Yamaka, a householder or a householder's son, prosperous, with great wealth, great property, and he is also possessed of protection. There emerges some person who is desirous of his ill-fare, desirous of non-well-being, desirous of non-release from commitment and who is desirous depriving him of his life. (113) To him this occurs: 'This householder or this householder's son, is prosperous, with great wealth, great property, and he is also possessed of protection. It is not easy to deprive him of his life by force. How now if I were to deprive him of life without getting close to him. He, having approached the householder or the householder's son would say thus to him: 'May I serve you, Sir!' That householder or the householder's son would get him to serve. He would serve by being one who rises early in the morning, going to sleep late, obediently carry out the assignments, of pleasant behavior and of lovely speech. That householder or the householder's son would treat him as a friend, treat him as a confidant and place trust on him. When, friend, it occurs to that person: 'This householder or householder's son has indeed confided in me.' Then having known that he was alone would deprive him of his life with a sharp sword.

"What do you think, friend Yamaka? When that person approached the householder or householder's son and said: 'May I serve you, Sir!' at that time indeed was a murderer. That person (the householder) did not know him, even though being a murderer: 'He is my murderer.'

"When that person served by being one who rises early in the morning, going to sleep late, obediently carry out the assignments, of pleasant behavior and of lovely speech, he was a murderer. That person (the householder) did not know him, even though being a murderer: 'He is my murderer.'

"When that person, having known that he (the householder) was alone and deprive him of his life with a sharp sword, he was a murderer. That person (the householder) did not know him, even though being a murderer: 'He is my murderer.'

"It is so, friend."

"Similarly, friend, an uneducated individualist, non-seer of the worthy ones, not adept in the doctrine of the noble ones, not trained in the morals[1] of the noble ones, non-seer of the genuine persons, not adept in the doctrine of the genuine persons, not trained in the morals of the genuine persons perceives material form as the self or the self as possessed of material form or material form as being in the self or self as being in material form. Feeling . . . Perception . . . Dispositions . . . Consciousness (114) as the self or the self as possessed of consciousness or consciousness as being in the self or self as being in consciousness.

"He does not know impermanent material form as it has become as: 'Impermanent is material form.' He does not know impermanent feeling as it has become as: 'Impermanent is feeling.' He does not know impermanent perception as it has become as: 'Impermanent is perception.' He does not know impermanent dispositions as they have become as: 'Impermanent are dispositions.' He does not know impermanent consciousness as it has become as: 'Impermanent is consciousness.'

"He does not know unsatisfactory material form as it has become as: 'Unsatisfactory is material form.' He does not know unsatisfactory feeling as it has become as: 'Unsatisfactory is feeling.' He does not know unsatisfactory perception as it has become as: 'Unsatisfactory is perception.' He does not know unsatisfactory dispositions as they have become as: 'Unsatisfactory are dispositions.' He does not know unsatisfactory consciousness as it has become as: 'Unsatisfactory is consciousness.'

"He does not know no-self material form as it has become as 'No-self is material form.' He does not know no-self feeling as it has become as: 'No-self is feeling.' He does not know no-self perception as it has become as: 'No-self is perception.' He does not know no-self dispositions as they have become as: 'No-self are dispositions.' He does not know no-self consciousness as it has become as: 'No-self is consciousness.'

"He does not know dispositionally conditioned material form as it has become as: 'Dispositionally conditioned is material form.' He does not know dispositionally conditioned feeling as it has become as: 'Dispositionally conditioned is feeling.' He does not know dispositionally conditioned perception as it has become as: 'Dispositionally conditioned is perception.' He does not know dispositionally conditioned dispositions as they have become as: 'Dispositionally conditioned are dispositions.' He does not know dispositionally conditioned consciousness as it has become as: 'Dispositionally conditioned is consciousness.'

"He does not know murderous material form as it has become as: 'Murderous is material form.' He does not know murderous feeling as it has become as: 'Murderous is feeling.' He does not know murderous perception as it has become as: 'Murderous is perception.' He does not know murderous dispositions as they have become as: 'Murderous are dispositions.' He does not know murderous consciousness as it has become as: 'Murderous is consciousness.'

"He approaches material form, grasps and determines as: 'My self.' He approaches feeling, . . . perception, . . . dispositions, . . . consciousness, grasps and determines as: 'My self.' The five aggregates of grasping of him, approached and grasped, contribute to non-well-being and suffering for a long time.

"An educated noble disciple, friend, a seer of the worthy ones, adept in the doctrine of the noble ones, trained in the morals of the noble ones, seer of the genuine persons, adept in the doctrine of the genuine persons, trained in the morals of the genuine persons does not perceive material form as the self or the self as possessed of material form or material form as being in the self or self as being in material form. Feeling . . . Perception . . . Dispositions . . . Consciousness as the self or the self as possessed of consciousness or consciousness as being in the self or self as being in consciousness.

(115) "He knows impermanent material form as it has become as: 'Impermanent is material form.' He knows impermanent feeling as it has become as: 'Impermanent is feeling.' He knows impermanent perception as it has become as: 'Impermanent is perception.' He knows impermanent dispositions as they have become as: 'Impermanent are dispositions.' He knows impermanent consciousness as it has become as: 'Impermanent is consciousness.'

"He knows unsatisfactory material form as it has become as: 'Unsatisfactory is material form.' He knows unsatisfactory feeling as it has become as: 'Unsatisfactory is feeling.' He knows unsatisfactory perception as it has become as: 'Unsatisfactory is perception.' He knows unsatisfactory dispositions as they have become as: 'Unsatisfactory are dispositions.' He knows unsatisfactory consciousness as it has become as: 'Unsatisfactory is consciousness.'

"He knows no-self material form as it has become as: 'No-self is material form.' He knows no-self feeling as it has become as: 'No-self is feeling.' He knows no-self perception as it has become as: 'No-self is perception.' He knows no-self dispositions as they have become as: 'No-self are dispositions.' He knows no-self consciousness as it has become as: 'No-self is consciousness.'

"He knows dispositionally conditioned material form as it has become as: 'Dispositionally conditioned is material form.' He knows dispositionally conditioned feeling as it has become as: 'Dispositionally conditioned is feeling.' He knows dispositionally conditioned perception as it has become as: 'Dispositionally conditioned is perception.' He knows dispositionally conditioned dispositions as they have become as: 'Dispositionally conditioned are dispositions.' He knows dispositionally conditioned consciousness as it has become as: 'Dispositionally conditioned is consciousness.'

"He knows murderous material form as it has become as: 'Murderous is material form.' He knows murderous feeling as it has become as: 'Murderous is feeling.' He knows murderous perception as it has become as: 'Murderous is perception.' He knows murderous dispositions as they have become as: 'Murderous are dispositions.' He knows murderous consciousness as it has become as: 'Murderous is consciousness.'

"He does not approach material form, does not grasp and does not determine as: 'My self.' He does not approach feeling, . . . perception, . . . dispositions, . . . consciousness, does not grasp and determine as: 'My self.' The five aggregates of grasping of him, not approached and not grasped, contribute to well-being and happiness for a long time."

"These, friend Sāriputta, indeed are. To whosoever venerable ones are such farers in the higher life, sympathetic, desirous of welfare, advisers and admonishers, and now having heard the preaching of the doctrine on the part of venerable Sāriputta my thought, without grasping, has been released from the influxes."

Venerable Sāriputta said thus. Delighted, venerable Yamaka, rejoiced in what venerable Sāriputta said.

---

[1]Note that the term *dhamma* is used in the first instance in the singular as *dhammassa* and in the second instance in the plural as *dhamme*.

HERBERT FINGARETTE

Immortality, Selflessness

IMMORTALITY

Should one call the idea of an afterlife, of an immortal soul, an image that reveals the meaning of death? I see it, rather, as an image that denies death. Some form of this denial of death is ubiquitous among human cultures. Souls, spirits, ghosts—these are among the mythic notions that embody this idea.

The idea of immortality is characteristically embedded in a larger mythic or theological context. In Christian theologies, for example, bodily death is a portentous event. The soul leaves the body forever and begins an eternal spiritual life. The quality of that life is determined by the Divine judgment of one's earthly sins and merits. However, in Asian reincarnation doctrines death takes on a radically different meaning. It is the moment when the soul casts off the old body, as we cast off an old garment, and takes on a new body and a new life on earth. The moral character of one's conduct in earlier lives determines one's moral fate in the current life, but the current life is in turn a chance to shape future lives. Each different mythic and theological doctrine has its effect in shaping the distinctive culture to which it belongs. But in spite of their no-table differences, each doctrine in one way or another denies death as a final end by centering around a doctrine of immortality.

Much as I wish I could believe some such doctrine, I cannot honestly tell myself that I do. There is no doubt in my mind that, if taken literally, such doctrines are not only false but are incoherent. The idea of a non-bodily consciousness such as the soul makes no sense because it is our physical being that locates us in time and space. For this reason all such doctrines are compelled to reify the "soul"—to give it, in short, a kind of quasi-body, and thus a location in space and time. The soul is conceived as an ethereal kind of matter located at some point in space (or in Heavenly space). Or it is conceived as a ghost-like entity. It has to be located in space because this ethereal en-tity presumably sees and hears—and how could "seeing" and "hearing" make sense un-less the one who sees and hears is located at some place in space? (What would a tree or a human being look like as seen from nowhere, or as seen from no particular point in time? Does a voice sound near or far, loud or soft, to one who has no physical loca-tion in relation to the speaker?)

For these and many other reasons one of the basic presuppositions on which all my thinking rests is that death is the end. There is no "afterlife," except in the sense in which the memory of me and of my objective achievements remains for those who survive men.

SELFLESSNESS

There is a way of dealing with one's death that denies death its sting while not deny-ing its reality. It is central to the major teachings of the East, but also has an important place in Western thought. It is the quest for "selflessness."

Many Eastern doctrines, and some Christian sects, attempt to remove the sense of self. The logic is easy to see: If one were truly selfless, what would be lost when death comes?—nothing. Or at least nothing of momentous importance. Death would not be seen as a negation of life—at least not a negation of one*self*.

Yet the goal of selflessness goes against the grain of the modern Westerner. Our grand aim is self-fulfillment rather than self-abnegation. It's true that in the Judeo-Christian tradition there is a teaching of selflessness: Thy Will, not mine, be done. But as a practical matter, and especially since the 19th century, this teaching has widely been abandoned and replaced by assertion and even glorification of the self. Empha-sis on the rights, the talents, the ambitions, and the achievements of the individual has become the hallmark of modern Western cultures.

This Western attitude contrasts sharply with the major Eastern teachings—Hin-duism, Buddhism, Confucianism, and Taoism. These share the idea that the individual self is the major obstacle to the freeing of the spirit. The individual self is seen as a mere delusion or impediment to be dispelled by one or another means. It is an intru-sive element that is the source of failure in human effort and disruption in Nature. In the East it is self-evident that the achievement of selflessness is liberation from fear of death. Even Confucius, who enjoins us to "cultivate the self," actually means that we should seek perfection in properly living our social role and status. He clearly opposes cultivating our personal, ego-motivated appetites.

The idea of selflessness is easily misunderstood and then unfairly condemned. To many people "selflessness" is equated with asceticism, and indeed in Asia it is regarded that way by some sects. But that equation need not hold true.

Suppose, for example, that I am completely taken up in playing a piece of music. I "lose myself" in it. My self disappears. This is a form of selflessness, but it is also self-fulfillment, not asceticism. If I'm totally absorbed in the proper execution of some significant task, perhaps writing a book that means much to me, I lose my self in it. This, too, is self-fulfillment. If I find joy in promoting the success or happiness of some other person, my attitude can be equally well characterized as selfless or as that of a caring self. Such an attitude would be selfless in the sense that my central aim is not my own personal gratification or profit, but the integrity of the action itself. I simply want to do "what should be done" (to use the language of the Bhagavad Gita). Yet this caring act is done joyously and is self-fulfilling.

As an ideal, selflessness is not utopian. We've all acted selflessly at times. Surely I can nourish and encourage this attitude in myself so that it increasingly fills my life. I would like to think it's true of a portion of my life already. To a great extent I do surrender myself to my love for my wife, my daughter, my grandsons, to my work, to my music.

The achievement of selflessness brings with it a kind of liberation. To the degree that this is one's stance in life, death would be, as Marcus Aurelius said long ago, merely a natural event, not necessarily welcome but certainly not ominous. The less concerned with oneself, the less can the end of the self loom as a personal threat. One is free from the anguish peculiar to those who must defend their ego. Candor requires me to confess my limits: Though selflessness might be a valid ideal, I don't see myself fully reaching that ideal in reality. Perhaps with a different upbringing—maybe in a family where some tradition of devotion to intense spiritual discipline played a major role—I might aspire to such a condition of total selflessness. (Maybe only saints and yogins achieve it.) But the reality is that my life has been too Western, too secular, for me to entertain such an expectation seriously.

There is still another important obstacle to a totally selfless life. Hindu, Buddhist, and some versions of the Judeo-Christian teachings make a basic assumption that we today cannot honestly make. The assumption is that each of us has a definite God-given or fate-given destiny.

The Bhagavad Gita, for example, teaches that I must replace personal, self-ish aims, and devote my efforts to my dharma, the destined and proper station and role in life that I have been born into. I must be a good and faithful husband, father, and philosopher—or, as the case might be, a good farmer, craftsman, soldier, ruler. If we give ourself to service in our station in life, we are free from the anxieties of the ego-centered life. When death comes, it is the natural close to a life lived as destined. There is nothing to regret.

Something of the same kind is true of Confucius's teaching. He assumed that we could live fully and adequately if we faithfully and sincerely follow the customs, traditions, and ceremonies handed down to us. He never doubted their adequacy. And for many Jews and Christians, the sacred writings and authoritative commentaries lay down all one needs to know about how to live one's life.

In Taoism it is Nature which supposedly shows us the right road for all contingencies. The essential is to follow Nature and not interfere by intruding our ego and its personal aims. I do believe that we often intrude, disturbing Nature, imposing our own ego, our own preconceptions, rather than being open to what the situation calls for. We can learn much from Taoism's sermon against human meddling.

The modern vision, however, is of a world with bona fide options, with choices that are often unavoidable. We cannot accept the presupposition that Nature, or tradition, or "Destiny" can decisively settle all questions for us. As we see it, choices are ineliminable from our world. So are the selves who must make those choices. The assumption of a world that presents us with complete answers for all occasions is not credible to modern Westerners.

In any case I know that total selflessness is not a practical option for me. That doesn't take away from the importance of achieving whatever degree of selflessness I can—and to that extent removing the terror aroused by that meaningless end of the self we call death.

I realize that what I need is an image of life and death that does not rely on supernaturalistic evasions of the reality of death. I need an image that does not require the unacceptable assumptions about a fixed path for each of us that are built into the Eastern doctrines of pure selflessness. I need an image that does not misrepresent the true meaning of death by analogizing it, for example, to separation or to sleep. The image I seek would have to recognize the variety, the uncertainties, the vicissitudes of life. It would have to be an image for modern times—an honest one.

CHAPTER 4

RELATIONSHIPS

INTRODUCTION

To the extent that living well involves achieving a standing higher than the standing of others, flourishing is a competitive undertaking. Goods like being the best runner or the best novelist are *competitive* goods, inasmuch as achieving them requires preventing others, who also badly want the goods (and who mean to deprive oneself of those goods), from achieving them. To the extent that living well involves achieving competitive goods, people value working *against* the interests of others, and thus making enemies, because each person values causing others the misfortune of being outdone. Needless to say, no one can identify with people who take an interest in working against her or his interests. Insofar as someone is an enemy, that person is decidedly not (one of) *us*. Hence, theorists who wish to portray the good life as one in which people share an identity, do not emphasize the importance of competitive goods. Instead, they emphasize aspects of life that bring people together, and nothing brings people together more closely than relationships among friends, lovers, married people, and families. To the extent that people are involved in such relationships (and avoid the opposite of friendship: the relationship between enemies), they fail to see their interests as separate from and incompatible with those of others. We come to share interests, and to that extent we come to share identities.

LOVE, FRIENDSHIP, AND SEX

Romantic love and friendship are related to each other, and to sexual desire, but each differs from the others. The first set of topics in this chapter focus on exactly what each is, how and why it is a good thing, and how each is related to the other.

1. LOVE: PLATO, NIETZSCHE, AND DE BEAUVOIR

The excerpt from Plato's *The Symposium* includes a selection from the speech of Aristophanes, who relates a myth about the origins of humanity, and a later selection from the speech of Socrates, who reports on the account of love he learned from Diotima.

According to the myth Aristophanes relates, people were originally round animals with four hands and four legs, two heads, and so on. When they attempted to climb to heaven and attack the gods, Zeus cut each in half. Ever since, each individual has yearned to be reunited with an appropriate half, once again to be one. This myth gives powerful expression to a common view about the nature of love. The identities of people in love overlap, and each comes to experience the other's well being as his or her own. Together, and from a united perspective, they happily face the world; returning to their perspectives as individuals, they feel incomplete and lonely, and they yearn to return to the united perspective. The myth makes another interesting speculation about identity: Sharing an identity is a *negative* condition. People share an identity when they *fail to* separate from others; and love is the urge to relax into a shared identity with another. To elaborate, human beings lived together intimately as their discriminatory faculties developed over time. They were at ease together long before they developed the ability to make sophisticated distinctions between themselves as individuals. As human beings became more sophisticated and more self-conscious, they were able to hold in memory all of the unique features they discovered or introduced. With effort, they could separate themselves from the rest, but thinking of themselves as individuals separate from others tended to go against the grain, and they easily chose to relax the effort of separation and rejoin the group. Perhaps at some level, people still yearn to relax and stop separating themselves off, and love is the desire to join with someone in this primordial way.

In his own account of love, Socrates does not endorse this powerful conception. He suggests that it limits the object of love artificially, when in fact love, or *eros,* ought to be equated with desire itself. Socrates suggests that love is the desire to possess the good and to do so forever. This statement does not imply that love has nothing to do with the way people yearn to shape their identities, however. Perhaps sharing an identity with another is one of the goods they want to possess forever. Moreover, since love is the desire to possess the good forever, love gives a powerful incentive to seek out and adopt ways of understanding identity such that one *can* live to enjoy the good forever. Unlike Gautama, Socrates thinks people should want to be selves with futures. For example, people are inclined to believe that identity is perpetuated along family lines. They believe this in spite of the fact that one human being is replaced by another, just as they believe that identity survives the body's gradual replacement of constituents and gradual changes of character over time. Since by procreating, people perpetuate themselves as families, the best available approximation to living forever, love inspires the desire to procreate.

Nietzsche returns to the conception of love suggested by Aristophanes' myth, adding interesting claims about the nature of the union that lovers desire. According to Nietzsche, the desire to possess is the desire to transform things into oneself and thus to deprive other people of those things no matter how badly they might want them. Hence the desire to possess is an expression of egoism. But romantic love is the desire to possess another, so it, too, is an expression of egoism. Furthermore, for men, romantic love is the desire to possess, while for women romantic love is the desire to *be* possessed. Nietzsche concedes the "immorality" of this asymmetry, but he suggests that it makes no sense for both male and female lovers to wish to be possessed (or, for that matter, to wish to possess): "If both partners felt impelled by love to renounce themselves, we should then get—I do not know what; perhaps an empty space?"

In *The Second Sex* (1949), Simon de Beauvoir (1908–1986), a French existentialist, refers back to Hegel's "Master and Slave." De Beauvoir suggests that as a subject, each individual is hostile to all others and wants to make objects of them, and men as a group have succeeded in making women as a group accept men as subjects and themselves as objects. Men are the "one" and women are the "other." This subordination pervades the relationship between the sexes. Thus while "the supreme goal of human love, as of mystical love, is identification with the loved one," or the formation of a "we," the identification is accomplished differently by members of opposite sexes, as Nietzsche claimed. When men are in love with women, for example, men want to "remain sovereign subjects" who "take possession of her," and men will not let women take possession of them. "For woman, on the contrary, to love is to relinquish everything for the benefit of a master." Thus, the male lover shares his identity with a female lover in the sense that he takes her identity as a component of his; for the female, "there is no other way out for her than to lose herself, body and soul, in him." Only he is free. All of this is unfortunate, de Beauvoir says, since "genuine love ought to be founded on the mutual recognition of two liberties; the lovers would then experience themselves both as self and as other."

2. FRIENDSHIP: ARISTOTLE

Aristotle notes that common usage suggests three forms of friendship: pleasure friendships, based on the pleasure each friend receives from the other, use friendships, based on the usefulness of each to the other, and character friendships, anchored in the characters of each friend. According to Aristotle, only character friends are really friends, for only they meet the four conditions for friendship:

1. Each wishes the other well.
2. In fact, each considers the other's well-being to be an intrinsic good.
3. Because each wishes the other well, each tries to help the other.
4. Each knows about the other's good will.

Friends do not regard each other as instrumental goods, as tools; instead, they consider their relationship to be fundamentally and intrinsically good, and hence central to self-realization. Aristotle also says that friendship is a reciprocal relationship; indeed, the view that a friend takes of one, and the way that view involves and incorporates one's own view of the friend, is a central reason why one values the friendship. Moreover, Aristotle strongly hints that one person does not regard another as a friend unless the other returns the friendly attitude *in kind,* which in large measure accounts for the worrisome character of the kind of stereotypic love Nietzsche and de Beauvoir see as common between the sexes: Stereotypic lovers do not want their love returned in kind, and hence they are not friends. Male love is (1) the desire to possess his lover and (2) the desire that his lover should want to be possessed by him, while female love is (1) the desire to be possessed by her lover and (2) the desire that her lover should want to possess her.

Insofar as Aristotle indicates that friends regard each other's well-being as intrinsically good, he hints that to some degree the identities of friends overlap, and they form a "we." Another reservation about stereotypic love emerges from a link between this point, that overlapping in identity is one object of friendship, with the earlier point that friends want their friendly attitudes returned in kind: Male love is the desire to add his lover to his identity and the desire that she should want to be added, while female love is the desire to add herself to his identity (thus losing herself in her lover) and the desire that he should want to add her. Once again, the two lovers do not want their attitudes returned in kind, hence they are not friends.

The premise that true romantic love is also friendship gives a reason to avoid the stereotypic pattern of love between the sexes and to understand love in such a way that it is possible between friends. As a beginning, consider the idea that the desire to merge identities with loved others includes a desire for the return of the attitude in kind; each wants the act of sharing identities to amount to the same thing for both. Hence, only friends can become romantic lovers, but at the extreme, romantic lovers are not mere friends. The identities of friends merely overlap, leaving separate individuals leading separate lives outside of the friendship, as well as the "we" that constitutes the friendship. But one (unattainable?) ideal of romantic love urges us to go beyond the overlapping "we" of the friendship ideal; it is the ideal by which "we" become *one*.

3. TRADITIONAL SEXUAL MORALITY: PAUL, CONFUCIUS, AND SCRUTON

People in the West are decidedly ambivalent about sex. On the one hand, some speak of it as a great good: Many say that it is so special that it should be saved for those in love. On the other hand, it carries a special stigma; to be associated with sex is to plummet in status, to which the examples of prostitution, the pornography industry, and indeed dating services attest. Sex is said to be beneath human beings, animalistic (yet eating and sleeping are equally animalistic without tainting the restaurant business or the hotel industry, and ranchers do not mind being associated with animals). The worst profanity in the English language refers to the act of sex. All these associations are very odd; if sex is so debasing, why would one want to save it for someone one loves?

The reasons why people might *value* sex are clear enough. It is enjoyable, and it is one essential step to bringing forth new life. So whence the stigma? One plausible speculation is that in the West, sex has long been thought to be an *anti*-spiritual, and hence evil, practice. People who came to identify themselves as nonphysical souls with afterlives ahead of them wanted to think that all good things were available in the afterlife. They thought that souls leave behind the physical world and physical things, and it is painful to leave behind valued things. Few obstacles interfere more with this transfer of concern from the physical to the spiritual than the desire for sex, for this extremely powerful desire can only be satisfied through physical bodies. So sex interferes with the project of adapting into spiritual beings. For that reason, it might be labeled anti-spiritual, and hence evil, and this attitude might leave its mark even on people who do not share its religious basis. This speculation can easily be backed by an examination of Platonism (especially the Socratic vision of souls in the *Phaedo*) and the Manichaean religion, which portrays the world as a struggle between the good-spiritual versus the evil-physical. Platonism and the Manichaean religion heavily influenced the early Christian church and Western culture as a whole.

People who view sex as a threat to spirituality might also say that sex is not evil when permitted by God, the apparent attitude expressed by the Apostle Paul in his letters. Paul counsels his readers to avoid sex altogether, as Christ did, but those who cannot should limit themselves to sex in the circumstances under which God permits it: the context of marriage.

A conservative attitude about sex is common in the East as well, but in China the attitude, although decidedly conservative, is often quite different, due to the widespread influence of Confucianism. For Confucius, the project was not to adapt oneself into a *spiritual* being. It was to adapt oneself into an exemplary *human* being, which requires shaping or civilizing oneself so as to participate in the human community with its sacred traditions and rites. Raw human nature can easily interfere with the process of civilizing people, and Confucius remarks several times that all too often, an overweening interest in sex prevents people from becoming an exemplary person. Sex does not carry the stigma of evil, but like everything else in life, sexuality should be shaped by ancient civilizing traditions.

In "Sexual Morality," Chapter II of his book *Sexual Desire* (1986), Roger Scruton articulates a conservative view of sexuality that is heavily influenced by Aristotle's ethics. Scruton argues that the capacity for erotic love is a virtue, and that to develop this capacity, people must properly shape sexual impulses, using a process of training and education that begins during childhood. For example, love is the fulfillment of desire, and training should shape impulses toward love and guard against habits that interfere with the capacity for love. The habit of promiscuity is especially dangerous, Scruton argues, because love is "prone to jealousy" and destroyed by infidelity. People should shape their sexual impulses with this danger in mind and form the habit of fidelity. Other practices prescribed by traditional sexual morality are also important to the development of the capacity for erotic love, according to Scruton, including heterosexuality.

4. RESPONSES TO TRADITIONAL SEXUAL MORALITY: GOLDMAN AND RICH

Traditional sexual morality takes an especially unfavorable attitude toward sex without love, promiscuity, and nonheterosexuality, but each of these practices has its proponents.

In his essay, Alan Goldman, a philosopher who teaches at the University of Miami, rebuts the charge that plain sex, or sex for its own sake, is a bad thing. Plain sex is condemned chiefly by those who insist that sex is, in its very nature, the means to an end. Such people say that sex is bad when it is not motivated by its proper purpose. For example, Aquinas suggests that the end or purpose of sex is reproduction, and many people say that sex is by its nature an expression of love. According to Goldman, plain sexual desire is simply the desire for contact with another person's body and the associated pleasure. Like eating dinner with someone, having sex might serve various purposes, but then again it might not; those ends are separable from sex. Having sex with those we love is surely better than having sex with strangers, but the same can be said about having dinner with those we love; sex with strangers should not be condemned as bad any more than having dinner with strangers. Goldman sees no morality intrinsic to sex. Sex acts, like other kinds of acts, are immoral only "when they are one-sided," "when the benefits are not mutual," or when "not freely and rationally endorsed by all parties." Moreover, sexual desire, unlike romantic love, does not limit itself to one other person, so one should not have the same expectations for sexuality as for love.

In her essay, Adrienne Rich, a contemporary feminist writer, suggests that women have been and usually still are "compelled" to adopt a heterosexual orientation. Moreover, the compulsion goes against the grain, since the earliest sources of emotional and physical nurturing are women, so both men's and women's search for love is directed toward women from the start. To make women heterosexuals, their search for love must be forcibly redirected.

MARRIAGE AND FAMILY

Marriage and family are absolutely central to the Confucian way of life. They are the central part of the traditional structure that defines the community with which the Confucian identifies. They are so much a part of how the community is ordered that Confucius thinks of the family as part of government. Over time, marriage and family have taken a particular shape that coordinates and harmonizes people's activities and appropriates love and sexuality in specified, predictable, reliable ways. Moreover, marriage and family are the primary instruments by which the community's traditions are perpetuated over time. By taking part in a traditional marriage and family, people adopt the ways of predecessors and fellow community members, and they pass those ways along to their children.

Conservatives in the West tend to take the same view concerning marriage and family, which is no surprise, since a conservative is someone who advocates conserving traditional values and ways. Marriage and the family play a crucial role in passing along traditional values and ways from one generation to the next.

1. THE CONSERVATIVE VIEW OF MARRIAGE AND FAMILY: CONFUCIUS, LIN YUTANG, AND HUTCHESON

In several passages in the *Analects,* Confucius underscores the importance of the patriarchal family and filial piety. Sons should love and obey their fathers and their older brothers, and all siblings should love and obey both parents. This pattern of obedience then helps shape people for participation in society, where they are to be obedient subjects or good rulers, and where they are to regard other people as members of their extended families.

The philosopher and novelist Lin Yutang points out some virtues of the Confucian family system, which ensures that helpless children receive care by people who love them and elderly people receive care by people who love and revere them. Reverence for the elderly is one of the most striking features of Chinese life, in contrast to life in the West, where youth is glorified. Reverence for the elderly is also more difficult to arrange for than is love for children, the author points out: "A natural man loves his children, but a cultured man loves his parents." Yet "how can any one deny that parents who have toiled for their children in their youth . . . have the right to be fed by them and loved and respected when they are old?"

In his *System of Moral Philosophy*, 18th-century British writer Francis Hutcheson (1694–1746) offers a defense of the traditional form of marriage and family. According to Hutcheson, people have a duty to contribute to "the continuance and good education of our race," but a couple should not have children unless they meet several conditions: (1) Together, they have the means to raise their children in the proper way. (2) Each mate has the virtues needed to raise children in the proper way. (3) They love each other (which ensures that they are friends who wish to remain together). (4) Finally, they will marry and remain together for life ("otherwise all true friendship and love must be banished"). Moreover, marriage should be monogamous (both partners should avoid sexual contact outside the marriage), so that fathers will know that the children they are raising are their own, and it should be a "state of equal partnership or friendship." Hutcheson rejects the traditional, patriarchal form of marriage. Hutcheson goes on to suggest that parents are permanently obligated to promote the welfare of their children, and children have the duties of obedience and gratitude, including the "sacred duty of supporting their aged parents, in their second infirmity."

2. ATTACKS ON THE CONSERVATIVE VIEW OF FAMILY AND MARRIAGE: DE BEAUVOIR AND FERGUSON

The traditional conservative view of marriage is increasingly resisted on various fronts. People who wish to view marriage as a contractual relationship press for the liberalization of marriage. If marriage is essentially a contractual relationship, married people should naturally feel free to settle the terms of their contract themselves, and they may well opt to abandon the traditional features of marriage. For example, they may opt for same sex marriages, marriages that involve more than two people, and so on.

Another group wishes to change the traditional marriage primarily because they see it as the source of inequities between women and men. De Beauvoir portrays the typical marriage as a "tragedy" which "mutilates" women: "At 20 or thereabouts, mistress of a home, bound permanently to a man, a child in her arms, she stands with her life virtually finished forever." For domestic activities are unappreciated and are not a form of self-realization for women, and the asymmetrical love typically involved in marriage turns women against their husbands. De Beauvoir seems to hold out some hope for a marriage that is "a combining of two whole, independent existences," taking place after "each individual [is] integrated as such in society at large, where each . . . could flourish without aid." But marriage will continue to oppress women as long as men are economically responsible for the couple, since the breadwinner, and the requirements of his job, will determine the course of life for the couple.

One way to overcome asymmetries among married people might be to encourage people to adopt androgyny as an ideal. Ann Ferguson argues that the ideal love relationship is impossible so long as traditional sex roles are maintained, for the feminine role subordinates women to men. Assuming that a heterosexual identity is acquired due to the structure of the traditional patriarchal family and social context, which involves many sorts of inequalities between the sexes, eliminating the inequalities in that structure by introducing a democratic socialist order might produce androgynous sexual identities.

Questions for Reflection

1. Scruton says that virtuous desire is made possible by moral education, and so "a whole section of traditional sexual morality must be upheld." But does traditional sexual morality answer to the needs of human nature, or does it demand conformity to a set of practices just because people have always conformed to those practices?

2. Is abstinence a natural choice? If not, is it a perversion?

3. Is Hutcheson right when he says that the ground for monogamy in marriage is the father's concern about raising his own children? How important is that concern? Are there other grounds for monogamy?

4. Do the identities of friends overlap? In what sense?

5. Critically assess Diotima's characterization of love. Is her characterization better than the characterization suggested by Aristophanes's myth?

6. Contrast Nietzsche's and de Beauvoir's characterizations of love between the sexes. Which is a more accurate description? Which states a better ideal toward which to strive?

7. Explain why sex carries a stigma in the West. Is Goldman right to suggest that plain sex should not be condemned? Is Scruton correct when he suggests that people should develop the habit of fidelity?

8. In "Philosophers against the Family" (a reading in *Person to Person,* cited in the Suggested Readings), Christina Hoff Sommers raises doubts about the project of reformulating marriage and family so as to make them gender-neutral institutions. Most importantly, she thinks that the advocates of this project do not adequately answer the question, "How can the benighted myriads . . . who do not wish to mesh together with other androgynous beings be reeducated?" How might de Beauvoir and Rich respond?

9. Friendship and romantic love seem to differ in that the former is not exclusive while the latter excludes other potential partners. Why is it good to have several friends but only one lover?

10. Can parents and their children be friends? Can lovers be friends? Explain.

11. Are people heterosexual due to the structure of the traditional patriarchal family, as Ferguson suggests? Is heterosexuality the cause of the traditional family? Or is neither the case? Would democratic socialism produce androgyny? Why?

Suggested Readings

Baker, R., and F. Elliston, *Philosophy and Sex.* Buffalo: Prometheus, 1984.

Blustein, Jeffrey. *Parents and Children: The Ethics of the Family.* New York: Oxford University Press, 1982.

Engels, F. *The Origin of the Family, Private Property, and the State.* New York: International Publishers, 1972.

Friedman, Marilyn. *What Are Friends For?* Ithaca, N.Y. Cornell University Press, 1993.

Graham, G. and H. LaFollette, eds. *Person to Person.* Philadelphia: Temple University Press, 1989.

Johnson, J. *Lesbian Nation: The Feminist Solution.* New York: Simon and Schuster, 1974.

Pakaluk, Michael, ed. *Other Selves: Philosophers on Friendship.* Indianapolis: Hackett, 1991.

Taylor, Richard. *Having Love Affairs.* Buffalo: Prometheus, 1982.

Weitzman, Lenore. *The Marriage Contract: Spouses, Lovers, and the Law.* New York: Free Press, 1981.

FRIENDSHIP, SEX, AND LOVE

CONFUCIUS

translated by Roger T. Ames and Henry Rosemont, Jr.

Analects

4.21 The Master said, "Children must know the age of their father and mother. On one hand, it is a source of joy; on the other, of trepidation."

9.18 The Master said, "I have yet to meet the person who is fonder of excellence (*de*) than of physical beauty."

9.31 "The flowers of the wild cherry tree
    Flutter and wave.
    How could I not be thinking of you?
    It is just that your home is so very far away."
The Master said, "He wasn't really thinking of her, or how could she be far away?"

14.7 The Master said, "Can you really love the people without urging them on? Can you do your utmost (*zhong*) for your lord without instructing him?"

16.4. Confucius said, "Having three kinds of friends will be a source of personal improvement; having three other kinds of friends will be a source of personal injury. One stands to be improved by friends who are true, who make good on their word, and who are broadly informed; one stands to be injured by friends who are ingratiating, who feign compliance, and who are glib talkers."

18.4 The Qi kinsmen made a gift of young singing and dancing girls to the throne. Ji Huanzi accepted them, and for three days he did not hold court, whereupon Confucius took his leave.

PLATO

The Symposium

. . . "Well, Eryximachus," began Aristophanes, ". . . [men] seem to me to be utterly insensible of the power of Love; otherwise he would have had the largest temples and
altars and the largest sacrifices. As it is, he has none of these things, though he deserves them most of all. For of all the gods he is the most friendly to man . . .

"First of all, you must learn the constitution of man and the modifications which it
has undergone, for originally it was different from what it is now. In the first place there
were three sexes, not, as with us, two, male and female; the third partook of the nature
of both the others and has vanished, though its name survives. The hermaphrodite was
a distinct sex in form as well as in name, with the characteristics of both male and female, but now the name alone remains, and that solely as a term of abuse. Secondly,
each human being was a rounded whole, with double back and flanks forming a complete circle; it had four hands and an equal number of legs, and two identically similar
faces upon a circular neck, with one head common to both the faces, which were
turned in opposite directions. It had four ears and two organs of generation and everything else to correspond. . . . The reason for the existence of three sexes and for their
being of such a nature is that originally the male sprang from the sun and the female
from the earth, while the sex which was both male and female came from the moon,
which partakes of the nature of both sun and earth. Their circular shape and their
hoop-like method of progression were both due to the fact that they were like their
parents. Their strength and vigour made them very formidable, and their pride was
overweening; they attacked the gods, and Homer's story of Ephialtes and Otus attempting to climb up to heaven and set upon the gods is related also to these beings.

"So Zeus and the other gods debated what was to be done with them. . . . At last,
after much painful thought, Zeus had an idea. 'I think,' he said, 'that I have found a way
by which we can allow the human race to continue to exist and also put an end to
their wickedness by making them weaker. I will cut each of them in two; in this way
they will be weaker, and at the same time more profitable to us by being more numerous. They shall walk upright upon two legs. If there is any sign of wantonness in them
after that, and they will not keep quiet, I will bisect them again, and they shall hop on
one leg.' With these words he cut the members of the human race in half, just like
fruit which is to be dried and preserved, or like eggs which are cut with a hair. As he
bisected each, he bade Apollo turn round the face and the half-neck attached to it towards the cut side, so that the victim, having the evidence of bisection before his
eyes, might behave better in future. . . .

"Man's original body having been thus cut in two, each half yearned for the half
from which it had been severed. When they met they threw their arms round one another and embraced, in their longing to grow together again, and they perished of
hunger and general neglect of their concerns, because they would not do anything
apart. When one member of a pair died and the other was left, the latter sought after
and embraced another partner, which might be the half either of a female whole
(what is now called a woman) or a male. So they went on perishing till Zeus took pity

on them, and hit upon a second plan. . . . By moving their genitals to the front, as they are now, Zeus made it possible for reproduction to take place by the intercourse of the male with the female. His object in making this change was twofold; if male coupled with female, children might be begotten and the race thus continued, but if male coupled with male, at any rate the desire for intercourse would be satisfied, and men set free from it to turn to other activities and to attend to the rest of the business of life. It is from this distant epoch, then, that we may date the innate love which human beings feel for one another, the love which restores us to our ancient state by attempting to weld two beings into one and to heal the wounds which humanity suffered. . . .

"No one can suppose that it is mere physical enjoyment which causes the one to take such intense delight in the company of the other. It is clear that the soul of each has some other longing which it cannot express, but can only surmise and obscurely hint at. Suppose Hephaestus with his tools were to visit them as they lie together, and stand over them and ask: 'What is it, mortals, that you hope to gain from one another?' Suppose too that when they could not answer he repeated his question in these terms: 'Is the object of your desire to be always together as much as possible, and never to be separated from one another day or night? If that is what you want, I am ready to melt and weld you together, so that, instead of two, you shall be one flesh; as long as you live you shall live a common life, and when you die, you shall suffer a common death, and be still one, not two, even in the next world. Would such a fate as this content you, and satisfy your longings?' We know what their answer would be; no one would refuse the offer; it would be plain that this is what everybody wants, and everybody would regard it as the precise expression of the desire which he had long felt but had been unable to formulate, that he should melt into his beloved, and that henceforth they should be one being instead of two. The reason is that this was our primitive condition when we were wholes, and love is simply the name for the desire and pursuit of the whole. . . . "

When Agathon had finished speaking, all his hearers, according to Aristodemus, loudly proclaimed that the young poet had acquitted himself in a way worthy of himself and of the god. Socrates looked at Eryximachus, and said:

"Do you still think, son of Acumenus, that my fear was a groundless fear? Admit that I prophesied truly when I said that Agathon would give a wonderful performance, and that I should be at a loss."

"I grant the prophetic nature of your remark about Agathon," replied Eryximachus, "but as for your being at a loss, I don't believe it."

"My dear sir, how can I fail to be at a loss? How could anyone who had to speak after so splendid and varied an oration as that which we have just heard? . . ."

"I realized how idiotic it was of me to agree to take part with you in praising Love, and to say that I was expert in love-matters, when, as it turned out, I was absolutely ignorant of the proper method of making a panegyric on any subject. I was stupid enough to suppose that the right thing was to speak the truth about the subject proposed for panegyric . . . But now it appears that this is not the right way to set about praising anything, and that the proper method is to ascribe to the subject of the panegyric all the loftiest and loveliest qualities, whether it actually possesses them or not . . . I'll no longer utter a panegyric, if it is to be after this fashion; I can't do it. I am quite willing to tell the truth in my own style, if you like; only I must not be regarded as competing with your speeches, or I shall be a laughing-stock. . . ."

Phaedrus and the rest encouraged him to make a speech in the way which he himself thought right. So he continued:

"Allow me also, Phaedrus, to ask Agathon a few small questions, so that I may obtain his agreement before I begin my speech." . . .

"Suppose a man wanted to be strong who was strong, or swift-footed who was swift-footed. . . . One might perhaps suppose in these and all similar cases that people who are of a certain character or who possess certain qualities also desire the qualities which they possess. But if you consider the matter, Agathon, you will see that these people must inevitably possess these qualities at the present moment, whether they like it or not, and no one presumably would desire what is inevitable. No, if a man says: 'I, who am healthy, or who am rich, nonetheless desire to be healthy or rich, as the case may be, and I desire the very qualities which I possess,' we should reply: 'My friend, what you, who are in possession of health and wealth and strength, really wish, is to have the possession of these qualities continued to you in the future, since at the present moment you possess them whether you wish it or not.' . . ."

"Yes," said Agathon.

"But this is to be in love with a thing which is not yet in one's power or possession, namely the continuance and preservation of one's present blessings in the future."

"Certainly."

"Such a man, then, and everyone else who feels desire, desires what is not in his present power or possession, and desire and love have for their object things or qualities which a man does not at present possess but which he lacks."

"Yes." . . .

"Now we have agreed that Love is in love with what he lacks and does not possess."

"Yes."

"So after all Love lacks and does not possess beauty?"

"Inevitably."

"Well then, would you call what lacks and in no way possesses beauty beautiful?"

"Certainly not."

"Do you still think then that Love is beautiful, if this is so?"

"It looks, Socrates, as if I didn't know what I was talking about when I said that."

"Still, it was a beautiful speech, Agathon. But there is just one more small point. Do you think that what is good is the same as what is beautiful?"

"I do."

"Then, if Love lacks beauty, and what is good coincides with what is beautiful, he also lacks goodness."

"I can't find any way of withstanding you, Socrates. Let it be as you say."

"Not at all, my dear Agathon. It is truth that you find it impossible to withstand; there is never the slightest difficulty in withstanding Socrates.

"But now I will leave you in peace, and try to give the account of Love which I once heard from a woman of Mantinea, called Diotima. She had other accomplishments as well—once; before the plague, when the Athenians had been sacrificing to avert it, she succeeded in postponing it for 10 years—but what concerns us at present is that she was my instructress in the art of love. I will try, taking the conclusions on which Agathon and I reached agreement as my starting-point, to give the best consecutive account I can of what she told me. As you were so careful to point out to us, Agathon, one must elucidate the essential nature and characteristics of Love before describing his effects. The easiest thing will be to go through the same questions and answers as she did with me. I had used very much the same language to her as Agathon used to me, and had said that Love is a great god and must be reckoned beautiful, but she employed against me the arguments by which I demonstrated to Agathon that to my way of thinking Love is neither beautiful nor good. 'What do you mean, Diotima?' I said. 'Is Love ugly and bad?' 'Don't say such things,' she answered; 'do you think that anything that is not beautiful is necessarily ugly?' 'Of course I do.' 'And that anything that is not wisdom is ignorance? Don't you know that there is a state of mind half-way between wisdom and ignorance?' 'What do you mean?' 'Having true convictions without being able to give reasons for them,' she replied. 'Surely you see that such a state of mind cannot be called understanding, because nothing irrational deserves the name; but it would be equally wrong to call it ignorance; how can one call a state of mind ignorance which hits upon the truth? The fact is that having true convictions is what I called it just now, a condition half-way between knowledge and ignorance.' 'I grant you that,' said I. 'Then do not maintain that what is not beautiful is ugly, and what is not good is bad. Do not suppose that because, on your own admission, Love is not good or beautiful, he must on that account be ugly and bad, but rather that he is something between the two.' 'And yet,' I said, 'everybody admits that he is a great god.' 'When you say everybody, do you mean those who don't know him, or do you include those who do?' 'I mean absolutely everybody.' She burst out laughing, and said: 'Well, Socrates, I don't see how he can be admitted to be a great god by those who say that he isn't even a god at all.' 'Who are they?' I asked. 'You are one of them and I'm another.' 'What can you mean?' 'It's perfectly easy; you'd say, wouldn't you, that all gods are happy and beautiful? You wouldn't dare to suggest that any of the gods is not?' 'Good heavens, no.' 'And by happy you mean in secure enjoyment of what is good and beautiful?' 'Certainly.' 'But you have agreed that it is because he lacks what is good and beautiful that Love desires these very things.' 'Yes, I have.' 'But a being who has no share of the good and beautiful cannot be a god?' 'Obviously not.' 'Very well then, you see that you are one of the people who believe that Love is not a god.'

" 'What can Love be then?' I said. 'A mortal?' 'Far from it.' 'Well, what?' 'As in my previous examples, he is half-way between mortal and immortal.' 'What sort of being is he then, Diotima?' 'He is a great spirit, Socrates; everything that is of the nature of a spirit is half-god and half-man.' 'And what is the function of such a being?' 'To interpret and convey messages to the gods from men and to men from the gods, prayers and sacrifices from the one, and commands and rewards from the other. Being of an intermediate nature, a spirit bridges the gap between them, and prevents the universe from falling into two separate halves. Through this class of being come all divination and the supernatural skill of priests in sacrifices and rites and spells and every kind of magic and wizardry. . . .'

" 'The truth of the matter is this. No god is a lover of wisdom or desires to be wise, for he is wise already, and the same is true of other wise persons, if there be any such. Nor on the other hand do the ignorant love wisdom and desire to be wise, for the tiresome thing about ignorance is precisely this, that a man who possesses neither beauty nor goodness nor intelligence is perfectly well satisfied with himself, and no one who does not believe that he lacks a thing desires what he does not believe that he lacks.'

" 'Who then,' I said, 'are the lovers of wisdom, if they are neither the wise nor the ignorant?' 'A child could answer that question. Obviously they are the intermediate class, of which Love among others is a member. Wisdom is one of the most beautiful of things, and Love is love of beauty, so it follows that Love must be a lover of wisdom, and consequently in a state half-way between wisdom and ignorance. . . . As for your thinking as you did about Love, there is nothing remarkable in that; to judge by what you said, you identified Love with the beloved object instead of with what feels love; that is why you thought that Love is supremely beautiful. The object of love is in all truth beautiful and delicate and perfect and worthy to be thought happy, but what feels love has a totally different character such as I have just described.'

" 'Tell me then, my friend,' I said, 'for your words carry conviction, what function Love performs among men, if this is his nature.' 'That is precisely what I am going to teach you, Socrates. . . . Love . . . is . . . , according to you, love of beauty. But suppose we were to be asked: In what does love of beauty consist, Socrates and Diotima? or, to put it more plainly, What is the aim of the love which is felt by the lover of beauty?' 'His aim is to attain possession of beautiful things,' I answered. 'But that merely raises a further question. What will have been gained by the man who is in possession of beauty?' I said that I could supply no ready answer to this question. 'Well,' she said, 'let us change our terms and substitute good for beautiful. Suppose someone asked you: Now, Socrates, what is the aim of the love felt by the lover of the good?' 'Possession of the good,' I replied. 'And what will have been gained by the man who is in possession of the good?' 'I find that an easier question to answer; he will be happy.' 'Presumably because happiness consists in the possession of the good, and once one has given that answer, the inquiry is at an end; there is no need to ask the further question Why does a man desire to be happy?' 'Quite so.'

" 'Now do you suppose that this desire and this love are characteristics common to all men, and that all perpetually desire to be in possession of the good, or what?' 'That is exactly what I mean; they are common to all men.' 'Why is it then, Socrates, if all men are always in love with the same thing, that we do not speak of all men as being in love, but say that some men are in love and others not?' 'I wonder what the reason can be.' 'There's no need to wonder; the truth is that we isolate a particular kind of love and appropriate for it the name of love, which really belongs to a wider whole, while we employ different names for the other kinds of love. . . . The generic concept embraces every desire for good and for happiness; that is precisely what almighty and all-ensnaring love is. But this desire expresses itself in many ways, and those with whom it takes the form of love of money or of physical prowess or of wisdom are not said to be in love or called lovers, whereas those whose passion runs in one particular channel usurp the name of lover, which belongs to them all, and are said to be lovers and in love.' 'There seems to be truth in what you say,' I remarked. 'There is indeed a theory,' she continued, 'that lovers are people who are in search of the other half of themselves, but according to my view of the matter, my friend, love is not desire either of the half or of the whole, unless that half or whole happens to be good. Men are quite willing to have their feet or their hands amputated if they believe those parts of themselves to be diseased. The truth is, I think, that people are not attached to what particularly belongs to them, except in so far as they can identify what is good with what is their own, and what is bad with what is not their own. The only object of men's love is what is good. Don't you agree?' 'Certainly I do.' 'May we then say without qualification that men are in love with what is good?' 'Yes.' 'But we must add, mustn't we, that the aim of their love is the possession of the good for themselves?' 'Yes.' 'And not only its possession but its perpetual possession?' 'Certainly.' 'To sum up, then, love is desire for the perpetual possession of the good.' 'Very true.'

" 'Now that we have established what love invariably is, we must ask in what way and by what type of action men must show their intense desire if it is to deserve the name of love. What will this function be? Can you tell me?' 'If I could, Diotima, I should not be feeling such admiration for your wisdom, or putting myself to school with you to learn precisely this.' 'Well,' she said, 'I will tell you. The function is that of procreation in what is beautiful, and such procreation can be either physical or spiritual.' 'What you say needs an interpreter. I don't understand.' 'I will put it more plainly. All men, Socrates, have a procreative impulse, both spiritual and physical, and when they come to maturity they feel a natural desire to beget children, but they can do so only in beauty and never in ugliness. There is something divine about the whole matter; in procreation and bringing to birth the mortal creature is endowed with a touch of immortality. But the process cannot take place in disharmony, and ugliness is out of harmony with everything divine, whereas beauty is in harmony with it. That is why Beauty is the goddess who presides over birth, and why, when a person in a state of desire comes into contact with beauty, he has a feeling of serenity and happy relaxation which make procreation possible. But, when ugliness is near, the effect is just the opposite. . . . The object of love, Socrates, is not, as you think, beauty.' 'What is it then?' 'Its object is to procreate and bring forth in beauty.' 'Really?' 'It is so, I assure you. Now, why is procreation the object of love? Because procreation is the nearest thing to perpetuity and immortality that a mortal being can attain. If, as we agreed, the aim of love is the perpetual possession of the good, it necessarily follows that it must desire immortality together with the good, and the argument leads us to the inevitable conclusion that love is love of immortality as well as of the good.' . . .

" 'The same argument holds good in the animal world as in the human, and mortal nature seeks, as far as may be, to perpetuate itself and become immortal. The only way in which it can achieve this is by procreation, which secures the perpetual replacement of an old member of the race by a new. Even during the period for which any living being is said to live and to retain his identity—as a man, for example, is called the same man from boyhood to old age—he does not in fact retain the same attributes, although he is called the same person; he is always becoming a new being and undergoing a process of loss and reparation, which affects his hair, his flesh, his bones, his blood, and his whole body. And not only his body, but his soul as well. No man's character, habits, opinions, desires, pleasures, pains, and fears remain always the same; new ones come into existence and old ones disappear. What happens with pieces of knowledge is even more remarkable; it is not merely that some appear and others disappear, so that we no more retain our identity with regard to knowledge than with regard to the other things I have mentioned, but that each individual piece of knowledge is subject to the same process as we are ourselves. When we use the word recollection we imply by using it that knowledge departs from us; forgetting is the departure of knowledge, and recollection, by implanting a new impression in the place of that which is lost, preserves it, and gives it a spurious appearance of uninterrupted identity. It is in this way that everything mortal is preserved; not by remaining for ever the same, which is the prerogative of divinity, but by undergoing a process in which the losses caused by age are repaired by new acquisitions of a similar kind. This device, Socrates, enables the mortal to partake of immortality, physically as well as in other ways; but the immortal enjoys immortality after another manner. So do not feel surprise that every creature naturally cherishes its own progeny; it is in order to secure immortality that each individual is haunted by this eager desire and love.'

"I was surprised at this account and said: 'You may be very wise, Diotima, but am I really to believe this?' 'Certainly you are,' she replied in true professional style; 'if you will only reflect you will see that the ambition of men provides an example of the same truth. You will be astonished at its irrationality unless you bear in mind what I have said, and remember that the love of fame and the desire to win a glory that shall never die have the strongest effects upon people. For this even more than for their children they are ready to run risks, spend their substance, endure every kind of hardships and even sacrifice their lives. . . . On the contrary; it is desire for immortal renown and a glorious reputation such as theirs that is the incentive of all actions, and the better a man is, the stronger the incentive; he is in love with immortality. Those whose creative instinct is physical have recourse to women, and show their love in this way, believing that by begetting children they can secure for themselves an immortal and blessed memory hereafter for ever; but there are some whose creative desire is of the soul, and who long to beget spiritually, not physically, the progeny which it is the nature of the soul to create and bring to birth. If you ask what that progeny is, it is wisdom and virtue in general. . . ."

ARISTOTLE

translated by J. F. Heil

Nicomachean Ethics, Book 8

ON FRIENDSHIP

CHAPTER 1

. . . Friendship is a virtue of sorts, or involves virtue, and is indispensable for life. After all, no one would choose to live without friends, even if he had everything else that is good. Indeed, it is the wealthy and those holding high offices and powerful positions who are thought to need friends most of all. What would be the benefit of such prosperity if it were stripped of good works, which arise most often and are most highly praised in relation to friends? And how could prosperity be guarded and maintained without friends? Indeed, the greater it is, the more precarious it becomes. In poverty too, and in all other misfortunes, people think friends are the only refuge.

For young people, friendship serves to keep them from error. For the elderly, to care and provide assistance to them when their actions fail because of weakness. For those in their prime, friendship is for fine actions. Indeed, "when two go together," they are more capable of thought and action.

Friendship seems to be implanted by nature in a parent toward a child and in a child toward a parent, not only among human beings, but also among birds and most animals. It exists between members of the same race, but especially between members of the human race, and that is why we praise lovers of humanity. We can also see in our travels how close and friendly every human being is to another.

Friendship seems to hold the state together, and legislators seem to take it more seriously than justice. Concord, after all, seems to be something like friendship, and concord is what they strive for above all, while faction, being a kind of hostility, is what they most try to drive off. Indeed, when people are friends there is no need for justice, but people who are just need the addition of friendship, and the most just things of all are thought to have the character of friendship.

Friendship, however, is not only necessary, but also fine. We praise those who love their friends, and it is thought to be a fine thing to have many friends. Furthermore, people think that the same men who are good are also friends. . . .

CHAPTER 2

Perhaps the nature and forms of friendship will be evident once we know what is lovable. It seems that not everything is loved, but only what is lovable, and this seems to be something either good or pleasant or useful. The useful, however, would seem to be a means to some good or some pleasure. Hence, the good and the pleasant would be lovable as ends.

Do people love what is good or what is good for *them?* These two are sometimes in disagreement, and likewise in the case of what is pleasant. Now, it seems that each person loves what is good for himself and, although in an unqualified sense the good is what is lovable, individually what is good to each person is what is lovable to him. Each person loves not what is, but what appears, good for himself. That will make no difference, however, since what appears good will be what appears lovable.

Although there are three reasons why people love things, the love of inanimate objects is not called friendship, since there is no *mutual* loving and no wish for their good. Presumably it is ridiculous to wish good things for wine. If anything, you wish it to keep so you can have it. For a friend, however, people say we should wish good things for his sake. They say that those who wish good things in this way have mere "goodwill," unless the same is returned to them from the other, since friendship lies in *reciprocated* goodwill. Perhaps we should add "if we are *aware* of it." After all, many of us have goodwill towards people we've never seen, but whom we suppose to be good or useful, one of these people may have the same feeling towards us. Here, then, we have a case where people appear to have mutual goodwill, but how could we call them friends if they are unaware of each other's disposition?

Friends, therefore, should have mutual goodwill, wish good things for each other, be aware of doing this, and do it for one of the three reasons given above.

CHAPTER 3

Now, these three reasons, and therefore the varieties of loving and friendship, differ in kind from one another. There are, then, three kinds of friendship, corresponding in number to the objects of love. Mutual loving (with awareness) occurs on the basis of each of these objects, and those who love each other wish good things for each other in precisely that respect in which they love each other.

Those who love each other because of their usefulness love each other not in themselves, but insofar as they get something good from the other, and likewise for those who love because of pleasure. It isn't for *his* having a certain character that we like the witty guy, but for the pleasure he gives *us*. So, those who love each other because of their usefulness do so because of the good they get for themselves, and those who love because of pleasure do so because of the pleasure they get for themselves, i.e., not insofar as the beloved is who he is, but insofar as he is useful or pleasant. These friendships, then, are *incidental*. The beloved is loved not insofar as he is who he is, but insofar as he provides some good, in the one case, some pleasure, in the other. Hence, such friendships are easily dissolved, when the parties don't remain like themselves: if they are no longer pleasant or useful, then they stop loving each other.

What is useful, however, does not remain the same, but is different at different times. When, therefore, the reason why they were friends is gone, the friendship is dissolved too, assuming that *that* was the reason for the friendship. This sort of friendship seems to occur most of all among the elderly, since people at that age are not pursuing what is pleasant, but what is beneficial. It also occurs among all those in their prime or youth who are pursuing their own advantage. Rarely do such people live together. Sometimes they do not even find each other pleasant. They have no further need, then, for this sort of association if they are not beneficial to each other. Indeed, they find each other pleasant only to the extent that they have expectations of some good from the other. The friendship of host and guest is put in this category too.

The friendship of young people seems to be for the reason of pleasure. After all, they live on the basis of emotion and pursue, above all, what is pleasant for themselves and right before them. As their age changes, however, the things they find pleasant also become different. This is why they are quick to become friends and quick to stop, since their friendship changes along with what is pleasant, and this sort of pleasure is quick to change. Young people also have erotic passion, since erotic love is for the most part based on emotion and pursued because of pleasure. Hence, they fall in and out of love quickly, often changing in the same day. Friends for pleasure, however, do wish to spend their days together and live together, since that is how they get what corresponds to their friendship.

Complete friendship, however, is the friendship between people who are good and similar in virtue. These people wish good things for each other in the same way, insofar as they are good people, and good in themselves. Those who wish good things for their *friends'* sake are friends most of all, since they have this disposition because of their friends *themselves* and not incidentally. Their friendship, then, remains for as long as they are good people, and virtue is an enduring thing. Each is good both in an unqualified sense and to his friend, because good people are both good in an unqualified sense and beneficial to each other. They are also pleasant in the same way, both in an unqualified sense and to each other, because each person finds his own actions and actions of the same sort pleasurable, and the actions of good people are the same or similar.

Now, it is reasonable that this sort of friendship is enduring. It combines in itself all that needs to belong to friends. Every friendship exists because of good or because of pleasure (whether in an unqualified sense or for the lover) and is based on a certain similarity. And all of the things we mentioned belong to this friendship on the basis of the people themselves. In this friendship, the partners are similar and the remaining features are present, both what is good in an unqualified sense and what is pleasant in an unqualified sense, and these are most lovable of all. Love and friendship, then, exist most of all and in their best form among these people.

Such friendships, however, are likely to be rare. Such people, after all, are few. Furthermore, time and familiarity are also required. As the proverb says, people cannot know each other before they have "shared the salt." They can neither accept one another nor be friends until each shows the other that he is lovable and can be trusted. . . .

PAUL

Sex, Marriage, and Divorce

1 CORINTHIANS 7.1–11

7. Now for the matters you wrote about. You say, "It is a good thing for a man not to have intercourse with a woman." Rather, in the face of so much immorality, let each man have his own wife and each woman her own husband. The husband must give the wife what is due to her, and equally the wife must give the husband his due. The wife cannot claim her body as her own; it is her husband's. Equally, the husband cannot claim his body as his own; it is his wife's. Do not deny yourselves to one another, except when you agree to devote yourselves to prayer for a time, and to come together again afterwards; otherwise, through lack of self-control, you may be tempted by Satan. I say this by way of concession, not command. I should like everyone to be as I myself am; but each person has the gift God has granted him, one this gift and another that.

To the unmarried and to widows I say this: it is a good thing if like me they stay as they are; but if they do not have self-control, they should marry. It is better to be married than burn with desire.

To the married I give this ruling, which is not mine but the Lord's: a wife must not separate herself from her husband—if she does, she must either remain unmarried or be reconciled to her husband—and the husband must not divorce his wife. . . .

1 THESSALONIANS 4.1–18

4. And now, friends, we have one thing to ask of you, as fellow-Christians. We passed on to you the tradition of the way we must live if we are to please God; you are indeed already following it, but we beg you to do so yet more thoroughly. You know the rules we gave you in the name of the Lord Jesus. This is the will of God, that you should be holy: you must abstain from fornication; each one of you must learn to gain mastery over his body, to hallow and honour it, not giving way to lust like the pagans who know nothing of God; no one must do his fellow-Christian wrong in this matter, or infringe on his rights. As we impressed on you before, the Lord punishes all such offences. For God called us to holiness, not to impurity. Anyone therefore who flouts these rules is flouting not man but the God who bestows on you his Holy Spirit.

About love of the brotherhood you need no words of mine, for you are yourselves taught by God to love one another, and you are in fact practising this rule of love towards all your fellow-Christians throughout Macedonia. Yet we appeal to you, friends, to do better still. Let it be your ambition to live quietly and attend to your own business; and to work with your hands, as we told you, so that you may command the respect of those outside your own number, and at the same time never be in want.

We wish you not to remain in ignorance, friends, about those who sleep in death; you should not grieve like the rest of mankind, who have no hope. We believe that Jesus died and rose again; so too will God bring those who died as Christians to be with Jesus.

This we tell you as a word from the Lord: those of us who are still alive when the Lord comes will have no advantage over those who have died; when the command is given, when the archangel's voice is heard, when God's trumpet sounds, then the Lord himself will descend from heaven; first the Christian dead will rise, then we who are still alive shall join them, caught up in clouds to meet the Lord in the air. Thus we shall always be with the Lord. Console one another, then, with these words.

FRIEDRICH NIETZSCHE

On Love and Friendship

THE THINGS PEOPLE CALL LOVE

Avarice and love: what different feelings these two terms evoke! Nevertheless it could be the same instinct that has two names—once deprecated by those who *have,* in whom the instinct has calmed down to some extent, and who are afraid for their "possessions," and the other time seen from the point of view of those who are not satisfied but still thirsty and who therefore glorify the instinct as "good." Our love of our neighbor—is it not a lust for new *possessions?* And likewise our love of knowledge, of truth, and altogether any lust for what is new? Gradually we become tired of the old, of what we safely possess, and we stretch out our hands again. Even the most beautiful scenery is no longer assured of our love after we have lived in it for 3 months, and some more distant coast attracts our avarice: possessions are generally diminished by possession.

Our pleasure in ourselves tries to maintain itself by again and again changing something new *into ourselves;* that is what possession means. To become tired of some possession means tiring of ourselves. (One can also suffer of an excess—the lust to throw away or to distribute can also assume the honorary name of "love.") When we see somebody suffer, we like to exploit this opportunity to take possession of him; those who become his benefactors and pity him, for example, do this and call the lust for a new possession that he awakens in them "love"; and the pleasure they feel is comparable to that aroused by the prospect of a new conquest.

Sexual love betrays itself most clearly as a lust for possession: the lover desires unconditional and sole possession of the person for whom he longs; he desires equally unconditional power over the soul and over the body of the beloved; he alone wants to be loved and desires to live and rule in the other soul as supreme and supremely desirable. If one considers that this means nothing less than *excluding* the whole world from a precious good, from happiness and enjoyment; if one considers that the lover aims at the impoverishment and deprivation of all competitors and would like to become the dragon guarding his golden hoard as the most inconsiderate and selfish of all "conquerors" and exploiters; if one considers, finally, that to the lover himself the whole rest of the world appears indifferent, pale, and worthless, and he is prepared to make any sacrifice, to disturb any order, to subordinate all other interests—then one comes to feel genuine amazement that this wild avarice and injustice of sexual love has been glorified and deified so much in all ages—indeed, that this love has furnished the concept of love as the opposite of egoism while it actually may be the most ingenuous expression of egoism.

As this point linguistic usage has evidently been formed by those who did not possess but desired. Probably, there have always been too many of these. Those to whom much possession and satiety were granted in this area have occasionally made some casual remark about "the raging demon," as that most gracious and beloved of all Athenians, Sophocles, did; but Eros has always laughed at such blasphemers; they were invariably his greatest favorites.

Here and there on earth we may encounter a kind of continuation of love in which this possessive craving of two people for each other gives way to a new desire and lust for possession—a *shared* higher thirst for an ideal above them. But who knows such love? Who has experienced it? Its right name is *friendship.*

HOW EACH SEX HAS ITS OWN PREJUDICE ABOUT LOVE

Despite all the concessions that I am willing to make to the prejudice in favor of monogamy, I will never admit the claim that man and woman have *equal* rights in love; these do not exist. For man and woman have different conceptions of love; and it is one of the conditions of love in both sexes that neither sex presupposes the same feeling and the same concept of "love" in the other. What woman means by love is clear enough: total devotion (not mere surrender) with soul and body, without any consideration or reserve, rather with shame and horror at the thought of a devotion that might be subject to special clauses or conditions. In this absence of conditions her love is a *faith;* woman has no other faith.

Man, when he loves a woman, wants precisely this love from her and is thus himself as far as can be from the presupposition of feminine love. Supposing, however, that there should also be men to whom the desire for total devotion is not alien; well, then they simply are—not men. A man who loves a woman becomes a slave; while a woman who loves like a woman becomes a *more perfect woman.*

A woman's passion in its unconditional renunciation of rights of her own presupposes precisely that on the other side there is no equal pathos, no equal will to renunciation; for if both partners felt impelled by love to renounce themselves, we should then get—I do not know what; perhaps an empty space?

Woman wants to be taken and accepted as a possession, wants to be absorbed into the concept of possession, possessed. Consequently, she wants someone who *takes,* who does not give himself or give himself away; on the contrary, he is supposed to become richer in "himself"—through the accretion of strength, happiness, and faith given him by the woman who gives herself. Woman gives herself away, man acquires more—I do not see how one can get around this natural opposition by means of social contracts or with the best will in the world to be just, desirable as it may be not to remind oneself constantly how harsh, terrible, enigmatic, and immoral this antagonism is. For love, thought of in its entirety as great and full, is nature, and being nature it is in all eternity something "immoral."

Faithfulness is accordingly included in woman's love; it follows from the definition. In man, it *can* easily develop in the wake of his love, perhaps as gratitude or as an idiosyncratic taste and so-called elective affinity; but it is not an *essential* element of his love—so definitely not that one might almost speak with some justification of a natural counterplay of love and faithfulness in man. For his love consists of wanting to *have* and not of renunciation and giving away; but *wanting* to have always comes to an end with *having.*

It is actually man's more refined and suspicious lust for possession that rarely admits his "having," and then only late, and thus permits his love to persist. It is even possible for his love to increase after the surrender; he will not readily concede that a woman should have nothing more to give him.

SIMONE DE BEAUVOIR

The Second Sex

INTRODUCTION

If her functioning as a female is not enough to define woman, if we decline also to explain her through "the eternal feminine," and if nevertheless we admit, provisionally, that women do exist, then we must face the question: what is a woman?

To state the question is, to me, to suggest, at once, a preliminary answer. The fact that I ask it is in itself significant. A man would never get the notion of writing a book on the peculiar situation of the human male. But if I wish to define myself, I must first of all say: "I am a woman"; on this truth must be based all further discussion. A man never begins by presenting himself as an individual of a certain sex; it goes without saying that he is a man. The terms *masculine* and *feminine* are used symmetrically only as a matter of form, as on legal papers. In actuality the relation of the two sexes is not quite like that of two electrical poles, for man represents both the positive and the neutral, as is indicated by the common use of *man* to designate human beings in general; whereas woman represents only the negative, defined by limiting criteria, without reciprocity. In the midst of an abstract discussion it is vexing to hear a man say: "You think thus and so because you are a woman"; but I know that my only defense is to reply: "I think thus and so because it is true," thereby removing my subjective self from the argument. It would be out of the question to reply: "And you think the contrary because you are a man," for it is understood that the fact of being a man is no peculiarity. A man is in the right in being a man; it is the woman who is in the wrong. It amounts to this: just as for the ancients there was an absolute vertical with reference to which the oblique was defined, so there is an absolute human type, the masculine. Woman has ovaries, a uterus; these peculiarities imprison her in her subjectivity, circumscribe her within the limits of her own nature. It is often said that she thinks with her glands. Man superbly ignores the fact that his anatomy also includes glands, such as the testicles, and that they secrete hormones. He thinks of his body as a direct and normal connection with the world, which he believes he apprehends objectively, whereas he regards the body of woman as a hindrance, a prison, weighed down by everything peculiar to it. "The female is a female by virtue of a certain *lack* of qualities," said Aristotle; "we should regard the female nature as afflicted with a natural defectiveness." And St. Thomas for his part pronounced woman to be an "imperfect man," an "incidental" being. This is symbolized in Genesis where Eve is depicted as made from what Bossuet called "a supernumerary bone" of Adam.

Thus humanity is male and man defines woman not in herself but as relative to him; she is not regarded as an autonomous being. Michelet writes: "Woman, the relative being. . . . " And Benda is most positive in his *Rapport d' Uriel:* "The body of man makes sense in itself quite apart from that of woman, whereas the latter seems wanting in significance by itself. . . . Man can think of himself without woman. She cannot think of herself without man." And she is simply what man decrees; thus she is called "the sex," by which is meant that she appears essentially to the male as a sexual being. For him she is sex—absolute sex, no less. She is defined and differentiated with reference to man and not he with reference to her; she is the incidental, the inessential as opposed to the essential. He is the Subject, he is the Absolute—she is the Other.

The category of the *Other* is as primordial as consciousness itself. In the most primitive societies, in the most ancient mythologies, one finds the expression of a duality—that of the Self and the Other. This duality was not originally attached to the division of the sexes; it was not dependent upon any empirical facts. It is revealed in such works as that of Granet on Chinese thought and those of Dumézil on the East Indies and Rome. The feminine element was at first no more involved in such pairs as Varuna-Mitra, Uranus-Zeus, Sun-Moon, and Day-Night than it was in the contrasts between Good and Evil, lucky and unlucky auspices, right and left, God and Lucifer. Otherness is a fundamental category of human thought.

Thus it is that no group ever sets itself up as the One without at once setting up the Other over against itself. . . .

Lévi-Strauss, at the end of a profound work on the various forms of primitive societies, reaches the following conclusion: "Passage from the state of Nature to the state of Culture is marked by man's ability to view biological relations as a series of contrasts; duality, alternation, opposition, and symmetry, whether under definite or vague forms, constitute not so much phenomena to be explained as fundamental and immediately given data of social reality."[1] These phenomena would be incomprehensible if in fact human society were simply a *Mitsein* or fellowship based on solidarity and friendliness. Things become clear, on the contrary, if, following Hegel, we find in consciousness itself a fundamental hostility toward every other consciousness; the subject can be posed only in being opposed—he sets himself up as the essential, as opposed to the other, the inessential, the object.

But the other consciousness, the other ego, sets up a reciprocal claim. The native traveling abroad is shocked to find himself in turn regarded as a "stranger" by the natives of neighboring countries. As a matter of fact, wars, festivals, trading, treaties, and contests among tribes, nations, and classes tend to deprive the concept *Other* of its absolute sense and to make manifest its relativity; willy-nilly, individuals and groups are forced to realize the reciprocity of their relations. How is it, then, that this reciprocity has not been recognized between the sexes, that one of the contrasting terms is set up as the sole essential, denying any relativity in regard to its correlative and defining the latter as pure otherness? Why is it that women do not dispute male sovereignty? No subject will readily volunteer to become the object, the inessential; it is not the Other who, in defining himself as the Other, establishes the One. The Other is posed as such by the One in defining himself as the One. But if the Other is not to regain the status of being the One, he must be submissive enough to accept this alien point of view. Whence comes this submission in the case of woman?

There are, to be sure, other cases in which a certain category has been able to dominate another completely for a time. Very often this privilege depends upon inequality of numbers—the majority imposes its rule upon the minority or persecutes it. But women are not a minority, like the American Negroes or the Jews; there are as many women as men on earth. . . .

The parallel drawn by Bebel between women and the proletariat is valid in that neither ever formed a minority or a separate collective unit of mankind. And instead of a single historical event it is in both cases a historical development that explains their status as a class and accounts for the membership of *particular individuals* in that class. But proletarians have not always existed, whereas there have always been women. They are women in virtue of their anatomy and physiology. Throughout history they have always been subordinated to men, and hence their dependency is not the result of a historical event or a social change—it was not something that *occurred*. The reason why otherness in this case seems to be an absolute is in part that it lacks the contingent or incidental nature of historical facts. A condition brought about at a certain time can be abolished at some other time, as the Negroes of Haiti and others have proved; but it might seem that a natural condition is beyond the possibility of change. In truth, however, the nature of things is no more immutably given, once for all, than is historical reality. If woman seems to be the inessential which never becomes the essential, it is because she herself fails to bring about this change. Proletarians say "We"; Negroes also. Regarding themselves as subjects, they transform the bourgeois, the whites, into "others." But women do not say "We," except at some congress of feminists or similar formal demonstration; men say "women," and women use the same word in referring to themselves. They do not authentically assume a subjective attitude.

. . . The bond that unites her to her oppressors is not comparable to any other. The division of the sexes is a biological fact, not an event in human history. Male and female stand opposed within a primordial *Mitsein,* and woman has not broken it. The couple is a fundamental unity with its two halves riveted together, and the cleavage of society along the line of sex is impossible. Here is to be found the basic trait of woman: she is the Other in a totality of which the two components are necessary to one another.

. . . To decline to be the Other, to refuse to be a party to the deal—this would be for women to renounce all the advantages conferred upon them by their alliance with the superior caste. Man-the-sovereign will provide woman-the-liege with material protection and will undertake the moral justification of her existence; thus she can evade at once both economic risk and the metaphysical risk of a liberty in which ends and aims must be contrived without assistance. Indeed, along with the ethical urge of each individual to affirm his subjective existence, there is also the temptation to forgo liberty and become a thing. This is an inauspicious road, for he who takes it—passive, lost, ruined—becomes henceforth the creature of another's will, frustrated in his transcendence and deprived of every value. But it is an easy road; on it one avoids the strain involved in undertaking an authentic existence. When man makes of woman the *Other,* he may, then, expect her to manifest deep-seated tendencies toward complicity. Thus, woman may fail to lay claim to the status of subject because she lacks definite resources, because she feels the necessary bond that ties her to man regardless of reciprocity, and because she is often very well pleased with her role as the *Other.*

THE NOMADS

. . . On the biological level a species is maintained only by creating itself anew; but this creation results only in repeating the same Life in more individuals. But man assures the repetition of Life while transcending Life through Existence; by this transcendence he creates values that deprive pure repetition of all value. In the animal, the freedom and variety of male activities are vain because no project is involved. Except for his service to the species, what he does is immaterial. Whereas in serving the species, the human male also remodels the face of the earth, he creates new instruments, he invents, he shapes the future. In setting himself up as sovereign, he is supported by the complicity of woman herself. For she, too, is an existent, she feels the urge to surpass, and her project is not mere repetition but transcendence toward a different future—in her heart of hearts she finds confirmation of the masculine pretensions. She joins the men in the festivals that celebrate the successes and the victories of the males. Her misfortune is to have been biologically destined for the repetition of Life, when even in her own view Life does not carry within itself its reasons for being, reasons that are more important than the life itself.

Certain passages in the argument employed by Hegel in defining the relation of master to slave apply much better to the relation of man to woman. The advantage of the master, he says, comes from his affirmation of Spirit as against Life through the fact that he risks his own life; but in fact the conquered slave has known this same risk. Whereas woman is basically an existent who gives Life and does not risk *her* life; between her and the male there has been no combat. Hegel's definition would seem to apply especially well to her. He says: "The other consciousness is the dependent consciousness for whom the essential reality is the animal type of life; that is to say, a mode of living bestowed by another entity." But this relation is to be distinguished from the relation of subjugation because woman also aspires to and recognizes the values that are concretely attained by the male. He it is who opens up the future to which she also reaches out. In truth women have never set up female values in opposition to male values; it is man who, desirous of maintaining masculine prerogatives, has invented that divergence. Men have presumed to create a feminine domain—the kingdom of life, of immanence—only in order to lock up women therein. But it is regardless of sex that the existent seeks self-justification through transcendence—the very submission of women is proof of that statement. What they demand today is to be recognized as existents by the same right as men and not to subordinate existence to life, the human being to its animality.

An existentialist perspective has enabled us, then, to understand how the biological and economic condition of the primitive horde must have led to male supremacy. The female, to a greater extent than the male, is the prey of the species; and the human race has always sought to escape its specific destiny. The support of life became for man an activity and a project through the invention of the tool: but in maternity woman remained closely bound to her body, like an animal. It is because humanity calls itself in question in the matter of the living—that is to say, values the reasons for living above mere life—that, confronting woman, man assumes mastery. Man's design is not to repeat himself in time: it is to take control of the instant and mold the future. It is male activity that in creating values has made of existence itself a value; this activity has prevailed over the confused forces of life; it has subdued Nature and Woman.

THE WOMAN IN LOVE

The word *love* has by no means the same sense for both sexes, and this is one cause of the serious misunderstandings that divide them. Byron well said: "Man's love is of man's life a thing apart; 'Tis woman's whole existence.". . .

Men have found it possible to be passionate lovers at certain times in their lives, but there is not one of them who could be called "a great lover"; in their most violent transports, they never abdicate completely; even on their knees before a mistress, what they still want is to take possession of her; at the very heart of their lives they remain sovereign subjects; the beloved woman is only one value among others; they wish to integrate her into their existence and not to squander it entirely on her. For woman, on the contrary, to love is to relinquish everything for the benefit of a master. . . .

It is the difference in their situations that is reflected in the difference men and women show in their conceptions of love. The individual who is a subject, who is himself, if he has the courageous inclination toward transcendence, endeavors to extend his grasp on the world: he is ambitious, he acts. But an inessential creature is incapable of sensing the absolute at the heart of her subjectivity; a being doomed to immanence cannot find self-realization in acts. Shut up in the sphere of the relative, destined to the male from childhood, habituated to seeing in him a superb being whom she cannot possibly equal, the woman who has not repressed her claim to humanity will dream of transcending her being toward one of these superior beings, of amalgamating herself with the sovereign subject. There is no other way out for her than to lose herself, body and soul, in him who is represented to her as the absolute, as the essential. Since she is anyway doomed to dependence, she will prefer to serve a god rather than obey tyrants—parents, husband, or protector. She chooses to desire her enslavement so ardently that it will seem to her the expression of her liberty; she will try to rise above her situation as inessential object by fully accepting it; through her flesh, her feelings, her behavior, she will enthrone him as supreme value and reality: she will humble herself to nothingness before him. Love becomes for her a religion.

. . . The adolescent girl wishes at first to identify herself with males; when she gives that up, she then seeks to share in their masculinity by having one of them in love with her; it is not the individuality of this one or that one which attracts her; she is in love with man in general. "And you, the men I shall love, how I await you!" writes Irène Reweliotty. "How I rejoice to think I shall know you soon: especially You, the first." Of course the male is to belong to the same class and race as hers, for sexual privilege is in play only within this frame. If man is to be a demigod, he must first of all be a human being, and to the colonial officer's daughter the native is not a man. If the young girl gives herself to an "inferior," it is for the reason that she wishes to degrade herself because she believes she is unworthy of love; but normally she is looking for a man who represents male superiority. She is soon to ascertain that many individuals of the favored sex are sadly contingent and earthbound, but at first her presumption is favorable to them; they are called on less to prove their worth than to avoid too gross a disproof of it—which accounts for many mistakes, some of them serious. A naïve young girl is caught by the gleam of virility, and in her eyes male worth is shown, according to circumstances, by physical strength, distinction of manner, wealth, cultivation, intelligence, authority, social status, a military uniform; but what she always wants is for her lover to represent the essence of manhood.

Familiarity is often sufficient to destroy his prestige; it may collapse at the first kiss, or in daily association, or during the wedding night. Love at a distance, however, is only a fantasy, not a real experience. The desire for love becomes a passionate love only when it is carnally realized. Inversely, love can arise as a result of physical intercourse;

in this case the sexually dominated woman acquires an exalted view of a man who at first seemed to her quite insignificant.

But it often happens that a woman succeeds in deifying none of the men she knows. Love has a smaller place in woman's life than has often been supposed. Husband, children, home, amusements, social duties, vanity, sexuality, career, are much more important. Most women dream of a *grand amour,* a soul-searing love. They have known substitutes, they have been close to it; it has come to them in partial, bruised, ridiculous, imperfect, mendacious forms; but very few have truly dedicated their lives to it. The *grandes amoureuses* are most often women who have not frittered themselves away in juvenile affairs; they have first accepted the traditional feminine destiny: husband, home, children; or they have known pitiless solitude; or they have banked on some enterprise that has been more or less of a failure. And when they glimpse the opportunity to salvage a disappointing life by dedicating it to some superior person, they desperately give themselves up to this hope. Mlle Aïssé, Juliette Drouet, and Mme d'Agoult were almost 30 when their love-life began, Julie de Lespinasse not far from 40. No other aim in life which seemed worth while was open to them, love was their only way out.

Even if they choose independence, this road seems the most attractive to a majority of women: it is agonizing for a woman to assume responsibility for her life. Even the male, when adolescent, is quite willing to turn to older women for guidance, education, mothering; but customary attitudes, the boy's training, and his own inner imperatives forbid him to content himself in the end with the easy solution of abdication; to him such affairs with older women are only a stage through which he passes. It is man's good fortune—in adulthood as in early childhood—to be obliged to take the most arduous roads, but the surest; it is woman's misfortune to be surrounded by almost irresistible temptations; everything incites her to follow the easy slopes; instead of being invited to fight her own way up, she is told that she has only to let herself slide and she will attain paradises of enchantment. When she perceives that she has been duped by a mirage, it is too late; her strength has been exhausted in a losing venture. . . .

The supreme goal of human love, as of mystical love, is identification with the loved one. The measure of values, the truth of the world, are in his consciousness; hence it is not enough to serve him. The woman in love tries to see with his eyes; she reads the books he reads, prefers the pictures and the music he prefers; she is interested only in the landscapes she sees with him, in the ideas that come from him; she adopts his friendships, his enmities, his opinions; when she questions herself, it is his reply she tries to hear; she wants to have in her lungs the air he has already breathed; the fruits and flowers that do not come from his hands have no taste and no fragrance. Her idea of location in space, even, is upset: the center of the world is no longer the place where she is, but that occupied by her lover; all roads lead to his home, and from it. She uses his words, mimics his gestures, acquires his eccentricities and his tics. "I am Heathcliff," says Catherine in *Wuthering Heights;* that is the cry of every woman in love; she is another incarnation of her loved one, his reflection, his double: she is *he.* She lets her own world collapse in contingence, for she really lives in his.

The supreme happiness of the woman in love is to be recognized by the loved man as a part of himself; when he says "we," she is associated and identified with him, she shares his prestige and reigns with him over the rest of the world; she never tires of repeating—even to excess—this delectable "we." As one necessary to a being who is absolute necessity, who stands forth in the world seeking necessary goals and who gives her back the world in necessary form, the woman in love acquires in her submission that magnificent possession, the absolute. It is this certitude that gives her lofty joys; she feels exalted to a place at the right hand of God. Small matter to her to have only second place if she has *her* place, forever, in a most wonderfully ordered world. So long as she is in love and is loved by and necessary to her loved one, she feels herself wholly justified: she knows peace and happiness. . . .

But this glorious felicity rarely lasts. No man really is God. The relations sustained by the mystic with the divine Absence depend on her fervor alone; but the deified man, who is not God, is present. And from this fact are to come the torments of the woman in love. Her most common fate is summed up in the famous words of Julie de Lespinasse: "Always, my dear friend, I love you, I suffer and I await you." To be sure, suffering is linked with love for men also; but their pangs are either of short duration or not overly severe . . .

It is not true that the loved man is absolutely necessary, above chance and circumstance, and the woman is not necessary to him; he is not really in a position to justify the feminine being who is consecrated to his worship, and he does not permit himself to be possessed by her.

An authentic love should assume the contingence of the other; that is to say, his lacks, his limitations, and his basic gratuitousness. It would not pretend to be a mode of salvation, but a human interrelation. Idolatrous love attributes an absolute value to the loved one, a first falsity that is brilliantly apparent to all outsiders. "*He* isn't worth all that love," is whispered around the woman in love . . . It is a searing disappointment to the woman to discover the faults, the mediocrity of her idol. Novelists, like Colette, have often depicted this bitter anguish. The disillusion is still more cruel than that of the child who sees the father's prestige crumble, because the woman has herself selected the one to whom she has given over her entire being.

Even if the chosen one is worthy of the profoundest affection, his truth is of the earth, earthy, and it is no longer this mere man whom the woman loves as she kneels before a supreme being; she is duped by that spirit of seriousness which declines to take values as incidental—that is to say, declines to recognize that they have their source in human existence. Her bad faith raises barriers between her and the man she adores. She offers him incense, she bows down, but she is not a friend to him since she does not realize that he is in danger in the world, that his projects and his aims are as fragile as he is; regarding him as the Faith, the Truth, she misunderstands his freedom—his hesitancy and anguish of spirit. This refusal to apply a human measuring scale to the lover explains many feminine paradoxes. The woman asks a favor from her lover. Is it granted? Then he is generous, rich, magnificent; he is kingly, he is divine. Is it refused? Then he is avaricious, mean, cruel; he is a devilish or a bestial creature. One might be tempted to object: if a "yes" is such an astounding and superb extravagance, should one be surprised at a "no"? If the "no" discloses such abject selfishness, why wonder so much at the "yes"? Between the superhuman and the inhuman is there no place for the human?

A fallen god is not a man: he is a fraud; the lover has no other alternative than to prove that he really is this king accepting adulation—or to confess himself a usurper. If he is no longer adored, he must be trampled on. In virtue of that glory with which she has haloed the brow of her beloved, the woman in love forbids him any weakness; she is disappointed and vexed if he does not live up to the image she has put in his place. If he gets tired or careless, if he gets hungry or thirsty at the wrong time, if he makes a mistake or contradicts himself, she asserts that he is "not himself" and she makes a grievance of it. In this indirect way she will go so far as to take him to task for any of his ventures that she disapproves; she judges her judge, and she denies him his liberty so that he may deserve to remain her master. Her worship sometimes finds better satisfaction in his absence than in his presence; as we have seen, there are women who devote themselves to dead or otherwise inaccessible heroes, so that they may never have to face them in person, for beings of flesh and blood would be fatally contrary to their dreams. Hence such disillusioned sayings as: "One must not believe in Prince Charming. Men are only poor creatures," and the like. They would not seem to be dwarfs if they had not been asked to be giants. . . .

Genuine love ought to be founded on the mutual recognition of two liberties; the lovers would then experience themselves both as self and as other: neither would give up transcendence, neither would be mutilated; together they would manifest values and aims in the world. For the one and the other, love would be revelation of self by the gift of self and enrichment of the world. . . .

But most often woman knows herself only as different, relative; her *pour-autrui*, relation to others, is confused with her very being; for her, love is not an intermediary "between herself and herself" because she does not attain her subjective existence; she remains engulfed in this loving woman whom man has not only revealed, but created. Her salvation depends on this despotic free being that has made her and can instantly destroy her. She lives in fear and trembling before this man who holds her destiny in his hands without quite knowing it, without quite wishing to. She is in danger through an other, and anguished and powerless onlooker at her own fate. Involuntary tyrant, involuntary executioner, this other wears a hostile visage in spite of her and of himself. And so, instead of the union sought for, the woman in love knows the most bitter solitude there is; instead of cooperation, she knows struggle and not seldom hate. For woman, love is a supreme effort to survive by accepting the dependence to which she is condemned; but even with consent a life of dependency can be lived only in fear and servility.

Men have vied with one another in proclaiming that love is woman's supreme accomplishment. "A woman who loves as a woman becomes only the more feminine," says Nietzsche; and Balzac: "Among the first-rate, man's life is fame, woman's life is love. Woman is man's equal only when she makes her life a perpetual offering, as that of man is perpetual action." But therein, again, is a cruel deception, since what she offers, men are in no wise anxious to accept. Man has no need of the unconditional devotion he claims, nor of the idolatrous love that flatters his vanity; he accepts them only on condition that he need not satisfy the reciprocal demands these attitudes imply. He preaches to woman that she should give—and her gifts bore him to distraction; she is left in embarrassment with her useless offerings, her empty life. On the day when it will be possible for woman to love not in her weakness but in her strength, not to escape herself but to find herself, not to abase herself but to assert herself—on that day love will become for her, as for man, a source of life and not of mortal danger. In the meantime, love represents in its most touching form the curse that lies heavily upon woman confined in the feminine universe, woman mutilated, insufficient unto herself. The innumerable martyrs to love bear witness against the injustice of a fate that offers a sterile hell as ultimate salvation.

---

[1][Some of de Beauvoir's notes have been omitted.—ed.] See C. Lévi-Strauss: *Les Structures élementaires de la parenté*. My thanks are due to C. Lévi-Strauss for his kindness in furnishing me with the proofs of his work, which, among others, I have used liberally in Part II.

ALAN H. GOLDMAN

Plain Sex

I

. . . I shall suggest here that sex continues to be misrepresented in recent writings, at least in philosophical writings, and I shall criticize the predominant form of analysis which I term "means–end analysis." Such conceptions attribute a necessary external goal or purpose to sexual activity, whether it be reproduction, the expression of love, simple communication, or interpersonal awareness. They analyze sexual activity as a means to one of these ends, implying that sexual desire is a desire to reproduce, to love or be loved, or to communicate with others. All definitions of this type suggest false views of the relation of sex to perversion and morality by implying that sex which does not fit one of these models or fulfill one of these functions is in some way deviant or incomplete.

The alternative, simpler analysis with which I will begin is that sexual desire is desire for contact with another person's body and for the pleasure which such contact produces; sexual activity is activity which tends to fulfill such desire of the agent. Whereas Aristotle and Butler were correct in holding that pleasure is normally a by-product rather than a goal of purposeful action, in the case of sex this is not so clear. The desire for another's body is, principally among other things, the desire for the pleasure that physical contact brings. On the other hand, it is not a desire for a particular sensation detachable from its causal context, a sensation which can be derived in other ways. This definition in terms of the general goal of sexual desire appears preferable to an attempt to more explicitly list or define specific sexual activities, for many activities such as kissing, embracing, massaging, or holding hands may or may not be sexual, depending upon the context and more specifically upon the purposes, needs, or desires into which such activities fit. The generality of the definition also represents a refusal (common in recent psychological texts) to overemphasize orgasm as the goal of sexual desire or genital sex as the only norm of sexual activity. . . .

Central to the definition is the fact that the goal of sexual desire and activity is the physical contact itself, rather than something else which this contact might express. By contrast, what I term "means–end analyses" posit ends which I take to be extraneous to plain sex, and they view sex as a means to these ends. Their fault lies not in defining sex in terms of its general goal, but in seeing plain sex as merely a means to other separable ends. I term these "means–end analyses" for convenience, although "means-separable-end analyses," while too cumbersome, might be more fully explanatory. The desire for physical contact with another person is a minimal criterion for (normal) sexual desire, but is both necessary and sufficient to qualify normal desire as sexual. Of course, we may want to express other feelings through sexual acts in various contexts; but without the desire for the physical contact in and for itself, or when it is sought for other reasons, activities in which contact is involved are not predominantly sexual. Furthermore, the desire for physical contact in itself, without the wish to express affection or other feelings through it, is sufficient to render sexual the activity of the agent which fulfills it. Various activities with this goal alone, such as kissing and caressing in certain contexts, qualify as sexual even without the presence of genital symptoms of sexual excitement. The latter are not therefore necessary criteria for sexual activity. . . .

Our definition of sex in terms of the desire for physical contact may appear too narrow in that a person's personality, not merely her or his body, may be sexually attractive to another, and in that looking or conversing in a certain way can be sexual in a given context without bodily contact. Nevertheless, it is not the contents of one's thoughts per se that are sexually appealing, but one's personality as embodied in certain manners of behavior. Furthermore, if a person is sexually attracted by another's personality, he or she will desire not just further conversation, but actual sexual contact. . . .

II

We may turn then to what sex is not, to the arguments regarding supposed conceptual connections between sex and other activities which it is necessary to conceptually distinguish. The most comprehensible attempt to build an extraneous purpose into the sex act identifies that purpose as reproduction, its primary biological function. While this may be "nature's" purpose, it certainly need not be ours (the analogy with eating, while sometimes overworked, is pertinent here). While this identification may once have had a rational basis which also grounded the identification of the value and morality of sex with that applicable to reproduction and childrearing, the development of contraception rendered the connection weak. Methods of contraception are by now so familiar and so widely used that it is not necessary to dwell upon the changes wrought by these developments in the concept of sex itself and in a rational sexual ethic dependent upon that concept. In the past, the ever present possibility of children rendered the concepts of sex and sexual morality different from those required at present. There may be good reasons, if the presence and care of both mother and father are beneficial to children, for restricting reproduction to marriage. Insofar as society has a legitimate role in protecting children's interests, it may be justified in giving marriage a legal status, although this question is complicated by the fact (among others) that children born to single mothers deserve no penalties. In any case, the point here is simply that these questions are irrelevant at the present time to those regarding the morality of sex and its potential social regulation. (Further connections with marriage will be discussed below.)

It is obvious that the desire for sex is not necessarily a desire to reproduce, that the psychological manifestation has become, if it were not always, distinct from its biological roots. There are many parallels, as previously mentioned, with other natural functions. The pleasures of eating and exercising are to a large extent independent of their roles in nourishment or health (as the junk-food industry discovered with a vengeance). Despite the obvious parallel with sex, there is still a tendency for many to think that sex acts which can be reproductive are, if not more moral or less immoral, at least more natural. These categories of morality and "naturalness," or normality, are not to be identified with each other, as will be argued below, and neither is applicable to sex by virtue of its connection to reproduction. The tendency to identify reproduction as the conceptually connected end of sex is most prevalent now in the pronouncements of the Catholic church. There the assumed analysis is clearly tied to a restrictive sexual morality according to which acts become immoral and unnatural when they are not oriented towards reproduction, a morality which has independent roots in the Christian sexual ethic as it derives from Paul. However, the means–end analysis fails to generate a consistent sexual ethic: homosexual and oral-genital sex is condemned while kissing or caressing, acts equally unlikely to lead in themselves to fertilization, even when properly characterized as sexual according to our definition, are not.

III

Before discussing further relations of means–end analyses to false or inconsistent sexual ethics and concepts of perversion, I turn to other examples of these analyses. One common position views sex as essentially an expression of love or affection between the partners. It is generally recognized that there are other types of love besides sexual, but sex itself is taken as an expression of one type, sometimes termed "romantic" love.[1] Various factors again ought to weaken this identification. First, there are other types of love besides that which it is appropriate to express sexually, and "romantic" love itself can be expressed in many other ways. I am not denying that sex can take on heightened value and meaning when it becomes a vehicle for the expression of feelings of love or tenderness, but so can many other usually mundane activities such as getting up early to make breakfast on Sunday, cleaning the house, and so on. Second, sex itself can be used to communicate many other emotions besides love, and, as I will argue below, can communicate nothing in particular and still be good sex.

On a deeper level, an internal tension is bound to result from an identification of sex, which I have described as a physical–psychological desire, with love as a long-term, deep emotional relationship between two individuals. As this type of relationship, love is permanent, at least in intent, and more or less exclusive. A normal person cannot deeply love more than a few individuals even in a lifetime. We may be suspicious that those who attempt or claim to love many love them weakly if at all. Yet, fleeting sexual desire can arise in relation to a variety of other individuals one finds sexually attractive. It may even be, as some have claimed, that sexual desire in humans naturally seeks variety, while this is obviously false of love. For this reason, monogamous sex, even if justified, almost always represents a sacrifice or the exercise of self-control on the part of the spouses, while monogamous love generally does not. There is no such thing as casual love in the sense in which I intend the term "love." It may occasionally happen that a spouse falls deeply in love with someone else (especially when sex is conceived in terms of love), but this is relatively rare in comparison to passing sexual desires for others; and while the former often indicates a weakness or fault in the marriage relation, the latter does not.

If love is indeed more exclusive in its objects than is sexual desire, this explains why those who view sex as essentially an expression of love would again tend to hold a repressive or restrictive sexual ethic. As in the case of reproduction, there may be good reasons for reserving the total commitment of deep love to the context of marriage and family—the normal personality may not withstand additional divisions of ultimate commitment and allegiance. There is no question that marriage itself is best sustained by a deep relation of love and affection; and even if love is not naturally monogamous, the benefits of family units to children provide additional reason to avoid serious commitments elsewhere which weaken family ties. It can be argued similarly that monogamous sex strengthens families by restricting and at the same time guaranteeing an outlet for sexual desire in marriage. But there is more force to the argument that recognition of a clear distinction between sex and love in society would help avoid disastrous marriages which result from adolescent confusion of the two when sexual desire is mistaken for permanent love, and would weaken damaging jealousies which arise in marriages in relation to passing sexual desires. The love and affection of a sound marriage certainly differs from the adolescent romantic variety, which is often a mere substitute for sex in the context of a repressive sexual ethic. . . .

I have now criticized various types of analysis sharing or suggesting a common means–end form. I have suggested that analyses of this form relate to attempts to limit moral or natural sex to that which fulfills some purpose or function extraneous to basic sexual desire. The attempts to brand forms of sex outside the idealized models as immoral or perverted fail to achieve consistency with intuitions that they themselves do not directly question. The reproductive model brands oral-genital sex a deviation, but cannot account for kissing or holding hands. . . .

The sex-love model makes most sexual desire seem degrading or base. These views condemn extramarital sex on the sound but irrelevant grounds that reproduction and deep commitment are best confined to family contexts. The romanticization of sex and the confusion of sexual desire with love operate in both directions: sex outside the context of romantic love is repressed; once it is repressed, partners become more difficult to find and sex becomes romanticized further, out of proportion to its real value for the individual.

What all these analyses share in addition to a common form is accordance with and perhaps derivation from the Platonic–Christian moral tradition, according to which the animal or purely physical element of humans is the source of immorality, and plain sex in the sense I defined it is an expression of this element, hence in itself to be condemned. . . .

Sexual desire lets us know that we are physical beings and, indeed, animals; this is why traditional Platonic morality is so thorough in its condemnation. Means–end analyses continue to reflect this tradition, sometimes unwittingly. They show that in conceptualizing sex it is still difficult, despite years of so-called revolution in this area, to free ourselves from the lingering suspicion that plain sex as physical desire is an expression of our "lower selves," that yielding to our animal natures is subhuman or vulgar.

VI

Having criticized these analyses for the sexual ethics . . . they imply, it remains to contrast my account along these lines. To the question of what morality might be implied by my analysis, the answer is that there are no moral implications whatever. Any analysis of sex which imputes a moral character to sex acts in themselves is wrong for that reason. There is no morality intrinsic to sex, although general moral rules apply to the treatment of others in sex acts as they apply to all human relations. We can speak of a sexual ethic as we can speak of a business ethic, without implying that business itself is either moral or immoral or that special rules are required to judge business practices which are not derived from rules that apply elsewhere as well. Sex is not in itself a moral category, although like business it invariably places us into relations with others in which moral rules apply. It gives us opportunity to do what is otherwise recognized as wrong, to harm others, deceive them or manipulate them against their wills. Just as the fact that an act is sexual in itself never renders it wrong or adds to its wrongness if it is wrong on other grounds (sexual acts towards minors are wrong on other grounds, as will be argued below), so no wrong act is to be excused because done from a sexual motive. If a "crime of passion" is to be excused, it would have to be on grounds of temporary insanity rather than sexual context (whether insanity does constitute a legitimate excuse for certain actions is too big a topic to argue here). Sexual motives are among others which may become deranged, and the fact that they are sexual has no bearing in itself on the moral character, whether negative or exculpatory, of the actions deriving from them. Whatever might be true of war, it is certainly not the case that all's fair in love or sex.

Our first conclusion regarding morality and sex is therefore that no conduct otherwise immoral should be excused because it is sexual conduct, and nothing in sex is immoral unless condemned by rules which apply elsewhere as well. The last clause requires further clarification. Sexual conduct can be governed by particular rules relating only to sex itself. But these precepts must be implied by general moral rules when these are applied to specific sexual relations or types of conduct. The same is true of rules of fair business, ethical medicine, or courtesy in driving a car. In the latter case, particular acts on the road may be reprehensible, such as tailgating or passing on the right, which seem to bear no resemblance as actions to any outside the context of highway safety. Nevertheless their immorality derives from the fact that they place others in danger, a circumstance which, when avoidable, is to be condemned in any context. This structure of general and specifically applicable rules describes a reasonable sexual ethic as well. To take an extreme case, rape is always a sexual act and it is always immoral. A rule against rape can therefore be considered an obvious part of sexual morality which has no bearing on nonsexual conduct. But the immorality of rape derives from its being an extreme violation of a person's body, of the right not to be humiliated, and of the general moral prohibition against using other persons against their wills, not from the fact that it is a sexual act.

The application elsewhere of general moral rules to sexual conduct is further complicated by the fact that it will be relative to the particular desires and preferences of one's partner (these may be influenced by and hence in some sense include misguided beliefs about sexual morality itself). This means that there will be fewer specific rules in the area of sexual ethics than in other areas of conduct, such as driving cars, where the relativity of preference is irrelevant to the prohibition of objectively dangerous conduct. More reliance will have to be placed upon the general moral rule, which in this area holds simply that the preferences, desires, and interests of one's partner or potential partner ought to be taken into account. This rule is certainly not specifically formulated to govern sexual relations; it is a form of the central principle of morality itself. But when applied to sex, it prohibits certain actions, such as molestation of children, which cannot be categorized as violations of the rule without at the same time being classified as sexual. I believe this last case is the closest we can come to an action which is wrong *because* it is sexual, but even here its wrongness is better characterized as deriving from the detrimental effects such behavior can have on the future emotional and sexual life of the naive victims, and from the fact that such behavior therefore involves manipulation of innocent persons without regard for their interests. Hence, this case also involves violation of a general moral rule which applies elsewhere as well.

Aside from faulty conceptual analyses of sex and the influence of the Platonic moral tradition, there are two more plausible reasons for thinking that there are moral dimensions intrinsic to sex acts per se. The first is that such acts are normally intensely pleasurable. According to a hedonistic, utilitarian moral theory they therefore should be at least prima facie morally right, rather than morally neutral in themselves. To me this seems incorrect and reflects unfavorably on the ethical theory in question. The pleasure intrinsic to sex acts is a good, but not, it seems to me, a good with much positive moral significance. Certainly I can have no duty to pursue such pleasure myself, and while it may be nice to give pleasure of any form to others, there is no ethical requirement to do so, given my right over my own body. The exception relates to the context of sex acts themselves, when one partner derives pleasure from the other and ought to return the favor. This duty to reciprocate takes us out of the domain of hedonistic utilitarianism, however, and into a Kantian moral framework, the central principles of which call for just such reciprocity in human relations. Since independent moral judgments regarding sexual activities constitute one area in which ethical theories are to be tested, these observations indicate here, as I believe others indicate elsewhere, the fertility of the Kantian, as opposed to the utilitarian, principle in reconstructing reasoned moral consciousness.

It may appear from this alternative Kantian viewpoint that sexual acts must be at least prima facie wrong in themselves. This is because they invariably involve at different stages the manipulation of one's partner for one's own pleasure, which might appear to be prohibited on the formulation of Kant's principle which holds that one ought not to treat another as a means to such private ends. A more realistic rendering of this formulation, however, one which recognizes its intended equivalence to the first universalizability principle, admits no such absolute prohibition. Many human relations, most economic transactions for example, involve using other individuals for personal benefit. These relations are immoral only when they are one-sided, when the benefits are not mutual, or when the transactions are not freely and rationally endorsed by all parties. The same holds true of sexual acts. The central principle governing them is the Kantian demand for reciprocity in sexual relations. In order to comply with the second formulation of the categorical imperative, one must recognize the subjectivity of one's partner (not merely by being aroused by her or his desire, as Nagel describes). Even in an act which by its nature "objectifies" the other, one recognizes a partner as a subject with demands and desires by yielding to those desires, by allowing oneself to be a sexual object as well, by giving pleasure or ensuring that the pleasures of the acts are mutual. It is this kind of reciprocity which forms the basis for morality in sex, which distinguishes right acts from wrong in this area as in others. (Of course, prior to sex acts one must gauge their effects upon potential partners and take these longer range interests into account.)

VII

I suggested earlier that in addition to generating confusion regarding the rightness or wrongness of sex acts, false conceptual analyses of the means–end form cause confusion about the value of sex to the individual. My account recognizes the satisfaction of desire and the pleasure this brings as the central psychological function of the sex act for the individual. Sex affords us a paradigm of pleasure, but not a cornerstone of value. For most of us it is not only a needed outlet for desire but also the most enjoyable form of recreation we know. Its value is nevertheless easily mistaken by being confused with that of love, when it is taken as essentially an expression of that emotion. Although intense, the pleasures of sex are brief and repetitive rather than cumulative. They give value to the specific acts which generate them, but not the lasting kind of value which enhances one's whole life. The briefness of these pleasures contributes to their intensity (or perhaps their intensity makes them necessarily brief), but it also relegates them to the periphery of most rational plans for the good life.

By contrast, love typically develops over a long term relation; while its pleasures may be less intense and physical, they are of more cumulative value. The importance of love to the individual may well be central in a rational system of value. And it has perhaps an even deeper moral significance relating to the identification with the interests of another person, which broadens one's possible relationships with others as well. Marriage is again important in preserving this relation between adults and children, which seems as important to the adults as it is to the children in broadening concerns which have a tendency to become selfish. Sexual desire, by contrast, is desire for another which is nevertheless essentially self-regarding. Sexual pleasure is certainly a good for the individual, and for many it may be necessary in order for them to function in a reasonably cheerful way. But it bears little relation to those other values just discussed, to which some analyses falsely suggest a conceptual connection. . . .

---

[1]Even Bertrand Russell, whose writing in this area was a model of rationality, at least for its period, tends to make this identification and to condemn plain sex in the absence of love: "sex intercourse apart from love has little value, and is to be regarded primarily as experimentation with a view to love." *Marriage and Morals* (New York: Bantam, 1959), p. 87.

ROGER SCRUTON

Sexual Morality

The weakness of the Kantian position lies in its attribution of a "motivating force" to reason—in its denial of Hume's principle that reason alone cannot be a motive to action. The Aristotelian position involves no commitment to the idea of a "pure practical reason." It recognises that practical reasoning concludes in action only because it begins in desire. The "practical syllogism" has a practical premise, and to the agent with evil desires no reason can be given that will, by its sheer force as a reason, suffice to make him good.

It might seem that, from such a realistic premise concerning the nature of practical reasoning, only moral subjectivism could emerge. For the premise suggests that practical reasoning does not change, but merely realises, the desires of the agent, and hence that it can concern itself only with means and never with ends. And indeed, from the immediate first-person point of view—the point of view of my present motives—such a conclusion is unavoidable. However, there is also the long-term point of view, and it is the distinctive feature of Aristotelian ethics that it makes this point of view central to its argument. It develops a kind of third-person reasoning which, while containing its own incontrovertible claim to validity, may also be applied by each agent to himself, so becoming practical, by transforming his desires.

The model for this reasoning is the practice of moral education. In educating a child I am concerned, not merely with what he does, but with what he feels and with his emerging character. Feeling and character, which provide his motives, determine what he will do. In moulding them, I mould his moral nature. I know that my child's desires will, if he is rational, determine his behaviour—for I know the truth enshrined in Aristotle's practical syllogism, according to which rational action is the realisation of desire. Moreover, I know that my child has (in normal circumstances) reason to be rational, for no other gift can compensate for the lack of this one. Hence I must, if I care for him, devote myself to the education both of his reason and of his desires.

Of course, given his present childish nature, I cannot easily persuade him to change in the preferred direction: only his love and my authority may elicit in him the disposition to do willingly that which is in his long-term interests. However, unlike him, I take an overview of his future life. I see that there is reason for him to have some desires rather than others, even if he cannot at present appreciate this fact. What, then, will guide me in his moral education?

We must note that the practical syllogism, which arises from the concrete circumstances of action, cannot be anticipated. I cannot solve now the specific practical problems that will encumber my child's existence. Nevertheless, I can anticipate, in a general way, the difficulties which any rational being must encounter on life's way, and I can consider the character which might generate fulfilment. To engage in such reflections is to invoke an idea of happiness, or *eudaimonia*. . . .

I suggest that Aristotle's invocation of happiness, as the final end of human conduct, is essentially correct. Happiness is the single final answer to the question "why do that?" the answer which survives the conflict with every rival interest or desire. In referring to happiness we refer, not to the satisfaction of impulses, but to the fulfilment of the person. We all have reason to want this fulfilment, and we want it reasonably, whatever our other desires, and whatever our circumstances. In moral education this alone is certain: that the child ought to be happy, and hence that whatever disposition is essential to happiness is a disposition that he has reason to acquire.

But what is happiness? Kant dismissed the idea as empty: happiness, he argued, simply stands for the generality of human desires: it means different things for different people, and provides no coherent motive of its own. Following Aristotle, however, I shall propose an idea of happiness as a kind of "flourishing." A gardener who tends a plant has reason to see that it flourishes. The unflourishing plant is one that tends towards non-existence. Flourishing pertains to the *being* of the plant, and to care for the plant is to care for its flourishing. . . .

It is clear that, if I have reason to do anything, I have reason to be successful in what I do. But success is not merely a matter of choosing the right means to my ends; it is also a matter of rightly choosing the end itself. Consequently, there is a distinction between virtue (which involves the disposition to make appropriate choices of ends) and skill (which involves mastery of the means whereby to accomplish them). This is the origin of Aristotle's distinction between *aretē* and *technē*.

Virtue is the disposition to choose those courses of action which contribute to my happiness: which cause me to flourish as a rational being. In educating my child I am educating his habits, and it is clear therefore that I shall always have reason to inculcate a habit of virtue, not for my sake, but for his own. At least, that is provided we accept that my main concern is what matters for *him*, in the future to which *he* is destined. At the same time, I do not think of virtue as a *means* only: it consists in the right choice of end. . . .

The thought of a person is self-conscious thought, expressing a rational conception of the world and of his place within it; his action is self-conscious action, stemming from practical reason. The "self" is a name for these distinctive thoughts and feelings, and in what follows I shall refer to "self-fulfilment," in order to denote the fulfilment of the rational being—the being with a first-person perspective. . . .

Derek Parfit has argued that personal identity ought not to matter in our practical reasoning: what matters, or ought to matter, he believes, is something else, which has been confused with identity on account of a metaphysical illusion. In what follows I shall be arguing that, from the first-person point of view, it is *precisely* identity that matters, for it is by virtue of a self-identifying thought that my practical reason engages with the future at all. This thought is, perhaps, an illusion. But so, as we have seen, is much else that informs our first-person view of ourselves.

I begin by introducing the "minimal self." This is a creature who has command of language, and in particular of the first-person case, sufficient to obey the rules of self-attribution concerning his present mental states. The difference between animality and selfhood is one of kind, and admits of no degrees: either a creature grasps self-attribution or he does not, and the conditions on grasping it are fairly stringent. However, the transition—which can be described, in Hegelian idiom, as the transition from object to subject—is built up of certain stages or "moments." That which begins in self-attribution leads towards intention and responsibility—towards the "maximal self" who projects himself forward and backward in time, and lives according to the logic of a human biography.

As we have seen, the minimal self is already the repository of authority. His voice is not the observer but the expression of his present mental state. He was a unique and irreplaceable authority in all matters relating to his own mental condition. Hence he may reveal himself to others, and also hide himself from them. He can pretend, just as he can be honest. He can also be argued with and learned from. All this creates . . . the foundation of interpersonal existence, by providing distinct responses and reactions, the subject and object of which are creatures with the first-person point of view.

Let us consider, now, the various attitudes that the minimal self may have towards his past and future. It is clear that, without a conception of my identity through time, many of my mental states would be strictly unintelligible to me. I cannot attribute to myself beliefs of a theoretical character, or moral beliefs, without also supposing that I endure long enough for such beliefs to make a difference in my behaviour. An instantaneous monad, who is no sooner born into the world than taken from it, has no time for serious belief, and to the extent that we see ourselves as theoretical and enquiring creatures, to that extent must we inevitably think of ourselves as enduring in time. The minimal self exists fully in the present, therefore, only by also asserting his identity over time. He attributes to himself both a past and a future, and although he may be mistaken in this attribution (as he may perhaps be mistaken in any assertion of identity over time) it is part of his nature to make it. On the basis of this attribution of self-identity, the present self may take up a variety of attitudes towards both past and future.

Consider, for example, remorse. If I say sincerely, "I am remorseful over what happened," not only do I assert my identity with a preceding person, I also incorporate the actions and omissions of that person into my own present accountability towards the world—my present sense of my debts and liabilities. The case should be contrasted with the sincere assertion "I regret what happened," which is more like a statement of wish, and makes no essential reference either to my own previous existence or to my present responsibility. . . .

However, just as a self-conscious being may have distinct attitudes to his past, so too may he have distinct attitudes to his own future. His outlook on the future ranges between two contrasting poles—which we may name, following Hampshire's seminal discussion, predicting and deciding. He may see himself in the future merely as the vehicle of impersonal forces which act through him but not from him, or else as an irreplaceable agent, the originator of actions of his own. As many philosophers have argued, intention involves a kind of certainty about one's future. In deciding, I lay claim now to a future event, and to the extent that I am sincere I must be certain that it will occur. An expression of the form "I intend to do it but I do not know if I will" cannot be sincere—unless it amounts to no more than the admission that I may change my mind.

Imagine now someone who never made decisions: the extreme case of the predictive person. We could never affect what he will do simply by arguing with him: no change of his view of the world will introduce a decision to alter it, and therefore nothing we say to him can give us grounds for thinking that he will do one thing rather than another. (After all, his *predictions* are no better than ours.) We cannot treat him as having any particular authority concerning his future conduct, nor will our desire to influence his conduct be furthered by consulting his expressed interests. If we are to engage with his future at all, it is only by steering him towards it independently of any expressed plan, intention, or resolve. Just as he sees himself in the future as the helpless vehicle of impersonal forces, so must we *treat* him as such: as a means whereby those forces seek expression and not as an "end in himself." So if he sees himself as an object, so too must we. (There begins a proof of a fundamental Hegelian and Marxian contention, that alienation from self is alienation from other.)

The example shows us how the self-conception of the minimal self may be enriched. In acquiring a decisive attitude towards his own future, as in acquiring a responsible attitude to his own past, the minimal self ceases to be merely a vehicle for the transmission of impersonal forces and becomes instead an active subject, whose relation to the world is one of freedom. He now *belongs* where he was previously an observer. However, there is more to the transition than the passage from predicting to deciding. He could make that transition merely by a few decisions, about matters of no importance. This alone will not amount to that full sense of the responsibility for his own future which is required of the mature rational agent. The truly decisive person also reasons about the future, and takes upon himself in the present the task of his remaining life.

How do we characterise this fully responsible being? One suggestion is that we suppose him, not merely to *have* desires, but also to stand in a critical relation towards them. We suppose him to engage in the reasoned criticism of desires, selecting those whose influence he would wish to prevail. Some philosophers have considered, therefore, that we should characterise the rational agent as the possessor of "second-order" desires. He desires some things, and desires to desire others. But again, it would be odd, and incomplete, if this were seen by the agent himself as simply another personal peculiarity, that he not only desired health, say, but also desired to desire it. Why should this new desire suffice to change his image of himself from that of a thing acted on to that of an agent who takes full responsibility for his future life?

What is required, I believe, is not a new order of desire, but a new conception of the object of desire—a conception that attributes to the object a specific importance, over and above the fact of being desired. In short, the subject should not only desire the object, but *see it as desirable.* He must attribute to it a *claim* over his desire, so that it becomes *right* to desire it. He must perceive the object of desire under the aspect not of desire only, but also of value. . . .

Many philosophers have argued that values are not objective properties of things, but subjective colourings, or (more usually) human artefacts. Such arguments are irrelevant to our purpose. They also tend to be based on peculiar assumptions: nobody ever thought that because a temple is an artefact it is therefore unreal. It does not matter that values are artefacts: what matters is that something vital to self-consciousness is omitted by those who fail to construct them. Whether there are rules (as Kant supposed) which constrain us to construct our values according to a certain pattern is a philosophical question that we may be unable to answer. But, to the extent that we have reason to pursue self-consciousness in its fullest form—and so enlarge the realms of subjectivity beyond those occupied by the minimal self—to that extent do we have reason to manufacture values. A world without values is one in which all activity has an ending, but no activity has an end. Consider the difference between the man who desires *x*, which he values, and the man who just desires *x*. The latter might satisfy his desire with no sense of improving his lot. He had a desire; now he has abolished it, and, if he is lucky, quietus falls. The first man, however, had a desire and, in abolishing it, obtains something of value—something which ministers to his sense of well-being. His lot has significantly improved; had it not improved, this would signify a change in his values.

To recognise the object of desire as desirable is to attribute to one's desire a new role in deliberation. In pursuing what he holds to be desirable, the agent is engaged, not merely in the calculation of means, but also in the rational choice of ends. It is this kind of deliberation that enables the present self to incorporate its own future into its practical reasoning, so as to pursue, not merely that which is presently desired, but also that which is conducive to satisfaction.

If values are artefacts, it is from the stuff of interpersonal emotion that they are constructed. Consider the emotion of pride. Someone who, upon obtaining the object of desire, feels proud of it, shows thereby that he regards it as desirable. The characteristic thought of such a person is that to obtain this object casts *credit* on himself. This thought grows from the personal interaction that leads us constantly to compare the actions of those around us with our own. In pride, as in remorse, the self is viewed from outside, as one among many social objects, defined in part by his relation to his kind. Implicit in these emotions is the idea of a rational community—the Kantian "Kingdom of Ends" to which all rational beings by nature belong.

It thus seems plausible to suppose that the minimal self advances towards responsibility for its past and future only by also enlarging its perspective, so as to confront itself as the object of interpersonal attitudes, one member of the class of beings who may be praised, blamed, and criticised. Let us now pose the Aristotelian question:

would it be better for my child to be a minimal or an "enlarged" self? Would it be better for him, overall, to avoid the sense of responsibility that causes him to answer now for his past and future, or to acquire it? The answer, I believe, is evident. In advance of any knowledge of the particular circumstances of his future, I must surely wish to inculcate in him the faculty of choice, and the outlook on himself that permits him, not only to desire things, but also to find fulfilment in obtaining them. For without such gifts my child cannot conceivably flourish according to his nature—which is that of a rational person.

This means, however, that I must wish also to prepare my child for interpersonal relations, and to inculcate in him the dispositions—pride, remorse, admiration, contempt—which are involved in constructing a concept of the desirable. The "maximal" self must not only acquire this concept, but also give it the place in practical reasoning necessary to secure an active attachment to his past and his future. Finally, he must learn to see as desirable only that which, in general human conditions, is the occasion of fulfilment. When he has learned that, he has learned virtue.

That brief sketch raises, of course, as many questions as it answers. But it suffices to suggest a way out of the impasse presented by Kantian ethics: a way of circumventing the paradoxes of the first-person case, while retaining the fundamental Kantian intuition that practical reason is built upon a concept of the self and its freedom. The Aristotelian strategy presents us with a view upon the self from a point of view outside it, and then derives conclusions—which, in principle at least, are of universal validity—concerning the well-being of that which it observes. This strategy provides us, I believe, with an important insight into the foundations of morality. It implies that the first-person perspective is fulfiled only when the world is seen in terms of value. On the Aristotelian principle, that *to telos phuseis estin* (the end is the essence), we might say that morality belongs to the *nature* of the self. The argument also implies that the building of the first-person perspective comes about precisely through the exercise of interpersonal responses—through a developing third-person perspective on the attitudes of others, which leads us to perceive both them and ourselves as belonging to a single moral kind, distinguished by the "self-hood" which makes this perception available. The building of the self is the building of a social context, in which the self takes its place beside the other, as object and subject of the universal attitudes of praise and blame—the attitudes which encapsulate the reality of "respect for persons." Thus the Aristotelian perspective that led us to seek for the grounds of morality in the third-person perspective of the moral educator leads us back to the Kantian subject, as the locus of moral existence.

We must now attempt to apply the Aristotelian strategy . . . and ask whether there is such a thing as sexual virtue, and, if so, what is it, and how is it acquired? Clearly, sexual desire, which is an interpersonal attitude with the most far-reaching consequences for those who are joined by it, cannot be morally neutral. On the contrary, it is in the experience of sexual desire that we are most vividly conscious of the distinction between virtuous and vicious impulses, and most vividly aware that, in the choice between them, our happiness is at stake.

The Aristotelian strategy enjoins us to ignore the actual conditions of any particular person's life, and to look only at the permanent features of human nature. We know that people feel sexual desire; that they feel erotic love, which may grow from desire; that they may avoid both these feelings, by dissipation or self-restraint. Is there anything to be said about desire, other than that it falls within the general scope of the virtue of temperance, which enjoins us to desire only what reason approves?

The first, and most important, observation to be made is that the capacity for love in general, and for erotic love in particular, is a virtue. . . . Erotic love involves an element of mutual self-enhancement; it generates a sense of the irreplaceable value, both of the other and of the self, and of the activities which bind them. To receive and to give this love is to achieve something of incomparable value in the process of self-fulfillment. It is to gain the most powerful of all interpersonal *guarantees;* in erotic love the subject becomes conscious of the full reality of his personal existence, not only in his own eyes, but in the eyes of another. Everything that he is and values gains sustenance from his love, and every project receives a meaning beyond the moment. All that exists for us as mere hope and hypothesis—the attachment to life and to the body—achieves under the rule of *eros* the aspect of a radiant certainty. Unlike the cold glances of approval, admiration, and pride, the glance of love sees value precisely in that which is the source of anxiety and doubt: in the merely contingent, merely "empirical," existence of the flesh, the existence which we did not choose, but to which we are condemned. It is the answer to man's fallen condition— to his *Geworfenheit.*

To receive erotic love, however, a person must be able to give it: or if he cannot, the love of others will be a torment to him, seeking from him that which he cannot provide, and directing against him the fury of a disappointed right. It is therefore unquestionable that we have reason to acquire the capacity for erotic love, and, if this means bending our sexual impulses in a certain direction, that will be the direction of sexual virtue. Indeed, the argument . . . has implied that the development of the sexual impulse towards love may be impeded: there are sexual habits which are vicious, precisely in neutralizing the capacity for love. The first thing that can be said, therefore, is that we all have reason to avoid those habits and to educate our children not to possess them. . . .

It is . . . the generality of the human condition that determines the basis of sexual morality. Tragedy and loss are the rare but necessary outcomes of a process which we all have reason to undergo. (Indeed, it is part of the point of tragedy that it divorces in our imagination the right and the good from the merely prudential: that it sets the value of life against the value of mere survival.) We wish to know, in advance of any particular experience, which dispositions a person must have if he is successfully to express himself in sexual desire and to be fulfiled in his sexual endeavours. Love is the fulfilment of desire, and therefore love is its *telos.* A life of celibacy may also be fulfiled; but, assuming the general truth that most of us have a powerful, and perhaps overwhelming, urge to make love, it is in our interests to ensure that love—and not some other thing—is made.

Love, I have argued, is prone to jealousy, and the object of jealousy is defined by the thought of the beloved's desire. Because jealousy is one of the greatest psychical catastrophes, involving the possible ruin of both partners, a morality based in the need for erotic love must forestall and eliminate jealousy. It is in the deepest human interest, therefore, that we form the habit of fidelity. This habit is natural and normal; but it is also easily broken, and the temptation to break it is contained in desire itself—in the element of generality which tempts us always to experiment, to verify, to detach ourselves from that which is too familiar in the interest of excitement and risk. Virtuous desire is faithful; but virtuous desire is also an artefact, made possible by a process of moral education which we do not, in truth, understand in its complexity.

If that observation is correct, a whole section of traditional sexual morality must be upheld. The fulfilment of sexual desire defines the nature of desire: *to telos phuseis estin.* And the nature of desire gives us our standard of normality. There are enormous varieties of human sexual conduct, and of "common-sense" morality: some societies permit or encourage polygamy, others look with indifference upon premarital intercourse, or regard marriage itself as no more than an episode in a relation that pre-exists and perhaps survives it. But no society, and no "common-sense" morality—not even, it seems, the morality of Samoa—looks with favour upon promiscuity or infidelity, unless influenced by a doctrine of "emancipation" or "liberation" which is dependent for its sense upon the very conventions which it defies. Whatever the institutional forms of human sexual union, and whatever the range of permitted partners, sexual desire is itself inherently "nuptial": it involves concentration upon the embodied existence of the other, leading through tenderness to the "vow" of erotic love. It is a telling observation that the civilisation which has most tolerated the institution of polygamy—the Islamic—has also, in its erotic literature, produced what are perhaps the intensest and most poignant celebrations of monogamous love, precisely through the attempt to capture, not the institution of marriage, but the human datum of desire.

The nuptiality of desire suggests, in its turn, a natural history of desire: a principle of development which defines the "normal course" of sexual education. "Sexual maturity" involves incorporating the sexual impulse into the personality, and so making sexual desire into an expression of the subject himself, even though it is, in the heat of action, a force which also overcomes him. If the Aristotelian approach to these things is as plausible as I think it is, the virtuous habit will also have the character of a "mean": it will involve the disposition to desire what is desirable, despite the competing impulses of animal lust (in which the intentionality of desire may be demolished) and timorous frigidity (in which the sexual impulse is impeded altogether). Education is directed towards the special kind of temperance which shows itself, sometimes as chastity, sometimes as fidelity, sometimes as passionate desire, according to the "right judgment" of the subject. In wanting what is judged to be desirable, the virtuous person wants what may also be loved, and what may therefore be obtained without hurt or humiliation.

Virtue is a matter of degree, rarely attained in its completion, but always admired. Because traditional sexual education has pursued sexual virtue, it is worthwhile summarising its most important features, in order to see the power of the idea that underlies and justifies it.

The most important feature of traditional sexual education is summarised in anthropological language as the "ethic of pollution and taboo." The child was taught to regard his body as sacred, and as subject to pollution by misperception or misuse.

The sense of pollution is by no means a trivial side-effect of the "bad sexual encounter": it may involve a penetrating disgust, at oneself, one's body, and one's situation, such as is experienced by the victim of rape. Those sentiments—which arise from our "fear of the obscene"—express the tension contained within the experience of embodiment. At any moment we can become "mere body," the self driven from its incarnation, and its habitation ransacked. The most important root idea of personal morality is that I am *in* my body, not (to borrow Descartes' image) as a pilot in a ship, but as an incarnate self. My body is identical with me, and sexual purity is the precious guarantee of this.

Sexual purity does not forbid desire: it simply ensures the status of desire as an interpersonal feeling. The child who learns "dirty habits" detaches his sex from himself, sets it outside himself as something curious and alien. His fascinated enslavement to the body is also a withering of desire, a scattering of erotic energy, and a loss of union with the other. Sexual purity sustains the *subject* of desire, making him present as a self in the very act which overcomes him. . . .

The purely human redemption which is offered to us in love is dependent, in the last analysis, upon public recognition of the value of chastity, and of the sacrilege involved in a sexual impulse that wanders free from the controlling impulse of respect. The "pollution" of the prostitute is not that she gives herself for money, but that she gives herself to those whom she hates or despises. This is the "wound" of unchastity, which cannot be healed in solitude by the one who suffers it, but only by his acceptance into a social order which confines the sexual impulse to the realm of intimate relations. The chaste person sustains the ideal of sexual innocence, by giving honourable form to chastity as a way of life. Through his example, it becomes not foolish but admirable to ignore the promptings of a desire that brings no intimacy or fulfilment. Chastity is not a private policy, followed by one individual alone for the sake of his peace of mind. It has a wider and more generous significance: it attempts to draw others into complicity, and to sustain a social order that confines the sexual impulse to the personal sphere. . . .

The cult of innocence is an attempt to *generate* rational conduct, by incorporating the sexual impulse into the self-activity of the subject. It is an attempt to impede the impulse, until such a time as it may attach itself to the interpersonal project that leads to its fulfilment: the project of union with another person, who is wanted not merely for his body, but for the person who *is* this body. Innocence is the disposition to avoid sexual encounter, except with the person whom one may fully desire. Children who have lost their innocence have acquired the habit of gratification through the body alone, in a state of partial or truncated desire. Their gratification is detached from the conditions of personal fulfilment and wanders from object to object with no settled tendency to attach itself to any, pursued all the while by a sense of the body's obscene dominion. "Debauching of the innocent" was traditionally regarded as a most serious offence, and one that offered genuine *harm* to the victim. The harm in question was not physical, but moral: the undermining of the process which prepares the child to enter the world of *eros*. (Thus Nabokov's Lolita, who passes with such rapidity from childish provocativeness to a knowing interest in the sexual act, finds, in the end, a marriage devoid of passion, and dies without knowledge of desire.)

The personal and the sexual can become divorced in many ways. The task of sexual morality is to unite them, to sustain thereby the intentionality of desire, and to prepare the individual for erotic love. Sexual morality is the morality of embodiment: the posture which strives to unite us with our bodies, precisely in those situations when our bodies are foremost in our thoughts. Without such a morality the human world is subject to a dangerous divide, a gulf between self and body, at the verge of which all our attempts at personal union falter and withdraw. Hence the prime focus of sexual morality is not the attitude to others, but the attitude to one's own body and its uses. Its aim is to safeguard the integrity of our embodiment. Only on that condition, it is thought, can we inculcate either innocence in the young or fidelity in the adult. Such habits are, however, only one part of sexual virtue. Traditional morality has combined its praise of them with a condemnation of other things—in particular of the habits of lust and perversion. And it is not hard to find the reason for these condemnations.

Perversion consists precisely in a diverting of sexual impulse from its interpersonal goal, or towards some act that is intrinsically destructive of personal relations and of the values that we find in them. The "dissolution" of the flesh, which the Marquis de Sade regarded as so important an element in the sexual aim, is in fact the dissolution of the soul; the perversions described by de Sade are not so much attempts to destroy the flesh of the victim as to rid his flesh of its personal meaning, to wring out, with the blood, the rival perspective. That is true in one way or another of all perversion, which can be simply described as the habit of finding a sexual release that avoids or abolishes the *other*, obliterating his embodiment with the obscene perception of his body. Perversion is narcissistic, often solipsistic, involving strategies of replacement which are intrinsically destructive of personal feeling. Perversion therefore prepares us for a life without personal fulfilment, in which no human relation achieves foundation in the acceptance of the other, as this acceptance is provided by desire.

Lust may be defined as genuine sexual desire, from which the goal of erotic love has been excluded, and in which whatever tends towards that goal—tenderness, intimacy, fidelity, dependence—is curtailed or obstructed. There need be nothing perverted in this. . . . Nevertheless, the traditional condemnation of lust is far from arbitrary, and the associated contrast between lust and love far from a matter of convention. Lust is also a habit, involving the disposition to give way to desire, without regard to any personal relation with the object. (Thus perversions are all forms of lust even though lust is not in itself a perversion.) Naturally, we all feel the promptings of lust, but the rapidity with which sexual acts become sexual habits, and the catastrophic effect of a sexual act which cannot be remembered without shame or humiliation, give us strong reasons to resist them . . .

In addition to the condemnation of lust and perversion, however, some part of traditional sexual education can be seen as a kind of sustained war against fantasy. It is undeniable that fantasy can play an important part in all our sexual doings, and even the most passionate and faithful lover may, in the act of love, rehearse to himself other scenes of sexual abandon than the one in which he is engaged. Nevertheless, there is truth in the contrast (familiar, in one version, from the writings of Freud) between fantasy and reality, and in the sense that the first is in some way destructive of the second.

Fantasy replaces the real, resistant, objective world with a pliant substitute—and that, indeed, is its purpose. Life in the actual world is difficult and embarrassing. Most of all it is difficult and embarrassing in our confrontation with other people, who, by their very existence, make demands that we may be unable or unwilling to meet. It requires a great force, such as the force of sexual desire, to overcome the embarrassment and self-protection that shield us from the most intimate encounters. It is tempting to take refuge in substitutes, which neither embarrass us nor resist the impulse of our spontaneous cravings. The habit grows, in masturbation, of creating a compliant world of desire, in which unreal objects become the focus of real emotions, and the emotions themselves are rendered incompetent to participate in the building of personal relations. The fantasy blocks the passage to reality, which becomes inaccessible to the will. . . .

ADRIENNE RICH

Compulsory Heterosexuality and Lesbian Existence

. . . Feminist theory can no longer afford merely to voice a toleration of "lesbianism" as an "alternative life style" or make token allusion to lesbians. A feminist critique of compulsory heterosexual orientation for women is long overdue. In this exploratory paper, I shall try to show why. . . . [1]

II

If women are the earliest sources of emotional caring and physical nurture for both female and male children, it would seem logical, from a feminist perspective at least, to pose the following questions: whether the search for love and tenderness in both sexes does not originally lead toward women; *why in fact women would ever redirect that search;* why species survival, the means of impregnation, and emotional/erotic relationships should ever have become so rigidly identified with each other; and why such violent strictures should be found necessary to enforce women's total emotional, erotic loyalty and subservience to men. I doubt that enough feminist scholars and theorists have taken the pains to acknowledge the societal forces which wrench woman's emotional and erotic energies away from themselves and other women and from woman-identified values. These forces, as I shall try to show, range from literal physical enslavement to the disguising and distorting of possible options.

I do not assume that mothering by women is a "sufficient cause" of lesbian existence. But the issue of mothering by women has been much in the air of late, usually accompanied by the view that increased parenting by men would minimize antagonism between the sexes and equalize the sexual imbalance of power of males over females. These discussions are carried on without reference to compulsory heterosexuality as a phenomenon, let alone as an ideology. I do not wish to psychologize here, but rather to identify sources of male power. I believe large numbers of men could, in fact, undertake child care on a large scale without radically altering the balance of male power in a male-identified society.

In her essay "The Origin of the Family," Kathleen Gough lists eight characteristics of male power in archaic and contemporary societies which I would like to use as a framework: "men's ability to deny women sexuality or to force it upon them; to command or exploit their labor to control their produce; to control or rob them of their children; to confine them physically and prevent their movement; to use them as objects in male transactions; to cramp their creativeness; or to withhold from them large areas of the society's knowledge and cultural attainments."[2] (Gough does not perceive these power characteristics as specifically enforcing heterosexuality, only as producing sexual inequality.) Below, Gough's words appear in italics; the elaboration of each of her categories, in brackets, is my own.

Characteristics of male power include *the power of men*

1. *to deny women* [their own] *sexuality*—[by means of clitoridectomy and infibulation; chastity belts; punishment, including death, for female adultery; punishment, including death, for lesbian sexuality; psychoanalytic denial of the clitoris; strictures against masturbation; denial of maternal and postmenopausal sensuality; unnecessary hysterectomy; pseudolesbian images in the media and literature; closing of archives and destruction of documents relating to lesbian existence]

2. *or to force it* [male sexuality] *upon them*—[by means of rape (including marital rape) and wife beating; father–daughter, brother–sister incest; the socialization of women to feel that male sexual "drive" amounts to a right;[3] idealization of heterosexual romance in art, literature, the media, advertising, etc.; child marriage; arranged marriage; prostitution; the harem; psychoanalytic doctrines of frigidity and vaginal orgasm; pornographic depictions of women responding pleasurably to sexual violence and humiliation (a subliminal message being that sadistic heterosexuality is more "normal" than sensuality between women)]

3. *to command or exploit their labor to control their produce*—[by means of the institutions of marriage and motherhood as unpaid production; the horizontal segregation of women in paid employment; the decoy of the upwardly mobile token woman; male control of abortion, contraception, sterilization, and child-birth; pimping; female infanticide, which robs mothers of daughters and contributes to generalized devaluation of women]

4. *to control or rob them of their children*—[by means of father right and "legal kidnaping";[4] enforced sterilization; systematized infanticide; seizure of children from lesbian mothers by the courts; the malpractice of male obstetrics; use of the mother as "token torturer"[5] in genital mutilation or in binding the daughter's feet (or mind) to fit her for marriage]

5. *to confine them physically and prevent their movement*—[by means of rape as terrorism, keeping women off the streets; purdah; foot binding; atrophying of women's athletic capabilities; high heels and "feminine" dress codes in fashion; the veil; sexual harassment on the streets; horizontal segregation of women in employment; prescriptions for "full-time" mothering at home; enforced economic dependence of wives]

6. *to use them as objects in male transactions*—[use of women as "gifts"; bride price; pimping; arranged marriage; use of women as entertainers to facilitate male deals—e.g., wife-hostess, cocktail waitress required to dress for male sexual titillation, call girls, "bunnies," geisha, *kisaeng* prostitutes, secretaries]

7. *to cramp their creativeness*—[witch persecutions as campaigns against midwives and female healers, and as pogrom against independent, "unassimilated" women;[6] definition of male pursuits as more valuable than female within any culture, so that cultural values become the embodiment of male subjectivity; restriction of female self-fulfillment to marriage and motherhood; sexual exploitation of women by male artists and teachers; the social and economic disruption of women's creative aspirations;[7] erasure of female tradition][8]

8. *to withhold from them large areas of the society's knowledge and cultural attainments*—[by means of noneducation of females; the "Great Silence" regarding women and particularly lesbian existence in history and culture;[9] sex-role tracking which deflects women from science, technology, and other "masculine" pursuits; male social/professional bonding which excludes women; discrimination against women in the professions]

These are some of the methods by which male power is manifested and maintained. Looking at the schema, what surely impresses itself is the fact that we are confronting not a simple maintenance of inequality and property possession, but a pervasive cluster of forces, ranging from physical brutality to control of consciousness, which suggests that an enormous potential counterforce is having to be restrained.

Some of the forms by which male power manifests itself are more easily recognizable as enforcing heterosexuality on women than are others. Yet each one I have listed adds to the cluster of forces within which women have been convinced that marriage and sexual orientation toward men are inevitable—even if unsatisfying or oppressive—components of their lives. The chastity belt; child marriage; erasure of lesbian existence (except as exotic and perverse) in art, literature, film; idealization of heterosexual romance and marriage—these are some fairly obvious forms of compulsion, the first two exemplifying physical force, the second two control of consciousness. While clitoridectomy has been assailed by feminists as a form of woman torture,[10] Kathleen Barry first pointed out that it is not simply a way of turning the young girl into a "marriageable" woman through brutal surgery. It intends that women in the intimate proximity of polygynous marriage will not form sexual relationships with each other, that—from a male, genital-fetishist perspective—female erotic connections, even in a sex-segregated situation, will be literally excised.[11]

The function of pornography as an influence of consciousness is a major public issue of our time, when a multibillion-dollar industry has the power to disseminate increasingly sadistic, women-degrading visual images. But even so-called soft-core pornography and advertising depict women as objects of sexual appetite devoid of emotional context, without individual meaning or personality—essentially as a sexual commodity to be consumed by males. (So-called lesbian pornography, created for the male voyeuristic eye, is equally devoid of emotional context or individual personality.) The most pernicious message relayed by pornography is that women are natural sexual prey to men and love it, that sexuality and violence are congruent, and that for women sex is essentially masochistic, humiliation pleasurable, physical abuse erotic. But along with this message comes another, not always recognized: that enforced submission and the use of cruelty, if played out in heterosexual pairing, is sexually "normal," while sensuality between women, including erotic mutuality and respect, is "queer," "sick," and either pornographic in itself or not very exciting compared with the sexuality of whips and bondage.[12] Pornography does not simply create a climate in which sex and violence are interchangeable; *it widens the range of behavior considered acceptable from men in heterosexual intercourse*—behavior which reiteratively strips women of their autonomy, dignity, and sexual potential, including the potential of loving and being loved by women in mutuality and integrity. . . .

III

I have chosen to use the terms *lesbian existence* and *lesbian continuum* because the word *lesbianism* has a clinical and limiting ring. *Lesbian existence* suggests both the fact of the historical presence of lesbians and our continuing creation of the meaning of that existence. I mean the term *lesbian continuum* to include a range—through each woman's life and throughout history—of woman-identified experience, not simply the fact that a woman has had or consciously desired genital sexual experience with another woman. If we expand it to embrace many more forms of primary intensity between and among women, including the sharing of a rich inner life, the bonding against male tyranny, the giving and receiving of practical and political support, if we can also hear it in such associations as *marriage resistance* and the "haggard" behavior identified with Mary Daly (obsolete meanings: "intractable," "willful," "wanton," and "unchaste," "a woman reluctant to yield to wooing"),[13] we begin to grasp breadths of female history and psychology which have lain out of reach as a consequence of limited, mostly clinical, definitions of *lesbianism.*

Lesbian existence comprises both the breaking of a taboo and the rejection of a compulsory way of life. It is also a direct or indirect attack on male right of access to women. But it is more than these, although we may first begin to perceive it as a form of naysaying to patriarchy, an act of resistance. It has, of course, included isolation, self-hatred, breakdown, alcoholism, suicide, and intrawoman violence; we romanticize at our peril what it means to love and act against the grain, and under heavy penalties; and lesbian existence has been lived (unlike, say, Jewish or Catholic existence) without access to any knowledge of a tradition, a continuity, a social underpinning. The destruction of records and memorabilia and letters documenting the realities of lesbian existence must be taken very seriously as a means of keeping heterosexuality compulsory for women, since what has been kept from our knowledge is joy, sensuality, courage, and community, as well as guilt, self-betrayal, and pain.[14]

Lesbians have historically been deprived of a political existence through "inclusion" as female version of male homosexuality. To equate lesbian existence with male homosexuality because each is stigmatized is to erase female reality once again. Part of the history of lesbian existence is, obviously, to be found where lesbians, lacking a coherent female community, have shared a kind of social life and common cause with homosexual men. But there are differences: women's lack of economic and cultural privilege relative to men; qualitative differences in female and male relationships—for example, the patterns of anonymous sex among male homosexuals, and the pronounced ageism in male homosexual standards of sexual attractiveness. I perceive the lesbian experience as being, like motherhood, a profoundly *female* experience, with particular oppressions, meanings, and potentialities we cannot comprehend as long as we simply bracket it with other sexually stigmatized existences. Just as the term *parenting* serves to conceal the particular and significant reality of being a parent who is actually a mother, the term *gay* may serve the purpose of blurring the very outlines we need to discern, which are of crucial value for feminism and for the freedom of women as a group.[15]

As the term *lesbian* has been held to limiting, clinical associations in its patriarchal definition, female friendship and comradeship have been set apart from the erotic, thus limiting the erotic itself. But as we deepen and broaden the range of what we define as lesbian existence, as we delineate a lesbian continuum, we begin to discover the erotic in female terms: as that which is unconfined to any single part of the body or solely to the body itself; as an energy not only diffuse but, as Audre Lorde has described it, omnipresent in "the sharing of joy, whether physical, emotional, psychic," and in the sharing of work; as the empowering joy which "makes us less willing to accept powerlessness, or those other supplied states of being which are not native to me, such as resignation, despair, self-effacement, depression, self-denial." . . .[16]

If we consider the possibility that all women—from the infant suckling at her mother's breast, to the grown woman experiencing orgasmic sensations while suckling her own child, perhaps recalling her mother's milk smell in her own, to two women, like Virginia Woolf's Chloe and Olivia, who share a laboratory,[17] to the woman dying at ninety, touched and handled by women—exist on a lesbian continuum, we can see ourselves as moving in and out of this continuum, whether we identify ourselves as lesbian or not.

We can then connect aspects of woman identification as diverse as the impudent, intimate girl friendships of 8 or 9 year olds and the banding together of those women of the 12th and 15th centuries known as Beguines who "shared houses, rented to one another, bequeathed houses to their room-mates . . . in cheap subdivided houses in the artisans' area of town," who "practiced Christian virtue on their own, dressing and living simply and not associating with men," who earned their livings as spinsters, bakers, nurses, or ran schools for young girls, and who managed— until the Church forced them to disperse—to live independent both of marriage and of conventual restrictions. . . .[18]

If we think of heterosexuality as *the* natural emotional and sensual inclination for women, lives such as these are seen as deviant, as pathological, or as emotionally and sensually deprived. Or, in more recent and permissive jargon, they are banalized as "life styles." And the work of such women, whether merely the daily work of individual or collective survival and resistance or the work of the writer, the activist, the reformer, the anthropologist, or the artist—the work of self-creation—is undervalued, or seen as the bitter fruit of "penis envy" or the sublimation of repressed eroticism or the meaningless rant of a "man-hater." But when we turn the lens of vision and consider the degree to which and the methods whereby heterosexual "preference" has actually been imposed on women, not only can we understand differently the meaning of individual lives and work, but we can begin to recognize a central fact of women's history: that women have always resisted male tyranny. A feminism of action, often though not always without a theory, has constantly re-emerged in every culture and in every period. We can then begin to study women's struggle against powerlessness, women's radical rebellion, not just in male-defined "concrete revolutionary situations"[19] but in all the situations male ideologies have not perceived as revolutionary—for example, the refusal of some women to produce children, aided at great risk by other women;[20] the refusal to produce a higher standard of living and leisure for men (Leghorn and Parker show how both are part of women's unacknowledged, unpaid, and ununionized economic contribution). We can no longer have patience with Dinnerstein's view that women have simply collaborated with men in the "sexual arrangements" of history. We begin to observe behavior, both in history and in individual biography, that has hitherto been invisible or misnamed, behavior which often constitutes, given the limits of the counterforce exerted in a given time and place, radical rebellion. And we can connect these rebellions and the necessity for them with the physical passion of woman for woman which is central to lesbian existence: the erotic sensuality which has been precisely, the most violently erased fact of female experience. . . .

---

[1]Rich's notes have been renumbered.–ed.

[2]Kathleen Gough, "The Origin of the Family," in *Toward an Anthropology of Women,* ed. Rayna [Rapp] Reiter (New York: Monthly Review Press, 1975), pp. 69-70.

[3]Kathleen Barry, *Female Sexual Slavery* (Englewood Cliffs, N.J.: Prentice-Hall, 1979), pp. 216-219.

[4]Anna Demeter, *Legal Kidnapping* (Boston: Beacon, 1977), pp. xx, 126-128.

[5]Mary Daly, *Gyn/Ecology: The Metaethics of Radical Feminism* (Boston: Beacon Press, 1978), pp. 139-141, 163-165.

[6]Barbara Ehrenreich and Deirdre English, *Witches, Midwives and Nurses: A History of Women Healers* (Old Westbury, N.Y.: Feminist Press, 1973); Andrea Dworkin, *Woman Hating* (New York: Dutton, 1974), pp. 118-154; Daly, *Gyn/Ecology,* pp. 178-222

[7]See Virginia Woolf, *A Room of One's Own* (London: Hogarth, 1929), and *Three Guineas* (New York: Harcourt Brace, [1938] 1966); Tillie Olsen, *Silences* (Boston: Delacorte, 1978); Michelle Cliff, "The Resonance of Interruption," *Chrysalis: A Magazine of Women's Culture* 8 (1979): 29-37.

[8]Mary Daly, *Beyond God the Father* (Boston: Beacon, 1973), pp. 347-351; Olsen, *Silences,* pp. 22-46.

[9]Daly, *Beyond God the Father,* p. 93.

[10]Fran P. Hosken, "The Violence of Power: Genital Mutilation of Females," *Heresies: A Feminist Journal of Art and Politics* 6 (1979): 28-35; Diana Russell and Nicole van de Van, eds., *Proceedings of the International Tribunal of Crimes against Women* (Millbrae, Calif.: Les Femmes, 1976), pp. 194-195. [A.R., 1986: See especially "Circumcision of Girls," in Nawal El Saadawi, *The Hidden Face of Eve: Women in the Arab World* (Boston: Beacon, 1982), pp. 33-43.]

[11]Barry, *Female Sexual Slavery,* pp. 163-164.

[12]The issue of "lesbian sadomasochism" needs to be examined in terms of dominant cultures' teachings about the relation of sex and violence. I believe this to be another example of the "double life" of women.

[13]Daly, *Gyn/Ecology,* p. 15.

[14]"In a hostile world in which women are not supposed to survive except in relation with and in service to men, entire communities of women were simply erased. History tends to bury what it seeks to reject" (Blanch W. Cook, " 'Women Alone Stir My Imagination': Lesbianism and the Cultural Tradition," *Signs: Journal of Women in Culture and Society* 4, no. 4 [Summer 1979]: 719-720). The Lesbian Herstory Archives in New York City is one attempt to preserve contemporary documents on lesbian existence—a project of enormous value and meaning, working against the continuing censorship and obliteration of relationships, networks, communities in other archives and elsewhere in the culture.

[15][A.R., 1986: The shared historical and spiritual "crossover" functions of lesbians and gay men in cultures past and present are traced by Judy Grahn in *Another Mother Tongue: Gay Words, Gay Worlds* (Boston: Beacon, 1984). I now think we have much to learn both from the uniquely female aspects of lesbian existence and from the complex "gay" identity we share with gay men.]

[16]Audre Lorde, "Uses of the Erotic: The Erotic as Power," in *Sister Outsider* (Trumansburg, N.Y.: Crossing Press, 1984).

[17]Woolf, *A Room of One's Own,* p. 126.

[18]Gracia Clark, "The Beguines: A Mediaeval Woman's Community," *Quest: A Feminist Quarterly* 1, no. 4 (1975): 73-80.

[19]See Rosalin Petchesky, "Dissolving the Hyphen: A Report on Marxist-Feminist Groups 1-5," in *Capitalist Patriarchy and the Case for Socialist Feminism,* ed. Zillah Eisenstein (New York: Monthly Review Press, 1979), p. 387.

[20][A.R., 1986: See Angela Davis, *Women, Race and Class* (New York: Random House, 1981), p. 102; Orlando Patterson, *Slavery and Social Death: A Comparative Study* (Cambridge: Harvard University Press, 1982), p. 133.]

MARRIAGE AND FAMILY

LIN YUTANG

On Growing Old Gracefully

The Chinese family system, as I conceive it, is largely an arrangment of particular provision for the young and the old, for since childhood and youth and old age occupy half of our life, it is important that the young and the old live a satisfactory life. It is true that the young are more helpless and can take less care of themselves, but on the other hand, they can get along better without material comforts than the old people. A child is often scarcely aware of material hardships, with the result that a poor child is often as happy as, if not happier than, a rich child. He may go barefooted, but that is a comfort, rather than a hardship to him, whereas going barefooted is often an intolerable hardship for old people. This comes from the child's greater vitality, the bounce of youth. He may have his temporary sorrows, but how easily he forgets them. He has no idea of money and no millionaire complex, as the old man has. At the worst, he collects only cigar coupons for buying a pop-gun, whereas the dowager collects Liberty Bonds. Between the fun of these two kinds of collection there is no comparison. The reason is the child is not yet intimidated by life as all grown-ups are. His personal habits are as yet unformed and he is not a slave to a particular brand of coffee, and he takes whatever comes along. He has very little racial prejudice and absolutely no religious prejudice. His thoughts and ideas have not fallen into certain ruts. Therefore, strange as it may seem, old people are even more dependent than the young because their fears are more definite and their desires are more delimited.

Something of this tenderness toward old age existed already in the primeval consciousness of the Chinese people, a feeling that I can compare only to the Western chivalry and feeling of tenderness toward women. If the early Chinese people had any chivalry, it was manifested not toward women and children, but toward the old people. That feeling of chivalry found clear expression in Mencius in some such saying as, "The people with grey hair should not be seen carrying burdens on the street," which was expressed as the final goal of a good government. Mencius also described the four classes of the world's most helpless people as: "The widows, widowers, orphans, and old people without children." Of these four classes the first two were to be taken care of by a political economy which should be so arranged that there would be no unmarried men and women. What was to be done about the orphans Mencius did not say, so far as we know, although orphanages have always existed throughout the ages, as well as pensions for old people. Every one realizes, however, that orphanages and old age pensions are poor substitutes for the home. The feeling is that the home alone can provide anything resembling a satisfactory arrangement for the old and the young. But for the young, it is to be taken for granted that not much need be said, since there is a natural paternal affection. "Water flows downwards and not upwards," the Chinese always say, and therefore the affection for parents and grandparents is something that stands more in need of being taught by culture. A natural man loves his children, but a cultured man loves his parents. In the end, the teaching of love and respect for old people became a generally accepted principle, and if we are to believe some of the writers, and desire to have the privilege of serving their parents in their old age actually became a consuming passion. The greatest regret a Chinese gentleman could have was the eternally lost opportunity of serving his old parents with medicine and soup on their deathbed, or not to be present when they died. For a high official in his fifties or sixties not to be able to invite his parents to come from their native village and stay with his family at the capital, "seeing them to bed every night and greeting them every morning," was to commit a moral sin of which he should be ashamed and for which he had constantly to offer excuses and explanations to his friends and colleagues. This regret was expressed in two lines by a man who returned too late to his home, when his parents had already died:

The tree desires repose, but the wind will not stop;
The son desires to serve, but his parents are already gone.

It is to be assumed that if man were to live this life like a poem, he would be able to look upon the sunset of his life as his happiest period, and instead of trying to postpone the much feared old age, be able actually to look forward to it, and gradually build up to it as the best and happiest period of his existence. In my efforts to compare and contrast Eastern and Western life, I have found no differences that are absolute except in this matter of the attitude towards age, which is sharp and clearcut and permits of no intermediate positions. The differences in our attitude towards sex, toward women, and toward work, play, and achievement are all relative. The relationship between husband and wife in China is not essentially different from that in the West, nor even the relationship between parent and child. Not even the ideas of individual liberty and democracy and the relationship between the people and their ruler are, after all, so very different. But in the matter of our attitude toward age, the difference is absolute, and the East and the West take exactly opposite points of view. This is clearest in the matter of asking about a person's age or telling one's own. In China, the first question a person asks the other on an official call, after asking about his name and surname is, "What is your glorious age?" If the person replies apologetically that he is 23 or 28, the other party generally comforts him by saying that he has still a glorious future, and that one day he may become old. But if the person replies that he is 35 or 38, the other party immediately exclaims with deep respect, "Good luck!"; enthusiasm grows in proportion as the gentleman is able to report a higher and higher age, and if the person is anywhere over 50, the inquirer immediately drops his voice in humility and respect. That is why all old people, if they can, should go and live in China, where even a beggar with a white beard is treated with extra kindness. People in middle age actually look forward to the time when they can celebrate their 51st birthday, and in the case of successful merchants and officials, they would celebrate even their 41st birthday with great pomp and glory. But the 51st birthday, or the half-century mark, is an occasion of rejoicing for people of all classes. The 61st is a happier and grander occasion that the 51st and the 71st is still happier and grander, while a man able to celebrate his 81st birthday is actually looked upon as one specially favored by heaven. The wearing of a beard becomes the special prerogative of those who have become grandparents, and a man doing so without the necessary qualifications, either of being a grandfather or being on the other side of 50, stands in danger of being sneered at behind his back. The result is that young men try to pass themselves off as older than they are by imitating the pose and dignity and point of view of the old people, and I have known young Chinese writers graduated from the middle schools, anywhere between 21 and 25, writing articles in the magazines to advise what "the young men ought and ought not to read," and discussing the pitfalls of youth with a fatherly condescension.

The desire to grow old and in any case to appear old is understandable when one understands the premium generally placed upon old age in China. In the first place, it is a privilege of the old people to talk, while the young must listen and hold their tongue. "A young man is supposed to have ears and no mouth," as a Chinese saying goes. Men of 20 are supposed to listen when people of thirty are talking, and these in turn are supposed to listen when men of 40 are talking. As the desire to talk and to be listened to is almost universal, it is evident that the further along one gets in years, the better chance he has to talk and to be listened to when he goes about in society. It is a game of life in which no one is favored, for everyone has a chance of becoming old in his time. Thus a father lecturing his son is obliged to stop suddenly and change his demeanor the moment the grandmother opens her mouth. Of course he wishes to be in the grandmother's place. And it is quite fair, for what right have the young to open their mouth when the old men can say, "I have crossed more bridges than you have crossed streets!" What right have the young got to talk? . . .

I have no doubt that the fact that the old men of America still insist on being so busy and active can be directly traced to individualism carried to a foolish extent. It is their pride and their love of independence and their shame of being dependent upon their children. But among the many human rights the American people have provided for in their Constitution, they have strangely forgotten about the right to be fed by their children, for it is a right and an obligation growing out of service. How can any one deny that parents who have toiled for their children in their youth, have lost many a good night's sleep when they were ill, have washed their diapers long before they could talk and have spent about a quarter of a century bringing them up and fitting them for life, have the right to be fed by them and loved and respected when they are old? Can one not forget the individual and his pride of self in a general scheme of home life in which men are justly taken care of by their parents and, having in turn taken care of their children, are also justly taken care of by the latter? The Chinese have not got the sense of individual independence because the whole conception of life is based upon mutual help within the home; hence there is no shame attached to the circumstance of one's being served by his children in the sunset of one's life. Rather it is considered good luck to have children who can take care of one. One lives for nothing else in China.

In the West, the old people efface themselves and prefer to live alone in some hotel with a restaurant on the ground floor, out of consideration for their children and an entirely unselfish desire not to interfere in their home life. But the old people *have* the right to interfere, and if interference is unpleasant, it is nevertheless natural, for all life, particularly the domestic life, is a lesson in restraint. Parents interfere with their children anyway when they are young, and the logic of non-interference is already seen in the results of the Behaviorists, who think that all children should be taken away from their parents. If one cannot tolerate one's own parents when they are old and comparatively helpless, parents who have done so much for us, whom else can one tolerate in the home? One has to learn self-restraint anyway, or even marriage will go on the rocks. And how can the personal service and devotion and adoration of loving children ever be replaced by the best hotel waiters?

The Chinese idea supporting this personal service to old parents is expressly defended on the sole ground of gratitude. The debts to one's friends may be numbered, but the debts to one's parents are beyond number. Again and again, Chinese essays on filial piety mention the fact of washing diapers, which takes on significance when one becomes a parent himself. In return, therefore, is it not right that in their old age, the parents should be served with the best food and have their favorite dishes placed before them? The duties of a son serving his parents are pretty hard, but it is sacrilege to make a comparison between nursing one's own parents and nursing a stranger in a hospital. For instance, the following are some of the duties of the junior at home, as prescribed by T'u Hsishih and incorporated in a book of moral instruction very popular as a text in the old schools:

> In the summer months, one should, while attending to his parents, stand by their side and fan them, to drive away the heat and the flies and mosquitoes. In winter, he should see that the bed quilts are warm enough and the stove fire is hot enough, and see that it is just right by attending to it constantly. He should also see if there are holes or crevices in the doors and windows, that there may be no draft, to the end that his parents are comfortable and happy.
>
> A child above ten should get up before his parents in the morning, and after the toilet go to their bed and ask if they have had a good night. If his parents have already gotten up, he should first curtsy to them before inquiring after their health, and should retire with another curtsy after the question. Before going to bed at night, he should prepare the bed, when the parents are going to sleep, and stand by until he sees that they have fallen off to sleep and then pull down the bed curtain and retire himself.

Who, therefore, wouldn't want to be an old man or an old father or grandfather in China?

This sort of thing is being very much laughed at by the proletarian writers of China as "feudalistic," but there is a charm to it which makes any old gentleman inland cling to it and think that modern China is going to the dogs. The important point is that *every man grows old in time,* if he lives long enough, as he certainly desires to. If one forgets this foolish individualism which seems to assume that an individual can exist in the abstract and be literally independent, one must admit that we must so plan our pattern of life that the golden period lies ahead in old age and not behind us in youth and innocence. For if we take the reverse attitude, we are committed without our knowing to a race with the merciless course of time, forever afraid of what lies ahead of us—a race, it is hardly necessary to point out, which is quite hopeless and in which we are eventually all defeated. No one can really stop growing old; he can only cheat himself by not admitting that he is growing old. And since there is no use fighting against nature, one might just as well grow old gracefully. The symphony of life should end with a grand finale of peace and serenity and material comfort and spiritual contentment, and not with the crash of a broken drum or cracked cymbals.

FRANCIS HUTCHESON

Monogamy

CHAP. I: CONCERNING THE ADVENTITIOUS STATES OR PERMANENT RELATIONS: AND FIRST MARRIAGE

BOOK III.

II

The first relation in order of nature is marriage. The several tribes of animals must soon have been extinct if nature had not providently implanted in them all the instinct and power of propagation. . . . No part of nature displays the goodness and wisdom of its author more fully, than the contrivance of the several instincts and passions in mankind subservient to this grand purpose. A careful attention to the frame of our nature in this respect, will clearly show our duties in this relation of marriage.

We have all attained to the knowledge of what is intended by nature in this instinct of propagation, before those years in which it arises: and a natural modesty or shame generally restrains us from gratifying it for some time further. We must also have observed that a long series of careful and troublesome attendance is absolutely necessary for preserving and educating the offspring; and that for this purpose nature has implanted that tenderest and most lasting parental affection in both parents, as their joint assistance is highly necessary. As this affection sweetens this labour to both, so it shows the strong obligation upon both to bear it. And thus all such as regard the voice of nature, and the obligation it imposes, or have any sense of humanity and virtue, must see that, if they gratify this inclination to procreate offspring, they must, both by sense of duty and by a strong affection toward the same objects, be united in intention and in a long course of labour and common care with the partner they choose for procreation. This joint counsel, care, and labour, can scarce be tolerable without a mutual affection and esteem between the parents; and to create this, we find that nature has wisely formed us in such a manner, that in all those who are under the restraints of the natural modesty, and of any sense of virtue, the inclination to procreate is excited, or at least generally regulated in its choice of a partner, by many delicate sentiments, and finer passions of the heart of the sweetest kind. The sense of beauty prepossesses in favour of a moral character, or acquaintance gives better assurance of it. The esteem of virtue and wisdom, the desire and love of innocence of manners, complacence, confidence, and the tenderest good-will, are the natural incitements and concomitants of the amorous desire; and almost obscure the brutal impulse toward the sensual gratification, which might be had with persons of any character. As we thus previously know the natural design of this impulse, and the obligations toward offspring thence to ensue, as we are endued with reason, we are obliged to restrain this impulse till we have obtained assurance of such harmony of minds as will make the long joint charge of education tolerable to both parents, and till we are in circumstances capable of supporting such offspring as may arise. . . .

This moral machinery of these instincts we find has appeared in all ages and nations, and generally prevailed; though, no doubt, vicious customs and habits can often weaken or almost extinguish many natural dispositions in some individuals. It will plainly show us almost all our obligations as to marriage and offspring, all the reasonable terms which should be stipulated in the marriage-contract, and the happy effects upon society, from following the intention of nature, and the mischiefs naturally ensuing from counteracting it, will further confirm our obligations.

III

And first, indulging the brutal impulse without entering into any social or friendly bond, without any regard to these tender and generous passions which naturally accompany this desire, beside its counteracting this beautiful contrivance of nature, must have many pernicious effects upon our bodies, our minds, and human society. To follow the brutal impulse, in opposition to the natural restraints of modesty, as early and as frequently as it appeared, would be pernicious to the bodies of the parents, as well as those of their posterity . . .

Again, unlimited indulgences in promiscuous fornication would have this effect, that the fathers would generally be uncertain about their own offspring, and have no other incitement to any cares about them than the general tie of humanity, which we know is not sufficient. They must want one of the most natural satisfactions in the knowledge and love of their offspring, and one of the chief incitements to labour and industry. The mothers, upon whom the whole burden of education would be cast, must find it intolerable. They would grow negligent, and give themselves up to brutal indulgences as well as the fathers. . . .

IV

As from the preceding observations it appears that mankind ought to be propagated by parents united in a friendly partnership for their education; we proceed to consider the reasonable terms of this partnership or contract; since 'tis plain there is a general duty incumbent on all with respect to our kind, which also is strongly recommended by our natural desires, that each one should contribute his part toward the continuance and good education of our race, unless he is ingaged in such important services to the public as are inconsistent with domestic cares, or in such circumstances that he cannot support a family. And without such just excuses it must be unnatural selfishness to decline our part of this necessary trouble.

I.

The first and most necessary article is that the fathers should have their offspring ascertained, and therefore the woman who professes to bear children to any man must give the strongest assurances that she will not at the same time cohabit with other men. The violation of this engagement is the greatest wrong imaginable, as it robs men of what is dearest to them, and the end of all their worldly cares, a certain offspring. In the marriage-contract therefore this is the first article.

'Tis necessary that women from their childhood should be so educated as shall best prevent such distressing injuries. 'Tis well known that their fornication before marriage, beside the dissolute habit it may occasion, founds such an intimacy with these persons they have gratified, and subjects their characters so much to them, and causes such proneness to future indulgences, or takes away their power of resisting their solicitations, that one is not well secured in having his own genuine posterity by marrying women of such conduct. . . .

The guilt therefore of fornication on the part of the man must also be very great, as he for a mean sensual gratification exposes his fellow-creature to a state of infamy, ruins the natural modesty and ingenuity of her mind, and makes her unworthy of that conjugal love and confidence upon which the greatest satisfaction of her life depends, nor can he obtain it but by falsehood and dissimulation, in which she cannot be assured of success.

We are all sensible how grievous this injury is, whether done by violence or fraudulent solicitations, to a sister or child of our own; the guilt is equal when others suffer by it. It must therefore be incumbent on all who have the charge of educating the young of either sex, to habituate them as much as possible to all modesty in speech and action, and restrain every contrary appearance. . . .

V

The second essential article in the marriage-contract, is that the husband should confine himself to one wife. 'Tis true the injury by the husband's infidelity is not so great as that by the wife's; he cannot deceive her by imposing on her a spurious brood. But in all other respects and moral turpitude is the same, and there are the same just reasons why a wife should demand this engagement from the husband. The natural passions of the woman as much require a friendly society, and unity of interest in the joint-education of the common offspring as those of the man.

'Tis the plainest injustice and inequality in this partnership, which all the finer sentiments of the heart declare should be an equal friendship, that a man and his offspring should be the sole objects of the woman's affections and tenderest cares, and all her world solicitudes, while his affections and cares are allowed to be divided among other women and their children, and probably wholly alienated from her. . . .

The effects upon the rising generation and upon society will be pernicious even from polygamy, as well as from the dissolute indulgences of husbands. The number of one man's children may be so great, that neither his care can suffice for their education, nor his flock or industry for their support. Many must be neglected, and all the care employed on a few favourites. As providence declares against this polygamy by preserving pretty nearly an equality in the numbers of the sexes, nay rather a surplus of the males; by allowing polygamy, many men must be excluded from all enjoyments of marriage and offspring; and thus disengaged from the natural bonds with mankind, and their natural cares, turn abandoned to all unsociable dispositions. Polygamy obstructs rather than promotes the increase of mankind. . . .

VI

As the joint charge of educating the common offspring requires that the marriage-contract should be for a long duration, since women are fruitful for one third of life and more, and generally the education of their younger children may require the joint attention of the parents for many years after the mother ceases to bear children: this bond must be intolerable without a mutual friendship. Now there can be no real friendship in a partnership merely entered into for propagation and the rearing of children, and that only for a certain term, and to expire with that term; or in one made dependent on contingencies or conditions not in the power of the parties. Both parties are allured into this contract, as into a society of love, by the tenderest sentiments of mutual esteem: the aim of all sincere friendship is perpetuity. And there can be none in contracts only for a term of years, or such as may be made void by accidents without any fault of the parties. The marriage-contract therefore must be for life, otherwise all true friendship and love must be banished, and that relation of marriage turned into a mere servile bargain for procreation and joint labour.

Again, how cruel is it on either side to divorce a person full of the fondest affection, on account of a bodily infirmity? . . .

There is such barbarity in casting off a dear friend without any demerit, that while there is no danger of a defect of offspring in a state, the allowance of divorces for this reason is not justifiable. . . .

VII

The tender sentiments and affections which engage the parties into this relation of marriage, plainly declare it to be a state of equal partnership or friendship, and not such a one wherein the one party stipulates to himself a right of governing in all domestic affairs, and the other promises subjection. Grant that there were generally superior strength both of body and mind in the males, this does not give any perfect right of government in any society. It could at best only oblige the other party to pay greater respect or honour to the superior abilities. And this superiority of the males in the endowments of mind does not at all hold universally. If the males more generally excel in fortitude, or strength or genius; there are other as amiable dispositions in which they are as generally surpassed by the females. . . .

Where husband and wife disagree in points of management; in smaller matters, this deference may be due to the one who has the greatest abilities, and manages the most important affairs, that the other should courteously yield, though against his or her private opinion. If ordinarily these superior abilities are in the husband, and his greater strength, and other circumstances of body, fit him to be employed in the more momentous affairs, it may more generally be the duty of the wife to submit. But in matters of great importance to the happiness of a family, if they cannot agree, nature suggests no other method of deciding such controversies, but a submission to common friends as arbitrators. . . .

CHAP. II: THE RIGHTS AND DUTIES OF PARENTS AND CHILDREN

The desire of posterity is natural to mankind, though in some instances it is restrained and overpowered by other desires. Such is the constitution of nature, that human offspring long continues in a very infirm state, needing the continual assistance and care of others, both on account of its weakness, and its want of all knowledge of the dangers it is surrounded with. A great deal of information and instruction, and many restraints upon their appetites, are necessary for preserving children to maturity, and fitting them for acting their part tolerably in human society. For all this indigence nature has provided a supply by implanting the tenderest affection in the breasts of the parents, exciting to and sweetening this long laborious attention. . . . Thus nature has constituted an amiable society, a permanent relation, by these lasting affections in the parents, and by the strongest motives of gratitude presented to the minds of the children to confirm the natural affection of their parts.

The intention of God in this matter, is manifest by this whole contrivance. The parental affection suggests the permanent obligation, on parents to preserve their children and consult their happiness to the utmost of their power. The weakly and ignorant state in which children long continue, suggests the parents right to an un-limited power of directing their actions for their safety and right education, and yet makes this power easy and safe to the children, by restraining all unnecessary fever-ity. The parental affection itself, when the children come to mature strength and knowledge, must procure the satisfaction of liberty to them, when they are thus capable of enjoying it, and exerting their own wisdom in the business of life; and yet will continue to them all the advantages of the counsel and other kind offices of parents. The children, on the other hand, as soon as they can know any thing of moral obligation, must see their duty of subjection and obedience in their early years, their duty of gratitude, and of making all returns they can to such tender benefactors; particularly, of complying with their inclinations, as far as they can consistently with their own natural satisfactions in life, nay, sacrificing, in their turn, to their parents, much of their own inclinations or pleasures not absolutely neces-sary to their happiness. They must discern the sacred duty of supporting their aged parents, in their second infirmity or childhood, and bearing with their weakly hu-mours and peevishness; as parents from a fond disinterested affection long bore with such manners of theirs in their childhood; without which they never could have attained to maturity; nor could any human laws or vigilance of civil governors have ensured their preservation, or compelled their parents to that faithful and labor-ious attendance to it.

II

The manifestly disinterested nature of this affection shows at once the nature and dura-tion of the parental power. The foundation of the right is the weakness and ignorance of childhood, which makes it absolutely necessary that they should be governed a long time by others: and the natural affection points out the parents as the proper governors, where no prudent civil institution has provided more effectually for their education. The generous nature of this affection shows that the power committed by nature is primar-ily intended for the good of the children, and, in consequence of their happiness, for the satisfaction also, and joy of the affectionate parent. The right therefore cannot ex-tend so far as to destroy the children, or keep them in a miserable state of slavery. When they attain to mature years, and the use of reason, they must obtain that liberty which is necessary to any rational enjoyment of life. The parental affection naturally secures to them this emancipation, as the reason God has given them intitles them to it.

SIMONE DE BEAUVOIR

The Married Woman

. . . It has been said that marriage diminishes man, which is often true; but almost al-ways it annihilates woman.

In the early years of marriage the wife often lulls herself with illusions, she tries to admire her husband wholeheartedly, to love him unreservedly, to feel herself indispensable to him and the children. And then her true sentiments become clear; she sees that her husband could get along very well without her, that her children are bound to get away from her and to be always more or less ungrateful. The home no longer saves her from empty liberty; she finds herself alone, forlorn, a subject; and she finds nothing to do with herself. Affectionate attachments and habitual ways may still be a great help, but not salvation. All sincere women writers have noted the melancholy in the heart of "the woman of 30"; it is a trait common to the heroines of Katherine Mansfield, Dorothy Parker, Virginia Woolf. . . .

The tragedy of marriage is not that it fails to assure woman the promised happiness—there is no such thing as assurance in regard to happiness—but that it mutilates her; it dooms her to repetition and routine. The first 20 years of woman's life are extraordinarily rich, as we have seen; she discovers the world and her destiny. At 20 or thereabouts mistress of a home, bound permanently to a man, a child in her arms, she stands with her life virtually finished forever. Real activities, real work, are the prerogative of her man: she has mere things to occupy her which are sometimes tiring but never fully satisfying. Her renunciation and devotion have been lauded, but it often seems to her bootless indeed to busy herself "with the care of two persons for life." It is all very fine to be forgetful of self, but still one must know for whom, for what. And the worst of it is that her very devotion often seems annoying, importunate; it is transformed for the husband into a tyranny from which he tries to escape; and yet he it is who imposes it upon his wife as her supreme, her unique justification. In marrying her he obliges her to give herself entirely to him; but he does not assume the corresponding obligation, which is to accept this gift and all its consequences.

It is the duplicity of the husband that dooms the wife to a misfortune of which he complains later that he is himself the victim. Just as he wants her to be at once warm and cool in bed, he requires her to be wholly his and yet no burden; he wishes her to establish him in a fixed place on earth and to leave him free, to assume the monotonous daily round and not to bore him, to be always at hand and never importunate; he wants to have her all to himself and not to belong to her; to live as one of a couple and to remain alone. Thus she is betrayed from the day he marries her. Her life through, she measures the extent of that betrayal. What D. H. Lawrence says of sexual love is generally valid: the union of two human beings is doomed to frustration if it is an attempt at a mutual completion which supposes an original mutilation; marriage should be a combining of two whole, independent existences, not a retreat, an annexation, a flight, a remedy. Ibsen's Nora understands this when she makes up her mind that before she can be a wife and mother she must first become a complete person. The couple should not be regarded as a unit, a closed cell; rather each individual should be integrated as such in society at large, where each (whether male or female) could flourish without aid; then attachments could be formed in pure generosity with another individual equally adapted to the group, attachments that would be founded upon the acknowledgment that both are free.

This balanced couple is not a utopian fancy: such couples do exist, sometimes even within the frame of marriage, most often outside it. Some mates are united by a strong sexual love that leaves them free in their friendships and in their work; others are held together by a friendship that does not preclude sexual liberty; more rare are those who are at once lovers and friends but do not seek in each other their sole reasons for living. Many nuances are possible in the relations between a man and a woman: in comradeship, pleasure, trust, fondness, co-operation, love, they can be for each other the most abundant source of joy, richness, and power available to human beings. Individuals are not to be blamed for the failure of marriage: it is—counter to the claims of such advocates as Comte and Tolstoy—the institution itself, perverted as it has been from the start. To hold and proclaim that a man and a woman, who may not even have chosen each other, *are in duty bound* to satisfy each other in every way throughout their lives is a monstrosity that necessarily gives rise to hypocrisy, lying, hostility, and unhappiness.

The traditional form of marriage is now undergoing modification, but it still involves oppression, which the two spouses feel in different ways. With regard only to the abstract, theoretical rights they enjoy, they are today almost equals; they are more free to choose one another than formerly, they can separate much more easily, especially in America, where divorce is no rarity; differences in age and culture between them are commonly less marked than they once were; the husband recognizes more willingly the independence his wife demands; they may share the cares of housekeeping equally; their diversions are enjoyed together: camping, bicycling, swimming, automobiling, and so on. The wife does not necessarily spend her days awaiting her husband's return; she may go in for sports, belong to clubs, associations, musical organizations, and the like, she is often busy outside the home, she may even have an occupation that brings her more or less money.

Many young households give the impression of being on a basis of perfect equality. But as long as the man retains economic responsibility for the couple, this is only an illusion. It is he who decides where they will live, according to the demands of his work; she *follows* him from city to country or vice versa, to distant possessions, to foreign countries; their standard of living is set according to his income; the daily, weekly, annual rhythms are set by his occupation; associations and friendships most often depend upon his profession. Being more positively integrated in society than his wife, he guides the couple in intellectual, political, and moral matters. Divorce is only a theoretical possibility for the woman who cannot earn her own living; if in America alimony is a heavy charge upon the man, in France the lot of the abandoned wife or mother, dependent upon a ridiculously small pension, is a scandal.

But the basic inequality still lies in the fact that the husband finds concrete self-realization in work and action, whereas for the wife, as such, liberty has only a negative aspect . . .

In France, even with the best will in the world on the part of the husband, once the young woman becomes a mother, the duties of the household overwhelm her no less surely than of yore.

It is a commonplace to say that in modern families, and especially in the United States, woman has reduced man to slavery. And this is nothing new. Since the times of the ancient Greeks males have always complained about Xantippe's tyranny. It is true, however, that woman now interferes in masculine domains that were formerly forbidden territory: I know, for example, university student couples in which the woman struggles madly for the success of her male, regulating his time schedule and diet and watching over his work in general; she deprives him of all amusement, almost puts him under lock and key. It is also true that the man is more defenseless than formerly against this despotism; he recognizes woman's theoretical rights and knows that she can concretely realize them only through him; he must compensate at his own expense for the impotence and sterility to which woman is condemned. In order to achieve an apparent equality in their association, it must be he who gives the most because he has more. But, precisely, if she receives, demands, it is because she is the poorer. The dialectic of master and slave here finds its most concrete application: in oppressing, one becomes oppressed. Men are enchained by reason of their very sovereignty; it is because they alone earn money that their wives demand checks, it is because they alone engage in a business or profession that their wives require them to be successful, it is because they alone embody transcendence that their wives wish to rob them of it by taking charge of their projects and successes.

Inversely, the tyranny exercised by woman only goes to show her dependence: she knows that the success of the couple, its future, its happiness, its justification rest in the hands of the other; if she seeks desperately to bend him to her will, it is because she is alienated in him—that is, her interests as an individual lie in him. She makes a weapon of her weakness; but the fact remains that she is weak. Conjugal slavery is chiefly a matter of daily irritation for the husband; but it is something more deep-seated for the woman; a wife who keeps her husband at her side for hours because she is bored certainly bothers him and seems burdensome; but in the last analysis he can get along without her much more easily than she can without him; if he leaves her, she is the one whose life will be ruined. The great difference is that with woman dependency is interiorized: she *is* a slave even when she behaves with apparent freedom; while man is essentially independent and his bondage comes from without. If he seems to be the victim, it is because his burdens are most evident: woman is supported by him like a parasite; but a parasite is not a conquering master. The truth is that just as—biologically—males and females are never victims of one another but both victims of the species, so man and wife together undergo the oppression of an institution they did not create. If it is asserted that *men* oppress *women,* the husband is indignant; he feels that *he* is the one who is oppressed—and he is; but the fact is that it is the masculine code, it is the society developed by the males and in their interest, that has established woman's situation in a form that is at present a source of torment for both sexes.

It is for their common welfare that the situation must be altered by prohibiting marriage as a "career" for woman. Men who declare themselves antifeminists, on the ground that "women are already bad enough as it is," are not too logical; it is precisely because marriage makes women into "praying mantises," "leeches," "poisonous" creatures, and so on, that it is necessary to transform marriage and, in consequence, the condition of women in general. Woman leans heavily upon man because she is not allowed to rely on herself; he will free himself in freeing her—that is to say, in giving her something to *do* in the world. . . .

ANN FERGUSON

Androgyny as an Ideal for Human Development

. . . Women and men develop their sexual identities, their sense of self, and their motivations through responding to the social expectations placed upon them. They develop the skills and personality traits necessary to carry out the productive and reproductive roles available to them in their sociohistorical context, given their sex, race, ethnic identity, and class background.

If we wish to develop a realistic ideal for human development, then, we cannot take the existing traits that differentiate men from women in this society as norms for behavior. Neither can we expect to find an ideal in some biological male and female substratum, after we strip away all the socialization processes we go through to develop our egos. Rather, with the present-day women's movement, we should ask: what traits are desirable and possible to teach people in order for them to reach their full individual human potential? And how would our society have to restructure its productive and reproductive relations in order to allow people to develop in this way?

AN IDEAL LOVE RELATIONSHIP

One argument for the development of androgynous personalities (and the accompanying destruction of the sexual division of labor in production and reproduction) is that without such a racial change in male and female roles an ideal love relationship between the sexes is not possible. The argument goes like this. An ideal love between two mature people would be love between equals. I assume that such an ideal is the only concept of love that is historically compatible with our other developed ideals of political and social equality. But, as Shulamith Firestone argues,[1] an equal love relationship requires the vulnerability of each partner to the other. There is today, however, an unequal balance of power in male–female relationships. . . . It is not possible for men and women to be equal while playing the complementary sex roles taught in our society. The feminine role makes a woman less equal, less powerful, and less free than the masculine role makes men. In fact, it is the emotional understanding of this lack of equality in love relations between men and women which increasingly influences feminists to choose lesbian love relationships.

Let us consider the vulnerabilities of women in a heterosexual love relationship under the four classifications Juliet Mitchell gives for women's roles:[2] production, reproduction, socialization of children, and sexuality.

1. *Women's role in production.* In the United States today, 42 percent of women work, and about 33 percent of married women work in the wage-labor force. This is much higher than the 6 percent of women in the wage-labor force around the turn of the century, and higher than in other industrialized countries. Nonetheless, sex-role socialization affects women's power in two important ways. First, because of job segregation by sex into part-time and low-paying jobs, women, whether single or married, are at an

economic disadvantage in comparison with men when it comes to supporting themselves. If they leave their husbands or lovers, they drop to a lower economic class, and many have to go on welfare. Second, women who have children and who also work in the wage-labor force have two jobs, not one: the responsibility for the major part of child-raising and housework, as well as the outside job. This keeps many housewives from seeking outside jobs, and makes them economically dependent on their husbands. Those who do work outside the home expend twice as much energy as the man and are less secure. Many women who try to combine career and motherhood find that the demands of both undermine their egos because they don't feel they can do both jobs adequately.[3]

2. *Women's role in reproduction.* Although women currently monopolize the means of biological reproduction, they are at a disadvantage because of the absence of free contraceptives, adequate health care, and free legal abortions. A man can enjoy sex without having to worry about the consequences the way a woman does if a mistake occurs and she becomes pregnant. Women have some compensation in the fact that in the United States today they are favored legally over the father in their right to control of the children in case of separation or divorce. But this legal advantage (a victory won by women in the early 20th century in the ongoing power struggle between the sexes for control of children, i.e. control over social reproduction) does not adequately compensate for the disadvantages to which motherhood subjects one in this society.

3. *Women's role in socialization: as wife and mother.* The social status of women, and hence their self-esteem, is measured primarily in terms of how successful they are in their relationships as lovers, wives, and mothers. Unlike men, who learn that their major social definition is success in work, women are taught from childhood that their ultimate goal is love and marriage. Women thus have more invested in a love relationship than men, and more to lose if it fails. The "old maid" or the "divorcee" is still an inferior status to be pitied, while the "swinging bachelor" is rather envied.

The fact than men achieve self- and social definition from their work means that they can feel a lesser commitment to working out problems in a relationship. Furthermore, men have more options for new relationships than do women. The double standard in sexuality allows a man to have affairs more readily than his wife. Ageism is a further limitation on women: an older man is considered a possible lover by both younger and older women, but an older woman, because she is no longer the "ideal" sex object, is not usually considered a desirable lover by either male peers or by younger men.

A woman's role as mother places her in a more vulnerable position than the man. Taking care of children and being attentive to their emotional needs is very demanding work. Many times it involves conflicts between the woman's own needs and the needs of the child. Often it involves conflict and jealousy between husband and children for her attention and emotional energy. It is the woman's role to harmonize this conflict, which she often does at the expense of herself, sacrificing her private time and interests in order to provide support for the projects of her husband and children.

No matter how devoted a parent a father is, he tends to see his time with the children as play time, not as work time. His job interests and hobbies take precedence over directing his energy to children. Thus he is more independent than the woman, who sees her job as making husband and children happy. This is the sort of job that is never completed, for there are always more ways to make people happy. Because a woman sees her job to be supporting her husband and mothering her children, the woman sees the family as her main "product." This makes her dependent on their activities, lives, and successes for her own success, and she lives vicariously through their activities. But as her "product" is human beings, when the children leave, as they must, to live independent lives, middle age brings an end to her main social function. The woman who has a career has other problems, for she has had to support her husband's career over hers wherever there was a conflict, because she knows male egos are tied up with success and "making it" in this competitive society. Women's egos, on the other hand, are primed for failure. Successful women, especially successful women with unsuccessful husbands, are considered not "true" women, but rather as deviants, "castrating bitches," "ball-busters," and "masculine women." For all these reasons, a woman in a love relationship with a man is geared . . . to put her interests last, to define herself in terms of husband and children, and therefore to be more dependent on them than they are on her.

A woman is also vulnerable in her role as mother because there are limited alternatives if, for example, she wishes to break off her relationship with the father of her children. As a mother, her social role in bringing up children is defined as more important, more essential for the well-being of the children than the man's. Therefore, she is expected to take the children to live with her, or else she is considered a failure as a mother. But the life of a divorced or single mother with children in a nuclear-family-oriented society is lonely and hard: she must now either do two jobs without the companionship of another adult, in a society where jobs for women are inadequate, or she must survive on welfare or alimony with a reduced standard of living. When this is the alternative, is it any wonder that mothers are more dependent on maintaining a relationship—even when it is not satisfying—than a man is?

4. *Women's role in sexuality.* A woman's sexual role is one in which she is both elevated by erotic romanticism and deflated to being a mere "cunt"—good for release of male sexual passions but interchangeable with other women. Because women play a subordinate role in society and are not seen as equal agents or as equally productive, men must justify a relationship with a particular woman by making her something special, mystifying her, making her better than other women. In fact, this idealization doesn't deal with her as a real *individual;* it treats her as either a beautiful object or as a mothering, supportive figure.

This idealization of women which occurs in the first stages of infatuation wears off as the couple settles into a relationship of some duration. What is left is the idea of woman as passive sex object whom one possesses and whose job as wife is to give the husband pleasure in bed. Since the woman is not seen as (and doesn't usually see herself as) active in sex, she tends to see sex as a duty rather than as a pleasure. She is not socially expected to take the active kind of initiative (even to the extent of asking for a certain kind of sex play) that would give her a sense of control over her sex life. The idea of herself as a body to be dressed and clothed in the latest media-advertised fashions "to please men" keeps her a slave to fashion and forces her to change her ego-ideal with every change in fashion. She can't see herself as an individual.

ANDROGYNY AS A PROGRESSIVE IDEAL

It is the sexual division of labor in the home and at work that perpetuates complementary sex roles for men and women. In underdeveloped societies with scarce material resources such an arrangement may indeed be the most rational way to allow for the most efficient raising of children and production of goods. But this is no longer true for developed societies. In this age of advanced technology, men's relative strength compared to women's is no longer important, either in war or in the production of goods. The gun and the spinning jenny have equalized the potential role of men and women in both repression and production. And the diaphragm, the pill, and other advances in the technology of reproduction have equalized the potential power of women and men to control their bodies and to reproduce themselves.[4] (The development of cloning would mean that men and women could reproduce without the participation of the opposite sex.)

We have seen how complementary sex roles and their extension to job segregation in wage labor make an ideal love relationship between equals impossible for men and women in our society. The questions that remain are: would the development of androgynous human beings through androgynous sex-role training be possible? If possible, would it allow for the development of equal love relationships? What other human potentials would androgyny allow to develop? And how would society have to be restructured in order to allow for androgynous human beings and equal love relationships?

There is good evidence that human babies are bisexual, and only *learn* a specific male or female identity by imitating and identifying with adult models. This evidence comes from the discovery that all human beings possess both male and female hormones (androgen and estrogen respectively), and also from concepts first developed at length by Freud. Freud argued that heterosexual identity is not achieved until the third stage of the child's sexual development. Sex identity is developed through the resolution of the Oedipus complex, in which the child has to give up a primary attachment to the mother and learn either to identify with, or love, the father. But Shulamith Firestone suggests that this process is not an inevitable one, as Freud presents it to be. Rather, it is due to the power dynamics of the patriarchal nuclear family.[5] Note that, on this analysis, if the sexual division of labor were destroyed, the mechanism that trains boys and girls to develop heterosexual sexual identities would also be destroyed. If fathers and mothers played equal nurturant roles in child-rearing and had equal social, economic, and political power outside the home, there would be no reason for the boy to have to reject his emotional side in order to gain the power associated with the male role. Neither would the girl have to assume a female role in rejecting her assertive, independent side in order to attain power indirectly through manipulation of males. As a sexual identity, bisexuality would then be the norm rather than the exception.

If bisexuality were the norm rather than the exception for the sexual identities that children develop,[6] androgynous sex roles would certainly be a consequence. For, as discussed above, the primary mechanism whereby complementary rather than androgynous sex roles are maintained is through heterosexual training, and through the socialization of needs for love and sexual gratification to the search for a love partner of the opposite sex. Such a partner is sought to complement one in the traits that one has repressed or not developed because in one's own sex such traits were not socially accepted.

THE ANDROGYNOUS MODEL

I believe that only androgynous people can attain the full human potential possible given our present level of material and social resources (and this only if society is radically restructured). Only such people can have ideal love relationships; and without such relationships, I maintain that none can develop to the fullest potential. Since human beings are social animals and develop through interaction and productive activity with others, such relationships are necessary.

Furthermore, recent studies have shown that the human brain has two distinct functions: one associated with analytic, logical, sequential thinking (the left brain), and the other associated with holistic, metaphorical, intuitive thought (the right brain). Only a person capable of tapping both these sides of him/herself will have developed to full potential. We might call this characteristic of the human brain "psychic bisexuality,"[7] since it has been shown that women in fact have developed skills which allow them to tap the abilities of the right side of the brain more than men, who on the contrary excel in the analytic, logical thought characteristic of the left side. The point is that men and women have the potential for using both these functions, and yet our socialization at present tends to cut off from one or the other of these parts of ourselves.[8]

What would an androgynous personality by like? My model for the ideal androgynous person comes from the concept of human potential developed by Marx in *Economic and Philosophical Manuscripts*. Marx's idea is that human beings have a need (or a potential) for free, creative, productive activity which allows them to control their lives in a situation of cooperation with others. Both men and women need to be equally active and independent; with an equal sense of control over their lives; equal opportunity for creative, productive activity; and a sense of meaningful involvement in the community.

Androgynous women would be just as assertive as men about their own needs in a love relationship: productive activity outside the home, the right to private time, and the freedom to form other intimate personal and sexual relationships. I maintain that being active and assertive—traits now associated with being "masculine"—are positive traits that all people need to develop. Many feminists are suspicious of the idea of self-assertion because it is associated with the traits of aggression and competitiveness. However, there is no inevitability to this connection: it results from the structural features of competitive, hierarchical economic systems, of which our own (monopoly capitalism) is one example. In principle, given the appropriate social structure, there is no reason why a self-assertive person cannot also be nurturant and cooperative.

Androgynous men would be more sensitive and aware of emotions then sex-role stereotyped "masculine" men are today. They would be more concerned with the feelings of all people, including women and children, and aware of conflicts of interests. Being sensitive to human emotions is necessary to an effective care and concern for others. Such sensitivity is now thought of as a "motherly," "feminine," or "maternal" instinct, but in fact it is a role and skill learned by women, and it can equally well be learned by men. Men need to get in touch with their own feelings in order to empathize with others, and, indeed, to understand themselves better so as to be more in control of their actions.

We have already discussed the fact that women are more vulnerable in a love relationship than men because many men consider a concern with feelings and emotions to be part of the woman's role. Women, then, are required to be more aware of everyone's feelings (if children and third parties are involved) than men, and they are under more pressure to harmonize the conflicts by sacrificing their own interests.

Another important problem with a non-androgynous love relationship is that it limits the development of mutual understanding. In general, it seems true that the more levels people can relate on, the deeper and more intimate their relationship is. The more experiences and activities they share, the greater their companionship and meaning to each other. And this is true for emotional experiences. Without mutual understanding of the complex of emotions involved in an ongoing love relationship, communication and growth on that level are blocked for both people. This means that, for both people, self-development of the sort that could come from the shared activity of understanding and struggling to deal with conflicts will not be possible.

In our society as presently structured, there are few possibilities for men and women to develop themselves through shared activities. Men and women share more activities with members of their own sex than with each other. Most women can't get jobs in our sexist, job-segregated society which allow them to share productive work with men. Most men just don't have the skills (or the time, given the demands of their wage-labor jobs) to understand the emotional needs of children and to share the activity of child-rearing equally with their wives.

How must our society be restructured to allow for the development of androgynous personalities? How can it be made to provide for self-development through the shared activities of productive and reproductive work? I maintain that this will not be possible (except for a small privileged elite) without the development of a democratic socialist society. In such a society no one would benefit from cheap labor (presently provided to the capitalist class by a part-time reserve army of women). Nor would anyone benefit from hierarchical power relationships (which encourage competition among the working class and reinforce male sex-role stereotypes as necessary to "making it" in society).

As society is presently constituted, the patriarchal nuclear family and women's reproductive work therein serve several crucial roles in maintaining the capitalist system. In the family, women do the unpaid work of social reproduction of the labor force (child-rearing). They also pacify and support the male breadwinner in an alienating society where men who are not in the capitalist class have little control of their product or work conditions. Men even come to envy their wives' relatively nonalienated labor in child-rearing rather than dealing with those with the real privilege, the capitalist class. Since those in power relations never give them up without a struggle, it is utopian to think that the capitalist class will allow for the elimination of the sexual division of labor without a socialist revolution with feminist priorities. Furthermore, men in the professional and working classes must be challenged by women with both a class and feminist consciousness to begin the process of change.

In order to eliminate the subordination of women in the patriarchal nuclear family and the perpetuation of sex-role stereotypes therein, there will need to be a radical reorganization of child-rearing. Father and mother must have an equal commitment to raising children. More of the reproductive work must be socialized—for example, by community child care, perhaps with parent cooperatives. Communal living is one obvious alternative which would de-emphasize biological parenthood and allow homosexuals and bisexuals the opportunity to have an equal part in relating to children. The increased socialization of child care would allow parents who are incompatible the freedom to dissolve their relationships without denying their children the secure, permanent loving relationships they need with both men and women. A community responsibility for child-rearing would provide children with male and female models other than their biological parent—models that they would be able to see and relate to emotionally.

Not only would men and women feel an equal responsibility to do reproductive work, they would also expect to do rewarding, productive work, in a situation where they had equal opportunity. Such a situation would of course require reduced workweeks for parents, maternity and paternity leaves, and the development of a technology of reproduction which would allow women complete control over their bodies.

As for love relationships, with the elimination of sex roles and the disappearance, in an overpopulated world, of any biological need for sex to be associated with procreation, there would be no reason why such a society could not transcend sexual gender. It would no longer matter what biological sex individuals had. Love relationships, and the sexual relationships developing out of them, would be based on the individual meshing-together of androgynous human beings.

---

[1] [Ferguson's notes have been renumbered—ed.] Shulamith Firestone, *The Dialectic of Sex* (New York: William Morrow, 1970), Chap. 6.

[2] Juliet Mitchell, *Woman's Estate* (New York: Random House, 1971).

[3] Socialization into complementary sex roles is responsible not only for job segregation practices' keeping women in low-paid service jobs which are extensions of the supportive work women do in the home as mothers, but also for making it difficult for women to feel confident in their ability to excel at competitive "male-defined" jobs.

[4] Thanks to Sam Bowles for this point.

[5] Firestone, *The Dialectic of Sex*. The boy and girl both realize that the father has power in the relationship between him and the mother, and that his role, and not the mother's, represents the possibility of achieving economic and social power in the world and over one's life. The mother, in contrast, represents nurturing and emotionality. Both boy and girl, then, in order to get power for themselves, have to reject the mother as a love object—the boy, because he is afraid of the father as rival and potential castrator; and the girl, because the only way as a girl she can attain power is through manipulating the father. So she becomes a rival to her mother for her father's love. The girl comes to identify with her mother and to choose her

father and, later, other men for love objects; while the boy identifies with his father, sublimates his sexual attraction to his mother into superego (will power), and chooses mother substitutes, other women, for his love objects.

[6]It should be understood here that no claim is being made that bisexuality is more desirable than homo- or heterosexuality. The point is that with the removal of the social mechanisms in the family that channel children into heterosexuality, there is no reason to suppose that most of them will develop in that direction. It would be more likely that humans with androgynous personalities would be bisexual, the assumption here being that there are no innate biological preferences in people for sexual objects of the same or opposite sex. Rather, this comes to be developed because of emotional connections of certain sorts of personality characteristics with the male and female body, characteristics which develop because of complementary sex-role training, and which would not be present without it.

The other mechanism which influences people to develop a heterosexual identity is the desire to reproduce. As long as the social institution for raising children is the heterosexual nuclear family, and as long as society continues to place social value on biological parenthood, most children will develop a heterosexual identity. Not, perhaps, in early childhood, but certainly after puberty, when the question of reproduction becomes viable. Radical socialization and collectivization of child-rearing would thus have to characterize a society before bisexuality would be the norm not only in early childhood, but in adulthood as well. For the purposes of developing androgynous individuals, however, full social bisexuality of this sort is not necessary. All that is needed is the restructuring of the sex roles of father and mother in the nuclear family so as to eliminate the sexual division of labor there.

[7]Charlotte Painter, Afterword to C. Painter and M. J. Moffet, eds., *Revelations: Diaries of Women* (New York: Random House, 1975).

[8]It is notable that writers, painters, and other intellectuals, who presumably would need skills of both sorts, have often been misfits in the prevalent complementary sex stereotyping. In fact, thinkers as diverse as Plato (in *the Symposium*) and Virginia Woolf (in *A Room of One's Own*) have suggested that writers and thinkers need to be androgynous to tap all the skills necessary for successful insight.

PART III

What Is Right?

■———■

INTRODUCTION

The introductory essay that opened the book noted fundamental differences between approaches to morality that focus on the concept of the good and approaches that focus on the concept of the right. Part 2 examined examples of the first kind of approach, working toward a clear idea of what sorts of things are good, according to various thinkers. Part 3 examines examples of the second kind of approach, working toward a clear grasp of the right. Some reminders and general comments might be helpful to consider at this time.

Early discussion noted the equivalence of "doing A is obligatory," "one must do A," "doing A is one's duty," "failing to do A is impermissible," and "failing to do A is not right (failing to do A is wrong)." When contemporary Westerners apply the concept of the right, they tend to presuppose a background of competing individuals or groups with conflicting interests. The right is understood to trump the interests of people, so that it limits the pursuit of these competing interests, creating limits that reasonable people willingly impose upon themselves. Reasonable people willingly do what is right, because the right is understood to be an *impartial*, hence reasonable, framework. The limits required by the right typically are expressed in the form of duties, usually paired with corresponding rights. Duties compel actions to accommodate the interests of others, and rights compel others to accommodate one's own interests. Thus, those who recognize a right not to be harmed also recognize a duty not to harm. But most people who recognize a duty to offer a reasonable amount of help to the needy do not recognize a corresponding right of the needy to receive help from those who can offer it. This difference results because the duty to aid is usually thought to carry leeway in choosing who shall receive one's aid.

Recall also that teleologists define the good independently from the right and then the right in terms of the good. They may or may not adopt this contemporary conception of the right as a framework that trumps the good or the interests of individuals or groups. It was largely absent in the ancient world, East and West, where philosophers preferred to eliminate conflicts by (re)shaping the self and what counts as self-interest.

Contemporary utilitarians, whose moral view is perhaps the most direct descendant of the ancient one, do not share the ancient assumption that people identify with the group and hence share the interests of the group. These theorists address themselves to a world of mostly separate individuals who do not accept the total good as part of their interests, offering instead the principle of utility maximization as an impartial hence reasonable basis for identifying individual duties and rights. The utilitarian formula holds that each individual's interests (or good) is important to me, yet these interests are in no sense *mine*.

In any case, the contemporary Western notion of right was strongly influenced by natural law tradition. According to the natural law tradition, obligations are set out by the commandments of God, who has legitimate authority. These commandments constitute an impartial perspective that absolutely trumps all other concerns, such as the pursuit of the interests of individuals and groups. In the seventeenth century, John Locke extended the natural law tradition by helping to develop the idea of (indefeasible) rights that correspond to (indefeasible) duties, thus introducing the natural *rights* tradition. Kant extended this tradition in important ways. He rejected the idea that duty can be considered entirely in terms of the force of God's commands. Kant believed that this theistic conception makes duty arbitrary and people unfree, so he attempted to reorient the notion of duties as commands of impartial reason itself and, insofar as people are (and identify themselves as) reasonable beings, as people's own commands to themselves.

Duties modeled on the notion of commands are rules, and modern Western philosophers tend to assume that obligations can be set out in the form of rules. These rules are the counterparts of the more ancient conception of virtues. Modern formulations of moral duties attempt to make explicit the contents of ancient virtues, and usually each of the virtues defended in the ancient world has a corresponding duty defended in the modern world.

Readings in Part III will examine some of the main duties attributed to people. They attempt to understand both the nature of the duties and their underlying rationales. The following list states these duties in general terms and notes corresponding virtues:

1. We must be true, both to ourselves and our community. (Virtues: integrity, honesty, faithfulness, loyalty, sincerity, candor, etc.)

2. We must not harm other people or living things. (Virtue: nonmaleficence)

3. We must offer a reasonable amount of help to those in need. (Virtue: beneficence)

4. We must deal fairly with people. (Virtue: justice)

Each of the four chapters in Part III is devoted to one of these four duties. Chapter 5 begins with the suggestion that people have a duty of fidelity.

FIDELITY

■━━━━━■

INTRODUCTION

The duty of fidelity might apply both to oneself and to others. This discussion begins with an examination of this duty as applied to oneself.

Do people have duties to themselves as opposed to duties to others? That is, must they do things for their own sakes? In the ancient world, thinkers suggested that various virtues and forms of conduct are crucial to self-realization, and hence in one's best interest. Perhaps this claim that certain virtues and conduct are conducive to self-realization can be associated with duties to the self. However, according to some ancient philosophers, backing away from self-realization extends beyond letting oneself down as an individual to include letting down one's true self (the community).

Assume that the role of the right is to limit competing individuals' pursuit of their own interests insofar as these conflict—limits that reasonable people willingly impose upon themselves. Then any suggestion of duties to the self may seem peculiar. Don't duties constrain people when they threaten or neglect the interests of others, not when they threaten or neglect their own interests? To go ahead with a harmful action that would otherwise be wrong, someone would have to secure the permission or the consent of the people whom the act would threaten. But each person automatically has her or his *own* permission. Others are likely to resist threats to or neglect of their interests, but no one faces such resistance in dealing only with herself or himself.

Nonetheless, Kant and other philosophers have carved out room for the notion of duties to the self, for certain ways of behaving toward oneself are considered prerequisites to treating *everyone* properly, as impartial moral principles require. Thus, the responsibility to act as a moral agent might entail the responsibility to improve oneself in whatever ways are necessary to become and remain a moral agent. This chapter examines two features that are commonly said to be central to becoming and remaining a moral agent: self-respect and integrity.

———

SELF-RESPECT

1. IMMANUEL KANT

Kant acknowledges the force of the point that those who neglect themselves have their own permission to do so. He acknowledges the impossibility of *unjust* treatment of oneself. Nonetheless, Kant says, conduct towards oneself may be morally *wrong*, violating a duty to believe in one's worth and to treat oneself consistently with that worth.

When animals act from inclination, the world remains orderly, since they are subjectively compelled to act in accordance with the natural order. But free beings are capable of acting contrary to the natural order, even while acting according to their inclinations. Yet to do so is to sink lower than animals—a degrading choice; since free beings ought to avoid such degradation, they ought not act disorderly, so they should restrict their freedom by following rules. "Man should take his stand upon maxims and restrain by rules the free actions which relate to himself. These are the rules of his self-regarding duties." The most basic rule of self-regard is "in all the actions which affect himself a man should so conduct himself that every exercise of his power is compatible with the fullest employment of them." Kant adds that people can act consistently with the worth of all people only through proper appreciation of their own worth, a proper degree of self-esteem. Therefore, he posits a duty to cultivate a sense of self-worth.

Kant speaks of (1) the central importance of self-respect and (2) the baseness of following inclination. But what, precisely, is the self one is supposed to respect? Kant's broad notion of "inclination" includes the projects and commitments in terms of which many define themselves. Being who we are—realizing ourselves—is very much a matter of following inclination. If being myself is largely a matter of following certain inclinations, and following inclinations is base, how can I respect myself? Should one understand the self entirely in terms of obeying the moral law? Shall we say that only as purely moral beings are we worthy of respect?

Duties to oneself rule out many types of action, according to Kant, including suicide, drunkenness, selling body parts, prostitution, and making oneself "an object of enjoyment for someone's sexual desire."

2. LAURENCE THOMAS

According to Laurence Thomas, a contemporary philosopher who teaches at Syracuse University, self-respect is not the same thing as self-esteem. Self-esteem is a sense of one's worth, which is determined by the ratio of successes to aspirations. On the other hand, a person has self-respect "if and only if he has the conviction that he is deserving of full moral status, and so the basic rights of that status, simply in virtue of the fact that he is a person." Thomas defends his account by drawing on the experiences of African Americans.

INTEGRITY

Broadly characterized, both Kantians and utilitarians think of the right as providing a reasonable perspective for adjudicating disputes among competing individuals and groups, because they think the right provides an impartial perspective. When interests clash with duties, so much the worse for the interests. But what if the interests that clash with duties are the basic commitments around which people define themselves? Might morality require a violation of these basic commitments? If so, people would be morally required to pull themselves apart, thus violating the integrity or unity of the self. Wouldn't that be tantamount to suicide? (Instead of speaking of suicide, should we say that people are expected to recreate themselves by identifying with new, morally sanitized projects, or by thinking of themselves as purely moral beings?) Can morality require people to destroy (or recreate) themselves because it is the optimal policy as assessed by an impartial perspective? Or should we instead say that people may never be required to violate the integrity of the self (as Kant himself hinted when he insisted upon the centrality to morality of self-respect)? Does that position affect the claim that impartial morality absolutely trumps all considerations of self-interest? Do such views of morality necessarily pit a person (as a moral agent) against the person (as a being with ties to particular people and projects), thus undermining the integrity of the self?

The writings of Bernard Williams provide a point of entry to these difficult issues. In "A Critique of Utilitarianism," Williams presses the point that utilitarianism, and consequentialism in general, might easily require action against one's defining interests, and thereby an attack on one's own integrity. Since meeting this kind of requirement is absurd, so is utilitarianism. Williams thinks that his criticisms of utilitarianism also undermine a principle that is the natural consequence of the utilitarian view, namely, the principle of negative responsibility: "that if I am ever responsible for anything, then I must be just as much responsible for things that I allow or fail to prevent, as I am for things that I myself, in the more everyday restricted sense, bring about."

HONESTY

Fidelity is a matter of being true or faithful. But it is one thing to be true to the facts as one perceives them, and another to be true to people. The former is honesty, while the latter is loyalty. Hence a duty to fidelity might entail a duty to be honest, or a duty to be loyal, or both.

When people think of honesty, they usually think of honesty toward others. But substantial arguments support the suggestion that we ought to be honest with ourselves as well as with others. This chapter examines both forms of honesty.

1. HONESTY WITH OTHERS

Deception, or intentionally producing false beliefs, might be motivated by self-aggrandizement or by a benevolent concern for the people thus deceived. However motivated, deception might take the form of intentionally making false claims, or the form of intentionally producing false beliefs, perhaps by withholding salient facts in a context in which full disclosure is expected.

Benevolent deception has been advocated in various contexts for a long time, particularly in the medical context. Both benevolent deception and deception designed to further the ends of state are often advocated as useful tools for politicians. But the appropriateness of benevolent deception remains a contested point. Francis Bacon and Immanuel Kant go so far as to condemn any form of deception as morally impermissible dishonesty. In "Of Truth"[1] Francis Bacon links truthful representation to the illumination of God, which, in turn, he equates with "the sovereign good of human nature." To lie, then, is to be "brave towards God and a coward towards men." Other writers, who admit that benevolent deception could be appropriate in imaginable circumstances, argue that those circumstances are rare indeed.

Confucius

In the *Analects,* Confucius clearly asserts that while truthfulness is an important attribute, it should take a back seat to benevolence in general and loyalty to one's family in particular. He is horrified to hear of a certain moral "paragon" who bore testimony against his father for stealing a sheep; upright fathers lie on behalf of their sons, says Confucius, and upright sons lie on behalf of their fathers:

> The Governor of She in conversation with Confucius said, "In our village there is someone called 'True Person.' When his father took a sheep on the sly, he reported him to the authorities." Confucius replied, "Those who are true in my village conduct themselves differently. A father covers for his son, and a son covers for his father. And being true lies in this." (13.18, Ames and Rosemont)

Elsewhere he adds:

> The master said, "Exemplary persons (*junzi*) are proper, but not fastidious." (15.37, Ames and Rosemont)

Plato

In his *Republic,* Plato acknowledges the importance of truthfulness but argues that the rulers or guardians of the state should carefully manipulate the beliefs of citizens. The rulers should make use of "convenient fictions" in educating the members of a just society. One of these useful lies is the claim that the earth literally gave birth to people, so that all citizens are born of the same soil and must protect the land that is their mother. Another of Plato's useful lies is the claim that different metals are mixed into people at birth, and these metals determine the places they should take in society.

Machiavelli

In *The Prince* the Italian political writer Niccolò Machiavelli (1469–1527) advises the politician to avoid rigid honesty in particular and morality in general, but this writer is somewhat cagey about the position he wants to take on the matter of honesty and rectitude. At first, he suggests that politicians should cultivate the *appearance* of honesty and rectitude, while avoiding *real* honesty and rectitude, so that they can "trick men with their cunning, and . . . overcome those abiding by honest principles." But then Machiavelli hedges his position. He says that the politician should not just appear to be honest and moral—the politician should really be honest and moral, *but* that the politician's "disposition should be such that, if he needs to be the opposite, he knows how." Can an official be honest and moral while standing ready to lie in order to achieve ends of state?

Should politicians operate with a relaxed moral framework, or indeed with no moral framework at all, so that they can act in the best interest of the state? Some suggest that politicians "must" sometimes "dirty their hands" and act immorally in order to avoid consequences that would be disastrous for the citizens or communities they represent. For example, lying or even killing some innocent citizens might be the only way to eliminate a substantial threat to the state, according to some political theorists.

Kant

Most people would say that while people have a *prima facie* duty to be honest, to avoid lying, a lie can be permissible in certain circumstances when they cannot meet other moral responsibilities without it. However, Immanuel Kant says honesty is "an unconditional duty which holds in all circumstances." In some places, Kant objects to lying on the grounds that it impugns the dignity of humanity. When a French philosopher named Benjamin Constant (1767–1830) condoned a lie to a murderer if it is necessary to protect the life of a friend, Kant countered with the response that lying undermines people's willingness to trust each other, and thereby undermines "all rights based on contracts," which harms everyone. He added that if you tell the murderer the truth about where your friend is, you are not the one who harms your friend; the murderer is the cause of your friend's death. However, since truthfulness is "the ground of all duties based on contract," justice demands that you be held responsible for all consequences of lying. If your lie sends the murderer outside your house, where he happens upon your friend and kills him, "you might justly be accused as the cause of his death."

Sidgwick

Henry Sidgwick (1838–1900), a British philosopher, points out that only some lies might be said to impugn the dignity of humanity, namely, lies for selfish ends. He also notes that some lies are endorsed by common-sense morality, such as lies that benefit the people who are deceived; for example, people sometimes lie to avoid dangerous shocks to children or invalids. A utilitarian, Sidgwick counsels benevolent deception when justified by appealing to "considerations of expediency." In addition to (a) benevolent deception, Sidgwick discusses (b) pious fraud, or lying for religious ends; and (c) turning questions aside by indirectly producing false beliefs.

Higgs and Honest Physicians

Should physicians ever lie to their patients? Suppose physicians think that the truth would give their patients dangerous shocks; may they conceal the truth, or even intentionally misrepresent the patients' conditions, or must they fully disclose the truth, albeit in a caring and supportive manner?

In order to think through this issue, it is necessary to consider the physician–patient relationship in its broader context. Some claim that people have a moral *right to bodily autonomy*, which is the right to decide what shall be done to their own bodies. The recognition of this right would seem to be necessitated by respect for *self-determination*. Self-determination is partly a matter of devising and revising one's life plan and values in light of changing circumstances and partly a matter of shaping one's life in accordance with our plans and values. Presumably everyone except certain individuals with severe mental impairments is capable of self-determination. However, no one can be self-determining in this sense without the right to bodily autonomy, and the courts have long recognized a legal right to bodily autonomy. Assuming that the self-determination of mentally competent people ought to be respected, affording patients such respect should be one of the goals of the physician. But, of course, the physician has another goal as well, namely, promoting the patient's well-being. In order to accomplish both goals, it is usually necessary for the physician to provide all information necessary for the patient to make an informed choice among treatment options (deemed effective by the physician) or to make an informed decision to refuse all treatment. However, which of the two goals should take priority in cases of conflict, respect for the mentally competent patient's self-determination or the promotion of the patient's well-being?

If respect for the patient's self-determination should always take priority, then perhaps physicians should always fully disclose the truth to patients even if the news will be a dangerous blow, although of course they ought to make the disclosure in the most gentle and supportive way possible. The patient has the final word on treatment options, and the patient cannot make an informed decision without the full disclosure of the truth. But might some patients transfer the right to make treatment decisions to the physician? And might some patients be rendered incapable of making rational decisions if given certain information?

In his essay, Higgs argues for a strong presumption for truth-telling in the medical context, but he also leaves some room for the acceptability of lies when "no acceptable alternative" remains.

2. HONESTY WITH ONESELF

Is it possible to deceive oneself? In "Self-Deception," an excerpt from his book *Being and Nothingness*, Jean-Paul Sartre argues that a lie to oneself is difficult to sustain. (He describes it as an "evanescent," "metastable," and "precarious" undertaking.) One must know the truth in order to conceal it from oneself, and Sartre assumes full awareness of the contents of one's consciousness, so an attempt to deceive oneself is easy to detect. However, the project of self-deception is apparently stable enough that "a person can live in self-deception, which does not mean that he does not have abrupt awakenings." So "we can neither reject nor comprehend self-deception."

Sartre goes on to give illuminating descriptions of some of the devices people use to deceive themselves. Principally they vacillate between seeing themselves as "facticities" and as "transcendences." That is, people vacillate between the perspective of the subjective self, or the self insofar as it is one's own creation, and the point of view of the natural self, or the self insofar as it is given by nature. Such vacillation allows one to disarm a repugnant truth by (1) saying that it is true only insofar as one is a natural self, when in fact one is a subjective self, or (2) saying that it is true only insofar as one is a subjective self when in fact one is a natural self. A second device people use is to vacillate between their own self-conceptions and the conceptions of them held by other people. A third is to chop their selves into different person stages and identify with some of these at one time, and with others at other times.

Thus, the desire to deceive oneself in various ways gives powerful grounds to leave the question of identity up in the air. If it were finally resolved, one could not continue to deceive oneself through caginess about self-image. Finally deciding on an identity is made difficult for another reason: According to Sartre, sincerity, "the antithesis of self-deception," is problematic because sincerity seems to require "that a man be for himself only what he is" which appears to entail identifying entirely with the objective view of the self. But that suggests that sincerity is itself a form of self-deception.

LOYALTY

Loyalty is a quality that is central to both friendship and patriotism. Loyalty in friendship means placing one's friend ahead of other people, and loyalty in patriotism means placing one's community or state ahead of other groups. In Chapter 5, Aristotle portrays friendship as an important element of a worthwhile life, and one might also take a similar view concerning patriotism. But perhaps friendship and patriotism are not unqualified goods. Indeed loyalty, which is an element of both, seems problematic if the right is identified as an impartial point of view that stands outside of and restricts all considerations of self-interest: Loyalty inclines people toward partiality, to develop and act upon special affections for particular people and groups, while the objective right seems to demand the impartial treatment of everyone.

1. KANTIAN COSMOPOLITAN

Because loyalty clashes with the impartiality that seems essential to the right, it is unsurprising to find Kant voicing reservations about friendship in his writings, as in the following passages from *Lectures on Ethics*:

> It is not man's way to embrace the whole world in his good-will; he prefers to restrict it to a small circle. He is inclined to form sects, parties, societies. The most primitive societies are those based on family connexion. . . .
>
> The more civilized man becomes, the broader his outlook and the less room there is for special friendships; civilized man seeks universal pleasures and a universal friendship, unrestricted by special ties. . . .
>
> To be the friend of everybody is impossible, for friendship is a particular relationship, and he who is a friend to everyone has no particular friend.

Clearly, Kant would prefer that we take the same favorable attitude to everyone without the restrictions of special ties to particular people of groups.

In "On the Relation of Theory to Practice in International Law—A General-Philanthropic, i.e., Cosmopolitan View," Part III of his 1793 book *On the Old Saw: That May be Right in Theory But it Won't Work in Practice*, Kant goes beyond voicing reservations about loyalty to particular persons and groups. He argues that morality requires no allegiance to a particular nation, but rather a "cosmopolitan view-point;" morality requires replacing the order of sovereign nation states with a federa-tion of nations linked together under a cosmopolitan constitution.

2. COMMUNITARIANS

Of course, people might favor some over others for more than one reason, and not all such reasons are consistent with friendship and patriotism. As Aristotle said, if I am in-terested in you solely because you can help me financially, or because you entertain me, then however kindly I feel toward you, I am not your friend. Something similar might be said of patriotism: If I am interested in my community solely because it is use-ful to me, I am not a patriot. The basis of well-wishing among friends is an overlap of identity, and the basis of the patriot's concern about her community is a failure to fully separate her identity from the community. This suggestion—that loyalty is a morally re-spectable offshoot of identification with the community—is defended by writers who call themselves "communitarians," such as Michael Sandel, by writers whose ideas the communitarians develop, such as Aristotle and G. W. F. Hegel, and by other writers who appeal to communitarian ideas, such as the conservative Roger Scruton and the self-styled "postmodernist bourgeois liberal" Richard Rorty, a philosopher at the University of Virginia. These thinkers question the idea that morality as equated with an impartial point of view ought to trump the interests of the community.

---

[1]In *Essays Civil and Moral* (London: Ward, Locke, 1910).

Questions for Reflection

1. How might Confucius respond to Kant's claim that "the most primitive societies are those based on family connexion"?

2. Are Plato and Machiavelli correct when they suggest that state officials may lie to the peo-ple whose interests they oversee? When people see through Plato's noble lies, won't they distrust state officials? What should state officials do to the people who see through the lies?

3. Under what circumstances, if any, should physicians lie to their patients? Could they morally lie to young children, whom the truth might frighten?

4. Why should one be honest with oneself? What is the relationship between honesty and in-tegrity? What is the relationship between honesty and being a particular self (as defined by commitments)?

5. What is loyalty? Do people face a duty to be loyal, or is loyalty incompatible with morality?

6. What ought you to do when your loyalty to your friend clashes with your loyalty to your community? What should you do if loyalty requires that you act against interests you con-sider essential to your identity?

7. What does Kant mean by *self-esteem*? Critically assess Kant's arguments for the claim that "self-esteem should be the principle of our duties towards ourselves."

8. How does Thomas distinguish between self-respect and self-esteem? How would Kant react? Critically assess Thomas's argument for the claim that "a person has self-respect . . . if and only if he has the conviction that he is deserving of full moral status, and so the basic rights of that status, simply in virtue of the fact that he is a person."

9. According to Williams, the claim that "each of us is specially responsible for what *he* does, rather than for what other people do," is "an idea closely connected with the value of integrity," and utilitarianism "makes integrity as a value more or less unintelligible." Explain, and assess, Williams's position.

Suggested Readings

On Integrity and Self-Respect
Frankfurt, Harry. *The Importance of What We Care About*. Cambridge: Cambridge University Press, 1988.
Nagel, Thomas. *The View from Nowhere*. New York: Oxford University Press, 1986.
Williams, Bernard. *Moral Luck*. Cambridge: Cambridge University Press, 1981.
——. *Problems of the Self*. Cambridge: Cambridge University Press, 1973.
Wolf, Susan. "Moral Saints." *Journal of Philosophy* 79, (1982) 419–39.
On Honesty
Bok, Sissela. *Lying: Moral Choice in Public and Private Life*. New York: Pantheon Books, 1978.
Fingarette, Herbert. *Self-Deception*. London: Routledge, 1979.
On Communitarianism
Bellah, Robert, et al. *Habits of the Heart*. Berkeley: University of California Press, 1985.
Crowley, B. *The Self, the Individual and the Community*. Oxford: Oxford Press, 1987.
Sandel, Michael. *Liberalism and the Limits of Justice*. Cambridge: Cambridge University Press, 1982.

INTEGRITY AND SELF-RESPECT

IMMANUEL KANT

Duties to Oneself

My duty towards myself cannot be treated juridically; the law touches only our relations with other men; I have no legal obligations towards myself; and whatever I do to myself I do to a consenting party; I cannot commit an act of injustice against myself. What we have to discuss is the use we make of liberty in respect of ourselves. . . .

Freedom is, on the one hand, that faculty which gives unlimited usefulness to all other faculties. It is the highest order of life, which serves as the foundation of all perfections and is their necessary condition. All animals have the faculty of using their powers according to will. But this will is not free. It is necessitated through the incitement of *stimuli*, and the actions of animals involve a *bruta necessitas*. If the will of all beings were so bound to sensuous impulse, the world would possess no value. The inherent value of the world, the *summum bonum*, is freedom in accordance with a will which is not necessitated to action. Freedom is thus the inner value of the world. But on the other hand, freedom unrestrained by rules of its conditional employment is the most terrible of all things. . . . I can conceive freedom as the complete absence of orderliness, if it is not subject to an objective determination. The grounds of this objective determination must lie in the understanding, and constitute the restrictions to freedom. Therefore the proper use of freedom is the supreme rule. What then is the condition under which freedom is restricted? It is the law. The universal law is therefore as follows: Let thy procedure be such that in all thine actions regularity prevails. What does this restraint imply when applied to the individual? That he should not follow his inclinations. The fundamental rule, in terms of which I ought to restrain my freedom, is the conformity of free behaviour to the essential ends of humanity. I shall not then follow my inclinations, but bring them under a rule. He who subjects his person to his inclinations, acts contrary to the essential end of humanity; for as a free being he must not be subjected to inclinations, but ought to determine them in the exercise of his freedom; and being a free agent he must have a rule, which is the essential end of humanity. In the case of animals inclinations are already determined by subjectively compelling factors; in their case, therefore, disorderliness is impossible. But if man gives free rein to his inclinations, he sinks lower than an animal because he then lives in a state of disorder which does not exist among animals. A man is then in contradiction with the essential ends of humanity in his own person, and so with himself. . . . The supreme rule is that in all the actions which affect himself a man should so conduct himself that every exercise of his power is compatible with the fullest employment of them. Let us illustrate our meaning by examples. If I have drunk too much I am incapable of using my freedom and my powers. Again, if I kill myself, I use my powers to deprive myself of the faculty of using them. That freedom, the principle of the highest order of life, should annul itself and abrogate the use of itself conflicts with the fullest use of freedom. But freedom can only be in harmony with itself under certain conditions; otherwise it comes into collision with itself. If there were no established order in Nature, everything would come to an end, and so is it with unbridled freedom. Evils are to be found, no doubt, in Nature, but the true moral evil, vice, only in freedom. We pity the unfortunate, but we hate the vicious and rejoice at their punishment. The conditions under which alone the fullest use of freedom is possible, and can be in harmony with itself, are the essential ends of humanity. It must conform with these. The principle of all duties is that the use of freedom must be in keeping with the essential ends of humanity. Thus, for instance, a human being is not entitled to sell his limbs for money, even if he were offered 10,000 thalers for a single finger. If he were so entitled, he could sell all his limbs. We can dispose of things which have no freedom but not of a being which has free will. A man who sells himself makes himself a thing and, as he has jettisoned his person, it is open to anyone to deal with him as he pleases. Another instance of this kind is where a human being makes himself a thing by making himself an object of enjoyment for some one's sexual desire. It degrades humanity, and that is why those guilty of it feel ashamed.

Not self-favour but self-esteem should be the principle of our duties towards ourselves. This means that our actions must be in keeping with the worth of man. . . . There are in us two grounds of action; inclinations, which belong to our animal nature, and humanity, to which the inclinations must be subjected. Our duties to ourselves are negative; they restrict our freedom in respect of our inclinations, which aim at our own welfare. Just as law restricts our freedom in our relations with other men, so do our duties to ourselves restrict our freedom in dealing with ourselves. All such duties are grounded in a certain love of honour consisting in self-esteem; man must not appear unworthy in his own eyes; his actions must be in keeping with humanity itself if he is to appear in his own eyes worthy of inner respect. To value approbation is the essential ingredient of our duties towards ourselves.

The better to appreciate our duties to ourselves, let us imagine the evil consequences of failure in these duties. They will be found to be most prejudicial to man. It is, of course, the inner baseness, and not the consequences, which is the principle of the action, but the consequences enable us to appreciate better the principle of the duties. Because we have freedom and the faculty to satisfy our inclinations by all manner of devices, if we did not restrain our freedom we should destroy ourselves. If it be argued that this is a rule of prudence, the answer is that the consequences must first be given before we can derive our prudence from them. There must, therefore, be a principle that man shall restrict his freedom, and this principle is a moral one.

We shall now examine separately the several duties man owes to himself, with particular reference to the conditions under which he lives as an intelligent being.

First there is the universal duty which devolves upon man of so ordering his life as to be fit for the performance of all moral duties. This demands that he should establish in himself principles and moral purity and strive to act in accordance with them. This in turn demands that he shall prove and examine himself to see whether his dispositions also are morally pure. The springs of disposition must be examined to discover whether they are honour or illusion, superstition or pure morality. Neglect to do this is exceedingly detrimental to morality. . . .

LAURENCE THOMAS

Self-Respect: Theory and Practice

We begin life as rather frail creatures who are quite unable to do much of anything for ourselves. If all goes well we end up as healthy adults with a secure sense of worth. At the outset of our lives, there are two things that are generally thought to enhance significantly the likelihood of our turning out to be adults of this sort: (i) our being a continuous object of parental love (or, of course, a permanent parental surrogate) and (ii) the acquisition of a strong sense of competence with respect to our ability to interact effectively with our social and physical environment.[1] It is obvious that whereas the latter continues to be important throughout our lives, the former does not. Of course, we may continue to value the love of our parents; the point, rather, is that as adults our sense of worth is not, if we develop normally, tied to our being loved by our parents. Does this mean, then, that the only important sense of worth to be countenanced among adults is that which turns upon their having a sense of competence? One reason to be skeptical that this is so is just that love, and therefore parental love, has so very little to do with a person's performances. I believe that self-respect can be seen as the social analogue, for adults, to the sense of worth that is generated by parental love. My aim in this essay is to show the importance which this line of reasoning has for both moral theory and social philosophy

I

. . . Whereas both parental love and praise both play a most important role in the child's life, the very fact that the child is very dependent upon his parents for food, shelter, and protection should make it obvious why parental love plays yet a more significant role in the child's life than parental praise. A child would be in an awful way if his being provided with these things were conditional upon his doing what his parents deemed praiseworthy. Because learning how to do as one's parents have instructed one is precisely what one does as a child, the fear of parental rejection would loom large in the life of a child for whom receiving these benefits was contingent upon his doing what his parents deemed praiseworthy; for he would be constantly fearful of failing to behave in this way. Moreover, if a child's receiving parental protection were made contingent upon this sort of thing, then out of fear he would be more reluctant to engage in exploratory behavior. This is because he would lack the assurance that his parents would protect him when things got out of hand for him. This would be unfortunate for the child, since engaging in exploratory behavior is one of the chief means by which the child acquires a strong sense of competence.[2]

As no doubt one has already surmised, the significance of parental love lies in the fact that, first of all, it allays, if not precludes entirely, the child's fear of parental rejection; second, it minimizes the child's fear of engaging in exploratory behavior. For, as a result of being the continuous object of parental love, the child comes to have the conviction that the reason why he matters to his parents is just that they love him, and not that he has this or that set of talents or that he behaves in this or that way. Parental praise, as important as it is,[3] could never instill in the child a conviction such as this. As a result of parental love, the child then comes to have a sense of worth that does not turn upon either his abilities or his behavior. This sense of worth is, I want to say, the precursor to self-respect.

To the fact that there are many ways in which persons can be treated is added morality, a conception of how persons ought to be treated. The primary way in which a rights-based moral theory does this is by postulating a set of basic rights, which each person has simply in virtue of being a person. . . . A person has self-respect, I shall say, if and only if he has the conviction that he is deserving of full moral status, and so the basic rights of that status, simply in virtue of the fact that he is a person. . . .

It is clear that, understood in this way, self-respect makes no reference at all to the abilities of persons, since a person is no less that in view of what her abilities are. . . . What is more, it follows, on my view, that in order to have self-respect, a person need not have a morally acceptable character. For the belief that one is deserving of full moral status is certainly compatible with the belief that one's moral character is not up to par. . . .

Thus far, I have merely offered an account of self-respect; I have not argued for its soundness. The argument that I shall offer will draw upon two examples from the black experience in the United States (§3); however, that argument will presuppose an appreciation for the difference between self-respect and self-esteem. So, before I begin it, a brief discussion about this latter concept is in order.

II

William James defined self-esteem as the ratio of a person's successes to his aspirations:[4]

$$\text{SELF-ESTEEM} = \frac{\text{SUCCESSES}}{\text{ASPIRATIONS}}$$

Contemporary psychologists have made no theoretical advances over James's notion of self-esteem.[5] They consider it to be the sense of worth that an individual has, which turns upon his evaluation of his ability to interact effectively with his environment, especially his social environment. It is of utmost importance to note that self-esteem is quite neutral between ends in that the successful pursuit of any end towards which a person aspires can contribute to his self-esteem. . . .

Now, as James's formula makes clear, the more (or less) in line our successes are with our aspirations, the higher (or lower) our self-esteem will be. From this it straightforwardly follows that, other things equal, the well-endowed are favored to have high self-esteem, since the well-endowed, in comparison to those whose assets are minimal, have fewer ends that are beyond their reach. . . . In any society where people are free to attempt to pursue the ends of their choosing, it is virtually inevitable that the talents of some will fail to match their aspirations and, therefore, that some will have low self-esteem. . . .

I have said that if a person has the appropriate aspirations, then the successful pursuit of any end can contribute significantly to his self-esteem. I want to conclude this section with the observation that the aim to lead a morally good life is no exception to this claim. A person's high self-esteem can turn just as much upon his moral accomplishments as it can upon his accomplishments in sports or the academy. Naturally enough, we may think of self-esteem that turns upon the former as moral self-esteem. And just as the failure to measure up to our nonmoral aspirations occasions nonmoral shame, the failure to measure up to our moral aspirations occasions moral shame. I have bothered to make this point explicit in order to show that we can capture an important Kantian insight in the absence of a Kantian conception of self-respect If we assume that everyone morally ought to aspire to lead a minimally decent moral life, then we can rightly say that there is a sense of shame—indeed, moral shame—that a person rightly feels in failing to do so. This we can say without saying that such a person must view herself or himself as not being deserving of full moral status. Thus, in order to experience moral shame a person need not lack self-respect. Self-respect, as I conceive of it, cannot be the source of moral shame; but, as these remarks make clear, the account of self-respect offered leaves room for such shame. I have not taken it out of the picture; rather, I have merely shifted its location.

III

I have offered an account of self-respect, which I have argued is distinct from self-esteem. I turn now to argue for the soundness of the account offered. As I remarked, I shall do this by drawing upon two examples from the black experience.

By definition (or so it seems) an Uncle Tom is a black who lacks self-respect. I do not know whether or not Booker T. Washington was an Uncle Tom; nor shall I be concerned to take a stand on the matter. I do know, however, that he has often been called an Uncle Tom.[6] What has been the force behind this epithet? Well, it is obvious that no one familiar with his life could have ever meant that he was lacking in talent or, in any case, that he set his sights too high. For this was a man who, though he was born a slave, went on to found an academic institution, The Tuskegee Institute. This is not something a minimally talented person is apt to do; and he did as much as any black could have reasonably hoped to do, life being what it was for blacks then. . . .

What had made him seem so vulnerable to the charge of being an Uncle Tom is that he appeared to be too accepting of the status quo. It was the prevailing view of whites back then that blacks were not socially prepared for full-fledged citizenship and, therefore, that social intercourse between blacks and whites, political participation on the part of blacks, and rights given to them should be kept to a minimum. It has seemed to a great many that, in his "Atlanta Exposition Address,"[7] it is precisely this view that Washington, himself, endorsed. If he did endorse this view, then the charge that he was an Uncle Tom seems fair enough. But, for all we know, and it is certainly not implausible to suppose this, Washington may have been a very shrewd and calculating black whose public stance was designed to appease the status quo in order to assure continued financial support from whites for the educational endeavors of blacks. If so, then I should think that a great deal more has to be said before one has a convincing case that he was an Uncle Tom. . . .

But, now, suppose that Washington did subscribe to the prevailing view about blacks then, why would this warrant the charge that he was an Uncle Tom and so lacked self-respect? . . .

If, in fact, he believed that blacks were not deserving of full-fledged citizenship; if, in particular, he believed that the franchise was something of which blacks should have to prove themselves worthy, then he is quite vulnerable to the charge that he was an Uncle Tom. As is the case now, the right to vote was not, during Washington's time, something that had to be earned: one needed only to be born in this country and to reach the age of majority. This is how whites were treated then; and Washington should have believed, regardless of what he maintained publicly, that considerations of fairness required that blacks be treated in the same way. If he, or anyone else, did not see that it was unfair that blacks should have to earn this fundamentally important right, when whites did not have to do so, then he failed to see that, even in the case of institutional rights, a person's claim to fair treatment is not secured by either his social standing as determined, say, by his wealth and mastery of the social graces or the hue of his skin. If so, then the charge that he was an Uncle Tom, and so lacked self-respect, would appear to be warranted. . . .

The Civil Rights Movement (CRM) of the 1960s provides us with another illustration from the black experience that supports the account of self-respect presented in this essay. At the outset, I should acknowledge that as a result of the CRM, the self-esteem of many blacks was enhanced as business and social institutions in the United States opened their more privileged positions to blacks in increasingly greater numbers and as various aspects of black culture and history gained greater appreciation in the American mainstream. And it is clear that both the collective pride and self-esteem of blacks was enhanced. I take as evidence of this change in hairstyles and, most importantly, the fact that the term "black," which hitherto had been considered a most disparaging term, replaced "coloured" and "Negro" as the accepted term for referring to persons of African descent.

Now, as significant as the changes that I have just described were, the CRM wrought yet a more fundamental change in the lives of blacks. It enhanced their self-respect. It secured or, in any event, made more secure the conviction on the part of the blacks that they are deserving of full moral status and, therefore, of the right to fair treatment. One must remember, after all, that the CRM did not straightaway result in the vast majority of blacks going on to pursue careers that greatly enhanced their self-esteem. Nor did it result in each black discovering in himself talents that hitherto had gone unnoticed by him. And although it is certainly true that the physical features of whites came to be a less important yardstick by which blacks measured their own physical attractiveness, the end result was not that all blacks got to be beautiful. Thus, if the success of the CRM were to be judged along these lines only, then it would have to be deemed a failure. But, in at least one very important respect a failure it was not.

A person did not need to acquire a new career, to discover new talents in himself, or to consider his physical appearance improved in order to feel the effects of the civil rights movement. For, the raison d'etre of this movement was not to secure these things as such. Rather, it was to stir the conscience of the American people, to arouse their sense of justice, and to move them to end the injustices that blacks have suffered.[8] *The* goal of the Civil Rights Movement was to secure the conviction on the part of both blacks and whites that blacks were deserving of full moral status and, therefore, of just and fair treatment. In order for blacks to see themselves in this light, a new career, or whatever, was far from necessary. Of course, given what the unjust treatment of blacks came to, the just treatment of blacks could not help but have a positive effect upon their self-esteem. (I take justice to be subsumable under fairness.[9] Nothing of substance turns on the talk about justice here.)

However, it would be a mistake to generalize from the Civil Rights Movement to the conclusion that whenever a group of people, who have been treated unjustly, are treated justly their self-esteem, as well as their self-respect, will be enhanced. For the unjust treatment of people does not, as a matter of logic, involve denying the fact that they have talents and abilities to pursue, with hope of success, and to appreciate the ends of the academy and the other professions. If it did, then we would be logically committed to the absurd view that we could not treat unjustly those who lack the natural endowment to pursue such ends. This last remark points to why self-respect is a more fundamental sense of worth than self-esteem. It could turn out, given our abilities, that so few ends are within our reach that our having low self-esteem is all but inevitable. But not so with self-respect, since it is not, in the first place, a sense of worth that turns upon what our abilities happen to be. Thus, observe that in the 1960s what blacks demanded, in the name of justice and fairness, is that they be allowed the freedoms, opportunities, and privileges to which others had been so long accustomed. What they did not demand, and rightly so, is that they be given the natural assets to do as others do. It is because blacks had a claim to the enhancement of their self-respect that they had a claim to the enhancement of their self-esteem. Sometimes the importance of the latter, as in the case at hand, is derivative upon the importance of the former; the importance of self-respect, however, is never derivative upon the importance of self-esteem. . . .

VI

In the introduction to this essay, I made the claim that self-respect is the social analogue to the sense of worth engendered by parental love. That must have seemed to be a quite controversial claim those many pages ago. I hope it is less so now. Self-respect, I have tried to show, is a sense of worth that is not in any way tied to a person's abilities. It is a moral sense of worth. It is among social institutions that we live; and these institutions can be conducive to our having self-respect. Not only that, it is of the utmost importance that social institutions are conducive to persons having self-respect, just as it is of the utmost importance that parents love their children. The reason why both of these claims are true has nothing whatsoever to do with the talents and abilities of persons. Now, if drawing upon the black experience has made it easier to see that self-respect is the social analogue to the sense of worth that is engendered by parental love, then our indebtedness to that experience may very well be greater than many have been inclined to suppose.

---

[1] [Thomas's notes have been renumbered—ed.] In connection with (i) see, e.g. John Bowlby, *Child Care and the Growth of Love* (Baltimore: Penguin Books, 1953), with (ii) see, e.g., Robert W. White, *Ego and Reality in Psychoanalytic Theory* (New York: International Universities Press, Inc., 1963). For arguments that support both (i) and (ii) see, among others, H. Rudolph Schaffer and Charles K. Crook, "The Role of the Mother in Early Social Development," in Harry McGurk (ed), *Issues in Childhood Social Development* (London: Metheun and Co., 1978) and M. Rutter, "Early Sources of Security and Competence," in Jerome Bruner and Alison Garton (eds), *Human Growth and Development* (Oxford: Oxford University Press, 1978).

[2] See White, ch. 3.

[3] For the way in which I have unpacked the difference between parental love and parental praise, I am much indebted to Gregory Vlastos, "Justice and Equality," in Richard Brandt (ed), *Social Justice* (Englewood Cliffs, N. J.: Prentice-Hall, 1962). See section II especially. I have also benefited from the following essays: Ann Swidler, "Love and Adulthood in American Culture" and Leonard I. Pearlin, "Life Strains and

Psychological Distress among Adults." Both are in Neil J. Smelser and Erik H. Erikson (eds), *Themes of Work and Love in Adulthood* (Cambridge, Mass.: Harvard University Press, 1980).

[4]*Principles of Psychology*, v. I, "The Consciousness of Self."

[5]Roger Brown in *Social Psychology* (New York: The Free Press, 1965) writes that James has "written, with unequaled sensitivity and wisdom, of the self as an object of knowledge, as a mental construction of the human organism" (648). Stanley Coopersmith, *The Antecedents of Self-Esteem* (San Francisco, Calif.: W. H. Freeman and Company, 1967) writes "Earlier psychologist and sociologists such as William James . . . provided major insights and guidelines for the study of self-esteem. Their formulations remain among the most cogent on the topic, particularly their discussions of the sources of high and low esteem" (27).

[6]For a discussion of the life of Booker T. Washington, see, among others, John Hope Franklin, *From Slavery to Freedom*, 3 ed. (New York: Random House, 1967), ch. 21, and Charles E. Silberman, *Crises in Black and White* (New York: Random House, 1964), ch. 5. And for the story of his life, see, of course, Washington's autobiography *Up from Slavery* (Boston, Mass.: Houghton, Mifflin, 1901).

[7]Consider the following passages from the address, which is to be found in Washington's autobiography, *Up from Slavery*, ch. 14:

—No race can prosper till it learns that there is as much dignity in tilling a field as in writing a poem. It is at the bottom of life we must begin, and not at the top.

—In all things that are purely social we can be as separate as the fingers, yet be one as the hand in all things essential to mutual progress.

—It is important and right that all privileges of the law be ours, but it is vastly more important that we be prepared for exercising these privileges.

[8]See Rawls' discussion on the role of civil disobedience in *A Theory of Justice* (Cambridge, MA: Harvard University Press, 1971) pp. 382–391.

[9]This is Rawls' insight, which is first stated in his "Justice as Fairness," *The Philosophical Review* 68 (1958). To put it most intuitively, justice is simply fairness backed up by rules of enforcement, especially legal ones. We speak of the sword of justice, not the sword of fairness. Talk about the virtue of justice, as exhibited in the just man, is not that much at odds with this point, if one supposes that the mark of the just man is that he does what should be required of him whether or not this is so. He does not treat others *unfairly* although he could easily get away with doing so. I owe this point to Paul Ziff.

BERNARD WILLIAMS

A Critique of Utilitarianism

NEGATIVE RESPONSIBILITY: AND TWO EXAMPLES

. . . Consequentialism is basically indifferent to whether a state of affairs consists in what I do, or is produced by what I do, where the notion is itself wide enough to include, for instance, situations in which other people do things which I have made them do, or allowed them to do, or encouraged them to do, or given them a chance to do. All that consequentialism is interested in is the idea of these doings being *consequences* of what I do, and that is a relation broad enough to include the relations just mentioned, and many others. . . .

For consequentialism, all causal connexions are on the same level, and it makes no difference, so far as that goes, whether the causation of a given state of affairs lies through another agent, or not.

Correspondingly, there is no relevant difference which consists *just* in one state of affairs being brought about by me, without intervention of other agents, and another being brought about through the intervention of other agents; although some genuinely causal differences involving a difference of value may correspond to that (as when, for instance, the other agents derive pleasure or pain from the transaction), that kind of difference will already be included in the specification of the state of affairs to be produced. Granted that the states of affairs have been adequately described in causally and evaluatively relevant terms, it makes no further comprehensible difference who produces them. It is because consequentialism attaches value ultimately to states of affairs, and its concern is with what states of affairs the world contains, that it essentially involves the notion of *negative responsibility*: that if I am ever responsible for anything, then I must be just as much responsible for things that I allow or fail to prevent, as I am for things that I myself, in the more everyday restricted sense, bring about.[1] Those things also must enter my deliberations, as a responsible moral agent, on the same footing. What matters is what states of affairs the world contains, and so what matters with respect to a given action is what comes about if it is done, and what comes about if it is not done, and those are questions not intrinsically affected by the nature of the causal linkage, in particular by whether the outcome is partly produced by other agents.

The strong doctrine of negative responsibility flows directly from consequentialism's assignment of ultimate value to states of affairs. Looked at from another point of view, it can be seen also as a special application of something that is favoured in many moral outlooks not themselves consequentialist—something which, indeed, some thinkers have been disposed to regard as the essence of morality itself: a principle of impartiality. Such a principle will claim that there can be no relevant difference from a moral point of view which consists just in the fact, not further explicable in general terms, that benefits or harms accrue to one person rather than to another—"it's me" can never in itself be a morally comprehensible reason. This principle, familiar with regard to the reception of harms and benefits, we can see consequentialism as extending to their production: from the moral point of view, there is no comprehensible difference which consists just in my bringing about a certain outcome rather than someone else's producing it. That the doctrine of negative responsibility represents in this way the extreme of impartiality, and abstracts from the identity of the agent, leaving just a locus of causal intervention in the world—that fact is not merely a surface paradox. It helps to explain why consequentialism can seem to some to express a more serious attitude than non-consequentialist views, why part of its appeal is to a certain kind of high-mindedness. Indeed, that is part of what is wrong with it. . . .

Let us look more concretely at two examples, to see what utilitarianism might say about them, what we might say about utilitarianism and, most importantly of all, what would be implied by certain ways thinking about the situations. . . .

(I) George, who has just taken his Ph.D. in chemistry, finds it extremely difficult to get a job. He is not very robust in health, which cuts down on the number of jobs he might be able to do satisfactorily. His wife has to go out to work to keep them, which itself causes a great deal of strain, since they have small children and there are severe problems about looking after them. The results of all this, especially on the children, are damaging. An older chemist, who knows about this situation, says that he can get George a decently paid job in a certain laboratory, which pursues research into chemical and biological warfare. George says that he cannot accept this, since he is opposed to chemical and biological warfare. The older man replies that he is not too keen on it himself, come to that, but after all George's refusal is not going to make the job or the laboratory go away; what is more, he happens to know that if George refuses the job, it will certainly go to a contemporary of George's who is not inhibited by any such scruples and is likely if appointed to push along the research with greater zeal than George would. Indeed, it is not merely concern for George and his family, but (to speak frankly and in confidence) some alarm about this other man's excess of zeal, which has led the older man to offer to use his influence to get George the job . . . George's wife, to whom he is deeply attached, has views (the details of which need not concern us) from which it follows that at least there is nothing particularly wrong with research into CBW. What should he do?

(2) Jim finds himself in the central square of a small South American town. Tied up against the wall are a row of 20 Indians, most terrified, a few defiant, in front of them several armed men in uniform. A heavy man in a sweat-stained khaki shirt turns out to be the captain in charge and, after a good deal of questioning of Jim which establishes that he got there by accident while on a botanical expedition, explains that the Indians are a random group of the inhabitants who, after recent acts of protest against the government, are just about to be killed to remind other possible protestors of the advantages of not protesting. However, since Jim is an honoured visitor from another land, the captain is happy to offer him a guest's privilege of killing one of the Indians himself. If Jim accepts, then as a special mark of the occasion, the other Indians will be let off. Of course, if Jim refuses, then there is no special occasion, and Pedro here will do what he was about to do when Jim arrived, and kill them all. Jim, with some desperate recollection of schoolboy fiction, wonders whether if he got hold of a gun, he could hold the captain, Pedro and the rest of the soldiers to threat, but it is quite clear from the set-up that nothing of that kind is going to work: any attempt at that sort of thing will mean that all the Indians will be killed, and himself. The men against the wall, and the other villagers, understand the situation, and are obviously begging him to accept. What should he do?

To these dilemmas, it seems to me that utilitarianism replies, in the first case, that George should accept the job, and in the second, that Jim should kill the Indian. Not only does utilitarianism give these answers but, if the situations are essentially as described and there are no further special factors, it regards them, it seems to me, as *obviously* the right answers. But many of us would certainly wonder whether, in (I), that could possibly be the right answer at all; and in the case of (2), even one who came to think that perhaps that was the answer, might well wonder whether it was obviously the answer. Nor is it just a question of the rightness or obviousness of these answers. It is also a question of what sort of considerations come into finding the answer. A feature of utilitarianism is that it cuts out a kind of consideration which for some others makes a difference to what they feel about such cases: a consideration involving the idea, as we might first and very simply put it, that each of us is specially responsible for what *he* does, rather than for what other people do. This is an idea closely connected with the value of integrity. It is often suspected that utilitarianism, at least in its direct forms, makes integrity as a value more or less unintelligible. I shall try to show that this suspicion is correct. Of course, even if that is correct, it would not necessarily follow that we should reject utilitarianism; perhaps, as utilitarians sometimes suggest, we should just forget about integrity, in favour of such things as a concern for the general good. However, if I am right, we cannot merely do that, since the reason why utilitarianism cannot understand integrity is that it cannot coherently describe the relations between a man's projects and his actions. . . .

INTEGRITY

The situations have in common that if the agent does not do a certain disagreeable thing, someone else will, and in Jim's situation at least the result, the state of affairs after the other man has acted, if he does, will be worse than after Jim has acted, if Jim does. The same, on a smaller scale, is true of George's case. I have already suggested that it is inherent in consequentialism that it offers a strong doctrine of negative responsibility: if I know that if I do X, O_1 will eventuate, and if I refrain from doing X, O_2 will, and that O_2 is worse than O_1, then I am responsible for O_2 if I refrain voluntarily from doing X. "You could have prevented it," as will be said, and truly, to Jim, if he refuses, by the relatives of the other Indians. (I shall leave the important question, which is to the side of the present issue, of the obligations, if any, that nest round the word "know": how far does one, under utilitarianism, have to research into the possibilities of maximally beneficent action, including prevention?)

In the present cases, the situation of O_2 includes another agent bringing about results worse than O_1. So far as O_2 has been identified up to this point—merely as the worse outcome which will eventuate if I refrain from doing X—we might equally have said that what that other brings about is O_2; but that would be to underdescribe the situation. For what occurs if Jim refrains from action is not solely 20 Indians dead, but *Pedro's killing 20 Indians*, and that is not a result which Pedro brings about, though the death of the Indians is. We can say: what one does is not included in the outcome of what one does, while what another does can be included in the outcome of what one does. For that to be so, as the terms are now being used, only a very weak condition has to be satisfied: for Pedro's killing the Indians to be the outcome of Jim's refusal, it only has to be causally true that if Jim had not refused, Pedro would not have done it.

That may be true enough for us to speak, in some sense, of Jim's responsibility for that outcome, if it occurs; but it is certainly not enough, it is worth noticing, for us to speak of Jim's *making* those things happen. For granted this way of their coming about, he could have made them happen only by making Pedro shoot, and there is no acceptable sense in which his refusal makes Pedro shoot. If the captain had said on Jim's refusal, "you leave me with no alternative," he would have been lying, like most who use that phrase. While the deaths, and the killing, may be the outcome of Jim's refusal, it is misleading to think, in such a case, of Jim having an *effect* on the world through the medium (as it happens) of Pedro's acts; for this is to leave Pedro out of the picture in his essential role of one who has intentions and projects, projects for realizing which Jim's refusal would leave an opportunity. Instead of thinking in terms of supposed effects of Jim's projects on Pedro, it is more revealing to think in terms of the effects of Pedro's projects on Jim's decision. This is the direction from which I want to criticize the notion of negative responsibility. . . .

What projects does a utilitarian agent have? As a utilitarian, he has the general project of bringing about maximally desirable outcomes; how he is to do this at any given moment is a question of what causal levers, so to speak, are at that moment within reach. The desirable outcomes, however, do not just consist of agents carrying out *that* project; there must be other more basic or lower-order projects which he and other agents have, and the desirable outcomes are going to consist, in part, of the maximally harmonious realization of those projects ("in part," because one component of a utilitarianly desirable outcome may be the occurrence of agreeable experiences which are not the satisfaction of anybody's projects). Unless there were first-order projects, the general utilitarian project would have nothing to work on, and would be vacuous. What do the more basic or lower-order projects comprise? Many will be the obvious kinds of desires for things for oneself, one's family, one's friends, including basic necessities of life, and in more relaxed circumstances, objects of taste. Or there may be pursuits and interests of an intellectual, cultural, or creative character. I introduce those as a separate class not because the objects of them lie in a separate class, and provide—as some utilitarians, in their churchy way, are fond of saying—"higher" pleasures. I introduce them separately because the agent's identification with them may be of a different order. It does not have to be: cultural and aesthetic interests just belong, for many, along with any other taste; but some people's commitment to these kinds of interests just is at once more thoroughgoing and serious than their pursuit of various objects of taste, while it is more individual and permeated with character than the desire for the necessities of life.

Beyond these, someone may have projects connected with his support of some cause: Zionism, for instance, or the abolition of chemical and biological warfare. Or there may be projects which flow from some more general disposition towards human conduct and character, such as a hatred of injustice, or of cruelty, or of killing.

It may be said that this last sort of disposition and its associated project do not count as (logically) "lower-order" relative to the higher-order project of maximizing desirable outcomes; rather, it may be said, it is itself a "higher-order" project. The vital question is not, however, how it is to be classified, but whether it and similar projects are to count among the projects whose satisfaction is to be included in the maximizing sum, and, correspondingly, as contributing to the agent's happiness. If the utilitarian says "no" to that, then he is almost certainly committed to a version of utilitarianism as absurdly superficial and shallow as Benthamite versions have often been accused of being. For this project will be discounted, presumably, on the ground that it involves, in the specification of its object, the mention of other people's happiness or interests: thus it is the kind of project which (unlike the pursuit of food for myself) presupposes a reference to other people's projects. . . . Utilitarianism would do well then to acknowledge the evident fact that among the things that make people happy is not only making other people happy, but being taken up or involved in any of a vast range of projects, or—if we waive the evangelical and moralizing associations of the word—commitments. One can be committed to such things as a person, a cause, an institution, a career, one's own genius, or the pursuit of danger.

Now none of these is itself the *pursuit of happiness*: by an exceedingly ancient platitude, it is not at all clear that there could be anything which was just that, or at least anything that had the slightest chance of being successful. Happiness, rather, requires being involved in, or at least content with, something else. . . .

Utilitarianism, then, should be willing to agree that its general aim of maximizing happiness does not imply that what everyone is doing is just pursuing happiness. On the contrary, people have to be pursuing other things. What those other things may be, utilitarianism, sticking to its professed empirical stance, should be prepared just to find out. No doubt some possible projects it will want to discourage, on the grounds that their being pursued involves a negative balance of happiness to others: though even there, the unblinking accountant's eye of the strict utilitarian will have something to put in the positive column, the satisfactions of the destructive agent. Beyond that, there will be a vast variety of generally beneficent or at least harmless projects; and some no doubt, will take the form not just of tastes or fancies, but of what I have called "commitments." It may even be that the utilitarian researcher will find that many of those with commitments, who have really identified themselves with objects outside themselves, who are thoroughly involved with other persons, or institutions, or activities, or causes, are actually happier than those whose projects and wants are not like that. If so, that is an important piece of utilitarian empirical lore. . . .

Let us now go back to the agent as utilitarian, and his higher-order project of maximizing desirable outcomes. At this level, he is committed only to that: what the outcome will actually consist of will depend entirely on the facts, on what persons with what projects and what potential satisfactions there are within calculable reach of the causal levers near which he finds himself. His own substantial projects and commitments come into it, but only as one lot among others—they potentially provide one set of satisfactions among those which he may be able to assist from where he happens to be. He is the agent of the satisfaction system who happens to be at a particular point at a particular time: in Jim's case, our man in South America. His own decisions as a utilitarian agent are a function of all the satisfactions which he can affect from where he is: and this means that the projects of others, to an indeterminately great extent, determine his decision.

This may be so either positively or negatively. It will be so positively if agents within the causal field of his decision have projects which are at any rate harmless, and so should be assisted. It will equally be so, but negatively, if there is an agent within the causal field whose projects are harmful, and have to be frustrated to maximize desirable outcomes. So it is with Jim and the soldier Pedro. On the utilitarian view, the undesirable projects of other people as much determine, in this negative way, one's decisions as the desirable ones do positively: if those people were not there, or had different projects, the causal nexus would be different, and it is the actual state of the causal nexus which determines the decision. The determination to an indefinite degree of my decisions by other people's projects is just another aspect of my unlimited responsibility to act for the best in a causal framework formed to a considerable extent by their projects.

The decision so determined is, for utilitarianism, the right decision. But what if it conflicts with some project of mine? This, the utilitarian will say, has already been dealt with: the satisfaction to you of fulfilling your project, and any satisfactions to others of your so doing, have already been through the calculating device and have been found inadequate. Now in the case of many sorts of projects, that is a perfectly reasonable sort of answer. But in the case of projects of the sort I have called "commitments," those with which one is more deeply and extensively involved and identified, this cannot just by itself be an adequate answer, and there may be no adequate answer at all. For, to take the extreme sort of case, how can a man, as a utilitarian agent, come to regard as one satisfaction among others, and a dispensable one, a project or attitude round which he has built his life, just because someone else's projects have so structured the causal scene that that is how the utilitarian sum comes out?

The point here is not, as utilitarians may hasten to say, that if the project or attitude is that central to his life, then to abandon it will be very disagreeable to him and great loss of utility will be involved. . . . On the contrary, once he is prepared to look at it like that, the argument in any serious case is over anyway. The point is that he is identified with his actions as flowing from projects and attitudes which in some cases he takes seriously at the deepest level, as what his life is about (or, in some cases, this section of his life—seriousness is not necessarily the same as persistence). It is absurd to demand of such a man, when the sums come in from the utility network which the projects of others have in part determined, that he should just step aside from his own project and decision and acknowledge the decision which utilitarian calculation requires. It is to alienate him in a real sense from his actions and the source of his action in his own convictions. It is to make him into a channel between the input of everyone's projects, including his own, and an output of optimistic decision; but this is to neglect the extent to which *his* actions and *his* decisions have to be seen as the actions and decisions which flow from the projects and attitudes with which he is most closely identified. It is thus, in the most literal sense, an attack on his integrity.

These sorts of considerations do not in themselves give solutions to practical dilemmas such as those provided by our examples; but I hope they help to provide other ways of thinking about them. In fact, it is not hard to see that in George's case, viewed from this perspective, the utilitarian solution would be wrong. Jim's case is different, and harder. But if (as I suppose) the utilitarian is probably right in this case, that is not to be found out just by asking the utilitarian's questions. Discussions of it— and I am not going to try to carry it further here—will have to take seriously the distinction between my killing someone, and its coming about because of what I do that someone else kills them: a distinction based, not so much on the distinction between action and inaction, as on the distinction between my projects and someone else's projects. At least it will have to start by taking that seriously, as utilitarianism does not; but then it will have to build out from there by asking why that distinction seems to have less, or a different, force in this case than it has in George's. One question here would be how far one's powerful objection to killing people just is, in fact, an application of a powerful objection to their being killed. Another dimension of that is the issue of how much it matters that the people at risk are actual, and there, as opposed to hypothetical, or future, or merely elsewhere.

There are many other considerations that could come into such a question, but the immediate point of all this is to draw one particular contrast with utilitarianism: that to reach a grounded decision in such a case should not be regarded as a matter of just discounting one's reactions, impulses and deeply held projects in the face of the pattern of utilities, nor yet merely adding them in—but in the first instance of trying to understand them.

Of course, time and circumstances are unlikely to make a grounded decision, in Jim's case at least, possible. It might not even be decent. . . . If we are not agents of the universal satisfaction system, we are not primarily janitors of any system of values, even our own: very often, we just act, as a possibly confused result of the situation in which we are engaged. That, I suspect, is very often an exceedingly good thing. To what extent utilitarians regard it as a good thing is an obscure question. . . .

---

[1][Williams's notes have been omitted—ed.]

HONESTY

PLATO

The Republic

It is our business to define, if we can, the natural gifts that fit men to be guardians of a commonwealth, and to select them accordingly. . . .

How are these Guardians to be brought up and educated? . . . Perhaps we shall hardly invent a system better than the one which long experience has worked out, with its two branches for the cultivation of the mind and of the body. And I suppose we shall begin with the mind, before we start physical training.

Naturally. . . .

Shall we simply allow our children to listen to any stories that anyone happens to make up, and so receive into their minds ideas often the very opposite of those we shall think they ought to have when they are grown up?

No, certainly not.

It seems, then, our first business will be to supervise the making of fables and legends, rejecting all which are unsatisfactory; and we shall induce nurses and mothers to tell their children only those which we have approved, and to think more of moulding their souls with these stories than they now do of rubbing their limbs to make them strong and shapely. Most of the stories now in use must be discarded. . . . If a poet writes of the gods in this way, we shall be angry and refuse him the means to produce his play. Nor shall we allow such poetry to be used in educating the young, if we mean our Guardians to be godfearing and to reproduce the divine nature in themselves so far as man may.

I entirely agree with your principles, he said, and I would have them observed as laws. . . .

Yes, he said; and I believe we have settled right.

We also want them to be brave. So the stories they hear should be such as to make them unafraid of death. A man with that fear in his heart cannot be brave, can he?

Surely not. . . .

Again, a high value must be set upon truthfulness. If we were right in saying that gods have no use for falsehood and it is useful to mankind only in the way of a medicine, obviously a medicine should be handled by no one but a physician.

Obviously.

If anyone, then, is to practise deception, either on the country's enemies or on its citizens, it must be the Rulers of the commonwealth, acting for its benefit; no one else may meddle with this privilege. . . .

Next, our young men will need self-control; and for the mass of mankind that chiefly means obeying their governors, and themselves governing their appetite for the pleasures of eating and drinking and sex. . . .

I agree.

Whereas we shall allow the poets to represent any examples of self-control and fortitude on the part of famous men. . . .

Nor again must these men of ours be lovers of money, or ready to take bribes. They must not hear that "gods and great princes may be won by gifts." . . .

Then we must not only compel our poets, on pain of expulsion, to make their poetry the express image of noble character; we must also supervise craftsmen of every kind. . . .

There could be no better upbringing than that. . . .

Good, said I; and what is the next point to be settled? Is it not the question, which of these Guardians are to be rulers and which are to obey?

No doubt.

Well, it is obvious that the elder must have authority over the young, and that the rulers must be the best.

Yes.

And as among farmers the best are those with a natural turn for farming, so, if we want the best among our Guardians, we must take those naturally fitted to watch over a commonwealth. They must have the right sort of intelligence and ability; and also they must look upon the commonwealth as their special concern—the sort of concern that is felt for something so closely bound up with oneself that its interests and fortunes, for good or ill, are held to be identical with one's own.

Exactly. . . .

We must watch them, I think, at every age and see whether they are capable of preserving this conviction that they must do what is best for the community, never forgetting it or allowing themselves to be either forced or bewitched into throwing it over. . . .

Now, said I, can we devise something in the way of those convenient fictions we spoke of earlier, a single bold flight of invention, which we may induce the community in general, and if possible the Rulers themselves, to accept?

What kind of fiction? . . .

I shall try to convince, first the Rulers and the soldiers, and then the whole community, that all that nurture and education which we gave them was only something they seemed to experience as it were in a dream. In reality they were the whole time down inside the earth, being moulded and fostered while their arms and all their equipment were being fashioned also; and at last, when they were complete, the earth sent them up from her womb into the light of day. So now they must think of the land they dwell in as a mother and nurse, whom they must take thought for and defend against any attack, and of their fellow citizens as brothers born of the same soil.

You might well be bashful about coming out with your fiction.

No doubt; but still you must hear the rest of the story. It is true, we shall tell our people in this fable, that all of you in this land are brothers; but the god who fashioned you mixed gold in the composition of those among you who are fit to rule so that they are of the most precious quality; and he put silver in the Auxiliaries and iron and brass in the farmers and craftsmen. Now, since you are all of one stock, although your children will generally be like their parents, sometimes a golden parent may have a silver child or a silver parent a golden one, and so on with all the other combinations. So the first and chief injunction laid by heaven upon the Rulers is that, among all the things of which they must show themselves good guardians, there is none that needs to be so carefully watched as the mixture of metals in the souls of children. If a child of their own is born with an alloy of iron or brass, they must, without the smallest pity, assign him the station proper to his nature and thrust him out among the craftsmen or the farmers. If, on the contrary, these classes produce a child with gold or silver in his composition, they will promote him, according to his value, to be a Guardian or an Auxiliary. They will appeal to a prophecy that ruin will come upon the state when it passes into the keeping of a man of iron or brass. Such is the story; can you think of any device to make them believe it?

Not in the first generation; but their sons and descendants might believe it, and finally the rest of mankind.

Well, said I, even so it might have a good effect in making them care more for the commonwealth and for one another; for I think I see what you mean.

NICCOLÒ MACHIAVELLI

The Prince

HOW PRINCES SHOULD HONOUR THEIR WORD

Everyone realizes how praiseworthy it is for a prince to honour his word and to be straightforward rather than crafty in his dealings; nonetheless contemporary experience shows that princes who have achieved great things have been those who have given their word lightly, who have known how to trick men with their cunning, and who, in the end, have overcome those abiding by honest principles.

You must understand, therefore, that there are two ways of fighting: by law or by force. The first way is natural to men, and the second to beasts. But as the first way often proves inadequate one must needs have recourse to the second. So a prince must understand how to make a nice use of the beast and the man. . . .

A prudent ruler cannot, and must not, honour his word when it places him at a disadvantage and when the reasons for which he made his promise no longer exist. If all men were good, this precept would not be good; but because men are wretched creatures who would not keep their word to you, you need not keep your word to them. And no prince ever lacked good excuses to colour his bad faith. One could give innumerable modern instances of this, showing how many pacts and promises have been made null and void by the bad faith of princes: those who have known best how to imitate the fox have come off best. But one must know how to colour one's actions and to be a great liar and deceiver. Men are so simple, and so much creatures of circumstance, that the deceiver will always find someone ready to be deceived. . . .

A prince, therefore, need not necessarily have all the good qualities I mentioned above, but he should certainly appear to have them. I would even go so far as to say that if he has these qualities and always behaves accordingly he will find them harmful; if he only appears to have them they will render him service. He should appear to be compassionate, faithful to his word, kind, guileless, and devout. And indeed he should be so. But his disposition should be such that, if he needs to be the opposite, he knows how. You must realize this: that a prince, and especially a new prince, cannot observe all those things which give men a reputation for virtue, because in order to maintain his state he is often forced to act in defiance of good faith, of charity, of kindness, of religion. And so he should have a flexible disposition, varying as fortune and circumstances dictate. As I said above, he should not deviate from what is good, if that is possible, but he should know how to do evil, if that is necessary. . . .

IMMANUEL KANT

On a Supposed Right to Lie from Altruistic Motives

In the journal *France*, for 1797, Part VI, No. 1, page 123, in an article entitled "On Political Reactions" by Benjamin Constant, there appears the following passage:

> The moral principle, "It is a duty to tell the truth," would make any society impossible if it were taken singly and unconditionally. We have proof of this in the very direct consequences which a German philosopher has drawn from this principle. This philosopher goes so far as to assert that it would be a crime to lie to a murderer who has asked whether our friend who is pursued by him had taken refuge in our house.

The French philosopher on page 124 refutes this principle in the following manner:

> It is a duty to tell the truth. The concept of duty is inseparable from the concept of right. A duty is that which in one being corresponds to the rights of another. Where

there are no rights, there are no duties. To tell the truth is thus a duty: but it is a duty only in respect to one who has a right to the truth. But no one has a right to a truth which injures others.

. . . Now the first question is: Does a man, in cases where he cannot avoid answering "Yes" or "No," have a right to be untruthful? The second question is: Is he not in fact bound to tell an untruth, when he is unjustly compelled to make a statement, in order to protect himself or another from a threatened misdeed?

Truthfulness in statements which cannot be avoided is the formal duty of an individual to everyone, however great may be the disadvantage accruing to himself or to another. If, by telling an untruth, I do not wrong him who unjustly compels me to make a statement, nevertheless by this falsification, which must be called a lie (though not in a legal sense), I commit a wrong against duty generally in a most essential point. That is, so far as in me lies I cause that declarations should in general find no credence, and hence that all rights based on contracts should be void and lose their force, and this is a wrong done to mankind generally.

Thus the definition of a lie as merely an intentional untruthful declaration to another person does not require the additional condition that it must harm another . . . For a lie always harms another; if not some other particular man, still it harms mankind generally, for it vitiates the source of law itself.

This benevolent lie, however, can become punishable under civil law through an accident (*casus*), and that which escapes liability to punishment only by accident can also be condemned as wrong even by external laws. For instance, if by telling a lie you have prevented murder, you have made yourself legally responsible for all the consequences; but if you have held rigorously to the truth, public justice can lay no hand on you, whatever the unforeseen consequences may be. After you have honestly answered the murderer's question as to whether this intended victim is at home, it may be that he has slipped out so that he does not come in the way of the murderer, and thus that the murder may not be committed. But if you had lied and said he was not at home when he had really gone out without your knowing it, and if the murderer had then met him as he went away and murdered him, you might justly be accused as the cause of his death. For if you had told the truth as far as you knew it, perhaps the murderer might have been apprehended by the neighbors while he searched the house and thus the deed might have been prevented. Therefore, whoever tells a lie, however well intentioned he might be, must answer for the consequences, however unforeseeable they were, and pay the penalty for them even in a civil tribunal. This is because truthfulness is a duty which must be regarded as the ground of all duties based on contract, and the laws of these duties would be rendered uncertain and useless if even the least exception to them were admitted.

To be truthful (honest) in all declarations, therefore, is a sacred and absolutely commanding decree of reason, limited by no expediency.

Mr. Constant . . . concludes (p. 125) that "a principle acknowledged to be true must never be abandoned, however obviously danger seems to be involved in it." (And yet the good man himself abandoned the unconditional principle of truthfulness on account of the danger which it involved for society. He did so because he could find no mediating principle which could serve to prevent this danger; and, in fact, there is no principle to be interpolated here.)

If we wish to preserve the names of the persons as they have been cited here, the "French philosopher" confuses the action by which someone does harm (*nocet*) to another in telling the truth when he cannot avoid making a statement, with the action whereby he does the other a wrong (*laedit*). It was only an accident (*casus*) that the truth of the statement harmed the occupant of the house; it was not a free act (in a juristic sense). For to demand of another that he should lie to one's own advantage would be a claim opposed to all lawfulness. Each man has not only a right but even the strict duty to be truthful in statements he cannot avoid making, whether they harm himself or others. In so doing, he does not do harm to him who suffers as a consequence; accident causes this harm. For one is not at all free to choose in such a case, since truthfulness (if he must speak) is an unconditional duty.

The "German philosopher" will not take as one of his principles the proposition (p. 124): "To tell the truth is a duty, but only to him who has a right to the truth." He will not do so, first, because of the ambiguous formulation of this proposition, for truth is not a possession the right to which can be granted to one and denied to another. But he will not do so chiefly because the duty of truthfulness (which is the only thing in question here) makes no distinction between persons to whom one has this duty and to whom one can exempt himself from this duty; rather, it is an unconditional duty which holds in all circumstances. . . .

The author says, "A principle recognized as true (I add, recognized as an a priori and hence apodictic principle) must never be abandoned, however obviously danger seems to be involved in it." But one must only understand the danger not as a danger of accidentally doing a harm but only as a danger of doing a wrong. This would happen if I made the duty of being truthful, which is unconditional and the supreme juridical condition in testimony, into a conditional duty subordinate to other considerations. Although in telling a certain lie I do not actually do anyone a wrong, I formally but not materially violate the principle of right with respect to all unavoidably necessary utterances. And this is much worse than to do injustice to any particular person, because such a deed against an individual does not always presuppose the existence of a principle in the subject which produces such an act.

If one is asked whether he intends to speak truthfully in a statement that he is about to make and does not receive the question with indignation at the suspicion it expressed that he might be a liar, but rather asks permission to consider possible exceptions, that person is already potentially a liar. That is because he shows that he does not acknowledge truthfulness as an intrinsic duty but makes reservations with respect to a rule which does not permit any exception, inasmuch as any exception would directly contradict itself.

All practical principles of right must contain rigorous truth, and the so-called "mediating principles" can contain only the more accurate definition of their application to actual cases (according to rules of policy), but they can never contain exceptions from the former. Such exceptions would nullify their universality, and that is precisely the reason that they are called principles.

HENRY SIDGWICK

The Classification of Duties—Veracity

It does not seem clearly agreed whether Veracity is an absolute and independent duty, or a special application of some higher principle. We find (*e.g.*) that Kant regards it as a duty owed to oneself to speak the truth, because "a lie is an abandonment or, as it were, annihilation of the dignity of man." And this seems to be the view in which lying is prohibited by the code of honour, except that it is not thought (by men of honour as such) that the dignity of man is impaired by *any* lying: but only that lying for selfish ends, especially under the influence of fear, is mean and base. In fact there seems to be circumstances under which the code of honour prescribes lying. Here, however, it may be said to be plainly divergent from the morality of Common Sense. Still, the latter does not seem to decide clearly whether truth-speaking is absolutely a duty, needing no further justification: or whether it is merely a general right of each man to have truth spoken to him by his fellows, which right however may be forfeited or suspended under certain circumstances. Just as each man is thought to have a natural right to personal security generally, but not if he is himself attempting to injure others in life and property: so if we may even kill in defence of ourselves and others, it seems strange if we may not lie, if lying will defend us better against a palpable invasion of our rights: and Common Sense does not seem to prohibit this decisively. And again, just as the orderly and systematic slaughter which we call war is thought perfectly right under certain circumstances, though painful and revolting: so in the word-contests of the law-courts, the lawyer is commonly held to be justified in untruthfulness within strict rules and limits: for an advocate is thought to be over-scrupulous who refuses to say what he knows to be false, if he is instructed to say it. Again, where deception is designed to benefit the person deceived, Common Sense seems to concede that it may sometimes be right: for example, most persons would not hesitate to speak falsely to an invalid, if this seemed the only way of concealing facts that might produce a dangerous shock: nor do I perceive that any one shrinks from telling fictions to children, on matters upon which it is thought well that they should not know the truth. But if the lawfulness of benevolent deception in any case be admitted, I do not see how we can decide when and how far it is admissible, except by considerations of expediency; that is, by weighing the gain of any particular deception against the imperilment of mutual confidence involved in all violation of truth.

The much argued question of religious deception ("pious fraud") naturally suggests itself here. It seems clear, however, that Common Sense now pronounces against the broad rule, that falsehoods may rightly be told in the interests of religion. But there is a subtler form in which the same principle is still maintained by moral persons. It is sometimes said that the most important truths of religion cannot be conveyed into the minds of ordinary men, except by being enclosed, as it were, in a shell of fiction; so that by relating such fictions as if they were facts, we are really performing an act of substantial veracity. Reflecting upon this argument, we see that it is not after all so clear wherein Veracity consists. For from the beliefs immediately communicated by any set of affirmations inferences are naturally drawn, and we may clearly foresee that they will be drawn. And though commonly we intend that both the beliefs immediately communicated and the inferences drawn from them should be true, and a person who always aims at this is praised as candid and sincere: still we find relaxation of the rule prescribing this intention claimed in two different ways by at least respectable sections of opinion. For first, as was just now observed, it is sometimes held that if a conclusion is true and important, and cannot be satisfactorily communicated otherwise, we may lead the mind of the hearer to it by means of fictitious premises. But the exact reverse of this is perhaps a commoner view: viz. that it is only an absolute duty to make our actual affirmations true: for it is said that though the ideal condition of human converse involves perfect sincerity and candour, and we ought to rejoice in exhibiting these virtues where we can, still in our actual world concealment is frequently necessary to the well-being of society, and may be legitimately effected by any means short of actual falsehood. Thus it is not uncommonly said that in defence of a secret we may not indeed *lie*, i.e. produce directly beliefs contrary to fact; but we may "turn a question aside," i.e., produce indirectly, by natural inference from our answer, a negatively false belief; or "throw the inquirer on a wrong scent," i.e., produce similarly a positively false belief. These two methods of concealment are known respectively as *suppressio veri* and *suggestio falsi*, and many think them legitimate under certain circumstances: while others say that if deception is to be practised at all, it is mere formalism to object to any one mode of effecting it more than another.

On the whole, then, reflection seems to show that the rule of Veracity, as commonly accepted, cannot be elevated into a definite moral axiom: for there is no real agreement as to how far we are bound to impart true beliefs to others: and while it is contrary to Common Sense to exact absolute candour under all circumstances, we yet find no self-evident secondary principle, clearly defining when it is not to be exacted.

ROGER HIGGS

On Telling Patients the Truth

. . . Plato was among the first to suggest that falsehood should be available to physicians as "medicine" for the good of patients (but not to lawyers who should have no part in it!). Sidgwick followed him in arguing that lies to invalids and children could sometimes be justified as being in the best interests of those deceived. But by and large, most early philosophers have looked to truthfulness as fundamental to trust between men.[1] There is a division of opinion between those who, with Kant, see no circumstances in which the duty to be truthful can be abrogated, "whatever the disadvantages accruing,"[2] and those who believe deception can be justifiably undertaken at times. . . .

Most modern thinkers in the field of medical ethics would hold that truthfulness is indeed a central principle of conduct, but that it is capable of coming into conflict with other principles, to which it must occasionally give way. On the other hand, the principle of veracity often receives support from other principles. For instance, it is hard to see how a patient can have autonomy, can make a free choice about matters concerning himself, without some measure of understanding of the facts as they influence the case; and that implies, under normal circumstances, some open, honest discussion with his advisers.[3] Equally, consent is a nonsense if it is not in some sense informed. The doctor's perspective, related to the patient's perceived needs and interests, is becoming less dominant over the patient's perspective, often expressed in terms of "rights." . . .

Once the central position of honesty has been established, we still need to examine whether doctors and nurses really do have, as has been suggested, special exemption from being truthful because of the nature of their work, and if so under what circumstances. The analogy with the discussion of the use of force may be helpful. Few would take the absolutist view here, and most would feel that some members of society, such as the police, have at times exemption from the usual prohibition against the use of physical force. The analogy reminds us, however, that the circumstances need to be carefully examined, and there is no blanket permission. The analogy is also helpful in that we can see that there may be circumstances at either end of the scale of importance when the issues, for most people, are clear cut. In a crisis, when there is absolutely no other alternative, we condone the use of force. At the other end of the scale, there may be occasions, such as controlling a good-natured crowd, in which the use of force is accepted by all for the smooth running of society, and that the "offence," in the sense of breaking the prohibition on the use of force against a person's will, is trivial—although the physical force required may be anything but! Similarly, there are arguments for lying at either end of the scale of importance. It may finally be decided that in a crisis there is no acceptable alternative, as when life is ebbing and truthfulness would bring certain disaster. Alternatively, the moral issue may appear so trivial as not to be worth considering (as, for example, when a doctor is called out at night by a patient who apologizes by saying, "I hope you don't mind me calling you at this time, doctor," and the doctor replies, "No, not at all."). However, the force analogy alerts us to the fact that occasions of these two types are few, fewer than those in which deliberate deceit would generally be regarded as acceptable in current medical practice, and should regularly be debated "in public" if abuses are to be avoided.[4] To this end it is necessary now to examine critically the arguments commonly used to defend lying to patients.

First comes the argument that it is enormously difficult to put across a technical subject to those with little technical knowledge and understanding, in a situation where so little is predictable. A patient has bowel cancer. With surgery it might be cured, or it might recur. Can the patient understand the effects of treatment? The symptom she is now getting might be due to cancer, there might be secondaries, and they in turn might be suppressible for a long time, or not at all. What future symptoms might occur, how long will she live, how will she die—all these are desperately important questions for the patient, but even for her doctor the answers can only be informed guesses, in an area where uncertainty is so hard to bear.

Yet to say we do not know anything is a lie. As doctors we know a great deal, and *can* make informed guesses or offer likelihoods. The whole truth may be impossible to attain, but truthfulness is not. "I do not know" can be a major piece of honesty. To deprive the patient of honest communication because we cannot know everything is, as we have seen, not only confused thinking but immoral. Thus deprived, the patient cannot plan, he cannot choose. . . .

The second argument for telling lies to patients is that no patient likes hearing depressing or frightening news. That is certainly true. There must be few who do. But in other walks of life no professional would normally consider it his or her duty to suppress information simply in order to preserve happiness. No accountant, foreseeing bankruptcy in his client's affairs, would chat cheerfully about the Budget or a temporarily reassuring credit account. Yet such suppression of information occurs daily in wards or surgeries throughout the country. Is this what patients themselves want?

In order to find out, a number of studies have been conducted over the past 30 years. In most studies there is a significant minority of patients, perhaps about a fifth, who, if given information, deny having been told. Sometimes this must be pure forgetfulness, sometimes it relates to the lack of skill of the informer, but sometimes with bad or unwelcome news there is an element of what is (perhaps not quite correctly) called "denial." The observer feels that at one level the news has been taken in, but at another its validity or reality has not been accepted. This process has been recognized as a buffer for the mind against the shock of unacceptable news, and often seems to be part of a process leading to its ultimate acceptance. But once this group has been allowed for, most surveys find that, of those who have had or who could have had a diagnosis made of, say, cancer, between two-thirds and three-quarters of those questioned were either glad to have been told, or declared that they would wish to know. Indeed, surveys reveal that most *doctors* would themselves wish to be told the truth, even though (according to earlier studies at least) most of those same doctors said they would not speak openly to their patients—a curious double standard! . . .

Why doctors have for so long misunderstood their patients' wishes is perhaps related to the task itself. Doctors don't want to give bad news, just as patients don't want it in abstract, but doctors have the choice of withholding the information, and in so doing protecting themselves from the pain of telling, and from the blame of being the bearer of bad news. . . .

Paternalism may be justifiable in the short term, and to "kid" someone, to treat him as a child because he is ill, and perhaps dying, may be very tempting. Yet true respect for that person (adult or child) can only be shown by allowing him allowable choices, by granting him whatever control is left, as weakness gradually undermines his hold on life. If respect is important then at the very least there must be no acceptable or effective alternative to lying in a particular situation if the lie is to be justified.

Staying with the assessment of consequences, however, a third argument for lying can be advanced, namely, that truthfulness can actually do harm. "What you don't know can't hurt you" is a phrase in common parlance (though it hardly fits with concepts of presymptomatic screening for preventable disease!). However, it is undeniable that blunt and unfeeling communication of unpleasant truths can cause acute distress, and sometimes long-term disability. The fear that professionals often have of upsetting people, of causing a scene, of making fools of themselves by letting unpleasant emotions flourish, seems to have elevated this argument beyond its natural limits. It is not unusual to find that the fear of creating harm will deter a surgical team from discussing a diagnosis gently with a patient, but not deter it from performing radical and mutilating surgery. Harm is a very personal concept. Most medical schools have, circulating in the refectory, a story about a patient who was informed that he had cancer and then leapt to his death. The intended moral for the medical student is, keep your mouth shut and do no harm. But that may not be the correct lesson to be learned from such cases (which I believe, in any case, to be less numerous than is commonly supposed). The style of telling could have been brutal, with no follow-up or support. It may have been the suggested treatment, not the basic illness. . . .

What these cases do, surely, is argue, not for no telling, but for better telling, for sensitivity and care in determining how much the patient wants to know, explaining carefully in ways the patient can understand, and providing full support and "aftercare" as in other treatments.

But even if it is accepted that the short-term effect of telling the truth may sometimes be considerable psychological disturbance, in the long term the balance seems definitely to swing the other way. The effects of lying are dramatically illustrated in "A Case of Obstructed Death?"[5] False information prevented a woman from returning to healthy living after a cancer operation, and robbed her of 6 months of active life. Also, the long-term effect of lies on the family and, perhaps most importantly, on society, is incalculable. If trust is gradually corroded, if the "wells are poisoned," progress is hard. Mistrust creates lack of communication and increased fear, and this generation has seen just such a fearful myth created around cancer.[6] Just how much harm has been done by this "demonizing" of cancer, preventing people coming to their doctors, or alternatively creating unnecessary attendances on doctors, will probably never be known.

There are doubtless many other reasons why doctors lie to their patients; but these can hardly be used to justify lies, even if we should acknowledge them in passing. Knowledge is power, and certainly doctors, though usually probably for reasons of work-load rather than anything more sinister, like to remain "in control." Health professionals may, like others, wish to protect themselves from confrontation, and may find it easier to coerce or manipulate than to gain permission. There may be a desire to avoid any pressure for change. And there is the constant problem of lack of time. But in any assessment, the key issues remain. Not telling the truth normally involves telling lies, and doctors and nurses have no "carte blanche" to lie. To do so requires a justification and this justification must be strong enough to overcome the negative moral weight of the lie itself. How can we set about this assessment in practical terms? . . .

There still seems to be a need to tell lies, [but] we must be able to justify them. That the person is a child, or "not very bright," will not do. Given the two ends of the spectrum of crisis and triviality, the vast middle range of communication requires honesty, so that autonomy and choice can be maintained. If lies are to be told, there really must be no acceptable alternative. The analogy with force may again be helpful here: perhaps using the same style of thinking as is used in the Mental Health Act, to test whether we are justified in removing someone's liberty against their will, may help us to see the gravity of what we are doing when we consider deception. It also suggests that the decision should be shared, in confidence, and be subject to debate, so that any alternative which may not initially have been seen may be considered. And it does not end there. If we break an important moral principle, that principle still retains its force, and its "shadow" has to be acknowledged. As professionals we shall have to ensure that we follow up, that we work through the broken trust or the disillusionment that the lie will bring to the patient, just as we would follow up and work through bad news, a major operation, or a psychiatric "sectioning." This follow-up may also be called for in our relationship with our colleagues if there has been major disagreement about what should be done.

In summary, there are *some* circumstances in which the health professions are probably exempted from society's general requirement for truthfulness. But not telling the truth is usually the same as telling a lie, and a lie requires strong justification. Lying must be a last resort, and we should act as if we were to be called upon to defend the decision in public debate, even if our duty of confidentiality does not allow this in practice. We should always aim to respect the other important principles governing interactions with patients, especially the preservation of the patient's autonomy. When all is said and done, many arguments for individual cases of lying do not hold water. Whether or not knowing the truth is essential to the patient's health, telling the truth is essential to the health of the doctor–patient relationship.

---

[1] [Higgs's notes have been renumbered—ed.]

[2] Immanuel Kant, "On a Supposed Right to Lie from Benevolent Motives," translated by T. K. Abbott, in Kant's *Critique of Practical Reason and Other Works on the Theory of Ethics* (London: Longmans, 1909).

[3] Alastair Campbell and Roger Higgs, *In That Case* (London: Darton, Longman and Todd, 1982).

[4] John Rawls, *A Theory of Justice* (Cambridge, Mass.: Harvard University Press, Belknap Press, 1971).

[5] Roger Higgs, "Truth at the Last—A Case of Obstructed Death?" *Journal of Medical Ethics* 8 (1982), 48–50; and Roger Higgs, "Obstructed Death Revisited," *Journal of Medical Ethics* 8 (1982), pp. 154–6.

[6] Susan Sontag, *Illness as Metaphor* (New York: Farrar, Straus and Giroux, 1978).

JEAN-PAUL SARTRE

Self-Deception

BAD FAITH AND FALSEHOOD

. . . We say indifferently of a person that he shows signs of bad faith or that he lies to himself. We shall willingly grant that bad faith is a lie to oneself, on condition that we distinguish the lie to oneself from lying in general. . . . The essence of the lie implies in fact that the liar actually is in complete possession of the truth which he is hiding. A man does not lie about what he is ignorant of; he does not lie when he spreads an error of which he himself is the dupe . . . The ideal description of the liar would be a cynical consciousness, affirming truth within himself, denying it in his words, and denying that negation as such. . . . The liar intends to deceive and he does not seek to hide this intention from himself nor to disguise the translucency of consciousness; on the contrary, he has recourse to it when there is a question of deciding secondary behavior. It explicitly exercises a regulatory control over all attitudes. . . .

The lie is also a normal phenomenon of what Heidegger calls the "*mit-sein*."[1] It presupposes my existence, the existence of the *Other*, my existence *for* the Other, and the existence of the Other *for* me. Thus there is no difficulty in holding that the liar must make the project of the lie in entire clarity and that he must possess a complete comprehension of the lie and of the truth which he is altering. It is sufficient that an over-all opacity hide his intentions from the *Other*; it is sufficient that the Other can take the lie for truth. By the lie consciousness affirms that it exists by nature as *hidden from the Other*; it utilizes for its own profit the ontological duality of myself and myself in the eyes of the Other.

The situation can not be the same for bad faith if this, as we have said, is indeed a lie to oneself. To be sure, the one who practices bad faith is hiding a displeasing truth or presenting as truth a pleasing untruth. Bad faith then has in appearance the structure of falsehood. Only what changes everything is the fact that in bad faith it is from myself that I am hiding the truth. Thus the duality of the deceiver and the deceived does not exist here. Bad faith on the contrary implies in essence the unity of a *single* consciousness. This does not mean that it can not be conditioned by the *mit-sein* like all other phenomena of human reality, but the *mit-sein* can call forth bad faith only by presenting itself as *a situation* which bad faith permits surpassing; bad faith does not come from outside to human reality. One does not undergo his bad faith; one is not infected with it; it is not a *state*. But consciousness affects itself with bad faith. There must be an original intention and a project of bad faith; this project implies a comprehension of bad faith as such and a pre-reflective apprehension (of) consciousness as affecting itself with bad faith. It follows first that the one to whom the lie is told and the one who lies are one and the same person, which means that I must know in my capacity as deceiver the truth which is hidden from me in my capacity as the one deceived. Better yet I must know the truth very exactly *in order* to conceal it more carefully—and this not at two different moments, which at a pinch would allow us to re-establish a semblance of duality—but in the unitary structure of a single project. How then can the lie subsist if the duality which conditions it is suppressed?

To this difficulty is added another which is derived from the total translucency of consciousness. That which affects itself with bad faith must be conscious (of) its bad faith since the being of consciousness is consciousness of being. It appears then that I must be in good faith, at least to the extent that I am conscious of my bad faith. But then this whole psychic system is annihilated. We must agree in fact that if I deliberately and cynically attempt to lie to myself, I fail completely in this undertaking; the lie falls back and collapses beneath my look; it is ruined *from behind* by the very consciousness of lying to myself which pitilessly constitutes itself well within my project as its very condition. We have here an *evanescent* phenomenon which exists only in and through its own differentiation. To be sure, these phenomena are frequent and we shall see that there is in fact an "evanescence" of bad faith, which, it is evident, vacillates continually between good faith and cynicism: Even though the existence of bad faith is very precarious, and though it belongs to the kind of psychic structures which we might call *metastable*, it presents nonetheless an autonomous and durable form. It can even be the normal aspect of life for a very great number of people. A person can *live* in bad faith, which does not mean that he does not have abrupt awakenings to cynicism or to good faith, but which implies a constant and particular style of life. Our embarrassment then appears extreme since we can neither reject nor comprehend bad faith. . . .

If we wish to get out of this difficulty, we should examine more closely the patterns of bad faith and attempt a description of them. This description will permit us perhaps to fix more exactly the conditions for the possibility of bad faith; that is, to reply to the question we raised at the outset: "What must be the being of man if he is to be capable of bad faith?"

Take the example of a woman who has consented to go out with a particular man for the first time. She knows very well the intentions which the man who is speaking to her cherishes regarding her. She knows also that it will be necessary sooner or later for her to make a decision. But she does not want to realize the urgency; she concerns herself only with what is respectful and discreet in the attitude of her companion. She does not apprehend this conduct as an attempt to achieve what we call "the first approach"; that is, she does not want to see possibilities of temporal development which his conduct presents. She restricts this behavior to what is in the present; she does not wish to read in the phrases which he addresses to her anything other than their explicit meaning. If he says to her, "I find you so attractive!" she disarms this phrase of its sexual background; she attaches to the conversation and to the behavior of the speaker, the immediate meanings, which she imagines as objective qualities. The man who is speaking to her appears to her sincere and respectful as the table is round or square, as the wall coloring is blue or gray. The qualities thus attached to the person she is listening to are in this way fixed in a permanence like that of things, which is no other than the projection of the strict present of the qualities into the temporal flux. This is because she does not quite know what she wants. She is profoundly aware of the desire which she inspires, but the desire cruel and naked would humiliate and horrify her. Yet she would find no charm in a respect which would be only respect. In order to satisfy her, there must be a feeling which is addressed wholly to her *personality*—i.e., to her full freedom—and which would be a recognition of her freedom. But at the same time this feeling must be wholly desire; that is, it must address itself to her body as object. This time then she refuses to apprehend the desire for what it is; she does not even give it a name; she recognizes it only to the extent that it transcends itself toward admiration, esteem, respect and that it is wholly absorbed in the more refined forms which it produces, to the extent of no longer figuring anymore as a sort of warmth and density. But then suppose he takes her hand. This act of her companion risks changing the situation by calling for an immediate decision. To leave the hand there is to consent in herself to flirt, to engage herself. To withdraw it is to break the troubled and unstable harmony which gives the hour its charm. The aim is to postpone the moment of decision as long as possible. We know what happens next; the young woman leaves her hand there, but she *does not notice* that she is leaving it. She does not notice because it happens by chance that she is at this moment all intellect. She draws her companion up to the most lofty regions of sentimental speculation; she speaks of Life, of her life, she shows herself in her essential aspect—a personality, a consciousness. And during this time the divorce of the body from the soul is accomplished; the hand rests inert between the warm hands of her companion—neither consenting nor resisting—a thing.

We shall say that this woman is in bad faith. But we see immediately that she uses various procedures in order to maintain herself in this bad faith. She has disarmed the actions of her companion by reducing them to being only what they are; that is, to existing in the mode of the in-itself. But she permits herself to enjoy his desire, to the extent that she will apprehend it as not being what it is, will recognize its transcendence. Finally while sensing profoundly the presence of her own body—to the point of being aroused, perhaps—she realizes herself as *not being* her own body, and she contemplates it as though from above as a passive object to which events can *happen* but which can neither provoke them nor avoid them because all its possibilities are outside of it. What unity do we find in these various aspects of bad faith? It is a certain art of forming contradictory concepts which unite in themselves both an idea and the negation of that idea. The basic concept which is thus engendered utilizes the double property of the human being, who is at once a *facticity* and a *transcendence*. These two aspects of human reality are and ought to be capable of a valid coordination. But bad faith does not wish either to coordinate them or to surmount them in a synthesis. Bad faith seeks to affirm their identity while preserving their differences. It must affirm facticity as *being* transcendence and transcendence as *being* facticity, in such a way that at the instant when a person apprehends the one, he can find himself abruptly faced with the other.

We can find the prototype of formulae of bad faith in certain famous expressions which have been rightly conceived to produce their whole effect in a spirit of bad faith. Take for example the title of a work by Jacques Chardonne, *Love Is Much More than Love*. We see here how unity is established between *present* love in its facticity— "the contact of two skins," sensuality, egoism, Proust's mechanism of jealousy, Adler's battle of the sexes, etc.—and love as transcendence—Mauriac's "river of fire," the longing for the infinite, Plato's *eros*, Lawrence's deep cosmic intuition, etc. Here we leave facticity to find ourselves suddenly beyond the present and the factual condition of man, beyond the psychological, in the heart of metaphysics. On the other hand, the title of a play by Sarment, *I Am Too Great for Myself*, which also presents characters in bad faith, throws us first into full transcendence in order suddenly to imprison us within the narrow limits of our factual essence. We will discover this structure again in the famous sentence: "He has become what he was" or in its no less famous opposite: "Eternity at last changes each man into himself." It is well understood that these various formulae have only the appearance of bad faith; they have been conceived in this paradoxical form explicitly to shock the mind and discountenance it by an enigma. But it is precisely this appearance which is of concern to us. What counts here is that the formulae do not constitute new, solidly structured ideas; on the contrary, they are formed so as to remain in perpetual disintegration and so that we may slide at any time from naturalistic present to transcendence and vice versa.

We can see the use which bad faith can make of these judgments which all aim at establishing that I am not what I am. If I were only what I *am*, I could, for example, seriously consider an adverse criticism which someone makes of me, question myself scrupulously, and perhaps be compelled to recognize the truth in it. But thanks to transcendence, I am not subject to all that I am. I do not even have to discuss the justice of the reproach. As Suzanne says to Figaro, "To prove that I am right would be to recognize that I can be wrong." I am on a plane where no reproach can touch me since what I really am is my transcendence. I flee from myself, I escape myself, I leave my tattered garment in the hands of the fault-finder. But the ambiguity necessary for bad faith comes from the fact that I affirm here that I *am* my transcendence in the mode of being of a thing. It is only thus, in fact, that I can feel that I escape all reproaches. It is in the sense that our young woman purifies the desire of anything humiliating by being willing to consider it only as pure transcendence, which she avoids even naming. . . .

But although this *metastable* concept of "transcendence–facticity" is one of the most basic instruments of bad faith, it is not the only one of its kind. We can equally well use another kind of duplicity derived from human reality which we will express roughly by saying that its being-for-itself implies complementarily a being-for-others. Upon any one of my conducts it is always possible to converge two looks, mine and that of the Other. . . . The equal dignity of being, possessed by my being-for-others and by my being-for-myself, permits a perpetually disintegrating synthesis and a perpetual game of escape from the for-itself to the for-others and from the for-others to the for-itself. We have seen also the use which our young lady made of our being-in-the-midst-of-the-world—i.e., of our inert presence as a passive object among other objects—in order to relieve herself suddenly from the functions of her being-in-the-world—that is, from the being which causes there to be a world by projecting itself beyond the world toward its own possibilities. Let us note finally the confusing syntheses which play on the nihilating ambiguity of these temporal ekstases, affirming at once that I am what I have been (the man who deliberately *arrests himself* at one period in his life and refuses to take into consideration the later changes) and that I am not what I have been (the man who in the face of reproaches or rancor dissociates himself from his past by insisting on his freedom and on his perpetual re-creation). In all these concepts, which have only a transitive role in the reasoning and which are eliminated from the conclusion (like the imaginaries in the computations of physicists), we find again the same structure. We have to deal with human reality as a being which is what it is not and which is not what it is.

But what exactly is necessary in order for these concepts of disintegration to be able to receive even a pretence of existence, in order for them to be able to appear for an instant to consciousness, even in a process of evanescence? A quick examination of the idea of sincerity, the antithesis of bad faith, will be very instructive in this connection. Actually sincerity presents itself as a demand and consequently is not a *state*. Now what is the ideal to be attained in this case? It is necessary that a man be *for himself* only what he *is*. But is this not precisely the definition of the in-itself—or if you prefer—the principle of identity? To posit as an ideal the being of things, is this not to assert by the same stroke that this being does not belong to human reality and that the principle of identity, far from being a universal axiom universally applied, is only a synthetic principle enjoying a merely regional universality? Thus in order that the concepts of bad faith can put us under illusion at least for an instant, in order that the candor of "pure hearts" (cf. Gide, Kessel) can have validity for human reality as an ideal, the principle of identity must not represent a constitutive principle of human reality and human reality must not be necessarily what it is but must be able to be what it is not. What does this mean?

If man is what he is, bad faith is forever impossible and candor ceases to be his ideal and becomes instead his being. But is man what he is? And more generally, how can he *be* what he is when he exists as consciousness of being? If candor or sincerity is a universal value, it is evident that the maxim "one must be what one is" does not serve solely as a regulating principle for judgments and concepts by which I express what I am. It posits not merely an ideal of knowing but an ideal of *being*; it proposes for us an absolute equivalence of being with itself as a prototype of being. In this sense it is necessary that we *make ourselves* what we are. But what *are we* then if we have the constant obligation to make ourselves what we are, if our mode of being is having the obligation to be what we are?

. . . To be sincere, we said, is to be what one is. That supposes that I am not originally what I am. But here naturally Kant's "You ought, therefore you can" is implicitly understood. I can *become* sincere; this is what my duty and my effort to achieve sincerity imply. But we definitely establish that the original structure of "not being what one is" renders impossible in advance all movement toward being in itself or "being what one is." And this impossibility is not hidden from consciousness; on the contrary, it is the very stuff of consciousness; it is the embarrassing constraint which we constantly experience; it is our very incapacity to recognize ourselves, to constitute ourselves as being what we are. It is this necessity which means that, as soon as we posit ourselves as a certain being, by a legitimate judgment, based on inner experience or correctly deduced from a priori or empirical premises, then by that very positing we surpass this being—and that not toward another being but toward emptiness, toward *nothing*.

How then can we blame another for not being sincere or rejoice in our own sincerity since this sincerity appears to us at the same time to be impossible? How can we in conversation, in confession, in introspection, even attempt sincerity since the effort will by its very nature be doomed to failure and since at the very time when we announce it we have a prejudicative comprehension of its futility? In introspection I try to determine exactly what I am, to make up my mind to be my true self without delay—even though it means consequently to set about searching for ways to change myself. But what does this mean if not that I am constituting myself as a thing? Shall I determine the ensemble of purposes and motivations which have pushed me to do this or that action? But this is already to postulate a causal determinism which constitutes the flow of my states of consciousness as a succession of physical states. Shall I uncover in myself "drives," even though it be to affirm them in shame? But is this not deliberately to forget that these drives are realized with my consent, that they are not forces of nature but that I lend them their efficacy by a perpetually renewed decision concerning their value? Shall I pass judgment on my character, on my nature? Is this not to veil from myself at that moment what I know only too well, that I thus judge a past to which by definition my present is not subject? The proof of this is that the same man who in sincerity posits that he is what in actuality he was, is indignant at the reproach of another and tries to disarm it by asserting that he can no longer be what he was. We are readily astonished and upset when the penalties of the court affect a man who in his new freedom *is no longer* the guilty person he was. But at the same time we require of this man that he recognize himself as *being* this guilty one. What then is sincerity except precisely a phenomenon of bad faith? Have we not shown indeed that in bad faith human reality is constituted as a being which is what it is not and which is not what it is?

In the final analysis the goal of sincerity and the goal of bad faith are not so different. . . . Here our concern is only with the sincerity which aims at itself in present immanence. What is its goal? To bring me to confess to myself what I am in order that I may finally coincide with my being; in a word, to cause myself to be, in the mode of the in-itself, what I am in the mode of "not being what I am." Its assumption is that fundamentally I am already, in the mode of the in-itself, what I have to be. Thus we find at the base of sincerity a continual game of mirror and reflection, a perpetual passage from the being which is what it is to the being which is not what it is and inversely from the being which is not what it is to the being which is what it is. And what is the goal of bad faith? To cause me to be what I am, in the mode of "not being what one is," or not to be what I am in the mode of "being what one is." We find here the same game of mirrors. In fact in order for me to have an intention of sincerity, I must at the outset simultaneously be and not be what I am. Sincerity does not assign to me a mode of being or a particular quality, but in relation to that quality it aims at making me pass from one mode of being to another mode of being. This second mode of being, the ideal of sincerity, I am prevented by nature from attaining; and at the very moment when I struggle to attain it, I have a vague prejudicative comprehension that I shall not attain it. But all the same, in order for me to be able to conceive an intention in bad faith, I must have such a nature that within my being I escape from my being. If I were sad or cowardly in the way in which this inkwell is an inkwell, the possibility of bad faith could not even be conceived. Not only should I be unable to escape from my being; I could not even imagine that I could escape from it. But if bad faith is possible by virtue of a simple project, it is because so far as my being is concerned, there is no difference between being and non-being if I am cut off from my project.

THE "FAITH" OF BAD FAITH

. . . The true problem of bad faith stems evidently from the fact that bad faith is *faith*. It can not be either a cynical lie or certainty—if certainty is the intuitive possession of the object. But if we take belief as meaning the adherence of being to its object when the object is not given or is given indistinctly, then bad faith is belief; and the essential problem of bad faith is a problem of belief.

How can we believe by bad faith in the concepts which we forge expressly to persuade ourselves? We must note in fact that the project of bad faith must be itself in bad faith. I am not only in bad faith at the end of my effort when I have constructed my two-faced concepts and when I have persuaded myself. In truth, I have not persuaded myself; to the extent that I could be so persuaded, I have always been so. And at the very moment when I was disposed to put myself in bad faith, I of necessity was in bad faith with respect to this same disposition. For me to have represented it to myself as bad faith would have been cynicism; to believe it sincerely innocent would have been in good faith. The decision to be in bad faith does not dare to speak its name; it believes itself and does not believe itself in bad faith; it believes itself and does not believe itself in good faith. It is this which, from the upsurge of bad faith, determines the later attitude and, as it were, the *Weltanshauung* of bad faith.

Bad faith does not hold the norms and criteria of truth as they are accepted by the critical thought of good faith. What it decides first, in fact, is the nature of truth. With bad faith a truth appears, a method of thinking, a type of being which is like that of objects; the ontological characteristic of the world of bad faith with which the subject suddenly surrounds himself is this: that here being is what it is not, and is not what it is. Consequently a peculiar type of evidence appears: *non-persuasive* evidence. Bad faith apprehends evidence but it is resigned in advance to not being fulfilled by this evidence, to not being persuaded and transformed into good faith. It makes itself humble and modest; it is not ignorant, it says, that faith is decision and that after each intuition, it must decide and *will what it is*. Thus bad faith in its primitive project and in its coming into the world decides on the exact nature of its requirements. It stands forth in the firm resolution *not to demand too much*, to count itself satisfied when it is barely persuaded, to force itself in decisions to adhere to uncertain truths. This original project of bad faith is a decision in bad faith on the nature of faith. Let us understand clearly that there is no question of a reflective, voluntary decision, but of a spontaneous determination of our being. One *puts oneself* in bad faith as one goes to sleep and one is in bad faith as one dreams. Once this mode of being has been realized, it is as difficult to get out of it as to wake oneself up; bad faith is a type of being in the world, like waking or dreaming, which by itself tends to perpetuate itself, although its structure is of the *metastable* type. But bad faith is conscious of its structure, and it has taken precautions by deciding that the metastable structure is the structure of being and that non-persuasion is the structure of all convictions. It follows that if bad faith is faith and if it includes in its original project its own negation (it determines itself to be not quite convinced in order to convince itself that I am what I am not), then to start with, a faith which wishes itself to be not quite convinced must be possible. What are the conditions for the possibility of such a faith?

I believe that my friend Pierre feels friendship for me. I believe it *in good faith*. I believe it but I do not have for it any self-evident intuition, for the nature of the object does not lend itself to intuition. I *believe it;* that is, I allow myself to give in to all impulses to trust it; I decide to believe in it, and to maintain myself in this decision; I conduct myself, finally, as if I were certain of it—and all this in the synthetic unity of one and the same attitude. . . . Belief is a particular consciousness of *the meaning* of Pierre's acts. But if I know that I believe, the belief appears to me as pure subjective determination without external correlative. This is what makes the very word "to believe" a term utilized indifferently to indicate the unwavering firmness of belief ("My God, I believe in you") and its character as disarmed and strictly subjective ("Is Pierre my friend? I do not know; I believe so"). . . . The subtle, total annihilation of bad faith by itself can not surprise me; it exists at the basis of all faith. What is it then? At the moment when I wish to believe myself courageous I *know* that I am a coward. And this certainly would come to destroy my belief. But *first*, I *am* not any more courageous than cowardly, if we are to understand this in the mode of being of the in-itself. In the second place, I do not *know* that I am courageous; such a view of myself can be accompanied only by *belief*, for it surpasses pure reflective certitude. In the third place, it is very true that bad faith does not succeed in believing what it wishes to believe. But it is precisely as the acceptance of not believing what it believes that it is bad faith. Good faith wishes to flee the "not-believing-what-one-believes" by finding refuge in being. Bad faith flees being by taking refuge in "not-believing-what-one-believes." It has disarmed all beliefs in advance—those which it would like to take hold of and, by the same stroke, the others, those which it wishes to flee. In *willing* this self-destruction of belief, from which science escapes by searching for evidence, it ruins the beliefs which are opposed to it, which reveal themselves as *being only* belief. Thus we can better understand the original phenomenon of bad faith.

In bad faith there is no cynical lie nor knowing preparation for deceitful concepts. But the first act of bad faith is to flee what it can not flee, to flee what it is. The very project of flight reveals to bad faith an inner disintegration in the heart of being, and it is this disintegration which bad faith wishes to be. In truth, the two immediate attitudes which we can take in the face of our being are conditioned by the very nature of this being and its immediate relation with the in-itself. Good faith seeks to flee the inner disintegration of my being in the direction of the in-itself which it should be and is not. Bad faith seeks to flee the in-itself by means of the inner disintegration of my being. But it denies this very disintegration as it denies that it is itself bad faith. Bad faith seeks by means of "not-being-what-one-is" to escape from the in-itself which I am not in the mode of being what one is not. It denies itself as bad faith and aims at the in-itself which I am not in the mode of "not-being-what-one-is-not." If bad faith is possible, it is because it is an immediate, permanent threat to every project of the human being; it is because consciousness conceals in its being a permanent risk of bad faith. The origin of this risk is the fact that the nature of consciousness simultaneously is to be what it is not and not to be what it is. . . .

---

[1] [Sartre's notes have been omitted—ed.]

LOYALTY AND COMMUNITY

IMMANUEL KANT

Cosmopolitanism

Are we to love the human race as a whole, or is it an object to be viewed with displeasure, an object that has our best wishes (lest we become misanthropic) but never our best expectations, and from which, therefore, we would rather avert our eyes?

The answer to this question depends on our answer to another question. Are there tendencies in human nature which allow us to infer that the species will always progress toward the better, and that the evil of present and past times will be lost in the good of the future? If so, we could love the species at least for its constant approach to the good; if not, we would have to loathe or despise it, no matter what the affectations of a universal love of mankind—which would then be, at most, a well-meaning love, not a love well pleased—may say to the contrary. What is and remains evil, notably the evil and deliberate mutual violation of the most sacred human rights, this we cannot avoid loathing, even when we try our hardest to love it. We hate it—not that we would harm people, but that we would have as little to do with them as possible. . . .

I may be allowed to assume, therefore, that our species, progressing steadily in civilization as is its natural end, is also making strides for the better in regard to the moral end of its existence, and that this progress will be *interrupted* now and then, but never *broken off*. I do not have to prove this assumption; the burden of proof is on its opponent. I rest my case on this: I have the innate duty (though in respect of moral character required I am not so good as I should and hence could be) so to affect posterity through each member in the sequence of generations in which I live, simply as a human being, that future generations will become continually better (which also must be assumed to be possible), and that this duty may thus rightfully be passed on from one generation to the next. Let any number of doubts be drawn from history to dispute my hopes, doubts which, if conclusive, might move me to abandon a seemingly futile labor; but as long as the futility cannot be made wholly certain, I cannot exchange my duty (as the *liquidum*) for the rule of prudence not to attempt the unfeasible (as the *illiquidum*, because it is a mere hypothesis). I may always be and remain unsure whether an improvement in the human race can be hoped for; but this can invalidate neither the maxim nor its necessary presupposition that in a practical respect it be feasible. . . .

Just as universal violence and the resulting distress were finally bound to make a people decide that they should submit to the coercion of public laws, which reason itself prescribes for them as remedy, and found a state under a *civil constitution*, even so the distress of ceaseless warfare, in which states in turn seek to reduce or subjugate each other, must eventually bring the states under a *cosmopolitan* constitution even against their will. Such general peace may pose an even greater threat to freedom from another quarter by leading to the most terrible despotism, as has repeatedly happened in the case of oversized states. Yet the distress of ceaseless warfare must compel them to adopt a condition which, although not a cosmopolitan community under one head, is still lawful—a *federation* under jointly agreed *international law*. . . .

"But states," it will be said, "will never submit to such coercive laws; and the proposal of a universal international state, whose authority all individual states should voluntarily accept and whose laws they should obey, may sound ever so nice in the theory of an Abbé de Saint-Pierre or a Rousseau, but it will not work in practice. Has it not always been ridiculed by great statesmen, and more yet by heads of state, as a pedantically childish academic idea?"

I for my part put my trust in the theory that proceeds from the principle of justice, concerning how relations between individuals and states *ought to be*. The theory commends to the earthly demigods the maxim to proceed so that each of their quarrels become the introduction to such a universal international state and, thus, to assume as a practical possibility that it *can be*.

At the same time, however, I trust (*in subsidium*) in the nature of things, which compels one to go where he would rather not (*fata volentem ducunt, nolentem trahunt*—fate guides the willing and drags the unwilling). In this I also take human nature into account. Since respect for right and duty is still alive in human nature, I cannot, or will not, consider it so steeped in evil that in the end, after many unsuccessful attempts, moral-practical reason should not triumph and show human nature also to be lovable. So, even from a cosmopolitan viewpoint my assertion stands: what is valid in theory, on rational grounds, is valid also in practice.

G. W. F. HEGEL

Philosophy of Right

ETHICAL LIFE

150. Virtue is the ethical order reflected in the individual character so far as that character is determined by its natural endowment. When virtue displays itself solely as the individual's simple conformity with the duties of the station to which he belongs, it is rectitude.

151. But when individuals are simply identified with the actual order, ethical life (*das Sittliche*) appears as their general mode of conduct, i.e. as custom (*Sitte*), while the habitual practice of ethical living appears as a second nature which, put in the place of the initial, purely natural will, is the soul of custom permeating it through and through, the significance and the actuality of its existence. It is mind living and present as a world, and the substance of mind thus exists now for the first time as mind.

152. In this way the ethical substantial order has attained its right, and its right its validity. That is to say, the self-will of the individual has vanished together with his private conscience which had claimed independence and opposed itself to the ethical substance. For, when his character is ethical, he recognizes as the end which moves him to act the universal which is itself unmoved but is disclosed in its specific determinations as rationality actualized. He knows that his own dignity and the whole stability of his particular ends are grounded in this same universal, and it is therein that he actually attains these. Subjectivity is itself the absolute form and existent actuality of the substantial order, and the distinction between subject on the one hand and substance on the other, as the object, end, and controlling power of the subject, is the same as, and has vanished directly along with, the distinction between them in form. . . .

153. The right of individuals to be subjectively destined to freedom is fulfilled when they belong to an actual ethical order, because their conviction of their freedom finds its truth in such an objective order, and it is in an ethical order that they are actually in possession of their own essence or their own inner universality. . . .

257. The state is the actuality of the ethical Idea. It is ethical mind *qua* the substantial will manifest and revealed to itself, knowing and thinking itself, accomplishing what it knows and in so far as it knows it. The state exists immediately in custom, mediately in individual self-consciousness, knowledge, and activity, while self-consciousness in virtue of its sentiment towards the state finds in the state, as its essence and the end and product of its activity, its substantive freedom. . . .

268. The political sentiment, patriotism pure and simple, is assured conviction with truth as its basis—mere subjective assurance is not the outcome of truth but is only opinion—and a volition which has become habitual. In this sense it is simply a product of the institutions subsisting in the state, since rationality is *actually* present in the state, while action in conformity with these institutions gives rationality its practical proof. This sentiment is, in general, trust (which may pass over into a greater or lesser degree of educated insight), or the consciousness that my interest, both substantive and particular, is contained and preserved in another's (i.e., in the state's) interest and end, i.e., in the other's relation to me as an individual. In this way, this very other is immediately not an other in my eyes, and in being conscious of this fact, I am free.

Patriotism is often understood to mean only a readiness for exceptional sacrifices and actions. Essentially, however, it is the sentiment which, in the relationships of our daily life and under ordinary conditions, habitually recognizes that the community is one's substantive groundwork and end. It is out of this consciousness, which during life's daily round stands the test in all circumstances, that there subsequently also arises the readiness for extraordinary exertions. . . .

269. The patriotic sentiment acquires its specifically determined content from the various members of the organism of the state. This organism is the development of the Idea to its differences and their objective actuality. Hence these different members are the various powers of the state with their functions and spheres of action, by means of which the universal continually engenders itself, and engenders itself in a necessary way because their specific character is fixed by the nature of the concept. Throughout this process the universal maintains its identity, since it is itself the presupposition of its own production. This organism is the constitution of the state.

ROGER SCRUTON

The Meaning of Conservatism

THE CONSERVATIVE ATTITUDE

THE DESIRE TO CONSERVE

It is a limp definition of conservatism to describe it as the desire to conserve; for although there is in every man and woman some impulse to conserve that which is safe and familiar, it is the nature of this "familiarity" that needs to be examined. To put it briefly, conservatism arises directly from the sense that one belongs to some continuing, and pre-existing social order, and that this fact is all important in determining what to do. The "order" in question may be that of a club, society, class, community, church, regiment, or nation—a man may feel towards all these things that institutional stance which it is the task of this book to describe and defend. In feeling it—in feeling thus engaged in the continuity of his social world—a man stands in the current of some common life. The important thing is that the life of a social arrangement may become mingled with the lives of its members. They may feel in themselves the persistence of the will that surrounds them. The conservative instinct is founded in that feeling: it is the enactment of historical vitality, the individual's sense of his society's will to live. Moreover, in so far as people love life they will love what has given them life; in so far as they desire to give life it is in order to perpetuate what they have. In that intricate entanglement of individual and society resides the "will to live" that constitutes conservatism. . . .

POLITICS AND PURPOSE

. . . Some human relations presuppose a common purpose, and fall apart when that purpose is fulfilled or discontinued. (Consider, for example, a business partnership.) But not all relations are of that nature. The pursuit of a certain mechanical analogy has led to the belief (widely held but seldom stated) that an activity without an aim is merely aimless. So that if we are to consider political activity as a form of rational conduct, we should ally it to certain aims—to a social ideal that translates immediately into policy. The rational politician must therefore be able to indicate the form of society at which he is aiming, why he is aiming at it, and what means he proposes for its realization.

Such a view is in fact confused. Most human activities, and most relations that are worthwhile, have no purpose. No purpose, that is, external to themselves. There is no "end in view," and to attempt to provide one is to do violence to the arrangement. Suppose I were to approach another in the spirit of a given purpose—there is something that I have in mind in, and hope to achieve through, my relations with him. And suppose that the sole interest of my relations with the other lies in this aim. Now there is a sense in which I can still treat him (in Kant's famous terminology) not as a means only, but also as an end. For I may try to accomplish my aim by seeking his concurrence in it. I reason with him, I try to persuade him to do what I want him to do. But, *if* that is my approach, then it is always possible that I shall not persuade him, or that he, in his turn, will dissuade me. A certain reciprocity arises, and the absolute authority of my aim—as the sole determining principle of what it is reasonable for me to do—must be abandoned. And there is nothing irrational in that. If my aim is abandoned in these circumstances it is because it has proved impossible or unjustifiable. In other words it has failed to become part of the fellowship upon which it was first imposed. It follows that, if I am to allow to another the degree of autonomy which his human nature demands of me, I simply cannot approach him with a clearly delimited set of aims for *him*, and expect the fulfilment of those aims to be the inevitable, natural, or even reasonable outcome of our intercourse. I might discover new ends, or even lapse into that state of "aimlessness" which is the norm of healthy human relations. Indeed, if friendship has a basis it is this: that a man may desire the company of someone for whom he has no specific purpose. The continuity of the friendship will generate its own passing aims and aspirations, but no one of them can ever come to dominate the arrangement without changing it from friendship to something else.

So too in politics. A statesman may have aims and ambitions for the society which he seeks to govern. But a society is more than a speechless organism. It has personality, and will. Its history, institutions, and culture are the repositories of human values—in short, it has the character of end as well as means. A politician who seeks to impose upon it a given set of purposes, and seeks no understanding of the reasons and values which the society proposes in return, acts in defiance of friendship. And yet, where else does the right to govern lie, if it is not in a man's fellowship with a social order? The subjection of politics to determining purposes, however "good in themselves" those purposes seem, is, on the conservative view, irrational. For it destroys the very relationship upon which government depends.

It is the mark of rational intercourse that aims are not all predetermined, that some ends—perhaps the most important ends—remain to be discovered rather than imposed. And in the life of society they are discovered not by the perusal of utopian treatises, but, primarily, through participation. And that means by sharing in the arrangements wherein the ends of political conduct have their life. (Likewise, the "ends" of friendship are alive in its continuity, and show themselves from day to day, but have no independent existence and die with the friendship.) To participate in a social arrangement is to possess not just a set of beliefs, expectations, and feelings towards one's fellow men; it is also to be availed of a *way of seeing*, through which the value of conduct may be recognized. . . . It is to recognize, therefore, that a society too has a will, and that a rational man must be open to its persuasion. This will lies, for the conservative, enshrined in history, tradition, culture, and prejudice. England, far from being a savage society that would justify the imposition of overarching decrees, is founded in the maturest of national cultures, and contains within itself all the principles of social life. The true conservative has his ear attuned to those principles, and tries to live, as a result, in friendship with the nation to which he owes his being. His own will to live, and the nation's will to live, are simply one and the same. . . .

ALLEGIANCE

It is allegiance which defines the condition of society, and which constitutes society as something greater than the "aggregate of individuals" that the liberal mind perceives. It is proper for a conservative to be sceptical of claims made on behalf of the value of the individual, if these claims should conflict with the allegiance necessary to society, even though he may wish the *state* (in the sense of the apparatus of government) to stand in a fairly loose relation to the activities of individual citizens. Individuality too is an artifact, an achievement which depends upon the social life of man. And indeed, as many historians have pointed out, it is a recent venture of the human spirit for men and women to define themselves as individuals, as creatures whose nature and value is summed up in their unique individual being. The condition of man requires that the individual, while he exists and acts as an autonomous being, does so only because he can first identify himself as something greater—as a member of a society, group, class, state, or nation, of some arrangement to which he may not attach a name, but which he recognizes instinctively as home. Politically speaking, this bond of allegiance—which, seen from the heights of intellectual speculation as "my station and its duties," is experienced as a peculiar certainty in the activity of day to day—is of a value which transcends the value of individuality. For the majority of men, the bond of allegiance has immediate authority, while the call to individuality is unheard. It is therefore wrong to consider that a statesman has some kind of duty to minister to the second of these, and ignore the first. If the two impulses are not in conflict, as they perhaps were not, for example, in the society described by Fielding (and defended by Burke), then well and good. But if the second threatens the first—as it must do in a society where individuality seeks to realize itself independently of the institutions and traditions that have nurtured it—then the civil order is threatened too. And the business of politics is to maintain the civil order, and to prevent the "dust and powder of individuality" that was once described as its ruin. . . .

The primary object of allegiance is . . . authority, which is to say power conceived as legitimate, and so bound by responsibility. In the family this authority and responsibility have their foundation and end in love, but from the beginning they transcend the personal love of individuals. . . . Authority and responsibility arise from and sustain the sense of the family as something greater than the aggregate of its members, an entity in which the members participate, so that its being and their being are intermingled. Man is increased and not diminished through his participation in such arrangements. Mere individuality, relinquished first to the family, and then to the whole social organism, is finally replaced by the mature allegiance which is the only politically desirable form of "freedom." It is obvious that such allegiance is a matter of degree, being fervent at some times, passive or failing at others. The possibility of conservatism supposes only that it exists to some degree, and in most active people.

It would seem, then, that the healthy state or nation must command the allegiance of its subjects. Patriotism of some kind—the individual's sense of his identity with a social order—is politically indispensable. . . .

The power of tradition is twofold. First, it makes history into reason, and therefore the past into a present aim (as the whole history of the nation is enacted in the ceremony of coronation). Secondly, tradition arises from every organization in society, and is no mere trapping of the exercise of power. Traditions arise and command respect wherever the individual seeks to relate himself to something transcendent. They arise in clubs and societies, in local life, in religion and family custom, in education, and in every institution where man is brought into contact with his kind. Later, in considering questions of politics, we must show how the state can bring authority, allegiance, and tradition together, in order to define the citizen as *subject*. . . .

There is no general explanation of *how* men re-create and accept traditions. Nor is it easy to draw the line between genuine re-creation and the establishment of new and divergent social forms. But in all attempts to restore, re-create and assimilate tradition, the feature of continuity remains. When a man acts from tradition he sees what he *now* does as belonging to a pattern that transcends the focus of his present interest, binding it to what has previously been done, and done successfully. (This is obvious from the case of artistic creation.) Naturally there are rival traditions, and it would be vain to pretend that there is reason to belong to *all* of them. There are traditions of torture, crime, and revolution. The traditions which the conservative fosters and upholds must therefore satisfy independent criteria. First, they must have the weight of a *successful* history—which is to say that they must be the palpable remainder of something that has flourished, and not the latest in a series of abortive starts. Secondly, they must engage the loyalty of their participants, in the deep sense of moulding their idea of what they are and should be. (Contrast the traditions of family life with those of torture.) Finally, they must point to something durable, something which survives and gives meaning to the acts that emerge from it.

But what does this tradition concretely amount to? No simple answer to this question can prove satisfactory: the task of dogma is to bridge the gap between philosophy and practice, and it is only in practice that the sum of our traditions can be understood. Nevertheless, it still belongs to dogma to delineate the *kind* of thing that is intended, and to present some partial exposition of its instances. Tradition, then, must include all those practices which serve to define the individual's "being in society." It constitutes his image of himself as a fragment of the greater social organism, and at the same time as the whole of that organism implicit in this individual part. . . .

RICHARD RORTY

The Unpatriotic Academy

Most of us, despite the outrage we may feel about governmental cowardice or corruption, and despite our despair over what is being done to the weakest and poorest among us, still identify with our country. We take pride in being citizens of a self-invented, self-reforming, enduring constitutional democracy. We think of the United States as having glorious—if tarnished—national traditions.

Many of the exceptions to this rule are found in colleges and universities, in the academic departments that have become sanctuaries for left-wing political views. I am glad there are such sanctuaries, even though I wish we had a left more broadly based, less self-involved and less jargon-ridden than our present one. But any left is better than none, and this one is doing a great deal of good for people who have gotten a raw deal in our society: women, African-Americans, gay men and lesbians. This focus on marginalized groups will, in the long run, help make our country much more decent, more tolerant and more civilized.

But there is a problem with this left: it is unpatriotic. In the name of "the politics of difference," it refuses to rejoice in the country it inhabits, it repudiates the idea of a national identity, and the emotion of national pride. This repudiation is the difference between traditional American pluralism and the new movement called multiculturalism. Pluralism is the attempt to make America what the philosopher John Rawls calls "a social union of social unions," a community of communities, a nation with far more room for difference than most. Multiculturalism is turning into the attempt to keep these communities at odds with one another.

Academic leftists who are enthusiastic about multiculturalism distrust the recent proposal by Sheldon Hackney, chairman of the National Endowment for the Humanities, to hold televised town meetings to "explore the meaning of American identity." Criticizing Mr. Hackney on this page on Jan. 30, Richard Sennett, a distinguished social critic, wrote that the idea of such an identity is just "the gentlemanly face of nationalism," and speaks of "the evil of a shared national identity."

It is too early to say whether the conversations Mr. Hackney proposes will be fruitful. But whether they are or not, it is important to insist that a sense of shared national identity is not an evil. It is an absolutely essential component of citizenship, of any attempt to take our country and its problems seriously. There is no incompatibility between respect for cultural differences and American patriotism.

Like every other country, ours has a lot to be proud of and a lot to be ashamed of. But a nation cannot reform itself unless it takes pride in itself—unless it has an identity, rejoices in it, reflects upon it, and tries to live up to it. Such pride sometimes takes the form of arrogant, bellicose nationalism. But it often takes the form of a yearning to live up to the nation's professed ideals.

That is the desire to which the Rev. Dr. Martin Luther King Jr. appealed, and he is somebody every American can be proud of. It is just as appropriate for white Americans to take pride in Dr. King and his (limited) success as for black Americans to take pride in Ralph Waldo Emerson and John Dewey and their (limited) successes. Cornel West wrote a book—"The American Evasion of Philosophy"—about the connections between Emerson, Dewey, W. E. B. DuBois and his own preaching in African-American churches. The late Irving Howe, whose "World of Our Fathers" did much to make us aware that we are a nation of immigrants, also tried to persuade us (in "The American Newness: Culture and Politics in the Age of Emerson") to cherish a distinctively American, distinctively Emersonian, hope.

Mr. Howe was able to rejoice in a country that had only in his lifetime started to allow Jews to be full-fledged members of society. Cornel West can still identify with a country that, by denying them decent schools and jobs, keeps so many black Americans humiliated and wretched.

There is no contradiction between such identification and shame at the greed, the intolerance, and the indifference to suffering that is widespread in the United States. On the contrary, you can feel shame over your country's behavior only to the extent to which you feel it is *your* country. If we fail in such identification, we fail in national hope. If we fail in national hope, we shall no longer even try to change our ways. If American leftists cease to be proud of being the heirs of Emerson, Lincoln, and King, Irving Howe's prophecy that "the 'newness' will come again"—that we shall once again experience the joyous self-confidence which fills Emerson's "American Scholar"—is unlikely to come true.

If in the interests of ideological purity, or out of the need to stay as angry as possible, the academic left insists on a "politics of difference," it will become increasingly isolated and ineffective. An unpatriotic left has never achieved anything. A left that refuses to take pride in its country will have no impact on that country's politics, and will eventually become an object of contempt.

CHAPTER 6

NONMALEFICENCE

INTRODUCTION

A pair of duties, one stated negatively and one stated positively, correspond to the virtue of beneficence. The first duty, sometimes called the *duty of nonmaleficence,* is the duty not to harm. The second duty, often called the *duty of beneficence,* is the duty to offer a reasonable amount of help to those in need. This chapter examines the requirements of nonmaleficence, and the next considers the requirements of beneficence. Some observations about the relationship between these two duties leads to a discussion of nonmaleficence and permissible harm.

BENEFICENCE VERSUS NONMALEFICENCE

The line between maleficence and beneficence is not always clear, since drawing it requires deciding whether something is a mere failure to harm as opposed to a positive benefit, and that decision can be difficult to reach. Nonetheless, the distinction between positive help on the one hand and failure to harm on the other is commonly made, and the duties of beneficence and nonmaleficence are treated differently in several ways.

1. The duty of nonmaleficence is often thought to take priority over beneficence; however important helping the needy might be, not (significantly) harming others is still more important. In fact, beneficence is controversial in a way that nonmaleficence is not, and while virtually everyone recognizes an extensive duty of nonmaleficence, many recognize only a limited further duty of beneficence or no such duty at all.

2. The distinction between nonmaleficence and beneficence can be aligned with an important distinction between positive and negative duties, but the point will take a bit of explaining. Recall, to begin with, that the correlative notions of duties and rights limit the pursuit of self-interest; while duties compel actions to accommodate the interests of others, rights compel actions by others to accommodate one's own interests. Now add that duties and rights might be construed in a negative way or in a positive way. A *negative* duty is an obligation not to in-

terfere with the interests and pursuits of others, while a *positive* duty is an obligation to provide others with assistance in meeting their interests. The distinction
between positive and negative duties corresponds to the distinction between
the duty of beneficence and the duty of nonmaleficence: Nonmaleficence would
be a negative duty, while beneficence would be a positive duty.

3. Add also that person *P*'s negative right to do (or have) *A* provides for a type of
   negative liberty, a liberty that consists in the fact that others are forbidden to
   interfere with *P*'s doing *A* (and in *P*'s having no duty to avoid *A*). Increasingly
   commonly, philosophers give liberty a positive sense, as well. A positive right
   to do *A* would provide for a *positive liberty,* a liberty based on others' duty to
   provide the means for *A*. But while the protection of negative liberty—and not
   positive liberty—would be a matter of nonmaleficence, the protection of positive liberty would be a matter of beneficence.

4. The duty of nonmaleficence is commonly said to restrict permissible behavior
   toward the nonhuman world. For example, most consider gratuitously hurting
   animals as an offense, whether through gratuitously subjecting them to physical harm or confining them in such a fashion that they cannot meet their needs.
   Far less often is the duty of beneficence applied to the nonhuman world.
   Rarely, for example, do people argue that a duty of beneficence enjoins humans to help animals that are not placed in special need by human action. Few
   people would claim that people must actively help wild animals confronted
   with natural threats, no matter how serious those threats might be.

Nonmaleficence restricts behavior toward the nonhuman world as well as the
human community. Nonetheless, how a person may and may not harm other people
is less controversial than how one may and may not harm the nonhuman world. Consider each form of harm in turn.

NONMALEFICENCE TOWARD PEOPLE

Begin with two observations about harm. First, actions that constitute harm are not always obvious to everyone. When they think of harm, most people think of bodily
damage, but physical harm is not the only known kind of harm. Actions can also harm
others by destroying their property or by interfering with (or thwarting) their attempts
to satisfy their desires. Also, harming people is sometimes a permissible choice. The
duty of nonmaleficence requires qualification to allow for exceptions in circumstances
with overriding moral concerns. For example, most people would say that killing is
sometimes permissible in self-defense.

As these two observations suggest, we need an account of impermissible harm;
fortunately, a standard account is available for consideration. Impermissibly harming
people can equate with violating their negative rights. This equation tends to be supported by one type of classical liberal, namely the *libertarian.* In fact, libertarians define *justice* entirely in terms of negative rights (and negative duties).

CLASSICAL LIBERALISM AND PROTECTION OF NEGATIVE RIGHTS

Appeals to *justice* apply the concept of the right to the social order: The social order is *just* when, and only when, it conforms to the requirements of the right. According to the libertarian, justice prevails when the social order effectively protects everyone's negative rights against violation; in this sense, justice requires that no one be harmed. Libertarians do not recognize any positive rights and duties; in fact, they say, governments that attempt to enforce positive rights are unjust because the enforcement of positive duties associated with positive rights would violate people's negative rights. Justice allows only minimal governments, or governments restricted to the protection of negative rights.

Perhaps the most influential advocate of limited government was the classical liberal John Locke, a seventeenth-century British philosopher whose writings had a profound impact on the founders of the United States. Locke wrote in the natural law tradition, and while he recognized the existence of some positive duties, he emphasized the fundamental importance of protecting negative rights as a restriction on legitimate, or just, government. According to Locke, negative rights or liberties are so extensive that only a limited form of government can achieve justice.

Locke and the Second Treatise

Locke sought to protect negative rights thought of as *natural* rights. Natural rights are rights (1) whose existence does not depend on facts about political arrangements, and (2) that are indefeasible, which means that they cannot be overridden by other pressing moral considerations. To justify the claim for natural rights, Locke appealed to the natural law theory, according to which people are morally bound by the natural law, which is the part of God's law that they can discover by drawing inferences from the evident facts of nature. The natural law confers various rights and responsibilities, including these: (1) Individuals bear the responsibility for deciding for themselves the content of the law of nature and acting according to its strictures. (2) By the natural law, all people are free and equal in that they may do anything they wish so long as they conform to the other conditions of the natural law, such as the (positive) duty to preserve their own lives and, under certain conditions, the lives of others.

People have an inviolable natural right to freedom within the limits imposed by the natural law, and they retain the right to judge whether others have transgressed the law of nature and violated their own rights. Coercive governmental authority receives little legitimacy in such a view. Locke states that government justly exercises only the authority to which everyone has given rational consent, and people would rationally consent only to a minimal state devoted almost entirely to protecting their rights.

Robert Nozick and Libertarianism

Harvard University professor Robert Nozick and other writers associated with the libertarian view accept many of the basic claims made by Locke. Like Locke, libertarians emphasize the importance of individual responsibility for one's life and for identifying and satisfying one's obligations. Property rights always play a fundamental role in libertarian schemes, as well, just as they did in Locke's scheme. Some libertarians are far more critical of extensive political authority than Locke was. Some, for example, defend anarchism on the grounds that individual autonomy is inconsistent with *any* sort of government authority, or on the grounds that people thrive best without coercion by centralized authority, or both. Other libertarians, such as Nozick, argue that a minimal state is legitimate, although a more extensive state would violate people's natural rights. Nozick differs substantially from Locke in his approach to justifying rights by avoiding theistic grounds for claims of natural rights. Nozick defends the natural rights doctrine on the basis of the second formulation of Kant's categorical imperative, which proscribes using people as a mere means. To violate people's negative rights is to use them as a mere means.

Unlike Locke, libertarians recognize the existence of negative rights only. Hence, they do not recognize the Lockean (positive) duty to preserve one's own life and sometimes the lives of others. Although acts that further one's own good are prudent, and acts that further the good of others are praiseworthy, neither is morally required. Competent adults have neither parentalistic nor humanitarian duties, and the corresponding sorts of laws are unjust infringements. Parentalistic laws would require competent adults to act in their own interests, and humanitarian laws would require people to aid competent adults; both are illegitimate in libertarian theory.

2. NONMALEFICENCE AND FUTURE GENERATIONS

Some virtue ethicists might assert a responsibility to create new human beings, so as to provide for the continued existence of the community. (Similarly, classical utilitarians might argue for a *prima facie* duty to reproduce, since, all things being equal, more people result in more utility.) However, no one is responsible for creating people for *their* sakes as individuals: Failure to create them cannot harm them, since they (and their sakes) do not then exist. Thus, philosophers who deploy the concept of the right *solely* as an impartial device for adjudicating clashes among the interests of individuals will not recognize a duty to create people, to have children. However, such philosophers may well argue that *having* children is not always permissible, for conception eventually produces a person whose interests command respect. Because conception would be harmful if it were to bring human beings into an unworthwhile life, perhaps duty demands not creating such beings. What about living human beings? Could others permissibly end their lives early on, either for their sakes or for the actors'? Would killing a human fetus in the early stages of development constitute harm to another, and if so would it be permissible anyway, at least in some circumstances?

Clearly, these questions raise two very different types of issues concerning nonmaleficence and future generations: (1) Issues concerning conception and initiation of human life, such as the potential duty to avoid bringing human beings into miserable lives. (2) Issues concerning abortion of human life. Readings in this chapter discuss both sorts of issues.

Abortion

Does abortion constitute harm to another, and if so is it permissible anyway, at least in some circumstances? Should this discussion speak of a *human being* during early development? Some facts about human development and about the way the courts have dealt with the abortion question may facilitate this debate.

Human Development

After conception, which involves the combining of an ovum and a spermatozoon, the resulting single-celled human organism is called a *zygote*. The zygote begins travelling through the fallopian tube, and at about 12 hours it splits into two cells, after which biologists speak of a *conceptus*. The conceptus continues to divide as it moves through the fallopian tube, attaching itself to the uterus about 8 days after conception. Each of the cells of the conceptus is biologically equivalent to the others in the sense that it could develop into a separate human being if separated from the others. At virtually any point during the first 2 weeks, twinning could occur. (Two four-celled organisms may also fuse to form a single individual, as has been done with mice.[1]) Since biology does not determine how many human beings the conceptus will develop into, *individual* is a somewhat misleading term for the conceptus.

Development has progressed far enough 2 weeks after conception for biologists to speak of an *embryo*. The embryo's heart begins to beat at about 5 weeks, and its first (extremely minimal) brain activity occurs at about 7 weeks. From 8 weeks on, biologists use the term *fetus* to refer to the developing human organism. At 3 months, the fetus shows sufficient brain activity for spontaneous movement; shortly thereafter, around 4 months, quickening, or perceptible movement by the fetus, occurs. At around 6 months the fetus becomes viable, or able to survive outside of the womb. Finally, signs of self-awareness, often used as a criterion for personhood, begin to occur long after birth, when the infant is about 2 years old.

The Legal Climate and Abortion

In the 1973 decision *Roe* v. *Wade,* the U.S. Supreme Court suggested that the abortion controversy involved a clash between a woman's constitutional right to privacy, the state's interest in protecting the woman's health, and the state's interest in protecting "potential life." In order to resolve this clash, the Court divided pregnancy into three trimesters, ruling that (1) during the first trimester "the abortion decision and its effectuation must be left to the medical judgment of the pregnant woman's attending physician;" (2) during the second trimester "the state . . . may . . . regulate the abortion procedure in ways that are reasonably related to maternal health;" and (3) during the third trimester "the state . . . may . . . proscribe abortion except where it is necessary . . . for the preservation of the life or health of the mother." About 20 years later, in the 1992 ruling *Planned Parenthood of Pennsylvania* v. *Casey, et al.,* the Court upheld the "central holding" of *Roe,* namely, that "viability marks the earliest point at which the state's interests in fetal life is constitutionally adequate to justify a legislative ban on nontherapeutic abortions." But the court noted that because viability is technology-relative, it might occur earlier than the end of the second trimester; if so, then states may proscribe earlier abortions. The court also introduced the undue burden test for acceptable state regulations of abortion: According to the court, a regulation is an undue burden, and hence invalid, when it "has the purpose or effect of placing a substantial obstacle in the path of a woman seeking an abortion of a nonviable fetus."

Humans, Human Beings, Life, Persons, and Potential Persons

Some people who reject the morally permissibility of abortions argue that killing a human being in the early stages of development is morally on a par with killing a fully mature human being: Except in certain circumstances (such as certain forms of self-defense) both are murder. But others defend the moral permissibility of abortions because speaking of a *human being* during early development is misleading, much as calling an acorn an *oak tree* would be; not speaking generically of killing "human beings" makes it easier to see that killing at early stages of development is of far less moral concern (if any) than killing later. Much of the confusion surrounding the abortion controversy is created by the language in which it is couched, and a discussion should pay attention to that language. Besides a *human being,* people speak of a *human, life, person,* and *potential person,* terms that differ considerably one from the others. Grass is an instance of "life," corpses are "human," and blood cells are both "human" and instances of "life," but most people are indifferent about destroying corpses and killing grass and blood cells; killing a "person," on the other hand, is of course a serious wrong, but is a fertilized egg or fetus clearly a "person"? A fetus is a "potential person," and a zygote is potentially several people, but in view of the possibility of cloning cells, isn't any human tissue a "potential person"? Besides, as philosophers such as Mary Anne Warren point out, the fact that something is a potential person(s) does not entail a duty to treat it like a person, any more than potential criminals or presidents must be treated like actual criminals or presidents.

Women's Rights

The abortion controversy would not disappear, even after a conclusion that killing a human being in the early stages of development is morally on par with killing a fully mature human being, so that a fetus would have the same right not to be killed as a 25 year-old woman. A second set of issues concerns apparent clashes between the rights of different people. In particular, resolving the question requires a conclusion about the relative importance of not killing a fetus versus not killing a woman or violating her bodily autonomy. In her well-known essay "A Defense of Abortion," Judith Jarvis Thomson argues that abortions in cases in which pregnancy threatens a woman's life are justifiable on the grounds that a woman may abort the fetus in self-defense. She also argues that respecting a woman's right to bodily autonomy is more important than not killing a fetus. Thomson's essay has generated considerable controversy. For instance, in an essay called "The Morality of Abortion," Baruch Brody suggests that no one may kill the innocent, either to save one's own life or to defend the autonomy of one's body. Thomson and Brody, like most people, would say that harming—even killing—someone who deliberately places one in substantial danger is permissible if doing so is the only way to protect one's life. But Thomson and Brody disagree about a much more controversial matter: Could one permissibly harm someone who is entirely blameless and in no way responsible for endangering one?

Many more questions remain. For example, courts have sometimes forced women to submit to surgical procedures such as Cesarean sections in order to avoid grave harm to fetuses. Can the apparatus of law morally permissibly coerce women into submitting to such procedures?

Refraining from Conceiving

People might refrain from conceiving and reproducing to prevent various forms of harm. The world's population was 5.7 billion in 1995, and at present fertility rates there would be 296 billion people in the year 2150. The potential disasters caused by overpopulation have been cited as grounds to restrict human reproduction. In an excerpt from her book *Reproducing Persons,* Laura Purdy discusses a more specific harm that counts against the permissibility of reproduction: the transmission of diseases or defects. Purdy sees a potential for moral wrong in reproducing "when we know there is a high risk of transmitting a serious disease or defect." Purdy does not discuss whether the moral wrong she describes should translate into legal restrictions. Should parents be legally restrained from reproducing when they are likely to transmit serious diseases or defects? The issue is a difficult one, especially in the wake of the troubled history of the state's attempts to limit reproduction. In the early part of the century, many states passed laws allowing the forcible sterilization of institutionalized people thought to have hereditary forms of mental deficiency, insanity, or criminality. In the case *Buck* v. *Bell* (1927) the Supreme Court declared such forcible sterilization to be constitutional, and the ruling stands to this day. Speaking on behalf of the Court, Justice Holmes said that "it is better for all the world, if instead of waiting to execute degenerate offspring for crime, or to let them starve for their imbecility, society can prevent those who are manifestly unfit from continuing their kind. . . . Three generations of imbeciles are enough."

Genetic Therapy

As the discussion so far suggests, opponents of conception and opponents of abortion cite the duty to avoid harm to future generations as their grounds. Nonmaleficence to future generations is also sometimes given as grounds for opposing a promising new medical technology: genetic therapy. By altering the genes of human beings, medical experts can theoretically eliminate genetic diseases such as Tay-Sachs disease, (so-called *negative* therapy), and make improvements in human beings (so-called *positive* therapy), such as, perhaps, increasing people's memory capacity or creativity. If this alteration is applied to an individual's reproductive cells, as in *germline* therapy, that individual's children will inherit the correction. If the alteration is applied to an individual's nonreproductive cells, as in *somatic* therapy, the correction will not be inherited. Many genetic diseases are extremely severe, so genetic therapy may well eliminate a great deal of human misery. But some argue that the new technology poses dangers so great that germline therapy must be avoided or postponed, in positive and perhaps even negative applications. The potential for misfortune is greater in the case of germline therapy than in somatic therapy since alterations are inherited. Some fear unanticipated dangers from somatic therapy, as well, but adults can take on the risks themselves, while germline therapy affects future generations who are in no position to give their consent.

NONMALEFICENCE TOWARD THE NONHUMAN WORLD

The traditional Confucian attitude about the moral importance of the nonhuman world is suggested by a succinct passage in the *Analects* (10.17):

> When his stables caught fire, the Master hurried back from court and asked, "Was anyone hurt?" He did not inquire after the horses.

However, the Daoist attitude concerning nature is quite different from the Confucian attitude. In his essay, Chung-ying Cheng describes the Daoist view and contrasts it with the approach to nature typical in the West. Westerners observe a fundamental contrast between the human and the inhuman: People stand outside of nature and exploit it as a resource. Westerners also tend to be atomistic, assuming that "everything in the world forms an entity on its own as a closed system, and therefore can be individually and separately dealt with." Easterners influenced by Daoism tend to take a more holistic view, assuming that people are part of nature and should cultivate harmony with nature as an extension of themselves.

Bernard Rollin suggests that traditional Western morality, with its emphasis on the rights of the individual, implies rights for individual animals, who should be shown moral concern. Individual animals have rights because they, like humans, are sentient beings with interests "arising out of *their* biologically given natures . . . , the infringement upon which matters greatly to them." Rollin goes on to cast doubt on the view that nonsentient natural objects and abstract objects such as rivers, species, and ecosystems have rights. Such items cannot be harmed in ways that matter to them, and their value, although considerable, is instrumental.

R. G. Frey doubts the case for animal rights, because animals cannot be said to have interests in any robust sense of the term *interests,* and they cannot suffer harm in any robust sense of the term *harm.* Something could be in X's interest in a very weak sense indeed: To say that something is in X's interest might just mean that something is conducive to X's being a good X. Similarly, to harm X might be to do something that is not in X's interest. Given this weak sense of *interest,* oil is in the interest of a tractor, for oil helps a tractor be a good instance of its kind; moreover, draining out its oil would harm the tractor. According to a much more robust sense of *interest,* something has interests when it has desires. Moreover, desires appear to be requisite for the attribution of rights, since tractors cannot have desires while people do. However, animals do not have desires, for animals do not have beliefs (since they do not have language), and beliefs are requisite for desires.

Utilitarians, beginning with Jeremy Bentham, would, of course, disagree with Frey. According to utilitarians, having desires is in fact not requisite for moral standing. The only feature relevant to moral standing is that a creature be able to experience pain, as animals can.

Questions for Reflection

1. Critically assess the view that impermissibly harming people is the same as violating their negative rights.

2. Do people have duties? What would the virtue ethicist say? What would the utilitarian say? Are duties limited to negative duties, or do positive duties constrain people, as well?

3. Purdy states her thesis this way: "It is morally wrong to reproduce when we know there is a high risk of transmitting a serious disease or defect," but she denies that it is an argument for legally restricting reproduction. If her thesis is correct, should government impose legal restrictions on reproduction? Why or why not?

4. Is Purdy right to reject as "moral minimalism" the view that "it is morally permissible to conceive individuals so long as we do not expect them to be so miserable that they wish they were dead"? Why or why not?

5. Is Thomson committed to the view that people may take whatever steps are necessary to protect their rights, including harming innocent persons? Is this view a correct one?

6. Do fertile people have a duty to bring people into the world? Why or why not?

7. Do potential people have the same rights as actual people? (Must potential presidents be treated the same way as actual presidents?)

8. Should people be required to obtain licenses before they are allowed to have children? If not, why not? If so, what sort of restrictions ought to be required of them?

9. Should all forms of genetic therapy be allowed? If not, which should be disallowed: negative somatic, positive somatic, negative germline, positive germline? If any should be disallowed, might they be allowed later, when circumstances change? What are those circumstances?

10. Should genetic therapy be used to increase cheerfulness? Why or why not?

11. Do any animals have rights? Which animals have rights, and what sort of rights do they have? Do plants have rights? Which plants and what sort of rights? How should people treat the nonhuman world according to the virtue ethicist?

12. Assess the following argument: Human overpopulation is unnecessarily harmful to the non-human world, so the human population ought to be drastically scaled back by forcible population control.

13. Assess the following argument: Human overpopulation is lowering the qualify of life for future generations by overcrowding and overconsumption of natural resources. In order to avoid violating rights of future generations, forcible population control ought to drastically scale back the population.

14. Is Frey correct when he says that animals do not have beliefs and, hence, do not have desires? If so, does it follow that animals lack rights?

Suggested Readings

On Libertarianism
Nozick, Robert. *Anarchy, State and Utopia.* New York: Basic Books, 1974.
On Abortion
Feinberg, Joel, ed. *The Problem of Abortion.* Belmont, Calif.: Wadsworth, 1984.
Sumner, L. W. *Abortion and Moral Theory.* Princeton: Princeton University Press, 1981.
Tooley, Michael. *Abortion and Infanticide.* Oxford: Oxford University Press, 1983.
On Environmental Ethics
Cooper, David, and Joy Palmer. *Just Environments.* London: Routledge, 1995.
Ehrlic, Paul. *The Population Explosion.* New York: Simon Schuster, 1990.
Frey, R. G. *Rights, Killing and Suffering.* Oxford: Blackwell, 1983.
Kleinig, J. *Valuing Life.* Princeton, N.J.: Princeton University Press, 1991.
Rollin, Bernard. *The Unheeded Cry.* Oxford: Oxford University Press, 1989.

---

[1]Clifford Grobstein, "Hereditary Constitution and Individual Life," *Society* 19 (1982): 54–58.

(NEGATIVE) RIGHTS AND NOT HARMING PEOPLE

JOHN LOCKE

Second Treatise of Government

OF THE STATES OF NATURE

§1. To understand political power right, and derive it from its original, we must consider what state all men are naturally in, and that is, a state of perfect freedom to order their actions and dispose of their possessions and persons, as they think fit, within the bounds of the law of nature; without asking leave, or depending upon the will of any other man.

A state also of equality, wherein all the power and jurisdiction is reciprocal, no one having more than another; there being nothing more evident than that creatures of the same species and rank, promiscuously born to all the same advantages of nature, and the use of the same faculties, should also be equal one amongst another without subordination or subjection; unless the Lord and Master of them all should, by any manifest declaration of his will, set one above another, and confer on him by an evident and clear appointment, an undoubted right to dominion and sovereignty. . . .

§6. But though this be a state of liberty, yet it is not a state of licence: though man in that state have an uncontrollable liberty to dispose of his person or possessions, yet he has not liberty to destroy himself, or so much as any creature in his possession, but where some nobler use than its bare preservation calls for it. The state of nature has a law of nature to govern it, which obliges every one: and reason, which is that law, teaches all mankind, who will but consult it, that being all equal and independent, no one ought to harm another in his life, health, liberty, or possessions: for men being all the workmanship of one omnipotent and infinitely wise Maker; all the servants of one sovereign Master, sent into the world by his order, and about his business; they are his property, whose workmanship they are, made to last during his, not another's pleasure: and being furnished with like faculties, sharing all in one community of nature, there cannot be supposed any such subordination among us that may authorize us to destroy another, as if we were made for one another's uses, as the inferior ranks of creatures are for ours. Every one, as he is bound to preserve himself, and not to quit his station willfully, so by the like reason, when his own preservation comes not in competition, ought he, as much as he can, to preserve the rest of mankind. . . .

§7. And that all men may be restrained from invading others' rights, and from doing hurt to one another, and the law of nature be observed, which willeth the peace and preservation of all mankind, the execution of the law of nature is, in that state, put into every man's hands, whereby every one has a right to punish the transgressors of that law to such a degree as may hinder its violation: for the law of nature would, as all other laws that concern men in this world, be in vain, if there were nobody that in the state of nature had a power to execute that law, and thereby preserve the innocent, and restrain offenders. And if any one in the state of nature may punish another for any evil he has done, every one may do so: for in that state of perfect equality, where naturally there is no superiority or jurisdiction of one over another, what any may do in prosecution of that law every one must needs have a right to do.

§8. And thus, in the state of nature, "one man comes by a power over another;" but yet no absolute or arbitrary power to use a criminal, when he has got him in his hands, according to the passionate heats or boundless extravagancy of his own will; but only to retribute to him, so far as calm reason and conscience dictate, what is proportionate to his transgression; which is so much as may serve for reparation and restraint: for these two are the only reasons why one man may lawfully do harm to another, which is that we call punishment. In transgressing the law of nature, the offender declares himself to live by another rule than that of reason and common equity. . . .

§15. To those that say, there were never any men in the state of nature, I . . . affirm, that all men are naturally in that state, and remain so, till by their own consents they make themselves members of some politic society; and I doubt not in the sequel of this discourse to make it very clear.

OF PROPERTY

§27. Though the earth, and all inferior creatures, be common to all men, yet every man has a property in his own person: this nobody has any right to but himself. The labour of his body, and the work of his hands, we may say, are properly his. Whatsoever then he removes out of the state that nature hath provided, and left it in, he hath mixed his labour with, and joined to it something that is his own, and thereby makes it his property. It being by him removed from the common state nature hath placed it in, it hath by this labour something annexed to it that excludes the common right of other men. For this labour being the unquestionable property of the labourer, no man but he can have a right to what that is once joined to, at least where there is enough, and as good, left in common for others.

§31. It will perhaps be objected to this, that "if gathering the acorns, or other fruits of the earth, &c. makes a right to them, then any one may engross as much as he will." To which I answer, Not so. The same law of nature, that does by this means give us property, does also bound that property too. "God has given us all things richly," 1 Tim. vi. 17, is the voice of reason confirmed by inspiration. But how far has he given it us? To enjoy. As much as any one can make use of to any advantage of life before it spoils, so much he may by his labour fix a property in: whatever is beyond this, is more than his share, and belongs to others. Nothing was made by God for man to spoil or destroy. And thus, considering the plenty of natural provisions there was a long time in the world, and the few spenders; and to how small a part of that provision the industry of one man could extend itself, and engross it to the prejudice of others; especially keeping within the bounds, set by reason, of what might serve for his use; there could be then little room for quarrels or contentions about property so established.

§32. But the chief matter of property being now not the fruits of the earth, and the beasts that subsist on it, but the earth itself; as that which takes in, and carries with it all the rest; I think it is plain, that property in that too is acquired as the former. As much land as a man tills, plants, improves, cultivates, and can use the product of, so much is his property.

§33. Nor was this appropriation of any parcel of land, by improving it, any prejudice to any other man, since there was still enough, and as good left; and more than the yet unprovided could use. So that, in effect, there was never the less left for others because of his enclosure for himself: for he that leaves as much as another can make use of, does as good as take nothing at all. . . .

§39. . . . Supposing the world given, as it was, to the children of men in common, we see how labour could make men distinct titles to several parcels of it, for their private uses; wherein there could be no doubt of right, no room for quarrel.

§40. Nor is it so strange, as perhaps before consideration it may appear, that the property of labour should be able to overbalance the community of land: for it is labour indeed that put the difference of value on every thing; and let any one consider what the difference is between an acre of land planted with tobacco or sugar, sown with wheat or barley, and an acre of the same land lying in common, without any husbandry upon it, and he will find, that the improvement of labour makes the far greater part of the value. . . .

§46. The greatest part of things really useful to the life of man, and such as the necessity of subsisting made the first commoners of the world look after, as it doth the Americans now, are generally things of short duration. . . . He that gathered a hundred bushels of acorns or apples, had thereby a property in them; they were his goods as soon as gathered. He was only to look that he used them before they spoiled, else he took more than his share, and robbed others. And indeed it was a foolish thing, as well as dishonest, to hoard up more than he could make use of. If he gave away a part to any body else, so that it perished not uselessly in his possession, these he also made use of. And if he also bartered away plums, that would have rotted in a week, for nuts that would last good for his eating a whole year, he did no injury; he wasted not the common stock; destroyed no part of the portion of the goods that belonged to others, so long as nothing perished uselessly in his hands. Again, if he would give his nuts for a piece of metal, pleased with its colour; or exchange his sheep for shells, or wool for a sparkling pebble or a diamond, and keep those by him all his life, he invaded not the right of others; he might heap as much of these durable things as he pleased; the exceeding of the bounds of his just property not lying in the largeness of his possession, but the perishing of any thing uselessly in it.

§47. And thus came in the use of money, some lasting thing that men might keep without spoiling, and that by mutual consent men would take in exchange for the truly useful, but perishable supports of life. . . .

§50. But since gold and silver, being little useful to the life of man in proportion to food, raiment, and carriage, has its value only from the consent of men, whereof labour yet makes, in great part, the measure; it is plain, that men have agreed to a disproportionate and unequal possession of the earth; they having, by a tacit and voluntary consent, found out a way how a man may fairly possess more land than he himself can use the product of, by receiving, in exchange for the overplus, gold and silver, which may be hoarded up without injury to any one; these metals not spoiling or decaying in the hands of the possessor. This partage of things in an inequality of private possessions, men have made practicable out of the bounds of society, and without compact; only by putting a value on gold and silver, and tacitly agreeing in the use of money: for in governments, the laws regulate the right of property, and the possession of land is determined by positive constitutions.

OF CIVIL GOVERNMENT

§87. . . . But because no political society can be, nor subsist, without having in itself the power to preserve the property, and, in order thereunto, punish the offences of all those of that society; there, and there only is political society, where every one of the members hath quitted this natural power, resigned it up into the hands of the community in all cases that exclude him not from appealing for protection to the law established by it. And thus all private judgment of every particular member being excluded, the community comes to be umpire, by settled standing rules, indifferent, and the same to all parties; and by men having authority from the community, for the execution of those rules, decides all the differences that may happen between any members of that society concerning any matter of right; and punishes those offences which any member hath committed against the society, with such penalties as the law has established: whereby it is easy to discern who are, and who are not, in political society together. Those who are united into one body, and have a common established law and judicature to appeal to, with authority to decide controversies between them, and punish offenders, are in civil society one with another: but those who have no such common appeal, I mean on earth, are still in the state of nature, each being, where there is no other, judge for himself, and executioner: which is, as I have before showed it, the perfect state of nature.

§88. And thus the commonwealth comes by a power to set down what punishment shall belong to the several transgressions which they think worthy of it, committed amongst the members of that society, (which is the power of making laws) as well as it has the power to punish any injury done unto any of its members, by any one that is not of it, (which is the power of war and peace:) and all this for the preservation of the property of all the members of that society, as far as is possible. But though every man who has entered into civil society, and is become a member of any commonwealth, has thereby quitted his power to punish offences against the law of nature, in prosecution of his own private judgment; yet with the judgment of offences, which he has given up to the legislative in all cases, where he can appeal to the magistrate, he has given a right to the commonwealth to employ his force, for the execution of the judgments of the commonwealth, whenever he shall be called to it; which indeed are his own judgments, they being made by himself, or his representative. And herein we have the original of the legislative and executive power of civil society, which is to judge by standing laws, how far offences are to be punished, when committed within the commonwealth; and also to determine, by occasional judgments founded on the present circumstances of the fact, how far injuries from without are to be vindicated; and in both these to employ all the force of all the members, when there shall be need. . . .

§**128.** In the state of nature, to omit the liberty he has of innocent delights, a man has two powers:

The first is to do whatsoever he thinks fit for the preservation of himself and others within the permission of the law of nature, by which law, common to them all, he and all the rest of mankind are one community, make up one society, distinct from all other creatures. And, were it not for the corruption and viciousness of degenerate men, there would be no need of any other, no necessity that men should separate from this great and natural community and by positive agreements combine into smaller and divided associations.

The other power a man has in the state of nature is the power to punish the crimes committed against that law. Both these he gives up when he joins in a private, if I may so call it, or particular politic society and incorporates into any commonwealth separate from the rest of mankind.

ROBERT NOZICK

Moral Constraints and the State

An ultraminimal state maintains a monopoly over all use of force except that necessary in immediate self-defense, and so excludes private (or agency) retaliation for wrong and exaction of compensation; but it provides protection and enforcement services *only* to those who purchase its protection and enforcement policies. . . .

A proponent of the ultraminimal state may seem to occupy an inconsistent position, even though he avoids the question of what makes protection uniquely suitable for redistributive provision. Greatly concerned to protect rights against violation, he makes this the sole legitimate function of the state; and he protests that all other functions are illegitimate because they themselves involve the violation of rights. Since he accords paramount place to the protection and nonviolation of rights, how can he support the ultraminimal state, which would seem to leave some persons' rights unprotected or ill-protected? How can he support this *in the name of* the nonviolation of rights?

MORAL CONSTRAINTS AND MORAL GOALS

This question assumes that a moral concern can function only as a moral *goal,* as an end state for some activities to achieve as their result. It may, indeed, seem to be a necessary truth that "right," "ought," "should," and so on, are to be explained in terms of what is, or is intended to be, productive of the greatest good, with all goals built into the good. Thus it is often thought that what is wrong with utilitarianism (which *is* of this form) is its too narrow conception of good. Utilitarianism doesn't, it is said, properly take rights and their nonviolation into account; it instead leaves them a derivative status. Many of the counterexample cases to utilitarianism fit under this objection, for example, punishing an innocent man to save a neighborhood from a vengeful rampage. But a theory may include in a primary way the nonviolation of rights, yet include it in the wrong place and the wrong manner. For suppose some condition about minimizing the total (weighted) amount of violations of rights is built into the desirable end state to be achieved. We then would have something like a "utilitarianism of rights"; violations of rights (to be *minimized*) merely would replace the total happiness as the relevant end state in the utilitarian structure. . . . This still would require us to violate someone's rights when doing so minimizes the total (weighted) amount of the violation of rights in the society. For example, violating someone's rights might deflect others from *their* mob rampaging through a part of town killing and burning *will* violate the rights of those living there. Therefore, someone might try to justify his punishing another *he* knows to be innocent of a crime that enraged a mob, on the grounds that punishing this innocent person would help to avoid even greater violations of rights by others, and so would lead to a minimum weighted score for rights violations in the society.

In contrast to incorporating rights into the end state to be achieved, one might place them as side constraints upon the actions to be done: don't violate constraints *C*. The rights of others determine the constraints upon your actions. (A *goal-directed* view with constraints added would be: among those acts available to you that don't violate constraints *C*, act so as to maximize goal *G*. Here, the rights of others would constrain your goal-directed behavior. I do not mean to imply that the correct moral view includes mandatory goals that must be pursued, even within the constraints.) This view differs from one that tries to build the side constraints *C into* the goal *G*. The side-constraint view forbids you to violate these moral constraints in the pursuit of your goals; whereas the view whose objective is to minimize the violation of these rights allows you to violate the rights (the constraints) in order to lessen their total violation in the society.

The claim that the proponent of the ultraminimal state is inconsistent, we now can see, assumes that he is a "utilitarian of rights." It assumes that his goal is, for example, to minimize the weighted amount of the violation of rights in the society, and that he should pursue this goal even through means that themselves violate people's rights. Instead, he may place the nonviolation of rights as a constraint upon action, rather than (or in addition to) building it into the end state to be realized. The position held by this proponent of the ultraminimal state will be a consistent one if his conception of rights holds that your being *forced* to contribute to another's welfare violates your rights, whereas someone else's not providing you with things you need greatly, including things essential to the protection of your rights, does not *itself* violate your rights, even though it avoids making it more difficult for someone else to violate them. (That conception will be consistent provided it does not construe the monopoly element of the ultraminimal state as itself a violation of rights.) That it is a consistent position does not, of course, show that it is an acceptable one.

WHY SIDE CONSTRAINTS?

Side constraints upon action reflect the underlying Kantian principle that individuals are ends and not merely means; they may not be sacrificed or used for the achieving of other ends without their consent. Individuals are inviolable. More should be said to illuminate this talk of ends and means. Consider a prime example of a means, a tool. There is no side constraint on how we may use a tool, other than the moral constraints on how we may use it upon others. There are procedures to be followed to preserve it for future use ("don't leave it out in the rain"), and there are more and less efficient ways of using it. But there is no limit on what we may do to it to best achieve our goals. Now imagine that there was an overrideable constraint *C* on some tool's use. For example, the tool might have been lent to you only on the condition that *C* not be violated unless the gain from doing so was above a certain specified amount, or unless it was necessary to achieve a certain specified goal. Here the object is not *completely* your tool, for use according to your wish or whim. But it is a tool nevertheless, even with regard to the overrideable constraint. If we add constraints on its use that may not be overridden, then the object may not be used as a tool *in those ways. In those respects,* it is not a tool at all. Can one add enough constraints so that an object cannot be used as a tool at all, in *any* respect?

Can behavior toward a person be constrained so that he is not to be used for any end except as he chooses? This is an impossibly stringent condition if it requires everyone who provides us with a good to approve positively of every use to which we wish to put it. Even the requirement that he merely should not object to any use we plan would seriously curtail bilateral exchange, not to mention sequences of such exchanges. It is sufficient that the other party stands to gain enough from the exchange so that he is willing to go through with it, even though he objects to one or more of the uses to which you shall put the good. Under such conditions, the other party is not being used solely as a means, in that respect. Another party, however, who would not choose to interact with you if he knew of the uses to which you *intend* to put his actions or goods, *is* being used as a means, even if he receives enough to choose (in his ignorance) to interact with you. . . .

Side constraints express the inviolability of others, in the ways they specify. These modes of inviolability are expressed by the following injunction: "Don't use people in specified ways." An end-state view, on the other hand, would express the view that people are ends and not merely means (if it chooses to express this view at all), by a different injunction: "Minimize the use in specified ways of persons as means." Following this precept itself may involve using someone as a means in one of the ways specified. Had Kant held this view, he would have given the second formula of the categorical imperative as, "So act as to minimize the use of humanity simply as a means," rather than the one he actually used: "Act in such a way that you always treat humanity, whether in your own person or in the person of any other, never simply as a means, but always at the same time as an end."

Side constraints express the inviolability of other persons. But why may not one violate persons for the greater social good? Individually, we each sometimes choose to undergo some pain or sacrifice for a greater benefit or to avoid a greater harm: we go to the dentist to avoid worse suffering later; we do some unpleasant work for its results; some persons diet to improve their health or looks; some save money to support themselves when they are older. In each case, some cost is borne for the sake of the greater overall good. Why not, *similarly,* hold that some persons have to bear some costs that benefit other persons more, for the sake of the overall social good? But there is no *social entity* with a good that undergoes some sacrifice for its own good. There are only individual people, different individual people, with their own individual lives. Using one of these people for the benefit of others, uses him and benefits the others. Nothing more. What happens is that something is done to him for the sake of others. Talk of an overall social good covers this up. (Intentionally?) To use a person in this way does not sufficiently respect and take account of the fact that he is a separate person, that his is the only life he has. *He* does not get some overbalancing good from his sacrifice, and no one is entitled to force this upon him—least of all a state or government that claims his allegiance (as other individuals do not) and that therefore scrupulously must be *neutral* between its citizens.

LIBERTARIAN CONSTRAINTS

The moral side constraints upon what we may do, I claim, reflect the fact of our separate existences. They reflect the fact that no moral balancing act can take place among us; there is no moral outweighing of one of our lives by others so as to lead to a greater overall *social* good. There is no justified sacrifice of some of us for others. This root idea, namely, that there are different individuals with separate lives and so no one may be sacrificed for others, underlies the existence of moral side constraints, but it also, I believe, leads to a libertarian side constraint that prohibits aggression against another. . . .

CONSTRAINTS AND ANIMALS

We can illuminate the status and implications of moral side constraints by considering living beings for whom such stringent side constraints (or any at all) usually are not considered appropriate: namely, nonhuman animals. Are there any limits to what we may do to animals? Have animals the moral status of mere *objects?* Do some purposes fail to entitle us to impose great costs on animals? What entitles us to use them at all?

Animals count for something. Some higher animals, at least, ought to be given some weight in people's deliberations about what to do. . . .

Consider the following (too minimal) position about the treatment of animals. So that we can easily refer to it, let us label this position "utilitarianism for animals, Kantianism for people." It says: (1) maximize the total happiness of all living beings; (2) place stringent side constraints on what one may do to human beings. Human beings may not be used or sacrificed for the benefit of others; animals may be used or sacrificed for the benefit of other people or animals *only if* those benefits are greater than the loss inflicted. (This inexact statement of the utilitarian position is close enough for our purposes, and it can be handled more easily in discussion.) One may proceed only if the total utilitarian benefit is greater than the utilitarian loss inflicted on the animals. This utilitarian view counts animals as much as normal utilitarianism does persons. . . .

Under "utilitarianism for animals, Kantianism for people," animals will be used for the gain of other animals and persons, but persons will never be used (harmed, sacrificed) against their will, for the gain of animals. Nothing may be inflicted upon persons for the sake of animals. (Including penalties for violating laws against cruelty to animals?) Is this an acceptable consequence? Can't one save 10,000 animals from excruciating suffering by inflicting some slight discomfort on a person who did not cause the animals' suffering? One may feel the side constraint is not absolute when it is *people* who can be saved from excruciating suffering. So perhaps the side constraint also relaxes, though not as much, when animals' suffering is at stake. The thoroughgoing utilitarian (for animals *and* for people, combined in one group) goes further and holds that, *ceteris paribus,* we may inflict some suffering on a person to avoid a (slightly) greater suffering of an animal. This permissive principle seems to me to be unacceptably strong, even when the purpose is to avoid greater suffering to a *person!*

Utilitarian theory is embarrassed by the possibility of utility monsters who get enormously greater gains in utility from any sacrifice of others than these others lose. For, unacceptably, the theory seems to require that we all be sacrificed in the monster's maw, in order to increase total utility. Similarly if people are utility devourers with respect to animals, always getting greatly counterbalancing utility from each sacrifice of an animal, we may feel that "utilitarianism for animals, Kantianism for people," in requiring (or allowing) that almost always animals be sacrificed, makes animals too subordinate to persons.

Since it counts only the happiness and suffering of animals, would the utilitarian view hold it all right to kill animals painlessly? Would it be all right, on the utilitarian view, to kill *people* painlessly, in the night, provided one didn't first announce it? . . . Is it all right to kill someone provided you immediately substitute another (by having a child or, in science-fiction fashion, by creating a full-grown person) who will be as happy as the rest of the life of the person you killed? After all, there would be no net diminution in total utility, or even any change in its profile of distribution. . . . Clearly, a utilitarian needs to supplement his view to handle such issues; perhaps he will find that the supplementary theory becomes the main one, relegating utilitarian considerations to a corner.

But isn't utilitarianism at least adequate for animals? I think not. But if not only the animals' felt experiences are relevant, what else is? Here a tangle of questions arises. How much does an animal's life have to be respected once it's alive, and how can we decide this? Must one also introduce some notion of a nondegraded existence? Would it be all right to use genetic-engineering techniques to breed natural slaves who would be contented with their lots? Natural animal slaves? Was that the domestication of animals? Even for animals, utilitarianism won't do as the whole story, but the thicket of questions daunts us.

JUDITH JARVIS THOMSON

A Defense of Abortion[1]

Most opposition to abortion relies on the premise that the fetus is a human being, a person, from the moment of conception. The premise is argued for, but, as I think, not well. Take, for example, the most common argument. We are asked to notice that the development of a human being from conception through birth into childhood is continuous; then it is said that to draw a line, to choose a point in this development and say "before this point the thing is not a person, after this point it is a person" is to make an arbitrary choice, a choice for which in the nature of things no good reason can be given. It is concluded that the fetus is, or anyway that we had better say it is, a person from the moment of conception. But this conclusion does not follow. Similar things might be said about the development of an acorn into an oak tree, and it does not follow that acorns are oak trees, or that we had better say they are. Arguments of this form are sometimes called "slippery slope arguments"—the phrase is perhaps self-explanatory—and it is dismaying that opponents of abortion rely on them so heavily and uncritically.

I am inclined to agree, however, that the prospects for "drawing a line" in the development of the fetus look dim. I am inclined to think also that we shall probably have to agree that the fetus has already become a human person well before birth. Indeed, it comes as a surprise when one first learns how early in its life it begins to acquire human characteristics. By the tenth week, for example, it already has a face, arms and legs, fingers and toes; it has internal organs, and brain activity is detectable.[2] On the other hand, I think that the premise is false, that the fetus is not a person from the moment of conception. A newly fertilized ovum, a newly implanted clump of cells, is no more a person than an acorn is an oak tree. But I shall not discuss any of this. For it seems to me to be of great interest to ask what happens if, for the sake of argument, we allow the premise. How, precisely, are we supposed to get from there to the conclusion that abortion is morally impermissible? Opponents of abortion commonly spend most of their time establishing that the fetus is a person, and hardly any time explaining the step from there to the impermissibility of abortion. Perhaps they think the step too simple and obvious to require much comment. Or perhaps instead they are simply being economical in argument. Many of those who defend abortion rely on the premise that the fetus is not a person, but only a bit of tissue that will become a person at birth; and why pay out more arguments than you have to? Whatever the explanation, I suggest that the step they take is neither easy nor obvious, that it calls for closer examination than it is commonly given, and that when we do give it this closer examination we shall feel inclined to reject it.

I propose, then, that we grant that the fetus is a person from the moment of conception. How does the argument go from here? Something like this, I take it. Every person has a right to life. So the fetus has a right to life. No doubt the mother has a right to decide what shall happen in and to her body; everyone would grant that. But surely a person's right to life is stronger and more stringent than the mother's right to decide what happens in and to her body, and so outweighs it. So the fetus may not be killed; an abortion may not be performed.

It sounds plausible. But now let me ask you to imagine this. You wake up in the morning and find yourself back to back in bed with an unconscious violinist. A famous unconscious violinist. He has been found to have a fatal kidney ailment, and the Society of Music Lovers has canvassed all the available medical records and found that you alone have the right blood type to help. They have therefore kidnapped you, and last night the violinist's circulatory system was plugged into yours, so that your kidneys can be used to extract poisons from his blood as well as your own. The director of the hospital now tells you, "Look, we're sorry the Society of Music Lovers did this to you—we would never have permitted it if we had known. But still, they did it, and the violinist now is plugged into you. To unplug you would be to kill him. But never mind, it's only for 9 months. By then he will have recovered from his ailment, and can safely be unplugged from you." Is it morally incumbent on you to accede to this situation? No doubt it would be very nice of you if you did, a great kindness. But do you *have* to accede to it? What if it were not 9 months, but 9 years? Or longer still? What if the director of the hospital says, "Tough luck, I agree, but you've now got to stay in bed, with the violinist plugged into you, for the rest of your life. Because remember this. All persons have a right to life, and violinists are persons. Granted you have a right to decide what happens in and to your body, but a person's right to life outweighs your right to decide what happens in and to your body. So you cannot ever be unplugged from him." I imagine you would regard this as outrageous, which suggests that something really is wrong with that plausible-sounding argument I mentioned a moment ago.

In this case, of course, you were kidnapped; you didn't volunteer for the operation that plugged the violinist into your kidneys. Can those who oppose abortion on the ground I mentioned make an exception for a pregnancy due to rape? Certainly. They can say that persons have a right to life only if they didn't come into existence because of rape; or they can say that all persons have a right to life, but that some have less of a right to life than others, in particular, that those who came into existence because of rape have less. But these statements have a rather unpleasant sound. Surely the question of whether you have a right to life at all, or how much of it you have, shouldn't turn on the question of whether or not you are the product of a rape. And in fact the people who oppose abortion on the ground I mentioned do not make this distinction, and hence do not make an exception in case of rape.

Nor do they make an exception for a case in which the mother has to spend the 9 months of her pregnancy in bed. They would agree that would be a great pity, and hard on the mother; but all the same, all persons have a right to life, the fetus is a person, and so on. I suspect, in fact, that they would not make an exception for a case in which, miraculously enough, the pregnancy went on for 9 years, or even the rest of the mother's life.

Some won't even make an exception for a case in which continuation of the pregnancy is likely to shorten the mother's life; they regard abortion as impermissible even to save the mother's life. Such cases are nowadays very rare, and many opponents of abortion do not accept this extreme view. All the same, it is a good place to begin: a number of points of interest come out in respect to it.

1. Let us call the view that abortion is impermissible even to save the mother's life "the extreme view." I want to suggest first that it does not issue from the argument I mentioned earlier without the addition of some fairly powerful premises. Suppose a woman has become pregnant, and now learns that she has a cardiac condition such that she will die if she carries the baby to term. What may be done for her? The fetus, being a person, has a right to life, but as the mother is a person too, so has she a right to life. Presumably they have an equal right to life. How is it supposed to come out that an abortion may not be performed? If mother and child have an equal right to life, shouldn't we perhaps flip a coin? Or should we add to the mother's right to life her right to decide what happens in and to her body, which everybody seems to be ready to grant—the sum of her rights now outweighing the fetus' right to life?

The most familiar argument here is the following. We are told that performing the abortion would be directly killing[3] the child, whereas doing nothing would not be killing the mother, but only letting her die. Moreover, in killing the child, one would be killing an innocent person, for the child has committed no crime, and is not aiming at his mother's death. And then there are a variety of ways in which this might be continued. (1) But as directly killing an innocent person is always and absolutely impermissible, an abortion may not be performed. Or, (2) as directly killing an innocent person is murder, and murder is always and absolutely impermissible, an abortion may not be performed.[4] Or, (3) as one's duty to refrain from directly killing an innocent person is more stringent than one's duty to keep a person from dying, an abortion may not be performed. Or, (4) if one's only options are directly killing an innocent person or letting a person die, one must prefer letting the person die, and thus an abortion may not be performed.[5]

Some people seem to have thought that these are not further premises which must be added if the conclusion is to be reached, but that they follow from the very fact that an innocent person has a right to life.[6] But this seems to me to be a mistake, and perhaps the simplest way to show this is to bring out that while we must certainly grant that innocent persons have a right to life, the thesis in (1) through (4) are all false. Take (2), for example. If directly killing an innocent person is murder, and thus is impermissible, then the mother's directly killing the innocent person inside her is murder, and thus impermissible. But it cannot seriously be thought to be murder if the mother performs an abortion on herself to save her life. It cannot seriously be said that she *must* refrain, that she *must* sit passively by and wait for her death. Let us look again at the case of you and the violinist. There you are, in bed with the violinist, and the director of the hospital says to you, "It's all most distressing, and I deeply sympathize, but you see this is putting an additional strain on your kidneys, and you'll be dead within the month. But you *have* to stay where you are all the same. Because unplugging you would be directly killing an innocent violinist, and that's murder, and that's impermissible." If anything in the world is true, it is that you do not commit murder, you do not do what is impermissible, if you reach around to your back and unplug yourself from that violinist to save your life.

The main focus of attention in writings on abortion has been on what a third party may or may not do in answer to a request from a woman for an abortion. This is in a way understandable. Things being as they are, there isn't much a woman can safely do to abort herself. So the question asked is what a third party may do, and what the mother may do, if it is mentioned at all, is deduced, almost as an afterthought, from what it is concluded that third parties may do. But it seems to me that to treat the matter in this way is to refuse to grant to the mother that very status of person which is so firmly insisted on for the fetus. For we cannot simply read off what a person may do from what a third party may do. Suppose you find yourself trapped in a tiny house with a growing child. I mean a very tiny house, and a rapidly growing child—you are already up against the wall of the house and in a few minutes you'll be crushed to death. The child on the other hand won't be crushed to death; if nothing is done to stop him from growing he'll be hurt, but in the end he'll simply burst open the house and walk out a free man. Now I could well understand it if a bystander were to say, "There's nothing we can do for you. We cannot choose between your life and his, we cannot be the ones to decide who is to live, we cannot intervene." But it cannot be concluded that you too can do nothing, that you cannot attack it to save your life. However innocent the child may be, you do not have to wait passively while it crushes you to death. Perhaps a pregnant woman is vaguely felt to have the status of house, to which we don't allow the right of self-defense. But if the woman houses the child, it should be remembered that she is a person who houses it.

I should perhaps stop to say explicitly that I am not claiming that people have a right to do anything whatever to save their lives. I think, rather, that there are drastic limits to the right of self-defense. If someone threatens you with death unless you torture someone else to death, I think you have not the right, even to save your life, to do so. But the case under consideration here is very different. In our case there are only two people involved, one whose life is threatened, and one who threatens it. Both are innocent: the one who is threatened is not threatened because of any fault, the one who threatens does not threaten because of any fault. For this reason we may feel that we bystanders cannot intervene. But the person threatened can.

In sum, a woman surely can defend her life against the threat to it posed by the unborn child, even if doing so involves its death. And this shows not merely that the theses in (1) through (4) are false; it shows also that the extreme view of abortion is false, and so we need not canvass any other possible ways of arriving at it from the argument I mentioned at the outset.

2. The extreme view could of course be weakened to say that while abortion is permissible to save the mother's life, it may not be performed by a third party, but only by the mother herself. But this cannot be right either. For what we have to keep in mind is that the mother and the unborn child are not like two tenants in a small house which has, by an unfortunate mistake, been rented to both: the mother *owns* the house. The fact that she does adds to the offensiveness of deducing that the mother can do nothing from the supposition that third parties can do nothing. But it does more than this: it casts a bright light on the supposition that third parties can do nothing. Certainly it lets us see that a third party who says "I cannot choose between you" is fooling himself if he thinks this is impartiality. If Jones has found and fastened on a certain coat, which he needs to keep him from freezing, but which Smith also needs to keep him from freezing, then it is not impartiality that says "I cannot choose between you" when Smith owns the coat. Women have said again and again "This body is *my* body!" and they have reason to feel angry, reason to feel that it has been like shouting into the wind. Smith, after all, is hardly likely to bless us if we say to him, "Of course it's your coat, anybody would grant that it is. But no one may choose between you and Jones who is to have it." . . .

3. Where the mother's life is not at stake, the argument I mentioned at the outset seems to have a much stronger pull. "Everyone has a right to life, so the unborn person has a right to life." And isn't the child's right to life weightier than anything other than the mother's own right to life, which she might put forward as ground for an abortion?

This argument treats the right to life as if it were unproblematic. It is not, and this seems to me to be precisely the source of the mistake.

For we should now, at long last, ask what it comes to, to have a right to life. In some views having a right to life includes having a right to be given at least the bare minimum one needs for continued life. But suppose that what in fact *is* the bare minimum a man needs for continued life is something he has no right at all to be given? If I am sick unto death, and the only thing that will save me is the touch of Henry Fonda's cool hand on my fevered brow, then all the same, I have no right to be given the touch of Henry Fonda's cool hand on my fevered brow. It would be frightfully nice of him to fly in from the West Coast to provide it. It would be less nice, though no doubt well meant, if my friends flew out to the West Coast and carried Henry Fonda back with them. But I have no right at all against anybody that he should do this for me. Or again, to return to the story I told earlier, the fact that for continued life that violinist needs the continued use of your kidneys does not establish that he has a right to be given the continued use of your kidneys. He certainly has no right against you that *you* should give him continued use of your kidneys. For nobody has any right to use your kidneys unless you give him such a right; and nobody has the right against you that you shall give him this right—if you do allow him to go on using your kidneys, this is a kindness on your part, and not something he can claim from you as his due. Nor has he any right against anybody else that *they* should give him continued use of your kidneys. Certainly he had no right against the Society of Music Lovers that they should plug him into you in the first place. And if you now start to unplug yourself, having learned that you will otherwise have to spend 9 years in bed with him, there is nobody in the world who must try to prevent you, in order to see to it that he is given something he has a right to be given. . . .

4. In the most ordinary sort of case, to deprive someone of what he has a right to is to treat him unjustly. Suppose a boy and his small brother are jointly given a box of chocolates for Christmas. If the older boy takes the box and refuses to give his brother any of the chocolates, he is unjust to him, for the brother has been given a right to half of them. But suppose that, having learned that otherwise it means 9 years in bed with that violinist, you unplug yourself from him. You surely are not being unjust to him, for you gave him no right to use your kidneys, and no one else can have given him any such right. But we have to notice that in unplugging yourself, you are killing him; and violinists, like everybody else, have a right to life, and thus in the view we were considering just now, the right not to be killed. So here you do what he supposedly has a right you shall not do, but you do not act unjustly to him in doing it.

The emendation which may be made at this point is this: the right to life consists not in the right not to be killed, but rather in the right not to be killed unjustly. This runs a risk of circularity, but never mind: it would enable us to square the fact that the violinist has a right to life with the fact that you do not act unjustly toward him in unplugging yourself, thereby killing him. For if you do not kill him unjustly, you do not violate his right to life, and so it is no wonder you do him no injustice.

But if this emendation is accepted, the gap in the argument against abortion stares us plainly in the face: it is by no means enough to show that the fetus is a person, to remind us that all persons have a right to life—we need to be shown also that killing the fetus violates its right to life, i.e., that abortion is unjust killing. And is it?

I suppose that we may take it as a datum that in a case of pregnancy due to rape the mother has not given the unborn person a right to the use of her body for food and shelter. Indeed, in what pregnancy could it be supposed that the mother has given the unborn person such a right? It is not as if there were unborn persons drifting about the world, to whom a woman who wants a child says "I invite you in."

But it might be argued that there are other ways one can have acquired a right to the use of another person's body than by having been invited to use it by that person. Suppose a woman voluntarily indulges in intercourse, knowing of the chance it will issue in pregnancy, and then she does become pregnant; is she not in part responsible for the presence, in fact the very existence, of the unborn person inside her? No doubt she did not invite it in. But doesn't her partial responsibility for its being there itself give it a right to the use of her body? If so, then her aborting it would be more like the boy's taking away the chocolates, and less like your unplugging yourself from the violinist—doing so would be depriving it of what it does have a right to, and thus would be doing it an injustice.

And then, too, it might be asked whether or not she can kill it even to save her own life: If she voluntarily called it into existence, how can she now kill it, even in self-defense?

. . . This argument would give the unborn person a right to its mother's body only if her pregnancy resulted from a voluntary act, undertaken in full knowledge of the chance a pregnancy might result from it. It would leave out entirely the unborn person whose existence is due to rape. Pending the availability of some further argument, then, we would be left with the conclusion that unborn persons whose existence is due to rape have no right to the use of their mothers' bodies, and thus that aborting them is not depriving them of anything they have a right to and hence is not unjust killing.

And we should also notice that it is not at all plain that this argument really does go even as far as it purports to. For there are cases and cases, and the details make a difference. If the room is stuffy, and I therefore open a window to air it, and a burglar climbs in, it would be absurd to say, "Ah, now he can stay, she's given him a right to the use of her house—for she is partially responsible for his presence there, having voluntarily done what enabled him to get in, in full knowledge that there are such things as burglars, and that burglars burgle." It would be still more absurd to say this if I had had bars installed outside my windows, precisely to prevent burglars from getting in, and a burglar got in only because of a defect in the bars. It remains equally absurd if we imagine it is not a burglar who climbs in, but an innocent person who blunders or falls in. Again, suppose it were like this: people-seeds drift about in the air like pollen, and if you open your windows, one may drift in and take root in your carpets or upholstery. You don't want children, so you fix up your windows with fine mesh screens, the very best you can buy. As can happen, however, and on very, very rare occasions does happen, one of the screens is defective; and a seed drifts in and takes root. Does the person-plant who now develops have a right to the use of your house? Surely not—despite the fact that you voluntarily opened your windows, you knowingly kept carpets and upholstered furniture, and you knew that screens were sometimes defective. Someone may argue that you are responsible for its rooting, that it does have a right to your house, because after all you *could* have lived out your life with bare floors and furniture, or with sealed windows and doors. But this won't do—for by the same token anyone can avoid a pregnancy due to rape by having a hysterectomy, or anyway by never leaving home without a (reliable!) army.

It seems to me that the argument we are looking at can establish at most that there are *some* cases in which the unborn person has a right to the use of its mother's body, and therefore *some* cases in which abortion is unjust killing. There is room for much discussion and argument as to precisely which, if any. But I think we should sidestep this issue and leave it open, for at any rate the argument certainly does not establish that all abortion is unjust killing.

5. There is room for yet another argument here, however. We surely must all grant that there may be cases in which it would be morally indecent to detach a person from your body at the cost of his life. Suppose you learn that what the violinist needs is not 9 years of your life, but only 1 hour: all you need do to save his life is to spend 1 hour in that bed with him. Suppose also that letting him use your kidneys for that 1 hour would not affect your health in the slightest. Admittedly you were kidnapped. Admittedly you did not give anyone permission to plug him into you. Nevertheless it seems to me plain you *ought* to allow him to use your kidneys for that hour—it would be indecent to refuse.

Again, suppose pregnancy lasted only an hour, and constituted no threat to life or health. And suppose that a woman becomes pregnant as a result of rape. Admittedly she did not voluntarily do anything to bring about the existence of a child. Admittedly she did nothing at all which would give the unborn person a right to the use of her body. All the same it might well be said, as in the newly emended violinist story, that she *ought* to allow it to remain for that hour—that it would be indecent of her to refuse.

Now some people are inclined to use the term "right" in such a way that it follows from the fact that you ought to allow a person to use your body for the hour he needs, that he has a right to use your body for the hour he needs, even though he has not been given that right by any person or act. They may say that it follows also that if you refuse, you act unjustly toward him. This use of the term is perhaps so common that it cannot be called wrong; nevertheless it seems to me to be an unfortunate loosening of what we would do better to keep a tight rein on. Suppose that box of chocolates I mentioned earlier has not been given to both boys jointly, but was given only to the older boy. There he sits, stolidly eating his way through the box, his small brother watching enviously. Here we are likely to say "You ought not to be so mean. You ought to give your brother some of those chocolates." My own view is that it just does not follow from the truth of this that the brother has any right to the chocolates. If the boy refuses to give his brother any, he is greedy, stingy, callous—but not unjust. I suppose that the people I have in mind will say it does follow that the brother has a right to some of the chocolates, and thus that the boy does act unjustly if he refuses to give his brother any. But the effect of saying this is to obscure what we should keep distinct, namely the difference between the boy's refusal in this case and the boy's refusal in the earlier case, in which the box was given to both boys jointly, and in which the small brother thus had what was from any point of view clear title to half.

A further objection to so using the term "right" that from the fact that A ought to do a thing for B, it follows that B has a right against A that A do it for him, is that it is going to make the question of whether or not a man has a right to a thing turn on how easy it is to provide him with it; and this seems not merely unfortunate, but morally unacceptable. Take the case of Henry Fonda again. I said earlier that I had no right to the touch of his cool hand on my fevered brow, even though I needed it to save my life. I said it would be frightfully nice of him to fly in from the West Coast to provide me with it, but that I had no right against him that he should do so. But suppose he isn't on the West Coast. Suppose he has only to walk across the room, place a hand briefly on my brow—and lo, my life is saved. Then surely he ought to do it, it would be indecent to refuse. Is it to be said "Ah, well, it follows that in this case she has a right to the touch of his hand on her brow, and so it would be an injustice in him to refuse"? So that I have a right to it when it is easy for him to provide it, though no right when it's hard? It's rather a shocking idea that anyone's rights should fade away and disappear as it gets harder and harder to accord them to him.

So my own view is that even though you ought to let the violinist use your kidneys for the 1 hour he needs, we should not conclude that he has a right to do so—we should say that if you refuse, you are, like the boy who owns all the chocolates and will give none away, self-centered and callous, indecent in fact, but not unjust. And similarly, that even supposing a case in which a woman pregnant due to rape ought to allow the unborn person to use her body for the hour he needs, we should not conclude that he has a right to do so; we should conclude that she is self-centered, callous, indecent, but not unjust, if she refuses. The complaints are no less grave; they are just different. However, there is no need to insist on this point. If anyone does wish to deduce "he has a right" from "you ought," then all the same he must surely grant that there are cases in which it is not morally required of you that you allow that violinist to use your kidneys, and in which he does not have a right to use them, and in which you do not do him an injustice if you refuse. And so also for mother and unborn child. Except in such cases as the unborn person has a right to demand it—and we were leaving open the possibility that there may be such cases—nobody is morally *required* to make large sacrifices, of health, of all other interests and concerns, of all other duties and commitments, for 9 years, or even for 9 months, in order to keep another person alive.

6. We have in fact to distinguish between two kinds of Samaritan: the Good Samaritan and what we might call the Minimally Decent Samaritan. The story of the Good Samaritan, you will remember, goes like this:

> A certain man went down from Jerusalem to Jericho, and fell among thieves, which stripped him of his raiment, and wounded him, and departed, leaving him half dead.
>
> And by chance there came down a certain priest that way; and when he saw him, he passed by on the other side.
>
> And likewise a Levite, when he was at the place, came and looked on him, and passed by on the other side.
>
> But a certain Samaritan, as he journeyed, came where he was; and when he saw · him he had compassion on him.
>
> And went to him, and bound up his wounds, pouring in oil and wine, and set him on his own beast, and brought him to an inn, and took care of him.
>
> And on the morrow, when he departed, he took out two pence, and gave them to the host, and said unto him, "Take care of him; and whatsoever thou spendest more, when I come again, I will repay thee."
>
> *(Luke 10:30-35)*

The Good Samaritan went out of his way, at some cost to himself, to help one in need of it. We are not told what the options were, that is, whether or not the priest and the Levite could have helped by doing less than the Good Samaritan did, but assuming they could have, then the fact they did nothing at all shows they were not even Minimally Decent Samaritans, not because they were not Samaritans, but because they were not even minimally decent.

. . . With one rather striking class of exceptions, no one in any country in the world is *legally* required to do anywhere near as much as this for anyone else. The class of exceptions is obvious. My main concern here is not the state of the law in respect to abortion, but it is worth drawing attention to the fact that in no state in this country is any man compelled by law to be even a Minimally Decent Samaritan to any person; there is no law under which charges could be brought against the thirty-eight who stood by while Kitty Genovese died. By contrast, in most states in this country women are compelled by law to be not merely Minimally Decent Samaritans, but Good Samaritans to unborn persons inside them. This doesn't by itself settle anything one way or the other, because it may well be argued that there should be laws in this country—as there are in many European countries—compelling at least Minimally Decent Samaritans.[7] But it does show that there is a gross injustice in the existing state of the law. And it shows also that the groups currently working against liberalization of abortion laws, in fact working toward having it declared unconstitutional for a state to permit abortion, had better start working for the adoption of Good Samaritan laws generally, or earn the charge that they are acting in bad faith.

I should think, myself, that Minimally Decent Samaritan laws would be one thing, Good Samaritan laws quite another, and in fact highly improper. But we are not here concerned with the law. What we should ask is not whether anybody should be compelled by law to be a Good Samaritan, but whether we must accede to a situation in which somebody is being compelled—by nature, perhaps—to be a Good Samaritan. We have, in other words, to look now at third-party interventions. I have been arguing that no person is morally required to make large sacrifices to sustain the life of another who has no right to demand them, and this even where the sacrifices do not include life itself; we are not morally required to be Good Samaritans or anyway Very Good Samaritans to one another. But what if a man cannot extricate himself from such a situation? What if he appeals to us to extricate him? It seems to me plain that there are cases in which we can, cases in which a Good Samaritan would extricate him. There you are, you were kidnapped, and 9 years in bed with that violinist lie ahead of you. You have your own life to lead. You are sorry, but you simply cannot see giving up so much of your life to the sustaining of his. You cannot extricate yourself, and ask us to do so. I should have thought that—in light of his having no right to the use of your body—it was obvious that we do not have to accede to your being forced to give up so much. We can do what you ask. There is no injustice to the violinist in our doing so.

7. Following the lead of the opponents of abortion, I have throughout been speaking of the fetus merely as a person, and what I have been asking is whether or not the argument we began with, which proceeds only from the fetus' being a person, really does establish its conclusion. I have argued that it does not.

But of course there are arguments and arguments, and it may be said that I have simply fastened on the wrong one. It may be said that what is important is not merely the fact that the fetus is a person, but that it is a person for whom the woman has a special kind of responsibility issuing from the fact that she is its mother. And it might be argued that all my analogies are therefore irrelevant—for you do not have that special kind of responsibility for that violinist, Henry Fonda does not have that special kind of responsibility for me. And our attention might be drawn to the fact that men and women both *are* compelled by law to provide support for their children.

I have in effect dealt (briefly) with this argument in Section 4 above; but a (still briefer) recapitulation now may be in order. Surely we do not have any such "special responsibility" for a person unless we have assumed it, explicitly or implicitly. If a set of parents do not try to prevent pregnancy, do not obtain an abortion, and then at the time of birth of the child do not put it out for adoption, but rather take it home with them, then they have assumed responsibility for it, they have given it rights, and they cannot *now* withdraw support from it at the cost of its life because they now find it difficult to go on providing for it. But if they have taken all reasonable precautions against having a child, they do not simply by virtue of their biological relationship to the child who comes into existence have a special responsibility for it. They may wish to assume responsibility for it, or they may not wish to. And I am suggesting that if assuming responsibility for it would require large sacrifices, then they may refuse. A Good Samaritan would not refuse—or anyway, a Splendid Samaritan, if the sacrifices that had to be made were enormous. But then so would a Good Samaritan assume responsibility for that violinist; so would Henry Fonda, if he is a Good Samaritan, fly in from the West Coast and assume responsibility for me.

8. My argument will be found unsatisfactory on two counts by many of those who want to regard abortion as morally permissible. First, while I do argue that abortion is not impermissible, I do not argue that it is always permissible. There may well be cases in which carrying the child to term requires only Minimally Decent Samaritanism of the mother, and this is a standard we must not fall below. I am inclined to think it a merit of my account precisely that it does *not* give a general yes or a general no. It allows for and supports our sense that, for example, a sick and desperately frightened 14-year-old schoolgirl, pregnant due to rape, may *of course* choose abortion, and that any law which rules this out is an insane law. And it also allows for and supports our sense that in other cases resort to abortion is even positively indecent. It would be indecent in the woman to request an abortion, and indecent in a doctor to perform it, if she is in her seventh month, and wants the abortion just to avoid the nuisance of postponing a trip abroad. The very fact that the arguments I have been drawing attention to treat all cases of abortion, or even all cases of abortion in which the mother's life is not at stake, as morally on a par ought to have made them suspect at the outset.

Secondly, while I am arguing for the permissibility of abortion in some cases, I am not arguing for the right to secure the death of the unborn child. It is easy to confuse these two things in that up to a certain point in the life of the fetus it is not able to survive outside the mother's body; hence removing it from her body guarantees its death. But they are importantly different. I have argued that you are not morally required to spend 9 months in bed, sustaining the life of that violinist; but to say this is by no means to say that if, when you unplug yourself, there is a miracle and he survives, you then have a right to turn round and slit his throat. You may detach yourself even if this costs him his life; you have no right to be guaranteed his death, by some other means, if unplugging yourself does not kill him. There are some people who will feel dissatisfied by this feature of my argument. A woman may be utterly devastated by the thought of a child, a bit of herself, put out for adoption and never seen or heard of again. She may therefore want not merely that the child be detached from her, but more, that it die. Some opponents of abortion are inclined to regard this as beneath contempt—thereby showing insensitivity to what is surely a powerful source of despair. All the same, I agree that the desire for the child's death is not one which anybody may gratify, should it turn out to be possible to detach the child alive.

At this place, however, it should be remembered that we have only been pretending throughout that the fetus is a human being from the moment of conception. A very early abortion is surely not the killing of a person, and so is not dealt with by anything I have said here.

---

[1] I am very much indebted to James Thomson for discussion, criticism, and many helpful suggestions.

[2] Daniel Callahan, *Abortion: Law, Choice and Morality* (New York, 1970), p. 373. This book gives a fascinating survey of the available information on abortion. The Jewish tradition is surveyed in David M. Feldman, *Birth Control in Jewish Law* (New York, 1968), Part 5; the Catholic tradition in John T. Noonan, Jr., "An Almost Absolute Value in History," in *The Morality of Abortion*, ed. John T. Noonan, Jr. (Cambridge, Mass., 1970)

[3] The term "direct" in the arguments I refer to is a technical one. Roughly, what is meant by "direct killing" is either killing as an end in itself, or killing as a means of some end, for example, the end of saving someone else's life. See footnote 6 for an example of its use.

[4]Cf. *Encyclical Letter of Pope Pius XI on Christian Marriage,* St. Paul Editions (Boston, n.d.), p. 32: "however much we may pity the mother whose health and even life is gravely imperiled in the performance of the duty allotted to her by nature, nevertheless what could ever be a sufficient reason for excusing in any way the direct murder of the innocent? This is precisely what we are dealing with here." Noonan (*The Morality of Abortion,* p. 43) reads this as follows: "What cause can ever avail to excuse in any way the direct killing of the innocent? For it is a question of that."

[5]The thesis in (4) is in an interesting way weaker than those in (1), (2), and (3): they rule out abortion even in cases in which both mother *and* child will die if the abortion is not performed. By contrast, one who held the previous view expressed in (4) could consistently say that one needn't prefer letting two persons die to killing one.

[6]Cf. the following passage from Pius XII, *Address to the Italian Catholic Society of Midwives:* "The baby in the maternal breast has the right to life immediately from God.—Hence there is no man, no human authority, no science, no medical, eugenic, social, economic or moral 'indication' which can establish or grant a valid juridical ground for a direct deliberate disposition of an innocent human life, that is a disposition which looks to its destruction either as an end or as a means to another end perhaps in itself not illicit.—The baby, still not born, is a man in the same degree and for the same reason as the mother" (quoted in Noonan, *The Morality of Abortion,* p. 45).

[7]For a discussion of the difficulties involved, and a survey of the European experience with such laws, see *The Good Samaritan and the Law,* ed. James M. Ratcliffe (New York, 1966).

LAURA M. PURDY

Can Having Children Be Immoral?

. . . There are many causes of misery in this world, and most of them are unrelated to genetic disease. In the general scheme of things, human misery is most efficiently reduced by concentrating on noxious social and political arrangements. Nonetheless, we should not ignore preventable harm just because it is confined to a relatively small corner of life. So the question arises, Can it be wrong to have a child because of genetic risk factors?

HUNTINGTON'S DISEASE

. . . I want to defend the thesis that it is morally wrong to reproduce when we know there is a high risk of transmitting a serious disease or defect. This thesis holds that some reproductive acts are wrong, and my argument puts the burden of proof on those who disagree with it to show why its conclusions can be overridden. Hence it denies that people should be free to reproduce mindless of the consequences.[2] However, as moral argument, it should be taken as a proposal for further debate and discussion. It is not, by itself, an argument in favor of legal prohibitions of reproduction.[3]

There is a huge range of genetic diseases. Some are quickly lethal; others kill more slowly, if at all. Some are mainly physical, some mainly mental; others impair both kinds of function. Some interfere tremendously with normal functioning, others less. Some are painful, some are not. There seems to be considerable agreement that rapidly lethal diseases, especially those, such as Tay-Sachs, accompanied by painful deterioration, should be prevented even at the cost of abortion. Conversely, there seems to be substantial agreement that relatively trivial problems, especially cosmetic ones, would not be legitimate grounds for abortion.[4] In short, there are cases ranging from low risk of mild disease or disability to high risk of serious disease or disability. Although it is difficult to decide where the duty to refrain from procreation becomes compelling, I believe that there are some clear cases. I have chosen to focus on Huntington's disease to illustrate the kinds of concrete issues such decisions entail. However, the arguments are also relevant to many other genetic diseases.[5]

The symptoms of Huntington's disease usually begin between the ages of 30 and 50:

> Onset is insidious. Personality changes (obstinacy, moodiness, lack of initiative) frequently antedate or accompany the involuntary choreic movements. These usually appear first in the face, neck, and arms, and are jerky, irregular, and stretching in character. Contradictions of the facial muscles result in grimaces; those of the respiratory muscles, lips, and tongue lead to hesitating, explosive speech. Irregular movements of the trunk are present; the gait is shuffling and dancing. Tendon reflexes are increased. . . . Some patients display a fatuous euphoria; others are spiteful, irascible, destructive, and violent. Paranoid reactions are common. Poverty of thought and impairment of attention, memory, and judgment occur. As the disease progresses, walking becomes impossible, swallowing difficult, and dementia profound. Suicide is not uncommon.[6]

The illness lasts about 15 years, terminating in death.

Huntington's disease is an autosomal dominant disease, meaning it is caused by a single defective gene located on a non-sex chromosome. It is passed from one generation to the next via affected individuals. Each child of such an affected person has a 50 percent risk of inheriting the gene and thus of eventually developing the disease, even if he or she was born before the parent's disease was evident.[7]

Until recently, Huntington's disease was especially problematic because most affected individuals did not know whether they had the gene for the disease until well into their childbearing years. So they had to decide about childbearing before knowing whether they could transmit the disease or not. . . . Then, in the 1980s . . . a genetic marker was found that, in certain circumstances, could tell people with a relatively high degree of probability whether or not they had the gene for the disease.[8] Finally, in March 1993, the defective gene itself was discovered.[9] Now individuals can find out whether they carry the gene for the disease, and prenatal screening can tell us whether a given fetus has inherited it. . . .

How serious are the risks involved in Huntington's disease? . . . There may still be considerable disagreement about the acceptability of a given risk. So it would be difficult in many circumstances to say how we should respond to a particular risk. Nevertheless, there are good grounds for a conservative approach, for it is reasonable to take special precautions to avoid very bad consequences, even if the risk is small. But the possible consequences here *are* very bad: a child who may inherit Huntington's disease has a much greater than average chance of being subjected to severe and prolonged suffering. And it is one thing to risk one's own welfare, but quite another to do so for others and without their consent.

Is this judgment about Huntington's disease really defensible? People appear to have quite different opinions. Optimists argue that a child born into a family afflicted with Huntington's disease has a reasonable chance of living a satisfactory life. After all, even children born of an afflicted parent still have a 50 percent chance of escaping the disease. And even if afflicted themselves, such people will probably enjoy some 30 years of healthy life before symptoms appear. It is also possible, although not at all likely, that some might not mind the symptoms caused by the disease. Optimists can point to diseased persons who have lived fruitful lives, as well as those who seem genuinely glad to be alive. One is Rick Donohue, a sufferer from the Joseph family disease: "You know, if my mom hadn't had me, I wouldn't be here for the life I have had. So there is a good possibility I will have children."[10] Optimists therefore conclude that it would be a shame if these persons had not lived.

Pessimists concede some of these facts but take a less sanguine view of them. They think a 50 percent risk of serious disease such as Huntington's is appallingly high. They suspect that many children born into afflicted families are liable to spend their youth in dreadful anticipation and fear of the disease. They expect that the disease, if it appears, will be perceived as a tragic and painful end to a blighted life. They point out that Rick Donohue is still young and has not experienced the full horror of his sickness. It is also well-known that some young persons have such a dilated sense of time that they can hardly envision themselves at 30 or 40, so the prospect of pain at that age is unreal to them.[11]

More empirical research on the psychology and life history of sufferers and potential sufferers is clearly needed to decide whether optimists or pessimists have a more accurate picture of the experiences of individuals at risk. But given that some will surely realize pessimists' worst fears, it seems unfair to conclude that the pleasures of those who deal best with the situation simply cancel out the suffering of those others when that suffering could be avoided altogether.

I think that these points indicate that the morality of procreation in such situations demands further investigation. I propose to do this by looking first at the position of the possible child, then at that of the potential parent.

POSSIBLE CHILDREN AND POTENTIAL PARENTS

. . . Now, what claims about children or possible children are relevant to the morality of childbearing in the circumstances being considered? Of primary importance is the judgment that we ought to try to provide every child with something like a minimally satisfying life. I am not altogether sure how best to formulate this standard, but I want clearly to reject the view that it is morally permissible to conceive individuals so long as we do not expect them to be so miserable that they wish they were dead.[12] I believe that this kind of moral minimalism is thoroughly unsatisfactory and that not many people would really want to live in a world where it was the prevailing standard. Its lure is that it puts few demands on us, but its price is the scant attention it pays to human well-being.

How might the judgment that we have a duty to try to provide a minimally satisfying life for our children be justified? It could, I think, be derived fairly straightforwardly from either utilitarian or contractarian theories of justice, although there is no space here for discussion of the details. The net result of such analysis would be to conclude that neglecting this duty would create unnecessary unhappiness or unfair disadvantage for some persons.

Of course, this line of reasoning confronts us with the need to spell out what is meant by "minimally satisfying" and what a standard based on this concept would require of us. . . . As we draw out what such a standard might require of us, it seems reasonable to retreat to the more limited claim that parents should try to ensure something like normal health for their children. . . . This conservative position would still justify efforts to avoid the birth of children at risk for Huntington's disease and other serious genetic diseases in virtually all societies.[13]

This view is reinforced by the following considerations. Given that possible children do not presently exist as actual individuals, they do not have a right to be brought into existence, and hence no one is maltreated by measures to avoid the conception of a possible person. Therefore, the conservative course that avoids the conception of those who would not be expected to enjoy a minimally satisfying life is at present the only fair course of action. The alternative is a laissez-faire approach that brings into existence the lucky, but only at the expense of the unlucky. Notice that attempting to avoid the creation of the unlucky does not necessarily lead to *fewer* people being brought into being; the question boils down to taking steps to bring those with better prospects into existence, instead of those with worse ones.

I have so far argued that if people with Huntington's disease are unlikely to live minimally satisfying lives, then those who might pass it on should not have genetically related children. This is consonant with the principle that the greater the danger of serious problems, the stronger the duty to avoid them. But this principle is in conflict with what people think of as the right to reproduce. How might one decide which should take precedence?

Expecting people to forego having genetically related children might seem to demand too great a sacrifice of them. But before reaching that conclusion we need to ask what is really at stake. One reason for wanting children is to experience family life, including love, companionship, watching kids grow, sharing their pains and triumphs, and helping to form members of the next generation. Other reasons emphasize the validation of parents as individuals within a continuous family line, children as a source of immortality, or perhaps even the gratification of producing partial replicas of oneself. Children may also be desired in an effort to prove that one is an adult, to try to cement a marriage, or to benefit parents economically.

Are there alternative ways of satisfying these desires? Adoption or new reproductive technologies can fulfill many of them without passing on known genetic defects. Sperm replacement has been available for many years via artificial insemination by donor. More recently, egg donation, sometimes in combination with contract pregnancy[14] has been used to provide eggs for women who prefer not to use their own. Eventually it may be possible to clone individual humans, although that now seems a long way off. All of these approaches to avoiding the use of particular genetic material are controversial and have generated much debate. I believe that tenable moral versions of each do exist.[15]

None of these methods permits people to extend both genetic lines or realize the desire for immortality or for children who resemble both parents; nor is it clear that such alternatives will necessarily succeed in proving that one is an adult, cementing a marriage, or providing economic benefits. Yet, many people feel these desires strongly. . . .

Fortunately, further scrutiny of the situation reveals that there are good reasons why people should attempt with appropriate social support to talk themselves out of the desires in question or to consider novel ways of fulfilling them. Wanting to see the genetic line continued is not particularly rational when it brings a sinister legacy of illness and death. The desire for immortality cannot be really satisfied anyway, and people need to face the fact that what really matters is how they behave in their own lifetimes. And finally, the desire for children who physically resemble one is understandable, but basically narcissistic, and its fulfillment cannot be guaranteed even by normal reproduction. There are other ways of proving one is an adult, and other ways of cementing marriages—and children don't necessarily do either. Children, especially prematurely ill children, may not provide the expected economic benefits anyway. Nongenetically related children may also provide benefits similar to those that would have been provided by genetically related ones, and expected economic benefits is, in many cases, a morally questionable reason for having children.

Before the advent of reliable genetic testing, the options of people in Huntington's families were cruelly limited. . . . Reliable genetic testing has opened up new possibilities. Those at risk who wish to have children can get tested. If they test positive, they know their possible children are at risk. Those who are opposed to abortion must be especially careful to avoid conception if they are to behave responsibly. Those not opposed to abortion can responsibly conceive children, but only if they are willing to test each fetus and abort those who carry the gene. If individuals at risk test negative, they are home free.

What about those who cannot face the test for themselves? . . . Prenatal testing can bring knowledge that enables one to avoid passing the disease to others, but only, in some cases, at the cost of coming to know with certainty that one will indeed develop the disease. This situation raises with peculiar force the question of whether parental responsibility requires people to get tested.

Some people think that we should recognize a right "not to know." It seems to me that such a right could be defended only where ignorance does not put others at serious risk. So if people are prepared to forego genetically related children, they need not get tested. By if they want genetically related children, then they must do whatever is necessary to ensure that affected babies are not the result. There is, after all, something inconsistent about the claim that one has a right to be shielded from the truth, even if the price is to risk inflicting on one's children the same dread disease one cannot even face in oneself.

In sum, until we can be assured that Huntington's disease does not prevent people from living a minimally satisfying life, individuals at risk for the disease have a moral duty to try not to bring affected babies into this world. There are now enough options available so that this duty needn't frustrate their reasonable desires. Society has a corresponding duty to facilitate moral behavior on the part of individuals. Such support ranges from the narrow and concrete (such as making sure that medical testing and counseling is available to all) to the more general social environment that guarantees that all pregnancies are voluntary, that pronatalism is eradicated, and that women are treated with respect regardless of the reproductive options they choose.

---

[2][The rest of Purdy's notes have been renumbered.—ed.] This is, of course, a very broad thesis. I defend an even broader version in Reproducing Persons: Issues in Feminist Bioethics (Ithaca: Cornell University Press, 1996), Chapter 2, "Loving Future People"

[3]Why would we want to resist legal enforcement of every moral conclusion? First, legal action has many costs, costs not necessarily worth paying in particular cases. Second, legal enforcement tends to take the matter out of the realm of debate and treat it as settled. But in many cases, especially where mores or technology are rapidly evolving, we don't want that to happen. Third, legal enforcement would undermine individual freedom and decision-making capacity. In some cases, the ends envisioned are important enough to warrant putting up with these disadvantages.

[4]Those who do not see fetuses as moral persons with a right to life may nonetheless hold that abortion is justifiable in these cases. I argue at some length elsewhere that lesser defects can cause great suffering. Once we are clear that there is nothing discriminatory about failing to conceive particular possible individuals, it makes sense, other things being equal, to avoid the prospect of such pain if we can. Naturally, other things rarely are equal. In the first place, many problems go undiscovered until a baby is born. Second, there are often substantial costs associated with screening programs. Third, although women should be encouraged to consider the moral dimensions of routine pregnancy, we do not want it to be so fraught with tension that it becomes a miserable experience. (See Reproducing Persons: Issues in Feminist Bioethics (Ithaca: Cornell University Press, 1996), Chapter 2, "Loving Future People.")

[5]It should be noted that failing to conceive a single individual can affect many lives: in 1916, 962 cases could be traced from six 17th-century arrivals in America. See Gordon Rattray Taylor, *The Biological Time Bomb* (New York: Penguin, 1968), p. 176.

[6]*The Merck Manual* (Rahway, N.J.: Merck, 1972), pp. 1363, 1346. We now know that the age of onset and severity of the disease are related to the number of abnormal replications of the glutamine code on the abnormal gene. See Andrew Revkin, "Hunting Down Huntington's," *Discover* (December 1993): 108.

[7]Hymie Gordon, "Genetic Counseling," *JAMA* 217, no. 9 (August 30, 1971): 1346.

[8]See Revkin, "Hunting Down Huntington's," 99–108.

[9]"Gene for Huntington's Disease Discovered," *Human Genome News* 5, no. 1 (May 1993): 5.

[10]*The New York Times*, September 30, 1975, p. 1. The Joseph family disease is similar to Huntington's disease except that symptoms start appearing in the 20s. Rick Donohue was in his early 20s at the time he made this statement.

[11]I have talked to college students who believe that they will have lived fully and be ready to die at those ages. It is astonishing how one's perspective changes over time and how ages that one once associated with senility and physical collapse come to seem the prime of human life.

[12]The view I am rejecting has been forcefully articulated by Derek Parfit, *Reasons and Persons* (Oxford: Clarendon, 1984). For more discussion, see Reproducing Persons: Issues in Feminist Bioethics (Ithaca: Cornell University Press, 1996), Chapter 2, "Loving Future People."

[13]Again, a troubling exception might be the isolated Venezuelan group Nancy Wexler found, where, because of inbreeding, a large proportion of the population is affected by Huntington's. See Revkin, "Hunting Down Huntington's."

[14]Or surrogacy, as it has been popularly known. I think that "contract pregnancy" is more accurate and more respectful of women. Eggs can be provided either by a woman who also gestates the fetus or by a third party.

[15]The most powerful objections to new reproductive technologies and arrangements concern possible bad consequences for women. However, I do not think that the arguments against them on these grounds have yet shown the dangers to be as great as some believe. So although it is perhaps true that new reproductive technologies and arrangements should not be used lightly, avoiding the conceptions discussed here is well worth the risk. For a series of viewpoints on this issue, including my own "Another Look at Contract Pregnancy" (Reproducing Persons: Issues in Feminist Bioethics (Ithaca: Cornell University Press, 1996), Chapter 12), see Helen B. Holmes, *Issues in Reproductive Technology 1: An Anthology* (New York: Garland, 1992).

SHERMAN ELIAS AND GEORGE J. ANNAS

Somatic and Germline Gene Therapy

Recent reports of human gene therapy experiments have been heralded worldwide with praise from the medical and scientific communities as well as the general public. A new medical journal, *Human Gene Therapy,* devoted entirely to this topic, has also been introduced. The stage is now set for more experiments involving human somatic cell genes, with the objective of ameliorating or correcting genetic defects.[1] In mid-1990 Steven Rosenberg and colleagues reported the use of retroviral-mediated gene transduction to introduce the gene coding for resistance to neomycin into human tumor-infiltrating lymphocytes before their infusion into five patients with metastatic melanoma.[2] The distribution and survival of these "gene-marked" lymphocytes were then studied, and for the first time, the feasibility and safety of introducing new genes into humans were demonstrated. We are now witnessing the transition from theoretical possibility to practical reality of the "dawn of a new age of cancer treatment" based on novel gene therapy strategies.[3] In September 1990, Michael Blaese and colleagues at the National Institute of Health (NIH) announced the first human gene experiment in a young girl with adenosine deaminase (ADA) deficiency, a very rare autosomal recessive genetic disorder resulting in severe combined immune deficiency.[4] Affected individuals usually die during childhood from chronic infections. The investigators obtained circulating lymphocytes from the patient, expanded the number of cells in culture, infected the cells with a recombinant retrovirus carrying the ADA gene, and then reinfused the cells into the patient.

SOMATIC CELL THERAPY

Some believe that somatic cell gene therapy is an unwise pursuit. Their underlying concern is that it will inevitably lead to the insertion of genes to change the character of people, reduce the human species to a technologically designed product, or even "change the meaning of being human."[5] These fears rest on the presupposition that somatic cell gene therapy differs in a significant way from accepted forms of treatment.[6]

This has not, however, been the consensus of panels of experts who have analyzed the issues. Both the President's Commission for the Study of Ethical Problems in Medicine and Biomedical and Behavioral Research[7] and the European Medical Research Councils[8] concluded that somatic cell gene therapy is not fundamentally different from other therapeutic procedures, such as organ transplantation or blood transfusion. The only important differences between somatic cell gene therapy and other treatments are the issues of safety and the possibility that viral vectors may also infect germ cells.

At present, among the various methods for introducing genetic material into cells, retroviral-based vectors appear to be the most promising approach for gene transfer in humans.[9] Concern has been raised that despite elaborate "built-in safety features" with redesigned mouse retroviral vectors, there is a finite risk that these vectors could recombine with undetected viruses or endogenous DNA sequences in the cell and so become infectious. This risk of "viral escape," as well as other potential risks that would be limited to the patient, such as activation of a proto-oncogene or disruption of an essential functioning gene, has resulted in society demanding very critical review and participation in any decisions to embark on human gene therapy.[10]

In the United States, recombinant DNA research funded by the NIH must first be reviewed by the local Institutional Review Board and local Institutional Biosafety Committee. In addition, the NIH has established the Recombinant DNA Advisory Committee (RAC) to review proposals to be funded by the NIH. An interdisciplinary subcommittee of RAC, called the Working Group on Human Gene Therapy, was formed that consisted of three laboratory scientists, three clinicians, three ethicists, three attorneys, two public-policy specialists, and one lay member. Based on a draft from this subcommittee, the RAC composed a document called "Points to Consider in the Design and Submission of Human Somatic-Cell Gene Therapy Protocols."[11] This document is intended to provide guidance in preparing proposals for NIH consideration, and focuses on: (1) objectives and rationale of the research, (2) research design, anticipated risks, and benefits, (3) selection of subjects, (4) informed consent, and (5) privacy and confidentiality. The RAC has deliberately limited its purview to somatic cell gene therapy, emphasizing that the "recombinant DNA is expected to be confined to the human subject" to be treated.[12]

W. French Anderson, a leading NIH investigator in the field of gene therapy, contends that "somatic cell gene therapy for the treatment of severe disease is considered ethical because it can be supported by the fundamental moral principle of beneficence: It would relieve human suffering."[13] He also argues that after the appropriate approval of therapeutic protocols by Institutional Review Boards and the NIH,

> it would be unethical to delay human trials. . . . Patients with serious genetic disease have little other hope at present for alleviation of their medical problems. Arguments that genetic engineering might someday be misused do not justify the needless perpetuation of human suffering that would result from unethical delay in the clinical application of this potentially powerful therapeutic procedure.[14]

And more recently, Anderson has insisted that it is time to be less tentative about somatic cell therapy, saying "What's the rush? The rush is the daily necessity to help sick people. Their (our) illnesses will not wait for a more convenient time."[15] A large majority of Americans seem to agree. According to a survey reported by the Office of

Technology Assessment, 83 percent of the public say they approve of human cell manipulation to cure usually fatal genetic diseases.[16]

It should be emphasized, however, that human experimentation regulation has a long history, and it is easy to forget even its basic lessons in the rush to research. We are unlikely to repeat Martin Cline's unapproved beta-thalassemia experiments, but we do continue to concentrate early experiments on children (who cannot consent for themselves) and the terminally ill (who are especially vulnerable to coercion), repeating many of the same ethical mistakes made with artificial heart and xenograft transplants in the 1980s. The point is that just because somatic cell experiments are not fundamentally different than transplant experiments, it does not mean that there are no ethical or legal problems of consequence involving these experiments, or that we have reached a consensus on how to resolve them.

GERMLINE CELL THERAPY

In contrast to somatic cell gene therapy, which is limited to the individual patient, germline gene therapy entails insertion of a gene into the reproductive cells of the patient in such a way that the disorder in his or her offspring would also be corrected. This can be interpreted either as the corrective genetic modification of gametes (sperm or ova) or their precursor cells, or insertion of genetic material into the totipotential cells of a human conceptus in refined variations of the techniques used for germline modification in the creation of transgenic animals.[17] As such, germline gene therapy constitutes a definitive qualitative departure from any previous medical interventions because the changes would not only affect the individual, but also would be deliberately passed on to future generations.[18]

Should human germline gene therapy be permitted? Until now there has been some comfort in the fact that technical difficulties would preclude consideration of such genetic engineering in human beings for many years to come. However, one need only look at the scientific advances presented at the First International Symposium on Preimplantation Genetics, held in Chicago in September 1990, to realize that the pace of technology in this area has become much faster than previously predicted. Although in the past it may have seemed politically prudent to avoid the subject, we must now begin to seriously discuss the ethical issues before germline gene experiments in humans are technically possible, in order to assist future policymakers in their deliberations.[19]

At the Workshop on International Cooperation for the Human Genome Project, in Valencia in October 1988, French researcher Jean Dausset suggested that the Genome Project posed such great potential hazards that it could open the door to Nazi-like atrocities. In an attempt to avoid such consequences, he suggested that the conferees agree on a moratorium on genetic manipulation of germline cells and a ban on gene transfer experiments on early embryos. The proposal won widespread agreement among the participants at the meeting and was only defeated after a watered-down resolution using "international cooperation" was suggested by Norton Zinder, who successfully argued that the group had no authority to enforce such a resolution. Leaving the question of authority for later debate, should we take Dausset's proposal for a moratorium on germline cell experimentation seriously?

ARGUMENTS AGAINST HUMAN GERMLINE GENE THERAPY

The ethical arguments against the use of a human germline gene therapy fall into three categories: (1) its potential clinical risks, (2) the broader concern of changing the gene pool, the genetic inheritance of the human population, and (3) social dangers.[20]

POTENTIAL CLINICAL RISKS

Major advances in knowledge must be made to overcome the significant technical obstacles for human germline gene therapy. Methods would have to be developed to stably integrate the new DNA precisely into the right chromosomal site in the appropriate tissues for adequate expression and proper regulation. The possibilities for dangerous mistakes are formidable: examples would include insertional mutagenesis, in which a normally functioning gene is disrupted or a proto-oncogene activated by the newly integrated gene, or the regulatory signals of the nonfunctional or dysfunctional gene could adversely affect the regulation of the new exogenous gene.[21] These safety concerns are compounded by practical problems, including loss of gametes or embryos by instrument manipulation and the inherent limitations and inefficiency of reproductive technologies such as in vitro fertilization (IVF). Of course, many medical experiments have significant risks, and in this respect, germline research is not unique. IVF itself was opposed on similar grounds in the late 1960s and early 1970s.

On the other hand, unless there is overwhelming evidence that the procedure will be successful and not cause harm to the resulting child, there is no justification for doing genetic experiments on an early embryo and then reimplanting it. The more reasonable position would be not to reimplant the genetically defective embryo in the first place. The same logic applies to gamete manipulation. This argument suggests that except in the vanishingly rare case in which both parents are homozygous, and thus all embryos produced will be affected with their condition, and this condition is seen as unacceptable by them, *and* they refuse to use either donor ovum or donor sperm, there will be no clinical role for genetic therapy to replace or substitute for defective genes in embryos. Even in this case, of course, such research may never be justifiable because of the significant risks of introducing even worse problems for the resulting child.

CHANGING THE GENE POOL

In germline gene therapy the objective would be to correct a genetic defect for future generations and hence restore the individual's lineage to the "normal" state. But what may be considered a harmful genetic trait today could be neutral in the future or could even conceivably serve a beneficial function, depending on environmental pressures in which the trait operates. Arno Motulsky has used the example of wearing eyeglasses. For primitive humans, genetically controlled myopia could prove fatal if one could not keep a sharp eye out for predators. The relatively high frequency of myopia and the need for some to wear eyeglasses represents loss of an adaptive biological trait in modern civilization. Nonetheless, myopia is never fatal, and some people, particularly ophthalmologists, optometrists, and eyeglass makers, might even say that the existence of myopia and other refractory deficits has been of benefit by creating a livelihood for them.[22] One danger is that we may wrongly eliminate a characteristic, such as sickle-cell trait, that by protecting against malaria has advantages for the carrier. On the other hand, much of medicine has the potential for altering the next generation by helping the current one survive to reproductive age. As Alexander Capron has noted:

> The major reasons for drawing a line between somatic-cell and germ-line interventions . . . are that germ-line changes not only run the risk of perpetuating any errors made into future generations of nonconsenting "subjects" but also go beyond ordinary medicine and interfere with human evolution. Again, it must be admitted that all of medicine obstructs evolution. But that is inadvertent, whereas with human germ-line genetic engineering, the interference is intentional.[23]

Capron continues the argument by noting that "the results produced by evolution at any points in time are hardly sacrosanct," producing, as they do, genetic diseases, and he concludes that intentionally interfering "in humankind's genetic inheritance is not a sufficient reason to foreswear the technique forever, though it is reason enough to distinguish it from somatic-cell interventions."[24] Robert Morison's warning is an appropriate note on which to close our gene pool discussion:

> The nominalist biological position is that there can be no such thing as an ideal man. Men are brothers simply because they all draw their assortment of genes from a common pool. Each individual owes his survival and general well-being partly to his own limited assortment of characters and partly to the benefits received through cultural interchange with other individuals representing other assortments. It follows that the brothers in such a human family have a sacred obligation to maintain the richness and variety of their heritage—their human gene pool and their common culture. Every man in a sense must become his brother's keeper, but the emphasis is on keeping and expanding what both hold in common, not on converting one brother to the ideal image held by the other.[25]

SOCIAL DANGERS

The intentional alteration of germline genes seems to be the real reason that some condemn it as presumptuously "playing God" and crossing a symbolic barrier beyond which medicine and mankind become involved not in treating disease, but in recreating ourselves. It is feared that we may begin to lose our footing on the slippery slope when we extend our notions of gene therapy toward "enhancement genetic engineering." This would involve insertion of a gene to enhance a specific characteristic: for example, adding an extra gene that codes for growth hormone into a normal child in an attempt to achieve a taller individual or, in the context of germline manipulation, to create taller future generations. From the medical perspective, French Anderson points out that adding a normal gene to correct the harmful effects of a nonfunctional or dysfunctional gene is different from inserting a gene to make more of an existing product. Selectively altering a characteristic might endanger the overall metabolic balance of individual cells or the body as a whole.[26] He has also warned:

> I fear that we might be like the young boy who loves to take things apart. He is bright enough to be able to disassemble a watch, and maybe even bright enough to get it back together again so that it works. But what if he tries to "improve" it? Maybe put on bigger hands so that the watch is "better" for viewing. But if the hands are too heavy for the mechanism, the watch will run slowly, erratically, or not at all. The boy can understand what he can see, but he cannot comprehend the precise engineering calculation that determined exactly how strong each spring should be, why the gears interact in the ways that they do, etc. Attempts on his part to improve the watch will probably only harm it. We will soon be able to provide a new gene so that a given property involved in a human life would be changed—e.g., a growth hormone gene. If we were to do so simply because we could, I feel that we would be like that young boy who changed the watch hands. We, like him, do not really understand what makes the object we are tinkering with tick. Since we do not understand, we should avoid meddling. Medicine is still so inexact that any modification (except perhaps one which returns towards normal a defective property) might cause severe short-term or long-term problems.[27]

The issues raised by such enhancement efforts are similar to those of athletes taking steroids, but with the added complication of perpetuating the effects to unborn generations. But assuming that all the medical concerns can be addressed, and even if such issues as scarcity of resources and equal access to care are resolved, one major ethical problem remains—the likelihood of genetic discrimination. Using the example of inserting the gene for growth hormone, if being tall were considered a social virtue, say for basketball players, it would only be an advantage if "opponents" could be kept relatively shorter by selectively limiting their access to the "treatment." What if a gene could be inserted to prevent a certain type of cancer in susceptible, yet otherwise normal, individuals? Could they lose their children's health insurance if they refused to have their gametes or embryos "treated"?[28] Will we be able to resist "encouraging" parents to decrease the "genetic burden" and thus not undermine individual autonomy and dignity?

The most troublesome of all forms of genetic engineering is "positive" eugenics. Human beings seem to have an urge to "improve" our own species by genetic manipulations. Throughout history men and women have practiced assortive mating based on physical characteristics, intelligence, artistic talent, disposition, and many other traits. It was the English aristocrat and mathematician Francis Galton, a cousin of Charles Darwin, who in 1883 coined the term "eugenics" from the Latin word meaning "wellborn." In his writings, Galton defined eugenics as the science of improving human condition through "judicious matings . . . to give the more suitable races or strains of blood a better chance of prevailing speedily over the less suitable."[29] Eugenic genetic engineering includes attempts to alter or "improve" complex human traits that are at least in part genetically determined—for example, intelligence, personality, or athletic ability. Because such traits are polygenic, purging the genome of undesirable genes and replacing them with an array of desirable genes would require technological advances that we cannot even foresee. Moreover, even if such replacement could be achieved, the interplay between the newly introduced genetic material and the recipient genome would result in entirely unpredictable results. Nonetheless, the scenario remains in the realm of remote possibility.

We need not envision a return to the "racial hygiene" totalitarianism of National Socialism under the Nazis to see that the genetic screening of preimplantation embryos might become popular, or even standard. As the U.S. Congress's Office of Technology Assessment (OTA) put the case in 1988, such screening need not be mandated by government at all, since individuals can be made to *want* it (as they are now made to want all sorts of things by advertising), even to insist on it as their right. In the words of the OTA report, "New technologies for identifying traits and altering genes make it possible for eugenic goals to be achieved through technological as opposed to social control."[30]

Sheldon Krimsky has persuasively argued that there are two potential moral boundaries for gene therapy: the boundary between somatic cells and germline cells, and the boundary between the amelioration of disease and the enhancement of traits. But as he has noted also, the first involves a clear distinction, but a dubious rule, whereas the second involves a desirable rule, but a fuzzy distinction. The problem is that the distinction between disease and enhancement has no objective, scientific basis; disease is constantly being redefined. Krimsky asks, for example, "is chemical hypersensitivity a disease? Any trait that has a higher association with the onset of a disease may itself be typed as a proto-disease, such as fibrocystic breasts."[31]

Thus the problem is that we want to use germline gene therapy only to correct devastating diseases to avoid, among other things, the creation of a "super class" of privileged and gene-enhanced individuals who have the advantage of both wealth and enhanced genetic endowment. But the solution is unlikely to be drawing a line between disease and enhancement, both because that line is inherently fuzzy and because once "treatment" techniques are established, it may be impossible, as a practical matter, to prevent these same techniques from being used for enhancement. Because many traits one might want to enhance, such as intelligence or beauty, are polygenic, we may also comfort ourselves that they may never actually be susceptible to predictable genetic manipulation.[32]

ARGUMENTS FOR HUMAN GERMLINE THERAPY

EFFICIENCY

Leroy Walters suggested two rationales for which human germline therapy is ethically defensible.[33] The first rationale is efficiency. Assuming that somatic cell gene therapy became a successful cure for disorders caused by single-gene abnormalities, such as cystic fibrosis or sickle-cell disease, treated patients would constitute a new group of phenotypically normal, homozygous "carriers" who could then transmit abnormal genes to their offspring. If a partner of such an individual had one normal copy for the gene and one abnormal one, there would be a 50 percent likelihood of an affected offspring. If two treated patients with the same genetic abnormality reproduced, all of the offspring would be affected. Each succeeding generation could be treated by means of somatic cell gene therapy; however, if available, some phenotypically cured patients would consider it more efficient, and in the long run less costly, to prevent transmission of the abnormal gene to their offspring via germline gene therapy. Andreas Gutierrez and colleagues appear to have accepted this efficiency rationale as well by suggesting that germline gene therapy might be used to *prevent* cancers in individuals carrying defective tumor suppressor genes (for example, the retinoblastoma gene in retinoblastoma and p53 in Li-Fraumeni syndrome).[34]

It has also been suggested that germline therapy would be needed to treat genetically defective embryos of couples who believe it is immoral to discard embryos (because they are human life) regardless of their genetic condition.[35] This argument, however, is not persuasive. First, individuals with this belief might not be able to justify putting their embryos at risk of extracorporeal existence in the first place, and even if they could, would find it even more difficult to justify manipulations of the embryos with germline gene therapy that may cause their demise. Further, even those who adamantly oppose abortion do not equate the failure to implant an extracorporeal human embryo with the termination of a pregnancy. Thus, germline gene therapy cannot be justified solely on the basis of the religious beliefs of those who hold that protectable human life begins at conception. Moreover, as has been argued previously, it cannot be justified solely on the basis of treating the embryos of homozygous parents, since alternatives, such as ovum and sperm donation, exist that put the potential child at no risk.

UNIQUE DISEASES

The second rationale for the germline approach would arise if some genetic diseases could only be treated by this method. For example, in hereditary diseases of the central nervous system, somatic cell gene therapy may be impossible because genes could not be introduced into nerve cells due to the blood-brain barrier. Early intervention that did not distinguish between somatic cells and germ cells may be the only means available for treating cells or tissues that are not amenable to genetic repair at a later stage of development or after birth.

On the surface, the efficiency argument seems reasonable if one is dealing with a genetic characteristic in all sperm and one could remove it from all sperm by manipulating testicular cells. On the other hand, if, as seems most likely, screening will be done on preimplantation embryos, and those with genetic "defects" identified, then the *most efficient* method of dealing with the defective embryos is to simply discard them, implanting only the "healthy" ones.

For now at least, it seems that the second rationale is the stronger one, but since we have no coherent theory for treating such diseases by germline therapy, actual experimentation is at best premature.

SHOULD GERMLINE THERAPY BE PERMITTED?

Even though Jean Dausset's moratorium proposal did not pass at Valencia, there is currently a de facto moratorium on germline therapy because it is unclear both how to do it and for what conditions it might be appropriate. Consequently, a formal moratorium seems unnecessary. It also seems unwise. A review of the literature and this summary of it make it clear that the issues have not been well thought-out or well debated. The arguments against germline gene therapy tend to be basically the same as those previously used against somatic cell therapy: work with genes seems to arouse greater concern primarily because of the "genetic theories" of the Nazis and their horrible acts to put them into practice, and the early work on recombinant DNA in the United States and the concern that it might create a dangerous strain of virus or an uncontrollable pathogen. The "future generation" argument is actually no different than the original arguments raised against IVF and any extracorporeal manipulation of the human embryo.

What seems most reasonable now is to continue the public debate on whether, and under what conditions, germline experimentation should be attempted. As a way to better focus this debate, we recommend the following prerequisites be met prior to attempting any human germline gene therapy:

1. Germline gene experimentation should only be undertaken to correct serious genetic disorders (for example, Tay-Sachs disease).

2. There should be considerable prior experience with human somatic cell gene therapy, which has clearly established its safety and efficacy.

3. There should be reasonable scientific evidence using appropriate animal models that germline gene therapy will cure or prevent the disease in question and not cause any harm.

4. Interventions should be undertaken only with the informed, voluntary, competent, and understanding consent of all individuals involved.

5. In addition to approval by expert panels such as the NIH's Working Group on Gene Therapy and local Institutional Review Boards, all proposals should have prior public discussion.

An international consensus is desirable, because germline gene manipulation is the area in which there is the most international concern. This presents us with the first real opportunity to develop an international forum for policy debate and perhaps even resolution. Since we are dealing with the future of the species, this does not seem like too much to expect.

---

[1]D. J. Weatherall, "Gene Therapy in Perspective," *Nature* 349:275-6, 1991; B. J. Culliton, "Gene Therapy on the Move," *Nature* 354-429, 1991; and M. Hoffman, "Putting New Muscle into Gene Therapy," *Science* 254:1455-6, 1991.

[2]S. A. Rosenberg, P. Aebersold, K. Cornetta, A. Kasid, R. A. Morgan, R. Moen, E. M. Karson, M. T. Lotze, J. C. Yang, S. L. Topalian, M. J. Merino, K. Culver, A. D. Miller, R. M. Blaese, and W. F. Anderson, "Gene Transfer into Humans—Immunotherapy of Patients with Advanced Melanomas, Using Tumor-Infiltrating Lymphocytes Modified by Retroviral Gene Transduction," *New England Journal of Medicine* 323:570-8, 1990.

[3]A. A. Gutierrez, N. R. Lemoine, and K. Sikora, "Gene Therapy for Cancer," *Lancet* 339:715-21, 1992; and A. Abbott, "Italians First to Use Stem Cells," *Nature* 356:465, 1992.

[4]L. Thompson, "Human Gene Therapy Debuts at NIH," *Washington Post,* September 15, 1990, p. A1. Other researchers may claim to have conducted the first human gene transfer experiments. In the early 1970s, German researchers conducted an experiment on German sisters who suffered from a rare metabolic error that caused them to develop high blood levels of arginine. Left uncorrected, this genetic defect

leads to metabolic abnormalities and mental retardation. Using Shope virus (which induces a low level of arginine in exposed humans), the researchers infected the girls in the hope that the virus would transfer its gene for the enzyme that the body needs to metabolize arginine. The attempt failed. The next experiments took place in 1980 in Italy and Israel. Turned down by the UCLA Institutional Review Board for an experiment to introduce the globin gene (by mixing the patient's bone marrow with cells with DNA coding for hemoglobin in the hope that a normal hemoglobin gene would stably incorporate into the bone marrow cells) in a patient with beta-thalassemia, Dr. Martin Cline later unsuccessfully performed this experiment on two children, one in Italy and one in Israel. He was sanctioned by the NIH for failure to obtain IRB approval and his case became notorious. See President's Commission for the Study of Ethical Problems in Medicine and Biomedical and Behavioral Research, *Splicing Life,* U.S. Government Printing Office, Stock no. 83-600500, Washington, D. C., 1982, pp. 44-5; and materials in J. Areen, P. King, S. Goldberg, and A. M. Capron, *Law, Science and Medicine,* Foundation Press, Mineola, NY, 1984, pp. 165-70.

[5]For example, "Gene Therapy (Editorial)," *Lancet* 1:193-4, 1989; G. Kolata, "Why Gene Therapy Is Considered Scary but Cell Therapy Isn't," *New York Times,* September 16, 1990, p. E5.

[6]E. K. Nichols, *Human Gene Therapy,* Institute of Medicine, National Academy of Science, Harvard Press, Cambridge, MA, 1988, p. 163.

[7]President's Commission for the Study of Ethical Problems in Medicine and Biomedical and Behavioral Research, *Splicing Life.*

[8]"Gene Therapy in Man. Recommendations of European Research Councils," *Lancet* 1:1271-2, 1988.

[9]W. F. Anderson, "Human Gene Therapy: Scientific and Ethical Considerations," *Journal of Medical Philosophy* 10:275-91, 1985.

[10]B. Culliton, "Gene Therapy: Into the Home Stretch," *Science* 249:974-6, 1990.

[11]Department of Health and Human Services, "National Institutes of Health Points to Consider in the Design and Submission of Human Somatic-Cell Gene Therapy Protocols," *Recombinant DNA Technical Bulletin* 9:221-42, 1986.

[12]Ibid.

[13]W. F. Anderson, "Human Gene Therapy: Why Draw a Line?" *Journal of Medical Philosophy* 14:681, 1989.

[14]Ibid.

[15]W. F. Anderson, "What's the Rush?" *Human Gene Therapy* 1:109-10, 1990.

[16]U.S. Congress, Office of Technology Assessment, "New Developments in Biotechnology—Background Paper," *Public Perceptions of Biotechnology,* OTA-BBP-BA-45, U.S. Government Printing Office, Washington, D.C., May 1987.

[17]G. Fowler, E. T. Juengst, and B. K. Zimmerman, "Germ-Line Gene Therapy and the Clinical Ethos of Medical Genetics," *Theoretical Medicine* 10:151-65, 1989.

[18]S. Elias and G. J. Annas, *Reproductive Genetics and the Law,* Year Book, New York, 1987.

[19]L. Walters, "The Ethics of Human Gene Therapy," *Nature* 320:225-7, 1986.

[20]Fowler et al., 1989, and Nichols, 1988. And see generally, on human embryo experiments, P. Singer and H. Kuhse, "The Ethics of Embryo Research," and G. J. Annas, "The Ethics of Embryo Research: Not as Easy as It Sounds," *Law, Medicine & Health Care* 14:133-40, 1987.

[21]Anderson, 1985.

[22]A. G. Motulsky, "Impact of Genetic Manipulation on Society and Medicine," *Science* 219:135-40, 1983.

[23]A. Capron, "Which Ills to Bear: Reevaluating the 'Threat' of Modern Genetics," *Emory Law Journal* 29:665-96, 1990.

[24]Ibid.

[25]R. Morison, "Darwinism: Foundation for an Ethical System?" *Zygon* 1:352, 1966.

[26]Anderson, 1985, 1989.

[27]W. F. Anderson, "Human Gene Therapy: Where to Draw the Line," unpublished draft, 1986, p. 607. Reprinted in 1987 supplement to Areen et al., 1984, p. 27.

[28]Anderson, 1985, 1989.

[29]D. Suzuki and P. Knudtson, *Genetics: The Clash between the New Genetics and Human Values,* Harvard Press, Cambridge, MA, 1989.

[30]U.S. Congress, Office of Technology Assessment, *Mapping Our Genes,* OTA-BA-373, U.S. Government Printing Office, Washington, D.C., April 1988.

[31]S. Krimsky, "Human Gene Therapy: Must We Know Where to Stop before We Start?" *Human Gene Therapy* 1:171-3, 1990.

[32]B. Davis, "Limits to Genetic Intervention in Humans: Somatic and Germline," in *Human Genetic Information: Science, Law and Ethics,* Ciba Foundation Symposium 149, John Wiley and Sons, New York, 1990.

[33]Walters, 1986.

[34]Gutierrez et al., 1992.

[35]R. M. Cook-Deegan, "Human Gene Therapy and Congress," *Human Gene Therapy* 1:163-70, 1990.

UNITED STATES SUPREME COURT

Roe v. *Wade (1973)*

The Constitution does not explicitly mention any right of privacy. In a line of decisions, however, going back perhaps as far as *Union Pacific R. Co.* v. *Botsford* (1891), the Court has recognized that a right of personal privacy, or a guarantee of certain areas or zones of privacy, does exist under the Constitution. In varying contexts the Court or individual Justices have indeed found at least the roots of that right in the First Amendment, . . . in the Fourth and Fifth Amendments, . . . in the penumbras of the Bill of Rights, . . . in the Ninth Amendment, . . . or in the concept of liberty guaranteed by the first section of the Fourteenth Amendment. . . .

This right of privacy . . . is broad enough to encompass a woman's decision whether or not to terminate her pregnancy. . . .

The Court's decisions recognizing a right of privacy also acknowledge that some state regulation in areas protected by that right is appropriate. As noted above, a state may properly assert important interests in safeguarding health, in maintaining medical standards, and in protecting potential life. At some point in pregnancy, these respective interests become sufficiently compelling to sustain regulation of the factors that govern the abortion decision. The privacy rights involved, therefore, cannot be said to be absolute. . . .

We therefore conclude that the right of personal privacy includes the abortion decision, but that this right is not unqualified and must be considered against important state interests in regulation. . . .

The state does have an important and legitimate interest in preserving and protecting the health of the pregnant woman . . . and . . . it has still *another* important and legitimate interest in protecting the potentiality of human life. These interests are separate and distinct. Each grows in substantiality as the woman approaches term and, at a point during pregnancy, each becomes "compelling."

With respect to the state's important and legitimate interest in the health of the mother, the "compelling" point, in the light of present medical knowledge, is at approximately the end of the first trimester. This is so because of the now established medical fact . . . that until the end of the first trimester mortality in abortion is less than mortality in normal childbirth. . . .

With respect to the state's important and legitimate interest in potential life, the "compelling" point is at viability. This is so because the fetus then presumably has the capability of meaningful life outside the mother's womb. State regulation protective of fetal life after viability thus has both logical and biological justifications. If the state is interested in protecting fetal life after viability, it may go so far as to proscribe abortion during that period except when it is necessary to preserve the life or health of the mother. . . .

To summarize and repeat:

A state criminal abortion statute of the current Texas type, that excepts from criminality only a *life-saving* procedure on behalf of the mother, without regard to pregnancy stage and without recognition of the other interests involved, is violative of the Due Process Clause of the Fourteenth Amendment.

(a) For the stage prior to approximately the end of the first trimester, the abortion decision and its effectuation must be left to the medical judgment of the pregnant woman's attending physician.

(b) For the stage subsequent to approximately the end of the first trimester, the state, in promoting its interest in the health of the mother, may, if it chooses, regulate the abortion procedure in ways that are reasonably related to maternal health.

(c) For the stage subsequent to viability the state, in promoting its interest in the potentiality of human life, may, if it chooses, regulate, and even proscribe, abortion except where it is necessary, in appropriate medical judgment, for the preservation of the life or health of the mother.

UNITED STATES SUPREME COURT

Planned Parenthood of Southeastern Pennsylvania v. *Robert P. Casey et al. (1992)*

Time has overtaken some of *Roe*'s factual assumptions: advances in maternal health care allow for abortions safe to the mother later in pregnancy than was true in 1973, see *Akron I, supra,* at 429, n. 11, and advances in neonatal care have advanced viability to a point somewhat earlier. . . . But these facts go only to the scheme of time limits on the realization of competing interests, and the divergences from the factual premises of 1973 have no bearing on the validity of *Roe*'s central holding, that viability marks the earliest point at which the State's interest in fetal life is constitutionally adequate to justify a legislative ban on nontherapeutic abortions. . . . Whenever it may occur, the attainment of viability may continue to serve as the critical fact, just as it has done since *Roe* was decided; which is to say that no change in *Roe*'s factual underpinning has left its central holding obsolete, and none supports an argument for overruling it. . . .

. . . Liberty must not be extinguished for want of a line that is clear. And it falls to us to give some real substance to the woman's liberty to determine whether to carry her pregnancy to full term.

We conclude the line should be drawn at viability, so that before that time the woman has a right to choose to terminate her pregnancy. We adhere to this principle for two reasons. First . . . is the doctrine of *stare decisis.* Any judicial act of line-drawing may seem somewhat arbitrary, but *Roe* was a reasoned statement, elaborated with great care. We have twice reaffirmed it in the face of great opposition. . . .

The second reason is that the concept of viability, as we noted in *Roe,* is the time at which there is a realistic possibility of maintaining and nourishing a life outside the womb, so that the independent existence of a second life can in reason and all fairness be the object of State protection that now overrides the rights of the woman. . . .

Roe v. *Wade* was express in its recognition of the State's "important and legitimate interest[s] in preserving and protecting the health of the pregnant woman [and] in protecting the potentiality of human life." 410 U.S., at 162. The trimester framework, however, does not fulfill *Roe*'s own promise that the State has an interest in protecting fetal life or potential life. *Roe* began the contradiction by using the trimester framework to forbid any regulation of abortion designed to advance that interest before viability. *Id.,* at 163. Before viability, *Roe* and subsequent cases treat all governmental attempts to influence a woman's decision on behalf of the potential life within her as unwarranted. This treatment is, in our judgment, incompatible with the recognition that there is a substantial state interest in potential life throughout pregnancy. Cf. *Webster,* 492 U.S., at 519 (opinion of Rehnquist, C. J.); *Akron I, supra,* at 461 (O'Connor, J., dissenting).

The very notion that the State has a substantial interest in potential life leads to the conclusion that not all regulations must be deemed unwarranted. Not all burdens on the right to decide whether to terminate a pregnancy will be undue. In our view, the undue burden standard is the appropriate means of reconciling the State's interest with the woman's constitutionally protected liberty. . . .

A finding of an undue burden is a shorthand for the conclusion that a state regulation has the purpose or effect of placing a substantial obstacle in the path of a woman seeking an abortion of a nonviable fetus. A statute with this purpose is invalid because the means chosen by the State to further the interest in potential life must be calculated to inform the woman's free choice, not hinder it. . . . That is to be expected in the application of any legal standard which must accommodate life's complexity. We do not expect it to be otherwise with respect to the undue burden standard.

UNITED STATES SUPREME COURT

Buck v. *Bell (1927)*

Mr. Justice Holmes delivered the opinion of the court:

This is a writ of error to review a judgment of the supreme court of appeals of the state of Virginia, affirming a judgment of the circuit court of Amherst county, by which the defendant in error, the superintendent of the State Colony for Epileptics and Feeble Minded, was ordered to perform the operation of salpingectomy upon Carrie Buck, the plaintiff in error, for the purpose of making her sterile. 143 Va. 310, 51 A.L.R. 855, 130 S.E. 516. The case comes here upon the contention that the statute authorizing the judgment is void under the 14th Amendment as denying to the plaintiff in error due process of law and the equal protection of the laws.

Carrie Buck is a feeble minded white woman who was committed to the State Colony above mentioned in due form. She is the daughter of a feeble minded mother in the same institution, and the mother of an illegitimate feeble minded child. She was 18 years old at the time of the trial of her case in the circuit court, in the latter part of 1924. An Act of Virginia approved March 20, 1924, recites that the health of the patient and the welfare of society may be promoted in certain cases by the sterilization of mental defectives, under careful safeguard, etc.: that the sterilization may be effected by males in vasectomy and in females by salpingectomy, without serious pain or substantial danger to life; that the Commonwealth is supporting in various institutions many defective persons who if now discharged would become a menace but if incapable of procreating might be discharged with safety and become self-supporting with benefit to themselves and to society; and that experience has shown that heredity plays an important part in the transmission of insanity, imbecility, etc. The statute then enacts that whenever the superintendent of certain institutions including the above named State Colony shall be of opinion that it is for the best interests of the patients and of society that an inmate under his care should be sexually sterilized, he may have the operation performed upon any patient afflicted with hereditary forms of insanity, imbecility, etc., on complying with the very careful provisions by which the act protects the patients from possible abuse. . . .

There can be no doubt that so far as procedure is concerned the rights of the patient are most carefully considered, and as every step in this case was taken in scrupulous compliance with the statute and after months of observation, there is no doubt that in that respect the plaintiff in error has had due process of law.

The attack is not upon the procedure but upon the substantive law. It seems to be contended that in no circumstances could such an order be justified. It certainly is contended that the order cannot be justified upon the existing grounds. The judgment finds the facts that have been recited and that Carrie Buck "is the probable potential parent of socially inadequate offspring, likewise afflicted, that she may be sexually sterilized without detriment to her general health and that her welfare and that of society will be promoted by her sterilization," and thereupon makes the order. In view of the general declarations of the legislature and the specific findings of the court obviously we cannot say as matter of law that the grounds do not exist, and if they exist they justify the result. We have seen more than once that the public welfare may call upon the best citizens for their lives. It would be strange if it could not call upon those who already sap the strength of the state for these lesser sacrifices, often not felt to be such by those concerned, in order to prevent our being swamped with incompetence. It is better for all the world, if instead of waiting to execute degenerate offspring for crime, or to let them starve for their imbecility, society can prevent those who are manifestly unfit from continuing their kind. The principle that sustains compulsory vaccination is broad enough to cover cutting the Fallopian tubes. Jacobson v Massachusetts, 197 U.S. 11. Three generations of imbeciles are enough.

But, it is said, however it might be if this reasoning were applied generally, it fails when it is confined to the small number who are in the institutions named and is not applied to the multitudes outside. It is the usual last resort of constitutional arguments to point out shortcomings of this sort. But the answer is that the law does all that is needed when it does all that it can, indicates a policy, applies it to all within the lines, and seeks to bring within the lines all similarly situated so far and so fast as its means allow. Of course so far as the operations enable those who otherwise must be kept confined to be returned to the world, and thus open the asylum to others, the equality aimed at will be more nearly reached.

Judgment affirmed.

Mr. Justice Butler dissents.

NONMALEFICENCE AND THE NONHUMAN WORLD

CHUNG-YING CHENG

On the Environmental Ethics of the *Tao* and the *Ch'i*

One central question for environmental ethics which must be raised before any other questions is what the term *environment* means or stands for. *Environment* is derived from *environs,* meaning "in circuit" or "turning around in" in Old French.[1] It is apparently a prepositional word, indicating an external relation without a context, also certainly devoid of a relationship of organic interdependence. Yet when we reflect on the experience of environment, we encounter many different things and different processes in the context of organic interdependence. We might say what we experience presupposes the existence of life and the living processes of many forms. This experience of environment is better expressed by the Chinese philosophical paradigm, *sheng-sheng-pu-yi* ("incessant activity of life creativity").[2] We must, therefore, make a distinction between a surface meaning and a depth meaning for *environment*. Without understanding life and the living process of life, we cannot understand the depth meaning of *environment*. On the other hand, without understanding the constituents and conditions of life, we cannot understand life and the living process of life. Hence, the very essence of environment requires an understanding of reality and the true identity of life in both its state and process aspects. This means we have to understand the *Tao* content and the *Tao* process in the environment, whereas *Tao* indicates the way of life-creativity in ceaseless movements and in a multitude of forms.

With the above analysis of the meaning of *environment,* it is clear that the essential depth meaning of *environment* was lost in modern man's conception of environment. The modern man's conception of environment is founded on the surface meaning of *environment,* which is typified by technology and science; with its underlying philosophy of modern-day materialism, Cartesian dualism, and mechanistic naturalism, the concept of environment of modern man was very much objectified, mechanized, rigidified, dehumanized, and possibly even de-enlivened, and so de-environmentalized.[3] Environment is no longer an environment at all; environment becomes simply "the surroundings," the physical periphery, the material conditions and the transient circumstances. The environment is conceived as a passive deadwood, and very often as only visible and tangible externalia. In fact, as the depth meaning of *environment* suggested above, environment is active life; it is not necessarily visible or tangible, and certainly it cannot be simply a matter of externality. Hence, it cannot be treated as an object, the material conditions, a machine tool, or a transient feature. Environment is more than the visible, more than the tangible, more than the external, more than a matter of quantified period of time or a spread of space. It has a deep structure as well as a deep process, as the concept of *Tao* indicates.

The distinction between the surface meaning and the depth meaning of *environment* also suggests a distinction between the Western and the Chinese approach to environment. Whereas the West focuses on the external relation of man to his surroundings based upon a qualitative separation and confrontation between the human and nonhuman worlds, the Chinese focus on the internal relation of man to his surroundings based upon an integrative interdependence and a harmony between man and the world. For modern Western man after Descartes, the nonhuman world is to be rationally studied, researched, and then scientifically manipulated and exploited for the maximum utility of serving man. This will to conquer and dominate nature is, of course, premised on the externality of nature to man, but there are two other rational principles or assumptions involved in exercising this will to conquer and dominate.

First, it is assumed that nature is a completed work of mechanical forces with one-dimensional natural laws controlling its workings. The one-dimensional natural laws are revealed in the physical sciences and the reductionistic methodology of physicalism. Hence, biological laws are very often reduced to laws of physics and chemistry, no other laws are permitted to stand on their own. Yet the relationship between various forms of life in the totality of nature cannot be said to be fully captured by physicalistic laws; nor can the relationship between man and the world of things be said to be regulated by these laws. The very fact of the breakdown of the environment in industrialized societies, as reflected, for example, in the problems of water-air-noise pollution precisely points to the lack of understanding of the relationship between various forms of life and man and his environment by way of modern science and technology.

There is a second assumption of the modern mechanical sciences: everything in the world forms an entity on its own as a closed system, and therefore can be individually and separately dealt with. This isolationist and atomistic assumption in the problem-solving methodology of modern science is strongly reflected in Western medical diagnostics and treatments. It was not until recent times that modern medical and health care researchers became aware of the potential limitations of this isolationist and atomistic approach, and became awakened to a holistic approach.

In contrast with the Western externalistic point of view on environment, the Chinese tradition, as represented by both Confucianism (with the *I Ching* as its metaphysical philosophy) and Taoism (with Chuang Tzu and Lao Tzu as its content), has developed an internalistic point of view on the environment. The internalistic point of view on the environment in Chinese philosophy focuses on man as the *consummator* of nature rather than man as the conqueror of nature, as a participant in nature rather than as a predator of nature. Man as the consummator of nature expresses continuously the beauty, truth, and goodness of nature; and articulates them in a moral or a natural cultivation of human life or human nature. This is paradigmatically well expressed in Confucius' saying "Man can enlarge the Way *(Tao)* rather than the Way enlarging man."[4] It is also expressed in Chuang Tzu's saying, "The *Tao* penetrates and forms a Unity."[5] As part and parcel of nature, man does not stand opposite nature in a hostile way. On the contrary, man has profound concern and care for nature at large, as befitting his own nature. For his own growth and well-being, man has to cultivate the internal link in him between himself and Mother Nature. To conquer nature and exploit it is a form of self-destruction and self-abasement for man. The material consequence of the conquest and exploitation must be forestalled by an awakening to what man really is or in what his nature really consists.

In contrast with the two Western assumptions about the environment, Chinese philosophy clearly asserts that nature, and therefore man's environment, is not a complete work of production by a transcendent God, but rather is a process of continuous production and reproduction of life. In Bruno's words, nature is *Natura naturans,* not merely *Natura naturata.* In other words, nature is an organism of continuous growth and decay, but never devoid of internal life. With this understanding men cannot treat nature as an isolated and atomic part without regard for the totality involving a past and a future. This leads to the second understanding contrary to the Western methodology of atomism: man has to interact with nature in a totalistic manner, realizing that there is no single linear chain of causality. There is always a many-to-many relationship between cause and effect. Hence, man has to consider a many-to-many level approach to relate the potential needs of man to nature. Man has to naturalize man as well as to humanize nature, treating nature as his equal and as a member within the family of the *Tao.* This approach to nature is reflected in the holistic approach of Chinese medicine in both its diagnostic and medical/health care aspects.

The modern mandarin translation for *environment* is *huan-chin,* meaning "world surroundings." This translation apparently reflects the surface meaning of *environment* correctly. But when embedded in the contexts of Chinese philosophy and Chinese cultural consciousness the "world of surroundings" does not simply denote individual things as entities in a microscopic structure: it also connotes a many-layered reality such as heaven and earth in a macroscopic enfoldment. This "world of surroundings" is generally conceived as something not static but dynamic, something not simply visible but invisible. It is in this sense of *environment* that we can speak of the *Tao* as the true environment of man: the true environment of man is also the true environment of nature or everything else in nature.

When asked about the presence of the *Tao,* Chuang Tzu had this to say: "(The *Tao* is) nowhere not present." Pressed as to where exactly the *Tao* lies, Chuang Tzu replied that the *Tao* is in the ants, in the weeds, in the ruins, and in the dungs.[6] The import of Chuang Tzu's message is that the *Tao* embraces everything, large or small, in the universe and imparts a unity of relationships in our environment, and that the *Tao* is a totality as well as a part of the totality pervading everything beyond our perception so that we cannot ignore what is hidden in our understanding of the environment. If understanding is the basis for action, this understanding of the environment in terms of the *Tao* is very essential for formulating an ethic of the environment, namely for articulating what human persons should do or attitudinize toward their world of surroundings. Two more observations have to be made in order to explicate the philosophy of the *Tao* for the purpose of the formulating an environmental ethics of the *Tao* or an ethics of the environment based on an understanding of the *Tao*.

The first observation concerns the *Tao* as the *tzu-jan*. *Tzu-jan* means "doing-something-on-its-own-accord," or natural spontaneity. In the *Tao Te Ching* it is said that "Man follows earth; earth follows heaven; heaven follows the *Tao* and the *Tao* follows *tzu-jan*."[7] But *tzu-jan* is not something beyond and above the *Tao*. It is the movement of the *Tao* as the *Tao,* namely as the underlying unity of all things as well as the underlying source of the life of all things. One important aspect of *tzu-jan* is that the movement of things must come from the *internal life* of things and never results from engineering or conditioning by an external power. That is why the life-creativity nature of the *Tao* is the only proper way of describing the nature of the movement of the *Tao*. However, to say this is not to say that only the *Tao* can have the movement of *tzu-jan*. In fact, all things can follow *tzu-jan* insofar as they follow the *Tao,* or in other words, act and move in the manner of the *Tao* and in unison and in accordance with the *Tao*. Perhaps a better way of expressing this is: things will move of their own accord *(tzu-jan)* insofar as they move by way of the *Tao* and the *Tao* moves by way of them. One has to distinguish between, on the one hand, *Tao*-oriented or *Tao*-founded movement and, on the other hand, thing-oriented or thing-founded movement. Only when the movement of a thing comes from the deep source of the thing—the *Tao* and its harmony with the totality of the movements of all other things—will the movement of things be genuinely of its own accord and, therefore, be spontaneous. Spontaneity *(tzu-jan)* is a matter of infinite depth and infinite breadth in an onto-cosmological sense.

One can, of course, speak of different degrees of *tzu-jan* in view of the different degrees of depth and breadth in harmonious relating and self-assertion among things. Just as things have their own histories and defining characteristics in form and substance, things also have their relative freedom of self-movement and life-creativity. Things, in fact, can be considered as conditions or preconditions of various forms of *tzu-jan* (spontaneity): insofar as things preserve their identity without destroying the identities of other things, and insofar as things change and transform without interfering with the process of change and transformation of other things, there is *tzu-jan*. This explains the mutual movement, rise and decline, ebb and flow, in things of nature.

For human beings, *tzu-jan* finds its rationale not only in the internal movement and life-creativity of human activity, but in the principle of least effort with maximum effect. Whatever produces maximum effect by minimum effort in human activity manifests natural spontaneity. One may, therefore, suggest that only in following natural spontaneity is there least effort and maximum effect. This can be called the *ecological principle of nature*.[8] Using this principle we can correctly interpret the most important point ever made about the nature of the *Tao:* "The *Tao* constantly does nothing and yet everything is being done" *(Tao-chang-wu-wei erh wu-pu-wei)*.[9] That the *Tao* constantly does nothing means that the *Tao* does not impose itself on things: the *Tao* only moves of its own accord. This also means that all things come into being on their own accord. The constant nonaction of the *Tao* is the ultimate cosmological principle of life-creativity and the only foundation for the evolution of the variety of life and the multitude of things. The nonaction of the *Tao* in this sense is an intrinsic principle of ultimate creativity; this intrinsic principle of ultimate creativity consists in an unlimitedness and an unlimitation of expression of life forms and life processes in a state of universal harmony and in a process of universal transformation.[10] In this ultimate sense of creativity, there is no effort made by the *Tao,* and yet there is an infinite effect, achieving life-creativity. The ecological principle reaches its ultimate limit in the principle of *chang-wu-wei.* Hence, we can conceive of the principle of least effort with maximum effect as an approximation to the *tzu-jan* of the *Tao* on the human plane.

With this principle correctly understood, we can resolve the dilemma and predicament arising from civilization and knowledge. The Taoist questions the value of knowledge and civilization, since they lead to greed, lust, and evil (tricks and treachery) in human society. In the same spirit, we can question the value of science and technology. In resolving many problems of man, do science and technology create more problems for man? Do science and technology seem to lead man to a purely pessimistic future? The Taoistic criticism here is that without an understanding of the *Tao* it is indeed possible and necessary that knowledge and civilization, science and technology, will doom man to self-slavery and self-destruction. Man simply falls into the bondage of his own conceptual prison and becomes a victim of his own desires. The Taoistic criticism of *wu-wei* is supposed to awaken man to self-examination and self-doubt; in this way man is awakened to a quest for self-surpassing and self-overcoming in an understanding of the totality of reality and its secret of creativity through *wu-wei* and reversion *(fan).*[11] With this awakening, man can still proceed with his knowledge and civilization, science and technology, if he is able to neutralize and temper his intellectual and intellectualistic efforts with a sense of the *Tao.* This means that man has to develop knowledge and civilization, science and technology, not out of pace with his efforts to relate to things, other humans and himself. His knowledge and civilization, science and technology, have to contribute to his relating to and integrating with the world of his surroundings. To do this he has to keep pace with his own growth as a sentient moral being, having regard and respect for his own identity and dignity of other beings, including his fellow man. Furthermore, he has to use his knowledge and hence, science and technology, in keeping with the order of things, with his best interests conceived and deferred in harmony with life and in preservation or promotion of universal creativity. He also has to closely follow the principle of least effort, if not the principle of no-effort, with maximum effect, if not infinite effect in terms of life and creativity—preservation and promotion—for his intellectual/scientific/technological/organizational activities.

As man is part and parcel of the *Tao,* it is only when man loses the sense of the *Tao* and respect for the *Tao* in his actual life that man becomes alienated from the *Tao* and his activities become a means of self-alienation which will inevitably result in losing the true identity of man by way of self-destruction. This is the natural and spontaneous reaction of the *Tao* to the self-alienation of man in his intellectual/scientific/exploitative en-grossment and obsession with himself. Hence, the remedy for knowledge and civilization, or for science and technology, is not more knowledge and more civilization, or more science and more technology, but a constant relating and integrating of these with the *Tao*. To do so is to naturalize as well as humanize knowledge and civilization, science and technology. It is to make these a part of the *Tao*. Although knowledge and civilization, science and technology, are man's forms for the appropriation of nature (the *Tao*), these forms should not remain apart: man should also let nature reappropriate them by integrating them into nature (the *Tao*). This is the essential point of an ethics of man's relation to the environment. To understand the *Tao* and to follow the *Tao* is the essence of the ethics of the environment; it is also the way to transform the artificiality and unnaturalness of knowledge and civilization, science and technology, into the spontaneity and naturalness of the *Tao*.

In light of this understanding, the conflict between the *Tao* and knowledge/civilization/science/technology can be resolved; the true ecology and life-creativity of nature can be restored with knowledge/civilization/science/technology. They can be seen as enhancing rather than obstructing, complementing rather than opposing, the actual spontaneity and harmony of the creativity of the *Tao*. This is the true wisdom of the Taoist critique of knowledge and civilization, science and technology. It is called *hsi-ming*, "hidden light," by Lao Tzu, and *liang-hsing*, "parallel understanding," by Chuang Tzu.[12] In this wisdom lies the most profound principle of both the ecology of nature and the ethics of the environment.

My second observation concerns the *Tao* as a process of the ramification and differentiation of the *ch'i*. Before I explain the meaning and reality of *ch'i* in Chinese philosophy, it is important to appreciate the significance of bringing in *ch'i* as an explanation of the depth structure and depth process of the environment. We have seen that the depth structure and depth process of the environment has been explained in terms of the *Tao* and its life-creativity (*sheng-sheng*). Even though this explanation is necessary in pinpointing the ontological being and becoming of the environment, it is not sufficient, on the one hand, to illuminate the dynamics and dialectics of the differentiation and ramifications of the *Tao* and, on the other hand, to manifest those dynamics and dialectics of the unification and integration of the *Tao*. In other words, there is a gap between the ontology of the *Tao* and the cosmology of the *Tao* which must be bridged.

It is when the *Tao* is seen in the form and activity of *ch'i* that this bridging takes place. It might be suggested that the *Tao* expresses itself in terms of three perspectives which result in three characterizations in the history of Chinese philosophy. The first perspective is derived from understanding the quality of the activity: it is the perspective of life-creativity as clearly formulated in the texts of the *I Ching*. This perspective has already been discussed above. The second perspective is derived from understanding the patterns of the activity: it is the perspective of the movement of internal spontaneity, reversion, and return, as clearly formulated in the texts of the *Tao Te Ching* as well as those of the *Chuang Tzu*. In fact, a concentration on the patterns of the movement of the *Tao* may lead one to see the *Tao* in terms of principles and reasons. The Neo-Confucianist metaphysics of *li* ("principle") is a logical result of this development. This development also leads to an epistemology of the *Tao*. In both the ontology of the *Tao* (life-creativity) and epistemology of the *Tao* (principles of nonaction, etc.), the *Tao* is always conceived as a totality and a unity; the nature of the unity and totality of the *Tao* is stressed above all. In fact, the very concept of the *Tao* carries with it a reference to its unity and totality. Yet the *Tao* is as much a distribution and diversification of being and becoming as a unity and totality of being and becoming. Hence, we need another explanation of this former aspect of the *Tao* which will also serve the purpose of cosmologizing the ontology and epistemology of the *Tao*. This is how the *Tao*-as-the-*ch'i* paradigm comes in. This is also how the concept of *ch'i* based on experience of the *Tao* as *ch'i* develops. We might therefore suggest that to understand environment in its depth meaning, one has to focus on both the totalistic and distributive aspects of the environment. Hence, one must focus on both the *Tao* as *tzu-jan* and the *Tao* as *ch'i*.

Another consideration with regard to the importance of the *Tao* as the *ch'i* is that whereas the *Tao* focuses on reality as a passage of dynamic processes, the *ch'i* focuses on reality as a presence of material—stuff which leads to an actualization of things and the concretization of events. Hence, for understanding the formation and transformation of the environment in its substantive structure, one has to understand *ch'i*. It is in understanding *ch'i* that one can see and grasp the subtleties of the environment *vis-à-vis* human beings. It is only on this basis (i.e., understanding the *Tao* as *ch'i*) that one is capable of formulating an ethics of the environment or an ethics of the *Tao* toward the environment.[13] For this reason, we may consider the discussion of the nature of *ch'i* as constituting a metaphysical inquiry into the depth structure and depth process of the environment. As the goal of an ethics of the environment is to understand how human beings should relate to the environment *via* a true understanding of environment, we may see how a metaphysical inquiry into the structure and process of the environment also constitutes a teleological inquiry into the nature of the environment in relation to man. It is only when we are able to understand the nature of the environment in its true identity that we are able to see what the end-values of our thinking about and acting toward the environment are. The end-values are provided by our understanding of reality: to act in accordance with reality and our true nature will be our end and ultimately will be the criterion of value. . . .

---

[1]Cf. Ernest Weekley, *An Etymological Dictionary of Modern English* (New York: Dover, 1967), p. 516 *(environ)*, p. 1583 *(veer)*.

[2]*Sheng-sheng* is derived from the Great Appendix of the *I Ching*, sec. 5, where it is said that "*Sheng-sheng* is called the change." "*Pu-yi*" is derived from the *Book of Poetry* in "Chou Sung," where it is said that "The mandate of Heaven is indeed profound and incessant *(pu-yi)*." This stanza is quoted in *Chung Yung* to describe the depth and width of the reality of Heaven and Earth. It is quite clear that the incessant activity of life-creativity is precisely what the *Tao* is. As a life-experience based concept of reality, *Tao* was universally conceived by ancient philosophers as a universal process of change and transformation as well as the fountainhead of all forms of life in the world. Therefore, *Tao* can be said to be the in-depth foundation, background, and context of the so-called *environment* for any sentient being. We shall see a more metaphysical consideration of the *Tao* in the writings of Lao Tzu.

[3]When I use the word *objectified*, I mean "being treated as an object"; when I use the word *mechanized*, I mean "being used merely as a machine"; when I use the word *rigidified*, I mean "being placed in the state of *rigor mortis*"; and when I use the word *de-enlivened*, I mean "being depleted of life and the living process"; when I use the word *dehumanized*, I mean "being given no consideration of human feeling and care"; finally, when I use the word *de-environmentalized*, I mean "being devalued as environment."

[4] *Analects,* 15: 28.

[5] *Chuang Tzu,* Chi Wu Lun.

[6] See the Chih Pei Yu chapter of *Chuang Tzu.*

[7] *Tao Te Ching,* 25.

[8] *Ecology* originally meant the economy of nature; when nature acts, it acts ecologically. The production of life and all things in nature can be said to come from the ecological movement of nature. In understanding the ecology of nature, one would naturally understand the *Tao,* but only when one independently sees the universality, unity, and life-creativity of the *Tao,* will one truly understand the ecology of nature. Hence, the *Tao* can be said to be the metaphysical foundation of the ecology of nature, whereas the ecology of nature is one principle of movement manifesting the *Tao,* corresponding to its spontaneity.

[9] Cf. *Tao Te Ching,* 37.

[10] This principle can be indeed expressed as the following equivalence: *cheng-wu-wei = tzu-jan = sheng-sheng = wu-pu-wie,* i.e., the constant self-restraining of externality = spontaneity = life-creativity = the natural harmony of all things.

[11] *Jan* ("reversion") refers to the fact that the *Tao* reverses what is done against the nature of things. But *jan* is also *fu* ("return"). If things are done according to their nature and of their own accord, things will return to their origin and their identity will be recurrently assured. See the distinction in the context of the *Tao Te Ching,* 40. "Reversion is the movement of the *Tao,*" 25, "The distance is the reversion," and 16. "All ten thousand things take place concurrently. I observe their recurrence *(fu) (via* their origin)."

[12] Cf. *Tao Te Ching* 2; *Chuang Tzu,* Chi W'u Lun.

[13] *Tao Te Ching,* 14.

BERNARD E. ROLLIN

The Moral Status of Nonhuman Things

As a bare minimum, environmental ethics comprises two fundamentally divergent concerns—namely, concern with individual nonhuman animals as direct objects of moral concern and concern with species, ecosystems, environments, wilderness areas, forests, the biosphere, and other nonsentient natural or even abstract objects as direct objects of moral concern. Usually, although with a number of major exceptions,[1] those who give primacy to animals have tended to deny the moral significance of environments and species as direct objects of moral concern, whereas those who give moral primacy to enviro-ecological concerns tend to deny or at least downplay the moral significance of individual animals.[2] Significant though these differences are, they should not cloud the dramatic nature of this common attempt to break out of a moral tradition that finds loci of value only in human beings and, derivatively, in human institutions.

Because of the revolutionary nature of these attempts, they also remain somewhat undeveloped and embryonic. Writings in this area by and large have tended to focus more on making the case for the attribution of moral status to these entities than in working out detailed answers to particular issues.[3] Thus, in order to assess these thrusts in relation to international justice, one must first attempt to articulate a consensus concerning the basic issue of attributing moral status to nonhumans, an attribution that, prima facie, flies in the face of previous moral tradition. In attempting such an articulation, one cannot hope to capture all approaches to these issues, but rather to glean what appears most defensible when assessed against the tribunal of common moral practice, moral theory attempting to explain that practice, and common moral discourse.

The most plausible strategy in attempting to revise traditional moral theory and practice is to show that the seeds of the new moral notions or extensions of old moral notions are, in fact, already implicit in the old moral machinery developed to deal with other issues. Only when such avenues are exhausted will it make sense to recommend major rebuilding of the machinery, rather than putting it to new uses. The classic examples of such extensions are obviously found in the extension of the moral/legal machinery of Western democracies to cover traditionally disenfranchised groups such as women and minorities. The relatively smooth flow of such applications owes much of its smoothness to the plausibility of a simple argument of the form:

> Our extant moral principles ought to cover all humans.
> _____Women are humans._____
> ∴ Our extant moral principles ought to cover women.

On the other hand, conceptually radical departures from tradition do not lend themselves to such simple rational reconstruction. Thus, for example, the principles of *favoring* members of traditionally disenfranchised groups at the expense of innocent members of nondisenfranchised groups for the sake of rectifying historically based injustice is viewed as much more morally problematic and ambivalent than simply according rights to these groups. Thus, it would be difficult to construct a simple syllogism in defense of this practice that would garner universal acquiescence with the ease of the one indicated previously.

Thus, one needs to distinguish between moral revolutionary thrusts that are ostensibly paradoxical to common sense and practice because they have been ignored in a wholesale fashion, yet are in fact logical extensions of common morality, and those revolutionary thrusts that are genuinely paradoxical to previous moral thinking and practice because they are not implicit therein. Being genuinely paradoxical does not invalidate a new moral thrust—it does, however, place upon its proponents a substantially greater burden of proof. Those philosophers, like myself, who have argued for a recognition of the moral status of individual animals and the rights and legal status that derive therefrom, have attempted to place ourselves in the first category. We recognize that a society that kills and eats billions of animals, kills millions more in research, and disposes of millions more for relatively frivolous reasons and that relies economically on animal exploitation as a mainstay of social wealth, considers talk of elevating the moral status of animals as impossible and paradoxical. But this does not mean that such an elevation does not follow unrecognized from moral principles we all hold. Indeed, the abolition of slavery or the liberation of women appeared similarly paradoxical and economically impossible, yet gradually both were perceived as morally necessary, in part because both were implicit, albeit unrecognized, in previously acknowledged assumptions.[4]

My own argument for elevating the status of animals has been a relatively straight-forward deduction of unnoticed implications of traditional morality. I have tried to show that no morally relevant grounds for excluding animals from the full application of our moral machinery will stand up to rational scrutiny. Traditional claims that rely on notions such as animals have no souls, are inferior to humans in power or intelligence or evolutionary status, are not moral agents, are not rational, are not possessed of free will, are not capable of language, are not bound by social contract to humans, and so forth, do not serve as justifiable reasons for excluding animals and their interests from the moral arena.

By the same token, morally relevant similarities exist between us and them in the case of the "higher" animals. Animals can suffer, as Jeremy Bentham said; they have interests; what we do to them matters to them; they can feel pain, fear, anxiety, loneliness, pleasure, boredom, and so on. Indeed, the simplicity and power of the argument calling attention to such morally relevant similarities has led Cartesians from Descartes to modern physiologists with a vested interest against attributing moral status to animals to declare that animals are machines with no morally relevant modes of awareness, a point often addressed today against moral claims such as mine. In fact, such claims have become a mainstay of what I have elsewhere called the "common sense of science." Thus, one who argues for an augmented moral status for animals finds it necessary to establish philosophically and scientifically what common sense takes for granted—namely, that animals *are* conscious.[5] Most people whose common sense is intact are not Cartesians and can see that moral talk cannot be withheld from animals and our treatment of them.

In my own work, appealing again to common moral practice, I have stressed our society's quasi-moral, quasi-legal notion of rights as a reflection of our commitment to the moral primacy of the individual, rather than the state. Rights protect what are hypothesized as the fundamental interests of human beings from cavalier encroachment by the common good—such interests as speech, assembly, belief, property, privacy, freedom from torture, and so forth. But those animals who are conscious also have fundamental interests arising out of *their* biologically given natures (or *teloi*), the infringement upon which matters greatly to them, and the fulfillment of which is central to their lives. Hence, I deduce the notion of animal rights from our common moral theory and practice and attempt to show that conceptually, at least, it is a deduction from the moral framework of the status quo rather than a major revision therein. Moral concern for individual animals follows from the hitherto ignored presence of morally relevant characteristics, primarily sentience, in animals. As a result, I am comfortable in attributing what Immanuel Kant called "intrinsic value," not merely use value, to animals if we attribute it to people.[6]

The task is far more formidable for those who attempt to make nonsentient natural objects, such as rivers and mountains, or, worse, quasi-abstract entities, such as species and ecosystems, into direct objects of moral concern. Interestingly enough, in direct opposition to the case of animals, such moves appear prima facie plausible to common morality, which has long expressed concern for the value and preservation of some natural objects, while condoning wholesale exploitation of others. In the same way, common practice often showed extreme concern for certain favored kinds of animals, while systematically exploiting others. Thus, many people in the United

States strongly oppose scientific research on dogs and cats, but are totally unconcerned about such use of rodents or swine. What is superficially plausible, however, quite unlike the case of animals, turns out to be deeply paradoxical given the machinery of traditional morality.

Many leading environmental ethicists have attempted to do for nonsentient natural objects and abstract objects the same sort of thing I have tried to do for animals—namely, attempted to elevate their status to direct objects of intrinsic value, ends in themselves, which are morally valuable not only because of their relations and utility to sentient beings, but in and of themselves.[7] To my knowledge, none of these theorists has attempted to claim, as I do for animals, that the locus of such value lies in the fact that what we do to these entities matters to them. No one has argued that we can harm rivers, species, or ecosystems in ways that matter to them.

Wherein, then, do these theorists locate the intrinsic value of these entities? This is not at all clear in the writings, but seems to come down to one of the following doubtful moves:

1. Going from the fact that environmental factors are absolutely essential to the well-being or survival of beings that are loci of intrinsic value to the conclusion that environmental factors therefore enjoy a similar or even higher moral status. Such a move is clearly fallacious. Just because I cannot survive without insulin, and I am an object of intrinsic value, it does not follow that insulin is, too. In fact, the insulin is a paradigmatic example of instrumental value.

2. Going from the fact that the environment "creates" all sentient creatures to the fact that its welfare is more important than theirs. This is really a variation on (1) and succumbs to the same sort of criticism, namely, that this reasoning represents a genetic fallacy. The cause of something valuable need not itself be valuable and certainly not necessarily more valuable than its effect—its value must be established independently of its result. The Holocaust may have caused the state of Israel; that does not make the Holocaust more valuable than the state of Israel.

3. Confusing aesthetic or instrumental value for sentient creatures, notably humans, with intrinsic value and underestimating aesthetic value as a category. We shall return to this shortly, for I suspect it is the root confusion in those attempting to give nonsentient nature intrinsic value.

4. Substituting rhetoric for logic at crucial points in the discussions and using a poetic rhetoric (descriptions of natural objects in terms such as "grandeur," "majesty," "novelty," "variety") as an unexplained basis for according them "intrinsic value."

5. Going from the metaphor that infringement on natural objects "matters" to them in the sense that disturbance evokes an adjustment by their self-regulating properties, to the erroneous conclusion that such self-regulation, being analogous to conscious coping in animals, entitles them to direct moral status.

In short, traditional morality and its theory do not offer a viable way to raise the moral status of nonsentient natural objects and abstract objects so that they are direct objects of moral concern on a par with or even higher than sentient creatures. Ordinary morality and moral concern take as their focus the effects of actions on beings who can be helped and harmed, in ways that matter to them, either directly or by implication. If it is immoral to wreck someone's property, it is because it is someone's; if it is immoral to promote the extinction of species, it is because such extinction causes aesthetic or practical harm to humans or to animals or because a species is, in the final analysis, a group of harmable individuals.

There is nothing, of course, to stop environmental ethicists from making a recommendation for a substantial revision of common and traditional morality. But such recommendations are likely to be dismissed or whittled away by a moral version of Occam's razor: Why grant animals rights and acknowledge in animals intrinsic value? Because they are conscious and what we do to them matters to them? Why grant rocks, or trees, or species, or ecosystems rights? Because these objects have great aesthetic value, or are essential to us, or are basic for survival? But these are paradigmatic examples of *instrumental* value. A conceptual confusion for a noble purpose is still a conceptual confusion.

There is nothing to be gained by attempting to elevate the moral status of nonsentient natural objects to that of sentient ones. One can develop a rich environmental ethic by locating the value of nonsentient natural objects in their relation to sentient ones. One can argue for the preservation of habitats because their destruction harms animals; one can argue for preserving ecosystems on the grounds of unforeseen pernicious consequences resulting from their destruction, a claim for which much empirical evidence exists. One can argue for the preservation of animal species as the sum of a group of individuals who would be harmed by its extinction. One can argue for preserving mountains, snail darters, streams, and cockroaches on aesthetic grounds. Too many philosophers forget the moral power of aesthetic claims and tend to see aesthetic reasons as a weak basis for preserving natural objects. Yet the moral imperative not to destroy unique aesthetic objects and even nonunique ones is an onerous one that is well ingrained into common practice—witness the worldwide establishment of national parks, preserves, forests, and wildlife areas.

Rather than attempting to transcend all views of natural objects as instrumental by grafting onto nature a mystical intrinsic value that can be buttressed only by poetic rhetoric, it would be far better to nurture public appreciation of subtle instrumental value, especially aesthetic value. People can learn to appreciate the unique beauty of a desert, or of a fragile ecosystem, or even of a noxious creature like a tick, when they understand the complexity and history therein and can read the story each life form contains. I am reminded of a colleague in parasitology who is loath to destroy worms he has studied upon completing his research because he has aesthetically learned to value their complexity of structure, function, and evolutionary history and role.

It is important to note that the attribution of value to nonsentient natural objects as a relational property arising out of their significance (recognized or not) for sentient beings does not denigrate the value of natural objects. Indeed, this attribution does not even imply that the interests or desires of individual sentient beings always trump concern for nonsentient ones. Our legal system has, for example, valuable and irreplaceable property laws that forbid owners of aesthetic objects, say a collection of Vincent Van Gogh paintings, to destroy them at will, say by adding them to one's funeral pyre. To be sure, this restriction on people's right to dispose of their own property arises out of a recognition of the value of these objects to other humans, but this is surely quite sensible. How else would one justify such a restriction? Nor, as we said earlier, need one limit the value of natural objects to their relationship to humans. Philosophically, one could, for example, sensibly (and commonsensically) argue for the preservation of acreage from the golf-course developer because failure to do so would mean the destruction of thousands of sentient creatures' habitats—a major infringement of their interests—while building the golf course would fulfill the rarefied and inessential interests of a few.

Thus, in my view, one would accord moral concern to natural objects in a variety of ways, depending on the sort of object being considered. Moral status for individual animals would arise from their sentience. Moral status of species and their protection from humans would arise from the fact that a species is a collection of morally relevant individuals; moral status also would arise from the fact that humans have an aesthetic concern in not letting a unique and irreplaceable aesthetic object (or group of objects) disappear forever from our *Umwelt* (environment). Concern for wilderness areas, mountains, deserts, and so on would arise from their survival value for sentient animals as well as from their aesthetic value for humans. (Some writers have suggested that this aesthetic value is so great as to be essential to human mental/physical health, a point perfectly compatible with my position.[8])

Nothing in what I have said as yet tells us how to weigh conflicting interests, whether between humans and other sentient creatures or between human desires and environmental protection. How does one weigh the aesthetic concern of those who oppose blasting away part of a cliff against the pragmatic concern of those who wish to build on a cliffside? But the problem of weighing is equally thorny in traditional ethics—witness lifeboat questions or questions concerning the allocation of scarce medical resources. Nor does the intrinsic value approach help in adjudicating such issues. How does one weigh the alleged intrinsic value of a cliffside against the interests of the (intrinsic-value-bearing) homebuilders?

Furthermore, the intrinsic value view can lead to results that are repugnant to common sense and ordinary moral consciousness. Thus, for example, it follows from what has been suggested by one intrinsic value theorist that if a migratory herd of plentiful elk were passing through an area containing an endangered species of moss, it would be not only permissible but obligatory to kill the elk in order to protect the moss because in one case we would lose a species, in another "merely" individuals.[9] In my view, such a case has a less paradoxical resolution. Destruction of the moss does not matter to the moss, whereas elk presumably care about living or being injured. Therefore, one would give prima facie priority to the elk. This might presumably be trumped if, for example, the moss were a substratum from which was extracted an ingredient necessary to stop a raging, lethal epidemic in humans or animals. But such cases—and indeed most cases of conflicting interests—must be decided on the actual occasion. These cases are decided by a careful examination of the facts of the situation. Thus, our suggestion of a basis for environmental ethics does not qualitatively change the situation from that of current ethical deliberation, whereas granting intrinsic value to natural objects would leave us with a "whole new ball game"—and one where we do not know the rules.

In sum, then, the question of environmental ethics . . . must be analyzed into two discrete components. First are those questions that pertain to direct objects of moral concern—nonhuman animals whose sentience we have good reason to suspect—and that require the application of traditional moral notions to a hitherto ignored domain of moral objects. Second are those questions pertaining to natural objects or abstract natural objects. Although it is nonsensical to attribute intrinsic or direct moral value to these objects, they nonetheless must become (and are indeed becoming) central to our social moral deliberations. This centrality derives from our increasing recognition of the far-reaching and sometimes subtle instrumental value these objects have for humans and animals. Knowing that contamination of remote desert areas by pollutants can destroy unique panoplies of fragile beauty, or that dumping wastes into the ocean can destroy a potential source of antibiotics, or that building a pipeline can have undreamed-of harmful effects goes a long way toward making us think twice about these activities—a far longer way than endowing them with quasimystical rhetorical status subject to (and begging for) positivistic torpedoing.

---

[1]See the chapters in Tom Regan, *All That Dwell Therein* (Berkeley: University of California Press, 1982).

[2]See Aldo Leopold, *A Sand County Almanac* (Oxford: Oxford University Press, 1949); J. Baird Callicott, "Animal Liberation: A Triangular Affair," *Environmental Ethics* 2 (1980): 311–338; Holmes Rolston III, *Philosophy Gone Wild* (Buffalo, N.Y.: Prometheus Books, 1986).

[3]There are exceptions to this generalization—for example, my own work in abolishing multiple use of animals as a standard teaching practice in medical and veterinary schools and my efforts in writing and promoting new legislation on proper care of laboratory animals.

[4]See the discussions of this point in Peter Singer, *Animal Liberation* (New York: New York Review of Books, 1975); and B. Rollin, *Animal Rights and Human Morality* (Buffalo, N.Y.: Prometheus Books, 1981).

[5]See my "Animal Pain," in M. Fox and L. Mickley (eds.), *Advances in Animal Welfare Science 1985* (The Hague: Martinus Nijhoff, 1985); and my "Animal Consciousness and Scientific Change," *New Ideas in Psychology* 4, no. 2 (1986): 141–152, as well as the replies to the latter by P. K. Feyerabend, H. Rachlin, and T. Leahey in the same issue, p. 153. See also my *Animal Consciousness, Animal Pain, and Scientific Change* (tentative title) (Oxford: Oxford University Press, forthcoming).

[6]See my *Animal Rights,* Part I.

[7]See the works mentioned in footnotes 1 and 2.

[8]This point is made with great rhetorical force in Edward Abbey, *Desert Solitaire* (New York: Ballantine Books, 1971).

[9]See Holmes Rolston, "Duties to Endangered Species," *Philosophy Gone Wild.*

R. G. FREY

Rights, Interests, Desires, and Beliefs

The question of whether nonhuman animals possess moral rights is once again being widely argued. . . . The major impetus to renewed interest in the subject of animal rights almost certainly stems from a heightened and more critical awareness, among philosophers and nonphilosophers alike, of the arguments for and against eating animals and using them in scientific research. For if animals *do* have moral rights, such as a right to live and to live free from unnecessary suffering, and if our present practices systematically tread upon these rights, then the case for eating and experimenting upon animals, especially when other alternatives are for the most part readily available, is going to have to be a powerful one indeed.

It is important, however, not to misconstrue the question: the question is not about which rights animals may or may not be thought to possess or about whether their alleged rights in a particular regard are on a par with the alleged rights of humans in this same regard but rather about the more fundamental issue of whether animals—or, in any event, the "higher" animals—are a kind of being which can be the logical subject of rights. It is this issue, and a particular position with respect to it, that I want critically to address here.

The position I have in mind is the widely influential one which links the possession of rights to the possession of interests. In his *System of Ethics,* Leonard Nelson is among the first, if not the first, to propound the view that all and only beings which have interests can have rights, a view which has attracted an increasingly wide following ever since. . . . Nelson himself is emphatic that animals as well as human beings are, as he puts it, "carriers of interests," and he concludes, accordingly, that animals possess rights, rights which both deserve and warrant our respect. For Nelson, then, it is because animals have interests that they can be the logical subject of rights, and his claim that animals *do have* interests forms the minor premiss, therefore, in an argument for the moral rights of animals:

> All and only beings which (can) have interests (can) have moral rights; Animals as well
> as humans (can) have interests; Therefore, animals (can) have moral rights. . . .

To say that "Good health is in John's interests" is not at all the same thing as to say that "John has an interest in good health." The former is intimately bound up with having a good or well-being to which good health is conducive, so that we could just as easily have said "Good health is conducive to John's good or well-being," whereas the latter—"John has an interest in good health"—is intimately bound up with wanting, with John's wanting good health. That these two notions of "interest" are logically distinct is readily apparent: good health may well be in John's interests, in the sense of being conducive to his good or well-being, even if John does not want good health, indeed, even if he wants to continue taking hard drugs, with the result that his health is irreparably damaged; and John may have an interest in taking drugs, in the sense of wanting to take them, even if it is apparent to him that it is not conducive to his good or well-being to continue to do so. In other words, something can be *in* John's interests without John's *having* an interest in it, and John can *have* an interest in something without its being *in* his interests.

If this is right, and there are these two logically distinct senses of "interest," we can go on to ask whether animals can have interests in either of these senses; and if they do, then perhaps the minor premiss of Nelson's argument for the moral rights of animals can be sustained.

Do animals, therefore, have interests in the first sense, in the sense of having a good or well-being which can be harmed or benefited? The answer, I think, is that they certainly do have interests in this sense; after all, it is plainly not good for a dog to be fed certain types of food or to be deprived of a certain amount of exercise. This answer, however, is of little use to the Nelsonian cause; for it yields the counter-intuitive result that manmade/manufactured objects and even things have interests, and, therefore, on the interest thesis, have or at least are candidates for having moral rights. For example, just as it is not good for a dog to be deprived of a certain amount of exercise, so it is not good for prehistoric cave drawings to be exposed to excessive amounts of carbon dioxide or for Rembrandt paintings to be exposed to excessive amounts of sunlight.

If, nevertheless, one is inclined to doubt that the notion of "not being good for" in the above examples shows that the object or thing in question "has a good," consider the case of tractors: anything, including tractors, can have a good, a well-being, I sub-mit, it is the sort of thing that can be good of its kind; and there are obviously good and bad tractors. A tractor which cannot perform certain tasks is not a good tractor, is not good of its kind; it falls short of those standards tractors must meet in order to be good ones. Thus, to say that it is in a tractor's interests to be well-oiled means only that it is conducive to the tractor's being a good one, good of its kind, if it is well-oiled. Just as John is good of his kind (i.e., human being) only if he is in health, so tractors are good of their kind only if they are well-oiled. Of course, farmers *have an interest* in their tractors being well-oiled; but this does not show that being well-oiled is not in a tractor's interest, in the sense of contributing to its being good of its kind. It *may* show that what makes good tractors good depends upon the purposes for which *we* make them; but the fact that we make them for certain purposes in no way shows that, once they are made, they cannot have a good of their own. Their good is being good of their kind, and being well-oiled is conducive to their being good of their kind and so, in this sense, in their interests. If this is right, if tractors do have interests, then on the interest thesis [that is, the claim that all and only beings which (can) have interests (can) have moral rights] they have or can have moral rights, and this is a counter-intuitive result.

It is tempting to object, I suppose, that tractors cannot be harmed and benefited and, therefore, cannot have interests. My earlier examples, however, suffice to meet this objection. Prehistoric cave drawings are (not benefited but) positively harmed by excessive amounts of carbon dioxide, and Rembrandt paintings are likewise certainly harmed through exposure to excessive amounts of sunlight. It must be emphasized that it is these objects themselves that are harmed, and that their owners are harmed only in so far as and to the extent that the objects themselves undergo harm. Accord-ingly, on the present objection, interests are present, and the interest thesis once again gives the result that objects or things have or can have moral rights. To accommodate those, should there be any, who just might feel that objects or things can have moral rights, when these objects or things are, e.g., significant works of art, the examples can be suitably altered, so that what is harmed is, e.g., a quite ordinary rug. But if drawings, paintings, and rugs can be harmed, why not tractors? Surely a tractor is harmed by prolonged exposure to rain? And surely the harm the tractor's owner suf-fers comes through and is a function of the harm to the tractor itself?

In short, it cannot be in this first sense of "interest" that the case for animals and for the truth of Nelson's minor premise is to be made; for though animals do have in-terests in this sense, so, too, do tractors, with awkward results.

Do animals, therefore, have interests in the second sense, in the sense of having wants which can be satisfied or left unsatisfied? In this sense, of course, it appears that tractors do not have interests; for though being well-oiled may be conducive to tractors being good of their kind, tractors do not *have an interest* in being well-oiled, since they cannot *want* to be well-oiled, cannot, in fact, have any wants whatever. But farmers can have wants, and they certainly have an interest in their tractors being well-oiled.

What, then, about animals? Can they have wants? By "wants," I understand a term that encompasses both needs and desires, and it is these that I shall consider.

If to ask whether animals can have wants is to ask whether they can have needs, then certainly animals have wants. A dog can need water. But *this* cannot be the sense of "want" on which having interests will depend, since it does not exclude things from the class of want-holders. Just as dogs need water in order to function normally, so tractors need oil in order to function normally; and just as dogs will die unless their need for water is satisfied, so trees and grass and a wide variety of plants and shrubs will die unless their need for water is satisfied. Though we should not give the fact undue weight, someone who in ordinary discourse says "The tractor wants oiling" certainly means the tractor needs oiling, if it is not to fall away from those standards which make tractors good of their kind. Dogs, too, need water, if they are not to fall away from the standards which make them good of their kind. It is perhaps worth emphasizing, moreover, as the cases of the tractor, trees, grass, etc., show, that needs do not require the presence either of consciousness or of knowledge of the lack which makes up the need. If, in sum, we are to agree that tractors, trees, grass, etc., do not have wants, and, therefore, interests, it cannot be the case that wants are to be construed as needs.

This, then, leaves desires, and the question of whether animals can have wants as desires. I may as well say at once that I do not think animals can have desires. My reasons for thinking this turn largely upon my doubts that animals can have beliefs, and my doubts in this regard turn partially, though in large part, upon the view that having beliefs is not compatible with the absence of language and linguistic ability. I realize that the claim that animals cannot have desires is a controversial one; but I think the case to be made in support of it, complex though it is, is persuasive. . . .

Suppose I am a collector of rare books and desire to own a Gutenberg Bible: my desire to own this volume is *to be traced* to my belief that I do not now own such a work and that my rare book collection is deficient in this regard. By "to be traced" here, what I mean is this: if someone were to ask *how* my belief that my book collection lacks a Gutenberg Bible is connected with my desire to own such a Bible, what better or more direct reply could be given that that, without this belief, I would not have this desire? For if I believed that my rare book collection *did* contain a Gutenberg Bible and so was complete in this sense, then I would not desire a Gutenberg Bible in order to make up what I now believe to be a notable deficiency in my collection. (Of course, I might desire to own more than one such Bible, but this contingency is not what is at issue here.)

Now what is it that I believe? I believe that my collection lacks a Gutenberg Bible; that is, I believe that the sentence "My collection lacks a Gutenberg Bible" is true. In constructions of the form "I believe that . . . ," what follows upon the "that" is a declarative sentence; and *what* I believe is that that sentence is true. The same is the case with constructions of the form "He believes that . . .": what follows upon the "that" is a declarative sentence, and what the "he" in question believes is that that sentence is true. The difficulty in the case of animals should be apparent: if someone were to say, e.g., "The cat believes the door is locked," then that person is holding, as I see it, that the cat holds the declarative sentence "The door is locked" to be true; and I can see no reason whatever for crediting the cat or any other creature which lacks language, including human infants, with entertaining declarative sentences and holding certain declarative sentences to be true.

Importantly, nothing whatever in this account is affected by changing the example, in order to rid it of sophisticated concepts like "door" and "locked," which in any event may be thought beyond cats, and to put in their place more rudimentary concepts. For the essence of this account is not about the relative sophistication of this or that concept but rather about the relationship between believing something and entertaining and regarding as true certain declarative sentences. If what is believed is that a certain declarative sentence is true, then no creature which lacks language can have beliefs; and without beliefs, a creature cannot have desires. And this is the case with animals, or so I suggest; and if I am right, not even in the sense, then, of wants as desires do animals have interests, which, to recall, is the minor premise in the Nelsonian argument for the moral rights of animals.

But is what is believed that a certain declarative sentence is true? I think there are three arguments of sorts that shore up the claim that this *is* what is believed.

First, I do not see how a creature could have the concept of belief without being able to distinguish between true and false beliefs. When I believe that my collection of rare books lacks a Gutenberg Bible, I believe that it is true that my collection lacks a Gutenberg Bible; put another way, I believe that it is false that my collection contains a Gutenberg Bible. I can distinguish, and do distinguish, between the sentences "My collection lacks a Gutenberg Bible" and "My collection contains a Gutenberg Bible," and it is only the former that I hold to be true. According to my view, what I believe in this case is that this sentence is true; and sentences are the sorts of things we regard as or hold to be true. As for the cat, and leaving aside now all questions about the relative sophistication of concepts, I do not see how it could have the belief that the door is locked unless it could distinguish this true belief from the false belief that the door is unlocked. But what is true or false are not states of affairs which correspond to or reflect or pertain to these beliefs; states of affairs are not true or false but either are or are not the case, either do or do not obtain. If, then, one is going to credit cats with beliefs, and cats must be able to distinguish true from false beliefs, and states of affairs are not true or false, then what exactly is it that cats are being credited with distinguishing as true or false? Reflection on this question, I think, forces one to credit cats with language, in order for there to be something that can be true or false in belief; and it is precisely because they lack language that we cannot make this move.

Second, if in order to have the concept of belief a creature must be possessed of the difference between true and false belief, then in order for a creature to be able to distinguish true from false beliefs that creature must—simply must, as I see it—have some awareness of, to put the matter in the most general terms, how language connects with, links up with the world; and I see no reason to credit cats with such an awareness. My belief that my collection lacks a Gutenberg Bible is true if and only if my collection lacks a Gutenberg Bible; that is, the *truth* of this belief cannot be entertained by me without it being the case that I am aware that the truth of the sentence "My collection lacks a Gutenberg Bible" is *at the very least* partially a function of how the world is. However difficult to capture, it is this relationship between language and the world a grasp of which is necessary if a creature is to grasp the difference between true and false belief, a distinction which it must grasp, if it is to possess the concept of belief at all.

Third, I do not see how a creature could have an awareness or grasp of how language connects with, links up with the world, to leave the matter at its most general, unless that creature was itself possessed of language; and cats are not possessed of language. If it were to be suggested, for example, that the sounds that cats make do amount to a language, I should deny it. This matter is far too large and complex to be tackled here; but the general line of argument I should use to support my denial can be sketched in a very few words. Can cats lie? If they cannot, then they cannot assert anything; and if they lack assertion, I do not see how they could possess a language. And I should be strict: I do not suggest that, lacking assertion, cats possess a language in some attenuated or secondary sense; rather, I suggest that, lacking assertion, they do not possess a language *at all.*

It may be suggested, of course, that there might possibly be a class of desires—let us call them simple desires—which do not involve the intervention of belief, in order to have them, and which do not require that we credit animals with language. Such simple desires, for example, might be for some object or other, and we as language-users might try to capture these simple desires in the case of a dog by describing its behavior in such terms as "The dog simply desires the bone." (This position may have to be complicated, as the result of questions about whether the dog possesses the concept "bone" or even more general concepts such as "material object," "thing," and "thing in my visual field"; but these questions I shall leave aside here.) If all the dog's desires are simple desires, and this is the point, then my arguments to show that dogs lack beliefs may well be beside the point.

A subsidiary argument is required, therefore, in order to cover this possibility. Suppose, then, the dog simply desires the bone: is the dog aware that it has this simple desire or not? If it is alleged to have this desire but to be unaware that it has it, to want but to be unaware that it wants, then a problem arises. In the case of human beings, unconscious desire can be made sense of, but only because we first make sense of conscious desire; but where no desires are conscious ones, where the creature in question is alleged to have only unconscious desires, what cash value can the use of the term "desire" have in such a case? This question must be appreciated against the backdrop of what appears to ensue as a result of the present claim. On the strength of the dog's behavior, it is claimed that the dog simply desires the bone; the desire we claim for it is one which, if we concede that it has it, it is unaware that it has; and no distinction between conscious and unconscious desire is to be drawn in the dog's case. Consider, then, a rubber plant which shuns the dark and through a series of movements, seeks the light: by parity of reasoning with the dog's case, we can endow the plant with an unconscious desire for the light, and claim as we do so that it, too, is a type of creature for whom no distinction between conscious and unconscious desire is possible. In other words, without an awareness-condition of some sort, it would seem that the world can be populated with an enormous number of unconscious desires in this way, and it no longer remains clear what, if anything, the cash value of the term "desire" is in such cases. If, however, the dog is alleged to have a simple desire for the bone and to be aware that it has this desire, then the dog is aware that it simply desires the bone; it is, in other words, self-conscious. Now my objection to regarding the dog as self-conscious is not merely founded upon the view that self-consciousness presupposes the possession of language, . . . upon the fact that there is nothing the dog can do which can express the difference between desiring the bone and being aware of desiring the bone. Yet, the dog would have to be capable of expressing this difference in its behavior, if one is going to hold, *on the basis of that behavior,* that the dog is aware that it has a simple desire for the bone, aware that it simply desires the bone.

Even, then, if we concede for the sake of argument that there are simple desires, desires which do not involve the intervention of belief in order to have them, the suggestion that we can credit animals with these desires, without also having to credit them with language, is at best problematic. . . .

I conclude, then, that the Nelsonian position on the moral rights of animals is not a sound one: the truth of the minor premiss in his argument—that animals have interests—is doubtful at best, and animals must have interests if, in accordance with the interest thesis, they are to be a logical subject of such rights. For animals either have interests in a sense which allows objects and things to have interests, and so, on the interest thesis, to have or to be candidates for having moral rights or they do not have interests at all, and so, on the interest thesis, do not have and are not candidates for having moral rights. I have reached this conclusion, moreover, without querying the correctness of the interest thesis itself, without querying, that is, whether the possession of interests *really is* a criterion for the possession of moral rights.

CHAPTER 7

BENEFICENCE

■ ━━━━ ■

INTRODUCTION

The duty of beneficence requires an offer of a reasonable amount of help to someone in need. Some people who recognize such a duty also think that this duty should take a back seat to a prior duty to help others with special ties, including family, marriage, friendship, and patriotism. The idea is that these special relationships create special obligations to promote the well-being of people linked in this way, and attempts to meet the needs of strangers should await the satisfaction of these special obligations. This type of prioritizing is a natural offshoot of the virtue ethics traditions in the East and West.

An important distinction separates help that a recipient welcomes and help that a recipient resists. The suggestion of a duty to provide "help" that people prefer not to receive might be called *parentalism* (or *paternalism*), and the aid provided might be called *parentalistic aid.* One example of this kind of aid is a coercive restriction designed to stop people from doing something that would be dangerous to their health. The suggestion of a duty to provide help welcomed by the recipient might be called *humanitarianism,* and the aid provided could be called *humanitarian aid.* One particularly controversial form of humanitarian aid is benevolent killing—killing people, or allowing them to die, when, for example, they have made competent decisions that their lives are no longer worthwhile, and they want medical treatment discontinued, or they request help in ending their lives. This chapter considers these forms of beneficence: parentalism and two types of humanitarianism, one directed at prolonging life and the other at ending life.

━━━━━━━━━━━━

HUMANITARIANISM

The chapter's first pair of readings provides two very different defenses of humanitarian aid. One extends the virtue ethics approach, and the other appeals to utilitarianism.

1. NODDINGS AND CARING

Nel Noddings, professor of child education at Stanford University, defends a virtue ethics approach in which two sentiments are the source of ethical behavior. The first is a natural human feeling of concern for the well-being of certain other people. The second sentiment comes to light through development of a personal ideal that Noddings calls a "vision of best self." This ideal is the conception of who, ideally, one should strive to be and how, ideally, one should strive to act. This ideal guides evaluations of natural feelings of concern for others, leading one to "accept and sustain the initial feeling rather than reject it." Under the guidance of a personal ideal, an individual comes to regard caring for certain others as a necessary act, because caring is the response of the person one strives to be. Caring enhances a personal, ethical ideal. But while we take on an obligation to care, "our obligation is limited and delimited by relation." Thus, "I am not obliged to care for starving children in Africa, because there is no way for this caring to be completed in the other unless I abandon the caring to which I am obligated," and "in connection with animals, . . . we may find it possible to refuse relation itself on the grounds of a species-specific impossibility of any form of reciprocity in caring." Noddings goes on to apply her ethics of caring to the issue of abortion, arguing that "abortions should be freely available in the first trimester, subject to medical determination in the second trimester, and banned in the third, when the fetus is viable."

2. SINGER AND PROMOTING THE COMMON GOOD

According to Peter Singer, professor of philosophy at Monash University in Australia, if people in affluent countries distributed grain and soybeans to people in poor countries instead of feeding this food to animals, the food supply would be more than sufficient to end hunger in the world. Singer also says that, morality demands redistribution of this food to the world's hungry. Singer realizes that people traditionally assume a morally crucial distinction between harming people and omitting to aid them. After making this distinction between an act and an omission, many people claim that killing others is almost always morally wrong, while they may permissibly refrain from saving people, allowing others to die. Deliberately allowing others to die when one has a special responsibility for their lives is morally wrong on the traditional view: Parents may not allow their children to starve if they can prevent it, and physicians charged with saving a life may not neglect that task. But neglecting the needs of strangers for whom one has no special responsibility can be permissible, even if those strangers die. This traditional reliance on the moral significance of the acts–omissions distinction is carried over into the classical liberal view of negative rights (as opposed to positive rights): My (negative) rights protect my pursuits from interference by others, but my rights do not entitle me to demand that others help me with my pursuits.

Consequentialist views such as utilitarianism reject many elements of this traditional view. For instance, utilitarians often reject the idea that special obligations to specific individuals restrict actions on behalf of strangers. Utilitarians also reject the moral significance of the act–omission distinction: An act and an omission are morally on a par if they generate the same consequences, so refraining from sending aid to people and allowing them to starve is just as bad as shooting people, or imprisoning them and allowing them to starve. Moreover, utilitarians tend to defend so-called *posi-*

tive rights which entitle needy people to the help of others. A utilitarian himself, Singer rejects the moral significance of the act–omission distinction and suggests that since "allowing someone to die is not intrinsically different from killing someone, it would seem that we are all murderers." Arguing on utilitarian grounds for an obligation to act in a way that maximizes the total good, Singer suggests that if people can prevent something bad without sacrificing anything of comparable significance, they must do so. On the basis of this comparable harm principle, Singer supports a moral requirement to sacrifice for others until they are no longer worse off than oneself.

PARENTALISM

John Stuart Mill mounted a powerful assault on parentalistic restrictions on people's behavior in his classic *On Liberty.* Nevertheless, these restrictions are commonplace, and they are still vigorously defended.

1. MILL AND LIBERTY

In *On Liberty,* Mill addresses a gap in the classical liberal view defended by John Locke. In claiming that rational people could consent to a form of majority rule, Locke had assumed that people could count on majoritarian rule not to violate individual moral rights. Mill questions this assumption when he suggests that "the will of the people . . . practically means the will of the . . . majority . . . ; the people, consequently, *may* desire to oppress a part of their number, and precautions are as much needed against this as against any other abuse of power." The precaution Mill defends, on utilitarian grounds, is the protection of a right to self-determination or personal liberty, as described in his famous *principle of liberty:* "The only purpose for which power can be rightfully exercised over any member of a civilized community, against his will, is to prevent harm to others. His own good, either physical or moral, is not a sufficient warrant." In fact, "over himself, over his own body and mind, the individual is sovereign."

Mill's principle of liberty is intended to rule out all *parentalistic* requirements. However, Mill clearly denies any intent to rule out humanitarian requirements, for he recognizes "many positive acts for the benefit of others, which he may rightfully be compelled to perform; such as, to give evidence in a court of justice; to bear his fair share in the common defence, or in any other joint work necessary to the interest of . . . society; and to perform certain acts of individual beneficence." Mill also notes that his principle of liberty does not apply to children, to the mentally impaired, to countries surrounded by enemies, or even to peoples who cannot be improved by education or free discussion.

On the basis of his principle of liberty, Mill suggests that several liberties merit protection: (1) liberty of conscience, freedom of thought and expression; (2) liberty of tastes and pursuits, doing as one chooses so long as those acts do not harm others; (3) freedom to unite for any purpose not involving harm to others.

Mill offers several grounds for the principle of liberty:

1. Individuals are more interested in their own well-being than others, and they know their own situations and feelings much better than anyone else.

2. The only conceivable duties to the self are self-respect and self-development, but the collective interest does not demand accountability to others for these duties.

3. Society has had "the whole period of childhood and nonage in which to try whether it could make [people] capable of rational conduct in life."

4. When the public does interfere with personal conduct, "the odds are that it interferes wrongly, and in the wrong place," because it usually simply enforces conformity to its preferences.

2. DWORKIN AND PARENTALISM

Gerald Dworkin suggests justifications for various forms of parentalism, or paternalism. Dworkin defines parentalism as "interference with a person's liberty of action justified by reasons referring exclusively to the welfare, good, happiness, needs, interests, or values of the person being coerced." According to Dworkin, Mill does not object to parentalism on strictly utilitarian grounds. Instead, Mill assumes that freedom of choice itself has absolute value. But if freedom of choice is the ground for protecting people against parentalism, then certain instances of parentalism are defensible on the grounds that they enhance an individual's freedom of choice. "We may argue for and against proposed paternalistic measures in terms of what fully rational individuals would accept as forms of protection." On this basis, Dworkin suggests promoting certain multipurpose goods such as health, even when individuals do not recognize their importance. Individuals should be protected from making irrevocable decisions when they are not thinking clearly about their situations.

BENEVOLENT KILLING

Some people face such tragically poor prospects that they decide they would rather not live on, and many of them commit suicide or request that others help them to die. As Jonathan Glover emphasizes in his essay "Suicide and Gambling with Life," many of these people reach their decisions through irrational thinking. For example, young people who have been jilted by their partners might be so emotionally distraught that they cannot appreciate the chances for improvement in their lives, so that in the long run they would be better off to live. For such people, a powerful case for preventing suicide attempts can be constructed on parentalistic grounds, as Glover suggests. However, the charge of irrationality does not hold against all who conclude that living on is not in their interests. People who face untreatable cancer that causes uncontrollable pain might well rationally conclude that living on is not in their interests, and they might well be rational in committing suicide or in asking others to help them die.

For such people, no clear parentalistic premise justifies intervention. Nonetheless, other moral grounds might support intervention. Someone might answer *no* to any of these questions and attempt to impose appropriate restrictions:

1. Would it ever be permissible for people to allow themselves to die after reaching a rational decision that living on is not in their best interests?
2. May they ever permissibly kill themselves?
3. Could those responsible for their medical treatment ever permissibly allow them to die?
4. Could those responsible for their medical treatment ever permissibly kill them?

The first and third questions concern omissions that permit death, while the second and fourth concern acts that bring about death. Consider omissions first and then acts.

1.   OMISSIONS: WITHHOLDING TREATMENT

Withholding life-sustaining medical treatment might result from a *patient's* decision to allow herself to die by refusing medical treatment. On the other hand, it might result from a *health-care provider's* decision to allow a patient to die by withholding (or withdrawing) medical treatment. Of course, the decision might also reflect a consensus of the health-care provider and either the patient or her family.

Patients

Virtually everyone agrees that a patient can morally decide to allow herself to die under certain circumstances. In perhaps the least controversial case, the patient might decide to allow herself to die because she knows that further treatment will be a *futile* exercise. But most people also agree that the futility of treatment is not the only requirement for a morally permissible decision to allow oneself to die. Most agree that a patient may legitimately consider her prospective quality of life in deciding to refuse life-sustaining treatment.

Basically, a reasonable decision to refuse a life-extending treatment requires an expectation that the additional life sacrificed probably will not be worthwhile, taking all things into consideration, including special responsibilities to others, such as children. A conception of the good features prominently in this decision. People assess the quality of their lives based on their conceptions of the good, and the value of a life-extending treatment is determined partly by the probability of its outcomes and partly by the quality of life given those outcomes. A person's conception of the good has two main elements:

1. First, it includes a *life plan* that sketches how, ideally, life ought to work out, together with values that underlie that plan. Obviously, some people's plans and values differ substantially from those of other people, and so conceptions of the good vary from person to person. In fact, health is only one of the important criteria on which people plan out their lives.
2. Second, *self-determination* is an element of a conception of the good. Self-determination is partly a matter of devising and revising one's life plan and

values in light of changing circumstances, and partly a matter of shaping one's life in accordance with one's plans and values. People desire that their lives reach certain goals, but they also want to specify those goals for themselves, and they want those goals to be reached through their own efforts.

Special responsibilities to others may prompt some to choose treatments that maintain lives they would otherwise judge unworthy of continuing. Indeed, some people might find fulfillment in meeting such responsibilities. However, some will decide that possible courses of treatment would leave them such poor lives that they could not summon the will to meet their special responsibilities. Consequently, people who feel required to extend their lives solely for others may ask whether the additional life would position them to meet their special responsibilities. If not, it hardly seems reasonable to let the sense of duty prevail.

Health-Care Professionals

An individual's decision to refuse life-sustaining treatment is usually one side of a joint evaluation process that involves health-care providers, as well, and these professionals do not necessarily share the patient's goals. Nonetheless, health-care professionals should treat two main goals as paramount considerations: respecting the patient's self-determination and promoting the patient's good or well-being.

Given these goals, the health-care decision-making process should allow the patient to make an informed choice among treatment options which, in the opinion of the health-care provider, might effectively promote the patient's good or well-being. In supporting the patient's informed choice and limiting the range of choices to effective treatments, the provider applies expertise at and interest in promoting the patient's well-being. Respect for patient self-determination requires that the provider then leave the next step in the decision process to the patient, who will take one of two actions:

1. Make an informed selection from among treatment options that the provider deems effective in promoting the patient's good (thus exercising a *right to informed consent*).

2. Make an informed decision to refuse all treatment, including life-sustaining treatment (thus exercising a *right to refuse treatment*).

Legal Rights to Informed Consent and to Refuse Treatment

Patients have legal rights to informed consent and to refuse treatment. The law requires a provider to ensure that a patient has all the information and understanding necessary to assess available treatment options. This finding is a matter of common law. Since the 1990 *Cruzan* decision of the U.S. Supreme Court, a competent patient has retained an unqualified legal right to refuse treatment.

Extending the Right to Refuse Treatment

The most straightforward type of decision to withdraw treatment is one in which a competent patient exercises the right to refuse treatment, and the health-care provider ensures that the patient makes an informed decision. But other withdrawal of treatment decisions involve less straightforward conditions.

First, the patient may refuse treatment that would otherwise occur after loss of the ability to make decisions. An adult can refuse such treatment by completing a living will, issuing a do not resuscitate order, or designating a surrogate by filing a durable power of attorney. In all three cases, the patient is exercising a right to refuse treatment, even though the patient is not competent at the time the treatment would otherwise occur.

But suppose that an unconscious patient has left no advance directives, yet in the presence of family or friends, the patient has made salient comments such as, "I do not want to end up like a vegetable." Presumably the importance of self-determination and the uncertainty concerning the patient's wishes call for reviving and questioning the patient if that is a feasible option. However, if the patient is in a persistent vegetative state or permanently demented, then the person who is most knowledgeable of the patient's values may still determine what the patient would have wanted; such a decision still may be a case of exercising the patient's right to refuse treatment. Evaluating treatment according to the patient's own values is known as the *subjective test*.

Matters are even more difficult for patients without known values and preferences, for then no one can evaluate treatment as the patient would. No one can sensibly ask what the patient would have wanted. When reviving and questioning such patients is feasible, that should be done, of course. But in other cases, families may justifiably apply a different sort of test, namely, the *reasonable person standard* or the *best interests standard*. In this way, others may decide to withdraw or withhold treatment from patients facing certain sorts of conditions after asking whether a reasonable person would want to be kept alive under the circumstances and whether keeping the person alive promotes her own best interests.

More difficult still are the cases of severely mentally deficient people who never had the level of sophistication necessary to form judgments about whether they would want to stay alive. Here again, the subjective test cannot be applied. But once again, the family might apply the *reasonable person standard* or the *best interests standard*. The same sort of test might support withholding or withdrawing treatment from infants facing certain dire conditions such as Tay-Sachs, a disease leading to a vegetative existence followed by death at about 3 years.

2.   ACTS: EUTHANASIA AND SUICIDE

The term *euthanasia* is sometimes used in a limited sense of killing motivated by mercy. In a more expansive usage, the term can mean both *active* euthanasia, which is mercy killing, and *passive* euthanasia, which is allowing people to die on the grounds that dying is in their best interests. The issue of whether a physician may respond to a patient's rational request for help in dying is intimately bound up with other issues, such as the issues discussed so far concerning the permissibility of withdrawing life-sustaining treatment, and the issue of the permissibility of suicide.

In considering this complex set of issues, two main positions emerge. First, a somewhat *conservative* view holds that letting patients die, and letting oneself die, are sometimes permissible acts, but killing patients, suicide, and assisted suicide are never permissible choices. Second, a more *liberal* view sometimes allows letting patients, including oneself, die, as well as killing patients, suicide, as well as assisted suicide.

Those who defend a conservative view concerning euthanasia and suicide and those who favor a more liberal view primarily clash over four topics: the value of life, the defining aim of the medical profession, the significance of the acts–omissions distinction, and the further consequences of allowing mercy killing.

Sanctity of Life

According to the conservative view, (innocent) human life is incomparably valuable, so it may not be sacrificed no matter what is at stake (with the possible exception of other human lives). Hence, both suicide and active euthanasia are impermissible acts. To this reasoning, proponents of the liberal view make two main responses:

1. If patients' lives are incomparably valuable, so that they must not be *ended,* then patients' lives must never be *allowed* to end; people must be kept alive no matter how much they suffer from and oppose continued treatment, and even if they are in a persistent vegetative state. This is an absurd position.

2. The reasoning that supports a patient's right to refuse treatment also supports a right to suicide and the permissibility of killing terminal patients upon their own request. Both are based on respect for self-determination. David Hume defends the permissibility of suicide largely on the grounds of respect for people's self-determination. Moreover, according to Carl Becker, "Buddhism has long recognized persons' rights to determine when they should move on from this existence to the next."

Defining Aim of the Health-Care Professions

Proponents of the conservative view suggest that the defining aim of the health-care profession—saving lives, in their view—implies that health-care providers must not kill. But according to liberals, a mission to save lives does not accurately capture the proper goal of health-care professions. In fact, they recognize dual goals: respecting patient self-determination *and* promoting patient well-being. Respect for the patient's self-determination supports the permissibility of responding to a rational request for help in dying.

Acts–Omissions Distinction

According to the conservative view, killing the innocent is intrinsically wrong, while allowing to die is sometimes an acceptable choice, so mercy killing and suicide (including assisted suicide) are moral offenses, while allowing a patient to die, including oneself, is not always prohibited. Many writers invoke the acts–omissions distinction in rejecting provisions for killing patients while permitting provisions that allow patients to die. One liberal response to this conservative view denies any morally significant distinction between an act and an omission, so circumstances that justify allowing someone to die also justify killing that person. Dan Brock, in his discussion "Death and Dying," defends a liberal stance partly by attacking the significance of the acts–omissions distinction.

Slippery Slope

Proponents of the conservative stance often suggest that if society fails to prohibit active euthanasia and suicide, then a host of unacceptable killings will be tolerated next, such as killing the chronically ill or the poor. Liberals often respond that a patient's *request* for help in dying constitutes a sharp, defensible line; that is, allowing *voluntary,* active euthanasia and suicide creates no reason to fear eventual tolerance of *involuntary,* active euthanasia and suicide.

Questions for Reflection

1. Noddings suggests that our obligations are "limited and delimited by relation." How might Singer respond? Whose view is most defensible?

2. On the surface, Mill's principle of liberty sounds like a principle that libertarians could defend. How would a libertarian react to Mill's own interpretation of his principle?

3. What is Mill's view concerning the importance of the acts–omissions distinction? How does his view compare to Singer's?

4. Is Mill correct when he says that humanity does not gain if individuals are held accountable for duties to the self? What if others have to step in and help those who fail in their duties to themselves?

5. According to Mill, "if grown persons are to be punished for not taking proper care of themselves, I would rather it were for their own sake, than under pretence of preventing them from impairing their capacity of rendering to society benefits which society does not pretend it has a right to exact." Given the principle of utility, why doesn't society have this right?

6. Mill seems to favor humanitarian restrictions while rejecting parentalistic restrictions. Clarify his position in this area. Does he define a justifiable position?

7. Having read the various discussions of the acts–omissions distinction, both in this chapter and in the Chapter 5 essay by Williams, do you believe that acts and omissions are morally on a par, or does a morally important distinction separate acts and omissions?

8. Singer says that if people can prevent something bad without sacrificing anything of comparable significance, they must do so. Do you agree with this position?

9. Suppose that I sneak into your hospital room and shut down your life-support equipment. Then you die. Have I allowed you to die (an omission), or have I killed you (an act)? If the latter, why shouldn't people say that physicians kill patients when they shut off life-support equipment?

10. What response does the virtue ethics approach suggest to a patient's request for help in dying?

Further Readings

On Humanitarian Aid

Aiken, William, and Hugh LaFollette, eds. *World Hunger and Moral Obligations.* Englewood Cliffs, N.J.: Prentice-Hall, 1977.

Dower, Nigel. *World Poverty Challenge and Response.* York, England: Ebor Press, 1983.

Held, Virginia, ed. *Justice and Care.* Boulder, CO.: Westview Press, 1995.

O'Neill, Onora. *Faces of Hunger.* London: Allen & Unwin, 1986.

Shue, Henry. *Basic Rights.* Princeton, N.J.: Princeton University Press, 1980.

Singer, Peter. *Practical Ethics.* Cambridge: Cambridge University Press, 1979.

On Autonomy and Parentalism

Dworkin, Gerald. *The Theory and Practice of Autonomy.* Cambridge: Cambridge University Press, 1988.

Feinberg, Joel. *Harmless Wrongdoing.* Oxford: Oxford University Press, 1988.

Young, R. *Personal Autonomy.* London: Coom Helm, 1986.

On Euthanasia

Kuhse, H. *The Sanctity-of-Life Doctrine in Medicine—A Critique.* Oxford: Oxford Press, 1987.

Steinbock, Bonnie, ed. *Killing and Letting Die.* Englewood Cliffs, N.J.: Prentice-Hall, 1980.

Rachels, James. *The End of Life.* Oxford: Oxford University Press, 1987.

HUMANITARIANISM

NEL NODDINGS

Ethics and Caring

FROM NATURAL TO ETHICAL CARING

David Hume long ago contended that morality is founded upon and rooted in feeling—that the "final sentence" on matters of morality, "that which renders morality an active virtue"—". . . this final sentence depends on some internal sense or feeling, which nature has made universal in the whole species. For what else can have an influence of this nature?"[1]

What is the nature of this feeling that is "universal in the whole species"? I want to suggest that morality as an "active virtue" requires two feelings and not just one. The first is the sentiment of natural caring. There can be no ethical sentiment without the initial, enabling sentiment. In situations where we act on behalf of the other because we want to do so, we are acting in accord with natural caring. A mother's caretaking efforts in behalf of her child are not usually considered ethical but natural. Even maternal animals take care of their offspring, and we do not credit them with ethical behavior.

The second sentiment occurs in response to a remembrance of the first. Nietzsche speaks of love and memory in the context of Christian love and Eros, but what he says may safely be taken out of context to illustrate the point I wish to make here:

> There is something so ambiguous and suggestive about the word love, something that speaks to the memory and to hope, that even the lowest intelligence and the coldest heart still feel something of the glimmer of this word. The cleverest woman and the most vulgar man recall the relatively least selfish moments of their whole life, even if Eros has taken only a low flight with them.[2]

This memory of our own best moments of caring and being cared for sweeps over us as a feeling—as an "I must"—in response to the plight of the other and our conflicting desire to serve our own interests. There is a transfer of feeling analogous to transfer of learning. In the intellectual domain, when I read a certain kind of mathematical puzzle, I may react by thinking, "That is like the sailors, monkey, and coconuts problem," and then, "Diophantine equations" or "modulo arithmetic" or "congruences." Similarly, when I encounter an other and feel the natural pang conflicted with my own desires—"I must—I do not want to"—I recognize the feeling and remember what has followed it in my own best moments. I have a picture of those moments in which I was cared for and in which I cared, and I may reach toward this memory and guide my conduct by it if I wish to do so.

Recognizing that ethical caring requires an effort that is not needed in natural caring does not commit us to a position that elevates ethical caring over natural caring. Kant has identified the ethical with that which is done out of duty and not out of love, and that distinction in itself seems right. But an ethic built on caring strives to maintain the caring attitude and is thus dependent upon, and not superior to, natural caring. The source of ethical behavior is, then, in twin sentiments—one that feels directly for the other and one that feels for and with that best self, who may accept and sustain the initial feeling rather than reject it.

We shall discuss the ethical ideal, that vision of best self, in some depth. When we commit ourselves to obey the "I must" even at its weakest and most fleeting, we are under the guidance of this ideal. It is not just any picture. Rather, it is our best picture of ourselves caring and being cared for. It may even be colored by acquaintance with one superior to us in caring, but, as I shall describe it, it is both constrained and attainable. It is limited by what we have already done and by what we are capable of, and it does not idealize the impossible so that we may escape into ideal abstraction. . . .

OBLIGATION

There are moments for all of us when we care quite naturally. We just do care; no ethical effort is required. "Want" and "ought" are indistinguishable in such cases. I want to do what I or others might judge I ought to do. But can there be a "demand" to care? There can be, surely, no demand for the initial impulse that arises as a feeling, an inner voice saying "I must do something," in response to the need of the cared-for. This impulse arises naturally, at least occasionally, in the absence of pathology. We cannot demand that one have this impulse, but we shrink from one who never has it. One who never feels the pain of another, who never confesses the internal "I must" that is so familiar to most of us, is beyond our normal pattern of understanding. Her case is pathological, and we avoid her.

But even if I feel the initial "I must," I may reject it. I may reject it instantaneously by shifting from "I must do something" to "Something must be done," and removing myself from the set of possible agents through whom the action should be accomplished. I may reject it because I feel that there is nothing I can do. If I do either of these things without reflection upon what I might do in behalf of the cared-for, then I do not care. Caring requires me to respond to the initial impulse with an act of commitment: I commit myself either to overt action on behalf of the cared-for (I pick up my crying infant) or I commit myself to thinking about what I might do. In the latter case, as we have seen, I may or may not act overtly in behalf of the cared-for. I may abstain from action if I believe that anything I might do would tend to work against the best interests of the cared-for. But the test of my caring is not wholly in how things turn out; the primary test lies in an examination of what I considered, how fully I received the other, and whether the free pursuit of his projects is partly a result of the completion of my caring in him.

But am I obliged to embrace the "I must"? In this form, the question is a bit odd, for the "I must" carries obligation with it. It comes to us as obligation. But accepting and affirming the "I must" are different from feeling it, and these responses are what I am pointing to when I ask whether I am obliged to embrace the "I must." The question nags at us; it is a question that has been asked, in a variety of forms, over and over by moralists and moral theorists. Usually, the question arises as part of the broader question of justification. We ask something of the sort: Why must I (or should I) do what suggests itself to reason as "right" or as needing to be done for the sake of some other? We might prefer to supplement "reason" with "and/or feeling." This question is, of course, not the only thorny question in moral theory, but it is one that has plagued theorists who see clearly that there is no way to derive an "I ought" statement from a chain of facts. I may agree readily that "things would be better"—that is, that a certain state of affairs commonly agreed to be desirable might be attained—if a certain chain of events were to take place. But there is still nothing in this intellectual chain that can produce the "I ought." I may choose to remain an observer on the scene.

Now I am suggesting that the "I must" arises directly and prior to consideration of what it is that I might do. The initial feeling is the "I must." When it comes to me indistinguishable from the "I want," I proceed easily as one-caring. But often it comes to me conflicted. It may be barely perceptible and it may be followed almost simultaneously by resistance. When someone asks me to get something for him or merely asks for my attention, the "I must" may be lost in a clamor of resistance. Now a second sentiment is required if I am to behave as one-caring. I care about myself as one-caring and, although I do not care naturally for the person who has asked something of me—at least not at this moment—I feel the genuine moral sentiment, the "I ought," that sensibility to which I have committed myself.

Let me try to make plausible my contention that the moral imperative arises directly. And, of course, I must try to explain how caring and what I am calling the "moral imperative" are related. When my infant cries in the night, I not only feel that I must do something but I want to do something. Because I love this child, because I am bonded to him, I want to remove his pain as I would want to remove my own. The "I must" is not a dutiful imperative but one that accompanies the "I want." If I were tied to a chair, for example, and wanted desperately to get free, I might say as I struggled, "I must do something; I must get out of these bonds." But this "must" is not yet the moral or ethical "ought." It is a "must" born of desire.

The most intimate situations of caring are, thus, natural. I do not feel that taking care of my own child is "moral" but, rather, natural. A woman who allows her own child to die of neglect is often considered sick rather than immoral; that is, we feel that either she or the situation into which she has been thrust must be pathological.

Otherwise, the impulse to respond, to nurture the living infant, is overwhelming. We share the impulse with other creatures in the animal kingdom. Whether we want to consider this response as "instinctive" is problematic, because certain patterns of response may be implied by the term and because suspension of reflective consciousness seems also to be implied (and I am not suggesting that we have no choice), but I have no difficulty in considering it as innate. Indeed, I am claiming that the impulse to act in behalf of the present other is itself innate. It lies latent in each of us, awaiting gradual development in a succession of caring relations. I am suggesting that our inclination toward and interest in morality derives from caring. In caring, we accept the natural impulse to act on behalf of the present other. We are engrossed in the other. We have received him and feel his pain or happiness, but we are not compelled by this impulse. We have a choice; we may accept what we feel, or we may reject it. If we have a strong desire to be moral, we will not reject it, and this strong desire to be moral is derived, reflectively, from the more fundamental and natural desire to be and to remain related. To reject the feeling when it arises is either to be in an internal state of imbalance or to contribute willfully to the diminution of the ethical ideal.

But suppose in a particular case that the "I must" does not arise, or that it whispers faintly and disappears, leaving distrust, repugnance, or hate. Why, then, should I behave morally toward the object of my dislike? Why should I not accept feelings other than those characteristic of caring and, thus, achieve an internal state of balance through hate, anger, or malice?

The answer to this is, I think, that the genuine moral sentiment (our second sentiment) arises from an evaluation of the caring relation as good, as better than, superior to, other forms of relatedness. I feel the moral "I must" when I recognize that my response will either enhance or diminish my ethical ideal. It will serve either to increase or decrease the likelihood of genuine caring. My response affects me as one-caring. In a given situation with someone I am not fond of, I may be able to find all sorts of reasons why I should not respond to his need. I may be too busy. He may be undiscerning. The matter may be, on objective analysis, unimportant. But, before I decide, I must turn away from this analytic chain of thought and back to the concrete situation. Here is this person with this perceived need to which is attached this importance. I must put justification aside temporarily. Shall I respond? How do I feel as a duality about the "I" who will not respond?

I am obliged, then, to accept the initial "I must" when it occurs and even to fetch it out of recalcitrant slumber when it fails to awake spontaneously.[3] The source of my obligation is the value I place on the relatedness of caring. This value itself arises as a product of actual caring and being cared-for and my reflection on the goodness of these concrete caring situations. . . .

I have identified the source of our obligation and have said that we are obligated to accept, and even to call forth, the feeling "I must." But what exactly must I do? Can my obligation be set forth in a list or hierarchy of principles? So far, it seems that I am obligated to maintain an attitude and, thus, to meet the other as one-caring and, at the same time, to increase my own virtue as one-caring. If I am advocating an ethic of virtue, do not all the usual dangers lie in wait: hypocrisy, self-righteousness, withdrawal from the public domain? . . .

Our obligation is limited and delimited by relation. We are never free, in the human domain, to abandon our preparedness to care; but, practically, if we are meeting those in our inner circles adequately as ones-caring and receiving those linked to our inner circles by formal chains of relation, we shall limit the calls upon our obligation quite naturally. We are not obliged to summon the "I must" if there is no possibility of completion in the other. I am not obliged to care for starving children in Africa, because there is no way for this caring to be completed in the other unless I abandon the caring to which I am obligated. I may still choose to do something in the direction of caring, but I am not obliged to do so. . . . Our obligation to animals . . . is even more sharply limited by relation. We cannot refuse obligation in human affairs by merely refusing to enter relation; we are, by virtue of our mutual humanity, already and perpetually in potential relation. Instead, we limit our obligation by examining the possibility of completion. In connection with animals, however, we may find it possible to refuse relation itself on the grounds of a species-specific impossibility of any form of reciprocity in caring.

Now, this is very important, and we should try to say clearly what governs our obligation. On the basis of what has been developed so far, there seem to be two criteria: the existence of or potential for present relation, and the dynamic potential for growth in relation, including the potential for increased reciprocity and, perhaps, mutuality. The first criterion establishes an absolute obligation and the second serves to put our obligations into an order of priority.

If the other toward whom we shall act is capable of responding as cared-for and there are no objective conditions that prevent our receiving this response—if, that is, our caring can be completed in the other—then we must meet that other as one-caring. If we do not care naturally, we must call upon our capacity for ethical caring. When we are in relation or when the other has addressed us, we must respond as one-caring. The imperative in relation is categorical. When relation has not yet been established, or when it may properly be refused (when no formal chain or natural circle is present), the imperative is more like that of the hypothetical: I must if I wish to (or am able to) move into relation.

The second criterion asks us to look at the nature of potential relation and, especially, at the capacity of the cared-for to respond. The potential for response in animals, for example, is nearly static; they cannot respond in mutuality, nor can the nature of their response change substantially. But a child's potential for increased response is enormous. If the possibility of relation is dynamic—if the relation may clearly grow with respect to reciprocity—then the possibility and degree of my obligation also grows. If response is imminent, so also is my obligation. This criterion will help us to distinguish between our obligation to members of the nonhuman animal world and, say, the human fetus. We must keep in mind, however, that the second criterion binds us in proportion to the probability of increased response and to the imminence of that response. Relation itself is fundamental in obligation. . . .

Now, let's consider an example: the problem of abortion. Operating under the guidance of an ethic of caring, we are not likely to find abortion in general either right or wrong. We shall have to inquire into individual cases. An incipient embryo is an information speck—a set of controlling instructions for a future human being.

Many of these specks are created and flushed away without their creators' awareness. From the view developed here, the information speck is an information speck; it has no given sanctity. There should be no concern over the waste of "human tissue," since nature herself is wildly prolific, even profligate.[4] The one-caring is concerned not with human tissue but with human consciousness—with pain, delight, hope, fear, entreaty, and response.

But suppose the information speck is mine, and I am aware of it. This child-to-be is the product of love between a man deeply cared-for and me. Will the child have his eyes or mine? His stature or mine? Our joint love of mathematics or his love of mechanics or my love of language? This is not just an information speck; it is endowed with prior love and current knowledge. It is sacred, but I—humbly, not presumptuously—confer sacredness upon it. I cannot, will not destroy it. It is joined to loved others through formal chains of caring. It is linked to the inner circle in a clearly defined way. I might wish that I were not pregnant, but I cannot destroy this known and potentially loved person-to-be. There is already relation albeit indirect and formal. My decision is an ethical one born of natural caring.

But suppose, now, that my beloved child has grown up; it is she who is pregnant and considering abortion. She is not sure of the love between herself and the man. She is miserably worried about her economic and emotional future. I might like to convey sanctity on this information speck; but I am not God—only mother to this suffering cared-for. It is she who is conscious and in pain, and I as one-caring move to relieve the pain. This information speck is an information speck and that is all. There is no formal relation, given the breakdown between husband and wife, and with the embryo, there is no present relation; the possibility of future relation—while not absent, surely—is uncertain. But what of this possibility for growing response? Must we not consider it? We must indeed. As the embryo becomes a fetus and, growing daily, becomes more nearly capable of response as cared-for, our obligation grows from a nagging uncertainty—an "I must if I wish"—to an utter conviction that we must meet this small other as one-caring.

If we try to formalize what has been expressed in the concrete situations described so far, we arrive at a legal approach to abortion very like that of the Supreme Court: abortions should be freely available in the first trimester, subject to medical determination in the second trimester, and banned in the third, when the fetus is viable. A woman under the guidance of our ethic would be likely to recognize the growing possibility of relation; the potential is clearly dynamic. Further, many women recognize the relation as established when the fetus begins to move about. It is not a question of when life begins but of when relation begins.

But what if relation is never established? Suppose the child is born and the mother admits no sense of relatedness. May she commit infanticide? One who asks such questions misinterprets the concept of relatedness that I have been struggling to describe. Since the infant, even the near-natal fetus, is capable of relation—of the sweetest and most unselfconscious reciprocity—one who encounters the infant is obligated to meet it as one-caring. Both parts of this claim are essential; it is not only the child's capability to respond but also the encounter that induces obligation. There must exist the possibility for our caring to be completed in the other. If the mother does not care naturally, then she must summon ethical caring to support her as one-caring. She may not ethically ignore the child's cry to live.

The one-caring, in considering abortion as in all other matters, cares first for the one in immediate pain or peril. She might suggest a brief and direct form of counseling in which a young expectant mother could come to grips with her feelings. If the incipient child has been sanctified by its mother, every effort must be made to help the two achieve a stable and hopeful life together; if it has not, it should be removed swiftly and mercifully with all loving attention to the woman, the conscious patient. Between these two clear reactions is a possible confused one: the young woman is not sure how she feels. The one-caring probes gently to see what has been considered, raising questions and retreating when the questions obviously have been considered and are now causing great pain. Is such a view "unprincipled"? If it is, it is boldly so; it is at least connected with the world as it is, at its best and at its worst, and it requires that we—in espousing a "best"—stand ready to actualize that preferred condition. The decision for or against abortion must be made by those directly involved in the concrete situation, but it need not be made alone. The one-caring cannot require everyone to behave as she would in a particular situation. Rather, when she dares to say, "I think you should do X," she adds, also, "Can I help you?" The one under her gaze is under her support and not her judgment.

One under the guidance of an ethic of caring is tempted to retreat to a manageable world. Her public life is limited by her insistence upon meeting the other as one-caring. So long as this is possible, she may reach outward and enlarge her circles of caring. When this reaching out destroys or drastically reduces her actual caring, she retreats and renews her contact with those who address her. If the retreat becomes a flight, an avoidance of the call to care, her ethical ideal is diminished. Similarly, if the retreat is away from human beings and toward other objects of caring—ideas, animals, humanity-at-large, God—her ethical ideal is virtually shattered. This is not a judgment, for we can understand and sympathize with one who makes such a choice. It is more in the nature of a perception: we see clearly what has been lost in the choice.

Our ethic of caring—which we might have called a "feminine ethic"—begins to look a bit mean in contrast to the masculine ethics of universal love or universal justice. But universal love is illusion. Under the illusion, some young people retreat to the church to worship that which they cannot actualize; some write lovely poetry extolling universal love; and some, in terrible disillusion, kill to establish the very principles which should have entreated them not to kill. Thus are lost both principles and persons.

---

[1][Noddings's notes have been renumbered—ed.] David Hume, "An Enquiry Concerning the Principles of Morals," in *Ethical Theories,* ed. A. I. Melden (Englewood Cliffs, N.J.: Prentice-Hall, 1967), p. 275.

[2]Friedrich Nietzsche, "Mixed Opinions and Maxims," in *The Portable Nietzsche,* ed. Walter Kaufmann (New York: Viking Press, 1954), p. 65.

[3]The question of "summonability" is a vital one for ethicists who rely on good or altruistic feelings for moral motivation. Note treatment of this problem in Lawrence R. Blum, *Friendship, Altruism, and Morality* (London: Routledge & Kegan Paul, 1980), pp. 20–23 and pp. 194–203. See, also, Henry Sidgwick, *The Methods of Ethics* (Indianapolis: Hackett, 1981); and Philip Mercer, *Sympathy and Ethics* (Oxford: Clarendon Press, 1962).

[4]Paul Ramsey raises this concern in *Fabricated Man* (New Haven, Conn.: Yale University Press, 1970).

PETER SINGER

Rich and Poor

SOME FACTS ABOUT POVERTY

Consider these facts: by the most cautious estimates, 400 million people lack the calories, protein, vitamins, and minerals needed to sustain their bodies and minds in a healthy state. Millions are constantly hungry; others suffer from deficiency diseases and from infections they would be able to resist on a better diet. Children are the worst affected. According to one study, 14 million children under 5 die every year from the combined effects of malnutrition and infection. In some districts half the children born can be expected to die before their fifth birthday.

Nor is lack of food the only hardship of the poor. To give a broader picture, Robert McNamara, when president of the World Bank, suggested the term "absolute poverty." The poverty we are familiar with in industrialized nations is relative poverty—meaning that some citizens are poor, relative to the wealth enjoyed by their neighbors. People living in relative poverty in Australia might be quite comfortably off by comparison with pensioners in Britain, and British pensioners are not poor in comparison with the poverty that exists in Mali or Ethiopia. Absolute poverty, on the other hand, is poverty by any standard. . . . McNamara has summed up absolute poverty as "a condition of life so characterized by malnutrition, illiteracy, disease, squalid surroundings, high infant mortality, and low life expectancy as to be beneath any reasonable definition of human decency."

Absolute poverty is, as McNamara has said, responsible for the loss of countless lives, especially among infants and young children. When absolute poverty does not cause death, it still causes misery of a kind not often seen in the affluent nations. Malnutrition in young children stunts both physical and mental development. According to the United Nations Development Programme, 180 million children under the age of 5 suffer from serious malnutrition. Millions of people on poor diets suffer from deficiency diseases, like goitre, or blindness caused by a lack of vitamin A. The food value of what the poor eat is further reduced by parasites such as hookworm and ringworm, which are endemic in conditions of poor sanitation and health education.

Death and disease apart, absolute poverty remains a miserable condition of life, with inadequate food, shelter, clothing, sanitation, health services, and education. The Worldwatch Institute estimates that as many as 1.2 billion people—or 23 percent of the word's population—live in absolute poverty. For the purposes of this estimate, absolute poverty is defined as "the lack of sufficient income in cash or kind to meet the most basic biological needs for food, clothing, and shelter." Absolute poverty is probably the principal cause of human misery today.

SOME FACTS ABOUT WEALTH

. . . The problem is not that the world cannot produce enough to feed and shelter its people. People in the poor countries consume, on average, 180 kilos of grain a year, while North Americans average around 900 kilos. The difference is caused by the fact that in the rich countries we feed most of our grain to animals, converting it into meat, milk, and eggs. Because this is a highly inefficient process, people in rich countries are responsible for the consumption of far more food than those in poor countries who eat few animal products. If we stopped feeding animals on grains and soybeans, the amount of food saved would—if distributed to those who need it—be more than enough to end hunger throughout the world.

These facts about animal food do not mean that we can easily solve the world food problem by cutting down on animal products, but they show that the problem is essentially one of distribution rather than production. The world does produce enough food. Moreover, the poorer nations themselves could produce far more if they made more use of improved agricultural techniques.

So why are people hungry? Poor people cannot afford to buy grain grown by farmers in the richer nations. Poor farmers cannot afford to buy improved seeds, or fertilizers, or the machinery needed for drilling wells and pumping water. Only by transferring some of the wealth of the rich nations to the poor can the situation be changed.

That this wealth exists is clear. Against the picture of absolute poverty that McNamara has painted, one might pose a picture of "absolute affluence." Those who are absolutely affluent are not necessarily affluent by comparison with their neighbors, but they are affluent by any reasonable definition of human needs. This means that they have more income than they need to provide themselves adequately with all the basic necessities of life. After buying (either directly or through their taxes) food, shelter, clothing, basic health services, and education, the absolutely affluent are still able to spend money on luxuries. The absolutely affluent choose their food for the pleasures of the palate, not to stop hunger; they buy new clothes to look good, not to keep warm; they move house to be in a better neighborhood or have a playroom for the children, not to keep out the rain; and after all this there is still money to spend on stereo systems, video-cameras, and overseas holidays.

At this stage I am making no ethical judgments about absolute affluence, merely pointing out that it exists. Its defining characteristic is a significant amount of income above the level necessary to provide for the basic human needs of oneself and one's dependents. By this standard, the majority of citizens of Western Europe, North America, Japan, Australia, New Zealand, and the oil-rich Middle Eastern states are all absolutely affluent. To quote McNamara once more:

> "The average citizen of a developed country enjoys wealth beyond the wildest dreams of the 1 billion Deonle in countries with per capita incomes under $200." These, therefore, are the countries—and individuals—who have wealth that they could, without threatening their own basic welfare, transfer to the absolutely poor.

At present, very little is being transferred. Only Sweden, the Netherlands, Norway, and some of the oil-exporting Arab states have reached the modest target, set by the United Nations, of 0.7 percent of gross national product (GNP). Britain gives 0.31 percent of its GNP in official development assistance and a small additional amount in unofficial aid from voluntary organizations. The total comes to about £2 per month per person, and compares with 5.5 percent of GNP spent on alcohol, and 3 percent on to-bacco. Other, even wealthier nations, give little more: Germany gives 0.41 percent and Japan 0.32 percent. The United States gives a mere 0.15 percent of its GNP.

THE MORAL EQUIVALENT OF MURDER?

If these are the facts, we cannot avoid concluding that by not giving more than we do, people in rich countries are allowing those in poor countries to suffer from absolute poverty, with consequent malnutrition, ill health, and death. This is not a conclusion that applies only to governments. It applies to each absolutely affluent individual, for each of us has the opportunity to do something about the situation; for instance, to give our time or money to voluntary organizations like Oxfam, Care, War on Want, Freedom from Hunger, Community Aid Abroad, and so on. If, then, allowing someone to die is not intrinsically different from killing someone, it would seem that we are all murderers.

Is this verdict too harsh? Many will reject it as self-evidently absurd. They would sooner take it as showing that allowing to die cannot be equivalent to killing than as showing that living in an affluent style without contributing to an overseas aid agency is ethically equivalent to going over to Ethiopia and shooting a few peasants. And no doubt, put as bluntly as that, the verdict is too harsh.

There are several significant differences between spending money on luxuries instead of using it to save lives, and deliberately shooting people.

First, the motivation will normally be different. Those who deliberately shoot others go out of their way to kill; they presumably want their victims dead, from malice, sadism, or some equally unpleasant motive. A person who buys a new stereo system presumably wants to enhance her enjoyment of music—not in itself a terrible thing. At worst, spending money on luxuries instead of giving it away indicates selfishness and indifference to the sufferings of others, characteristics that may be undesirable but are not comparable with actual malice or similar motives. Second, it is not difficult for most of us to act in accordance with a rule against killing people; it is, on the other hand, very difficult to obey a rule that commands us to save all the lives we can. To live a comfortable, or even luxurious life it is not necessary to kill anyone; but it is necessary to allow some to die whom we might have saved, for the money that we need to live comfortably could have been given away. Thus the duty to avoid killing is much easier to discharge completely than the duty to save. Saving every life we could would mean cutting our standard of living down to the bare essentials needed to keep us alive.[1] To discharge this duty completely would require a degree of moral heroism utterly different from that required by mere avoidance of killing.

A third difference is the greater certainty of the outcome of shooting when compared with not giving aid. If I point a loaded gun at someone at close range and pull the trigger, it is virtually certain that the person will be killed; whereas the money that I could give might be spent on a project that turns out to be unsuccessful and helps no one.

Fourth, when people are shot there are identifiable individuals who have been harmed. We can point to them and to their grieving families. When I buy my stereo system, I cannot know who my money would have saved if I had given it away. In a time of famine I may see dead bodies and grieving families on television reports, and I might not doubt that my money would have saved some of them; even then it is impossible to point to a body and say that had I not bought the stereo, that person would have survived.

Fifth, it might be said that the plight of the hungry is not my doing, and so I cannot be held responsible for it. The starving would have been starving if I had never existed. If I kill, however, I am responsible for my victims' deaths, for those people would not have died if I had not killed them.

These differences . . . are extrinsic differences, that is, differences normally but not necessarily associated with the distinction between killing and allowing to die. We can imagine cases in which someone allows another to die for malicious or sadistic reasons; we can imagine a world in which there are so few people needing assistance, and they are so easy to assist, that our duty not to allow people to die is as easily discharged as our duty not to kill; we can imagine situations in which the outcome of not helping is as sure as shooting; we can imagine cases in which we can identify the person we allow to die. We can even imagine a case of allowing to die in which, if I had not existed, the person would not have died—for instance, a case in which If I had not been in a position to help (though I don't help) someone else would have been in my position and would have helped. . . .

The extrinsic differences that *normally* mark off killing and allowing to die . . . explain why we *normally* regard killing as much worse than allowing to die.

To explain our conventional ethical attitudes is not to justify them. Do the five differences not only explain, but also justify, out attitudes? Let us consider them one by one:

1. Take the lack of an identifiable victim first. Suppose that I am a traveling salesperson, selling tinned food, and I learn that a batch of tins contains a contaminant, the known effect of which, when consumed, is to double the risk that the consumer will die from stomach cancer. Suppose I continue to sell the tins. My decision may have no identifiable victims. Some of those who eat the food will die from cancer. The proportion of consumers dying in this way will be twice that of the community at large, but who among the consumers died because they ate what I sold, and who would have contracted the disease anyway? It is impossible to tell; but surely this impossibility makes my decision no less reprehensible than it would have been had the contaminant had more readily detectable, though equally fatal, effects.

2. The lack of certainty that by giving money I could save a life does reduce the wrongness of not giving, by comparison with deliberate killing; but it is insufficient to show that not giving is acceptable conduct. The motorist who speeds through pedestrian crossings, heedless of anyone who might be on them, is not a murderer. She may never actually hit a pedestrian; yet what she does is very wrong indeed.

3. The notion of responsibility for acts rather than omissions is more puzzling. On the one hand, we feel ourselves to be under a greater obligation to help those whose misfortunes we have caused. (It is for this reason that advocates of overseas aid often argue that Western nations have created the poverty of third world nations, through forms of economic exploitation that go back to the colonial system.) On the other hand, any consequentialist would insist that we are responsible for all the consequences of our actions, and if a consequence of my spending money on a luxury item is that someone dies, I am responsible for that death. It is true that the person would have died even if I had never existed, but what is the relevance of that? The fact is that I do exist, and the consequentialist will say that our responsibilities derive from the world as it is, not as it might have been.

One way of making sense of the nonconsequentialist view of responsibility is by basing it on a theory of rights of the kind proposed by John Locke or, more recently, Robert Nozick. If everyone has a right to life, and this right is a right *against* others who might threaten my life, but not a right to assistance from others when my life is in danger, then we can understand the feeling that we are responsible for acting to kill but not for omitting to save. The former violates the rights of others, the latter does not. Should we accept such a theory of rights? If we build up our theory of rights by imagining, as Locke and Nozick do, individuals living independently from each other in a "state of nature," it may seem natural to adopt a conception of rights in which as long as each leaves the other alone, no rights are violated. I might, on this view, quite properly have maintained my independent existence if I had wished to do so. So if I do not make you any worse off than you would have been if I had had nothing at all to do with you, how can I have violated your rights? But why start from such an unhistorical, abstract, and ultimately inexplicable idea as an independent individual? Our ancestors were—like other primates—social beings long before they were human beings, and could not have developed the abilities and capacities of human beings if they had not been social beings first. In any case, we are not, now, isolated individuals. So why should we assume that rights must be restricted to rights against interference? We might, instead, adopt the view that taking rights to life seriously is incompatible with standing by and watching people die when one could easily save them.

4. What of the difference in motivation? That a person does not positively wish for the death of another lessens the severity of the blame she deserves; but not by as much as our present attitudes to giving aid suggest. The behavior of the speeding motorist is again comparable, for such motorists usually have no desire at all to kill anyone. They merely enjoy speeding and are indifferent to the consequences. Despite their lack of malice, those who kill with cars deserve not only blame but also severe punishment.

5. Finally, the fact that to avoid killing people is normally not difficult, whereas to save all one possibly could save is heroic, must make an important difference to our attitude to failure to do what the respective principles demand. Not to kill is a minimum standard of acceptable conduct we can require of everyone; to save all one possibly could is not something that can realistically be required,

especially not in societies accustomed to giving as little as ours do. Given the generally accepted standards, people who give, say, $1,000 a year to an overseas aid organization are more aptly praised for above average generosity than blamed for giving less than they might. The appropriateness of praise and blame is, however, a separate issue from the rightness or wrongness of actions. The former evaluates the agent: the latter evaluates the action. Perhaps many people who give $1,000 really ought to give at least $5,000, but to blame them for not giving more could be counterproductive. It might make them feel that what is required is too demanding, and if one is going to be blamed anyway, one might as well not give anything at all.

(That an ethic that put saving all one possibly can on the same footing as not killing would be an ethic for saints or heroes should not lead us to assume that the alternative must be an ethic that makes it obligatory not to kill, but puts us under no obligation to save anyone. There are positions in between these extremes, as we shall soon see.)

Here is a summary of the five differences that normally exist between killing and allowing to die, in the context of absolute poverty and overseas aid. The lack of an identifiable victim is of no moral significance, though it may play an important role in explaining our attitudes. The idea that we are directly responsible for those we kill, but not for those we do not help, depends on a questionable notion of responsibility and may need to be based on a controversial theory of rights. Differences in certainty and motivation are ethically significant, and show that not aiding the poor is not to be condemned as murdering them; it could, however, be on a par with killing someone as a result of reckless driving, which is serious enough. Finally the difficulty of completely discharging the duty of saving all one possibly can makes it inappropriate to blame those who fall short of this target as we blame those who kill; but this does not show that the act itself is less serious. Nor does it indicate anything about those who, far from saving all they possibly can, make no effort to save anyone.

These conclusions suggest a new approach. Instead of attempting to deal with the contrast between affluence and poverty by comparing not saving with deliberate killing, let us consider afresh whether we have an obligation to assist those whose lives are in danger, and if so, how this obligation applies to the present world situation.

THE OBLIGATION TO ASSIST

THE ARGUMENT FOR AN OBLIGATION TO ASSIST

The path from the library at my university to the humanities lecture theatre passes a shallow ornamental pond. Suppose that on my way to give a lecture I notice that a small child has fallen in and is in danger of drowning. Would anyone deny that I ought to wade in and pull the child out? This will mean getting my clothes muddy and either canceling my lecture or delaying it until I can find something dry to change into; but compared with the avoidable death of a child this is insignificant.

A plausible principle that would support the judgment that I ought to pull the child out is this: if it is in our power to prevent something very bad from happening, without thereby sacrificing anything of comparable moral significance, we ought to do it. This principle seems uncontroversial. . . .

Nevertheless the uncontroversial appearance of the principle that we ought to prevent what is bad when we can do so without sacrificing anything of comparable moral significance is deceptive. If it were taken seriously and acted upon, our lives and our world would be fundamentally changed. For the principle applies, not just to rare situations in which one can save a child from a pond, but to the everyday situation in which we can assist those living in absolute poverty. In saying this I assume that absolute poverty, with its hunger and malnutrition, lack of shelter, illiteracy, disease, high infant mortality, and low life expectancy, is a bad thing. And I assume that it is within the power of the affluent to reduce absolute poverty, without sacrificing anything of comparable moral significance. If these two assumptions and the principle we have been discussing are correct, we have an obligation to help those in absolute poverty that is no less strong than our obligation to rescue a drowning child from a pond. Not to help would be wrong, whether or not it is intrinsically equivalent to killing. Helping is not, as conventionally thought, a charitable act that it is praiseworthy to do, but not wrong to omit; it is something that everyone ought to do.

This is the argument for an obligation to assist. Set out more formally, it would look like this.

> *First premise:* If we can prevent something bad without sacrificing anything of comparable significance, we ought to do it.
>
> *Second premise:* Absolute poverty is bad.
>
> *Third premise:* There is some absolute poverty we can prevent without sacrificing anything of comparable moral significance.
>
> *Conclusion:* We ought to prevent some absolute poverty. . . .

OBJECTIONS TO THE ARGUMENT

Taking Care of Our Own

Anyone who has worked to increase overseas aid will have come across the argument that we should look after those near us, our families, and then the poor in our own country, before we think about poverty in distant places.

No doubt we do instinctively prefer to help those who are close to us. Few could stand by and watch a child drown; many can ignore a famine in Africa. But the question is not what we usually do, but what we ought to do, and it is difficult to see any sound moral justification for the view that distance, or community membership, makes a crucial difference to our obligations. . . .

Property Myths

Do people have a right to private property, a right that contradicts the view that they are under an obligation to give some of their wealth away to those in absolute poverty?

According to some theories of rights (for instance, Robert Nozick's), provided one has acquired one's property without the use of unjust means like force and fraud, one may be entitled to enormous wealth while others starve. This individualistic conception of rights is in contrast to other views, like the early Christian doctrine to be found in the works of Thomas Aquinas, which holds that since property exists for the satisfaction of human needs, "whatever a man has in superabundance is owed, of natural right, to the poor for their sustenance." A socialist would also, of course, see wealth as belonging to the community rather than the individual, while utilitarians, whether socialist or not, would be prepared to override property rights to prevent great evils.

Does the argument for an obligation to assist others therefore presuppose one of these other theories of property rights, and not an individualistic theory like Nozick's? Not necessarily. A theory of property rights can insist on our *right* to retain wealth without pronouncing on whether the rich *ought* to give to the poor. Nozick, for example, rejects the use of compulsory means like taxation to redistribute income, but suggests that we can achieve the ends we deem morally desirable by voluntary means. So Nozick would reject the claim that rich people have an "obligation" to give to the poor, in so far as this implies that the poor have a right to our aid, but might accept that giving is something we ought to do and failing to give, though within one's rights, is wrong—for there is more to an ethical life than respecting the rights of others.

The argument for an obligation to assist can survive, with only minor modifications, even if we accept an individualistic theory of property rights. In any case, however, I do not think we should accept such a theory. It leaves too much to chance to be an acceptable ethical view. . . .

Population and the Ethics of Triage

Perhaps the most serious objection to the argument that we have an obligation to assist is that since the major cause of absolute poverty is overpopulation, helping those now in poverty will only ensure that yet more people are born to live in poverty in the future.

In its most extreme form, this objection is taken to show that we should adopt a policy of "triage." The term comes from medical policies adopted in wartime. With too few doctors to cope with all the casualties, the wounded were divided into three categories: those who would probably survive without medical assistance, those who might survive if they received assistance, but otherwise probably would not, and those who even with medical assistance probably would not survive. Only those in the middle category were given medical assistance. . . . In support of this view Garrett Hardin has offered a metaphor: we in the rich nations are like the occupants of a crowded lifeboat adrift in a sea full of drowning people. If we try to save the drowning by bringing them aboard, our boat will be overloaded and we shall all drown. Since it is better that some survive than none, we should leave the others to drown. In the world today, according to Hardin, "lifeboat ethics" apply. The rich should leave the poor to starve, for otherwise the poor will drag the rich down with them.

Against this view, some writers have argued that overpopulation is a myth. The world produces ample food to feed its population, and could, according to some estimates, feed ten times as many. People are hungry not because there are too many but because of inequitable land distribution, the manipulation of third world economies by the developed nations, wastage of food in the West, and so on. Putting aside the controversial issue of the extent to which food production might one day be increased, it is true, as we have already seen, that the world now produces enough to feed its inhabitants—the amount lost by being fed to animals itself being enough to meet existing grain shortages. Nevertheless population growth cannot be ignored. Bangladesh could, with land reform and using better techniques, feed its present population of 115 million; but by the year 2000, according to the United Nations Population Division estimates, its population will be 150 million. The enormous effort that will have to go into feeding an extra 35 million people, all added to the population within a decade, means that Bangladesh must develop at full speed to stay where it is. Other low-income countries are in similar situations. By the end of the century, Ethiopia's population is expected to rise from 49 to 66 million; Somalia's from 7 to 9 million, India's from 853 to 1,041 million, Zaire's from 35 to 49 million.[2]

What will happen if the world population continues to grow? It cannot do so indefinitely. It will be checked by a decline in birth rates or a rise in death rates. Those who advocate triage are proposing that we allow the population growth of some countries to be checked by a rise in death rates—that is, by increased malnutrition, and related diseases; by widespread famines; by increased infant mortality; and by epidemics of infectious diseases. . . .

Advocates of triage are rightly concerned with the long-term consequences of our actions. They say that helping the poor and starving now merely ensures more poor and starving in the future. When our capacity to help is finally unable to cope—as one day it must be—the suffering will be greater than it would be if we stopped helping now. If this is correct, there is nothing we can do to prevent absolute starvation and poverty, in the long run, and so we have no obligation to assist. Nor does it seem reasonable to hold that under these circumstances people have a right to our assistance. If we do accept such a right, irrespective of the consequences, we are saying that, in Hardin's metaphor, we should continue to haul the drowning into our lifeboat until the boat sinks and we all drown. If triage is to be rejected it must be tackled on its own ground, within the framework of consequentialist ethics. Here it is vulnerable. . . .

The policy of triage involves a certain, very great evil: population control by famine and disease. Tens of millions would die slowly. Hundreds of millions would continue to live in absolute poverty, at the very margin of existence. Against this prospect, advocates of the policy place a possible evil that is greater still: the same process of famine and disease, taking place in, say, 50 years' time, when the world's population may be three times its present level, and the number who will die from famine, or struggle on in absolute poverty, will be that much greater. The question is: how probable is this forecast that continued assistance now will lead to greater disasters in the future?

Forecasts of population growth are notoriously fallible, and theories about the factors that affect it remain speculative. One theory, at least as plausible as any other, is that countries pass through a "demographic transition" as their standard of living rises. When people are very poor and have no access to modern medicine their fertility is high, but population is kept in check by high death rates. The introduction of sanitation, modern medical techniques, and other improvements reduces the death rate, but initially has little effect on the birth rate. Then population grows rapidly. Some poor countries, especially in sub-Saharan Africa, are now in this phase. If standards of living continue to rise, however, couples begin to realize that to have the same number of children surviving to maturity as in the past, they do not need to give birth to as many children as their parents did. The need for children to provide economic support in old age diminishes. Improved education and the emancipation and employment of women also reduce the birth-rate, and so population growth begins to level off. Most rich nations have reached this stage, and their populations are growing only very slowly, if at all. If this theory is right, there is an alternative to the disasters accepted as inevitable by supporters of triage. We can assist poor countries to raise the living standards of the poorest members of their population. We can encourage the governments of these countries to enact land reform measures, improve education, and liberate women from a purely child-bearing role. We can also help other countries to make contraception and sterilization widely available. There is a fair chance that these measures will hasten the onset of the demographic transition and bring population growth down to a manageable level. According to United Nations estimates, in 1965 the average woman in the third world gave birth to six children, and only 8 percent were using some form of contraception; by 1991 the average number of children had dropped to just below four, and more than half the women in the third world were taking contraceptive measures. Notable successes in encouraging the use of contraception had occurred in Thailand, Indonesia, Mexico, Columbia, Brazil, and Bangladesh. This achievement reflected a relatively low expenditure in developing countries—considering the size and significance of the problem—of $3 billion annually, with only 20 percent of this sum coming from developed nations. So expenditure in this area seems likely to be highly cost-effective. Success cannot be guaranteed; but the evidence suggests that we can reduce population growth by improving economic security and education, and making contraceptives more widely available. This prospect makes triage ethically unacceptable. We cannot allow millions to die from starvation and disease when there is a reasonable probability that population can be brought under control without such horrors.

Population growth is therefore not a reason against giving overseas aid, although it should make us think about the kind of aid to give. Instead of food handouts, it may be better to give aid that leads to a slowing of population growth. . . . One awkward question remains. What should we do about a poor and already overpopulated country that, for religious or nationalistic reasons, restricts the use of contraceptives and refuses to slow its population growth? Should we nevertheless offer development assistance? Or should we make our offer conditional on effective steps being taken to reduce the birth rate? To the latter course, some would object that putting conditions on aid is an attempt to impose our own ideas on independent sovereign nations. So it is—but is this imposition unjustifiable? If the argument for an obligation to assist is sound, we have an obligation to reduce absolute poverty; but we have no obligation to make sacrifices that, to the best of our knowledge, have no prospect of reducing poverty in the long run. Hence we have no obligation to assist countries whose governments have policies that will make our aid ineffective. This could be very harsh on poor citizens of these countries—for they may have no say in the government's policies—but we will help more people in the long run by using our resources where they are most effective. (The same principles may apply, incidentally, to countries that refuse to take other steps that could make assistance effective—like refusing to reform systems of land holding that impose intolerable burdens on poor tenant farmers.) . . .

Too High a Standard?

The final objection to the argument for an obligation to assist is that it sets a standard so high that none but a saint could attain it. This objection comes in at least three versions. The first maintains that, human nature being what it is, we cannot achieve so high a standard, and since it is absurd to say that we ought to do what we cannot do, we must reject the claim that we ought to give so much. The second version asserts that even if we could achieve so high a standard, to do so would be undesirable. The third version of the objection is that to set so high a standard is undesirable because it will be perceived as too difficult to reach, and will discourage many from even attempting to do so.

Those who put forward the first version of the objection are often influenced by the fact that we have evolved from a natural process in which those with a high degree of concern for their own interests, or the interests of their offspring and kin, can be expected to leave more descendants in future generations, and eventually to completely replace any who are entirely altruistic. Thus the biologist Garrett Hardin has argued, in support of his "lifeboat ethics," that altruism can only exist "on a small scale, over the short term, and within small, intimate groups"; while Richard Dawkins has written, in his provocative book *The Selfish Gene*: "Much as we might wish to believe otherwise, universal love and the welfare of the species as a whole are concepts which simply do not make evolutionary sense." . . . When we have money to spend on luxuries and others are starving, however, it is clear that we can all give much more than we do give. . . . Nor is there, as we approach closer to this standard, any barrier beyond which we cannot go. For that reason there is no basis for saying that the impartial standard is mistaken because "ought" implies "can" and we cannot be impartial.

The second version of the objection has been put by several philosophers during the past decade, among them Susan Wolf in a forceful article entitled "Moral Saints." Wolf argues that if we all took the kind of moral stance defended in this chapter, we would have to do without a great deal that makes life interesting: opera, gourmet cooking, elegant clothes, and professional sport, for a start. The kind of life we come to see as ethically required of us would be a single-minded pursuit of the overall good, lacking that broad diversity of interests and activities that, on a less demanding view, can be part of our ideal of a good life for a human being. To this, however, one can respond that while the rich and varied life that Wolf upholds as an ideal may be the most desirable form of life for a human being in a world of plenty, it is wrong to assume that it remains a good life in a world in which buying luxuries for oneself means accepting the continued avoidable suffering of others. . . . The life-or-death needs of others must take priority. . . .

The third version of the objection asks: might it not be counterproductive to demand that people give up so much? Might not people say: "As I can't do what is morally required anyway, I won't bother to give at all." . . .

Is it true that the standard set by our argument is so high as to be counterproductive? There is not much evidence to go by, but discussions of the argument, with students and others have led me to think it might be. Yet, the conventionally accepted standard—a few coins in a collection tin when one is waved under your nose—is obviously far too low. What level should we advocate? Any figure will be arbitrary, but there may be something to be said for a round percentage of one's income like, say, 10 percent—more than a token donation, yet not so high as to be beyond all but saints. . . .

---

[1]Strictly, we would need to cut down on the minimum level compatible with earning the income which, after providing for our needs, left us most to give away. Thus if my present position earns me, say, $40,000 a year, but requires me to spend $5,000 a year on dressing respectably and maintaining a car, I cannot save more people by giving away the car and clothes if that will mean taking a job that, although it does not involve me in these expenses, earns me only $20,000.

[2]Ominously, . . . the signs are that the situation is becoming even worse than was then predicted. In 1979 Bangladesh had a population of 80 million and it was predicted that by 2000 its population would reach 146 million; Ethiopia's was only 29 million, and was predicted to reach 54 million; and India's was 620 million and predicted to reach 958 million.

PARENTALISM

J. S. MILL

On Liberty

CHAPTER IV

What, then, is the rightful limit to the sovereignty of the individual over himself? Where does the authority of society begin? How much of human life should be assigned to individuality, and how much to society?

Each will receive its proper share, if each has that which more particularly concerns it. To individuality should belong the part of life in which it is chiefly the individual that is interested; to society, the part which chiefly interests society.

Though society is not founded on a contract, and though no good purpose is answered by inventing a contract in order to deduce social obligations from it, every one who receives the protection of society owes a return for the benefit, and the fact of living in society renders it indispensable that each should be bound to observe a certain line of conduct towards the rest. This conduct consists, first, in not injuring the interests of one another; (or rather certain interests, which, either by express legal provision or by tacit understanding, ought to be considered as rights); and secondly, in each person's bearing his share (to be fixed on some equitable principle) of the labours and sacrifices incurred for defending the society or its members from injury and molestation. These conditions society is justified in enforcing at all costs to those who endeavour to withhold fulfilment. Nor is this all that society may do. The acts of an individual may be hurtful to others, or wanting in due consideration for their welfare, without going the length of violating any of their constituted rights. The offender may then be justly punished by opinion, though not by law. As soon as any part of a person's conduct affects prejudicially the interests of others, society has jurisdiction over it, and the question whether the general welfare will or will not be promoted by interfering with it, becomes open to discussion. But there is no room for entertaining any such question when a person's conduct affects the interests of no persons besides himself, or needs not affect them unless they like (all the persons concerned being of full age, and the ordinary amount of understanding). In all such cases there should be perfect freedom, legal and social, to do the action and stand the consequences.

I fully admit that the mischief which a person does to himself may seriously affect, both through their sympathies and their interests, those nearly connected with him, and in a minor degree, society at large. When, by conduct of this sort, a person is led to violate a distinct and assignable obligation to any other person or persons, the case is taken out of the self-regarding class, and becomes amenable to moral disapprobation in the proper sense of the term. If, for example, a man, through intemperance or extravagance, becomes unable to pay his debts, or, having undertaken the moral responsibility of a family, becomes from the same cause incapable of supporting or educating them, he is deservedly reprobated, and might be justly punished; but it is for the breach of duty to his family or creditors, not for the extravagance. . . . No person ought to be punished simply for being drunk; but a soldier or a policeman should be punished for being drunk on duty. Whenever, in short, there is a definite damage, or a definite risk of damage, either to an individual or to the public, the case is taken out of the province of liberty, and placed in that of morality or law.

But with regard to the merely contingent, or, as it may be called, constructive injury which a person causes to society, by conduct which neither violates any specific duty to the public, nor occasions perceptible hurt to any assignable individual except himself; the inconvenience is one which society can afford to bear, for the sake of the greater good of human freedom. If grown persons are to be punished for not taking proper care of themselves, I would rather it were for their own sake, than under pretence of preventing them from impairing their capacity of rendering to society benefits which society does not pretend it has a right to exact. But I cannot consent to argue the point as if society had no means of bringing its weaker members up to its ordinary standard of rational conduct, except waiting till they do something irrational, and then punishing them, legally or morally, for it. Society has had absolute power over them during all the early portion of their existence: it has had the whole period of childhood and nonage in which to try whether it could make them capable of rational conduct in life. The existing generation is master both of the training and the entire circumstances of the generation to come; it cannot indeed make them perfectly wise and good, because it is itself so lamentably deficient in goodness and wisdom; and its best efforts are not always, in individual cases, its most successful ones; but it is perfectly well able to make the rising generation, as a whole, as good as, and a little better than, itself. If society lets any considerable number of its members grow up

mere children, incapable of being acted on by rational consideration of distant motives, society has itself to blame for the consequences. . . .

But the strongest of all the arguments against the interference of the public with
purely personal conduct, is that when it does interfere, the odds are that it interferes
wrongly, and in the wrong place. On questions of social morality, of duty to others,
the opinion of the public, that is, of an overruling majority, though often wrong, is
likely to be still oftener right; because on such questions they are only required to
judge of their own interests; of the manner in which some mode of conduct, if allowed to be practised, would affect themselves. But the opinion of a similar majority,
imposed as a law on the minority, on questions of self-regarding conduct, is quite as
likely to be wrong as right; for in these cases public opinion means, at the best, some
people's opinion of what is good or bad for other people; while very often it does not
even mean that; the public, with the most perfect indifference, passing over the pleasure or convenience of those whose conduct they censure, and considering only their
own preference. There are many who consider as an injury to themselves any conduct
which they have a distaste for, and resent it as an outrage to their feelings; as a religious bigot, when charged with disregarding the religious feelings of others, has been
known to retort that they disregard his feelings, by persisting in their abominable worship or creed. . . .

GERALD DWORKIN

Paternalism

Neither one person, nor any number of persons, is warranted in saying to another
human creature of ripe-years, that he shall not do with his life for his own benefit
what he chooses to do with it. [Mill]

I do not want to go along with a volunteer basis. I think a fellow should be compelled
to become better and not let him use his discretion whether he wants to get smarter,
more healthy or more honest. [General Hershey]

I take as my starting point the "one very simple principle" proclaimed by Mill *On
Liberty* . . .

That principle is, that the sole end for which mankind are warranted, individually
or collectively, in interfering with the liberty of action of any of their number, is self-
protection. That the only purpose for which power can be rightfully exercised over
any member of a civilized community, against his will, is to prevent harm to others.
He cannot rightfully be compelled to do or forbear because it will be better for him to
do so, because it will make him happier, because, in the opinion of others, to do so
would be wise, or even right.

This principle is neither "one" nor "very simple." It is at least two principles; one
asserting that self-protection or the prevention of harm to others is sometimes a sufficient warrant and the other claiming that the individual's own good is *never* a suffi-

cient warrant for the exercise of compulsion either by the society as a whole or by its individual members. I assume that no one, with the possible exception of extreme pacifists or anarchists, questions the correctness of the first half of the principle. This essay is an examination of the negative claim embodied in Mill's principle—the objection to paternalistic interferences with a man's liberty.

By paternalism I shall understand roughly the interference with a person's liberty of action justified by reasons referring exclusively to the welfare, good, happiness, needs, interests or values of the person being coerced. One is always well-advised to illustrate one's definitions by examples but it is not easy to find "pure" examples of paternalistic interferences. For almost any piece of legislation is justified by several different kinds of reasons and even if historically a piece of legislation can be shown to have been introduced for purely paternalistic motives, it may be that advocates of the legislation with an antipaternalistic outlook can find sufficient reasons justifying the legislation without appealing to the reasons which were originally adduced to support it. Thus, for example, it may be that the original legislation requiring motorcyclists to wear safety helmets was introduced for purely paternalistic reasons. But the Rhode Island Supreme Court recently upheld such legislation on the grounds that it was "not persuaded that the legislature is powerless to prohibit individuals from pursuing a course of conduct which could conceivably result in their becoming public charges," thus clearly introducing reasons of a quite different kind. Now I regard this decision as being based on reasoning of a very dubious nature but it illustrates the kind of problem one has in finding examples. The following is a list of the kinds of interferences I have in mind as being paternalistic.

1. Laws requiring motorcyclists to wear safety helmets when operating their machines.

2. Laws forbidding persons from swimming at a public beach when lifeguards are not on duty.

3. Laws making suicide a criminal offense.

4. Laws making it illegal for women and children to work at certain types of jobs.

5. Laws regulating certain kinds of sexual conduct, for example, homosexuality among consenting adults in private.

6. Laws regulating the use of certain drugs which may have harmful consequences to the user but do not lead to antisocial conduct.

7. Laws requiring a license to engage in certain professions with those not receiving a license subject to fine or jail sentence if they do engage in the practice.

8. Laws compelling people to spend a specified fraction of their income on the purchase of retirement annuities (Social Security).

9. Laws forbidding various forms of gambling (often justified on the grounds that the poor are more likely to throw away their money on such activities than the rich who can afford to).

10. Laws regulating the maximum rates of interest for loans.

11. Laws against duelling.

In addition to laws which attach criminal or civil penalties to certain kinds of action there are laws, rules, regulations, decrees which make it either difficult or impossible for people to carry out their plans and which are also justified on paternalistic grounds. Examples of this are:

1. Laws regulating the types of contracts which will be upheld as valid by the courts, for example, . . . no man may make a valid contract for perpetual involuntary servitude.

2. Not allowing assumption of risk as a defense to an action based on the violation of a safety statute.

3. Not allowing as a defense to a charge of murder or assault the consent of the victim.

4. Requiring members of certain religious sects to have compulsory blood transfusions. This is made possible by not allowing the patient to have recourse to civil suits for assault and battery and by means of injunctions.

5. Civil commitment procedures when these are specifically justified on the basis of preventing the person being committed from harming himself. The D.C. Hospitalization of the Mentally Ill Act provides for involuntary hospitalization of a person who "is mentally ill, and because of that illness, is likely to injure himself or others if allowed to remain at liberty." The term injure in this context applies to unintentional as well as intentional injuries.

All of my examples are of existing restrictions on the liberty of individuals. Obviously one can think of interferences which have not yet been imposed. Thus one might ban the sale of cigarettes. . . .

Bearing these examples in mind, let me return to a characterization of paternalism. I said earlier that I meant by the term, roughly, interference with a person's liberty for his own good. But, as some of the examples show, the class of persons whose good is involved is not always identical with the class of persons whose freedom is restricted. Thus, in the case of professional licensing it is the practitioner who is directly interfered with but it is the would-be patient whose interests are presumably being served. Not allowing the consent of the victim to be a defense to certain types of crime primarily affects the would-be aggressor but it is the interests of the willing victim that we are trying to protect. Sometimes a person may fall into both classes as would be the case if we banned the manufacture and sale of cigarettes and a given manufacturer happened to be a smoker as well.

Thus we may first divide paternalistic interferences into "pure" and "impure" cases. In "pure" paternalism the class of persons whose freedom is restricted is identical with the class of persons whose benefit is intended to be promoted by such restrictions. Examples: the making of suicide a crime, requiring a Christian Scientist to receive a blood transfusion. In the case of "impure" paternalism in trying to protect the welfare of a class of persons we find that the only way to do so will involve restricting the freedom of other persons besides those who are benefitted. Now it might be thought that there are no cases of "impure" paternalism since any such case could always be justified on nonpaternalistic grounds, that is, in terms of preventing harm to others. Thus we might ban cigarette manufacturers from continuing to manufacture their product on the grounds that we are preventing them from causing illness to others in the same way that we prevent other manufacturers from releasing pollutants into the atmosphere, thereby causing danger to the members of the community. The difference is, however, that in the former but not the latter case the harm is of such a nature that it could be avoided by those individuals affected if they so chose. The incurring of the harm requires, so to speak, the active cooperation of the victim. It would be mistaken theoretically and hypocritical in practice to assert that our interference in such cases is just like our interference in standard cases of protecting others from harm. At the very least someone interfered with in this way can reply that no one is complaining about his activities. It may be that impure paternalism requires arguments or reasons of a stronger kind in order to be justified, since there are persons who are losing a portion of their liberty and they do not even have the solace of having it done "in their own interest." Of course in some sense, if paternalistic justifications are ever correct, then we are protecting others, we are preventing some from injuring others, but it is important to see the differences between this and the standard case.

Paternalism then will always involve limitations on the liberty of some individuals in their own interest but it may also extend to interferences with the liberty of parties whose interests are not in question.

Finally, by way of some more preliminary analysis, I want to distinguish paternalistic interference with liberty from a related type with which it is often confused. Consider, for example, legislation which forbids employees to work more than, say, 40 hours per week. It is sometimes argued that such legislation is paternalistic for if employees desired such a restriction on their hours of work they could agree among themselves to impose it voluntarily. But because they do not the society imposes its own conception of their best interests upon them by the use of coercion. Hence this is paternalism.

Now it may be that some legislation of this nature is, in fact, paternalistically motivated. I am not denying that. All I want to point out is that there is another possible way of justifying such measures which is not paternalistic in nature. It is not paternalistic because, as Mill puts it in a similar context, such measures are "required not to overrule the judgment of individuals respecting their own interest, but to give effect to that judgment: they being unable to give effect to it except by concert, which concert again cannot be effectual unless it receives validity and sanction from the law" (*Principles of Political Economy*).

The line of reasoning here is a familiar one first found in Hobbes and developed with great sophistication by contemporary economists in the last decade or so. There are restrictions which are in the interests of a class of persons taken collectively but are such that the immediate interest of each individual is furthered by his violating the rule when others adhere to it. In such cases the individuals involved may need the use of compulsion to give effect to their collective judgment of their own interest by guaranteeing each individual compliance by the others. In these cases compulsion is not used to achieve some benefit which is not recognized to be a benefit by those concerned, but rather because it is the only feasible means of achieving some benefit which *is* recognized as such by all concerned. This way of viewing matters provides us with another characterization of paternalism in general. Paternalism might be thought of as the use of coercion to achieve a good which is not recognized as such by those persons for whom the good is intended. Again while this formulation captures the heart of the matter—it is surely what Mill is objecting to in *On Liberty*—the matter is not always quite like that. For example, when we force motorcyclists to wear helmets we are trying to promote a good—the protection of the person from injury—which is surely recognized by most of the individuals concerned. It is not that a cyclist doesn't value his bodily integrity; rather, as a supporter of such legislation would put it, he either places, perhaps irrationally, another value or good (freedom from wearing a helmet) above that of physical well-being or, perhaps, while recognizing the danger in the abstract, he either does not fully appreciate it or he underestimates the likelihood of its occurring. But now we are approaching the question of possible justifications of paternalistic measures and the rest of this essay will be devoted to that question.

I shall begin for dialectical purposes by discussing Mill's objections to paternalism and then go on to discuss more positive proposals.

An initial feature that strikes one is the absolute nature of Mill's prohibitions against paternalism. It is so unlike the carefully qualified admonitions of Mill and his fellow utilitarians on other moral issues. He speaks of self-protection as the *sole* end warranting coercion, of the individual's own goals as *never* being a sufficient warrant. Contrast this with his discussion of the prohibition against lying in *Utilitarianism*:

> Yet that even this rule, sacred as it is, admits of possible exception, is acknowledged by all moralists, the chief of which is where the with-holding of some fact . . . would save an individual . . . from great and unmerited evil.

The same tentativeness is present when he deals with justice:

> It is confessedly unjust to break faith with any one: to violate an engagement, either express or implied, or disappoint expectations raised by our own conduct, at least if we have raised these expectations knowingly and voluntarily. Like all the other obligations of justice already spoken of, this one is not regarded as absolute, but as capable of being overruled by a stronger obligation of justice on the other side.

This anomaly calls for some explanation. The structure of Mill's argument is as follows:

1. Since restraint is an evil the burden of proof is on those who propose such restraint.

2. Since the conduct which is being considered is purely self-regarding, the normal appeal to the protection of the interests of others is not available.

3. Therefore we have to consider whether reasons involving reference to the individual's own good, happiness, welfare, or interests are sufficient to overcome the burden of justification.

4. We either cannot advance the interests of the individual by compulsion, or the attempt to do so involves evils which outweigh the good done.

5. Hence the promotion of the individual's own interests does not provide a sufficient warrant for the use of compulsion.

Clearly the operative premise here is (4), and it is bolstered by claims about the status of the individual as judge and appraiser of his welfare, interests, needs, et cetera:

> With respect to his own feelings and circumstances, the most ordinary man or woman has means of knowledge immeasurable surpassing those that can be possessed by any one else.
>
> He is the man most interested in his own well-being: the interest which any other person, except in cases of strong personal attachment, can have in it is trifling, compared to that which he himself has.
>
> These claims are used to support the following generalizations concerning the utility of compulsion for paternalistic purposes.
>
> The interferences of society to overrule his judgment and purposes in what only regards himself must be grounded on general presumptions; which may be altogether wrong, and even if right, are as likely as not to be misapplied to individual cases.
>
> But the strongest of all the arguments against the interference of the public with purely personal conduct is that when it does interfere, the odds are that it interferes wrongly and in the wrong place.
>
> All errors which the individual is likely to commit against advice and warning are far outweighed by the evil of allowing others to constrain him to what they deem his good.

Performing the utilitarian calculation by balancing the advantages and disadvantages, we find that: "Mankind are greater gainers by suffering each other to live as seems good to themselves, than by compelling each other to live as seems good to the rest." Ergo, (4).

This classical case of a utilitarian argument with all the premises spelled out is not the only line of reasoning present in Mill's discussion. There are asides, and more than asides, which look quite different and I shall deal with them later. But this is clearly the main channel of Mill's thought and it is one which has been subjected to vigorous attack from the moment it appeared—most often by fellow utilitarians. The link that they have usually seized on is, as Fitzjames Stephen put it in *Liberty, Equality, Fraternity,* the absence of proof that the "mass of adults are so well acquainted with their own interests and so much disposed to pursue them that no compulsion or restraint put upon them by any others for the purpose of promoting their interest can really promote them." Even so sympathetic a critic as H. L. A. Hart is forced to the conclusion that:

> In Chapter 5 of his essay [On Liberty] Mill carried his protests against paternalism to lengths that may now appear to us as fantastic. . . . No doubt if we no longer sympathise with this criticism this is due, in part, to a general decline in the belief that individuals know their own interest best.
>
> Mill endows the average individual with "too much of the psychology of a middle-aged man whose desires are relatively fixed, not liable to be artificially stimulated by external influences; who knows what he wants and what gives him satisfaction or happiness; and who pursues these things when he can."

Now it is interesting to note that Mill himself was aware of some of the limitations on the doctrine that the individual is the best judge of his own interests. In his discussion of government intervention in general (even where the intervention does not interfere with liberty but provides alternative institutions to those of the market) after making claims which are parallel to those just discussed, for example, "People understand their own business and their own interests better, and care for them more, than the government does, or can be expected to do," he goes on to an intelligent discussion of the "very large and conspicuous exceptions" to the maxim that:

> Most persons take a juster and more intelligent view of their own interest, and of the means of promoting it than can either be prescribed to them by a general enactment of the legislature, or pointed out in the particular case by a public functionary.

Thus there are things

> of which the utility does not consist in ministering to inclinations, nor in serving the daily uses of life, and the want of which is least felt where the need is greatest. This is peculiarly true of those things which are chiefly useful as tending to raise the character of human beings. The uncultivated cannot be competent judges of cultivation. Those who most need to be made wiser and better, usually desire it least, and, if they desire it, would be incapable of finding the way to it by their own lights.
>
> . . . A second exception to the doctrine that individuals are the best judges of their own interest, is when an individual attempts to decide irrevocably now what will be best for his interest at some future and distant time. The presumption in favor of individual judgment is only legitimate, where the judgement is grounded on actual, and especially on present, personal experience; not where it is formed antecedently to experience, and not suffered to be reversed even after experience has condemned it.

The upshot of these exceptions is that Mill does not declare that there should never be government interference with the economy but rather that

> . . . in every instance, the burden of making out a strong case should be thrown not on those who resist but those who recommend government interference. Letting alone, in short, should be the general practice; every departure from it, unless required by some great good, is a certain evil.

In short, we get a presumption, not an absolute prohibition. The question is why doesn't the argument against paternalism go the same way?

I suggest that the answer lies in seeing that in addition to a purely utilitarian argument Mill uses another as well. As a utilitarian, Mill has to show, in Fitzjames Stephen's words, that: "Self-protection apart, no good object can be attained by any compulsion which is not in itself a greater evil than the absence of the object which the compulsion obtains." To show this is impossible, one reason being that it isn't true. Preventing a man from selling himself into slavery (a paternalistic measure which Mill himself accepts as legitimate), or from taking heroin, or from driving a car without wearing seat belts may constitute a lesser evil than allowing him to do any of these things. A consistent utilitarian can only argue against paternalism on the grounds that it (as a matter of fact) does not maximize the good. It is always a contingent question that may be returned by the evidence. But there is also a non-contingent argument which runs through *On Liberty.* When Mill states that "there is a part of the life of every person who has come to years of discretion, within which the individuality of that person ought to reign uncontrolled either by any other person or by the public collectively," he is saying something about what it means to be a person, an autonomous agent. It is because coercing a person for his own good denies this status as an independent entity that Mill objects to it so strongly and in such absolute terms. To be able to choose is a good that is independent of the wisdom of what is chosen. A man's "mode of laying out his existence is the best, not because it is the best in itself, but because it is his own mode." It is the privilege and proper condition of a human being, arrived at the maturity of his faculties, to use and interpret experience in his own way.

As further evidence of this line of reasoning in Mill, consider the one exception to his prohibition against paternalism:

> In this and most civilized countries, for example, an engagement by which a person should sell himself, or allow himself to be sold, as a slave, would be null and void; neither enforced by law nor by opinion. The ground for thus limiting his power of voluntarily disposing of his own lot in life, is apparent, and is very clearly seen in this extreme case. The reason for not interfering, unless for the sake of others, with a person's voluntary acts, is consideration for his liberty. His voluntary choice is evidence that what he so chooses is desirable, or at least endurable, to him, and his good is on the whole best provided for by allowing him to take his own means of pursuing it. But by selling himself as a slave, he abdicates his liberty; he foregoes any future use of it beyond that single act. He therefore defeats, in his own case, the very purpose which is the justification of allowing him to dispose of himself. He is no longer free; but is thenceforth in a position which has no longer the presumption in its favour, that would be afforded by his voluntarily remaining in it. The principle of freedom cannot require that he should be free not to be free. It is not freedom to be allowed to alienate his freedom.

Now leaving aside the fudging on the meaning of freedom in the last line, it is clear that part of this argument is incorrect. While it is true that *future* choices of the slave are not reasons for thinking that what he chooses then is desirable for him, what is at issue is limiting his immediate choice; and since this choice is made freely, the individual may be correct in thinking that his interests are best provided for by entering such a contract. But the main consideration for not allowing such a contract is the need to preserve the liberty of the person to make future choices. This gives us a principle—a very narrow one—by which to justify some paternalistic interferences. Paternalism is justified only to preserve a wider range of freedom for the individual in question. How far this principle could be extended, whether it can justify all the cases in which we are inclined upon reflection to think paternalistic measures justified, remains to be discussed. What I have tried to show so far is that there are two strains of argument in Mill—one a straightforward utilitarian mode of reasoning and one which relies not on the goods which free choice leads to but on the absolute value of the choice itself. The first cannot establish any absolute prohibition but at most a presumption and indeed a fairly weak one given some fairly plausible assumptions about human psychology; the second, while a stronger line of argument, seems to me to allow on its own grounds a wider range of paternalism than might be suspected. I turn now to a consideration of these matters.

We might begin looking for principles governing the acceptable use of paternalistic power in cases where it is generally agreed that it is legitimate. Even Mill intends his principles to be applicable only to mature individuals, not those in what he calls "non-age." What is it that justifies us in interfering with children? The fact that they lack some of the emotional and cognitive capacities required in order to make fully rational decisions. It is an empirical question to just what extent children have an adequate conception of their own present and future interests but there is not much doubt that there are many deficiencies. For example, it is very difficult for a child to defer gratification for any considerable period of time. Given these deficiencies and given the very real and permanent dangers that may befall the child, it becomes not only permissible but even a duty of the parent to restrict the child's freedom in various ways. There is however an important moral limitation on the exercise of such parental power which is provided by the notion of the child eventually coming to see the correctness of his parent's interventions. Parental paternalism may be thought of as a wager by the parent on the child's subsequent recognition of the wisdom of the restrictions. There is an emphasis on what could be called future-oriented consent—on what the child will come to welcome, rather than on what he does welcome.

The essence of this idea has been incorporated by idealist philosophers into various types of "real-will" theory as applied to fully adult persons. Extensions of paternalism are argued for by claiming that in various respects, chronologically mature individuals share the same deficiencies in knowledge, capacity to think rationally, and the ability to carry out decisions that children possess. Hence in interfering with such people we are in effect doing what they would do if they were fully rational. Hence we are not really opposing their will, hence we are not really interfering with their freedom. . . . Still the basic notion of consent is important and seems to me the only acceptable way of trying to delimit an area of justified paternalism.

Let me start by considering a case where the consent is not hypothetical in nature. Under certain conditions it is rational for an individual to agree that others should force him to act in ways which, at the time of action, the individual may not see as desirable. If, for example, a man knows that he is subject to breaking his resolves when temptation is present, he may ask a friend to refuse to entertain his requests at some later stage.

A classical example is given in the *Odyssey* when Odysseus commands his men to tie him to the mast and refuse all future orders to be set free, because he knows the power of the Sirens to enchant men with their songs. Here we are on relatively sound ground in later refusing Odysseus' request to be set free. He may even claim to have changed his mind but, since it is *just* such changes that he wished to guard against we are entitled to ignore them.

A process analogous to this may take place on a social rather than individual basis. An electorate may mandate its representatives to pass legislation which when it comes time to "pay the price" may be unpalatable. I may believe that a tax increase is necessary to halt inflation though I may resent the lower pay check each month. However in both this case and that of Odysseus, the measure to be enforced is specifically requested by the party involved and at some point in time there is genuine consent and agreement on the part of those persons whose liberty is infringed. Such is not the case for the paternalistic measures we have been speaking about. What must be involved here is not consent to specific measures but rather consent to a system of government, run by elected representatives, with an understanding that they may act to safeguard our interests in certain limited ways.

I suggest that since we are all aware of our irrational propensities, deficiencies in cognitive and emotional capacities, and avoidable and unavoidable ignorance, it is rational and prudent for us to in effect take out "social insurance policies." We may argue for and against proposed paternalistic measures in terms of what fully rational individuals would accept as forms of protection. Now clearly, since the initial agreement is not about specific measures we are dealing with a more-or-less blank check and therefore there have to be carefully defined limits. What I am looking for are certain kinds of conditions which make it plausible to suppose that rational men could reach agreement to limit their liberty even when other men's interests are not affected.

Of course as in any kind of agreement schema there are great difficulties in deciding what rational individuals would or would not accept. Particularly in sensitive areas of personal liberty, there is always a danger of the dispute over agreement and rationality being a disguised version of evaluative and normative disagreement.

Let me suggest types of situations in which it seems plausible to suppose that fully rational individuals would agree to having paternalistic restrictions imposed upon them. It is reasonable to suppose that there are "goods" such as health which any person would want to have in order to pursue his own good—no matter how that good is conceived. This is an argument used in connection with compulsory education for children but it seems to me that it can be extended to other goods which have this character. Then one could agree that the attainment of such goods should be promoted even when not recognized to be such, at the moment, by the individuals concerned.

An immediate difficulty arises from the fact that men are always faced with competing goods and that there may be reasons why even a value such as health—or indeed life—may be overridden by competing values. Thus the problem with the Christian Scientist and blood transfusions. It may be more important for him to reject "impure substances" than to go on living. The difficult problem that must be faced is whether one can give sense to the notion of a person irrationally attaching weights to competing values.

Consider a person who knows the statistical data on the probability of being injured when not wearing seat belts in an automobile and knows the types and gravity of the various injuries. He also insists that the inconvenience attached to fastening the belt every time he gets in and out of the car outweighs for him the possible risks to himself. I am inclined in this case to think that such a weighing is irrational. Given his life plans, which we are assuming are those of the average person, his interests and commitments already undertaken, I think it is safe to predict that we can find inconsistencies in his calculations at some point. I am assuming that this is not a man who for some conscious or unconscious reasons is trying to injure himself nor is he a man who just likes to "live dangerously." I am assuming that he is like us in all the relevant respects but just puts an enormously high negative value on inconvenience—one which does not seem comprehensible or reasonable.

It is always possible, of course, to assimilate this person to creatures like myself. I, also, neglect to fasten my seat belt and I concede such behavior is not rational but not because I weigh the inconvenience differently from those who fasten the belts. It is just that having made (roughly) the same calculation as everybody else, I ignore it in my actions. . . . A plausible explanation for this deplorable habit is that although I know in some intellectual sense what the probabilities and risks are I do not fully appreciate them in an emotionally genuine manner.

We have two distinct types of situation in which a man acts in a nonrational fashion. In one case he attaches incorrect weights to some of his values; in the other he neglects to act in accordance with his actual preferences and desires. Clearly there is a stronger and more persuasive argument for paternalism in the latter situation. Here we are really not—by assumption—imposing a good on another person. But why may we not extend our interference to what we might call evaluative delusions? After all, in the case of cognitive delusions we are prepared, often, to act against the expressed will of the person involved. If a man believes that when he jumps out the window he will float upwards—Robert Nozick's example—would not we detain him, forcibly if necessary? The reply will be that this man doesn't wish to be injured and if we could convince him that he is mistaken as to the consequences of his action, he would not wish to perform the action. But part of what is involved in claiming that the man who doesn't fasten his seat-belts is attaching an incorrect weight to the inconvenience of fastening them is that if he were to be involved in an accident and severely injured he would look back and admit that the inconvenience wasn't as bad as all that. So there is a sense in which, if I could convince him of the consequences of his action, he also would not wish to continue his present course of action. Now the notion of consequences being used here is covering a lot of ground. In one case it's being used to indicate what will or can happen as a result of a course of action and in the other it's making a prediction about the future evaluation of the consequences—in the first sense—of a course of action. And whatever the difference between facts and values—whether it be hard and fast or soft and slow—we are genuinely more reluctant to consent to interferences where evaluative differences are the issue. Let me now consider another factor which comes into play in some of these situations which may make an important difference in our willingness to consent to paternalistic restrictions.

Some of the decisions we make are of such a character that they produce changes which are in one or another way irreversible. Situations are created in which it is difficult or impossible to return to anything like the initial stage at which the decision was made. In particular, some of these changes will make it impossible to continue to make reasoned choices in the future. I am thinking specifically of decisions which involve taking drugs that are physically or psychologically addictive and those which are destructive of one's mental and physical capacities.

I suggest we think of the imposition of paternalistic interferences in situations of this kind as being a kind of insurance policy which we take out against making decisions which are far-reaching, potentially dangerous, and irreversible. Each of these factors is important. Clearly there are many decisions we make that are relatively irreversible. In deciding to learn to play chess, I could predict in view of my general interest in games that some portion of my free time was going to be preempted and that it would not be easy to give up the game once I acquired a certain competence. But my whole life style was not going to be jeopardized in an extreme manner. Further it might be argued that even with addictive drugs such as heroin one's normal life plans would not be seriously interfered with if an inexpensive and adequate supply were readily available. So this type of argument might have a much narrower scope than appears to be the case at first.

A second class of cases concerns decisions which are made under extreme psychological and sociological pressures. I am not thinking here of the making of the decision as being something one is pressured into—for example, a good reason for making duelling illegal is that unless this is done many people might have to manifest their courage and integrity in ways in which they would rather not do so—but rather of decisions, such as that to commit suicide, which are usually made at a point where the individual is not thinking clearly and calmly about the nature of his decision. In addition, of course, this comes under the previous heading of all-too-irrevocable decisions. Now there are practical steps which a society could take if it wanted to decrease the possibility of suicide—for example not paying social security benefits to the survivors or, as religious institutions do, not allowing persons to be buried with the same status as natural deaths. I think we may count these as interferences with the liberty of persons to attempt suicide and the question is whether they are justifiable.

Using my argument schema the question is whether rational individuals would consent to such limitations. I see no reason for them to consent to an absolute prohibition but I do think it is reasonable for them to agree to some kind of enforced waiting period. Since we are all aware of the possibility of temporary states, such as great fear of depression, that are inimical to the making of well-informed and rational decisions, it would be prudent for all of us if there were some kind of institutional arrangement whereby we were restrained from making a decision which is so irreversible. What this would be like in practice is difficult to envisage and it may be that if no practical arrangements were feasible we would have to conclude that there should be no restriction at all on this kind of action. But we might have a "cooling off" period, in much the same way that we now require couples who file for divorce to go through a waiting period. Or, more far-fetched, we might imagine a Suicide Board composed of a psychologist and another member picked by the applicant. The Board would be required to meet and talk with the person proposing to take his life, though its approval would not be required.

A third class of decisions—these classes are not supposed to be disjoint—involves dangers which are either not sufficiently understood or appreciated correctly by the persons involved. Let me illustrate, using the example of cigarette smoking, a number of possible cases.

1. A man may not know the facts—for example, smoking between one and two packs a day shortens life expectancy 6.2 years, the costs and pain of the illness caused by smoking, et cetera.

2. A man may know the facts, wish to stop smoking, but not have the requisite will-power.

3. A man may know the facts but not have them play the correct role in his calculation because, say, he discounts the danger psychologically since it is remote in time and/or inflates the attractiveness of other consequences of his decision which he regards as beneficial.

In Case 1 what is called for is education, the posting of warnings, et cetera. In Case 2 there is no theoretical problem. We are not imposing a good on someone who rejects it. We are simply using coercion to enable people to carry out their own goals. (Note: There obviously is a difficulty in that only a subclass of the individuals affected wish to be prevented from doing what they are doing.) In Case 3 there is a sense in which we are imposing a good on someone in that given his current appraisal of the facts he doesn't wish to be restricted. But in another sense we are not imposing a good since what is being claimed—and what must be shown or at least argued for—is that an accurate accounting on his part would lead him to reject his current course of action. Now we all know that such cases exist, that we are prone to disregarding dangers that are only possibilities, that immediate pleasures are often magnified and distorted.

If in addition the dangers are severe and far-reaching, we could agree to allow the state a certain degree of power to intervene in such situations. The difficulty is in specifying in advance, even vaguely, the class of cases in which intervention will be legitimate.

A related difficulty is that of drawing a line so that it is not the case that all ultra-hazardous activities are ruled out, for example, mountain-climbing, bull-fighting, sports-car racing, et cetera. There are some risks—even very great ones—which a person is entitled to take with his life.

A good deal depends on the nature of the deprivation—for example, does it prevent the person from engaging in the activity completely or merely limit his participation—and how important to the nature of the activity is the absence of restriction when this is weighed against the role that the activity plays in the life of the person. In the case of automobile seat belts, for example, the restriction is trivial in nature, interferes not at all with the use or enjoyment of the activity, and does, I am assuming, considerably reduce a high risk of serious injury. Whereas, for example, making mountain-climbing illegal completely prevents a person from engaging in an activity which may play an important role in his life and his conception of the person he is.

In general, the easiest cases to handle are those which can be argued about in the terms which Mill thought to be so important—a concern not just for the happiness or welfare, in some broad sense, of the individual but rather a concern for the autonomy and freedom of the person. I suggest that we would be most likely to consent to paternalism in those instances in which it preserves and enhances for the individual his ability to rationally consider and carry out his own decisions.

I have suggested in this essay a number of types of situations in which it seems plausible that rational men would agree to granting the legislative powers of a society the right to impose restrictions on what Mill calls "self-regarding" conduct. However, rational men knowing something about the resources of ignorance, ill-will, and stupidity available to the lawmakers of a society—a good case in point is the history of drug legislation in the United States—will be concerned to limit such intervention to a minimum. I suggest in closing two principles designed to achieve this end.

In all cases of paternalistic legislation there must be a heavy and clear burden of proof placed on the authorities to demonstrate the exact nature of the harmful effects (or beneficial consequences) to be avoided (or achieved) and the probability of their occurrence. The burden of proof here is two-fold—what lawyers distinguish as the burden of going forward and the burden of persuasion. That the authorities have the burden of going forward means that it is up to them to raise the question and bring forward evidence of the evils to be avoided. Unlike the case of new drugs, where the manufacturer must produce some evidence that the drug has been tested and found not harmful, no citizen has to show with respect to self-regarding conduct that it is not harmful or promotes his best interest. In addition the nature and cogency of the evidence for the harmfulness of the course of action must be set at a high level. To paraphrase a formulation of the burden of proof for criminal proceedings—better ten men ruin themselves than one man be unjustly deprived of liberty.

Finally, I suggest a principle of the least restrictive alternative. If there is an alternative way of accomplishing the desired end without restricting liberty although it may involve great expense, inconvenience, et cetera, the society must adopt it.

BENEVOLENT KILLING

Dan Brock

Death and Dying

AN ETHICAL FRAMEWORK
FOR LIFE-SUPPORT DECISIONS

It is widely agreed that it was common historically to view the physician–patient relationship as one in which the physician directed care and made decisions about treatment and the patient's role was to comply with the "Doctor's orders." Patients were told only as much about their condition and treatment as was necessary to comply effectively with treatment.

This is sometimes called the authoritarian or paternalist model of the physician–patient relationship. . . . Yet the weight of argument and opinion has shifted substantially toward securing an enlarged, indeed principal, role in treatment decision making for the patient. Why has this happened? One reason is a new concept of the ends of medicine and of the proper form of the physician–patient relationship (Katz 1984; President's Commission 1982; Siegler 1981).

There are many ways of more precisely formulating the new concept. One prominent version sees the goals of health-care decision making as the promotion of patients' well-being while respecting their self-determination. How is this different from promoting and preserving patients' health and life? What best promotes health and life is naturally thought to be an objective factual matter, an empirical question, one not dependent on a particular patient's preferences and values. So understood, what best promotes patients' health and preserves their lives is a factual matter about which the physician, not the patient, possesses expertise. Why then is a central role necessary for the patient in deciding on treatment?

To view the end point of the health-care process as the patient's well-being, instead of as health and life in general, is not to deny that physicians seek to beneficially affect patients' health and life. Rather, it is to stress that health and life extension are ultimately of value in the service of the broader, overall well-being of the patient. They are of value insofar as they facilitate the patient's pursuit of his or her overall plan of life—the aims, goals, and values important to the particular patient. In many instances the decision of which alternative treatment best promotes a patient's well-being, including the alternative of no treatment, cannot be objectively determined independent of the patient's own preference and values.

In the case of life-support decisions, when the forgoing of life support is under serious consideration, it is usually because (1) the patient is critically or terminally ill and likely to die soon no matter what is done, and (2) because the quality of the patient's life is seriously limited by the effects of disease, disability, and sometimes the treatment itself. Whether treatment and continued life under such severely constrained conditions are better than no more life must depend in significant part on how the particular patient views his or her life under those conditions. The physician is in the best position to predict the specific outcomes of different treatment alternatives and their effects on the patient, but the patient is in the best position to evaluate what importance should be given to any particular effect, such as the discomfort and restrictions on communication caused by intubation, or the restrictions on activities caused by dialysis. It is well established that different persons evaluate the importance of such burdens significantly differently—some tolerate intubation or dialysis relatively well if it allows their lives to be prolonged; others find that the limitations make life no longer worth living.

There is no single right answer to how such conditions should be valued; there are only the actual answers that real persons give for themselves. This is why many have urged that health-care decision making should be a process of shared decision making between physician and patient (Katz 1984; President's Commission 1982; Siegler 1981). Each brings something to the decision-making process that the other lacks, and the communication is necessary to decisions that best serve the patient's well-being: The physician brings knowledge about the likely outcomes of alternative treatments; the patient brings knowledge of the personal aims, ends, and values by which to evaluate those outcomes. Thus, even if treatment decision making aims only to serve the patient's well-being, shared decision making (a process of conversation between the physician and patient) is necessary to identify the best alternative.

In this . . . view of health-care decision making, the other value that should guide the process is the patient's self-determination or autonomy. Self-determination can be understood as the interest each person has in making important decisions that shape and affect one's life for oneself and according to one's own aims and values. Respecting people's self-determination helps give them control and responsibility for the lives they lead and the kind of persons they become. In health care, involving patients in important treatment decisions and leaving them free to refuse any proffered treatment respects their self-determination. If people's interest in self-determination is important in ordinary medical care, surely it is more important in decisions about life support that determine when and under what conditions their lives will end. Valuing self-determination requires respecting both patients' own concept of their well-being (the subjective aspect of well-being noted above) and patients' interest in participating in the decision-making process about their care.

Both values of patient well-being and self-determination support a process of shared decision making between physician and patient in which the patient retains the right to refuse any offered treatment. Shared decision making does not preclude, but instead can foster, the important trust traditionally and commonly bestowed by patients on their physicians; nor is it incompatible with patients asking their physicians to make some decisions for them. . . .

It should be noted that, in this view, carefully limited quality of life considerations *do* quite properly and inevitably play a role in the assessment of alternatives and of their overall benefits and burdens. For most persons, whether the continued life made possible by a particular life-sustaining treatment is, on balance, wanted and a benefit will depend at least in part on the quality of that life. What is important is that the assessment should be of the quality of life *to the patient*. This view does not sanction giving weight to how the patient's continued life may affect the quality of other's lives, for example by making the patient a burden to others. Nor does it sanction any judgments that some people's lives are not socially or economically worth sustaining because they are of low quality. The proper question is whether the patient's present and anticipated quality of life is sufficiently bad to make it, according to him or her, worse than no more life at all. This is a very narrowly constrained role for quality-of-life considerations that is fully compatible with respecting patients' self-determination and their own view of their well-being.

THE INCOMPETENT PATIENT

Our account of life-support decision making thus far largely assumes that the patient is competent to make such decisions. Of course, this is often or even usually not the case when forgoing life-sustaining treatment is seriously at issue. The effects of illness and disease, as well as of treatments themselves, commonly compromise or eliminate patients' abilities to participate in decision making. Someone else then has to decide for them. . . .

The most direct way for incompetent patients to participate in decisions about their care in a manner serving their well-being and self-determination is through use of advance directives. There are two principal forms of advance directives: instructional directives, which state the patient's wishes about treatment; and proxy directives, which name a surrogate to decide for the patient. Living wills are the best known form of instructional directive. Durable Powers of Attorney for Health Care combine the functions of designating a surrogate and giving instructions to the surrogate about the patient's wishes concerning treatment. Nearly all states in the United States now give legal force to advance directives, and the federal Patient Self-Determination Act requires all health-care institutions to inform patients about their rights to have them. Nevertheless, advance directives are at best only a partial solution to the problem of decision making for incompetent patients for several reasons. First, and probably most important, only a small proportion of incompetent patients for whom such decisions must be made now have advance directives, and even with increased efforts to publicize advance directives and their value, most patients will probably not have them in the foreseeable future.

Second, to ensure the patient's competence when they are made, advance directives are usually made well in advance of the circumstances in which they are to be applied. Thus, they are inevitably framed in somewhat vague and general terms, and commonly make use of phrases like "if I am terminally ill and death is imminent, no further artificial or extraordinary means to prolong my life shall be employed," and so forth. Although such instructions can provide others with general guidance as to the patient's wishes regarding life support, they inevitably leave much discretion to those who must interpret them in the patient's specific circumstances. At what point is death imminent? Are antibiotics extraordinary means? Even when patients have advance directives, others must unavoidably play the important role of interpreting them. This has led many persons to conclude that Durable Powers of Attorney for Health Care are more helpful than Living Wills.

A third difficulty is that, as a way to guard against possible well-intentioned misuse or ill-intentioned abuse by others of advance directives, the conditions bringing the directives into legal effect are sometimes narrowly limited. For example, the condition that death be imminent on many natural interpretations restricts the directive so that it does not apply in many of the circumstances in which decisions about life support must be made. . . .

In the absence of any advance directive, others must decide for the incompetent patient. The principle guiding such decisions most in accord with promoting the patient's well-being, as he or she views it, while also respecting his or her self-determination, is the principle of substituted judgment. This principle directs the surrogate decision maker to attempt to decide as the patient would have decided in the circumstances that now obtain if he or she were competent. This essentially directs the surrogate to use his or her knowledge of the patient's preferences and values relevant to this decision, even if these preferences and values are different from most people's or the surrogate's, in determining what the patient would have wanted.

In the absence of any information about what the particular patient would have wanted, for example, because there are no available family or friends of the patient, it is generally accepted that the principle guiding decisions should be the best interests principle. This principle directs the surrogate to decide about life support in a manner that best serves the patient's interests. Lacking any knowledge of this particular patient's wishes, such decisions inevitably involve asking what most reasonable persons would want for themselves in the circumstances.

It is widely agreed that the surrogate decision maker who is to apply these principles should usually be the patient's closest family member. The presumption for the family member as surrogate is usually based on at least three reasons. First, in most instances the family member is the person whom the patient would have wanted to make necessary decisions. Second, in most cases the family member both knows the patient best and cares most about the patient and, thus, is usually the person best able to secure what the patient would have wanted. Finally, the family in our society is commonly accorded a significant degree of authority to care for its dependent members. . . .

SOME ADDITIONAL CONTROVERSIAL MORAL CONSTRAINTS ON FORGOING LIFE SUPPORT

Many of the principal moral disputes about life-sustaining treatment do not focus on the broad issues discussed above of the proper role of patients or surrogates in health-care decision making and of the proper form of the physician–patient relationship. Instead, the disputes are more specific to life-sustaining treatment and reflect the important fact that death is typically the direct and expected result of forgoing such treatment. . . .

WITHHOLDING AND WITHDRAWING LIFE SUPPORT

Some people believe that although patients or their surrogates may refuse to start any life-sustaining treatment they judge to be excessively burdensome or without benefit, it is not morally permissible to stop life support once it has begun. Alternatively, even if such treatments can sometimes be stopped once begun, it is often held that it is a graver matter requiring weightier reasons to stop; stopping is at least sometimes not permissible in circumstances in which it would be permissible not to start. This accurately reflects some medical practice in which, for example, physicians who are prepared to honor patients' or their families' requests for Do Not Resuscitate or Do Not Intubate orders nevertheless, in similar circumstances, are reluctant to stop respirators on which patients are dependent for life. Physicians commonly feel more responsible for a patient's death that results from stopping the patient's respirator than from not starting it. But is there good reason to treat withdrawal of life-sustaining treatment as morally different and more serious than withholding such treatment? Consider Case 12.1.

Case 12.1

A very gravely ill patient is brought into a hospital emergency room from a nursing home and sent to the intensive care unit (ICU). The patient begins to develop respiratory failure that is likely to require intubation very soon. At that point, the patient's family members and longstanding attending physician arrive at the ICU and inform the ICU staff that there had been extensive discussion about future care with the patient when he was unquestionably competent. Given his grave and terminal illness, as well as his state of debilitation, the patient had firmly rejected being placed on a respirator under any circumstances, and the family and physician produce the patient's advance directive to show this.

Most would hold that this patient should not be intubated and placed on a respirator against his will, and most ICUs would probably not do so. Suppose now that the situation is exactly the same except that the attending physician and family are slightly delayed in traffic and arrive 15 minutes after the patient has been intubated and placed on the respirator. Can this difference be of any moral importance? Could it possibly justify ethically a refusal by the staff to remove the patient from the respirator? Do not the very same circumstances that justified not placing the patient on the respirator now justify taking him off it? Do not factors like the patient's condition, prognosis, and firmly expressed competent wishes morally determine what should be done, not whether we do not start, or 15 minutes later stop, the respirator? Why should the stop/not start difference matter morally at all?

Cases such as this have led many to conclude that the difference between not starting and stopping, or withholding and withdrawing, life-sustaining treatment is not in itself of any moral importance. . . .

KILLING AND ALLOWING TO DIE

The distinction between stopping and not starting a life-sustaining treatment corresponds in general to the distinction between acts and omissions leading to death. Ambiguities also abound about whether decisions to forgo a life-sustaining treatment should be classified as an act or an omission. Does the positive decision to forgo treatment make it an omission? However these distinctions are more precisely drawn, if there is no moral importance to whether a life-sustaining treatment is stopped or not started, it would seem to follow that it is not morally significant according to this view whether it is an act or omission of the physician that leads to death. This implication is increasingly widely accepted (*Barber and Nedjl* 1983; *Conroy* 1985; Wanzer et al. 1985; Hastings Center 1988). Yet the distinction between acts and omissions leading to death is also commonly understood to be the basis for the distinction between killing and allowing to die. Some commentators have gone on to accept, or to explicitly argue, that killing is in itself no different morally than allowing to die, although, of course, that position remains controversial (Glover 1977; Steinbock 1980; Kamm 1993). The "no difference" position is compatible with many or most actual acts of killing being morally worse, all things considered, than most cases of allowing to die.

Although this view has been accepted by many philosophers and bioethicists, many health-care personnel, patients, and their families strongly resist it. For many, the view that killing is both wrong and also worse than allowing to die is a deeply and powerfully held view. But the positive decision actively to turn off a life-sustaining treatment such as a respirator seems to be an action, not an omission, which leads to death, and so, in this view, it is considered a killing, not a case of allowing to die. This line of reasoning uncovers a more general concern about whether all stopping of life support might be killing and therefore morally wrong. In assessing this question, it is important to be clear, first, about the meaning of the claim that killing is *in itself* no different morally than allowing to die. The claim is that the mere fact that one case is an instance of killing, another of allowing to die, does not make one any worse morally than the other, or make one justified or permissible but the other not. This is not to say that any particular instance of killing may not be morally worse than some instance of allowing to die. It *is* to say that if the killing is worse, it is because of its other properties such as the motives of the killer, whether the victim consented, and so forth, that differentiate it morally from the particular instance of allowing to die. Second, it is important to distinguish whether common instances of stopping life support should be understood as killing or as allowing to die from whether, if they are killings, they are for that reason morally wrong. Most commentators who have argued that stopping life-sustaining treatment is killing have insisted as well that it is not therefore wrong; some killing, including stopping life support, is morally permissible and justified.

Are standard cases of stopping life-sustaining treatment killing or allowing to die (Brock 1993; Raches 1975)? A physician who stops a respirator at the voluntary request of a clearly competent patient who is terminally ill and undergoing unrelievable suffering would commonly be understood by all involved as allowing the patient to die, with the patient's underlying disease the cause of death. If done with the consent of the patient, and with the intent of respecting his self-determination while promoting his well-being as he views it, it would be held by many to be morally justified. Let us agree that it can be morally justified, but is it allowing to die? Suppose the patient has a greedy nephew who stands to inherit his money and who has become impatient for the old man to die so that he will get the money. Thinking that his uncle is prepared to continue on the respirator indefinitely, that his physicians would not be willing to stop it in any case, and that his inheritance will be exhausted by a lengthy and expensive hospitalization, he slips into the room, turns off the respirator, and his uncle dies. The nephew is found out, confronted, and replies, "I didn't kill him, I merely allowed him to die; his underlying disease caused his death." Surely this would be dismissed as specious nonsense. The nephew deliberately killed his uncle. However, it does seem that he did exactly what the physician did in the other case. Both acted in a manner that caused the patient's death, expected it to do so, and might have performed the very same bodily movements in doing so.

If the nephew killed his uncle, doesn't the physician kill his patient as well? Of course, the physician acts with a different and proper motive, with the patient's consent, and in a professional role in which he is authorized to carry out the patient's wishes concerning treatment. The differences in motive, consent, and social role make what he does, but not what the nephew does, morally justified. That is not to say, however, that what he does, and whether he kills or allows to die, is any different from the nephew—only that his killing is justified, but the nephew's was not. One can kill or allow to die with or without consent, with a good or bad motive, and in or not in a social or legal role that authorizes doing so. This general line of reasoning, then, accepts that standard cases of stopping life-sustaining treatment are sometimes correctly understood as killing, but rejects any inference that they therefore must be wrong.

One explanation of why this account is resisted is that many physicians and others use the concept of killing as a normative concept to refer to unjustified actions causing death. In this view, killing may occur in medicine accidentally or negligently, but physicians do not knowingly and deliberately kill their patients; put flippantly, physicians do not understand killing patients to be part of their job description. Yet, of course, physicians do stop life support in cases like the above and believe, quite rightly, that they can be justified in doing so. Thus, there is a powerful motive to understand what is done as allowing to die, not as killing. Common though this way of thinking may be, it is mistaken. It is a mistake to suppose that all killing must be unjustified, either morally or in the law. Killing in self-defense is an example of justified killing outside of medicine, and stopping life support appears to be one within medicine.

There is another explanation of why standard cases of stopping life support are thought to be allowing to die and not killing. In the case of a terminally ill patient, a lethal disease process is already present. A life-sustaining treatment such as use of a respirator may then be thought of as holding back or blocking the normal progress of the patient's disease. Removing the artificial intervention is then viewed as standing aside and allowing the patient to die by letting the disease process proceed unimpeded. This may be a plausible explanation of why stopping life-support is commonly understood to be allowing to die, but if it is to be any more than a metaphorical account, it must at the least explain why the nephew does not allow to die. It is not clear how this is to be done consistent with the way of killing and allowing to die are distinguished over a broad range of cases. Even if stopping life support is understood as allowing to die along these lines, killing may still not be, in itself, morally different from allowing to die.

IS FORGOING LIFE SUPPORT SUICIDE?

Parallel to the concern that stopping life-support systems is killing and therefore wrong is the concern that any forgoing of life support is suicide or assisted suicide and therefore wrong. Courts in particular try to distinguish forgoing life support from suicide, probably to insulate physicians, families, and other health-care personnel from possible liability under laws prohibiting assisting in a suicide. The 1985 New Jersey Supreme Court decision in *Conroy* summarizes well the reasoning of many courts and others:

> . . . declining life-sustaining medical treatment may not properly be viewed as an attempt to commit suicide. Refusing medical intervention merely allows the disease to take its natural course; if death were eventually to occur, it would be the result, primarily, of the underlying disease, and not the result of a self-inflicted injury. In addition, people who refuse life-sustaining medical treatment may not harbor a specific intent to die, rather, they may fervently wish to live, but to do so free of unwanted medical technology, surgery, or drugs, and without protracted suffering. . . . Recognizing the right of a terminally ill person to reject medical treatment respects that person's intent, not to die, but to suspend medical intervention at a point consonant with the "individual's view respecting a personally preferred manner of concluding life." The difference is between self-infliction or self-destruction and self-determination (*Conroy* 1985).

Although this way of distinguishing forgoing life support from suicide may seem plausible, it is at least problematic in some cases. The judgment of a person who competently decides to commit suicide is essentially that "my expected future life, under the best conditions possible for me, is so bad that I judge it to be worse than no further continued life at all." This seems to be in essence exactly the same judgment that some persons who decide to forgo life-sustaining treatment make. The refusal of life-sustaining treatment is their means of ending their life; their intent is to end their life because of its unacceptable prospects. Their death now when they otherwise would not have died *is* self-inflicted, whether they take a lethal poison or disconnect a respirator. There need be, of course, no underlying lethal disease process present when a person commits suicide, whereas there must be when life-sustaining treatment is refused, but that need only mean that the person with a lethal disease thereby has an additional means of ending his or her life; there is no reason to think that a person subject to a lethal disease process therefore could not commit suicide.

The court's reasoning, at the most, distinguishes some but not all cases of forgoing life-sustaining treatment from suicide, although it should be adequate to protect all instances from falling under legal statutes concerning assisting in suicide. Even if at least some instances of forgoing life-sustaining treatment are suicide, it does not follow that they are morally wrong. The very same reasoning offered earlier in support of a competent patient's moral right to refuse any life-sustaining medical treatment applies in any case in which doing so may be suicide. The patient's self-determination and well-being support the moral permissibility of his or her declining *any* life-sustaining treatment, including any instance that might reasonably be construed as suicide. Cases of competent decisions to decline life-sustaining treatment that constitute suicide are commonly instances of rational and morally permissible suicide. Moreover, in virtually all states, committing or attempting suicide is not legally prohibited. . . .

PHYSICIAN-ASSISTED SUICIDE AND VOLUNTARY ACTIVE EUTHANASIA

If competent patients are morally entitled to refuse any life-sustaining treatment, should they also be permitted in similar circumstances to have others, such as their physicians or family members, directly end their lives, or assist them in directly ending their lives, by a lethal injection or medication? We have deliberately avoided using until now the term *euthanasia* because of its strong emotionally laden connotations, but it is this sort of direct and active killing that is commonly understood as euthanasia. The very same values of patient well-being and self-determination that support a patient's right to refuse any life-sustaining treatment appear also to support physician-assisted suicide or voluntary euthanasia in some circumstances. Does this show that if one accepts that forgoing life support is morally permissible, one must accept physician-assisted suicide and voluntary euthanasia as well?

In the increasingly intense public and professional debates on the issue, many have endorsed physician-assisted suicide but not euthanasia. Are the two importantly different morally? The only difference between them need be who performs the final physical act of administering the lethal dose—the physician or the patient. In both, the choice should rest fully with the patient, who can change his or her mind until the time the process is irreversible. This small difference in the parts played by the physician and the patient seems not to support a substantial moral difference between them. At most, physician-assisted suicide might provide in some cases slightly stronger evidence of the patient's resolve. Of course, some believe there is an obvious and important moral difference—in assisted suicide, the patient kills himself or herself, whereas, in euthanasia, the physician kills the patient. But this is misleading at best. In physician-assisted suicide, the patient and physician collaborate in a joint effort to kill the patient for which both are responsible. Physician-assisted suicide and voluntary euthanasia are not substantially different morally—the arguments for and against them generally apply equally to both.

It is important to distinguish two levels at which the morality of assisted suicide and euthanasia can arise. The first is whether any specific instances of euthanasia are morally permissible. The second is whether public and legal policy should permit euthanasia. Many opponents of a public policy making euthanasia legally permissible nevertheless grant that there are particular cases in which it is morally permissible. For example, consider the case of a terminally ill and imminently dying patient with a form of cancer that causes him very great and unrelievable suffering. With his competence not in question, the patient implores his physician to end his suffering by giving him a lethal injection. It seems cruelly perverse to hold that if a life-sustaining treatment were in place we should honor the patient's request to remove it and let him die, but that otherwise we cannot intervene and must leave him to suffer in pain until nature takes its course. How could assisted suicide or voluntary euthanasia be morally wrong in a case such as this?

Some would respond that deliberate or intentional killing of innocent persons is always wrong, even if done for an otherwise good end, such as relieving suffering. If our argument above was correct, that some cases of stopping life support are both intentional killing and morally justified, then we have already established that some killing of persons is not morally wrong. But even if all forgoing of life support is allowing to die, but all euthanasia is deliberate killing, it does not follow that euthanasia must be wrong. To see this, we need to ask why killing is morally wrong in cases that are uncontroversially wrong. A plausible answer is that it deprives the victim of a very great and desired good—future life, and all that the person killed would have been able to do in that future life. But in cases of assisted suicide or voluntary euthanasia, the patient wants death, not future life, and judges the best future life possible for him or her to be a burden, not a good. The values of patient self-determination and well-being do not oppose, but support, assisted suicide and euthanasia. Thus, the reasons that make paradigm cases of wrongful killing wrongful do not apply to assisted suicide and euthanasia. Nevertheless, even if assisted suicide and euthanasia are morally justified in some cases, it could be bad public policy to permit them.

There is space here to give only examples of some of the more important good and bad consequences likely from making assisted suicide and voluntary euthanasia legally permissible. What are the more important good consequences? One has already been cited, the relief of dying patients' suffering when only death will provide that relief; James Rachels called this the argument from mercy (Rachels 1975). But there are not great numbers of patients undergoing severe suffering that can only be relieved by directly killing them. Modern methods of pain management make it possible to control the pain of nearly all such patients without the use of lethal means, though sometimes at the cost of so sedating the patient that interaction and communication with others is limited or no longer possible. Most cases in which such suffering is not in fact relieved are due to wrongful failure to employ effective methods of available pain management, not to a prohibition of assisted suicide or euthanasia. But even with adequate pain relief, some dying patients would prefer active steps to end their lives to "letting nature take its course." Moreover, public opinion polls consistently show that a majority believes assisted suicide and euthanasia should be available to patients who want it. Although few people would ever exercise the choice to use assisted suicide or euthanasia, many more would get the important reassurance that, should they want them, they would be available. Finally, some patients would have a more peaceful, humane, and dignified death. Denying this alternative to patients who want it has a cost that should not be borne lightly in a society that values self-determination highly in its moral, political, and legal traditions.

Opponents of permitting assisted suicide or euthanasia cite a number of potential bad consequences. For example, they argue that assisted suicide and euthanasia are incompatible with the fundamental moral and professional commitments of physicians as healers to care for patients and protect life (Gaylin et al. 1988). Public trust in the profession's commitment to fight with the patient against disease and death might be undermined if physicians also became "the angels of death." Physicians themselves might also find the role of administrator of euthanasia in uneasy conflict with their role as medical caregivers to the sick and dying, and their capacity to care effectively for the dying might be undermined. Moreover, opponents fear that permitting assisted suicide and euthanasia would weaken society's commitment to provide optimal care for dying patients, especially frail and vulnerable elderly patients, in an era of cost containment in health care. But perhaps the most common and influential worry of opponents is expressed in the so-called slippery slope argument (Kamisar 1958). Even if we begin by permitting assisted suicide and euthanasia in the few cases in which such direct killing might be justified, we would inevitably end up permitting it in a great many other cases in which it would be wrong. It is the first step on the path to the Nazi policy of killing the old and the weak and the socially disfavored and must be firmly resisted. Since this path is slippery and steep, we must stay off it altogether.

What is to be made of this argument? If the factual claim is true that any relaxation of the prohibition of assisted suicide or euthanasia must inevitably lead to the Nazis' final solution, then all will agree that the prohibition must be firmly maintained. What is controversial, however, is how serious and likely is the risk of abuse. There are few data regarding such risks and what data there are are controversial. For example, both proponents and opponents of assisted suicide and euthanasia cite the example of the Netherlands, the only country in which the practices are legally permitted, in support of claims that the practices can or cannot be adequately limited and controlled (Van der Maas 1991). It is uncontroversial, however, that the likelihood of abuse depends on the procedures and safeguards that are built into any policy proposal and practice. More extreme versions of the slippery slope, those that see the practice as leading to the Nazi euthanasia program, lack credibility; we can and do make very clear and firm distinctions, for example, between voluntary and involuntary euthanasia, and the values supporting the former in no way support the latter. More likely is that over time the practice might be extended from competent patients to surrogates choosing for incompetent patients, just as has happened with forgoing life support. But even if this occurred, it would not be all bad, just as extending authority to surrogates to forgo life support for incompetent patients has not been entirely, or even overall, for the worse.

Reasonable people disagree both about the likelihood of these and other good and bad effects occurring from an authorization of assisted suicide or voluntary active euthanasia, as well as about the relative moral importance of them. I believe that these and other considerations, on balance, do support a carefully controlled practice permitting physician-assisted suicide and voluntary euthanasia. Different persons, however, can reasonably reach different conclusions about whether this trade-off, on balance, argues in favor of or against permitting suicide and euthanasia, but it is on the basis of such considerations that the policy question ought to be decided.

INTENDED VERSUS MERELY FORESEEN CONSEQUENCES

Some have seen a different issue at stake in assisted suicide and euthanasia. They argue that the intentional killing of innocent human beings is morally wrong, but actions from which a person's death is foreseen, though not intended, may sometimes be morally permissible (Fried 1978). This is the distinction embodied in the Roman Catholic Doctrine of Double Effect, sometimes also characterized as the difference between direct and indirect intention (Frey 1975). It is important not merely in its potential implications for active euthanasia but also for the issue of providing adequate relief of suffering to the dying. The following cases illustrate both implications. It sometimes happens that, in the final stages of some terminal cancers, levels of medication (usually morphine) necessary to control pain reach levels that seriously risk depressing the patient's respiration and hastening his or her death. In such cases physicians often administer morphine at a patient's request with the intention or goal of relieving the patient's suffering, but foresee, though not intend, the patient's likely earlier death from respiratory depression. Most physicians, on the other hand, would not give a lethal injection of potassium chloride (which causes cardiac arrest and death) at the patient's request to end the patient's suffering if morphine were unavailable or unavailing. Apart from what is legally permitted, is there an important moral difference between the two cases?

Many think that the important difference lies in the physician's intentions. No fully adequate analysis exists of the concept of intention. Nevertheless, it does seem that the patient's earlier death is intended only in the morphine, not in the potassium chloride, case. In each case, however, the physician's aim is to respond to the patient's request to end his suffering. The difference appears to be that in the potassium chloride case the means used to do so is to kill the patient; only through his death is the suffering ended. In the morphine case the administration of morphine is the means to the end of relieving the suffering and earlier death is merely a foreseen side effect. The end sought is the same in each case, and the difference is that the death is the means to the end in one case and the foreseen consequence of achieving the end in the other.

Can this difference be of sufficient moral importance to make the one morally permissible and the other prohibited? Many have argued that it cannot (Bennett 1981). In each case, the physician's end or motive of relieving suffering at the request of the patient is the same. In each case, it is causally impossible to end the patient's suffering without acting in a way that will cause his death. In each case, both the patient and physician are prepared to end the suffering even at the cost of the patient's earlier death. The relief of suffering is judged to be of sufficient importance to justify acting in a way that leads to death. These seem to be the essential value judgments involved and they do not differ in the two cases. The difference in intention seems to be one of causal and temporal structure—in one, the death precedes and brings about the end and relief of suffering; in the other, it temporally follows and is a causal consequence of achieving the end. It is hard to see why this difference in causal and temporal structure should have much, or any, moral importance. It is tempting to reply that in the morphine case one would have given the morphine even if respiratory depression and death would not have followed, but that the point of the potassium chloride was to cause death. However, if somehow potassium chloride would have relieved the suffering without causing death, one would have given it as well. In each case, in the circumstances that existed, it was necessary to act in a way that the physician knew would lead to the patient's death as a way to relieve his suffering.

There is a difference in the two cases in the certainty with which the earlier death will occur. It may never be completely certain that the dosage level of morphine is sufficient to cause death, and none would deny that this is a morally significant difference in the two cases. However, in some instances this difference in probability may be extremely small and so not support a great moral difference between the two cases. In any event, this is a difference in the risk of a bad outcome and not of intentions. Critics of the foreseen/intended distinction have argued that physicians are reasonably held equally morally responsible for all the foreseen consequences of their actions, regardless of whether intended, because all such consequences are under their control. In this perspective, in both cases it is a matter of weighing the relative benefits and burdens to the patient of relieving his suffering and shortening his life. If the patient judges that relief of suffering is paramount, the physician would be morally justified in acting in either the morphine or potassium chloride case. For the reasons of public policy discussed above it may be wise, nevertheless, not legally to authorize the performance of direct voluntary euthanasia as in the potassium chloride case. It is important to emphasize that this would not be because the two cases are in themselves significantly different morally, but because of public policy concerns about the one and not the other. It is important to emphasize also that the general right of the patient to decide about treatment includes the right to have adequate pain medication, even if that may shorten his life. The relief of suffering is a longstanding, central, and fully legitimate aim of medicine. . . .

References

Bennett, J. "Morality and Consequences." In S. M. McMurrin, Ed., *The Tanner Lectures in Human Value II*. Salt Lake City: University of Utah Press, 1981.

Brock, D. W. *Life and Death: Philosophical Essays in Biomedical Ethics*. New York: Cambridge University Press, 1993.

Buchanan, A. E., Brock. D. W. *Deciding for Others: The Ethics of Surrogate Decision-Making*. New York: Cambridge University Press, 1989.

Dworkin, G. *The Theory and Practice of Autonomy.* Cambridge, MA: Cambridge University Press, 1988.

Frey, R. "Some Aspects to the Doctrine of Double Effect." *Can J Philos* 5 (1975): 259-283.

Fried, C. *Right and Wrong.* Cambridge: Harvard University Press, 1978.

Gaylin, W., Kass, L., Pellegrino, E., Siegler, M. "Doctors Must Not Kill." *JAMA* 259 (1988): 2139-2140.

Glover, J. *Causing Death and Saving Lives.* New York: Penguin Books, 1977.

Green, M., Wikler, D. "Brain Death and Personal Identity." *Philos Public Affairs* 9 (1980): 105-133.

Hastings Center. *Guidelines for the Termination of Treatment and Care of the Dying.* Briarcliff Manor, NY: The Hastings Center, 1988.

Kamisar, Y. "Some Non-Religious Views Against Proposed Mercy Killing Legislation." *Minn L Rev* 42 (1958): 969-1042.

Kamm, F. *Morality/Mortality.* Oxford: Oxford University Press, 1993.

Kass, L. *Toward a More Natural Science: Biology and Human Affairs.* New York: Free Press, 1985.

Katz, J. *The Silent World of Doctor and Patient.* New York: Free Press, 1984.

President's Commission for Ethical Problems in Medicine. *Defining Death.* Washington, DC: U.S. Government Printing Office, 1981.

———. *Making Health-Care Decisions.* Washington, DC: U.S. Government Printing Office, 1982.

———. *Deciding to Forgo Life-Sustaining Treatment.* Washington, DC: U.S. Government Printing Office, 1983a.

———. *Securing Access to Health Care.* Washington, DC: U.S. Government Printing Office, 1983b.

Rachels, J. "Active and Passive Euthanasia." *N Engl J Med* 292 (1975): 78-80.

Rosner, F. "Hospital Medical Ethics Committees: A Review of Their Development." *JAMA* 253 (1985): 2693-2697.

Siegler, M., Weisbard, A. "Against the Emerging Stream." *Arch Intern Med* 145 (1985): 129-131.

Singer, P., Kuhse, H. *Should This Baby Live?* New York: Oxford University Press, 1986.

Steinbock, B., Ed. *Killing and Letting Die.* Englewood Cliffs, NJ: Prentice Hall, 1980.

Tomlinson, T., Brody, H. "Futility and the Ethics of Resuscitation." *JAMA* 264 (1990): 1276-1280.

Van der Maas, P., et al. "Euthanasia and Other Medical Decisions Concerning the End of Life," *Lancet* 338 (1991): 669-674.

Veatch, R. M. "The Whole-Brain Oriented Concept of Death: An Outmoded Philosophical Formulation." *J Thanatol* 13 (1975): 13-30.

Wanzer, S., et al. "The Physicians' Responsibility Toward Hopelessly Ill Patients." *N Engl J Med* 310 (1984): 955-959.

Weir, R. *Selective Non-Treatment of Handicapped Newborns.* New York: Oxford University Press, 1984.

CARL B. BECKER

Buddhist Views of Suicide and Euthanasia

. . . Japan has long been more aware of and sensitive to the dying process than modern Western cultures. Moreover, Japan already has its own good philosophical and experiential background to deal effectively with "new" issues of bioethics, such as euthanasia. Japanese Buddhists have long recognized what Westerners are only recently rediscovering: that the manner of dying at the moment of death is very important. This fundamental premise probably predates Buddhism itself, but is made very explicit in the teachings of the Buddha.[1] In his meditations, the Buddha noticed that even people with good karma were sometimes born into bad situations, and even those with bad karma were sometimes found inordinately pleasant rebirths. Buddha declared that the crucial variable governing rebirth was the nature of the consciousness at the moment of death. Thereafter, Buddhists placed high importance on holding the proper thoughts at the moment of death. Many examples of this idea can be found in two works of the Theravāda canon, the *Petavatthu* and the *Vimānavatthu* ("Stories of the Departed"). Indeed, in many sutras, monks visit laymen on their deathbeds to ensure that their dying thoughts are wholesome,[2] and the Buddha recommends that lay followers similarly encourage each other on such occasions.[3]

Buddhism sees death as not the end of life, but simply a transition; suicide is therefore no escape from anything. Thus, in the early *sangha* (community of followers of the Buddha), suicide was in principle condemned as an inappropriate action.[4] But the early Buddhist texts include many cases of suicide of Vakkali[5] and of Channa[6] were committed in the face of painful and irreversible sickness. It is significant, however, that the Buddha's praise of the suicides is *not* based on the fact that they were in terminal states, but rather that their minds were selfless, desireless, and enlightened at the moments of their passing.

This theme is more dramatically visible in the example of Godhika. This disciple repeatedly achieved an advanced level of *samādhi,* bordering on *parinirvāṇa,* and then slipped out of the state of enlightenment into normal consciousness again. After this happened six times, Godhika at last vowed to pass on to the next realm while enlightened, and quietly committed suicide during his next period of enlightenment. While cautioning his other disciples against suicide, the Buddha nonetheless blessed and praised Godhika's steadiness of mind and purpose, and declared that he had passed on to *nirvāṇa.* In short, the acceptability of suicide, even in the early Buddhist community, depended not on terminal illness alone, but upon the state of selfless equanimity with which one was able to pass away. It is interesting in passing that all these suicides were committed by the subject knifing himself, a technique which came to be standardized in later Japanese ritual suicide.

When asked about the morality of committing suicide to move on to the next world, the Buddha did not criticize it.[7] He emphasized that only the uncraving mind would be able to move on towards *nirvāṇa,* and that, conversely, minds desiring to get free of or flee something by their death might achieve nothing. Similarly, there are stories in the Jātaka tales of the Buddha giving his own body (in former lives) to save other beings, both animals and humans. Thus death out of compassion for others is also lauded in the scriptures.[8] It is also well known that in the Jain tradition, saints were expected to fast until their deaths,[9] and thereafter there have been those in both China and Japan who have followed this tradition.[10]

In China, it is believed that a disciple of Zendō's jumped out of a tree in order to kill himself and reach the Pure Land. Zendō's response was not that the action of suicide was right or wrong in and of itself, but that the disciple who wanted so strongly to see the Pure Land was doubtless ready to reach it.[11] Other more recent examples may be found in the Buddhist suicides of the Vietnamese monks protesting against the Vietnam government.[12] Whether or not these stories are all historical fact is not at issue here. The point is that they demonstrate the consistent Buddhist position toward suicide: there is nothing intrinsically wrong with taking one's own life, if it is not done in hate, anger, or fear. Equanimity or preparedness of mind is the main issue.

In summary, Buddhism realizes that death is not the end of anything, but a transition. Buddhism has long recognized persons' rights to determine when they should move on from this existence to the next. The important consideration here is not whether the body lives or dies, but whether the mind can remain at peace and in harmony with itself. The Jōdo (Pure Land) tradition tends to stress the continuity of life, while the Zen tradition tends to stress the importance of the time and manner of dying. Both of these ideas are deeply rooted in the Japanese consciousness. . . .

---

[1][Becker's notes have been renumbered—ed.] Cf. *Hastings Encyclopedia of Religion,* vol. 4, p. 448.

[2]*Majhima Nikāya* II, 91; III, 258.

[3]*Samyutta Nikāya* V, 408.

[4]Tamaki Koshirō, "Shi no oboegaki": (Memoranda on death), in *Bukkyō shisō,* vol. 10, ed. Bukkyō Shisō Kenkyūkai, Tokyo (September 1988), pp. 465–475.

[5]*Sūtta Vibhaṅga, Vinaya* III, 74; cf. *Samyutta Nikāya* III. 119-124.

[6]*Majhima Nikaya* III, 263-266 (*Channovada-sūtta*); *Samyutta Nikāya* IV, 55-60 (*Channavaga*).

[7]*Samyutta Nikāya* I, 121.

[8]*Jataka Suvarṇa Prabhāsa* 206ff.

[9]*Ācāranga Sūtra* I, 7, 6.

[10]A mummified body of one such monk is preserved in the Myorenji temple, close to Tsukuba University.

[11]Ogasawara Senshū, *Chūgoku Jōdokyō no kenkyū* (Researches in Chinese Pure Land Buddhism) (Kyoto: Heirakuji, 1951), pp. 60ff.

[12]Thich Nhat Hanh. *The Lotus in the Sea of Fire* (London, S. C. M. Press, 1967).

U.S. SUPREME COURT

Cruzan v. Director, Missouri Department of Health (1990)

At common law, even the touching of one person by another without consent and without legal justification was a battery. . . . Before the turn of the century, this Court observed that "[n]o right is held more sacred, or is more carefully guarded, by the common law, than the right of every individual to the possession and control of his own person, free from all restraint or interference of others, unless by clear and unquestionable authority of law." *Union Pacific R. Co.* v. *Botsford,* 141 US 250, 251 (1891). This notion of bodily integrity has been embodied in the requirement that informed consent is generally required for medical treatment. . . .

The logical corollary of the doctrine of informed consent is that the patient generally possesses the right not to consent, that is, to refuse treatment.

For purposes of this case, we assume that the United States Constitution would grant a competent person a constitutionally protected right to refuse lifesaving hydration and nutrition.

Petitioners . . . assert that an incompetent person should possess the same right in this respect as is possessed by a competent person.

The difficulty with petitioners' claim is that in a sense it begs the question: an incompetent person is not able to make an informed and voluntary choice to exercise a hypothetical right to refuse treatment or any other right. Such a "right" must be exercised for her, if at all, by some sort of surrogate. Here, Missouri has in effect recognized that under certain circumstances a surrogate may act for the patient in electing to have hydration and nutrition withdrawn in such a way as to cause death, but it has established a procedural safeguard to assure that the action of the surrogate conforms as best it may to the wishes expressed by the patient while competent. Missouri requires that evidence of the incompetent's wishes as to the withdrawal of treatment be proved by clear and convincing evidence. The question, then, is whether the United States Constitution forbids the establishment of this procedural requirement by the State. We hold that it does not.

Whether or not Missouri's clear and convincing evidence requirement comports with the United States Constitution depends in part on what interests the State may properly seek to protect in this situation. Missouri relies on its interest in the protection and preservation of human life, and there can be no gainsaying this interest. As a general matter, the States—indeed, all civilized nations—demonstrate their commitment to life by treating homicide as serious crime. Moreover, the majority of States in this country have laws imposing criminal penalties on one who assists another to commit suicide. We do not think a State is required to remain neutral in the face of an informed and voluntary decision by a physically-able adult to starve to death.

But in the context presented here, a State has more particular interests at stake. The choice between life and death is a deeply personal decision of obvious and overwhelming finality. We believe Missouri may legitimately seek to safeguard the personal element of this choice through the imposition of heightened evidentiary requirements. It cannot be disputed that the Due Process Clause protects an interest in life as well as an interest in refusing life-sustaining medical treatment. Not all incompetent patients will have loved ones available to serve as surrogate decisionmakers. And even where family members are present "[t]here will, of course, be some unfortunate situations in which family members will not act to protect a patient." *In re Jobes,* 108 NJ 394, 419, 529 A2d 434, 477 (1987). A State is entitled to guard against potential abuses in such situations. Similarly, a State is entitled to consider that a judicial proceeding to make a determination regarding an incompetent's wishes may very well not be an adversarial one, with the added guarantee of accurate factfinding that the adversary process brings with it. See *Ohio* v. *Akron Center for Reproductive Health,* 111 L Ed 2d 405 (1990). Finally, we think a State may properly decline to make judgments about the "quality" of life that a particular individual may enjoy, and simply assert an unqualified interest in the preservation of human life to be weighed against the constitutionally protected interests of the individual.

In our view, Missouri has permissibly sought to advance these interests through the adoption of a "clear and convincing" standard of proof to govern such proceedings.

CHAPTER 8

FAIRNESS

■══════■

INTRODUCTION

The final duty to be discussed is the duty to treat others fairly. Fair treatment is intimately associated with equal treatment; hence often the requirement of fair treatment is expressed as the duty to treat others as equals. Like the duty of nonmaleficence (which libertarians fashion into a complete moral framework) and the duty of beneficence (which Noddings fashioned into a moral framework in Chapter 7), the duty of fairness is sometimes considered the essential ingredient in an entire theory of right or justice. The view that justice is essentially fairness may be sustained on the basis of two main assumptions: (1) society is composed of individuals and groups of individuals with conflicting interests, and (2) it is just to regulate the pursuit of these competing interests on the basis of rules that treat everyone *fairly.*

This chapter examines the leading attempt to develop the concept of fairness into a general theory of justice, namely, Rawls's theory of justice as fairness. It then considers fairness as applied to social opportunities such as employment, and as applied to punishment for capital crimes.

JUSTICE AS FAIRNESS

1. THE ARISTOTELIAN BACKGROUND

Insofar as a particular virtue corresponds to the duty of fairness, that virtue would presumably be *justice.* Aristotle discusses justice in Book V of his *Nicomachean Ethics* (not reproduced here). He notes that sometimes the term *just* is simply a synonym of *moral,* and sometimes it means something more specific, namely *fairness.* Justice as fairness takes two main forms: distributive justice and rectificatory justice. Distributive justice concerns assets held jointly, such as a business owned by two or more people, and it consists in equality for equals. Thus if two people have made equal contributions to a business enterprise, they should receive equal returns on their joint endeavor, but if one person makes a greater investment, the returns should be distributed in proportion to contributions. Rectificatory justice concerns unjust gains and losses, and it consists in restoring the victim's losses and eliminating the aggressor's improper gains.

2. RAWLS

In his book *A Theory of Justice,* John Rawls, a philosopher at Harvard University, defends a theory he calls "justice as fairness." Rawls does not maintain that justice is exactly the same thing as fairness, but he sees a substantial overlap between the two. Rawls identifies his view as a contractarian theory, which is a theory that uses the device of a contract to help illuminate the concept of justice. In this characterization, Rawls aligns himself with theorists such as Thomas Hobbes (1588–1679), John Locke, Jean-Jacques Rousseau (1712–1778), and Immanuel Kant. Of these, Rawls's view is most comparable to that of Kant.

Rawls suggests that injustice is "simply inequalities that are not to the benefit of all." However, he qualifies this claim in several ways. First, he limits the scope of his thesis. He addresses the issue of justice for normal, fully cooperating members of society only, and simply declines to discuss the demands of justice for groups such as the mentally deficient or the physically handicapped. He also declines to discuss the issue of criminal justice. Second, Rawls focuses on the main institutions of society, which he calls the *basic structure,* and he declines to discuss what justice might demand in specific cases. Finally, Rawls revises his view substantially in later writings. Most importantly, he replaces his liberty principle with one that requires the protection of a much less extensive set of liberties. In their most current form, his revisions appear in his book *Political Liberalism* (New York: Columbia University Press, 1993).

Rawls's main idea is to assess principles of justice using a conceptual device he calls the *original position.* The original position is a hypothetical situation that corresponds in some ways to the state of nature imagined by Locke and other contractarians. In the original position, Rawls conceives a representative of each person in society. My representative evaluates alternative conceptions of justice on my behalf and attempts to serve my interests. Rawls designs the original position with restrictions on the representatives that ensure fair representation, expecting that the representatives will then choose fair principles of justice. Some salient features define the original position:

1. The representatives have equal powers.

2. The representatives have the same motivation: Each wants to serve the interests of the person represented (and that person alone) as well as possible.

3. The representatives choose rationally, ranking options according to how well they serve the people represented.

4. The representatives are situated behind a "veil of ignorance." They do not know various facts about the people they represent, such as their social positions, genders, races, natural assets, psychological propensities, or even the particulars about their conceptions of the good.

3. KURT VONNEGUT, JR.

In "Harrison Bergeron," Kurt Vonnegut parodies the idea that society should be arranged so that in every way people are equals. He invites the reader to ask how important equality is and how extensively it should prevail.

NONDISCRIMINATION

1. WASSERSTROM

In his essay Richard A. Wasserstrom, a philosopher at the University of California, Santa Cruz, attempts to clarify the requirements of justice concerning racism, sexism, and preferential treatment. He discusses these topics from three perspectives. The perspective of *social realities* concerns itself with the facts about how race and sex affect people in society. Second, the perspective of *ideals* is concerned with how race and sex *ought* to affect people. Third, the perspective of *instrumentalities* is concerned with the means by which the ideal may be achieved.

According to Wasserstrom, the social reality is that our society is racist and sexist. He says that "in our culture to be nonwhite—and especially to be black—is to be treated and seen to be a member of a group that is different from and inferior to the group of standard, fully developed persons, the adult white males." Moreover, in today's culture "it is more advantageous to be a male rather than a female." When he discusses the perspective of ideals, Wasserstrom notes substantial disagreement concerning how sex and race ought to affect people in a just society. According to the assimilationist ideal, sex and race would have no more affect on the way people are treated than does eye color. But this requires the elimination of all sex-role differentiation: if a nonsexist society is one in which a person's sex has no more significance than one's eye color, then laws requiring such things as same sex marriages would be sexist. Indeed, "bisexuality, not heterosexuality or homosexuality, would be the norm for intimate, sexual relationships in the ideal society that was assimilationist in respect to sex." Some people might prefer to develop an ideal other than the assimilationist ideal, such as the diversity ideal or the ideal of toleration. Wasserstrom goes on to defend affirmative action programs from various charges, including racism or sexism.

2. STEELE

Shelby Steele's essay "Affirmative Action" is Chapter 7 of his book *The Content of Our Character.* Steele argues that affirmative action programs are Faustian bargains. He acknowledges powerful arguments in favor of affirmative action, but he raises the concern that such programs lead people to suppose that African Americans are inferior people, which is demoralizing to them. He also suggests that these programs encourage blacks to "exploit their own past victimization as a source of power and privilege," which encourages blacks to "become invested in the view of one's self as a victim," and provides them an incentive to be "reliant on others just as we are struggling for self-reliance." Affirmative action programs also help to prevent African Americans from reaching top positions of authority, since they contribute to reputations of advancement by color as much as by competence. At some point, corporations "shift the emphasis from color to competence" and "preference backfires for blacks and becomes a taint that holds them back." Instead of affirmative action, Steele would prefer economic development for all disadvantaged people, supported by measures to eradicate racial and gender discrimination.

(CAPITAL) PUNISHMENT

Should society punish people for serious breaches of morality or crimes? In particular, is the death penalty an appropriate punishment? Several leading positions have emerged concerning the moral acceptability of punishment in general and the death penalty in particular. A position called *rehabilitationism* rejects punishment altogether, while two others, called *deterrentism* and *retributionism,* defend the appropriateness of punishment in substantially different ways.

1. VIEWS CONCERNING PUNISHMENT

Rehabilitationists

Some argue that people are not really responsible for their behavior, since it results in the final analysis from their genetic inheritances or social environments or both, and not the autonomous choices of the individuals. In effect, this position claims that people are incapable of acting immorally *or* morally. Consequently, no one deserves punishment, even murderers, and the sensible response to behavior that seriously harms people is rehabilitation of those who have caused the harm, or confinement to protect others if rehabilitation is not possible.

Deterrentists

A second position argues that punishment is appropriate regardless of whether people are in the final analysis responsible for their behavior. Punishment is appropriate because people, like other animals, respond to threats, and the threat of punishment is a necessary and effective deterrent to serious crimes or breaches of morality. The death penalty, in particular, is an appropriate deterrent to potential murderers, thus saving the lives of innocent people who otherwise would die. Utilitarians tend to favor the deterrentist stance, viewing punishment as an evil, since it causes pain for some, but a necessary one, since it increases overall utility in society. A common reservation charges that the utilitarian approach to punishment appears to countenance unfair, undeserved punishments: If punishing wrongdoers far more than they deserve would boost the effectiveness of a deterrent, why not inflict extraordinarily harsh punishments? If punishing the innocent would also deter certain acts of wrongdoing, why not do so? On the other hand, if punishing certain acts of wrongdoing, however grave, would have no deterrent effect, why do it?

Retributionists

Perhaps the most common view concerning punishment presupposes that society can reasonably hold most people responsible for their behavior most of the time. Given that people are responsible for their improper acts, they deserve punishment for these acts: To give punishment comparable to the seriousness of wrongful behavior is to treat offenders with fairness and hence morality or justice. As Jeffrey Reiman says in his essay, both the Golden Rule (do unto others as you would have them do unto you) and *lex talionis* (an eye for an eye) seem to call for fair treatment of others, that is, treatment as equals. *Lex talionis* in particular suggests that when others cause harm, those injured can justly pay them back with comparable harm. Given the seriousness of certain acts of murder, the fair punishment is execution, according to many retributionists.

Retributionists and utilitarian defenders of the deterrence view seem to offer deeply conflicting approaches to punishment. While the point of punishment on the retributionist view is to give wrongdoers what they deserve, which is a backwards looking view, proponents of the deterrentist view say that concern over the past ignores the important point, which is the future consequences of punishment.

2. REIMAN

Jeffrey Reiman, professor of philosophy at American University, sees value in both the deterrentist and the retributionist views. Agreeing with retributionists, he says that in principle, the death penalty is a just punishment for some murderers, inasmuch as some murderers deserve to be killed. Agreeing with deterrentists, Reiman says that the death penalty should probably be maintained if needed to deter future murderers, "since otherwise we would be sacrificing the future victims of potential murderers whom we could have deterred." But Reiman does not believe that the death penalty is needed to deter future murderers, citing evidence that suggests that long prison sentences are as effective as the death penalty. He adds that justice can result from less severe punishments than the ones murderers deserve, or else jailers would have to rape rapists and torture torturers. Reiman suggests replacing the death penalty with a less severe penalty because "in refraining from imposing the death penalty, the state, by its vivid and impressive example, contributes to reducing our tolerance for cruelty and thereby fosters the advance of human civilization as we understand it."

3. NATHANSON

Stephen Nathanson, professor of philosophy at Northeastern University, questions the retributionist claim that the death penalty is appropriate because some murderers deserve to die. The claim that the death penalty is an appropriate sanction presupposes that it can be applied accurately and fairly, but it cannot be, according to Nathanson. He notes that complex, imprecise, and controversial criteria determine what people deserve, which makes likely unfair and inaccurate applications of penalties in general and the death penalty in particular. He cites the Supreme Court decision in *Furman* v. *Georgia* (1972) that the death penalty was being applied so unfairly that it violated the constitution. Nathanson asserts that in *Gregg* v. *Georgia* (1976), the Supreme Court incorrectly allowed the penalty once again after states took steps to alleviate the problem of unfair applications.

4. VAN DEN HAAG

Ernest van den Haag, Professor Emeritus of Jurisprudence and Public Policy at Fordham University, makes a case in favor of capital punishment. Elsewhere (see, for example, his book, *The Death Penalty: A Debate*) he argues on common-sense grounds that the death penalty is a stronger deterrent for crimes than life imprisonment, and he adds that even under uncertainty about its deterrent effect, society should continue to impose the death penalty and gamble with the lives of convicted murderers rather than with the lives of innocent victims. The death penalty is especially appropriate in special cases, such as the case of criminals who are already serving life sentences. In the essay printed here, van den Haag responds to Reiman and Nathanson.

Questions for Reflection

1. Suppose that Reiman is correct in saying that when the state, which is uniquely positioned and visible, refuses to torture the torturers who deserve that punishment and refuses to kill murderers who deserve to be killed, it helps reduce people's tolerance for cruelty. How does this argument apply to people other than the state? Should victims' relatives be allowed to provide the punishment that, Reiman admits, is a just response to torturers and murderers?

2. Does Reiman make a convincing case that the death penalty is an especially horrible punishment? His main point is that the death brought about by execution is unavoidable and foreseen by its victim. But with some qualifications, does everyone face such a death?

3. In "Capital Punishment and Deterrence" (*Philosophy & Public Affairs* 3 (1974): 431–443), D. A. Conway argues that van den Haag's argument about gambling with lives is invalid because capital punishment guarantees that convicted murderers will die, but eliminating it leaves only a probability that more innocent people will die. Assess Conway's criticism.

4. Should society be arranged to encourage bisexuality, given the assimilationist idea discussed by Wasserstrom? If not, should society not be arranged so that a person's sex has no more significance than eye color?

5. Does a view of justice as fairness require that society prevent conservative religious parents from raising their children to embrace sexist values? Why or why not? Would doing so violate the parents' rights?

6. According to Aristotle, people who make a greater contribution to a joint enterprise should receive correspondingly greater returns. Would Rawls agree? Why or why not?

7. What would Rawls's theory of justice as fairness require if it were extended to the case of people who need extremely expensive medical treatment? What would it require if extended to the case of people with severe handicaps?

8. How would Nietzsche react to Rawls's theory of justice as fairness? How might Rawls respond?

9. Is the society Vonnegut sketches more just than yours? Would justice as Rawls understands it condemn the society Vonnegut imagines?

10. Which policy is more just: (1) completely banning liver transplants, so that they are equally unavailable; (2) allowing a free-market of livers, so that liver transplants go to recipients chosen by donors—usually the highest bidders; (3) distribution by lottery; (4) distribution by need; (5) distribution by moral merit.

11. Is the right thing to do always to act fairly? (Is fairness our only duty?) Or are there competing duties that sometimes require departures from fairness?

Selected Readings

On Rawls

Blocker, H, and Elizabeth Smith, eds. *John Rawls's Theory of Social Justice*. Athens: Ohio University Press, 1980.

Daniels, Norman. *Reading Rawls*. New York: Basic Books, 1976.

On Discrimination

Banton, Michael. *International Action against Racial Discrimination*. Oxford: Clarendon Press, 1996.

Boxill, Bernard. *Blacks and Social Justice*. Totowa: Rowman and Allenheld, 1984.

Bubeck, Diemut. *Care, Gender, and Justice*. Oxford: Clarendon Press, 1995.

Fullinwider, Robert. *The Reverse Discrimination Controversy*. Totowa: Rowman and Littlefield, 1980.

Goldman, Alan. *Justice and Reverse Discrimination*. Princeton: Princeton University Press, 1979.

On Punishment

Ewing, A. C. *The Morality of Punishment*. London: Kegan Paul, 1929.

Hart, H. L. A. *Punishment and Responsibility*. New York: Oxford University Press, 1968.

Honderich, Ted. *Punishment: The Supposed Justifications*. Harmondsworth, England: Penguin, 1984.

Hood, Roger. *Death Penalty*. Oxford: Clarendon Press, 1996.

Duff, R. A. *Trials and Punishments*. Cambridge: Cambridge University Press, 1986.

Mello, Michael. *Against the Death Penalty*. Boston: Northeastern University Press, 1996.

Ten, C. L. *Crime, Guilt, and Punishment*. Oxford: Clarendon Press, 1987.

EQUALITY

JOHN RAWLS

A Theory of Justice

1.   THE ROLE OF JUSTICE

. . . Let us assume, to fix ideas, that a society is a more or less self-sufficient association of persons who in their relations to one another recognize certain rules of conduct as binding and who for the most part act in accordance with them. Suppose further that these rules specify a system of cooperation designed to advance the good of those taking part in it. Then, although a society is a cooperative venture for mutual advantage, it is typically marked by a conflict as well as by an identity of interests. There is an identity of interests since social cooperation makes possible a better life for all than any would have if each were to live solely by his own efforts. There is a conflict of interests since persons are not indifferent as to how the greater benefits produced by their collaboration are distributed, for in order to pursue their ends they each prefer a larger to a lesser share. A set of principles is required for choosing among the various social arrangements which determine this division of advantages and for underwriting an agreement on the proper distributive shares. These principles are the principles of social justice: they provide a way of assigning rights and duties in the basic institutions of society and they define the appropriate distribution of the benefits and burdens of social cooperation.

. . . Men disagree about which principles should define the basic terms of their association. Yet we may still say, despite this disagreement, that they each have a conception of justice. That is, they understand the need for, and they are prepared to affirm, a characteristic set of principles for assigning basic rights and duties and for determining what they take to be the proper distribution of the benefits and burdens of social cooperation. Thus it seems natural to think of the concept of justice as distinct from the various conceptions of justice and as being specified by the role which these different sets of principles, these different conceptions, have in common.[1] . . .

2.   THE SUBJECT OF JUSTICE

Many different kinds of things are said to be just and unjust: not only laws, institutions, and social systems, but also particular actions of many kinds, including decisions, judgments, and imputations. We also call the attitudes and dispositions of persons, and persons themselves, just and unjust. Our topic, however, is that of social justice. For us the primary subject of justice is the basic structure of society, or more exactly, the way in which the major social institutions distribute fundamental rights and duties and determine the division of advantages from social cooperation. By major institutions I understand the political constitution and the principle economic and social arrangements. . . . The basic structure is the primary subject of justice because its effects are so profound and present from the start. . . .

The scope of our inquiry is limited in two ways. First of all, I am concerned with a special case of the problem of justice. I shall not consider the justice of institutions and social practices generally, nor except in passing the justice of the law of nations and of relations between states. . . .

The other limitation on our discussion is that for the most part I examine the principles of justice that would regulate a well-ordered society. Everyone is presumed to act justly and to do his part in upholding just institutions. Though justice may be, as Hume remarked, the cautious, jealous virtue, we can still ask what a perfectly just society would be like. Thus I consider primarily what I call strict compliance as opposed to partial compliance theory. . . . The latter studies the principles that govern how we are to deal with injustice.

3.   THE MAIN IDEA OF THE THEORY OF JUSTICE

My aim is to present a conception of justice which generalizes and carries to a higher level of abstraction the familiar theory of the social contract as found, say, in Locke, Rousseau, and Kant. In order to do this we are not to think of the original contract as one to enter a particular society or to set up a particular form of government. Rather, the guiding idea is that the principles of justice for the basic structure of society are the object of the original agreement. They are the principles that free and rational persons concerned to further their own interests would accept in an initial position of equality as defining the fundamental terms of their association. These principles are to regulate all further agreements; they specify the kinds of social cooperation that can be entered into and the forms of government that can be established. This way of regarding the principles of justice I shall call justice as fairness.

Thus we are to imagine that those who engage in social cooperation choose together, in one joint act, the principles which are to assign basic rights and duties and to determine the division of social benefits. . . . The choice which rational men would make in this hypothetical situation of equal liberty, assuming for the present that this choice problem has a solution, determines the principles of justice.

In justice as fairness the original position of equality corresponds to the state of nature in the traditional theory of the social contract. This original position is not, of course, thought of as an actual historical state of affairs, much less as a primitive condition of culture. It is understood as a purely hypothetical situation characterized so as to lead to a certain conception of justice. Among the essential features of this situation is that no one knows his place in society, his class position or social status, nor does any one know his fortune in the distribution of natural assets and abilities, his intelligence, strength, and the like. I shall even assume that the parties do not know their conceptions of the good or their special psychological propensities. The principles of justice are chosen behind a veil of ignorance. This ensures that no one is advantaged or disadvantaged in the choice of principles by the outcome of natural chance or the contingency of social circumstances. Since all are similarly situated and no one is able to design principles to favor his particular condition, the principles of justice are the result of a fair agreement or bargain. For given the circumstances of the original position, the symmetry of everyone's relations to each other, this initial situation is fair between individuals as moral persons, that is, as rational beings with their own ends and capable, I shall assume, of a sense of justice. The original position is, one might say, the appropriate initial status quo, and thus the fundamental agreements reached in it are fair. This explains the propriety of the name "justice as fairness": it conveys the idea that the principles of justice are agreed to in an initial situation that is fair. The name does not mean that the concepts of justice and fairness are the same, any more than the phrase "poetry as metaphor" means that the concepts of poetry and metaphor are the same.

Justice as fairness begins, as I have said, with one of the most general of all choices which persons might make together, namely, with the choice of the first principles of a conception of justice which is to regulate all subsequent criticism and reform of institutions. Then, having chosen a conception of justice, we can suppose that they are to choose a constitution and a legislature to enact laws, and so on, all in accordance with the principles of justice initially agreed upon. Our social situation is just if it is such that by this sequence of hypothetical agreements we would have contracted into the general system of rules which defines it. . . .

It seems reasonable to suppose that the parties in the original position are equal. That is, all have the same rights in the procedure for choosing principles; each can make proposals, submit reasons for their acceptance, and so on. Obviously the purpose of these conditions is to represent equality between human beings as moral persons, as creatures having a conception of their good and capable of a sense of justice. The basis of equality is taken to be similarity in these two respects. Systems of ends are not ranked in value; and each man is presumed to have the requisite ability to understand and to act upon whatever principles are adopted. Together with the veil of ignorance, these conditions define the principles of justice as those which rational persons concerned to advance their interests would consent to as equals when none are known to be advantaged or disadvantaged by social and natural contingencies.

There is, however, another side to justifying a particular description of the original position. This is to see if the principles which would be chosen match our considered convictions of justice or extend them in an acceptable way. We can note whether applying these principles would lead us to make the same judgments about the basic structure of society which we now make intuitively and in which we have the greatest confidence; or whether, in cases where our present judgments are in doubt and given with hesitation, these principles offer a resolution which we can affirm on reflection. . . .

In searching for the most favored description of this situation we work from both ends. We begin by describing it so that it represents generally shared and preferably weak conditions. We then see if these conditions are strong enough to yield a significant set of principles. . . . By going back and forth, sometimes altering the conditions of the contractual circumstances, at others withdrawing our judgments and conforming them to principle, I assume that eventually we shall find a description of the initial situation that both expresses reasonable conditions and yields principles which match our considered judgments duly pruned and adjusted. This state of affairs I refer to as reflective equilibrium. . . .

11.   TWO PRINCIPLES OF JUSTICE

I shall now state in a provisional form the two principles of justice that I believe would be chosen in the original position. . . .

The first statement of the two principles reads as follows.

First: each person is to have an equal right to the most extensive basic liberty compatible with a similar liberty for others.

Second: social and economic inequalities are to be arranged so that they are both (a) reasonably expected to be to everyone's advantage, and (b) attached to positions and offices open to all. . . .

As their formulation suggests, these principles presuppose that the social structure can be divided into two more or less distinct parts, the first principle applying to the one, the second to the other. They distinguish between those aspects of the social system that define and secure the equal liberties of citizenship and those that specify and establish social and economic inequalities. The basic liberties of citizens are, roughly speaking, political liberty (the right to vote and to be eligible for public office) together with freedom of speech and assembly; liberty of conscience and freedom of thought; freedom of the person along with the right to hold (personal) property; and freedom from arbitrary arrest and seizure as defined by the concept of the rule of law. These liberties are all required to be equal by the first principle, since citizens of a just society are to have the same basic rights.

The second principle applies, in the first approximation, to the distribution of income and wealth and to the design of organizations that make use of differences in authority and responsibility, or chains of command. While the distribution of wealth and income need not be equal, it must be to everyone's advantage, and at the same time, positions of authority and offices of command must be accessible to all. One applies the second principle by holding positions open, and then, subject to this constraint, arranges social and economic inequalities so that everyone benefits.

These principles are to be arranged in a serial order with the first principle prior to the second. . . .

It should be observed that the two principles (and this holds for all formulations) are a special case of a more general conception of justice that can be expressed as follows.

> All social values—liberty and opportunity, income and wealth, and the bases of self-respect—are to be distributed equally unless an unequal distribution of any, or all, of these values is to everyone's advantage.

Injustice, then, is simply inequalities that are not to the benefit of all.

----

[1]Rawls's notes have been omitted—ed.

Kurt Vonnegut, Jr.

Harrison Bergeron

The year was 2081, and everybody was finally equal. They weren't only equal before God and the law. They were equal every which way. Nobody was smarter than anybody else. Nobody was better looking than anybody else. Nobody was stronger or quicker than anybody else. All this equality was due to the 211th, 212th, and 213th Amendments to the Constitution, and to the unceasing vigilance of agents of the United States Handicapper General.

Some things about living still weren't quite right, though. April, for instance, still drove people crazy by not being springtime. And it was in that clammy month that the H-G men took George and Hazel Bergeron's 14-year-old son, Harrison, away.

It was tragic, all right, but George and Hazel couldn't think about it very hard. Hazel had a perfectly average intelligence, which meant she couldn't think about anything except in short bursts. And George, while his intelligence was way above normal, had a little mental handicap radio in his ear. He was required by law to wear it at all times. It was tuned to a government transmitter. Every 20 seconds or so, the transmitter would send out some sharp noise to keep people like George from taking unfair advantage of their brains.

George and Hazel were watching television. There were tears on Hazel's cheeks, but she'd forgotten for the moment what they were about.

On the television screen were ballerinas.

A buzzer sounded in George's head. His thoughts fled in panic, like bandits from a burglar alarm.

"That was a real pretty dance, that dance they just did," said Hazel.

"Huh?" said George.

"The dance—it was nice," said Hazel.

"Yup," said George. He tried to think a little about the ballerinas. They weren't really very good—no better than anybody else would have been, anyway. They were burdened with sash-weights and bags of birdshot, and their faces were masked, so that no one, seeing a free and graceful gesture or a pretty face, would feel like something the cat drug in. George was toying with the vague notion that maybe dancers shouldn't be handicapped. But he didn't get very far with it before another noise in his ear radio scattered his thoughts.

George winced. So did two out of the eight ballerinas.

Hazel saw him wince. Having no mental handicap herself, she had to ask George what the latest sound had been.

"Sounded like someone hitting a milk bottle with a ball peen hammer," said George.

"I'd think it would be real interesting, hearing all the different sounds," said Hazel, a little envious. "All the things they think up."

"Um," said George.

"Only, if I was Handicapper General, you know what I would do?" said Hazel. Hazel, as a matter of fact, bore a strong resemblance to the Handicapper General, a woman named Diana Moon Glampers. "If I was Diana Moon Glampers," said Hazel, "I'd have chimes on Sunday—just chimes. Kind of in honor of religion."

"I could think, if it was just chimes," said George.

"Well—maybe make 'em real loud," said Hazel. "I think I'd make a good Handicapper General."

"Good as anybody else," said George.

"Who knows better'n I do what normal is?" said Hazel.

"Right," said George. He began to think glimmeringly about his abnormal son who was now in jail, about Harrison, but a 21-gun salute in his head stopped that.

"Boy!" said Hazel, "that was a doozy, wasn't it?"

It was such a doozy that George was white and trembling, and tears stood on the rims of his red eyes. Two of the eight ballerinas had collapsed to the studio floor, were holding their temples.

"All of a sudden you look so tired," said Hazel. "Why don't you stretch out on the sofa, so's you can rest your handicap bag on the pillows, honeybunch." She was referring to the 47 pounds of birdshot in a canvas bag, which was padlocked around George's neck. "Go on and rest the bag for a little while," she said. "I don't care if you're not equal to me for a while."

George weighed the bag with his hands. "I don't mind it," he said. "I don't notice it any more. It's just a part of me."

"You've been so tired lately—kind of wore out," said Hazel. "If there was just some way we could make a little hole in the bottom of the bag, and just take out a few of them lead balls. Just a few."

"Two years in prison and $2,000 fine for every ball I took out," said George. "I don't call that a bargain."

"If you could just take a few out when you came home from work," said Hazel. "I mean—you don't compete with anybody around here. You just sit around."

"If I tried to get away with it," said George, "then other people'd get away with it—and pretty soon we'd be right back to the dark ages again, with everybody competing against everybody else. You wouldn't like that, would you?"

"I'd hate it," said Hazel.

"There you are," said George. "The minute people start cheating on laws, what do you think happens to society?"

If Hazel hadn't been able to come up with an answer to this question, George couldn't have supplied one. A siren was going off in his head.

"Reckon it'd fall all apart," said Hazel.

"What would?" said George blankly.

"Society," said Hazel uncertainly. "Wasn't that what you just said?"

"Who knows?" said George.

The television program was suddenly interrupted for a news bulletin. It wasn't clear at first as to what the bulletin was about, since the announcer, like all announcers, had a serious speech impediment. For about half a minute, and in a state of high excitement, the announcer tried to say, "Ladies and gentlemen—"

He finally gave up, handed the bulletin to a ballerina to read.

"That's all right—" Hazel said of the announcer, "he tried. That's the big thing. He tried to do the best he could with what God gave him. He should get a nice raise for trying so hard."

"Ladies and gentlemen—" said the ballerina, reading the bulletin. She must have been extraordinarily beautiful, because the mask she wore was hideous. And it was easy to see that she was the strongest and most graceful of the dancers, for her handicap bags were as big as those worn by 200-pound men.

And she had to apologize at once for her voice, which was a very unfair voice for a woman to use. Her voice was a warm, luminous, timeless melody. "Excuse me—" she said, and she began again, making her voice absolutely uncompetitive.

"Harrison Bergeron, age 14," she said in a grackle squawk, "has just escaped from jail, where he was held on suspicion of plotting to overthrow the government. He is a genius and an athlete, is under-handicapped, and should be regarded as extremely dangerous."

A police photograph of Harrison Bergeron was flashed on the screen—upside down, then sideways, upside down again, then right side up. The picture showed the full length of Harrison against a background calibrated in feet and inches. He was exactly 7 feet tall.

The rest of Harrison's appearance was Halloween and hardware. Nobody had ever borne heavier handicaps. He had outgrown hindrances faster than the H-G men could think them up. Instead of a little ear radio for a mental handicap, he wore a tremendous pair of earphones, and spectacles with thick wavy lenses. The spectacles were intended to make him not only half blind, but to give him whanging headaches besides.

Scrap metal was hung all over him. Ordinarily, there was a certain symmetry, a military neatness to the handicaps issued to strong people, but Harrison looked like a walking junkyard. In the race of life, Harrison carried 300 pounds.

And to offset his good looks, the H-G men required that he wear at all times a red rubber ball for a nose, keep his eyebrows shaved off, and cover his even white teeth with black caps at snaggle-tooth random.

"If you see this boy," said the ballerina, "do not—repeat, do not—try to reason with him."

There was the shriek of a door being torn from its hinges.

Screams and barking cries of consternation came from the television set. The photograph of Harrison Bergeron on the screen jumped again and again, as though dancing to the tune of an earthquake.

George Bergeron correctly identified the earthquake, and well he might have—for many was the time his own home had danced to the same crashing tune. "My God—" said George, "that must be Harrison!"

The realization was blasted from his mind instantly by the sound of an automobile collision in his head.

When George could open his eyes again, the photograph of Harrison was gone. A living, breathing Harrison filled the screen.

Clanking, clownish, and huge, Harrison stood in the center of the studio. The knob of the uprooted studio door was still in his hand. Ballerinas, technicians, musicians, and announcers cowered on their knees before him, expecting to die.

"I am the Emperor!" cried Harrison. "Do you hear? I am the Emperor! Everybody must do what I say at once!" He stamped his foot and the studio shook.

"Even as I stand here—" he bellowed, "crippled, hobbled, sickened—I am a greater ruler than any man who ever lived! Now watch me become what I *can* become!"

Harrison tore the straps of his handicap harness like wet tissue paper, tore straps guaranteed to support 5,000 pounds.

Harrison's scrap-iron handicaps crashed to the floor.

Harrison thrust his thumbs under the bar of the padlock that secured his head harness. The bar snapped like celery. Harrison smashed his headphones and spectacles against the wall.

He flung away his rubber-ball nose, revealed a man that would have awed Thor, the god of thunder.

"I shall now select my Empress!" he said, looking down on the cowering people. "Let the first woman who dares rise to her feet claim her mate and her throne!"

A moment passed, and then a ballerina arose, swaying like a willow.

Harrison plucked the mental handicap from her ear, snapped off her physical handicaps with marvelous delicacy. Last of all, he removed her mask.

She was blindingly beautiful.

"Now—" said Harrison, taking her hand, "shall we show the people the meaning of the word dance? Music!" he commanded.

The musicians scrambled back into their chairs, and Harrison stripped them of their handicaps, too. "Play your best," he told them, "and I'll make you barons and dukes and earls."

The music began. It was normal at first—cheap, silly, false. But Harrison snatched two musicians from their chairs, waved them like batons as he sang the music as he wanted it played. He slammed them back into their chairs.

The music began again and was much improved.

Harrison and his Empress merely listened to the music for a while—listened gravely, as though synchronizing their heartbeats with it.

They shifted their weights to their toes.

Harrison placed his big hands on the girl's tiny waist, letting her sense the weightlessness that would soon be hers.

And then, in an explosion of joy and grace, into the air they sprang!

Not only were the laws of the land abandoned, but the law of gravity and the laws of motion as well.

They reeled, whirled, swiveled, flounced, capered, gamboled, and spun.

They leaped like deer on the moon.

The studio ceiling was 30 feet high, but each leap brought the dancers nearer to it.

It became their obvious intention to kiss the ceiling.

They kissed it.

And then, neutralizing gravity with love and pure will, they remained suspended in air inches below the ceiling, and they kissed each other for a long, long time.

It was then that Diana Moon Glampers, the Handicapper General, came into the studio with a doubled-barreled 10-gauge shotgun. She fired twice, and the Emperor and the Empress were dead before they hit the floor.

Diana Moon Glampers loaded the gun again. She aimed it at the musicians and told them they had 10 seconds to get their handicaps back on.

It was then that the Bergeron's television tube burned out.

Hazel turned to comment about the blackout to George. But George had gone out into the kitchen for a can of beer.

George came back in with the beer, paused while a handicap signal shook him up. And then he sat down again. "You been crying?" he said to Hazel.

"Yup," she said.

"What about?" he said.

"I forget," she said. "Something real sad on television."

"What was it?" he said.

"It's all kind of mixed up in my mind," said Hazel.

"Forget sad things," said George.

"I always do," said Hazel.

"That's my girl," said George. He winced. There was the sound of a rivetting gun in his head.

"Gee—I could tell that one was a doozy," said Hazel.

"You can say that again," said George.

"Gee—" said Hazel, "I could tell that one was a doozy."

NONDISCRIMINATION

RICHARD A. WASSERSTROM

Racism, Sexism, and Preferential Treatment: An Approach to the Topics

INTRODUCTION

Racism and sexism are two central issues that engage the attention of many persons living within the United States today. But while there is relatively little disagreement about their importance as topics, there is substantial, vehement, and apparently intractable disagreement about what individuals, practices, ideas, and institutions are either racist or sexist—and for what reasons. In dispute are a number of related questions concerning how individuals and institutions ought to regard and respond to matters relating to race or sex.

One particularly contemporary example concerns those programs variously called programs of "affirmative action," "preferential treatment," or "reverse discrimination" that are a feature of much of our institutional life. Attitudes and beliefs about these programs are diverse. Some persons are convinced that all such programs in virtually all of their forms are themselves racist and sexist and are for these among other reasons indefensible.[1] The programs are causally explicable, perhaps, but morally reprehensible. Other persons—a majority, I suspect—are sorely troubled by these programs. They are convinced that some features of some programs, e.g., quotas, are indefensible and wrong. Other features and programs are tolerated, but not with fervor or enthusiasm. They are seen as a kind of moral compromise, as, perhaps, a lesser evil among a set of unappealing options.[2] They are reluctantly perceived and implemented as a covert, euphemistic way to do what would clearly be wrong—even racist or sexist—to do overtly and with candor. And still a third group has a very different view. They think these programs are important and appropriate. They do not see these programs, quotas included, as racist or sexist, and they see much about the dominant societal institutions that is.[3] They regard the racism and sexism of the society as accounting in substantial measure for the failure or refusal to adopt such programs willingly and to press vigorously for their full implementation.

I think that much of the confusion in thinking and arguing about racism, sexism, and affirmative action results from a failure to see that there are three different perspectives within which the topics of racism, sexism, and affirmative action can most usefully be examined. The first of these perspectives concentrates on what in fact is true of the culture, on what can be called the social realities. Here the fundamental question concerns the way the culture is: What are its institutions, attitudes and ideologies in respect to matters of race and sex?[4]

The second perspective is concerned with the way things ought to be. From this perspective, analysis focuses very largely on possible, desirable states of affairs. Here the fundamental question concerns ideals: What would the good society—in terms of its institutions, its attitudes, and its values—look like in respect to matters involving race and sex?[5]

The third perspective looks forward to the means by which the ideal may be achieved. Its focus is on the question: What is the best or most appropriate way to move from the existing social realities, whatever they happen to be, to a closer approximation of the ideal society? This perspective is concerned with instrumentalities. . . .[6]

1. SOCIAL REALITIES

One way to think and talk about racism and sexism is to concentrate upon the perspective of the social realities. Here one must begin by insisting that to talk about either is to talk about a particular social and cultural context. In this section I concentrate upon two questions that can be asked about the social realities of our culture. First, I consider the position of blacks and females in the culture vis-à-vis the position of those who are white, and those who are male. And second, I provide an analysis of the different ways in which a complex institution, such as our legal system, can be seen to be racist or sexist. The analysis is offered as a schematic account of the possible types of racism or sexism.

A. THE POSITION OF BLACKS AND WOMEN

In our own culture the first thing to observe is that race and sex are socially important categories. They are so in virtue of the fact that we live in a culture which has, throughout its existence, made race and sex extremely important characteristics of and for all the people living in the culture.

It is surely possible to imagine a culture in which race would be an unimportant, insignificant characteristic of individuals. In such a culture race would be largely if not exclusively a matter of superficial physiology; a matter, we might say, simply of the way one looked. And if it were, then any analysis of race and racism would necessarily assume very different dimensions from what they do in our society. In such a culture, the meaning of the term "race" would itself have to change substantially. This can be seen by the fact that in such a culture it would literally make no sense to say of a person that he or she was "passing." This is something that can be said and understood in our own culture and it shows at least that to talk of race is to talk of more than the way one looks.

Sometimes when people talk about what is wrong with affirmative action programs, or programs of preferential hiring, they say that what is wrong with such programs is that they take a thing as superficial as an individual's race and turn it into something important.[7] They say that a person's race doesn't matter; other things do, such as qualifications. Whatever else may be said of statements such as these, as descriptions of the social realities they seem to be simply false. One complex but true empirical fact about our society is that the race of an individual is much more than a fact of superficial physiology. It is, instead, one of the dominant characteristics that affects both the way the individual looks at the world and the way the world looks at the individual. . . .

I can put the point another way: Race does not function in our culture as does eye color. Eye color is an irrelevant category; nobody cares what color people's eyes are; it is not an important cultural fact; nothing turns on what eye color you have. It is important to see that race is not like that at all. And this truth affects what will and will not count as cases of racism. In our culture to be nonwhite—and especially to be black—is to be treated and seen to be a member of a group that is different from and inferior to the group of standard, fully developed persons, the adult white males. To be black is to be a member of what was a despised minority and what is still a disliked and oppressed one.[8] That is simply part of the awful truth of our cultural and social history, and a significant feature of the social reality of our culture today.

We can see fairly easily that the two sexual categories, like the racial ones, are themselves in important respects products of the society. Like one's race, one's sex is not merely or even primarily a matter of physiology. To see this we need only realize that we can understand the idea of a transsexual. A transsexual is someone who would describe himself or herself either as a person who is essentially a female but through some accident of nature is trapped in a male body, or a person who is essentially a male but through some accident of nature is trapped in the body of a female. His (or her) description is some kind of a shorthand way of saying that he (or she) is more comfortable with the role allocated by the culture to people who are physiologically of the opposite sex. The fact that we regard this assertion of the transsexual as intelligible seems to me to show how deep the notion of sexual identity is in our culture and how little it has to do with physiological differences between males and females. Because people do pass in the context of race and because we can understand what passing means; because people are transsexuals and because we can understand what transsexuality means, we can see that the existing social categories of both race and sex are in this sense creations of the culture.

It is even clearer in the case of sex than in the case of race that one's sexual identity is a centrally important, crucially relevant category within our culture. I think, in fact, that it is more important and more fundamental than one's race. It is evident that there are substantially different role expectations and role assignments to persons in accordance with their sexual physiology, and that the positions of the two sexes in the culture are distinct. We do have a patriarchal society in which it matters enormously whether one is a male or a female.[9] By almost all important measures it is more advantageous to be a male rather than a female.

Women and men are socialized differently. We learn very early and forcefully that we are either males or females and that much turns upon which sex we are. The evidence seems to be overwhelming and well-documented that sex roles play a fundamental role in the way persons think of themselves and the world—to say nothing of the way the world thinks of them.[10] Men and women are taught to see men as independent, capable, and powerful; men and women are taught to see women as dependent, limited in abilities, and passive. A woman's success or failure in life is defined largely in terms of her activities within the family. It is important for her that she marry, and when she does she is expected to take responsibility for the wifely tasks: the housework, the child care, the general emotional welfare of the husband and children. Her status in society is determined in substantial measure by the vocation and success of her husband. Economically, women are substantially worse off than men. They do not receive any pay for the work that is done in the home. As members of the labor force their wages are significantly lower than those paid to men, even when they are engaged in similar work and have similar educational backgrounds. The higher the prestige or the salary of the job, the less present women are in the labor force. And, of course, women are conspicuously absent from most positions of authority and power in the major economic and political institutions of our society.

As is true for race, it is also a significant social fact that to be a female is to be an entity or creature viewed as different from the standard, fully developed person who is male as well as white. But to be female, as opposed to being black, is not to be conceived of as simply a creature of less worth. That is one important thing that differentiates sexism from racism: The ideology of sex, as opposed to the ideology of race, is a good deal more complex and confusing. Women are both put on a pedestal and deemed not fully developed persons. They are idealized; their approval and admiration is sought; and they are at the same time regarded as less competent than men and less able to live fully developed, fully human lives—for that is what men do. . . .

Viewed from the perspective of social reality it should be clear, too, that racism and sexism should not be thought of as phenomena that consist simply in taking a person's race or sex into account, or even simply in taking a person's race or sex into account in an arbitrary way. Instead, racism and sexism consist in taking race and sex into account in a certain way, in the context of a specific set of institutional arrangements and a specific ideology which together create and maintain a *system* of unjust institutions and unwarranted beliefs and attitudes. That system is and has been one in which political, economic, and social power and advantage are concentrated in the hands of those who are white and male.

One way to bring this out, as well as to show another respect in which racism and sexism are different, concerns segregated bathrooms—a topic that may seem silly and trivial but which is certainly illuminating and probably important. We know, for instance, that it is wrong, clearly racist, to have racially segregated bathrooms. There is, however, no common conception that it is wrong, clearly sexist, to have sexually segregated ones. How is this to be accounted for? The answer to the question of why it was and is racist to have racially segregated bathrooms can be discovered through a consideration of the role that this practice played in that system of racial segregation we had in the United States—from, in other words, an examination of the social realities. For racially segregated bathrooms were an important part of that system. And that system had an ideology; it was complex and perhaps not even wholly internally consistent. A significant feature of the ideology was that blacks were not only less than fully developed humans, but that they were also dirty and impure. . . .

It is worth observing that the social reality of sexually segregated bathrooms appears to be different. The idea behind such sexual segregation seems to have more to do with the mutual undesirability of the use by both sexes of the same bathroom at the same time. There is no notion of the possibility of contamination; or even directly of inferiority and superiority. What seems to be involved—at least in part—is the importance of inculcating and preserving a sense of secrecy concerning the genitalia of the opposite sex. What seems to be at stake is the maintenance of that same sense of mystery or forbiddenness about the other sex's sexuality which is fostered by the general prohibition upon public nudity and the unashamed viewing of genitalia.

Sexually segregated bathrooms simply play a different role in our culture than did racially segregated ones. But that is not to say that the role they play is either benign or unobjectionable—only that it is different. Sexually segregated bathrooms may well be objectionable, but here too, the objection is not on the ground that they are prima facie capricious or arbitrary. Rather, the case against them now would rest on the ground that they are, perhaps, one small part of that scheme of sex-role differentiation which uses the mystery of sexual anatomy, among other things, to maintain the primacy of heterosexual sexual attraction central to that version of the patriarchal system of power relationships we have today. Whether sexually segregated bathrooms would be objectionable, because irrational, in the good society depends once again upon what the good society would look like in respect to sexual differentiation.

B. TYPES OF RACISM OR SEXISM

Another recurring question that can profitably be examined within the perspective of social realities is whether the legal system is racist or sexist. Indeed, it seems to me essential that the social realities of the relationships and ideologies concerning race and sex be kept in mind whenever one is trying to assess claims that are made about the racism or sexism of important institutions such as the legal system. It is also of considerable importance in assessing such claims to understand that even within the perspective of social reality, racism or sexism can manifest itself, or be understood, in different ways. That these are both important points can be seen through a brief examination of the different, distinctive ways in which our own legal system might plausibly be understood to be racist. . . .

The first type of racism is the simplest and the least controversial. It is the case of overt racism, in which a law or a legal institution expressly takes into account the race of individuals in order to assign benefits and burdens in such a way as to bestow an unjustified benefit upon a member or members of the racially dominant group or an unjustified burden upon members of the racial groups that are oppressed. We no longer have many, if any, cases of overt racism in our legal system today, although we certainly had a number in the past. . . .

The second type of racism is very similar to overt racism. It is covert, but intentional, racism, in which a law or a legal institution has as its purpose the allocation of benefits and burdens in order to support the power of the dominant race, but does not use race specifically as a basis for allocating these benefits and burdens. One particularly good historical example involves the use of grandfather clauses which were inserted in statutes governing voter registration in a number of states after passage of the 15th amendment.[11]

Covert racism within the law is not entirely a thing of the past. Many instances of de facto school segregation in the North and West are cases of covert racism. At times certain school boards—virtually all of which are overwhelmingly white in composition—quite consciously try to maintain exclusively or predominantly white schools within a school district. The classifications such school boards use are not ostensibly racial, but are based upon the places of residence of the affected students. These categories provide the opportunity for covert racism in engineering the racial composition of individual schools within the board's jurisdiction.[12]

What has been said so far is surely neither novel nor controversial. What is interesting, however, is that a number of persons appear to believe that as long as the legal system is not overtly or covertly racist, there is nothing to the charge that it is racist. So, for example, Mr. Justice Powell said in a speech a few years ago:

> It is of course true that we have witnessed racial injustice in the past, as has every other country with significant racial diversity. But no one can fairly question the present national commitment to full equality and justice. Racial discrimination, by state action, is now proscribed by laws and court decisions which protect civil liberties more broadly than in any other country. But laws alone are not enough. Racial prejudice in the hearts of men cannot be legislated out of existence; it will pass only in time, and as human beings of all races learn in humility to respect each other—a process not furthered by recrimination or undue self-accusation.[13]

I believe it is a mistake to think about the problem of racism in terms of overt or covert racial discrimination by state action, which is now banished, and racial prejudice, which still lingers, but only in the hearts of persons. For there is another, more subtle kind of racism—unintentional, perhaps, but effective—which is as much a part of the legal system as are overt and covert racist laws and practices. It is what some critics of the legal system probably mean when they talk about the "institutional racism" of the legal system.[14]

There are at least two kinds of institutional racism. The first is the racism of subinstitutions within the legal system such as the jury, or the racism of practices built upon or countenanced by the law. These institutions and practices very often, if not always, reflect in important and serious ways a variety of dominant values in the operation of what is apparently a neutral legal mechanism. The result is the maintenance and reenforcement of a system in which whites dominate over nonwhites. One relatively uninteresting (because familiar) example is the case of de facto school segregation. . . .

A less familiar, and hence perhaps more instructive, example concerns the question of the importance of having blacks on juries, especially in cases in which blacks are criminal defendants. The orthodox view within the law is that it is unfair to try a black defendant before an all-white jury if blacks were overtly or covertly excluded from the jury rolls used to provide the jury panel, but not otherwise.[15] One reason that is often given is that the systematic exclusion of blacks increases too greatly the chance of racial prejudice operating against the black defendant.[16] The problem with this way of thinking about things is that it does not make much sense. If whites are apt to be prejudiced against blacks, then an all-white jury is just as apt to be prejudiced against a black defendant, irrespective of whether blacks were systematically excluded from the jury rolls. I suspect that the rule has developed in the way it has because the courts think that many, if not most, whites are not prejudiced against blacks, unless, perhaps, they happen to live in an area where there is systematic exclusion of blacks from the jury rolls. Hence prejudice is the chief worry, and a sectional, if not historical, one at that.

White prejudice against blacks is, I think, a problem, and not just a sectional one. However, the existence or nonexistence of prejudice against blacks does not go to the heart of the matter. It is a worry, but it is not the chief worry. A black person may not be able to get a fair trial from an all-white jury even though the jurors are disposed to be fair and impartial, because the whites may unknowingly bring into the jury box a view about a variety of matters which affects in very fundamental respects the way they will look at and assess the facts. Thus, for example, it is not, I suspect, part of the experience of most white persons who serve on juries that police often lie in their dealings with people and the courts. Indeed, it is probably not part of their experience that persons lie about serious matters except on rare occasions. And they themselves tend to take truth telling very seriously. As a result, white persons for whom these facts about police and lying are a part of their social reality will have very great difficulty taking seriously the possibility that the inculpatory testimony of a police witness is a deliberate untruth. However, it may also be a part of the social reality that many black persons, just because they are black, have had encounters with the police in which the police were at best indifferent to whether they, the police, were speaking the truth. And even more black persons may have known a friend or a relative who has had such an experience. As a result, a black juror would be more likely than his or her white counterpart to approach skeptically the testimony of ostensibly neutral, reliable witnesses such as police officers. . . .

The second type of institutional racism is what I will call "conceptual" institutional racism. We have a variety of ways of thinking about the legal system, and we have a variety of ways of thinking within the legal system about certain problems. We use concepts. Quite often without realizing it, the concepts used take for granted certain objectionable aspects of racist ideology without our being aware of it. The second *Brown* case *(Brown II)* provides an example.[17] There was a second *Brown* case because, having decided that the existing system of racially segregated public education was unconstitutional *(Brown I),*[18] the Supreme Court gave legitimacy to a second issue—the nature of the relief to be granted—by treating it as a distinct question to be considered and decided separately. That in itself was striking because in most cases, once the Supreme Court has found unconstitutionality, there has been no problem about relief (apart from questions of retroactivity): The unconstitutional practices and acts are to cease. As is well known, the Court in *Brown II* concluded that the desegregation of public education had to proceed "with all deliberate speed."[19] The Court said that there were "complexities arising from the transition to a system of public education freed from racial discrimination."[20] More specifically, time might be necessary to carry out the ruling because of

> problems related to administration, arising from the physical condition of the school plant, the school transportation system personnel, revision of school districts and attendance areas into compact units to achieve a system of determining admission to the public school on a non-racial basis, and revision of local laws and regulations which may be necessary in solving the foregoing problems.[21]

Now, I do not know whether the Court believed what it said in this passage, but it is a fantastic bit of nonsense that is, for my purposes, most instructive. Why? Because there was nothing complicated about most of the dual school systems of the southern states. Many counties, especially the rural ones, had one high school, typically called either "Booker T. Washington High School" or "George Washington Carver High School," where all the black children in the county went; another school, often called "Sidney Lanier High School" or "Robert E. Lee High School," was attended by all the white children in the county. There was nothing difficult about deciding that—as of the day after the decision—half of the children in the county, say all those who lived in the southern part of the county, would go to Robert E. Lee High School, and all those who lived in the northern half would go to Booker T. Washington High School. *Brown I* could have been implemented the day after the Court reached its decision. But it was also true that the black schools throughout the South were utterly wretched when compared to the white schools. There never had been any system of separate but equal education. In almost every measurable respect, the black schools were inferior. One possibility is that, without being explicitly aware of it, the members of the Supreme Court made use of some assumptions that were a significant feature of the dominant racist ideology. If the assumptions had been made explicit, the reasoning would have gone something like this: Those black schools are wretched. We cannot order white children to go to those schools, especially when they have gone to better schools in the past. So while it is unfair to deprive blacks, to make them go to these awful, segregated schools, they will have to wait until the black schools either are eliminated or are sufficiently improved so that there are good schools for everybody to attend.

What seems to me to be most objectionable, and racist, about *Brown II* is the uncritical acceptance of the idea that during this process of change, black schoolchildren would have to suffer by continuing to attend inadequate schools. The Supreme Court's solution assumed that the correct way to deal with this problem was to continue to have the black children go to their schools until the black schools were brought up to par or eliminated. That is a kind of conceptual racism in which the legal system accepts the dominant racist ideology, which holds that the claims of black children are worth less than the claims of white children in those cases in which conflict is inevitable.[22] It seems to me that any minimally fair solution would have required that during the interim process, if anybody had to go to an inadequate school, it would have been the white children, since they were the ones who had previously had the benefit of the good schools. But this is simply not the way racial matters are thought about within the dominant ideology. . . .

2. IDEALS

A second perspective is also important for an understanding and analysis of racism and sexism. It is the perspective of the ideal. Just as we can and must ask what is involved today in our culture in being of one race or of one sex rather than the other, and how individuals are in fact viewed and treated, we can also ask different questions: What would the good or just society make of race and sex, and to what degree, if at all, would racial and sexual distinctions ever be taken into account? Indeed, it could plausibly be argued that we could not have an adequate idea of whether a society was racist or sexist unless we had some conception of what a thoroughly nonracist or nonsexist society would look like. This perspective is an extremely instructive as well as an often neglected one. Comparatively little theoretical literature dealing with either racism or sexism has concerned itself in a systematic way with this perspective.[23] Moreover, as I shall try to demonstrate, it is on occasion introduced in an inappropriate context, e.g., in discussions of the relevance of the biological differences between males and females.

To understand more precisely what some of the possible ideals are in respect to racial or sexual differentiation, it is necessary to distinguish in a crude way among three levels or areas of social and political arrangements and activities.[24] First, there is the area of basic political rights and obligations, including the right to vote and to travel and the obligation to pay taxes. Second, there is the area of important, nongovernmental institutional benefits and burdens. Examples are access to and employment in the significant economic markets, the opportunity to acquire and enjoy housing in the setting of one's choice, the right of persons who want to marry each other to do so, and the duties (nonlegal as well as legal) that persons acquire in getting married. Third, there is the area of individual, social interaction, including such matters as whom one will have as friends, and what aesthetic preferences one will cultivate and enjoy.

As to each of these three areas we can ask whether in a nonracist society it would be thought appropriate ever to take the race of the individuals into account. Thus, one picture of a nonracist society is that which is captured by what I call the assimilationist ideal: A nonracist society would be one in which the race of an individual would be the functional equivalent of the eye color of individuals in our society today.[25] In our society no basic political rights and obligations are determined on the basis of eye color. No important institutional benefits and burdens are connected with eye color. Indeed, except for the mildest sort of aesthetic preferences, a person would be thought odd who even made private, social decisions by taking eye color into account. And for reasons that we could fairly readily state, we could explain why it would be wrong to permit anything but the mildest, most trivial aesthetic preference to turn on eye color. The reasons would concern the irrelevance of eye color for any political or social institution, practice or arrangement. It would, of course, be equally odd for a person to say that while he or she looked blue-eyed, he or she regarded himself or herself as really a brown-eyed person. That is, because eye color functions differently in our culture than does race or sex, there is no analogue in respect to eye color to passing or transsexuality. According to the assimilationist ideal, a nonracist society would be one in which an individual's race was of no more significance in any of these three areas than is eye color today.

The assimilationist ideal is not, however, the only possible plausible ideal. There are two others that are closely related, but distinguishable. One is the ideal of diversity; the other, the ideal of tolerance. Both can be understood by considering how religion, rather than eye color, tends to be thought about in our culture. According to the ideal of diversity, heterodoxy in respect to religious belief and practice is regarded as a positive good. In this view there would be a loss—it would be a worse society— were everyone to be a member of the same religion. According to the other view, the ideal of tolerance, heterodoxy in respect to religious beliefs and practice would be seen more as a necessary, lesser evil. In this view there is nothing intrinsically better about diversity in respect to religion, but the evils of achieving anything like homogeneity far outweigh the possible benefits.

Now, whatever differences there might be between the ideals of diversity and tolerance, the similarities are more striking. Under neither ideal would it be thought that the allocation of basic political rights and duties should take an individual's religion into account. We would want equalitarianism or nondiscrimination even in respect to most important institutional benefits and burdens—for example, access to employment in the desirable vocations. Nonetheless, on both views it would be deemed appropriate to have some institutions (typically those which are connected in an intimate way with these religions) which do in a variety of ways take the religion of members of the society into account. For example, it might be thought permissible and appropriate for members of a religious group to join together in collective associations which have religious, educational, and social dimensions. And on the individual, interpersonal level, it might be thought unobjectionable, or on the diversity view, even admirable, were persons to select their associates, friends, and mates on the basis of their religious orientation. So there are two possible and plausible ideals of what the good society would look like in respect to religion in which religious differences would be to some degree maintained because the variety of religions was seen either as a valuable feature of the society, or as one to be tolerated. The picture is a more complex, less easily describable one than that of the assimilationist ideal.

The point of all this is its relevance to the case of sexism. One central and difficult question is what the ideal society would look like in respect to sex. The assimilationist ideal does not seem to be as readily plausible and obviously attractive here as it is in the case of race. Many persons invoke the possible realization of the assimilationist ideal as a reason for rejecting the equal rights amendment and indeed the idea of women's liberation itself. My view is that the assimilationist ideal may be just as good and just as important an ideal in respect to sex as it is in respect to race.[26] But many persons think there are good reasons why an assimilationist society in respect to sex would not be desirable. One reason for their view might be that to make the assimilationist ideal a reality in respect to sex would involve more profound and fundamental revisions of our institutions and our attitudes than would be the case in respect to race. It is certainly true that on the institutional level we would have to alter radically our practices concerning the family and marriage. If a nonsexist society is a society in which one's sex is no more significant than eye color in our society today, then laws which require the persons who are being married to be of different sexes would clearly be sexist laws. Insofar as they are based upon the desirability of unifying the distinctive features of one male and one female, laws and institutions which conceive of the nuclear family as ideally composed of two and only two adults should also be thought of as anachronistic as well as sexist laws and institutions.

On the attitudinal and conceptual level, the assimilationist ideal would require the eradication of all sex-role differentiation. It would never teach about the inevitable or essential attributes of masculinity or femininity; it would never encourage or discourage the ideas of sisterhood or brotherhood; and it would be unintelligible to talk about the virtues as well as disabilities of being a woman or a man. Were sex like eye color, these things would make no sense. A nonsexist world might conceivably tolerate both homosexuality and heterosexuality (as peculiar kinds of personal erotic preference), but any kind of sexually *exclusive* preference would be either as anomalous or as statistically fortuitous as is a sexual preference connected with eye color in our society today. Just as the normal, typical adult is virtually oblivious to the eye color of other persons for all major interpersonal relationships, so the normal, typical adult in this kind of nonsexist society would be indifferent to the sexual, physiological differences of other persons for all interpersonal relationships. Bisexuality, not heterosexuality or homosexuality, would be the norm for intimate, sexual relationships in the ideal society that was assimilationist in respect to sex.

All of this seems to me to be worth talking about because unless and until we are clear about issues such as these we cannot be wholly certain about whether, from the perspective of the ideal, some of the institutions in our own culture are or are not sexist. We know that racially segregated bathrooms are racist. We know that laws that prohibit persons of different races from marrying are racist. But throughout our society we have sexually segregated bathrooms, and we have laws which prohibit individuals of the same sex from marrying. As I have argued above, from the perspective of the existing social reality there are important ways to distinguish the racial from the sexual cases and to criticize both practices. But that still leaves open the question of whether in the good society these sexual distinctions, or others, would be thought worth preserving either because they were meritorious, or at least to be tolerated because they were necessary.

As I have indicated, it may be that the problem is with the assimilationist ideal. It may be that in respect to sex (and conceivably, even in respect to race) something more like either of the ideals in respect to religion—pluralistic ideals founded on diversity or tolerance—is the right one. But the problem then—and it is a very substantial one—is to specify with a good deal of precision and care what that ideal really comes to. Which legal, institutional, and personal differentiations are permissible and which are not? Which attitudes and beliefs concerning sexual identification and difference are properly introduced and maintained and which are not?

3. INSTRUMENTALITIES

The instrumental perspective does not require much theoretical attention beyond what has already been said. It is concerned with the question of what would be the best way to move from the social realities to the ideal. The most salient considerations are, therefore, empirical ones—although of a complex sort.

Affirmative action programs, even those which require explicit racial and sexual minimum quotas, are most plausibly assessed from within this perspective.[27] If the social reality is one of racial and sexual oppression—as I think it is—and if, for example, the most defensible picture of a nonracist, nonsexist society is the one captured by the assimilationist ideal, then the chief and perhaps only question to be asked of such programs is whether they are well suited to bring about movement from the existing state of affairs to a closer approximation of the assimilationist ideal. If it turns out, for example, that explicit racial quotas will in fact exacerbate racial prejudice and hostility,[28] thereby making it harder rather than easier to achieve an assimilationist society, that is a reason which counts against the instrumental desirability of racial quotas. This would not settle the matter, of course, for there might also be respects in which racial quotas would advance the coming of the assimilationist society, e.g., by redistributing wealth and positions of power and authority to blacks, thereby creating previously unavailable role models, and by putting persons with different perspectives and interests in a position more directly to influence the course of social change.

But persons might be unhappy with this way of thinking about affirmative action—and especially about quotas. They might have three different but related objections. The first objection would be that there are more questions to be asked about means or instruments than whether they will work to bring about a certain end. In particular, there is also the question of the *way* they will work as means to bring about the end. Some means may be morally objectionable as means, no matter how noble or desirable the end. That is the good sense in the slogan: The ends do not justify the means.

I certainly agree with this general point. It is the application to particular cases, for example this one, that vitiates the force of the objection. Indeed, given the way I have formulated the instrumental perspective, I have left a good deal of room for the moral assessment of means to be built in. That is to say, I have described the question as one of the instrumental "desirability," not just the "efficaciousness" in any narrow sense, of the means that are selected.

The second objection is rather more sophisticated. Someone might say something like this: it is just wrong in principle ever to take an individual's race or sex into account. Persons just have a right never to have race or sex considered. No reasons need be given; we just know they have that right. This is a common way of talking today in moral philosophy,[29] but I find nothing persuasive or attractive about it. I do not know that persons have such a right. I do not "see" it. Instead, I think I can give and have given reasons in my discussion of the social realities as well as my discussion of ideals for why they might be said to have rights not to be treated in certain ways. That is to say, I have tried to show something of what was wrong about the way blacks and women were and are treated in our culture.[30] I have not simply proclaimed the existence of a right.

Another form of this objection is more convincing. The opponent of quotas and affirmative action programs might argue that any proponent of them is guilty of intellectual inconsistency, if not racism or sexism. At times past, employers, universities, and many social institutions did have racial or sexual quotas, when they did not practice overt racial or sexual exclusion, and it was clear that these quotas were pernicious.

What is more, many of those who were most concerned to bring about the eradication of those racial quotas are now untroubled by the new programs which reinstitute them. And this is just a terrible sort of intellectual inconsistency which at worst panders to the fashion of the present moment and at best replaces intellectual honesty and integrity with understandable but misguided sympathy. The assimilationist ideal requires ignoring race and sex as distinguishing features of people.

Such an argument is a useful means by which to bring out the way in which the analysis I am proposing can respond. The racial quotas and practices of racial exclusion that were an integral part of the fabric of our culture, and which are still to some degree a part of it, were pernicious. They were a grievous wrong and it was and is important that all morally concerned individuals work for their eradication from our social universe. The racial quotas that are a part of contemporary affirmative action programs are, I think, commendable and right. But even if I am mistaken about the latter, the point is that there is no inconsistency involved in holding both views. For even if contemporary schemes of racial quotas are wrong, they are wrong for reasons very different from those that made quotas against blacks wrong.

As I have argued, the fundamental evil of programs that discriminated against blacks or women was that these programs were a part of a larger social universe which systematically maintained an unwarranted and unjust scheme which concentrated power, authority, and goods in the hands of white males. Programs which excluded or limited the access of blacks and women into these institutions were wrong both because of the direct consequences of these programs on the individuals most affected and because the system of racial and sexual superiority of which they were constituents was an immoral one in that it severely and without any adequate justification restricted the capacities, autonomy, and happiness of those who were members of the less favored categories.

Whatever may be wrong with today's affirmative action programs and quota systems, it should be clear that the evil, if any, is not the same. Racial and sexual minorities do not constitute the dominant social group. Nor is the conception of who is a fully developed member of the moral and social community one of an individual who is either female or black. Quotas which prefer women or blacks do not add to the already relatively overabundant supply of resources and opportunities at the disposal of white males. If racial quotas are to be condemned or if affirmative action programs are to be abandoned, it should be because they will not work well to achieve the desired result. It is not because they seek either to perpetuate an unjust society or to realize a corrupt ideal. . . .

There is finally the third objection: that affirmative action programs are wrong because they take race and sex into account rather than the only thing that matters—an individual's qualifications. Someone might argue that what is wrong with these programs is that they deprive persons who are more qualified by bestowing benefits on those who are less qualified in virtue of their being either black or female.

There are many things wrong with the objection based on qualifications. Not the least of them is that we do not live in a society in which there is even the serious pretense of a qualification requirement for many jobs of substantial power and authority. Would anyone claim that the persons who comprise the judiciary are there because they are the most qualified lawyers or the most qualified persons to be judges? Would anyone claim that Henry Ford II was the head of the Ford Motor Company because he was the most qualified person for the job? Or that the 100 men who are Senators are the most qualified persons to be Senators? Part of what is wrong with even talking about qualifications and merit is that the argument derives some of its force from the erroneous notion that we would have a meritocracy were it not for affirmative action.

But there is a theoretical difficulty as well, which cuts much more deeply into the argument about qualifications. The argument cannot be that the most qualified ought to be selected because the most qualified will perform most efficiently, for this instrumental approach was what the opponent of affirmative action thought was wrong with taking the instrumental perspective in the first place. To be at all persuasive, the argument must be that those who are the most qualified *deserve* to receive the benefits (the job, the place in law school, etc.) because they are the most qualified. And there is just no reason to think that this is a correct premise. There is a logical gap in the inference that the person who is most qualified to perform a task, e.g., be a good student, deserves to be admitted as a student. Of course, those who deserve to be admitted should be admitted. But why do the most qualified deserve anything? . . .

Someone might reply that the most able students deserve to be admitted to the university because all of their earlier schooling was a kind of competition, with university admission being the prize awarded to the winners. They deserve to be admitted because that is what the rule of the competition provides. . . .

There are several problems with this argument. The most substantial of them is that it is an empirically implausible picture of our social world. Most of what are regarded as the decisive characteristics for higher education have a great deal to do with things over which the individual has neither control nor responsibility: such things as home environment, socioeconomic class of parents, and, of course, the quality of the primary and secondary schools attended. Since individuals do not deserve having had any of these things vis-à-vis other individuals, they do not, for the most part, deserve their qualifications. And since they do not deserve their abilities they do not in any strong sense deserve to be admitted because of their abilities.

To be sure, if there is a rule which connects, say, performance at high school with admission to college, then there is a weak sense in which those who do well at high school deserve, for that reason alone, to be admitted to college. But then, as I have said, the merits of this rule need to be explored and defended. In addition, if persons have built up or relied upon their reasonable expectations concerning performance and admission, they have a claim to be admitted on this ground as well. But it is certainly not obvious that these claims of desert are any stronger or more compelling than competing claims based upon the needs of or advantages to women or blacks. . . .[31]

I do not think I have shown programs of preferential treatment to be right and desirable, because I have not sought to answer all of the empirical questions that may be relevant. But I have, I hope, shown that it is wrong to think that contemporary affirmative action programs are racist or sexist in the centrally important sense in which many past and present features of our society have been and are racist and sexist. The social realities do make a fundamental difference. It is also wrong to think that these programs are in any strong sense either unjust or unprincipled. The case for programs of preferential treatment can plausibly rest on the view that the programs are not un-fair (except in the weak sense described above) to white males, and on the view that it is unfair to continue the present set of unjust—often racist and sexist—institutions that comprise the social reality. The case for these programs also rests on the thesis that it is fair, given the distribution of power and influence in the United States, to re-distribute in this way, and that such programs may reasonably be viewed as useful means by which to achieve very significant social ideals.

CONCLUSION

I do not think that the topics of racism, sexism, and preferential treatment are easily penetrable. Indeed, I have tried to show that they contain complicated issues which must be carefully distinguished and discussed. But I also believe, and have tried to show, that the topics are susceptible to rational analysis. There is a difference between problems that are difficult because confusion is present, and problems that are diffi-cult because a number of distinct ideas and arguments must be considered. It is my ambition to have moved thinking about the topics and issues in question some dis-tance from the first to the second of these categories.

---

[1][Some of Wasserstrom's notes have been omitted, and others are renumbered—ed.]

[2]See, e.g., Nagel "Equal Treatment and Compensatory Discrimination," 2 *Phil. & Pub. Aff.* 348, 362 (1973).

[3]Among those who have defended such programs, in one form or another, are Askin, *The Case for Compensatory Treatment,* 24 Rut. L. Rev. 65 (1964); Bell, *In Defense of Minority Admissions Programs: A Reply to Professor Graglia,* 119 U. Pa. L. Rev. 364 (1970); Ely, *The Constitutionality of Reverse Discrimi-nation,* 41 U. Chi. L. Rev. 723 (1974); Hughes, *Reparations for Blacks,* 43 N. Y. U. L. Rev. 1063 (1968). The precise programs defended vary greatly, as do the reasons offered to justify them.

[4]This perspective is discussed in Part 1.

[5]This perspective is discussed in Part 2.

[6]This perspective is discussed in Part 3.

[7]Mr. Justice Douglas suggests something like this in his dissent in *DeFunis:* "The consideration of race as a measure of an applicant's qualification normally introduces a capricious and irrelevant factor working an invidious discrimination." *DeFunis* v. *Odegaard,* 416 U. S. 312, 333 (1974).

[8]See, e.g., J. Baldwin, *The Fire Next Time* (1963); W. E. B. DuBois, *The Souls of Black Folks* (1903); R. Ellison, *Invisible Man* (1952); J. Franklin, *From Slavery to Freedom* (3rd ed. 1968); C. Hamilton and S. Carmichael, *Black Power* (1967); Report of the U.S. Commission on Civil Disorders (1968); Kilson, "Whither Integration?", 45 *Am. Scholar* 360 (1976); and hundreds, if not thousands of other books and arti-cles, both literary and empirical. . . .

[9]The best general account I have read of the structure of patriarchy and of its major dimensions and attributes is that found in *Sexual Politics* in the chapter, "Theory of Sexual Politics." K. Millett, *Sexual Poli-tics* 23–58 (1970). The essay seems to me to be truly a major contribution to an understanding of the sub-ject. . . .

[10]See, e.g., Hochschild, "A Review of Sex Role Research," 78 *Am. J. Soc.* 1011 (1973), which reviews and very usefully categorizes the enormous volume of literature on this topic. See also Stewart, "Social Influ-ences of Sex Differences in Behavior," in *Sex Differences* 138 (M. Teitelbaum ed. 1976); Weitzman, "Sex-Role Socialization," in *Women: A Feminist Perspective* 105 (J. Freeman ed. 1975). . . .

[11]See, e.g., *Guinn* v. *United States*, 238 U. S. 347 (1915). . . .

[12]See, e.g., *Crawford* v. *Board of Educ.*, 17 Cal. 3d 280 (1976); *Jackson* v. *Pasadena City School Dist.*, 59 Cal. 2d 876, 382 P.2d 878, 31 Cal. Rptr. 606 (1963).

[13]N.Y. Times, Aug. 31, 1972, § 1, at 33, col. 3.

[14]. . . A perceptive account of the differences between prejudice and racism, and of the different kinds of racism, including institutional racism of the sorts I discuss below, can be found in M. Jones, *Prejudice and Racism* (1972). *See especially* pp. 60–115 (Ch. 4, "Perspectives on Prejudice"), and pp. 116–67 (Ch. 5, "Realities of Racism"). A somewhat analogous set of distinctions concerning sexism is made in Jaggar, "On Sexual Equality," 84 *Ethics* 275, 276–77 (1974).

[15]*Whitus* v. *Georgia*, 385 U.S. 545 (1967), *Avery* v. *Georgia*, 345 U.S. 559 (1953), and *Strauder* v. *West Virginia*, 100 U.S. 303 (1880), are three of the many cases declaring it unconstitutional to exclude blacks systematically from the jury rolls when the defendant is black. *Swain* v. *Alabama*, 380 U.S. 202 (1963), is one of the many cases declaring that it is not unconstitutional that no blacks were in fact on the jury that tried the defendant.

[16]See, e.g., *Peters* v. *Kiff*, 407 U.S. 493, 508–09 (Burger, C. J., dissenting).

[17]*Brown* v. *Board of Educ.*, 349 U.S. 294 (1955).

[18]*Brown* v. *Board of Educ.*, 347 U.S. 483 (1954).

[19]349 U.S. at 301.

[20]Ibid., at 299.

[21]Ibid., at 300–01.

[22]The unusual character of *Brown II* was recognized by Mr. Justice Goldberg in *Watson* v. *City of Memphis*, 373 U.S. 526 (1963). . . .

[23]One thorough and very valuable exploration of this and a number of the other topics discussed in this section is Alison Jaggar's "On Sexual Equality," note 14. The article also contains a very useful analysis of the views of a number of other feminists who have dealt with this issue.

[24]An analysis of the social realities of an existing society can also divide things up into these three areas.

[25]There is a danger in calling this ideal the "assimilationist" ideal. That term suggests the idea of incorporating oneself, one's values, and the like into the dominant group and its practices and values. I want to make it clear that no part of that idea is meant to be captured by my use of this term. Mine is a stipulative definition.

[26]Jaggar describes something fairly close to the assimilation view in this way: "The traditional feminist answer to this question [of what the features of a nonsexist society would be] has been that a sexually egalitarian society is one in which virtually no public recognition is given to the fact that there is a physiological sex difference between persons. This is not to say that the different reproductive function of each sex should be unacknowledged in such a society nor that there should be no physicians specializing in female and male complaints, etc. But it is to say that, except in this sort of context, the question whether someone is female or male should have no significance. . . . In the mainstream tradition, the non-sexist society is one which is totally integrated sexually, one in which sexual differences have ceased to be a matter of public concern." Jaggar, note 14, at 276–77.

[27]Although ostensibly empirical, the question of whether and to what extent affirmative action programs "work" has a substantial nonempirical component. There are many variables that can plausibly be taken into account, and many differing weights to be assigned to these variables. Consequently, how one marshalls and assesses the "evidence" concerning which programs "work" and which do not, has at least as much to do with whether one believes that the programs are or are not justifiable on other grounds as it does with a disinterested marshalling of the "facts." See, e.g., T. Sowell, *Affirmative Action Reconsidered* 34–40 (1975); N. Glazer, *Affirmative Discrimination: Ethnic Inequality and Public Policy* (1975). This also is a feature of Mr. Justice Mosk's analysis where he asserts, for example, that "[t]he overemphasis upon race as a criterion will *undoubtedly* be counterproductive." *Bakke* v. *Regents of the Univ. of Cal.*, 18 Cal. 3d 34, 62, 553 P.2d 1152, 1171, 132 Cal. Rptr. 680, 699 (1976) (emphasis added), *cert. granted*, L.A. Daily Jour., Feb. 23, 1977, at 1, col. 2 (No. 76–811). . . .

[28]See *Bakke* v. *Regents of the Univ. of Cal.,* 18 Cal. 3d 34, 62, 553 P.2d 1152, 1171, 132 Cal. Rptr. 680, 699, (1976), *cert. granted,* 45 U.S.L.W. 3437 (U.S. Dec. 14, 1976) (No. 76–811).

[29]For example, such an approach seems, at least at times, to underlie the writings of R. Nozick, *Anarchy, State, and Utopia* (1974).

[30]I have also tried to discuss some of these matters, although not with anything like complete success, in Wasserstrom, "Rights, Human Rights, and Racial Discrimination," 61 *J. Phil.* 628 (1964).

[31]. . . For a discussion of some of the literature that discusses the issues of compensation and reparation, see, e.g., Boxill, "The Morality of Reparation," 2 *Soc. Theory & Prac.* 113 (1972).

Shelby Steele

Affirmative Action

THE PRICE OF PREFERENCE

In a few short years, when my two children will be applying to college, the affirmative action policies by which most universities offer black students some form of preferential treatment will present me with a dilemma. I am a middle-class black, a college professor, far from wealthy, but also well-removed from the kind of deprivation that would qualify my children for the label "disadvantaged." Both of them have endured racial insensitivity from whites. They have been called names, have suffered slights, and have experienced firsthand the peculiar malevolence that racism brings out in people. Yet, they have never experienced racial discrimination, have never been stopped by their race on any path they have chosen to follow. Still, their society now tells them that if they will only designate themselves as black on their college applications, they will likely do better in the college lottery than if they conceal this fact. I think there is something of a Faustian bargain in this.

Of course, many blacks and a considerable number of whites would say that I was sanctimoniously making affirmative action into a test of character. They would say that this small preference is the meagerest recompense for centuries of unrelieved oppression. And to these arguments other very obvious facts must be added. In America, many marginally competent or flatly incompetent whites are hired everyday—some because their white skin suits the conscious or unconscious racial preference of their employer. The white children of alumni are often grandfathered into elite universities in what can only be seen as a residual benefit of historic white privilege. Worse, white incompetence is always an individual matter, while for blacks it is often confirmation of ugly stereotypes. The Peter Principle was not conceived with only blacks in mind. Given that unfairness cuts both ways, doesn't it only balance the scales of history that my children now receive a slight preference over whites? Doesn't this repay, in a small way, the systematic denial under which their grandfather lived out his days?

So, in theory, affirmative action certainly has all the moral symmetry that fairness requires—the injustice of historical and even contemporary white advantage is offset with black advantage; preference replaces prejudice, inclusion answers exclusion. It is reformist and corrective, even repentent and redemptive. And I would never sneer at these good intentions. Born in the late forties in Chicago, I started my education (a charitable term in this case) in a segregated school and suffered all the indignities that come to blacks in a segregated society. My father, born in the South, only made it to the third grade before the white man's fields took permanent priority over his formal education. And though he educated himself into an advanced reader with an almost professorial authority, he could only drive a truck for a living and never earned more than $90 a week in his entire life. So yes, it is crucial to my sense of citizenship, to my ability to identify with the spirit and the interests of America, to know that this country, however imperfectly, recognizes its past sins and wishes to correct them.

Yet good intentions, because of the opportunity for innocence they offer us, are very seductive and can blind us to the effects they generate when implemented. In our society, affirmative action is, among other things, a testament to white goodwill and to black power, and in the midst of these heavy investments, its effects can be hard to see. But after 20 years of implementation, I think affirmative action has shown itself to be more bad than good and that blacks—whom I will focus on in this essay— now stand to lose more from it than they gain.

In talking with affirmative action administrators and with blacks and whites in general, it is clear that supporters of affirmative action focus on its good intentions while detractors emphasize its negative effects. Proponents talk about "diversity" and "pluralism"; opponents speak of "reverse discrimination," the unfairness of quotas and set-asides. It was virtually impossible to find people outside either camp. The closest I came was a white male manager at a large computer company who said, "I think it amounts to reverse discrimination, but I'll put up with a little of that for a little more diversity." I'll live with a little of the effect to gain a little of the intention, he seemed to be saying. But this only makes him a halfhearted supporter of affirmative action. I think many people who don't really like affirmative action support it to one degree or another anyway.

I believe they do this because of what happened to white and black Americans in the crucible of the 60s when whites were confronted with their racial guilt and blacks tasted their first real power. In this stormy time white absolution and black power coalesced into virtual mandates for society. Affirmative action became a meeting ground for these mandates in the law, and in the late 60s and early 70s it underwent a remarkable escalation of its mission from simple anti-discrimination enforcement to social engineering by means of quotas, goals, timetables, set-asides, and other forms of preferential treatment.

Legally, this was achieved through a series of executive orders and EEOC guidelines that allowed racial imbalances in the workplace to stand as proof of racial discrimination. Once it could be assumed that discrimination explained racial imbalances, it became easy to justify group remedies to presumed discrimination, rather than the normal case-by-case redress for proven discrimination. Preferential treatment through quotas, goals, and so on is designed to correct imbalances based on the assumption that they always indicate discrimination. This expansion of what constitutes discrimination allowed affirmative action to escalate into the business of social engineering in the name of anti-discrimination, to push society toward statistically proportionate racial representation, without any obligation of proving actual discrimination.

What accounted for this shift, I believe, was the white mandate to achieve a new racial innocence and the black mandate to gain power. Even though blacks had made great advances during the 60s without quotas, these mandates which came to a head in the very late 60s, could no longer be satisfied by anything less than racial preferences. I don't think these mandates in themselves were wrong, since whites clearly needed to do better by blacks and blacks needed more real power in society. But, as they came together in affirmative action, their effect was to distort our understanding of racial discrimination in a way that allowed us to offer the remediation of preference on the basis of mere color rather than actual injury. By making black the color of preference, these mandates have reburdened society with the very marriage of color and preference (in reverse) that we set out to eradicate. The old sin is reaffirmed in a new guise.

But the essential problem with this form of affirmative action is the way it leaps over the hard business of developing a formerly oppressed people to the point where they can achieve proportionate representation on their own (given equal opportunity) and goes straight for the proportionate representation. This may satisfy some whites of their innocence and some blacks of their power, but it does very little to truly uplift blacks.

A white female affirmative action officer at an Ivy League university told me what many supporters of affirmative action now say: "We're after diversity. We ideally want a student body where racial and ethnic groups are represented according to their proportion in society." When affirmative action escalated into social engineering, diversity became a golden word. It grants whites an egalitarian fairness (innocence) and blacks an entitlement to proportionate representation (power). *Diversity* is a term that applies democratic principles to races and cultures rather than to citizens, despite the fact that there is nothing to indicate that real diversity is the same thing as proportionate representation. Too often the result of this on campuses (for example) has been a democracy of colors rather than of people, an artificial diversity that gives the appearance of an educational parity between black and white students that has not yet been achieved in reality. Here again, racial preferences allow society to leapfrog over the difficult problem of developing blacks to parity with whites and into a cosmetic diversity that covers the blemish of disparity—a full 6 years after admission, only about 26 percent of black students graduate from college.

Racial representation is not the same thing as racial development, yet affirmative action fosters a confusion of these very different needs. Representation can be manufactured; development is always hard-earned. However, it is the music of innocence and power that we hear in affirmative action that causes us to cling to it and to its distracting emphasis on representation. The fact is that after 20 years of racial preferences, the gap between white and black median income is greater than it was in the 70s. None of this is to say that blacks don't need policies that ensure our right to equal opportunity, but what we need more is the development that will let us take advantage of society's efforts to include us.

I think that one of the most troubling effects of racial preferences for blacks is a kind of demoralization, or put another way, an enlargement of self-doubt. Under affirmative action the quality that earns us preferential treatment is an implied inferiority. However this inferiority is explained—and it is easily enough explained by the myriad deprivations that grew out of our oppression—it is still inferiority. There are explanations, and then there is the fact. And the fact must be borne by the individual as a condition apart from the explanation, apart even from the fact that others like himself also bear this condition. In integrated situations where blacks must compete with whites who may be better prepared, these explanations may quickly wear thin and expose the individual to racial as well as personal self-doubt.

All of this is compounded by the cultural myth of black inferiority that blacks have always lived with. What this means in practical terms is that when blacks deliver themselves into integrated situations, they encounter a nasty little reflex in whites, a mindless, atavistic reflex that responds to the color black with alarm. Attributions may follow this alarm if the white cares to indulge them, and if they do, they will most likely be negative—one such attribution is intellectual ineptness. I think this reflex and the attributions that may follow it embarrass most whites today, therefore, it is usually quickly repressed. Nevertheless, on an equally atavistic level, the black will be aware of the reflex his color triggers and will feel a stab of horror at seeing himself reflected in this way. He, too, will do a quick repression, but a lifetime of such stabbings is what constitutes his inner realm of racial doubt. . . .

The point here is that the implication of inferiority that racial preferences engender in both the white and black mind expands rather than contracts this doubt. Even when the black sees no implication of inferiority in racial preferences, he knows that whites do, so that—consciously or unconsciously—the result is virtually the same. The effect of preferential treatment—the lowering of normal standards to increase black representation—puts blacks at war with an expanded realm of debilitating doubt, so that the doubt itself becomes an unrecognized preoccupation that undermines their ability to perform, especially in integrated situations. On largely white campuses, blacks are five times more likely to drop out than whites. Preferential treatment, no matter how it is justified in the light of day, subjects blacks to a midnight of self-doubt, and so often transforms their advantage into a revolving door.

Another liability of affirmative action comes from the fact that it indirectly encourages blacks to exploit their own past victimization as a source of power and privilege. Victimization, like implied inferiority, is what justifies preference, so that to receive the benefits of preferential treatment one must, to some extent, become invested in the view of one's self as a victim. In this way, affirmative action nurtures a victim-focused identity in blacks. The obvious irony here is that we become inadvertently invested in the very condition we are trying to overcome. Racial preferences send us the message that there is more power in our past suffering than our present achievements—none of which could bring us a *preference* over others.

When power itself grows out of suffering, then blacks are encouraged to expand the boundaries of what qualifies as racial oppression, a situation that can lead us to paint our victimization in vivid colors, even as we receive the benefits of preference.

The same corporations and institutions that give us preference are also seen as our oppressors. At Stanford University minority students—some of whom enjoy as much as $15,000 a year in financial aid—recently took over the president's office demanding, among other things, more financial aid. The power to be found in victimization, like any power, is intoxicating and can lend itself to the creation of a new class of super-victims who can feel the pea of victimization under 20 mattresses. Preferential treatment rewards us for being underdogs rather than for moving beyond that status—a misplacement of incentives that, along with its deepening of our doubt, is more a yoke than a spur.

But, I think, one of the worst prices that blacks pay for preference has to do with an illusion. I saw this illusion at work recently in the mother of a middle-class black student who was going off to his first semester of college. "They owe us this, so don't think for a minute that you don't belong there." This is the logic by which many blacks, and some whites, justify affirmative action—it is something "owed," a form of reparation. But this logic overlooks a much harder and less digestible reality, that it is impossible to repay blacks living today for the historic suffering of the race. If all blacks were given $1 million tomorrow morning it would not amount to a dime on the dollar of three centuries of oppression, nor would it obviate the residues of that oppression that we still carry today. The concept of historic reparation grows out of man's need to impose a degree of justice on the world that simply does not exist. Suffering can be endured and overcome, it cannot be repaid. Blacks cannot be repaid for the injustice done to the race, but we can be corrupted by society's guilty gestures of repayment.

Affirmative action is such a gesture. It tells us that racial preferences can do for us what we cannot do for ourselves. The corruption here is in the hidden incentive *not* to do what we believe preferences will do. This is an incentive to be reliant on others just as we are struggling for self-reliance. And it keeps alive the illusion that we can find some deliverance in repayment. The hardest thing for any sufferer to accept is that his suffering excuses him from very little and never has enough currency to restore him. To think otherwise is to prolong the suffering.

Several blacks I spoke with said they were still in favor of affirmative action because of the "subtle" discrimination blacks were subject to once on the job. One photojournalist said, "They have ways of ignoring you." A black female television producer said, "You can't file a lawsuit when your boss doesn't invite you to the insider meetings without ruining your career. So we still need affirmative action." Others mentioned the infamous "glass ceiling" through which blacks can see the top positions of authority but never reach them. But I don't think racial preferences are a protection against this subtle discrimination; I think they contribute to it.

In any workplace, racial preferences will always create two-tiered populations composed of preferreds and unpreferreds. This division makes automatic a perception of enhanced competence for the unpreferreds and of questionable competence for the preferreds—the former earned his way, even though others were given preference, while the latter made it by color as much as by competence. Racial preferences implicitly mark white with an exaggerated superiority just as they mark blacks with an exaggerated inferiority. They not only reinforce America's oldest racial myth but, for blacks, they have the effect of stigmatizing the already stigmatized.

I think that much of the "subtle" discrimination that blacks talk about is often (not always) discrimination against the stigma of questionable competence that affirmative action delivers to blacks. In this sense, preferences scapegoat the very people they seek to help. And it may be that at a certain level employers impose a glass ceiling, but this may not be against the race so much as against the race's reputation for having advanced by color as much as by competence. Affirmative action makes a glass ceiling virtually necessary as a protection against the corruptions of preferential treatment. This ceiling is the point at which corporations shift the emphasis from color to competency and stop playing the affirmative action game. Here preference backfires for blacks and becomes a taint that holds them back. Of course, one could argue that this taint, which is, after all, in the minds of whites, becomes nothing more than an excuse to discriminate against blacks. And certainly the result is the same in either case— blacks don't get past the glass ceiling. But this argument does not get around the fact that racial preferences now taint this color with a new theme of suspicion that makes it even more vulnerable to the impulse in others to discriminate. In this crucial yet gray area of perceived competence, preferences make whites look better than they are and blacks worse, while doing nothing whatever to stop the very real discrimination that blacks may encounter. I don't wish to justify the glass ceiling here, but only to suggest the very subtle ways that affirmative action revives rather than extinguishes the old rationalizations for racial discrimination.

In education, a revolving door; in employment, a glass ceiling.

I believe affirmative action is problematic in our society because it tries to function like a social program. Rather than ask it to ensure equal opportunity we have demanded that it create parity between the races. But preferential treatment does not teach skills, or educate, or instill motivation. It only passes out entitlement by color, a situation that in my profession has created an unrealistically high demand for black professors. The social engineer's assumption is that this high demand will inspire more blacks to earn Ph.D.s and join the profession. In fact, the number of blacks earning Ph.D.s has declined in recent years. A Ph.D. must be developed from preschool on. He requires family and community support. He must acquire an entire system of values that enables him to work hard while delaying gratification. There are social programs, I believe, that can (and should) help blacks *develop* in all these areas, but entitlement by color is not a social program; it is a dubious reward for being black.

It now seems clear that the Supreme Court, in a series of recent decisions, is moving away from racial preferences. It has disallowed preferences except in instances of "identified discrimination," eroded the precedent that statistical racial imbalances are *prima facie* evidence of discrimination, and in effect granted white males the right to challenge consent degrees that use preference to achieve racial balances in the workplace. One civil rights leader said, "Night has fallen on civil rights." But I am not so sure. The effect of these decisions is to protect the constitutional rights of everyone rather than take rights away from blacks. What they do take away from blacks is the special entitlement to more rights than others that preferences always grant. Night has fallen on racial preferences, not on the fundamental rights of black Americans. The reason for this shift, I believe, is that the white mandate for absolution from past racial sins has weakened considerably during the 80s. Whites are now less willing to endure unfairness to themselves in order to grant special entitlements to blacks, even when these entitlements are justified in the name of past suffering. Yet the black mandate for more power in society has remained unchanged. And I think part of the anxiety that many blacks feel over these decisions has to do with the loss of black power they may signal. We had won a certain specialness and now we are losing it.

But the power we've lost by these decisions is really only the power that grows out of our victimization—the power to claim special entitlements under the law because of past oppression. This is not a very substantial or reliable power, and it is important that we know this so we can focus more exclusively on the kind of development that will bring enduring power. There is talk now that Congress will pass new legislation to compensate for these new limits on affirmative action. If this happens, I hope that their focus will be on development and anti-discrimination rather than entitlement, on achieving racial parity rather than jerry-building racial diversity.

I would also like to see affirmative action go back to its original purpose of enforcing equal opportunity—a purpose that in itself disallows racial preferences. We cannot be sure that the discriminatory impulse in America has yet been shamed into extinction, and I believe affirmative action can make its greatest contribution by providing a rigorous vigilance in this area. It can guard against constitutional rather than racial rights, and help institutions evolve standards of merit and selection that are appropriate to the institution's needs yet as free of racial bias as possible (again, with the understanding that racial imbalances are not always an indication of racial bias). One of the most important things affirmative action can do is to define exactly what racial discrimination is and how it might manifest itself within a specific institution. The impulse to discriminate *is* subtle and cannot be ferreted out unless its many guises are made clear to people. Along with this there should be monitoring of institutions and heavy sanctions brought to bear when actual discrimination is found. This is the sort of affirmative action that America owes to blacks and to itself. It goes after the evil of discrimination itself, while preferences only sidestep the evil and grant entitlement to its *presumed* victims.

But if not preferences, then what? I think we need social policies that are committed to two goals: the educational and economic development of disadvantaged people, regardless of race, and the eradication from our society—through close monitoring and severe sanctions—of racial, ethnic, or gender discrimination. Preferences will not deliver us to either of these goals, since they tend to benefit those who are not disadvantaged—middle-class white women and middle-class blacks—and attack one form of discrimination with another. Preferences are inexpensive and carry the glamour of good intentions—change the numbers and the good deed is done. To be against them is to be unkind. But I think the unkindest cut is to bestow on children like my own an undeserved advantage while neglecting the development of those disadvantaged children on the East Side of my city who will likely never be in a position to benefit from a preference. Give my children fairness; give disadvantaged children a better shot at development—better elementary and secondary schools, job training, safer neighborhoods, better financial assistance for college, and so on. Fewer blacks go to college today than 10 years ago; more black males of college age are in prison or under the control of the criminal justice system than in college. This despite racial preferences.

The mandates of black power and white absolution out of which preferences emerged were not wrong in themselves. What was wrong was that both races focused more on the goals of these mandates than on the means to the goals. Blacks can have no real power without taking responsibility for their own educational and economic development. Whites can have no racial innocence without earning it by eradicating discrimination and helping the disadvantaged to develop. Because we ignored the means, the goals have not been reached, and the real work remains to be done.

U.S. SUPREME COURT

Brown v. Board of Education of Topeka, Kansas I (1954)

Chief Justice Warren delivered the opinion of the Court.

These cases came to us from the States of Kansas, South Carolina, Virginia, and Delaware. . . .

In each of the cases, minors of the Negro race, through their legal representatives, seek aid of the courts in obtaining admission to the public schools of their community on a non-segregated basis. . . . In each of the cases other than the Delaware case, a three-judge federal district court denied relief to the plaintiffs on the so-called "separate but equal" doctrine announced by the Court in *Plessy* v. *Ferguson*. . . .

We come then to the question presented: Does segregation of children in public schools solely on the basis of race, even though the physical facilities and other "tangible" factors may be equal, deprive the children of the minority group of equal educational opportunities? We believe that it does.

In *Sweatt* v. *Painter* . . . in finding that a segregated law school for Negroes could not provide them equal educational opportunities, this Court relied in large part on "those qualities which are incapable of objective measurement but which make for greatness in a law school." In *McLaurin* v. *Oklahoma State Regents* . . . the Court, in requiring that a Negro admitted to a white graduate school be treated like all other students, again resorted to intangible considerations: ". . . his ability to study, to engage in discussion and exchange views with other students, and, in general, to learn his profession." Such considerations apply with added force to children in grade and high schools. To separate them from others of similar age and qualifications solely because of their race generates a feeling of inferiority as to their status in the community that may affect their hearts and minds in a way unlikely ever to be undone.

Whatever may have been the extent of psychological knowledge at the time of *Plessy* v. *Ferguson,* this finding is amply supported by modern authority. Any language in *Plessy* v. *Ferguson* contrary to this finding is rejected.

We conclude that in the field of public education the doctrine of "separate but equal" has no place. Separate educational facilities are inherently unequal. Therefore, we hold that the plaintiffs and others similarly situated for whom the actions have been brought are, by the reason of the segregation complained of, deprived of the equal protection of the laws guaranteed by the 14th Amendment. This disposition makes unnecessary any discussion whether such segregation also violates the Due Process Clause of the 14th Amendment.

U.S. SUPREME COURT

Regents of The University of California v. Bakke (1978)

Mr. Justice Powell announced the judgment of the Court. . . .

Allan Bakke is a white male who applied to the Davis Medical School in both 1973 and 1974. In both years Bakke's application was considered by the general admissions program, and he received an interview. His 1973 interview was with Dr. Theodore H. West, who considered Bakke "a very desirable applicant to [the] medical school." Despite a strong benchmark score of 468 out of 500, Bakke was rejected. His application had come late in the year, and no applicants in the general admissions process with scores below 470 were accepted after Bakke's application was completed. There were four special admissions slots unfilled at that time, however, for which Bakke was not considered. . . .

Bakke's 1974 application was completed early in the year. . . . Again, Bakke's application was rejected. . . . In both years, applicants were admitted under the special program with grade point averages, MCAT scores, and benchmark scores significantly lower than Bakke's. . . .

The special admissions program is undeniably a classification based on race and ethnic background. To the extent that there existed a pool of at least minimally qualified minority applicants to fill the 16 special admissions seats, white applicants could compete only for 84 seats in the entering class, rather than the 100 open to minority applicants. Whether this limitation is described as a quota or a goal, it is a line drawn on the basis of race and ethnic status.

. . . The guarantee of equal protection cannot mean one thing when applied to one individual and something else when applied to a person of another color. If both are not accorded the same protection, then it is not equal. . . .

It is evident that the Davis special admission program involves the use of an explicit racial classification never before countenanced by this Court. It tells applicants who are not Negro, Asian, or "Chicano" that they are totally excluded from a specific percentage of the seats in an entering class. No matter how strong their qualifications, quantitative and extracurricular, including their own potential for contribution to educational diversity, they are never afforded the chance to compete with applicants from the preferred groups for the special admission seats. At the same time, the preferred applicants have the opportunity to compete for every seat in the class.

The fatal flaw in petitioner's preferential program is its disregard of individual rights as guaranteed by the 14th Amendment. Such rights are not absolute. But when a State's distribution of benefits or imposition of burdens hinges on the color of a person's skin or ancestry, that individual is entitled to a demonstration that the challenged classification is necessary to promote a substantial state interest. Petitioner has failed to carry this burden. For this reason, that portion of the California court's judgment holding petitioner's special admissions program invalid under the 14th Amendment must be affirmed.

In enjoining petitioner from ever considering the race of any applicant, however, the courts below failed to recognize that the State has a substantial interest that legitimately may be served by a properly devised admissions program involving the competitive consideration of race and ethnic origin. For this reason, so much of the California court's judgment as enjoins petitioner from any consideration of the race of any applicant must be reversed.

With respect to respondent's entitlement to an injunction directing his admission to the Medical School, petitioner has conceded that it could not carry its burden of proving that, but for the existence of its unlawful special admissions program, respondent still would not have been admitted. Hence, respondent is entitled to the injunction, and that portion of the judgment must be affirmed.

(CAPITAL) PUNISHMENT

STEPHEN NATHANSON

Is the Death Penalty What Murderers Deserve?

THE ARGUMENT FROM DESERT

In this paper, I am going to focus on one issue in the debate about the death penalty. The issue is whether we ought to have the death penalty because people who commit murder deserve to die.

In focusing on this one issue, I will be ignoring many other important aspects of the death penalty debate.[1] Still, because this issue is so central to many people's thinking, it deserves careful attention, and making progress in understanding it can help us to decide whether the death penalty is a morally justified form of punishment.

Many people think it is obvious that at least certain people who are guilty of murder deserve to die. In addition, they think it is obvious that if some people deserve to die for their crimes, then we ought to institute the death penalty as the legal punishment for them.

Indeed, the truth of these claims seems so obvious to some people that they often don't feel a need to state their argument. Instead, they think they can prove their case simply by reciting the names of particularly evil and horrifying people—whether they be political leaders like Hitler, Stalin, and Pol Pot or especially vile murderers like Jeffrey Dahmer, Theodore Bundy, or Timothy McVeigh. Simply to recall these names and the crimes perpetrated by these people is supposed to be enough to show that the death penalty is a morally justified form of punishment.

I assume that when people recall these names, they are implicitly appealing to the argument from desert, the view that the death penalty is legitimate and desirable because some murderers deserve to die. In the pages that follow, I will try to show that this argument and the conclusion it supports are mistaken.

TWO BAD REPLIES

Opponents of the death penalty sometimes respond to this argument by charging that it simply expresses a desire for vengeance and that vengeful desires are base and unworthy—especially for those who claim to be civilized and to respect the value of human life.

This is not an effective reply. First, while it charges advocates of the death penalty with an undesirable motive, it does not show that they actually have such a motive. After all, people who favor the death penalty, even if they are mistaken about what justice requires, may still be motivated by a desire for justice. They may cherish human life and think that killing is the only punishment that responds appropriately to the evil of unjustifiably taking a life. Even if they are mistaken about this, there is no justification for assuming that undesirable motives underlie their support for the death penalty.

A second bad reply might try to show that even people who commit the vilest acts are essentially good and hence that they deserve no evil. It is hard to see how this argument could be persuasively developed. If the only way to show that murderers do not deserve to die is by arguing that they are really good people, then the argument would be doomed to failure. Just as it is implausible to argue that no actions are wrong, so is it implausible to argue that all people are fundamentally good.

WHY THE ARGUMENT FROM DESERT IS FLAWED

One of the main problems with the argument that the death penalty is required because (at least some) murderers deserve to die is that it oversimplifies and takes as obvious what is actually a very complex matter. It says: Some murderers deserve to die, and we, acting through our legal system, should kill them. End of discussion.

The argument assumes (a) that we know with certainty what people deserve and (b) that what people deserve is the only consideration that matters in the debate about capital punishment. Each of these assumptions is false. It is often difficult to know what people deserve, and there are other matters that need to be considered when deciding on the appropriate legal punishment for murder and other crimes.

The argument ignores other relevant matters because it thinks of the death penalty only as an act of ending a convicted criminal's life. But the death penalty is also an institution. It is a set of legal rules and practices that authorize certain people to take legal steps that can lead to the killing of a convicted criminal. Once we start to think about the death penalty as an institution and not as an individual act, we are less likely to overlook the fact that other things may matter in addition to whether a particular person deserves death.

There are often reasons why we don't institutionalize a particular practice, even if we would like certain people to be treated in a particular way. For example, some people oppose the institution of "physician-assisted suicide" even though they think that some individuals would be better off if someone helped them to die. Yet, fears about the impact of this practice on the doctor/patient relationship and about possible abuses of this practice lead some people to oppose it, even though they might want it to be permitted in particular cases.[2]

What this example shows is that we cannot move automatically from judgments that an act would be good in a particular case to judgments that we ought to establish a practice to carry out that act. Advocates of the death penalty who appeal to the argument from desert are generally thinking about the execution of a particular person, but they neglect the difficult institutional issues that arise in writing the death penalty into our laws and legal practices.

DETERMINING WHAT PEOPLE DESERVE

We have the illusion that it is easy to tell what people deserve because in some cases, what people deserve depends entirely on two things: (1) their actions or traits and (2) some set of accepted criteria. If, for example, a student answers all the questions on a test correctly and if getting a perfect score is the criterion for an "A" grade, then the student deserves an A. Or, if a prize is offered to the tallest person at a party, the one who is tallest deserves the prize. In each case, the combination of an action or a trait and a criterion yields a simple determination of what people deserve. People who think it obvious that murderers deserve to die may have this model in mind, and this may explain their confidence in their judgment.

There are several sources of complications, however. In some cases, deciding whether the person has performed the required action may not be so easy. So, for example, a student who writes an excellent essay may deserve an "A" grade, but the criteria for an excellent essay are more complicated that the criteria for a perfect score on a multiple choice test. Coherence, clarity, originality, understanding, etc. (which are some of the features of an excellent essay) are matters of degree, and competent evaluators may differ on the degree to which a particular essay exhibits these qualities. Even if everyone agrees that some essays are in the good-to-excellent range and that others are poor, competent evaluators may still disagree about whether a particular essay merits an A, an A-, or a B+. Likewise, determining who is the most beautiful person in a group is trickier than determining who is the tallest one, even if there is general agreement about who the top contenders are.

These cases may seem irrelevant to judging murderers, but in fact they are quite analogous. Judging whether the action of a particular murderer deserves death, life in prison, or some other punishment is more like evaluating an essay than it is like grading a multiple choice test, more like deciding who is most beautiful than it is like deciding who is tallest.

Things would be simpler, of course, if we believed that everyone who illegally kills another human being deserves to die. If, for example, we really believed in the maxim "an eye for an eye," that would give us a criterion that would permit killing everyone who kills another human being. But that is not what we think, and it is not the rule on which our legal system is based. (If we really accepted the "eye for an eye" principle, we would have to accept the idea that executioners ought to be executed.)

Some killings are not illegal at all—for example, those done in self-defense. Even among those that are crimes, we distinguish between manslaughter and murder, and murders are classified as first or second degree, while cases of manslaughter may be divided into various categories: voluntary, involuntary, reckless, etc.

Because we differentiate among types of killings, prosecutors have to decide not just whether there is evidence that Tom killed Dick; they also have to decide what degree of homicide to charge Tom with. Their charge is extremely important because only people who are charged with first degree murder are eligible for the death penalty.[3] Likewise, juries must decide not only that there is evidence beyond a reasonable doubt that Tom killed Dick; they must also decide if the circumstances were such that Tom is guilty of first degree murder, second degree murder, or some other grade of homicide. Finally, even if Tom is convicted of first degree murder, the jury and/or the judge must decide whether Tom satisfies the legal criteria for being sentenced to death or whether he ought to be sentenced to prison.

In one sense, of course, all homicides are equally serious, since all involve the death of a human being. But we do not actually judge all of them to be equally bad. If a person was severely provoked or acted in a rage, we may not think his deed is as terrible as it would be if he had coldly planned the murder in advance. Even cases of prior planning differ among themselves. Think of the woman who, after years of cruelty and abuse, makes a plan to kill her husband and then carries it out.

So, deciding whether someone deserves to die is quite different from deciding that all the answers on a multiple choice test are correct or that one person is the tallest in a room. For this reason, prosecutors, juries, and judges often end up treating people who have committed apparently similar crimes in very different ways. Some are sentenced to die while others are given prison terms. Others of us might judge these same cases in different ways entirely, just as different evaluators might disagree about the degree of excellence in a particular piece of writing or the beauty of a particular contestant.[4]

Notice that there are at least two different sources of disparities. People may judge the particular cases differently, but they may also understand the criteria differently. Where criteria are unclear, so many different understandings may be possible that the criteria don't provide genuine guidance. People may feel that they are following them, but each follows his or her own understanding of them. The legal scholar Charles Black, Jr., has argued that the legal criteria for determining who should be executed are so unclear that they are not genuine rules or guidelines at all.[5]

WHY DISPARITIES ARE TROUBLING

The fact that people who have committed similar crimes often receive different punishments is troubling for a number of reasons. Even if a person who is executed does deserve to die, it is troubling if other people who are equally deserving are treated more leniently. This is because whether a person's punishment is just or not depends not simply on what he or she deserves but also on how the punishment compares with the punishments of others. So, what a person deserves is not the only factor that determines whether that person's punishment is just. A punishment can be deserved and still be unjust.[6]

If one student in a class receives a failing grade for cheating while another is simply warned not to do it again, then even if the first student deserved to fail, the infliction of this punishment is unjust. Or, to take an example from recent news reports, if low-ranking members of the military are typically imprisoned or receive dishonorable discharges for committing adultery while high-ranking officers are generally reprimanded, the punishment of those with lower rank seems unfair, even if (given military rules), they deserve a severe punishment.

What is common to both these cases is that arbitrary reasons—reasons that have nothing to do with the criteria of desert—play an important role in determining whether people will be treated as they deserve. In the case of military personnel who are guilty of adultery, the arbitrary reasons may by systematic, creating a system of advantaged and disadvantaged parties.

Similar charges, supported by considerable research, have been made about the death penalty. The severity of the punishment imposed on people convicted of homicide depends not just on the awfulness of their crimes but also on factors like their race, the race of their victims, and whether they have the money to acquire skillful legal representation. Yet none of these factors is relevant to what they deserve.[7]

In 1972, the Supreme Court thought these problems were so serious that, by a vote of 5–4 in *Furman* v. *Georgia,* it ruled the death penalty unconstitutional. Four years later, in *Gregg* v. *Georgia,* it ruled that some new state laws that authorize the death penalty were consistent with the Constitution. These new laws, the Court argued, provided clear guidelines for jurors to use and thus insured that the sentencing of murderers would no longer be arbitrary or capricious.

In reinstating the death penalty, the justices in the majority seemed to be making two false assumptions. First, they assumed that changing the laws could succeed in weeding out the influence of arbitrary factors from the judicial process. Second, they also mistakenly assumed that judgments of desert could be made with an extraordinary degree of precision.

To see why these are false, imagine that two people are guilty of first degree murder and that juries are asked to determine whether they deserve to die or whether they deserve life imprisonment. Both have committed terrible crimes so if one is justifiably sentenced to prison and the other is justifiably sentenced to death, there must be some fairly precise scale that can be used to distinguish them. It is as if there were a point system and everyone who commits first degree murder has at least 95 out of a potential 100 points. Only those who score 98 or more, however, deserve to die. Juries then are judging where between 95 and 100 a particular murderer falls. Such judgments are totally different from the judgments about desert that we make in ordinary life. In ordinary circumstances, our judgments about what people deserve are quite crude and rough. We have no experience with the kind of precise calculations of desert that are required in these kinds of sentencing decisions.

Even if we are confident that we can classify some murders as worse than others, we should not feel confident that we can make precise discriminations between different people who have committed dreadful crimes. As the judgments required become more and more complex (not just judging that Tom killed Dick but rather that Tom's killing Dick should be rated as a 97 rather than a 98), our degree of confidence should diminish. Human fallibility becomes a more significant feature. Prejudices and irrelevant factors can play a role because the criteria are so murky. The punishment people receive begins to look more like the result of the "luck of the draw" rather than the result of a reasoned assessment of desert. It is this randomness that led Supreme Court Justice Stewart to write in *Furman* v. *Georgia* that receiving a death sentence was like "being struck by lightening."[8] It happened to some people who committed murders but not to others, even though there was no discernible difference between their crimes. This degree of fallibility and randomness may be acceptable in the evaluating of essays or beauty contests, but it is not acceptable on a matter of life and death.

Why is it not acceptable? Because death penalty advocates claim that they only want to execute those who deserve to die. They also claim that they have the highest respect for life and that this respect is what motivates their support of the most severe punishment for taking a life. This is a contradictory view, however, once one recognizes the fallibility of these judgments and the impossibility of meaningful, precise standards of desert. To recognize the likelihood of error and arbitrariness here is to recognize the possibility that people will be executed who do not deserve to die, and this must be something that people who have the highest respect for life must oppose. Only if we could make judgments about what people deserve in a precise, reliable way can support of the death penalty be compatible with a proper respect for human life.

Consider one other factor. Juries and judges don't actually get to examine the murder itself in order to determine the degree of guilt and blameworthiness. What they get to consider is the account of the murder that is presented and described by the prosecutor, the defense lawyer, and the witnesses who are called to testify. Yet the ability of lawyers to present a case effectively varies considerably, and impoverished defendants are often represented by inexperienced lawyers who are assigned to the case and who may lack both the resources and the skills to represent the defendant effectively.

The judgment about what a particular murderer deserves, then, is not directly based on the nature of the crime and the killer themselves. Rather, it is based on these factors as they are filtered through the abilities of the lawyer who represents the defendant, adding one more element of complexity to the context in which these judgments are made.

The simple model of judging desert, then, does not really fit what goes on in death penalty cases, even if we look primarily at the actions that people perform. For reasons that I will now explain, the situation is even more murky than I have so far suggested.

IT'S NOT JUST ACTIONS THAT MATTER

Judgments of desert are even more complicated than I have so far discussed. We can see this in the following kind of case.

Suppose that Jill has written a paper that everyone thinks is excellent, while Jack wrote a paper that everyone agrees is weak. Looking at the papers alone, the teacher gives Jill an A and Jack a C. Jill, however, wrote her paper in a very short time and put very little effort into it, while Jack put in long hours doing research, wrote a first draft, consulted with his teacher, edited and revised his paper, and did everything in his power to write an excellent paper. While it is perhaps proper that Jill gets a higher grade, it is not so obvious that she is morally more deserving of a high grade than Jack. He worked hard (a morally relevant factor), while she took advantage of natural gifts or superior earlier schooling (both of which are matters of luck).

Or consider the beauty contest participants. Even if we had a precise scale of beauty so that everyone agreed on who was most beautiful, would it follow that the winner really deserves the prize? Isn't the winner's beauty just a matter of luck and not really deserved at all?

Similar issues arise in criminal cases. Even if a person has committed a brutal murder, we may still have reason to wonder whether he or she actually deserves the punishment for that crime.

In one area, the law recognizes this. When murders are committed by people who are judged to be criminally insane, the judgment is made that they are not responsible for their actions. People who are criminally insane cannot be held responsible for their actions and hence cannot deserve to be punished. We may confine them to protect others from them, but this is a misfortune, since it involves imposing severe limits on the liberty of people who do not deserve such deprivations.

What makes people criminally insane? Two criteria that have traditionally been important are (a) the inability to tell right from wrong or to appreciate the wrongness of the action they commit and (b) the inability to control one's impulses.[9]

In fact, only a small number of people are judged to be so lacking in their moral capacities that they are thought to be beyond being judged to deserve punishment. But the case of the criminally insane makes it clear that we cannot tell what someone deserves simply on the basis of what they do. We also have to know that they have the capacities to act as moral agents. In particular, they have to be able to know that their action is wrong, and they have to be able to exercise control over their impulses.

So, when we judge that a particular murderer deserves to die, we are judging not just the awfulness of the kind of murder that this person committed; we are also making a judgment about the capacity of this person to act as a moral agent.

Critics of the death penalty often suggest that judges and juries are not very good at making these complex judgments, and they believe that persons who are undeserving of death are sometimes executed. In making this argument, they are not denying the dreadfulness of the crime the person committed. Rather, they are claiming that we cannot tell what people morally deserve just by looking at features of their actions. Even where the action is genuinely horrific, there may be facts about the person that diminish responsibility and blameworthiness. These facts may not be taken seriously enough within the legal process.

That is the conclusion reached in a study of the death penalty in the United States published by Amnesty International, the international human rights organization. This study claimed that many of these who have been executed have in fact been mentally ill or had features that diminished their personal blameworthiness for their deeds. Here are the report's descriptions of some of the people who have been executed in the United States:

> Arthur Goode: Mentally unstable; documented history of mental illness since age of three.

> David Funchess: Vietnam veteran; . . . Left army with heroin addiction. Several years after conviction was found to be suffering from post-traumatic stress syndrome, a psychological disorder not properly understood at [the] time of his trial.

> John Young: His psychiatric trauma from witnessing [his] mother's murder at age three and subsequent neglected childhood [were] not mentioned at his trial; . . . Young [was] alleged to have been under the influence of drugs at [the] time of crime.

> Jerome Bowden: Diagnosed as mentally retarded, with IQ of 65.

> David Martin: History of drug/alcohol addiction. Reportedly suffered mental/physical abuse as a child . . .

> James Terry Roach—Minor at [the] time of crime. Trial record acknowledged Roach acting under [the] domination of [an] older man, and that he was mentally retarded. Later evidence that he was suffering from hereditary degenerative disease that could have affected mental state.[10]

What shall we say about these people? Admittedly, our picture of them is limited, but if we reflect on the features of these people, we may come to doubt that people with these features could truly deserve to die, even if there is no doubt that they committed terrible crimes.

And once we realize that we cannot fully tell what someone deserves just by knowing what dreadful acts they committed, then we can see that no recitation of the names of terrible murderers is sufficient to prove anything. A person can fail to be fully blameworthy, even if he has intentionally and maliciously committed the most vile crimes.

This does not mean that people should not be punished or held responsible. The defense of social order and personal security seems to require the institution of punishment, and punishment can be at least partly defended on this basis. But we ought not to feel confident that we can judge the precise degree of punishment that people morally deserve, and even if we could do this, we ought not to feel confident that our criminal justice system actually does so.

To affirm that the people listed above deserved to die, we would have to judge that factors like a history of mental illness, mental retardation, post-traumatic stress syndrome, childhood trauma, and abuse are irrelevant to determinations of what people deserve. Yet our legal system appears to sanction just such judgments, raising strong doubts that it takes seriously the questions of determining what people deserve in all its complexity. It is hard to imagine, for example, that if there is an infinitely wise God who judges such people for their crimes, such a God would dismiss mental illness, retardation, and trauma as irrelevant to what people deserve. Once we recognize their relevance, however, it becomes clear that the snap judgments we sometimes make about what people deserve do not do justice to the complexity of the factors that are relevant to judging what people morally deserve.

A SERIOUS OBJECTION

Faced with arguments of the sort I have raised, some people simply stand pat. They reaffirm their confidence in their own and other people's judgments about what murderers deserve, and they dismiss as irrelevant the flaws in our legal system and the influence of arbitrary factors on the imposition of the death penalty. I have tried throughout this paper to argue against this mindset and have nothing further to add.

There is another response, however, which is important for me to acknowledge and reply to briefly. Some people hear these arguments, recognize the inadequacy of our judgments about what people deserve, and acknowledge the role that race, poverty, and other irrelevant factors play in the death penalty system.

But, they say, these same factors play a role throughout our system of judicial punishment. If showing the complexity of desert judgments and the influence of arbitrary factors is a good argument against the death penalty, then isn't it a good argument against the whole system of punishment? Doesn't my argument reduce itself to absurdity when we see that it implies the illegitimacy of all punishment?

Nonetheless, we cannot and should not abolish the system of punishment. At least at present, it plays a necessary role in sustaining and enforcing the rules of civilized life. Without it, we would be likely to see more widespread violations of people's rights and a serious loss of security for most people. So, punishment is a necessary institution and one which we should retain.[11]

In responding to this objection, let me first agree that the factors I have discussed do operate at all levels and that they do indeed raise serious worries about our system of justice. Putting people in prison for long periods is a grievous punishment, and no one should be happy about the influence of race, social status, and wealth on the distribution of punishment.

It does not follow, however, that we should retain the death penalty. There are two reasons for this, which I will simply state without defending fully. First, punishing by death is a significantly more severe punishment than imprisonment and so needs to be treated differently from other punishments by people who claim to have civilized and humane values. One reason, though not the only one, for this is that the death penalty cannot be corrected in any way. Any errors, any executions of innocent people cannot be undone or compensated for, while imprisonment permits reversals and at least partial corrections.

Second, while the argument above assumes that we need punishment to protect people's lives and safety, the same cannot be said for the death penalty. There is no solid evidence that the death penalty provides greater safety or security than long term imprisonment or life imprisonment without parole.[12]

Because of the extraordinary severity of the death penalty, then, and because it provides no extra measure of safety for our citizens, the arguments raised in this paper count against it with special force. They should, in addition, spur us on to seek greater justice throughout our legal system, but only in the case of the death penalty do they constitute such a powerful case for abolition.

THE BASIC QUESTION

I have been discussing the question of what people morally deserve because advocates of the death penalty say that moral justice will only be done if the law takes the lives of (at least some) murderers. Advocates of the death penalty say that they care about doing what is morally right and that they want the law to be patterned on the demands of morality. Thinking that it is obvious that murderers morally deserve to die, they want death to be the legal punishment for murder.

I have tried to show that the belief on which this argument rests—the belief that murderers deserve to die—is far from obviously true. Even if it is true of some murderers, the judgment that it is true of them is complicated, and there is much room for error in arriving at that judgment.

In addition, the legal system as it actually operates is a kind of filtering device that deeply influences the kinds of facts that emerge about particular people, and the set of social attitudes prevalent in society deeply influences the way in which different kinds of murderers and their victims are regarded.

People who favor the death penalty often overlook the fact that they are approving a system that may execute some murderers who they themselves would not judge to be deserving of death. Once the system is in place, death penalty supporters don't get to pick and choose who will live and who will die. Other people, with perhaps different criteria, get to make those decisions.[13]

It is very difficult to know about a particular murderer that he or she deserves to die, and it is impossible to design a system that makes such judgments in a reliable way. Recognizing the fallibility of our judgments in individual cases and of the system as a whole, we would do best to express our commitment to respecting human life and human dignity by forsaking the practice of killing those who kill. Every legitimate social need for the defense of human life can be accomplished with other punishments that are sufficiently severe and that allow for the correction of error and injustice.[14]

---

[1]In *An Eye for an Eye?—The Immorality of Punishing by Death* (Lanham, Md.: Rowman and Littlefield, 1987), I try to consider all of the major arguments both for and against the death penalty. For a valuable source of much relevant information, see the various editions of Hugo Bedau, ed., *The Death Penalty in America* (New York: Oxford University Press, various years).

[2]I don't mean to take any stand here on physician-assisted suicide. The example is only intended to bring out the distinction between an individual act and a general practice.

[3]For an interesting description that brings out some of these classification problems see Steven Phillips, *No Heroes, No Villains* (New York: Random House, 1977).

[4]For a discussion of these problems that includes many examples of similar cases handled differently, see Ursula Bentele, "The Death Penalty in Georgia: Still Arbitrary," *Washington University Law Quarterly* 62 (1985): 573–646.

[5]This argument is put forward by Black in *Capital Punishment: The Inevitability of Caprice and Mistake*, 2d ed. (New York: W. W. Norton, 1981), pp. 26–29.

[6]On this point, see my article, "Does It Matter If the Death Penalty Is Arbitrarily Administered?" *Philosophy and Public Affairs* 14 (1985): 149–64. For a contrary view, see Ernest van den Haag, "The Collapse of the Case against Capital Punishment," *National Review*, March 31, 1978.

[7]For studies of the influence of race on sentencing, see William Bowers and Glenn Pierce, "Racial Discrimination and Criminal Homicide under Post-Furman Capital Statutes," *Crime and Delinquency* 26 (1980): 563–635; and Samuel Gross and Robert Mauro, *Death and Discrimination* (Boston: Northeastern University Press, 1989).

[8]Reprinted in Hugo Bedau, ed., *The Death Penalty in America,* 3d ed. (New York: Oxford University Press, 1982), p. 263.

[9]For a philosophical analysis of criminal insanity, see Herbert Fingarette, *The Meaning of Criminal Insanity* (Berkeley: University of California Press, 1972).

[10]From Amnesty International, *United States of America: The Death Penalty* (London: Amnesty International Publications, 1987), pp. 198–203.

[11]My argument here echoes familiar points whose classic expression can be found in Thomas Hobbes's *Leviathan,* especially Chapters 13–17. For a contrary view by a defender of anarchism, see Peter Kropotkin, "Law and Authority," in Roger Baldwin, ed., *Kropotkin's Revolutionary Pamphlets* (New York: Dover Books, 1970).

[12]For a brief survey of the evidence on the deterrent power of the death penalty, see Chapter 2 of my book, *An Eye for an Eye?* For fuller overviews of this debate, see the third and fourth editions of Bedau, ed., *Death Penalty in America.*

[13]For other points about the systematic nature of the death penalty, see my "How (Not) to Think about the Death Penalty," *The International Journal of Applied Philosophy* 11 (Winter/Spring 1997): 7–10.

[14]I'd like to express my appreciation to Bill Bowers and Ben Steiner for insightful comments on an earlier draft and for sharing their research on the process of jury deliberations, to Ursula Bentele for keeping me accurate on legal matters, and to Steven Luper for the invitation to write the paper and for helpful feedback on an earlier draft.

JEFFREY REIMAN

Against the Death Penalty

My position about the death penalty as punishment for murder can be summed up in the following four propositions:

1. Though the death penalty is a just punishment for some murder, it is not unjust to punish murderers less harshly (down to a certain limit);

2. Though the death penalty would be justified if needed to deter future murders, we have no good reason to believe that it is needed to deter future murders; and

3. In refraining from imposing the death penalty, the state, by its vivid and impressive example, contributes to reducing our tolerance for cruelty and thereby fosters the advance of human civilization as we understand it.

Taken together, these three propositions imply that we do no injustice to actual or potential murder victims, and we do some considerable good, in refraining from executing murderers. This conclusion will be reinforced by another argument, this one for the proposition:

4. Though the death penalty is *in principle* a just penalty for murder, it is unjust *in practice* in America because it is applied in arbitrary and discriminatory ways, and this is likely to continue into the foreseeable future.

This fourth proposition conjoined with the prior three imply the overall conclusion that it is good in principle to avoid the death penalty and bad in practice to impose it. In what follows, I shall state briefly the arguments for each of these propositions.[1] For ease of identification, I shall number the first paragraph in which the argument for each proposition begins.

1. Before showing that the death penalty is just punishment for some murders, it is useful to dispose of a number of popular but weak arguments against the death penalty. One such popular argument contends that, if murder is wrong, then death penalty is wrong as well. But this argument proves too much! It would work against all punishments since all are wrong if done by a regular citizen under normal circumstances. (If I imprison you in a little jail in my basement, I am guilty of kidnapping; if I am caught and convicted, the state will lock me up in jail and will not have committed the same wrong that I did). The point here is that what is wrong about murder is not merely that it is killing per se, but the killing of a legally innocent person by a nonauthorized individual—and this doesn't apply to executions that are the outcome of conviction and sentencing at a fair trial.

Another argument that some people think is decisive against capital punishment points to the irrevocability of the punishment. The idea here is that innocents are sometimes wrongly convicted and if they receive the death penalty there is no way to correct the wrong done to them. While there is some force to this claim, its force is at best a relative matter. To be sure, if someone is executed and later found to have been innocent, there is no way to give him back the life that has been taken. Whereas, if someone is sentenced to life in prison and is found to have been innocent, she can be set free and perhaps given money to make up for the years spent in prison—however, those years cannot be given back. On the other hand, the innocent person who has been executed can at least be compensated in the form of money to his family and he can have his name cleared. So, it's not that the death penalty is irrevocable and other punishments are revocable; rather, all punishments are irrevocable though the death penalty is, so to speak, relatively more irrevocable than the rest. In any event, this only makes a difference in cases of mistaken conviction of the innocent, and the evidence is that such mistakes—particularly in capital cases—are quite rare. And, further, since we accept the death of innocents elsewhere, on the highways, as a cost of progress, as a necessary accompaniment of military operations, and so on, it is not plausible to think that the execution of a small number of innocent persons is so terrible as to outweigh all other considerations, especially when every effort is made to make sure that it does not occur.

Finally, it is sometimes argued that if we use the death penalty as a means to deter future murderers, we kill someone to protect others (from different people than the one we have executed), and thus we violate the Kantian prohibition against using individuals as means to the welfare of others. But the Kantian prohibition is not against using others as means, it is against using others as *mere* means (that is, in total disregard of their own desires and goals). Though you use the bus driver as a means to your getting home, you don't use her as a mere means because the job pays her a living and thus promotes her desires and goals as it does yours. Now, if what deters criminals is the existence of an effective system of deterrence, then criminals punished as part of that system are not used as a mere means since their desires and goals are also served, inasmuch as they have also benefited from deterrence of other criminals. Even criminals don't want to be crime victims. Further, if there is a right to threaten punishment in self-defense, then a society has the right to threaten punishment to defend its members, and there is no more violation of the Kantian maxim in imposing such punishment than there is in carrying out any threat to defend oneself against unjust attack.[2]

One way to see that the death penalty is a just punishment for at least some murders (the cold-blooded, premeditated ones) is to reflect on the *lex talionis*, an eye for an eye, a tooth for a tooth, and all that. Some regard this as a primitive rule, but it has I think an undeniable element of justice. And many who think that the death penalty is just punishment for murder are responding to this element. To see what the element is consider how similar the *lex talionis* is to the Golden Rule. The Golden Rule tells us to do unto others what we would have others do unto us, and the *lex talionis* counsels that we do to others what they have done to us. Both of these reflect a belief in the equality of all human beings. Treating others as you *would* have them treat you means treating others as equal to you, because it implies that you count their suffering to be as great a calamity as your own suffering, that you count your right to impose suffering on them as no greater than their right to impose suffering on you, and so on. The Golden Rule would not make sense if it were applied to two people, one of whom was thought to be inherently more valuable than the other. Imposing a harm on the more valuable one would be worse than imposing the same harm on the less valuable one—and neither could judge her actions by what she would have the other do to her. Since *lex talionis* says that you are rightly paid back for the harm you have caused another with a similar harm, it implies that the value of what you have done to another is the same as the value of having it done to you—which, again, would not be the case if one of you were thought inherently more valuable than the other. Consequently, treating people according to the *lex talionis* (like treating them according to the Golden Rule) affirms the equality of all concerned—and this supports the idea that punishing according to *lex talionis* is just.

Furthermore, on the Kantian assumption that a rational individual implicitly endorses the universal form of the intention that guides his action, a rational individual who kills another implicitly endorses the idea that he may be killed, and thus, he authorizes his own execution thereby absolving his executioner of injustice. What's more, much as above we saw that acting on *lex talionis* affirms the equality of criminal and victim, this Kantian-inspired argument suggests that acting on *lex talionis* affirms the rationality of criminal and victim. The criminal's rationality is affirmed because he is treated as if he had willed the universal form of his intention. The victim's rationality is affirmed because the criminal only authorizes his own killing if he has intended to kill another rational being like himself—then, he implicitly endorses the universal version of that intention, thereby authorizing his own killing. A person who intentionally kills an animal does not implicitly endorse his own being killed; only someone who kills someone like himself authorizes his own killing. In this way, the Kantian argument also invokes the equality of criminal and victim.

On the basis of arguments like this, I maintain that the idea that people deserve having done to them roughly what they have done (or attempted to do) to others affirms both the equality and rationality of human beings and for that reason is just. Kant has said: "No one has ever heard of anyone condemned to death on account of murder who complained that he was getting too much [punishment] and therefore was being treated unjustly; everyone would laugh in his face if he were to make such a statement."[3] If Kant is right, then even murderers recognize the inherent justice of the death penalty.

However, while the justice of the *lex talionis* implies the justice of executing some murderers, it does not imply that punishing less harshly is automatically unjust. We can see this by noting that the justice of the *lex talionis* implies also the justice of torturing torturers and raping rapists. I am certain and I assume my reader is as well that we need not impose these latter punishments to do justice (even if there were no other way of equaling the harm done or attempted by the criminal). Otherwise the price of doing justice would be matching the cruelty of the worst criminals, and that would effectively price justice out of the moral market. It follows that justice can be served with lesser punishments. Now, I think that there are two ways that punishing less harshly than the *lex talionis* could be unjust; it could be unjust to the actual victim of murder or to the future victims of potential murderers. It would be unjust to the actual victim if the punishment we mete out instead of execution were so slight that it trivialized the harm that the murderer did. This would make a sham out of implicit affirmation of equality that underlies the justice of the *lex talionis*. However, life imprisonment, or even a lengthy prison sentence—say, 20 years or more without parole—is a very grave punishment and not one that trivializes the harm done by the murderer. Punishment would be unjust to future victims if it were so mild that it failed to be a reasonable deterrent to potential murderers. Thus, refraining from executing murderers could be wrong if executions were needed to deter future murderers. In the following section, I shall say why there is no reason to think that this is so.

2. I grant that, if the death penalty were needed to deter future murderers, that would be a strong reason in favor of using the death penalty, since otherwise we would be sacrificing the future victims of potential murderers whom we could have deterred. And I think that this is a real injustice to those future victims, since the we in question is the state. Because the state claims a monopoly of the use of force, it owes its citizens protection, and thus does them injustice when it fails to provide the level of pro-

tection it reasonably could provide. However, there is no reason to believe that we need the death penalty to deter future murderers. The evidence we have strongly supports the idea that we get the same level of deterrence from life imprisonment, and even from substantial prison terms, such as 20 years without parole.

Before 1975, the most important work on the comparative deterrent impact of the capital punishment versus life in prison was that of Thorsten Sellin. He compared the homicide rates in states with the death penalty to the rates in similar states without the death penalty, and found no greater incidence of homicide in states without the death penalty than in similar states with it. In 1975, Isaac Ehrlich, a University of Chicago econometrician, reported the results of a statistical study which he claimed proved that, in the period from 1933 to 1969, each execution deterred as many as eight murders. This finding was, however, widely challenged. Ehrlich found a deterrent impact of executions in the period from 1933 to 1969, which includes the period of 1963 to 1969, a time when hardly any executions were carried out and crime rates rose for reasons that are arguably independent of the existence or nonexistence of capital punishment. When the 1963–1969 period is excluded, no significant deterrent effect shows. This is a very serious problem since the period from 1933 through to the end of the 1930s was one in which executions were carried out at the highest rate in American history—before or after. That no deterrent effect turns up when the study is limited to 1933 to 1962 almost seems evidence *against* the deterrent effect of the death penalty!

Consequently, in 1978, *after Ehrlich's study*, the editors of a National Academy of Sciences study of the impact of punishment wrote: "In summary, the flaws in the earlier analyses (i.e., Sellin's and others) and the sensitivity of the more recent analyses to minor variation in model specification and the serious temporal instability of the results lead the panel to conclude that the available studies provide no useful evidence on the deterrent effect of capital punishment."[4] Note that, while the deterrence research commented upon here generally compares the deterrent impact of capital punishment with that of life imprisonment, the failure to prove that capital punishment deters murder more than does incarceration goes beyond life in prison. A substantial proportion of people serving life sentences are released on parole before the end of their sentences. Since this is public knowledge, we should conclude from these studies that we have no evidence that capital punishment deters murder more effectively than prison sentences that are less than life, though still substantial, such as 20 years.

Another version of the argument for the greater deterrence impact of capital punishment compared to lesser punishments is called *the argument from common sense*. It holds that, whatever the social science studies do or don't show, it is only common sense that people will be more deterred by what they fear more, and since people fear death more than life in prison, they will be deterred more by execution than by a life sentence. This argument for the death penalty, however, assumes without argument or evidence that deterrence increases continuously and endlessly with the fearfulness of threatened punishment rather than leveling out at some threshold beyond which increases in fearfulness produce no additional increment of deterrence. That being tortured for a year is worse than being tortured for 6 months doesn't imply that a year's torture will deter you from actions that a half-year's torture would not deter— since a half-year's torture may be bad enough to deter you from all the actions that you can be deterred from doing. Likewise, though the death penalty may be worse than life in prison, that doesn't imply that the death penalty will deter acts that a life sentence won't because a life sentence may be bad enough to do all the deterring that can be done—and that is precisely what the social science studies seem to show. And, as I suggested above, what applies here to life sentences applies as well to substantial prison sentences.

I take it then that there is no reason to believe that we save more innocent lives with the death penalty than with less harsh penalties such as life in prison or some lengthy sentence, such as 20 years without parole. But then we do no injustice to the future victims of potential murderers by refraining from the death penalty. And, in conjunction with the argument of the previous section, it follows that we do no injustice to actual or potential murder victims if we refrain from executing murderers and sentence them instead to life in prison or to some substantial sentence, say, 20 or more years in prison without parole. But it remains to be seen what good will be served by doing the latter instead of executing.

3. Here I want to suggest that, in refraining from imposing the death penalty, the state, by its vivid and impressive example, contributes to reducing our tolerance for cruelty and thereby fosters the advance of human civilization as we understand it. To see this, note first that it has been acknowledged that the state, and particularly the criminal justice system, plays an educational role in society as a model of morally accepted conduct and an indicator of the line between morally permissible and impermissible actions. Now, consider the general repugnance that is attached to the use of torture—even as a punishment for criminals who have tortured their victims. It seems to me that, by refraining from torturing even those who deserve it, our state plays a role in promoting that repugnance. That we will not torture even those who have earned it by their crimes conveys a message about the awfulness of torture, namely, that it is something that civilized people will not do even to give evil people their just deserts. Thus it seems to me that in this case the state advances the cause of human civilization by contributing to a reduction in people's tolerance for cruelty. I think that the modern state is uniquely positioned to do this sort of thing because of its size (representing millions, even hundreds of millions of citizens) and its visibility (starting with the printing press that accompanied the birth of modern nations, increasing with radio, television, and the other media of instantaneous communication). And because the state can do this, it should. Consequently, I contend that if the state were to put execution in the same category as torture, it would contribute yet further to reducing our tolerance for cruelty and to advancing the cause of human civilization. And because it can do this, it should.

To make this argument plausible, however, I must show that execution is horrible enough to warrant its inclusion alongside torture. I think that execution is horrible in a way similar to (though not identical with) the way in which torture is horrible. Torture is horrible because of two of its features, which also characterize execution: intense pain and the spectacle of one person being completely subject to the power of another.[5] This latter is separate from the issue of pain, since it is something that offends people about unpainful things, such as slavery (even voluntarily entered) and prostitution (even voluntarily chosen as an occupation). Execution shares this separate feature. It enacts the total subjugation of one person to his fellows, whether the individual to be executed is strapped into an electric chair or bound like a laboratory animal on a hospital gurney awaiting lethal injection.

Moreover, execution, even by physically painless means, is characterized by a special and intense psychological pain that distinguishes it from the loss of life that awaits us all. This is because execution involves the most psychologically painful features of death. We normally regard death from human causes as worse than death from natural causes, since a humanly caused shortening of life lacks the consolation of unavoidability. And we normally regard death whose coming is foreseen by its victim as worse than sudden death because a foreseen death adds to the loss of life the terrible consciousness of that impending loss. An execution combines the worst of both. Its coming is foreseen, in that its date is normally already set, and it lacks the consolation of unavoidability, in that it depends on the will of one's fellow human beings not on natural forces beyond human control. Indeed, it was on just such grounds that Albert Camus regarded the death penalty as itself a kind of torture: "As a general rule, a man is undone by waiting for capital punishment well before he dies. Two deaths are inflicted on him, the first being worse than the second, whereas he killed but once. Compared to such torture, the penalty of retaliation [the *lex talionis*] seems like a civilized law."[6]

4. However just in principle the death penalty may be, it is applied unjustly in practice in America and is likely to be so for the foreseeable future. The evidence for this conclusion comes from various sources. Numerous studies show that killers of whites are more likely to get the death penalty than killers of blacks, and that black killers of whites are far more likely to be sentenced to death than white killers of blacks. Moreover, just about everyone recognizes that poor people are more likely to be sentenced to death and to have those sentences carried out than well-off people. And these injustices persist even after all death penalty statutes were declared unconstitutional in 1972[7] and only those death penalty statutes with provisions for reducing arbitrariness in sentencing were admitted as constitutional in 1976.[8] In short, injustice in the application of the death penalty persists even after legal reform, and this strongly suggests that it is so deep that it will not be corrected in the foreseeable future.

It might be objected that discrimination is also found in the handing out of prison sentences and thus that this argument would prove that we should abolish prison as well as the death penalty. But I accept that we need some system of punishment to deter crime and mete out justice to criminals, and for that reason even a discriminatory punishment system is better than none. Then, the objection based on discrimination works only against those elements of the punishment system that are not needed either to deter crime or to do justice, and I have shown above that this is true of the death penalty. Needless to say we should also strive to eliminate discrimination in the parts of the criminal justice that we cannot do without.

Other, more subtle, kinds of discrimination also affect the way the death penalty is actually carried out. There are many ways in which the actions of well-off people lead to death which are not counted as murder. For example, many more people die as a result of preventable occupational diseases (due to toxic chemicals, coal and textile dust, and the like, in the workplace) or preventable environmental pollution than die as a result of what is treated legally as homicide.[9] So, in addition to all the legal advantages that money can buy a wealthy person accused of murder, the law also helps the wealthy by not defining as murder many of the ways in which the wealthy are responsible for the deaths of fellow human beings. Add to this that many of the killings that we do treat as murders, the ones done by the poor in our society, are the predictable outcomes of remediable social injustice—the discrimination and exploitation that, for example, have helped to keep African Americans at the bottom of the economic ladder for centuries. Those who benefit from injustice and who could remedy it bear some of the responsibility for the crimes that are predictable outcomes of injustice—and that implies that plenty of well-off people share responsibility with many of our poor murderers. But since these more fortunate folks are not likely to be held responsible for murder, it is unfair to hold only the poor victims of injustice responsible—and wholly responsible to boot!

Finally, we already saw that the French existentialist, Albert Camus, asserted famously that life on death row is a kind of torture. Recently, Robert Johnson has studied the psychological effects on condemned men on death row and confirmed Camus's claim. In his book *Condemned to Die*, Johnson recounts the painful psychological deterioration suffered by a substantial majority of the death row prisoners he studied.[10] Since the death row inmate faces execution, he is viewed as having nothing to lose and thus is treated as the most dangerous of criminals. As a result, his confinement and isolation are nearly total. Since he has no future for which to be rehabilitated, he receives the least and the worst of the prison's facilities. Since his guards know they are essentially warehousing him until his death, they treat him as something less than human—and so he is brutalized, taunted, powerless, and constantly reminded of it. The effect of this on the death row inmate, as Johnson reports it, is quite literally the breaking down of the structure of the ego—a process not unlike that caused by brainwashing. Since we do not reserve the term "torture" only for processes resulting in physical pain, but recognize processes that result in extreme psychological suffering as torture as well (consider sleep deprivation or the so-called Chinese water torture), Johnson's and Camus's application of this term to the conditions of death row confinement seems reasonable.

It might be objected that some of the responsibility for the torturous life of death row inmates is the inmates' own fault, since in pressing their legal appeals, they delay their executions and thus prolong their time on death row. Capital murder convictions and sentences, however, are reversed on appeal with great frequency, nearly ten times the rate of reversals in noncapital cases. This strongly supports the idea that such appeals are necessary to test the legality of murder convictions and death penalty sentences. To hold the inmate somehow responsible for the delays that result from his appeals, and thus for the (increased) torment he suffers as a consequence, is effectively to confront him with the choice of accepting execution before its legality is fully tested or suffering torture until it is. Since no just society should expect (or even want) a person to accept a sentence until its legal validity has been established, it is unjust to torture him until it has and perverse to assert that he has brought the torture on himself by his insistence that the legality of his sentence be fully tested before it is carried out.

The worst features of death row might be ameliorated, but it is unlikely that its torturous nature will be eliminated, or even that it is possible to eliminate it. This is, in part, because it is linked to an understandable psychological strategy used by the guards in order to protect themselves against natural, painful, and ambivalent feelings of sympathy for a person awaiting a humanly inflicted death. Johnson writes: "I think it can also be argued . . . that humane death rows will not be achieved in practice because the purpose of death row confinement is to facilitate executions by dehumanizing both the prisoners and (to a lesser degree) their executioners and thus make it easier for both to conform to the etiquette of ritual killing."[11]

If conditions on death row are and are likely to continue to be a real form of psychological torture, if Camus and Johnson are correct, then it must be admitted that the death penalty is in practice not merely a penalty of death—it is a penalty or torture until death. Then the sentence of death is more than the *lex talionis* allows as a just penalty for murder—and thus it is unjust in practice.

I think that I have proven that it would be good in principle to refrain from imposing the death penalty and bad in practice to continue using it. And, I have proven this while accepting the two strongest claims made by defenders of capital punishment, namely, that death is just punishment for at least some murderers, and that, if the death penalty were a superior deterrent to murder than imprisonment, that would justify using the death penalty.

---

[1]The full argument for these propositions, along with supporting data, references, and replies to objections, is in Louis Pojman and Jeffrey Reiman, *The Death Penalty: For and Against* (Lanham, Md: Rowman & Littlefield, 1998), pp. 67-132, 151-163. My essay in that book is based upon and substantially revises my "Justice, Civilization, and the Death Penalty: Answer van den Haag," *Philosophy and Public Affairs* 14, no. 2 (Spring 1985): 115-148; and my "The Justice of the Death Penalty in an Unjust World," in *Challenging Capital Punishment: Legal and Social Science Approaches*, ed. by K. Haas & J. Inciardi (Beverly Hills, Calif.: Sage, 1988), pp. 29-48.

[2]Elsewhere I have argued at length that punishment needed to deter reasonable people is *deserved* by criminals. See Pojman and Reiman, *Death Penalty*, pp. 79-85.

[3]Immanuel Kant, "The Metaphysical Elements of Justice," Part 1 of *The Metaphysics of Morals*, trans. by J. Ladd (Indianapolis: Bobbs-Merrill, 1965; originally published 1797), p. 104, see also p. 133.

[4]Alfred Blumstein, Jacqueline Cohen, and Daniel Nagin, eds., *Deterrence and Incapacitation: Estimating the Effects of Criminal Sanctions on Crime Rates* (Washington, D.C.: National Academy of Sciences, 1978), p. 9.

[5]Hugo Bedau has developed this latter consideration at length with respect to the death penalty. See Hugo A. Bedau, "Thinking about the Death Penalty as a Cruel and Unusual Punishment," *U.C. Davis Law Review* 18 (Summer 1985): 917. This article is reprinted in Hugo A. Bedau, *Death Is Different: Studies in the Morality, Law, and Politics of Capital Punishment* (Boston: Northeastern University Press, 1987); and Hugo A. Bedau, ed., *The Death Penalty in America: Current Controversies* (New York: Oxford University Press, 1997).

[6]Albert Camus, "Reflections on the Guillotine," in Albert Camus, *Resistance, Rebellion, and Death* (New York: Knopf, 1961), p. 205.

[7]*Furman* v. *Georgia*, 408 U.S. 238 (1972).

[8]*Gregg* v. *Georgia*, 428 U.S. 153 (1976).

[9]Jeffrey Reiman, *The Rich Get Richer and the Poor Get Prison: Ideology, Class, and Criminal Justice*, 5th ed. (Boston: Allyn and Bacon, 1998), pp. 71–78, 81–87.

[10]Robert Johnson, *Condemned to Die: Life under Sentence of Death* (New York: Elsevier, 1981), p. 129.

[11]Robert Johnson, personal correspondence.

ERNEST VAN DEN HAAG

A Response to Reiman and Nathanson

I had the pleasure on prior occasions to respond to essays on the death penalty by Messrs. Reiman and Nathanson. Here they have greatly enriched their arguments. (I hope to have done the same.) Neither, however, has changed his basic view. Which goes to show that my attempt to rehabilitate them was futile—as I have long believed most such attempts are. If two mild mannered professors of philosophy cannot be reformed, what chance do we have with hardened criminals? Since it may not be obvious from my response let me make it explicit now that I have respect and affection for Jeffrey Reiman. However wrong his views be they are always interesting and original in their wrongness.

RESPONSE TO REIMAN: SHOULD HUMANENESS REPLACE JUSTICE?

Reiman believes that the death penalty is just, because deserved for murder (via the *lex talionis*). But, he thinks it would not be unjust to punish murderers less harshly, and, for various reasons, of which anon, it would be more humane to do so. Being humane, Reiman opposes the death penalty.

Reiman has an odd notion of "deserved" which allows him to think it justice to give less than what is deserved as a punishment, or, I presume, as a reward. But it is not justice to give anyone less, or more, than is deserved. If you won a race you deserve the trophy promised and should get no less, even if you are morally repugnant. Nor should you get the trophy merely because you have moral merits irrelevant to the race. If you have done something wrong you get the deserved (and prescribed) punishment. *Suum cuique tribue.* To everyone what he deserves. It is not just to give less than what is deserved. Charity is desirable as other forms of love are, but is not justice, precisely because it need not be deserved. So with generosity, or "humanness." The murderer knew what his punishment would be and volunteered to risk suffering it. (If he didn't volunteer he didn't commit a crime.)

I do not mean to suggest that he calculates his risk. Thank God he doesn't, because the risk of suffering the death penalty is exceedingly small. What deters most people is a generalized dread both of the crime and of the punishment. That dread ultimately goes back to the death penalty. Probability calculations are no more involved than they are when people buy a lottery ticket. The size of the punishment, or of the reward, seems to matter more than the probability of receiving it, in determining deterrence or attractiveness. A case for clemency can be made in some cases. But clemency (Reiman's humaneness?) cannot take the place of justice and should not be confused with it.

Because the death penalty is applied arbitrarily and discriminatorily, Reiman says it is unjust in practice. *Non sequitur.* The arbitrary or discriminatory application of the penalty does not make those who receive it less guilty, or less deserving of the penalty, than they would be if everyone (or no one) else in their position also would receive it. How does any murderer become less deserving of execution because other murderers are not executed, whether because of luck (they were not caught or the evidence was insufficient) or because of discrimination? Unequal punishment is not unjust, if those who deserve it get the punishment they deserve. Unequal justice is justice still and the only justice available to us. The inequality of distribution is undesirable and unconstitutional if deliberate but not remedied by abolishing just punishments.

By not imposing the death penalty, Reiman contends, we would reduce social intolerance for cruelty. One could as well say: By not imposing the death penalty we display more tolerance for the cruelty of murderers than we should and thereby we encourage it.[1] (Incidentally, Reiman confuses reversing and revoking penalties. Except for fines, penalties cannot be reversed. The death penalty is not exceptional in this. It is exceptional only because it cannot be revoked as other penalties can.)

If the death penalty is morally deserved for murder, it should be imposed even if it does not deter future murderers (as long as it does not encourage them). However, I disagree with Reiman on the empirical question of deterrence. I don't think it has been shown, or can be shown, that the death penalty does not, or cannot, deter more than imprisonment. What has been shown is that its greater deterrent effect has not been proven beyond controversy. But not proving deterrence is not the same as disproving it, as Reiman comes perilously close to contending. He also argues that the threat of imprisonment anyway will deter all those that can be deterred. Maybe. But it seems quite possible that some prospective murderers not deterred by the threat of life imprisonment will be deterred by the threat of execution. Even if not probable surely this is possible. And the possibility is enough to make it prudent as well as just to execute those who deserve the death penalty.

Reiman also believes that execution is painful and undignified because it totally subjects one person to the power of another. Both these arguments seem weak. If, as it is currently done in most states, the criminal receives first an injection that anesthetizes him and then two lethal injections, he cannot feel pain any more than an anesthetized patient does during a surgical operation. Actually his death is likely to be less painful than the death of most persons; and he is not more, or less, in the power of his executioner than a patient is in the power of his surgeon.

Finally on the matter of poverty. It is true, as Reiman contends, that the poor commit proportionately more violent crimes than the rich. There are many reasons for this, the main one being that the rich can obtain most of what they want by buying it whereas the poor, by definition, cannot. They are more tempted therefore to obtain what they want by violence. Reiman assumes that somehow this is the fault of the rich, which is not much better than assuming that the suffering of the ill is the fault of the healthy. There are rich and poor in any system. Even if everyone, diligent or lazy, were to get the same income, some will impoverish themselves by spending it immediately, and others will enrich themselves by saving. Motives for crime will remain abundant.

In any case temptation is an explanation, not a justification. The purpose of the criminal law is to dissuade people who are tempted from committing crimes. There is no point in threatening the untempted. Unlike compulsion, temptation can be resisted and is not exculpatory.

RESPONSE TO NATHANSON: SHOULD EQUALITY REPLACE JUSTICE?

Professor Nathanson promises to focus on whether "people who commit murder deserve to die." He does not keep his promise. On the contrary, his paper is so unfocussed I found it hard to follow. He describes desert as difficult to determine and complex, but never tells whether, if desert were simple and easy to determine, it could justify the death penalty. He never suggests what he means by "deserve" beyond simply "should get." He also insists that the death penalty is not an individual act but an institution. It is both, but so what? What follows? I know of no philosopher who neglects (as Nathanson implies) the obvious, that we cannot move from a particular act to a general practice.

Professor Nathanson's favorite analogy is between sentencing and grading a true and false test on the one hand or an essay test on the other. He never tires of reiterating that sentencing is more like grading an essay test. I don't know of anyone who would contest his point. Analogies are not proofs but, at best, helpful illustrations. But many of Nathanson's analogies are misleading or themselves based on error. This is true of his arguments as well. He writes "If we really accepted the eye for an eye principle we would have to accept the idea that executioners ought to be executed." Not so. A few lines before Nathanson indicates that he is aware that the *lex talionis* was applicable only to murder (illegal killing) but not to execution (legal killing). Otherwise it would justify the infinite vendettas it was meant to avoid.

Elsewhere Nathanson asserts that whether a person's punishment is just or not does not depend simply on what is deserved, but also on how "the punishment compares with the punishment of others." Not so. If others got a different punishment for the same crime it merely follows that the punishments were unequal, both may be unjust, or one of them may be just and the other not. The just punishment is the one deserved, whether or not it is also received by others.

Nathanson also asserts "a punishment can be deserved and still be unjust." I can't see that at all. If the punishment is deserved it is just by definition. "To give everyone what is deserved is to do justice" (Domitianus Ulpianus). Nathanson illustrates his point "if one student receives a failing grade for cheating while another is simply warned, then even if the first student deserved to fail, the infliction of this punishment is unjust." Why? The fact that someone else who deserved the same punishment did not get it does not make the deserved punishment unjust. Nathanson also objects to the fact (and it is a fact) that two murderers having committed the same crime may get different sentences. This inequality is regrettable but unavoidable and true for all punishments. The two murderers appear before different courts evaluating different evidence have different prosecutors and defense lawyers and different juries. Our system of justice rests on the belief that we can punish people as nearly as they deserve as can be done. Nathanson's demand, that punishment be exactly what is deserved and that we somehow must find ways of determining desert precisely, seems bizarre. It is impossible to do that whether we are dealing with a burglary or a murder.[2] Only God can have the kind of judgment Nathanson would like all of us to have. That is no reason for giving up the justice system, including the death penalty. We exclude hearsay evidence, insist that jurors have no detectable bias and require them to be unanimous in finding a defendant guilty only if none has a reasonable doubt of his guilt. I do not see how we can do more to avoid error, except by giving up punishment.

Nathanson also points out that courts do not directly witness crimes but must rely on testimony and circumstances reported by witnesses and analyzed by attorneys. Quite so. For the greater part of our life we have to rely on indirect experiences. When he teaches, Professor Nathanson expects his students to rely on indirect experiences and reports.

Returning to his favorite analogy Professor Nathanson laments that two students get the grades they get when one of them writes a brilliant paper with little effort and the other writes a not so brilliant paper, although he spends much more effort and time on it. Somehow, Nathanson feels the first student should not get an A and the second a C because, after all, the second student made more efforts. But the task of the teacher (after kindergarten) is not to grade students according to the efforts they made but rather to grade the results of their efforts. We cannot grade efforts nor should we. As Nathanson notes, the winner of a beauty contest may be morally inferior to the loser. And beauty or talent are largely matters of luck. But beauty is what the contest judges are to grade. In a sense this applies to crime as well. The judges (or professors) do not have the task of correcting the injustices of life but a more restricted one of determining who wins or loses according to the preestablished rules. Is the defendant guilty as charged? The court determines this and the sentence as well, on the basis not of the defendant's beauty or efforts or wealth or talent but on the basis of the gravity of his crime and his culpability in committing it. This is what is meant by equality before the law.

Professor Nathanson is certainly right in affirming that it is difficult to determine more merit, but fortunately we are called upon mostly to determine what people deserve for specific acts. Did he run faster than the others? He deserves to win—even though other runners may be more deserving in other respects, and made greater efforts.

The vagueness of Professor Nathanson's criteria of desert becomes apparent when we consider the instances of misjudgment he cites. (These misjudgments were listed by Amnesty International, an organization opposed to the death penalty. Nathanson seems to rely entirely on the arguments of the defense; he does not mention what prosecutors, or courts, contended. He also accepts unquestioningly all facts alleged by the defense.) Consider some of Nathanson's instances.

Arthur Goode, "mentally unstable, documented history of mental illness at the age of three." Wherein does that show that Goode should not suffer the death penalty? Obviously the courts held that he was mentally competent when he committed the act for which he was tried. The court may have been wrong, but wherein does mental instability at the age of three show this?

David Funchess, "Vietnam veteran, left army with heroin addiction, suffering post traumatic stress syndrome, a psychological disorder not properly understood at the time of trial." It is still not properly understood and may not exist. If it does, how does it exculpate?

John Young, "His psychiatric trauma from witnessing his mother's murder at the age of three and subsequent neglected childhood were not mentioned at the trial. Alleged to have been under the influence of drugs at the time of the crime." The court found that these things, mentioned or not mentioned in the trial, were no reasons for not imposing the death penalty. Nathanson never shows wherein the court is wrong.

Jerome Borden, "Diagnosed as mentally retarded with an IQ of 65." An IQ of 65 is not sufficient to indicate that the person did not understand what he was doing or did not know or could not know that it was wrong.

David Martin, "History of drug/alcohol addiction. Reportedly (!) suffered from mental, physical abuse as a child." Abuse is regrettable but why should it exempt from the death penalty? Many people unfortunately are abused as children but do not become criminals and many criminals have never been abused. Thus abuse is neither a necessary nor a sufficient reason for not punishing crimes.

Reading the essay to which I am responding has persuaded me that Professor Nathanson is opposed to the death penalty. The arguments he offers have not persuaded me that he should be.

---

[1]Theologians and philosophers such as Thomas Aquinas, Immanuel Kant, G. F. W. Hegel, John St. Mill, and Thomas Jefferson have felt that we have a duty to execute murderers for the sake of their human dignity which is affirmed by recognizing their responsibility.

[2]Criminals in Pakistan get different punishments than they do in the United States, and punishments in Manhattan differ from the sentences judges mete out in Alabama. Some states have the death penalty, others don't.

U.S. SUPREME COURT

Furman v. *Georgia* (1972)

. . . Certiorari was granted limited to the following question: "Does the imposition and carrying out of the death penalty in [these cases] constitute cruel and unusual punishment in violation of the 8th and 14th Amendments?" 403 U.S. 952 (1971). The Court holds that the imposition and carrying out of the death penalty in these cases constitute cruel and unusual punishment in violation of the 8th and 14th Amendments. The judgment in each case is therefore reversed insofar as it leaves undisturbed the death sentence imposed, and the cases are remanded for further proceedings.

So ordered.

Mr. Justice Douglas, concurring.

In these three cases the death penalty was imposed, one of them for murder, and two for rape. . . .

The high service rendered by the "cruel and unusual" punishment clause of the 8th Amendment is to require legislatures to write penal laws that are evenhanded, nonselective, and nonarbitrary, and to require judges to see to it that general laws are not applied sparsely, selectively, and spottily to unpopular groups.

A law that stated that anyone making more than $50,000 would be exempt from the death penalty would plainly fall, as would a law that in terms said that blacks, those who never went beyond the fifth grade in school, those who made less than $3,000 a year or those who were unpopular or unstable should be the only people executed. A law which in the overall view reaches that result in practice has no more sanctity than a law which in terms provides the same.

Thus, these discretionary statutes are unconstitutional in their operation. They are pregnant with discrimination and discrimination is an ingredient not compatible with the idea of equal protection of the laws that is implicit in the ban on "cruel and un- usual" punishment.

Any law which is nondiscriminatory on its face may be applied in such a way as to violate the Equal Protection Clause of the 14th Amendment. . . . Such conceivably might be the fate of a mandatory death penalty, where equal or lesser sentences were imposed on the elite, a harsher one on the minorities or members of the lower castes. Whether a mandatory death penalty would otherwise be constitutional is a question I do not reach.

I concur in the judgments of the Court.

Mr. Justice Brennan, concurring.

. . . There are . . . four principles by which we may determine whether a particular punishment is "cruel and unusual." The primary principle, which I believe supplies the essential predicate for the application of the others, is that a punishment must not by its severity be degrading to human dignity. The paradigm violation of this principle would be the infliction of a torturous punishment of the type that the Clause has al- ways prohibited. Yet "[i]t is unlikely that any State at this moment in history," *Robinson* v. *California,* 370 U.S., at 666, would pass a law providing for the infliction of such a punishment. Indeed, no such punishment has ever been before this Court. The same may be said of the other principles. It is unlikely that this Court will confront a severe punishment that is obviously inflicted in wholly arbitrary fashion; no State would en- gage in a reign of blind terror. Nor is it likely that this Court will be called upon to re- view a severe punishment that is clearly and totally rejected throughout society; no legislature would be able even to authorize the infliction of such a punishment. Nor, finally, is it likely that this Court will have to consider a severe punishment that is patently unnecessary; no State today would inflict a severe punishment knowing that there was no reason whatever for doing so. In short, we are unlikely to have occasion to determine that a punishment is fatally offensive under any one principle.

. . . The question, then, is whether the deliberate infliction of death is today consistent with the command of the Clause that the State may not inflict punishments that do not comport with human dignity. I will analyze the punishment of death in terms of the principles set out above and the cumulative test to which they lead: It is a denial of human dignity for the State arbitrarily to subject a person to an unusually severe punishment that society has indicated it does not regard as acceptable, and that cannot be shown to serve any penal purpose more effectively than a significantly less drastic punishment. Under these principles and this test, death is today a "cruel and unusual" punishment.

Death is a unique punishment in the United States. In a society that so strongly affirms the sanctity of life, not surprisingly the common view is that death is the ultimate sanction. This natural human feeling appears all about us. There has been no national debate about punishment, in general or by imprisonment, comparable to the debate about the punishment of death. No other punishment has been so continuously restricted, nor has any State yet abolished prisons, as some have abolished this punishment. . . .

The only explanation for the uniqueness of death is its extreme severity. Death is today an unusually severe punishment, unusual in its pain, in its finality, and in its enormity. No other existing punishment is comparable to death in terms of physical and mental suffering. Although our information is not conclusive, it appears that there is no method available that guarantees an immediate and painless death. Since the discontinuance of flogging as a constitutionally permissible punishment, . . . death remains as the only punishment that may involve the conscious infliction of physical pain. In addition, we know that mental pain is an inseparable part of our practice of punishing criminals by death for the prospect of pending execution exacts a frightful toll during the inevitable long wait between the imposition of sentence and the actual infliction of death. . . .

In comparison to all other punishments today, then, the deliberate extinguishment of human life by the State is uniquely degrading to human dignity. I would not hesitate to hold, on that ground alone, that death is today a "cruel and unusual" punishment, were it not that death is a punishment of longstanding usage and acceptance in this country. I therefore turn to the second principle—that the State may not arbitrarily inflict an unusually severe punishment.

. . . When the punishment of death is inflicted in a trivial number of the cases in which it is legally available, the conclusion is virtually inescapable that it is being inflicted arbitrarily. Indeed, it smacks of little more than a lottery system. The States claim, however, that this rarity is evidence not of arbitrariness, but of informed selectivity: Death is inflicted, they say, only in "extreme" cases.

Informed selectively, of course, is a value not to be denigrated. Yet presumably the States could make precisely the same claim if there were 10 executions per year, or five, or even if there were but one. That there may be as many as 50 per year does not strengthen the claim. When the rate of infliction is at this low level, it is highly implausible that only the worst criminals or the criminals who commit the worst crimes are selected for this punishment. . . .

I turn . . . to the third principle. An examination of the history and present operation of the American practice of punishing criminals by death reveals that this punishment has been almost totally rejected by contemporary society. . . . The progressive
decline in, and the current rarity of, the infliction of death demonstrate that our society seriously questions the appropriateness of this punishment today.

The final principle to be considered is that an unusually severe and degrading punishment may not be excessive in view of the purposes for which it is inflicted. This
principle, too, is related to the others. When there is a strong probability that the State
is arbitrarily inflicting an unusually severe punishment that is subject to grave societal
doubts, it is likely also that the punishment cannot be shown to be serving any penal
purpose that could not be served equally well by some less severe punishment.

The States' primary claim is that death is a necessary punishment because it prevents the commission of capital crimes more effectively than any less severe punishment. The first part of this claim is that the infliction of death is necessary to stop the
individuals executed from committing further crimes. The sufficient answer to this is
that if a criminal convicted of a capital crime poses a danger to society, effective administration of the State's pardon and parole laws can delay or deny his release from
prison, and techniques of isolation can eliminate or minimize the danger while he remains confined.

The more significant argument is that the threat of death prevents the commission of capital crimes because it deters potential criminals who would not be deterred
by the threat of imprisonment. The argument is not based upon evidence that the
threat of death is a superior deterrent. Indeed, as my Brother Marshall establishes, the
available evidence uniformly indicates, although it does not conclusively prove, that
the threat of death has no greater deterrent effect that the threat of imprisonment.

U. S. SUPREME COURT

Gregg v. *Georgia* (1976)

Mr. Justice Stewart, Mr. Justice Powell, and Mr. Justice Stevens announced the judgment of the Court and filed an opinion delivered by Mr. Justice Stewart.

The issue in this case is whether the imposition of the sentence of death for the
crime of murder under the law of Georgia violates the 6th and 14th Amendments. . . .
We address initially the basic contention that the punishment of death for the crime
of murder is, under all circumstances, "cruel and unusual" in violation of the 8th and
14th Amendments of the Constitution. . . .

The Court on a number of occasions has both assumed and asserted the constitutionality of capital punishment. In several cases that assumption provided a necessary
foundation for the decision, as the Court was asked to decide whether a particular
method of carrying out a capital sentence would be allowed to stand under the 8th
Amendment. But until *Furman* v. *Georgia,* the Court never confronted squarely the

fundamental claim that the punishment of death always, regardless of the enormity of the offense or the procedure followed in imposing the sentence, is cruel and unusual punishment in violation of the Constitution. Although this issue was presented and addressed in *Furman,* it was not resolved by the Court. Four Justices would have reached the opposite conclusion; and three Justices, while agreeing that the statutes then before the Court were invalid as applied, left open the question whether such punishment may ever be imposed. We now hold that the punishment of death does not invariably violate the Constitution. . . .

The imposition of the death penalty for the crime of murder has a long history of acceptance both in the United States and in England. The common-law rule imposed a mandatory death sentence on all convicted murderers. . . . And the penalty continued to be used into the 20th century by most American States, although the breadth of the common-law rule was diminished, initially by narrowing the class of murders to be punished by death and subsequently by widespread adoption of laws expressly granting juries the discretion to recommend mercy. . . .

It is apparent from the text of the Constitution itself that the existence of capital punishment was accepted by the Framers. . . . The 5th Amendment, adopted at the same time as the 8th, contemplated the continued existence of the capital sanction by imposing certain limits on the prosecution of capital cases. . . . And the 14th Amendment, adopted over three-quarters of a century later, similarly contemplates the existence of the capital sanction in providing that no State shall deprive any person of "life, liberty, or property" without due process of law. . . .

The petitioners . . . before the Court today renew the "standards of decency" argument, but developments during the 4 years since *Furman* have undercut substantially the assumptions upon which their argument rested. Despite the continuing debate, dating back to the 19th century, over the morality and utility of capital punishment, it is now evident that a large proportion of American society continues to regard it as an appropriate and necessary criminal sanction.

The most marked indication of society's endorsement of the death penalty for murder is the legislative response to *Furman.* The legislatures of at least 35 States have enacted new statutes that provide for the death penalty for at least some crimes that result in the death of another person. And the Congress of the United States, in 1974, enacted a statute providing the death penalty for aircraft piracy that results in death. . . .

The death penalty is said to serve two principal social purposes: retribution and deterrence of capital crimes by prospective offenders.

In part, capital punishment is an expression of society's moral outrage at particularly offensive conduct. This function may be unappealing to many, but it is essential in an ordered society that asks its citizens to rely on legal processes rather than self-help to vindicate their wrongs. . . . "Retribution is no longer the dominant objective of the criminal law," *Williams* v. *New York,* 337 U.S. 241, 248 (1949), but neither is it a forbidden objective or one inconsistent with our respect for the dignity of men. . . . Indeed, the decision that capital punishment may be the appropriate sanction in extreme cases is an expression of the community's belief that certain crimes are themselves so grievous an affront to humanity that the only adequate response may be the penalty of death.

Statistical attempts to evaluate the worth of the death penalty as a deterrent to crimes by potential offenders have occasioned a great deal of debate. The results simply have been inconclusive. . . .

In sum, we cannot say that the judgment of the Georgia legislature that capital punishment may be necessary in some cases is clearly wrong. Considerations of federalism, as well as respect for the ability of a legislature to evaluate, in terms of its particular state the moral consensus concerning the death penalty and its social utility as a sanction, require us to conclude, in the absence of more convincing evidence, that the infliction of death as a punishment for murder is not without justification and thus is not unconstitutionally severe.

Finally, we must consider whether the punishment of death is disproportionate in relation to the crime for which it is imposed. There is no question that death as a punishment is unique in its severity and irrevocability. . . . When a defendant's life is at stake, the Court has been particularly sensitive to insure that every safeguard is observed. . . . But we are concerned here only with the imposition of capital punishment for the crime of murder, and when a life has been taken deliberately by the offender, we cannot say that the punishment is invariably disproportionate to the crimes. . . .

We now turn to consideration of the constitutionality of Georgia's capital-sentencing procedures. In the wake of *Furman,* Georgia amended its capital punishment statute, but chose not to narrow the scope of its murder provisions. . . .

These procedures require the jury to consider the circumstances of the crime and the criminal before it recommends sentence. No longer can a Georgia jury do as *Furman's* jury did: reach a finding of the defendant's guilt and then, without guidance or direction, decide whether he should live or die. . . .

. . . Georgia's new sentencing procedures require as a prerequisite to the imposition of the death penalty, specific jury findings as to the circumstances of the crime or the character of the defendant. Moreover to guard further against a situation comparable to that presented in *Furman,* the Supreme Court of Georgia compares each death sentence with the sentences imposed on similarly situated defendants to ensure that the sentence of death in a particular case is not disproportionate. On their face these procedures seem to satisfy the concerns of *Furman.*

CREDITS

Chapter 1

"Aristotelianism." Copyright 1998 John F. Heil. Selections from Book 1 of Aristotle's *Nicomachean Ethics*. Translation by J. F. Heil. Copyright 1998 John F. Heil.

"Utilitarianism." Copyright 1998 Judith Norman. Reprinted by permission of the author.

From "Themes in Kant's Moral Philosophy" by John Rawls. Reprinted from *Kant's Transcendental Deductions: The Three Critiques* and *The Opus Postumum* (1989), edited by Eckart Forster, with the permission of the publishers, Stanford University Press. © 1989 by the Board of Trustees of the Leland Stanford Junior University.

Kant, Immanuel, *Grounding for the Metaphysics of Morals*, translation by James W. Ellington—By permission of Hackett Publishing Company. All rights reserved.

"Confucius and the *Analects*." Copyright 1998 Henry Rosemont, Jr.

From Roger T. Ames and Henry Rosemont, Jr., translators, *The Analects of Confucius: A Philosophical Tradition,* Ballantine Books, 1998. Reprinted by permission of the authors.

"Daoism." Copyright 1998 Philip J. Ivanhoe.

Daodejing. Copyright 1998 Philip J. Ivanhoe.

"Buddhist Moral Philosophy." Copyright 1998 David J. Kalupahana.

"Discourse on Non-conflict," translated by David J. Kalupahana. Copyright 1998 David J. Kalupahana.

"Discourse on the Perfection of Wisdom the Cutting with the Diamond," translated by David J. Kalupahana. Copyright 1998 David J. Kalupahana.

Chapter 2

Oliver Sacks, "A Matter of Identity." Reprinted with the permission of Simon & Schuster from *The Man Who Mistook His Wife for a Hat* by Oliver Sacks. Copyright © 1970, 1981, 1983, 1984, 1985 by Oliver Sacks.

Friedrich Nietzsche, "Schopenhaur as Educator," from *Untimely Meditations,* translated by R. J. Hollingdale. Reprinted by permission of Cambridge University Press.

The Genealogy of Morals by F. Nietzsche, translated by Kaufman & Hollingdale. From *On the Genealogy of Morals* by Friedrich Nietzsche, translated by Kaufman & Hollingdale. Copyright © 1967 by Random House. Reprinted by permission of Random House.

Existentialism and Humanism by Sartre. From *Existentialism and Humanism* by Jean-Paul Sartre, translated by P. Mariet. Reprinted by permission of Methuen & Co.

"Master and Slave" by G. W. F. Hegel, translated by Judith Norman. Copyright 1998 Judith Norman.

"The Focus-Field Self in Classical Confucianism" by Roger T. Ames. Excerpt from *The Focus-Field Self in Classical Confucianism*. Reprinted by permission of the State University of New York Press, from *Self as Person in Asian Theory and Practice* by Roger T. Ames, Wimal Dissanayake, and

From "Androgyny as an Ideal for Human Development" by Ann Ferguson from *Feminism and Philosophy,* ed. by Mary Vetterling-Braggin et al. Copyright © 1977 by Rowman & Littlefield. Reprinted by permission of the publisher.

Chapter 5

From "Duties to Oneself" from *Lectures on Ethics* by Immanuel Kant, translated by Louis Infield. Reprinted by permission of Methuen & Co.

From "Self-Respect: Theory and Practice" by Laurence Thomas in *Philosophy Born of Struggle: Anthology of Afro-American Philosophy from 1917* by Leonard Harris. Reprinted by permission of Methuen & Co and Laurence Thomas.

"A Critique of Utilitarianism" by Bernard Williams, from *Utilitarianism: For and Against* by J. J. C. Smart and Bernard Williams. Reprinted with the permission of Cambridge University Press.

Excerpts from *The Republic* by Plato, translated by Francis Macdonald Cornford, reprinted by permission of Oxford University Press.

"How Princes Should Honor Their Word" from *The Prince* by Niccolò Machiavelli, translated by George Bull (Penguin Classics 1961, Second revised edition 1981) copyright © George Bull, 1961, 1975, 1981. Reproduced by permission of Penguin Books Ltd.

Excerpt from "On a Supposed Right to Lie from Atruistic Motives" by Immanuel Kant, from *Critique of Practical Reason and Other Writings in Moral Philosophy*, by Immanuel Kant, edited and translated by Lewis White Beck. Reprinted with permission of the Estate of Lewis White Beck.

"On Telling Patients the Truth" by Roger Higgs from *Moral Dilemmas in Modern Medicine* ed. Michael Lockwood. Reprinted from *Moral Dilemmas in Modern Medicine* edited by Michael Lockwood (1985) by permission of Oxford University Press.

Selected sections of "Bad Faith" from *Being and Nothingness*, translated by Hazel E. Barnes. Used by permission of Philosophical Library, New York.

Parts I and II, On the Relation of Theory to Practice in International Law from *On the Old Saw That May Be Right in Theory but It Won't Work in Practice* by Immanuel Kant, trans. E. B. Ashton. From *On the Old Saw* by Immanuel Kant. Translated by E. B. Ashton. Copyright 1974 University of Pennsylvania Press. Reprinted by permission of the publisher.

"Ethical Life" and "The State" by G. W. F. Hegel from *Hegel's Philosophy of Right*, translated by T. M. Knox 1978 ed. Reprinted by permission of Oxford University Press.

From *The Meaning of Conservatism* by Roger Scruton. Copyright © 1980 by Roger Scruton. Reprinted by permission of Macmillan Press Ltd.

From "The Unpatriotic Academy" by Richard Rorty. Copyright © 1994 by the New York Times Co. Reprinted by permission.

Chapter 6

From "Moral Constraints and the State" from *Anarchy, State and Utopia* by Robert Nozick. Copyright © 1974 by Basic Books, Inc. Reprinted by permission of Basic Books, a subsidiary of Perseus Books Group, LLC.

From "A Defense of Abortion" by Judith Jarvis Thomson. Copyright 1971 by Princeton University Press. Reprinted by permission of Princeton University Press.

"Genetics and Reproductive Risk" from *Reproducing Persons: Issues in Feminist Bioethics* by Laura M. Purdy. Copyright © 1996 by Cornell University Press. Used by permission of Cornell University Press.

"Somatic and Germline Gene Therapy" by Sherman Elias and G. Annas, from *Gene Mapping: Using Law and Ethics As Guides,* edited by George J. Annas and Sherman Elias. Copyright © 1992 by Oxford University Press Inc. Used by permission of Oxford University Press, Inc.

Exerpt from "On the Environmental Ethics of the Tao and the *Ch'i*" by Chung-ying Cheng